ORGANIZATION
THEORY

THIRD EDITION

B.J. Hodge
William P. Anthony

The Florida State University

Boston ■ London ■ Sydney ■ Toronto

Allyn and Bacon, Inc.

TO MICHAEL

Copyright © 1988, 1984, 1979 by Allyn and Bacon, Inc.
A Division of Simon & Schuster
160 Gould Street
Needham Heights, Massachusetts 02194-2310

Library of Congress Cataloging-in-Publication Data

Hodge, Billy J.
  Organization theory / B. J. Hodge, William P. Anthony.
    p.   cm.
  Includes bibliographies and indexes.
  ISBN 0-205-11325-7
  1. Organization. 2. Management. I. Anthony, William P.
II. Title.
HD31.H542   1988
658.4—dc19   87-26024
                                                      CIP

Series editor: Jack Peters
Production administrator: Annette Joseph
Production coordinator: Helyn Pultz
Editorial-production service: Sally Stickney
Cover administrator: Linda K. Dickinson

Printed in the United States of America

10 9 8 7 6 5 4 3 2 1   92 91 90 89 88

C O N T E N T S

3 Macro-Environmental Components 89

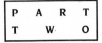

PART TWO

THE ORGANIZATION'S LINKAGE SYSTEMS 119

4 The Organization's External Linkages 121

P R E F A C E

This is a book about organization theory. It is the product of our continuing evolution of thought about what organizations are and how they work. The content of this edition reflects a rethinking of material contained in the two previous editions, together with the inclusion of four new chapters that are products of this rethinking process.

This edition, like the previous two, retains the environmental focus or perspective. We examine this environmental context through the use of the systems approach. This is done to achieve a perspective of totality and interconnectedness of and among its components that are necessary to understand contemporary organization theory. Additionally, we take a rather static approach; that is, we concentrate on structure and process as opposed to treating behavioral topics. There are some exceptions, as in the discussion of power, politics, conflict, and culture, which recognize current developments in the field.

The material is intended to be a primer in the field of organization theory and is aimed at upper-division and graduate-level courses. To make the material more relevant, we have introduced and closed each chapter with a "real-life" case example. The text itself also contains many examples from actual organizations to help pin down concepts in practical terms and ideas. These concepts are defined in a glossary located at the end of the text. At the beginning of each chapter, we have provided a convenient list of key concepts contained in each chapter. This list can be a handy reminder for each chapter's content.

There are sixteen chapters divided into four major parts. We begin with Chapter 1, "Organization Theory and the Manager," in which we tie organization theory to the manager's role and look at some of the major early contributors and schools of thought. Chapter 2, "Organizations as Systems," examines the organization as a total system and analyzes it in systems terms and concepts. Chapter 3, "Macro-Environmental Components," looks at the macro environment and its components. These three chapters constitute Part One, "Introduction."

Part Two, "The Organization's Linkage Systems," is comprised of Chapters 4, 5, and 6. Chapter 4, "The Organization's External Linkages," treats the various linkage networks and other mechanisms the organization utilizes for coping with its environment.

The concept of information processing as it aids in decision making makes up Chapter 5, "Information Processing and Organizational Choices." Chapter 6, "Interorganizational Relationships," examines the enactment process and the forms of interorganizational cooperation as well as the various restrictions on them.

The next six chapters form Part Three, "The Organization's Internal Environment." They contain much of the traditional material in organization theory about which there is general agreement as to the concepts discussed.

Chapter 7, "Organizational Strategy: Coping with the External Environment," treats strategic planning and how it is used to deal with environmental threats and opportunities. We also include a brief look at the various types of strategies that an organization can adopt.

Chapter 8 is entitled "Organizational Effectiveness and Goals," and here we show the relationship between these two important concepts. Additionally, classes of goals and a normative hierarchy are discussed, as are various classes of work needed to attain desirable goals. The chapter also discusses some means to measure an organization's effectiveness in seeking to attain its goals.

Chapter 9, "Organization Design: An Overview," is devoted to the general concept of organization design. We discuss four key concepts of organization design—differentiation, integration, decentralization, and span of control—and show how they are integral parts of organization theory. This discussion is followed by Chapter 10, "Patterns of Organization Design," in which we talk about bases and types of design and how to distinguish effective structures.

"Organization Size and Complexity" is Chapter 11. An organization's growth stages are presented here. We look at size and its consequences and how it relates to the concept of delegation. The last part of the chapter examines organizational complexity and why it is important to organization theory.

Today, we are surrounded by a technological revolution that affects our personal and organizational lives. We look at this important phenomenon in Chapter 12, "The Role of Technology." Types of technology, their relationship to organizations, and how job design and sociotechnical systems fit into organization theory are discussed.

We conclude the text proper with Part Four, "Organizational Dynamics," which contains the final four chapters. We treat a vital and central topic in Chapter 13, "Organizational Culture." What it is and how to diagnose an organization's culture are covered, as is the process of changing/managing an organization's culture.

Chapter 14, "Power, Authority, and Politics in Organizations" is concerned with three significant elements of organization theory. In addition to providing concise definitions, the chapter looks at power sources; how to assess power; and the politics of organization life. This is a dynamic segment of organization theory that deserves a careful analysis.

We all experience conflict in our daily lives and the same situations happen in organizational life as well. Therefore, we discuss the concept of conflict in a new chapter, "Conflict in Organizations" (Chapter 15). In this discussion, we examine the bases of conflict, its stages, and some models of conflict management. The intent of the material is to provide a foundation for understanding and dealing with this important organization theory concept from a management point of view.

Like conflict, change invariably occurs in all organizations as they mature. In recognition of this, Chapter 16, "Organizational Renaissance," presents change topics as they relate to the organization, its environment, and strategy. The management of change is a must for the management of today's organization. This chapter can help in that endeavor.

We end the book with six integrative cases based on actual events that occurred within real organizations. The purpose of these cases is twofold: (1) to demonstrate the applicability of organization theory concepts and principles to real-life organizations; and (2) to permit the student to use these concepts and principles as problem-solving tools.

Once again, there is an instructor's manual to accompany the text. We believe it contains material that instructors can productively use in teaching and evaluating.

Many students, colleagues, and friends helped and supported our efforts. To all of them, we say "thanks." Though impossible to list everyone, we would like to mention the following who did yeoman work on the project: Ralph Catalanello of Northern Illinois University; Thomas L. Keon of the University of Missouri at Columbia; Pamela Specht of the University of Nebraska at Omaha; Daniel F. Twomey of West Virginia University; Robert F. Allison of Wayne State University; Gregory G. Dess of Arizona State University; Ricky W. Griffin of Texas A & M University; Shaker A. Zahra of Old Dominion University; and James Swenson of Moorhead State University. Very special thanks go to Sally Stickney, our editorial-production service. Her incomparable work made a major contribution to this edition.

We wish to thank The Florida State University for its unswerving support in many and varied forms and Jack Peters and the entire staff at Allyn and Bacon for their much-needed assistance. We appreciate it very much.

Finally, to Michael D. Hankin, Assistant to the Vice President for Finance and Administration at The Florida State University, we express our deepest appreciation for making this edition possible by his research and writing. It is to him that we dedicate this edition.

PART ONE

Introduction

The first part of the text answers three important questions: (1) What is organization theory, how is it related to management, and how did the field develop? (2) What is the systems approach to studying organizations? and (3) What are the external forces that exist outside an organization's structure and why do they play such an integral role in studying organization theory?

Organization theory and management theory are closely related concepts. A manager must understand the workings of an organization in order to be effective in the managerial role. Therefore, an understanding of organization theory serves as a foundation for studying management. The concepts that underlie organization theory developed hand in hand with management concepts. As people understood more about how organizations operate, they learned how managers could operate more efficiently. Moreover, although the development of organization theory is rather eclectic, it is closely related to management theory. Concepts, ideas, and research from such diverse areas as economics, engineering, psychology, sociology, political science, and social psychology appear in organization theory literature.

How do we gain an understanding of these concepts? How can we place boundaries on them and arrange them in some logical fashion? To answer these questions, we use the systems approach. In Chapter 2, we explain what this approach is, why it is a good one to use in understanding organization theory, and how it can actually be used. We also present our basic analytical framework of the micro–intermediate–macro environments in this chapter.

Finally, it is the premise of this text that organizations interact with the external environment in which they exist. Chapter 3 studies the forces in this environment, such as politics, culture, competition, technology, customer/client groups, the skill mix of the general population, and the economic system. Examining these forces will reveal that an organization's efficiency, effectiveness, and even its survival depend on understanding why and how these environmental forces operate.

Chapters 1, 2, and 3 set the stage for Part Two, "The Organization's Linkage Systems," and for the remainder of the text.

1

Organization Theory and the Manager

A New View at General Motors

In 1984, General Motors Corporation realized that, because the world of auto manufacturing had become so complex and changeable, it was in danger of being left in the dust of its U.S. and international competitors. To become more competitive, Roger B. Smith, chairman of GM, set a new course for the company that was comprised of two major strategic thrusts—acquiring partners to provide the technological strengths it lacked and redesigning the company's management structure and operations for automobile manufacturing.

Smith sought partners to provide GM with high technology and electronic data processing that would not only bring in new revenues, but also enable it to build better cars. The partnership aspects of this new strategy involved deals with such foreign firms as Daewoo Corporation of South Korea, which, beginning in 1987, will provide GM with subcompact Pontiacs. Additionally, in 1984, GM purchased Electronic Data Systems (EDS) from Texas millionaire H. Ross Perot, ostensibly to lay the foundation for a GM information-processing company and to enhance its own internal information-processing capabilities. With Perot on the GM board, a different management perspective was added to the GM outlook, one which advocates a more responsive and flexible organization instead of the old GM style of decentralized, bureaucratic conservatism.

Under Smith's leadership, GM sought to end its "go-it-alone" attitude. Making the organization externally oriented would permit it to act more flexibly and react faster to the changing environment. New safety, pollution-control, and fuel-economy laws, in addition to intense foreign competition, forced GM to revamp its philosophical outlook as well as its management structure and manufacturing methods. This revamping, in turn, is changing GM's corporate culture from one characterized by in-house conservatism to one characterized by risk taking and innovation.

Perhaps the most striking example of GM's new attitude is the construction of its Saturn plant in Tennessee. Utilizing high-tech design, innovative management, and improved labor relations, the corporation hopes that this new plant will enable GM to once again be the world leader in automobile manufacturing and sales.

Saturn, which represents a radical departure from GM's change-resistant corporate culture, will rely not only on new manufacturing technology to build better automobiles, but also on high-tech marketing. For example, in 1989, when the first Saturns roll off the assembly line, Chevrolet dealers will be offered "first dibs" at selling them; however, long-range plans call for separate Saturn dealerships. Plans are in the works to develop and use a new computer system that will enable customers to purchase a Saturn by punching buttons on a computer at the dealership. The customer-generated order, complete with options, will be entered into the computer at the Spring Hill, Tennessee, Saturn plant. Within hours, the factory will begin to build the car specially ordered by a customer from anywhere in the world. Should this new system work as planned, customers will be actively and directly involved with Saturn operations, thus bypassing all the delays and red tape associated with the "old" GM when a customer wished to special order a car.

Even the company's old adversary, the United Auto Workers, is cooperating with

Sources: "GM Moves into a New Era," *Business Week* (July 16, 1984): 48–54; Anne B. Fisher, "Behind the Hype at GM's Saturn," *Fortune* (November 11, 1985), 34–36; C. Woods, "GM Changes Models," *Management Today* (January 1986): 56–63; Todd Mason, Russell Mitchell, and William J. Hampton, "Ross Perot's Crusade: He's Begun a One-Man Campaign to Make GM Competitive Again," *Business Week* (October 6, 1986): 60–65.

GM on the Saturn project. Automation does, however, concern the union, because increased automation may lead to fewer jobs if massive retraining is not implemented.

A different form of conflict might develop as GM applies its "new view" to Saturn operations. In the past, GM's design engineers developed new car blueprints without first consulting manufacturing engineers. Likewise, the design and manufacturing engineers rarely consulted the organization's marketing professionals. At Saturn, a new process called "simultaneous engineering" will be instituted whereby everybody will work together at the outset of a project. Some old GM veterans claim that simultaneous engineering will cause "turf battles" as various organization groups and members try to maintain their old spheres of influence.

Diversification and high technology at GM are also being matched by the development of new organization structures. In the 1970s and early 1980s, GM found out the hard way that downsizing automobiles could not be effectively managed through its traditional five-division system. Engineering, design, and overall management control for small-car development became a nightmare, a situation reflected in the poor-quality cars GM produced and the resultant decline in sales.

Borrowing management techniques and structures from Adam-Opel in West Germany, GM has, for design, engineering, and manufacturing purposes, placed its five divisions into two groups—one for the expensive, big cars and one for the generally sportier, smaller, and less expensive models. This restructuring should streamline the way each model is conceived, designed, and developed. The five-division system, however, will remain intact for marketing purposes.

General Motors's new direction is long-term. New high-tech partnerships and acquisitions as well as new car models beyond Saturn are in the works. Although it took some time, GM now realizes that the world it exists in today, and the one it will exist in tomorrow, is radically different from yesterday.

The above case is a real-life application of the components of organization theory, particularly in view of the environmental perspective we emphasize throughout the text. As you read the subsequent chapters and analyze the material contained therein, you will realize that the various components of organization theory are not just theoretical, abstract concepts. Rather, they are real dimensions of real organizations, as evidenced in the GM narrative. You will discover that academic theories and concepts have concrete counterparts in today's organizations, and that they are practiced by organizations of all types to resolve their problems and improve their performance.

CHAPTER PLAN

This first chapter begins by defining organizations, telling why they exist, and explaining the relationship between organization theory and practice.

The next major portion of the chapter explains the various components of organization theory: boundary and environment; information processing and choices; adaptation and change; goals; work; organization design; size and complexity; technology; culture; and power and authority.

When studying any subject, it is important to have a historical perspective; therefore, the next major portion of the chapter provides a brief history of the development of organization theory, including some of the early contributors to the field and the various schools of thought they have provided: the Classical School, the Behavioral School, the Systems School, and the Contingency School.

This chapter will provide you with a basic understanding of what organization theory is and of what the various schools of thought have put forward to explain it. This first chapter, then, is a short primer on the foundation of organization theory that will be the basis for the remainder of the text.

We truly live in a world of organizations today. Literally, every aspect of our daily activities is affected in some way by organizations. We work in organizations, play in organizations, and live in one of the oldest forms of organization, the family. Although we are so involved in and with them, we perhaps have given little thought to what organizations really are and how they work. This book takes a close look at the world of organizations with the intention of examining why they exist, how they are designed, how they function, and how they grow and survive over time. We hope its contents will help you more fully appreciate today's world of organizations.

WHAT ARE ORGANIZATIONS AND WHY DO THEY EXIST?

Most likely, we humans, like our animal relatives the great apes, have always lived in organized groups. The earliest group activities were probably no more complex than gathering food, migrating, or defending the group. This group effort enabled people to combine talents and efforts into attaining larger goals such as building and protecting their communities. Labor specialization made it possible for individuals to concentrate on tasks they did best without having to do every task necessary for survival and progress. Thus a community could have, say, one baker who would bake for the whole community while another member could spend time on sewing or farming.

Group activity requires cooperation, else members can find themselves working at cross-purposes and therefore losing the benefits of association. In order to attain this cooperation and so to achieve desired complex goals, some system of structural relationships had to be established. Such a system of group relationships built on and fostering cooperation, then, is basically the meaning of an organization. Thus, an organization can be thought of as two or more people working cooperatively toward a common objective or set of objectives.

This *system of cooperation* is made up of several parts: the *human element*, the *physical element*, the *work element*, and the *coordination element*. All these elements, taken collectively, can be thought of as an organization.

Therefore, organizations can be thought of as social systems of cooperation that are designed to enhance individual effort aimed at goal accomplishment. In order to continue to refine and improve organizational activity, management must develop an explanation of how organizations form, function, and survive. Such an explanation is termed *organization theory*.

This theory must explain component parts and their relationships so that some prediction can be made about how they are likely to behave under given conditions.[1] Theory, then, contains assumptions that are relevant and that are based on empirically tested definitions. Thus, it is imperative that theorists base both their assumptions and definitions upon the real world.

HOW ARE THEORY AND PRACTICE RELATED?

There has been a good deal of controversy and debate over the relationship between theory and practice. Much of this debate has been the tempest-in-a-teapot variety because it stems from a lack of appreciation of either concept. Where time and effort are taken to define terms and show their applicability, much of the heat of debate is removed.

Theory can be defined as an explanation of some phenomenon, and it consists of principles that describe relationships observed in association with the phenomenon.[2] In other words, theory explains practice and in so doing helps to improve it. In light of this, theory and practice cannot be properly viewed as contradictory; rather, they must be viewed as complementary. For the purpose of this book, therefore, the concepts will be considered as twin dimensions of an organization.

How Is Management Theory Related to Organization Theory?

Management theory is an explanation of management practice. In other words, it explains how managers behave. Here, once again, there has been debate and controversy much like the general debate over the relationship between theory and practice.

Management behavior consists of the things a manager does in carrying out his or her responsibility. There are many accounts of what managers do, but they all seem to center around the basic work that can be termed *decision making* and *influence*. There are those who use different terms (e.g., planning and controlling) or who add to the list (e.g., organizing, staffing, and directing). If one carefully examines these lists, however, one can group all the activities into the basic functions of decision making and influence.

Organization theory, on the other hand, can be thought of as a group of related concepts, principles, and hypotheses that is used to explain the components of organizations and how they behave. This means that organization theory can help us understand what organizations are and how they behave in a given environment.

All organizations require the exercise of managerial functions. Thus, as an integral part of explaining the organization, it is necessary to devise an explanation of managerial work. Taken together, management and organization theory help explain total organization action.

For an individual to understand organizations and how they work, a general knowledge of both management theory and organization theory must be applied. This book is concerned primarily with the latter, an examination of organization theory and how it can be used to explain the activity of today's organization world, but we do take a managerial approach throughout.

COMPONENTS OF ORGANIZATION THEORY

It is important to examine the various parts or components of organization theory in order to understand its broad scope. The following components must be understood individually and collectively if the proper perspective of organization theory is to be established. These parts are the basic building blocks for constructing an explanation of how organizations behave. They are discussed briefly below and then given more complete treatment in later chapters. In addition, where applicable, we will refer to the introductory case in this chapter to demonstrate real-life applications of these theoretical components.

Boundary and Environment

Every organization exists within an extensive and complex environmental network. *Organization environment*, as used here, refers to all groups, norms, and conditions with which an organization must deal. It includes such things as the political, cultural, economic, competitive, technological, skill mix, consumer/client groups, and like systems that affect an organization and which are in turn affected by it. The environment is the total set of outside forces surrounding and shaping the behavior of the organization and its members.[3]

In order to be successful the organization must interact with this environment because it supplies the organization with inputs (in the form of resources, information, and so forth) that are necessary to determine the products and services to be furnished to components of that environment. It also receives the output (products and services) produced by the organization. To maintain this harmony with its environment, the organization must carefully define and maintain a means of gathering the necessary inputs for effective decision making and implementation and for distributing organizational outputs. Such a system is termed the *boundary network*. The boundary network can be thought of as a kind of membrane through which passes organization inputs and outputs and which helps keep the organization in harmony with the environment surrounding it.

Within the boundary network, it is necessary to establish *sensors* to monitor change and trends. Among these early warning devices are all of the critical control points that can tell a management group what is happening in the environment. For example, customer complaints or buying habits can be an invaluable source of input about what the organization should be doing in terms of marketing, pricing, product mix, and so on. Sensors can take the form of mechanical devices, organization units (e.g., market research), or individual work assignments (e.g., salespersons' reports).

Information Processing and Choices

Organizations must obtain relevant information about their environments in order to properly interact with them. This means that the environment must be scanned, or read, and important trends and issues be examined by the organization. These issues should deal with all important aspects of the environment—political, legal, economic, technological, and so on—but most important of all, with the market. This information is then acted on by the organization. Choices (decisions) are made with respect to what the organization should or should not do in dealing with the environment. Should a new product be introduced? Should a plant be expanded? Should an office be relocated?

In our introductory case, we read how GM purchased EDS. General Motors decided to purchase EDS in order to enhance its own information-processing capabilities, and thus to make better decisions (choices). Only by obtaining adequate information on the environment and efficiently processing it can an organization make proper choices in answering the questions posed above.

Adaptation and Change

Today's organization exists in a turbulent environment characterized by what has been termed by some as *discontinuous change*.[4] If it is to survive and prosper, the organization must be capable of adjusting all its component parts to accommodate this change. This means that it must process the inputs brought to it from its boundary system in an effective and efficient manner. Even though a *particular* organization (e.g., a conservative church) may exist in a relatively stable environment where change and adaptation are rather minor, this organization may in the future face the kind of environment characterized by turbulence; therefore, adaptation and change should be considered a facet of an organization's *actual* or *potential* environment.

The management group must be aware of this need and must build flexibility into every facet of the organization. Additionally, it must adopt a philosophy and strategy to support the processes of adaptation and change. In the absence of these conditions, decay, deterioration, and eventual demise await the unsuspecting organization.

STRATEGY. As environments change, so must organizations. Organizations must adapt to changing requirements and opportunities found in their environment. A stagnant organization in a dynamic environment significantly increases the chances that it will soon lose touch with its market and subsequently wither and die. Note the serious problems that faced GM because of its insulated point of view during the late 1970s through mid-1980s.

The method the organization uses to deal with its environment is called *strategy*. This is the unique approach an organization brings to bear on its environmental opportunities and threats, and it reflects the mission, goals, strengths, and weaknesses of the organization. Strategy reflects the particular approach the organization will use to beat out competition while capitalizing on market opportunities. As exemplified in our introductory case, GM has embarked upon a two-pronged strategy of internal restructuring and external technology acquisition in order to meet the threats and opportunities posed in the external environment.

Goals

It was stated earlier that organizations were established to enable individuals to accomplish more in a group than they could as individuals. In other words, organizations are devices for pooling talent and ability into an effective whole that can reach some desired objective.[5]

Every organization is initially built to accomplish some goal. This goal or purpose thus becomes the starting point for building the organization and the benchmark for measuring its success. A *goal* or *purpose* is an unrealized state or condition that the members deem desirable. For example, the members might decide that they would like to manufacture and distribute a food product, say peanut butter in an aerosol can, so that they can earn an acceptable rate of return on their investment. This product, when sold for an appropriate price, will yield this rate of return and so satisfy individual member goals. It is important to note, however, that the organization will have a network of goals, some of which might be contradictory. The problem then becomes one of balance among goals in order to avoid pursuing those that are at cross-purposes. For instance, some people in the organization may feel it is important to be a leader in product innovation, while others might believe in being more conservative in product marketing strategy. Balancing these conflicting points of view is one of the prime responsibilities of management.

For example, we read in the introductory case that GM has established a primary goal of once again being the world's leader in automobile manufacturing and sales. In turn, there are secondary goals to be accomplished, such as technology acquisition, improved labor relations, new model development, and so on. Although these goals are not mutually exclusive, they must be balanced against each other. Should GM have to lay off workers in order to streamline its operations, this would, on the surface, seem to conflict with the goal of improving labor relations. Through high-tech retraining programs, GM plans to accomplish its secondary goal of improving labor relations while simultaneously improving its assembly operations. These measures, in turn, should help accomplish the primary goal.

Work

Once the goal structure of an organization is established, it is time for the members to decide on the type of work that will be necessary to accomplish these goals. Basically, any organization must perform two fundamental types of work: primary and secondary.[6] The *primary work* consists of *production and distribution* of the goods or services that will satisfy consumer needs. These needs, remember, are the basis for defining organization goals. That is to say, the needs of the consumer group with which the organization is concerned will determine its goals, and these, in turn, will serve as the basis for defining the kind and amount of work necessary to accomplish them.

Secondary work* consists of all those activities that *support and extend* the operations of primary work. For example, in a manufacturing firm, the secondary work would include accounting, personnel, and quality control. These are by no means all of the types of secondary work; rather, they represent the kind of work that must be performed in order to enhance the execution of primary work.

In the case of General Motors, the primary work is the manufacture and sale of automobiles. Secondary work there would be information processing, labor relations, technical training for employees, and so on, because these activities are not primarily concerned with the major GM objective, but offer much-needed support instead.

A sound theory of organizations must enable the manager and student of organizations alike to understand these relationships and how they fit the goal structure if they are to be successful in predicting and controlling organization behavior.

Organization Design

As indicated above, an organization is basically a system of coordinated social units concerned with accomplishing certain goals. In order for this system to be effective, decisions have to be made about its form and how its pieces fit together. These decisions, which are among the most important managerial choices, result in the design of the organization. Organization design is primarily concerned with two major variables: structure

---

*Primary work is also commonly referred to as *line work*, and secondary work is often termed *staff work*. We will use the primary and secondary classifications in this book simply because they seem to be more descriptive and are less confusing.

and process. Inherent in these variables are such issues as differentiation, integration, and complexity.

ORGANIZATION STRUCTURE. The geometric patterns of work divisions and their hierarchical arrangements constitute the basic components of structure. These patterns should be used as the primary guide for making decisions about selecting and grouping the other components of structure (such as personnel, physical assets, responsibility, authority, and accountability).* *Structure* is basically a managerial tool that aids in guiding the organization toward its goals and can be considered the skeleton of the organization body.

The form the organization structure takes can be depicted in its *design*. This is merely the outward or physical manifestation of the structure. Note, however, that not all components of the structure can be shown in its design. For example, it is not possible to show the nature of responsibility in a design of structure. The closest approximation to an understanding of responsibility can be seen in titles, and these can be quite misleading, to say the least. So, structure, while being a narrower concept than design, is the foundation for design. Stated simply, structure is a determinant of design rather than vice versa.

Structure and design go hand in hand in the study of organizations. Structure is the hierarchy of work, authority, and responsibility that orders the components of the organization into some logical arrangement. Design, on the other hand, has two meanings, one as a verb, and the other as a noun. When used as a verb, design means the *process of deciding* the shape or form these arrangements will take. As a noun, it means the existing shape or form of the organization, its structure, policies, procedures, rules, and so on.

STRUCTURAL CONCEPTS. An organization may properly be thought of as a set of *role elaborations*. In other words, the members of the organization are assigned to perform certain duties or responsibilities that can be thought of as roles. There must be some order established for these roles; otherwise, there would be chaos in place of efficiency. The basis for this complex of role sets is work division. This means that management must make decisions regarding how the work of the organization is to be divided among its members. This process of decision making about work divisions is termed *differentiation*.[7]

Differentiation essentially involves separating a unit of work from its original location and making it the basis for another unit of work. It is the forces that split up the work to be done in the organization. It is similar to

---

*These factors will be discussed in more detail in later chapters, especially Chapters 9 and 10.

specialization. For example, when a supervisor in the shipping department of a manufacturing concern hires a clerk and assigns him the responsibility of keeping records of goods shipped from the company, she has engaged in work differentiation; she has separated a function—record-keeping—that she previously performed herself and assigned that function to the clerk. The role of the clerk, then, has its foundation in the separation of the record-keeping function. Although the above example is a simple one, it is representative of the process of work differentiation that produces the total set of roles that constitute the organization.

In order to tie the various differentiations together, management must devise integration mechanisms. These devices serve to help hold the various roles in an effective pattern so that organizational efficiency does not suffer. Among these devices are such things as the direction function, authority and power, the communications and control system, organization and job design, selection and training, reward systems, and appraisal and development.[8]

The manager uses these mechanisms to bring the necessary information and other forms of input required to hold all the pieces of the organization in an effective form for dealing with all its environmental influences. So, in a sense, these mechanisms are the internal adhesives that help hold the various departments and divisions in the organization together.

Integration is the condition in which all parts of the total organization are held together in a state of dynamic equilibrium.[9] General Motors, by redesigning its organization structure from five-car divisions to two groups (one for big cars and one for small cars), is attempting to achieve better overall integration and coordination of automobile manufacturing.

The matter of complexity also arises when one discusses the twin issues of differentiation and integration. *Complexity* can be defined, at least informally, as task specialization within the organization. In other words, to the extent that there has been extensive differentiation of highly technical work units, the requirements for specialized talent increase. This brings to the organization a group of individuals who possess special skills and who might well possess a narrowly focused education. As a result, these individuals might tend to concentrate unduly on their particular role assignment and not take the global perspective required for total organization integration. The accountant is a good example of such a person; the same could be said for lawyers, doctors, and other professional personnel.

There are other situations in which *horizontal differentiation* (the process of lateral division of work) results in work units that require little talent. For example, such a highly complex operation as automobile assembly can be differentiated into such work units as lug-nut installation and lug-nut tightening, neither of which requires highly skilled talent.

Consequently, the notion of differentiation and integration must be considered from a situation-specific perspective. The extent, nature, and means for attaining integration must be considered from a prescriptive (as opposed to a patent) point of view.

Complexity, then, is a term that describes the degree of sophistication and specialization that results from the separation of work units for the purpose of establishing units of responsibility. These three variables, differentiation, integration, and complexity, must be taken into account when constructing a theory of organizations.

Size and Complexity

Organizations that enjoy any measure of success find it necessary to increase their membership and to assign duties to these additional members. The process that is used to add members to the organization will result in the necessity of dividing the work of the organization into subunits or groups, each under the direction of a manager or managers. In order for these managers to perform their managerial duties properly, they must be granted appropriate responsibility and authority. The means for making these assignments is termed *delegation*.[10] Delegation may be defined as the process of sharing an obligation (responsibility) and an accompanying right (authority) of a superior with a subordinate in the organization. It is this basic process that enables an organization to grow.

As the organization grows and develops and becomes more complex, it tends to become more formalized. Written procedures, policies, and rules evolve, replacing the unwritten but usually understood ways of operating. When the organization becomes so large that face-to-face interaction among organization members is reduced, then written policies, procedures, and rules are used to achieve consistency of action. Hence, the organization becomes more complex.

Indeed, one of the problems facing GM as it tries to revitalize itself is its sheer size and complexity. With over 800,000 employees, Chairman Smith cannot implement changes with lightning-like speed. Therefore, certain GM production and assembly systems are still being run the "old way" while Smith and his associates experiment with new methods.

Technology

Another component of organization theory is *technology*. This we briefly define as the art and science that are employed in the production and distribution of goods and services. Technology is the way the organization goes about converting its inputs into outputs that are desired by components of the environment.

Technology is a pervasive component of organization theory because the way an organization carries out its production and distribution functions affects organization structure, design, strategy, culture, size, and so on. In other words, virtually every other component of organization theory is affected by technology.

Technology may also be viewed as a component part of the environment in that the basis of a society is the way in which it goes about acquiring and distributing the goods and services needed by its members. So, for our purposes, we will consider technology both an internal and an external component of organization theory, although we will concentrate most of our efforts in explaining the role that it plays within organizations.

Culture

All organizations can be identified by their own distinct character or culture. When we use the term *culture*, we are referring to the common values, beliefs, and behaviors exhibited by organization members. Culture is also symbolic, and it is expressed in such products and processes as myths, company logos, rituals, anecdotes, heroes, ceremonies, office furnishings, building design, and so on. Culture is an important cornerstone of organization theory because it pervades all aspects of an organization's operations—it affects how goals are formulated, how work is performed, and the nature and strength of relationships. Most importantly, culture is a critical variable affecting an organization's ability to adapt to its environment through strategy. Because culture reflects what has worked in the past, it can inhibit the organization as it attempts to change in view of environmental threats or opportunities. Conversely, culture can be an enabling factor for change and adaptability if its manifested values and subsequent behaviors encourage flexibility and creativity.

General Motors's culture was conservative and introspective, inhibiting the organization as it attempted to revitalize itself in the face of global competition. General Motors is now attempting to build a new organization culture, one characterized by openness, innovation, and flexibility.

Power and Authority

No theory of organizations would be complete without a discussion of the roles that power and authority play in organization activity. *Power* is the ability to influence others successfully. It comes from any single source or from a combination of possible sources.[11] For example, one can have power over others because of one's intelligence, skill, or money. Regardless of its source, power enables one to exercise one's will over others. Thus, in order to understand the total workings of an organization, the role that power plays in these workings must be appreciated.

Authority can be defined as power that has been officially recognized by the organization.[12] Once an organization legally authorizes an individual to act on its behalf, that person is said to possess authority. The concern of the theorist is to understand how authority comes to be officially recognized by the organization and what considerations should be made regarding its use.

Power and authority must be considered components of a theory of organizations because they enable the manager to take actions to initiate the performance of work and to accomplish goals.

POLITICS. Concomitant with the components of power and authority is the subcomponent of politics. Within organizations, politics involves those activities that organization members undertake to acquire, develop, and use power. A political view sees the organization from the basis of decisions that stem from power, rather than those based on authority. In addition, such a political view maintains that political activities, such as bargaining and conflict, are the essence of organization life.

Referring again to General Motors, H. Ross Perot, former owner of Electronic Data Systems, became a GM director when he sold EDS to that company. As a director, Perot had very little formal authority; nevertheless, because of a variety of personal and business reasons, he had considerable power in the GM organization. This often put him at loggerheads with GM Chairman Roger Smith, who possessed considerable formal authority.

In sum, we consider organization theory to be composed of ten cornerstones:

boundary and environment
information processing and choices
adaptation and change
goals
work
organization design
size and complexity
technology
culture
power and authority

We believe that this rather simple, but integrated, scheme will allow the student of organizations to conveniently classify and see the relationships between the various concepts and principles necessary to understand not only how organizations come to be but how they sustain themselves and prosper. Be aware that this scheme applies not only to business organizations, but to other types as well—political (government agencies), moral (churches), intensive-technology (NASA), adaptive (research and development companies), and mutual benefit (trade associations). The rest of the book is based on an explanation of these individual concepts and how they are related to one another in a theory of organizations at work.

HISTORY OF ORGANIZATION THEORY

In this section we trace the development of organization theory in order to develop an appreciation of the present state of knowledge about how and why organizations work. Much of what follows is closely related to the development of management theory. This is partially due to the fact that part of what was once considered to be in the domain of management theory has subsequently been reclassified as organization theory. Also, some component parts (e.g., authority, delegation, and goals) can be properly classified as belonging to both disciplines as they are known today.

In the present discussion, however, we stress organization theory and its development even though there is some overlap with the evolution of management thought. Although many of the concepts of organization are traceable to antiquity, the Industrial Revolution marked the beginning of what we know today as the modern organization, so it seems appropriate to begin our discussion with this major event.

One of the early contributors to what is now known as organization theory was Adam Smith with his major work, *An Inquiry into the Nature and Causes of the Wealth of Nations*.[13] Smith's work brought a much needed framework to the knowledge about organizations that was available at the time. His was one of the few reflective approaches to organization until the end of the nineteenth century. This was due largely to the dynamic changes that were occurring in business practices and to the technological innovations that were associated with them. Crises left little time for the kind of effort required to build a coherent system of thought about how organizations worked.[14]

Early Contributors

Among the most important early contributors to a theory of organizations was Max Weber (1864–1920), whose monumental work analyzed bureaucracy. This major work has led some to refer to Weber as the "father of organization theory."[15] Weber's concentration was largely on bureaucracy as the "ideal" form of organization, which was built around rational decision making. Knowledge and ability were seen as superior to favoritism as the basis for organization. The bureaucratic organization that Weber envisioned was based on the following tenets:

1. A division of labor existed in which authority and responsibility were clearly defined for each member and were legitimized as official duties.
2. The offices or positions would be organized in a hierarchy of authority resulting in a chain of command.
3. All organizational members were to be selected on the basis of technical qualifications through formal examinations or by virtue of training or education.
4. Officials were appointed, not elected.
5. Administrative officials worked for fixed salaries and were career officials.
6. The administrative official was not an owner of the unit being administered.
7. The administrator would be subject to strict rules, discipline, and controls regarding his conduct while performing the official duties. These rules and controls would be impersonal and uniformly applied in all cases.[16]

An organization based on these tenets, argued Weber, would overcome the inefficiency and cumbersomeness found in the typical organization of his time. It was not uncommon for positions to be filled by favoritism, rather than by demonstrated competence. Subjectivity and opinion took precedence over objectivity and order in the hiring and placement of employees.

The separation of management and ownership would allow the hiring of professional career administrators who would be responsible for administering the affairs of the organization on a day-to-day basis. This would enable these administrators to concentrate on devoting their "job-related" talents to making decisions based on careful analyses of the facts in the situation. Efficiency would thus be improved, according to Weber.

More objective personnel selection was complemented by the imposition of rules based on work requirements that were strictly followed. These rules would bring consistency both to performance and decision making, so the organization would be more consistent and, supposedly, more efficient.

Although his contributions to organization theory were landmarks, they went almost unnoticed in the United States until 1940. As Wren notes, however, when the search for the explanation of how large organizations work began in earnest, attention focused on Weber and his work.[17]

It was not until the 1920s that a concerted effort to study organizations formally began. Contributions in this era were of two major types: (1) the compilation of scattered bits of knowledge into one source treated from a historical perspective[18] and (2) the building of a comprehensive theory of organization management for the first time.[19]

The writings of this time concentrated on organization work or functions. A central theme was that if work could be studied properly and if principles could be drawn about how best to perform it, then these principles could be taught to managers who would thus be able to perform more effectively and efficiently.

From this start has come the development of organization theory as it is known today. The early studies were more micro than macro; that is, attention was centered on the organization itself rather than on the relationship of the organization to its environment. This is not to say that the latter was not important; rather, attention was given to the area of concern that appeared to be most critical: how to achieve an effectively functioning organization capable of attaining its objectives. Concentration on the work of the organization appeared to provide the most promise.

Many disciplines have contributed to the development of organization theory. For example, political science, economics, psychology, and engineering have all helped improve our understanding of organizations. As a result, organization theorists have approached the study of organizations from a wide range of perspectives. This diversity of approach has resulted in several major schools of thought, which we discuss briefly below.

The Classical School

The Classical School attempted to create a set of rational techniques that would help in building both structure and process and so provide a coordinated set of relationships among the components of the organization. It was believed that if there could be rational approaches and techniques, the organization could be better able to attain the goals for which it was established.

The focus for the work of the Classicists was the business organization because it was easily available for study and because it was the kind of organization that required rational structure and process that could produce efficiency, a hallmark of the business organization. Since the initial investigations, however, the scope has been expanded to include every type of organization, but with the same emphasis—to build rationality into the operation of the organization. The Classicists believed that rationality in structure and process could be attained by building a theory around what they defined as the "one best way" of doing things. The theory, thus, was founded on four pillars: *division of labor, scalar and functional processes, structure,* and *span of control.*[20]

The school concentrated its attention on the proper allocation of work to people and machines. The divisions of work became the foundation for the selection, placement, and development of personnel. Both the structure and the process employed were built on these divisions of labor that were aimed at achieving the advantages of specialization. With each person performing a limited task for which he or she had been properly trained and being supervised by a management group also specializing in task performance, the entire organization was thought to be optimally coordinated.

It was from this pillar that the others evolved and on which they are based. The proper division of labor has been called the most important economic concept ever devised.[21]

Scalar and functional processes refer to vertical and horizontal growth, respectively. As the organization experiences growth, personnel need to be added to perform the additional tasks that must be accomplished. In order to accommodate them, the organization must expand and add more supervisors. When the work load of any one manager is determined to be excessive, more people are added to the unit by delegating the authority and responsibility to them for the added work of the unit. If it is necessary to add more levels of supervision, a new level is created in the structure. This process results in vertical growth (the scalar process). If no additional levels of structure are required, however, the growth is horizontal (the functional process). For example, if a manager merely adds additional personnel at the same level as present subordinates, growth is horizontal. These two processes account for all organization growth, and it can be seen that they are based on the first pillar, division of labor.

Structure refers to the vertical arrangement of jobs in the organization. Again, it is evident that this pillar is founded on the division of labor. The essence of structure is a hierarchical pattern of authority and responsibility relationships aimed at coordinating the work of the organization. Classical theory centered its focus around the line and staff organization structure. The line structure is concerned with accomplishing the basic work with which the organization is primarily concerned. The staff structure, on the other hand, is concerned with those functions that facilitate or expedite the performance of this basic work. In this connection, it can be thought of as special work divisions that are aimed at providing economy and effectiveness to the line structure.

The subordinates who immediately report to a given superior constitute the superior's *span of control.* Getting a group of subordinates who can be effectively supervised by a manager is of primary importance to

Classical theory. There are, of course, limits to how many subordinates a manager can effectively supervise. The determination of that number was the concern of V. A. Graicunas, who developed a numerical table of limits that gained wide acceptance in the Classical School.[22]

Graicunas contended that spans of control were limited by the fact that the complexity and the number of possible contacts increased geometrically when personnel were added arithmetically to a span of control. Thus, any given span should be relatively small, depending on the nature of the work being done, the ability of the superior, and the ability of the subordinates. Graicunas's theory was a major contribution to the Classical School.

The structure can be considered to be made up of all spans of control taken collectively. Therefore, the shape of the structure is determined by the number and size of its spans of control. The shape can be basically tall with narrow spans of control (few subordinates reporting to a superior) or flat with wide spans of control (many subordinates reporting to a superior).[23] The span of control concept is key in Classical theory because it points up the limitations of managerial ability while at the same time it treats the matter of complexity of relationships and the need to provide coordination among them.

The four pillars of the Classical School are of central importance to the theory. Virtually every facet of the theory can be traced to one or more of them. The theory thus concentrates on the anatomy of formal organizations with a view to building rational, well-coordinated relationships among them.

Among the many contributors to Classical theory, the name of Frederick Taylor must be counted as one of the most important. Taylor made countless contributions to both management and organization theory based on his work at the shop level in the steel industry. His experience there convinced him that there was a major need to develop the "one best way" to perform a task, to make that way standard practice, to find a first-class person to perform it, and to provide that person with the best tools and equipment available. Both the person and the organization would benefit as a result.

Taylor devised many special tools and techniques that brought more efficient operations, developed a piece-rate incentive pay plan, and created a functional organization structure, among other things. Basically, he argued for the application of science to the practice of management. In fact, he maintained that management must engage in a mental revolution—a new way of viewing things—that he called *scientific management*. Today, it is considered to be one of the most important contributions to management ever made.

Frank and Lillian Gilbreth made many significant contributions to what has come to be known as Classical theory. Their work was centered on the study of time and motion as the primary means for finding the "one best way." J. D. Mooney and Alan C. Reiley's *Onward Industry!*[24] is a major addition to the study of organizations, while Carl Barth and Henry Gantt added mathematical dimensions to scientific management.

There are countless other Americans who helped nurture the new movement. They all were, however, concerned with operational problems that occurred at the lower levels of the organization.

At about the same time that Taylor and his colleagues were developing their theories and practices in this country, Henri Fayol was beginning his study of organizations in France. Unlike Taylor, Fayol concentrated his efforts on explaining the workings of the administrative levels of the organization. He maintained that it was possible to devise a set of principles of administration that could be universally applied to improve the practice of management. As a result of his belief and study (conducted primarily in the coal mining industry), Fayol formulated fourteen principles of management that he believed would improve the state of the art of management practice. He held that these principles could be applied in any type of organization. This was, perhaps, the first notion of *universality* introduced into the literature of management and organization theory.

The application of these principles, which can be found in almost any basic text on management theory, was considered to be at the heart of improved management practice. In other words, if managers would apply these principles, they would improve the quality of their management practice to the benefit of their organization as a whole. Fayol's work can properly be considered a complement to that of Taylor and his colleagues. Taken together, all these contributions increased the understanding of both the shop and the administrative levels of the organization.

It should be noted here that the Classical School is a body of thought, as opposed to a period of time. Accordingly, there are writers and researchers today who hold its basic tenets. For example, writers and researchers in recent years have extended the principles that were developed in the earlier part of this century.

These Classicists all concentrated in some fashion on how to build an organization that was based on proper principles of work and the processing of information needed to carry out that work in the most efficient manner. Theirs was a micro view based on task performance that held the human element virtually constant. There were those who held that this was too narrow a view of how organizations should be built and operated. There evolved a group that was concerned with how the human element should be accounted for in a theory of organizations. This group has come to be known as the Behavioral School.

The Behavioral School

The Behavioral School is primarily composed of investigators from psychology, social psychology, and sociology. These students of organizations have sought to improve the understanding of organization behavior by studying in a scientific manner why and how people behave in a certain way in organization settings. Their contributions are ultimately aimed at enabling management to understand behavior in order to be capable of modifying it in a manner deemed effective for the organization.

The Behavioral School largely accepted the theory put forth by the Classicists but modified it by stressing the importance of the social group to organization efficiency. Where the Classicists, for the most part, held the human element relatively constant in the form of Taylor's "one best man" who would be a model for performance, the Behaviorists explored the role of group membership as a factor in organization theory. Group norms and customs were viewed as helping shape behavior and thus productivity.

The Behaviorists examined both the micro (e.g., motivation and leadership) and the macro (e.g., social and technical systems analysis) aspects of group membership.[25] They attempted, in short, to study people as behaving individuals in an organized setting (the organization). So attention was given not only to how the individual is motivated and behaves but to how social groups interact with one another and with the technology of the organization. This view perhaps is more complicated and more dynamic than the view of the Classicists.

Although the movement began before this experiment,* the most notable study the Behaviorists conducted was the Hawthorne Experiment. It was carried out in Western Electric's Hawthorne plant outside Chicago during the period between 1927 and 1932 under the direction of Elton Mayo and Fritz Roethlisberger of Harvard University. The studies centered around the effect of physical factors (such as lighting, working conditions, and the length of the work period) on output of workers in various sections of the plant. These conditions and factors were altered considerably from standard, and the result was that production continued to increase under these stress conditions.[26] The reason posed by the researchers for this result was that the close-knit social conditions among the workers caused them to band together under these conditions and to continue to produce in spite of adversity.

This demonstrated an important factor of group productivity—it was not solely a function of what had been considered prime determinants such as pay, working conditions, and so on. This meant that the scientific method, which concentrated on such issues, would have to be rethought by management; that is, although the ideas were important,

---

*See, for example, the works of Robert Owen and Hugo Münsterberg.

there were other equally important determinants of productivity. This discovery was a hallmark in organization theory.

Both Mary Parker Follett and Chester Barnard must be counted among the notables of the Behavioral School. Mary Parker Follett stressed the group principle in her works because she believed the group took precedence over the individual, and this emphasis would enable the individual to develop fully. Participation, cooperation, communication, coordination, and the sharing of authority were themes that characterized her writings.

Follett's ideas were, indeed, quite a departure from the basic foundations of the Classical School. Her belief in the sharing of authority with subordinates was a clear break with the Classicists, as was her concern with the role and importance of the group (as opposed to the individual). Concentrating on how groups form and perform and how involvement of subordinates could improve organization success were her signal contributions to organization theory.

Chester Barnard's *The Functions of the Executive*[27] has become a classic in organization literature. Barnard expanded the experience he had as president of New Jersey Bell into an explanation of human behavior at work. His writing stressed cooperation as the main way to achieve both individual and organization success. He tied the needs of the formal organization to the needs of the individual and of informal groups within it and so provided new insight into how organizations work.

Another of the major contributors to the Behavioral School was Douglas McGregor, whose ideas about human motivation were based on the proposition that a person's assumptions about others have a significant impact on the way that person behaves toward them. For example, if a person assumes that work is undesirable, that one must spend a lifetime at work doing only enough to avoid punishment, and thus the best motivation is fear of job loss, that worker operates from what McGregor called the *Theory X* set of assumptions. The role of the manager would be to create an atmosphere of dependency and fear if the workers were to produce at their maximum. Current thinking, of course, rejects this role for the manager.

Instead, the manager is encouraged to assume that work is natural, that creativity is widely spread throughout the population, that people can be taught to accept responsibility, and that fear is only one way (and not a very good one) to inspire behavior. McGregor termed these assumptions *Theory Y*. Today, most basic courses in human behavior seem to be based on these assumptions. Thus, McGregor's Theory X and Theory Y symbolize what, at that time, was a new approach to motivation and interpersonal relationships.

Another major contribution to motivation theory was made by Abraham Maslow, who formulated a *hierarchy of human needs*.[28] He maintained that humans have five levels of needs, and their behavior is determined by the levels of needs which are given attention at a particular time. The most basic need, according to Maslow, is physiological—the need for food, clothing, and shelter. This need dominates people's attention until it is perceived to be satisfied. Then attention shifts to the safety need—the need to be safe from injury and the concern for the preservation of the means for satisfying the physiological need. The third-level need is social—the need to be a member of a group. This is followed by the ego or self-esteem need, which deals with the necessity to develop and maintain a healthy self-concept. The highest-order need is self-actualization, the need to realize one's fullest potential. The recognition of this hierarchy and the effect that it has on behavior is an important facet of understanding human behavior and its part in the development of a theory of organizations.

Frederick Herzberg's *two-factor theory of motivation* is also a key contribution to the Behavioral School.[29] Herzberg's research led him to conclude that job enrichment is the core of motivation. He found that there are two sets of determinants of behavior: *job context* (working conditions, pay, quality of supervision, and so on) and *job content* (recognition, promotion, professional growth, and so on). Management's role is to build jobs or tasks that bring about a sense of accomplishment and appreciation rather than to construct motivation efforts solely on the traditional tools of pay, fear, and so on.

George Homans with his classic, *The Human Group*,[30] increased understanding of the effects of group membership on behavior and productivity. Kurt Lewin made a similarly important contribution to understanding group behavior with his *field theory*, the expression of social and psychological concepts and events in terms of physical science concepts.

There have been other contributors to the Behavioral School; the ones singled out are but representative of the quality and importance of the work of the entire group. Certainly they have increased our understanding of behavior and improved our efforts to develop a general theory of organizations.

The work of the Behaviorists was based on acceptance of the scientific approach of the Classicists but with the recognition that, in order to develop a complete theory of organizations, additional emphasis must be given to the interpersonal relationships among members of the organization. The Hawthorne studies broke new ground for this belief, and today much of the work of organization analysis is based on these findings. Even such scientific approaches as time and motion study have been enlarged to recognize the impact of behavior on production and performance.

The Behaviorists also gave attention to group dynamics, role performance, motivation, leadership, and human relationships in general. These studies have done much to enlighten the understanding of why people behave as they do. Through all these findings runs the notion that people do, indeed, have a variety of needs, ambitions, and expectations, and they form groups to aid in realizing and satisfying them. The tasks they perform in these groups, although they might be structured scientifically, cannot be carried out effectively using *only* the precepts of science as the basic guideline.

Recently, the so-called Japanese style of management and organization has received a great deal of attention from theorists and practitioners alike. This style is, in reality, a variation on a theme, so to speak. Whereas the Behaviorists emphasized the human element and involvement in the organization's processes, the Japanese style has taken this emphasis one step further.

The essence of this approach is that people will work harder and with more of a sense of commitment if they have job security (most Japanese workers have a guarantee of lifetime employment) and feel they have a significant part to play in decision making and group activity. The work groups are organized around large job assignments rather than the monotonous, routine snippets of work that characterize the assembly-line approach of the Classical School. General Motors plans to implement this approach in its Saturn plant in Tennessee, and has already experimented with it at its joint-venture-with-Toyota plant, NUMMI, in California. This human resources climate is well founded in the basic tenets of the Behavioral School.

The Behaviorists have been faulted for the incompleteness of their approach: critics have seen the contributions as incomplete in that the Behaviorists did not take the total set of functional relationships of the organization into account. Critics felt that many of the works of the Classicists were not given sufficient attention. For example, work methods, technology, and work design were assumed, according to critics. Nevertheless, it is safe to say that the present understanding of organization theory is in large measure a result of the work of the Behaviorists.

The Systems School

General systems theory has improved the appreciation of not only how the organization functions but also how it interacts with its environment. General systems theorists, among them Kenneth Boulding and Ludwig von Bertalanffy,[31] have suggested that organizations be considered as systems of resources combined in a fashion aimed at accomplishing some purpose. Thus, they saw organizations as being made up of an integrated set of components, each with a particular job to do.

These theorists argued that there were two views of systems: closed and open. A *closed system* is one that operates independently from its environment. In other words, the system is considered an entity unto itself without regard to outside influences. It has been said that the Classical view of organizations was essentially a closed-system view in that the organization analysis centered on the formal structure and its role without considering how its environment affected and was affected by it. On the other hand, the *open-systems* view holds that an analysis of organizations must take into account the ecology of the organization—how well it accommodates to its outside world.

The systems approach provides a macro perspective to the analysis and study of organizations by furnishing a framework for such an approach. This means that the approach makes it possible for the theorist to consider the effect that environmental dynamics (the turbulence and change that characterize today's society) are likely to have on the organization.

By using a general systems approach, the organization theorist can not only examine how component parts of the organization function together as a unit but also appreciate interorganization linkages.

One aspect of organization equilibrium is control, and the execution of this function has been greatly enhanced by the application of *cybernetics*, an essential component of systems theory. Norbert Weiner[32] and Stafford Beer[33] are two notable contributors to the application of cybernetics, the notion of the control of a system through the use of feedback from the environment of the system itself. For example, a thermostat regulates an air conditioner based on the air temperature around the thermostat. If the thermostat is set at seventy degrees Fahrenheit, it will allow the air conditioner to operate until that temperature is reached, then will automatically shut off the air conditioner. Once it is set, the thermostat regulates the air conditioning unit.

Jay Forrester has done research in an attempt to simulate the workings of an entire organization, and Martin Starr has been instrumental in using mathematical techniques for solving organization problems. These and other researchers have helped move organization theory to its present state of development.

The systems view, in short, is a means of appreciating how organization parts fit together and how organizations interact with their environment and with other organizations. It is a broad perspective that makes room for the application of both behavioral and quantitative methods to the study of the components of organizations traceable to the work of the Classicists and modified by the Behaviorists. Thus, the Systems School can be considered a contribution in itself and also a means of more fully using the contributions of the Classical and Behavioral Schools.

Application of systems concepts and principles to the study of organizations must be counted as a valuable aid to management and organization alike. The approach helps provide the orientation needed to keep the organization in a state of dynamic equilibrium with its environment—a condition essential for the modern organization.

The Contingency School

As its name implies, the Contingency School maintains that organization theory must be based on the open-systems concept, in contrast to the static view held by the Classicists. So, in a sense, contingency theory is built on the constructs devised by the Systems School.

The essence of the school is based on the proposition that an organization's relationship to other organizations, as well as to its total environment, "depends on the situation." Such a view requires both theorists and managers to be more adaptable, flexible, and even more ingenious in their decision-making processes. Thus, the contingency theory rejects the all-purpose principles and constructs espoused by the Classicists and substitutes for them a prescriptive, adaptive view of the organization.

One pioneer who was instrumental in moving organization theory to the contingency approach was Joan Woodward, who studied the effect of technology on the organization. Her empirical study was aimed at understanding why firms whose organization structures were built on classical foundations were not always the most successful from a commercial point of view. Woodward found that many variations in organization structure were associated with differences in manufacturing techniques. As Woodward pointed out:

> Different technologies imposed different kinds of demands on individuals and organizations, and these demands had to be met through an appropriate structure. Commercially successful firms seemed to be those in which function and form were complementary.[34]

In her research she found that many firms had established departments simply to appease an individual manager or to copy other firms in the industry that had already set up similar departments. There did not appear to be much objective thinking or justification for such arrangements.

Woodward's research demonstrated that the rules of the Classical School did not always work in practice.[35] Organization structure appeared to be a product of many more variables than the early Classicists had thought. Her testing of well-established practices and ideas meant that Woodward's research approach had set an important precedent in the evolution of organization theory. She argued that *knowledge* must replace *beliefs* and that such a replacement should be based on research.[36]

Woodward's ideas have left a lasting imprint on today's state of knowledge about how organizations work. The demonstration of a direct relationship between technology and the social structure of the organization was the main finding of Woodward's research. Organizations making technical advances tended to develop direct relationships between these advances and the similarities in their structures, for example, the length of chains of command, the spans of control of the chief executive, and the ratios of managers to total personnel.

Woodward's challenge to the unthinking application of the rules and guides of early Classical writers and her emphasis on empirical testing and analyses of organizations are among her most lasting contributions to contingency theory. She must be counted among those few researchers who have helped alter the evolution of organization theory into a more rational science.

Jay Galbraith also must be considered a major architect of organization theory as we know it today. He conducted studies of how the organization was established on the basis of the predictability of its tasks. The more certain the task, he found, the more the amount of activity that could be planned and the less was the need for continuous information flows through the organization.

Galbraith viewed the organization as a processor that kept in tune with the demands of its basic task environment by properly processing decision information. Coordination among the various components of the organization was necessary if it was to deal effectively with its task environment. Change in this environment required the addition of more coordinating devices to process information for tying the organization to its environment.[37] Organization structures were viewed as information processors designed to achieve coordination and integration among their component parts. This is now a well-established idea in contemporary organization thought.

Several authors have further developed some of the ideas of contingency thinking. One of these recent important contributors is James D. Thompson, whose work in the area of technology's effect on organizations is already a classic. His ideas are important because his work is not limited to business organizations, but is applicable to a wide variety of organizations. Thompson argued that organizations that experience similar technological and environmental problems will engage in similar behavior.[38]

This suggests that there should be similarities in organizing patterns among such organizations. This idea provides a point of departure for studying organizations; it should be fruitful to study organizations facing similar technological and environmental forces in order to determine how these organizations have been structured to accommodate to these forces.

Thompson was also a pioneer in stressing the necessity for analyzing the organization as an open system. It is simply not prudent to build an organization without considering how such forces as technology and the environment will affect the organization. Although it might be considered commonplace today, Thompson's concept of the organization as an open system is a landmark in the evolution of organization theory.

The concepts of an organization as an open system and the effect of technology on organizing efforts are key contributions to the evolution of organization theory. Thus, Thompson's work has helped us understand how the forces of technology and open environmental systems affect the organization.

Jay W. Lorsch and Paul R. Lawrence were among the first researchers to discover the contingent relationship between an organization and its environment. Their research demonstrated that successful organizations appear to be structured in a pattern that was consistent with environmental demands. This pattern of relationships was evident in the amount and nature of differentiation occurring in the organization.

Lorsch and Lawrence measured differentiation in terms of four basic components:

1. Formality of structure (reliance on rules, procedures, and so on)
2. Goal orientation (concern with market targets contrasted with concern with scientific goals)
3. Time orientation (short-term versus long-term)
4. Interpersonal orientation (concern for task accomplishment versus concern for interpersonal relationships)[39]

Thus, successful technical organizations would have structures with a minimum amount of formality, a scientific rather than a market goal orientation, and managers who have a long-term perspective coupled with a task orientation. These conditions, according to Lorsch and Lawrence, seem to best fit an organization to a highly technical task environment.

On the other hand, an organization such as a social club might have a market orientation, a considerable amount of formality in the form of ritual, a short-term perspective, and a concern for interpersonal relationships.

Successful organizations were found by Lorsch and Lawrence to have orientations consistent with their environments.[40] There was a contingent relationship, in other words, between these organizations and how they were structured to deal with their environments. These contingent relations resulted in more differentiation of the various parts of the organization. Environmental demands were thus formally recognized as an important factor in decisions about how to structure an organization.

Once the various components were differentiated, it was necessary to tie them together into an effective whole. This is the role of integration. A highly differentiated organization structure places a serious need on the organization to develop a coordination network among the many subunits. Thus, the real challenge for management is how to achieve a balance and an integrated pattern of relationships among the differentiated parts.

Lorsch and Lawrence stated the challenge to management well:

> ... organizations, to be economically successful, needed to meet environmental demands for both differentiation and integration, but they had to do this in spite of the fact that these two states were opposed to each other.[41]

In other words, the more differentiation required by the environment, the more necessary is the integration that, by the very nature of the differentiation, is difficult to achieve.

The significance of Lorsch and Lawrence's work is that it puts forth in clear perspective the effect of the environment on organizations and how they must differentiate and integrate activities and orientations to cope with this effect in a particular or contingent fashion. There are simply no ironclad formulas for structuring organizations, a point that is well established in modern organization theory.

TABLE 1.1

Evolution of Organization Theory

School	Major Concepts	Theoretical Foundations	Primary Writers
Classical (1890–1930)	Division of labor Scalar and functional processes Structure Span of control	Engineering Economics	Taylor, Mooney and Reiley, Weber, Gantt, Fayol, F. and L. Gilbreth, Graicunas
Behavioral (1930–1960)	Motivation/needs theory Communications Leadership theory Group dynamics Human relations	Psychology Sociology Social psychology	Follet, Barnard, McGregor, Maslow, Herzberg, Homans, Lewin
Systems (1960–Present)	Quantitative techniques Holism Open/closed Macro perspective Functionalism	Mathematics Engineering Computer science	von Bertalanffy, Boulding, Ackoff, Forrester, Kast and Rosenzweig
Contingency (1965–Present)	Open systems Prescriptive approach Dynamic relationships	Sociology Management and leadership studies Industrial engineering	Woodward, Thompson, Lorsch and Lawrence, Galbraith

In this section we have examined four schools of thought about organizations. The treatment was necessarily a survey because the intent was to highlight major developments and advances rather than to catalog them in detail. It is necessary to have this backdrop of historical perspective in order to appreciate more fully the present state of development of organization theory. Table 1.1 shows a summary of this evolution.

PLAN OF THE BOOK

The book is divided into five parts as depicted in Table 1.2. The first four parts consist of text material. The fifth part consists of comprehensive cases that require you to integrate and synthesize various concepts we de-

TABLE 1.2

Plan of the Book

Part One Introduction	Part Two The Organization's Linkage Systems	Part Three The Organization's Internal Environment	Part Four Organizational Dynamics	Integrative Cases
(Chapter 1) Organization Theory and the Manager	(Chapter 4) The Organization's External Linkages	(Chapter 7) Organizational Strategy: Coping with the External Environment	(Chapter 13) Organizational Culture	(Case 1) NASA: Mission Aborted
(Chapter 2) Organizations as Systems	(Chapter 5) Information Processing and Organizational Choices	(Chapter 8) Organizational Effectiveness and Goals	(Chapter 14) Power, Authority, and Politics in Organizations	(Case 2) IBM: Blue Skies
(Chapter 3) Macro-Environmental Components	(Chapter 6) Interorganizational Relationships	(Chapter 9) Organization Design: An Overview	(Chapter 15) Conflict in Organizations	(Case 3) Chrysler: You *Would* Buy a Used Car from This Man
		(Chapter 10) Patterns of Organization Design	(Chapter 16) Organizational Renaissance	(Case 4) Eastern Airlines: Clipped Wings
		(Chapter 11) Organization Size and Complexity		(Case 5) Shearson/American Express: A Leg to Stand On
		(Chapter 12) The Role of Technology		(Case 6) Bayer: Take Two Aspirin and . . .

scribe in the book and apply them to resolving organizational problems. In the book we move from a macro to a micro orientation, and conclude the text material with the concept of organization renewal and change.

SUMMARY

The job of the manager in today's complex organization is a complicated one indeed. The manager must not only deal with more involved issues but make quality decisions in a highly charged atmosphere characterized by discontinuous change. No longer is experience enough background to manage an organization. Instead, the manager must be able to call on an arsenal of sophisticated tools and techniques based on a sound knowledge of organizations—how they are put together and how they operate. Otherwise, the organization must surely suffer.

The potentially disastrous consequences can be avoided, however, if the manager commands a sound knowledge of organization theory. This theory can help him or her make quality decisions and successfully influence others to carry them out. It can help improve decision quality by making the manager aware of the various components of organization theory. To understand how they fit together as an explanation of the activity of the organization provides a perspective for seeing a decision's consequences.

The student of organization theory today should have a clear understanding of the four basic schools of thought on the subject. The Classical School first brought attention to the subject by its concentration on the nature of work and how it fits into building and maintaining an organization structure, seen as the cornerstone to understanding organizations.

The Behavioral School added to this base by stressing the necessity for understanding not only individual but group behavior and the role that the group plays in organization performance.

It was left to the Systems School to combine the findings and arguments of both the Classical and Behavioral Schools into what is termed a total understanding of organizations and how they work.

Finally, the Contingency theorists put forth the idea that the organization's relationship with its environment is properly viewed as flexible and prescriptive rather than as static and patent. This approach, indeed, represents one of the most productive developments in organization theory in the last decade.

Managerial effectiveness will improve as a result of the appreciation of how organizations function. Organization theory should then be included in the preparation of those who would assume managerial positions. Better quality decisions coupled with more effective implementation through better understanding of individual and group behavior can only bring improved performance to the organization.

QUESTIONS FOR REVIEW AND DISCUSSION

1. There has been considerable debate about the general relationship between theory and practice. How would you reconcile this debate in the field of organizations?
2. Describe and justify the components of organization theory. What other components would you add to the theory? Why?
3. How is organization theory related to management theory?
4. Why is an appreciation of the evolution of the field important to a student of organization theory today?
5. What are the essential foundations of the Classical School?
6. How did the Behavioral School view the works of the Classical School?
7. Who were the main contributors to the Behavioral School? What was the nature of their work?
8. What is the essence of the Systems School of organization theory?
9. What is meant by the term *contingency theory*?
10. How can a knowledge of organization theory improve the practice of management?

ENDNOTES

1. H. M. Blaylock, *Theory Building* (Englewood Cliffs, N.J.: Prentice-Hall, 1971).

2. Robert Dubin, *Theory Building* (New York: Free Press, 1969), 3.

3. Anant R. Negandhi, "Socio-Cultural Variables in Organizational Studies: A Critical Appraisal," in *Modern Organizational Theory*, ed. Anant Negandhi (Kent, Ohio: Kent State University Press, 1973), 313–342.

4. F. E. Emery and E. L. Trist, "The Causal Texture of Organizational Environments," *Human Relations* 18 (February 1965): 24.

5. James L. Gibson, John M. Ivancevich, and James H. Donnelly, Jr., *Organizations: Behavior, Structure and Processes* (Dallas: Business Publications, 1976), 4.

6. R. C. Davis, *The Fundamentals of Top Management* (New York: Harper & Row, 1951), 95–109.

7. Paul R. Lawrence and Jay W. Lorsch, "Differentiation and Integration in Complex Organizations," *Administrative Science Quarterly* (June 1967): 1–47.

8. Raymond E. Miles, *Theories of Management: Implications for Organizational Behavior and Development* (New York: McGraw-Hill, 1975), 21–24.

9. Lawrence and Lorsch, "Differentiation and Integration," 12.

10. Gerald G. Fisch, "Toward Effective Delegation," *CPA Journal* 46 (July 1976): 66–67.

11. John R. P. French and Bertram Raven, "The Bases of Social Power," in *Group Dynamics*, 2d ed., ed. Dorwin Cartwright and A. F. Zander (Evanston, Ill.: Row Peterson, 1960), 607–623.

12. Daniel Katz and Robert L. Kahn. *The Social Psychology of Organizations* (New York: John Wiley & Sons, 1966), 203.

13. Adam Smith, *An Inquiry Into the Nature and Causes of the Wealth of Nations*, in Great Books of the Western World, Vol. 39, *Encyclopedia Britannica*, 1952 (originally published in 1776).

14. Billy J. Hodge and Herbert J. Johnson, *Management and Organizational Behavior* (New York: John Wiley & Sons, 1970), 17.

15. Daniel A. Wren, *The Evolution of Management Thought* (New York: Ronald Press, 1972), 230.

16. A. M. Henderson and Talcott Parsons, eds. and trans., *Max Weber: The Theory of Social and Economic Organization* (New York: Free Press, 1947).

17. Wren, *Management Thought*, 234.

18. L. Anderson and F. T. Schwenning, *The Science of Production Organization* (New York: Wiley, 1938); and James D. Mooney and Alan C. Reiley, *Onward Industry!* (New York: Harper, 1931).

19. R. C. Davis, *The Fundamentals of Top Management* (New York: Harper & Row, 1951). This work was the culmination of work begun by Davis in the 1920s.

20. William G. Scott and Terence R. Mitchell, *Organization Theory: A Structural and Behavioral Analysis*, 3d ed. (Homewood, Ill.: Richard D. Irwin, 1976), 31–35.

21. Dexter S. Kimball, *Principles of Industrial Organization*, 3d ed. (New York: McGraw-Hill, 1925), xi and 20.

22. V. A. Graicunas, "Relationships in Organization," *Papers on the Science of Administration* (New York: Columbia University Press, 1937).

23. Theo Haimann and William G. Scott, *Management in the Modern Organization* (Boston: Houghton Mifflin, 1970), Chapter 15.

24. Mooney and Reiley, *Onward Industry!*

25. Wren, *Management Thought*, 439.

26. Elton Mayo, *The Human Problems of an Industrial Civilization* (New York: Macmillan, 1933); and Fritz Roethlisberger and William J. Dickenson, *Management and the Worker* (Cambridge, Mass.: Harvard University Press, 1939).

27. Chester I. Barnard, *The Functions of the Executive* (Cambridge, Mass.: Harvard University Press, 1938).

28. A. H. Maslow, "A Theory of Human Motivation," *Psychological Review* 50 (1943): 370–396.

29. Frederick Herzberg, Barnard Mausner, and Barbara B. Synderman, *The Motivation to Work* (New York: John Wiley & Sons, 1959).

30. George C. Homans, *The Human Group* (New York: Harcourt Brace, 1950).

31. Kenneth E. Boulding, "General Systems Theory—The Skeleton of Science," *Management Science* (April 1956): 197–208; and Ludwig von Bertalanffy,

"General Systems Theory—A Critical Review," in *Modern Systems Research for the Behavioral Scientist*, ed. Walter Buckley (Chicago: Aldine, 1968).

32. Norbert Weiner, *The Human Use of Human Beings*, rev. ed. (New York: Doubleday Anchor Books, 1954).

33. Stafford Beer, *Cybernetics and Management* (New York: John Wiley & Sons, 1959).

34. Joan Woodward, *Industrial Organization: Theory and Practice* (Oxford University Press, 1965), vi.

35. Ibid., 242.

36. Ibid., 25.

37. Jay Galbraith, "Environmental and Technological Determinants of Organization Design," in *Studies in Organization Design*, ed. Jay W. Lorsch and Paul R. Lawrence (Homewood, Ill.: Richard D. Irwin and the Dorsey Press, 1970), 113–139.

38. James D. Thompson, *Organizations in Action* (New York: McGraw-Hill, 1967), 1 and 39–65.

39. Jay W. Lorsch and Paul R. Lawrence, *Studies in Organization Design* (Homewood, Ill.: Richard D. Irwin and the Dorsey Press, 1970), 6.

40. Ibid., 6–7.

41. Ibid., 8.

ANNOTATED BIBLIOGRAPHY

Barnard, Chester. *The Functions of the Executive*. Cambridge, Mass.: Harvard University Press, 1939.

This is a landmark book by a top executive dealing with the essentials of running an organization. The content is not dated. Particular attention is paid to communication and the proper use and understanding of authority.

Bolman, Lee G., and Deal, Terrence F. *Modern Approaches to Understanding and Managing Organizations*. San Francisco: Jossey-Bass, 1984.

This book makes a significant contribution to the literature. Not only does it provide an interesting historical sketch, but it also provides a valuable synthesis of management concepts. The authors feel that many organizational problems result from managers who possess personal theories that are either too simplistic or too narrow in scope. Successful managers are people who are able to blend differing viewpoints about organizations into a comprehensive framework.

Boulding, Kenneth E. "General Systems Theory—The Skeleton of Science." *Management Science* (April 1956): 197–208.

Boulding's article is a concise and enduring statement of the concept, meaning, and intent of general systems theory. The importance and usefulness of this powerful idea shine through clearly in this work from the early years of this theory.

Breeze, John D. "Henri Fayol's Basic Tools of Administration." In *Academy of Management Proceedings* 81, edited by Kae H. Chung, 101–105. San Diego, Calif.: Academy of Management, 1981.

In 1923, Henri Fayol advocated five basic tools for successful administration. This paper traces the development of the particular techniques that he subsequently decided were of the greatest importance to successful management.

Carroll, Stephen J., and Gellen, Dennis J. "The Classical Management Functions: Are They Really Outdated?" *Academy of Management Proceedings* 84, edited by John A. Pearce, II and Richard B. Robinson, Jr., 132–136. Boston: Academy of Management, 1984).

This paper argues that the classical management functions are not "folklore," but represent valid abstractions about what managers actually do and should do. The authors conclude that the descriptions of the classical management functions have relevance for managerial work description. Moreover, the skills associated with these functions are directly related to organization effectiveness.

Daft, Richard L. *Organization Theory and Design*. St. Paul, Minn.: West, 1983.

This book is written for the student, teacher, or manager who wants to understand organizations and work effectively in them. The text makes effective use of examples from real organizations, focuses exclusively on organization theory concepts, and makes effective use of current research in order to describe the usefulness, interest, and applicability of organization theory concepts.

Dale, Earnest; Greenwood, Regina S.; and Greenwood, Ronald G. "Donaldson Brown: GM's Pioneer Management Theorist and Practitioner." In *Academy of Management Proceedings* 80, edited by Richard C. Huseman, 119–124. Detroit, Mich.: Academy of Management, 1980.

Donaldson Brown was the originator of ROI, an architect of General Motors's management structure, and one of the conceptualizers of the decentralization and coordinated control concept. He was one of the most influential management and organization theorists at GM, and this paper presents some of his contributions.

Davis, R. C. *The Fundamentals of Top Management*. New York: Harper & Row, 1951.

This book represents a culmination of previous organization theory to the date of its publication. Davis sets down the basics of organization structure and process in a way that serves as the skeleton of modern organization theory. Much thought is also given to the management of the properly designed organization.

Dubin, Robert. *Handbook of Work, Organization and Society*. Chicago: Rand McNally, 1976.

This book must rank as one of the finest readings concerning the subject of work. Work is explored as it relates to individuals within the organization and as it relates to the organization itself within society.

Hill, Walter A. *Readings in Organizational Theory: A Behavioral Approach*. Boston, Mass.: Allyn and Bacon, 1976.

Extensive attention is directed toward the external and the internal environment of the organization. Also discussed is how the organization's internal social variables and the external environment variables act on the administrative processes of the organization.

Homans, George C. *The Human Group*. New York: Harcourt, Brace, Jovanovich, 1950.

This book is a synthesis of behavioral knowledge to its date of publication, and it represents the pioneering work on the relationship of organizations, productivity, and group membership. It is interesting and useful because it is a forerunner of modern organization behavior thinking.

Koontz, Harold. "The Management Theory Jungle Revisited." *Academy of Management Review* 5, no. 2 (April 1980): 475–487.

The various schools and approaches to management theory identified by Dr. Koontz twenty years ago and called "The Management Theory Jungle" are revisited. He now finds eleven distinct approaches compared to the original six, and implies that the jungle may be getting more diverse and impenetrable. However, certain developments are occurring that may indicate that there might be some movement toward a unified and practical theory of management.

Locke, Edwin A. "The Ideas of Frederick W. Taylor: An Evaluation." *Academy of Management Review* 7, no. 1 (January 1982): 14–24.

The ideas and techniques of Frederick W. Taylor are examined with respect to their validity and acceptance by modern management. Concerning the principles of scientific decision making and techniques such as time study, standardization, goal setting, money as a motivator, scientific selection, and rest pauses, Taylor's views were fundamentally correct and have been generally accepted.

Martin, Lowell G. "A View of Work Toward the Year 2000." *Personnel Journal* 56 (October 1977): 502–505.

This article reveals the effects of technological change on work functions. It discusses modification in managerial philosophies as a result of organizational change and the resulting influence on the individual within the organization.

Miller, Danny, and Friesen, Peter H. *Organizations: A Quantum View*. Englewood Cliffs, N.J.: Prentice-Hall, 1984.

This book is a recent contribution to contingency theories of organization structure. It extends the earlier work of Burns and Stalker (1961), Woodward (1965), Lawrence and Lorsch (1967), and Mintzberg (1979), both theoretically and methodologically. Further, it summarizes an ambitious and successful program of research on organization structure, strategy, structural change, and entrepreneurial behavior.

Osborn, Richard N.; Hunt, James G.; and Jauch, Lawrence R. *Organization Theory: An Integrated Approach*. New York: John Wiley & Sons, 1980.

Macro aspects of organization theory are discussed through a top-down organization of the chapters, starting at the environment and total organization, moving down into the organization, and ending at the work unit level.

Robbins, Steven P. *Organization Theory: The Structure and Design of Organizations*. Englewood Cliffs, N.J.: Prentice-Hall, 1983.

This contemporary text on organization theory covers the contemporary material in a rigorous fashion while being interesting and relevant to the reader. The text identifies the essential issues of organization theory in clear and concise English, relies heavily upon the use of examples, and gives particular attention to the political factors affecting structural decisions in organizations.

Thompson, James D. *Organizations in Action*. New York: McGraw-Hill, 1967.
Thompson's little book on organization theory is a landmark in the field. It is primarily a collection of propositions about the behavior of organizations, backed up by thought-provoking, if tantalizingly spare, discussion of applicable concepts.

Wren, Daniel A. *The Evolution of Management Thought*. 2d ed. New York: Ronald Press, 1979.
An outstanding work in the field of management history, comprehensive in all respects and written in a readable and witty style. Pertinent information and citation on all areas of evolving managerial theory and practice is included. It is a master source book.

ADDITIONAL REFERENCES

Baker, C. R. "Personnel and Organizational Structure Factors in Planning." *Managerial Plan* 25 (May 1977): 26–28.

Bedeian, Arthur G. *Organizations: Theory and Analysis*. Hinsdale, Ill.: Dryden Press, 1980.

Cappa and Avery, Consultants. *Contingency Planning and Management: A Bibliographical Guide*. Monticello, Ill.: Vance Bibliographies, 1985.

Chandler, Alfred, Jr. *Strategy and Structure*. Cambridge, Mass.: MIT Press, 1963.

Dornbush, Sanford M., and Scott, Richard W. *Evolution and the Exercise of Authority*. San Francisco: Jossey-Bass, 1975.

Freeland, J. R., and Moore, J. H. "Implications of Resource Directive Allocation Models for Organizational Design." *Management Science* 23 (June 1977): 1050–1059.

Gerloff, Edwin A. *Organization Theory and Design: A Strategic Approach for Management*. New York: McGraw-Hill, 1985.

Graicunas, V. A. "Relationships in Organization." *Papers on the Science of Administration*. New York: Columbia University Press, 1937.

La Porte, Todd R. *Organized Social Complexity*. Princeton: Princeton University Press, 1975.

Lawrence, Barbara S. "Historical Perspective: Using the Past to Study the Present." *Academy of Management Review* 9, no. 2 (April 1984): 307–312.

Miner, John B. *Theories of Organizational Structure and Processes*. Hinsdale, Ill.: Dryden Press, 1982.

Mooney, James D., and Reiley, Alan C. *Onward Industry!* New York: Harper & Row, 1931.

Pfeffer, Jeffrey. *Organizations and Organization Theory*. Marshfield, Mass.: Pitman, 1983.

Roethlisberger, Fritz, and Dickson, William J. *Management and the Worker*. Cambridge, Mass.: Harvard University Press, 1937.

Scott, William G., and Mitchell, Terence R. *Organization Theory: A Structural and Behavioral Analysis*. 3d ed. Homewood, Ill.: Richard D. Irwin, 1976.

Simon, Herbert. *The New Science of Management Decision*. New York: Harper & Row, 1960.

Steers, R. M. "When Is an Organization Effective? A Process Approach to Understanding Effectiveness." *Organizational Dynamics* 5 (August 1976): 50–63.

Veiga, John F., and Yanouzas, John N. *The Dynamics of Organization Theory: Gaining a Macro Perspective*. 2d ed. St. Paul, Minn.: West, 1984.

Warren, J. R. "Diagnosis of the Potential for Organizational Improvement." *Personnel Journal* 56 (June 1977): 302–304.

Weiner, Norbert. *Cybernetics*. Cambridge, Mass.: MIT Press, 1948.

Weiner, Norbert. *The Human Use of Human Beings*. Boston: Houghton Mifflin, 1950.

Woodward, Joan. *Industrial Organization: Theory and Practice*. London: Oxford University Press, 1965.

C A S E

New Luster at Johnson Wax

Like many other large organizations, S. C. Johnson and Son (Johnson Wax) had become set in its ways, and, until recent business reversals "awakened" the company, it had been operating in a stagnation mode since the late 1970s.

From its founding in 1886 until the late 1970s, the company had become a giant in the home products field, becoming famous for such products as Johnson Wax, Pledge furniture polish, Raid bug spray, and so on. In fact, aggressiveness and innovation were company watchwords as product after product was introduced into the marketplace. Moreover, the company had a philosophy of never introducing a new product that did not have a demonstrable point of superiority over that of its competitors. If the product was not superior, then it simply would not be introduced into the marketplace.

However, a cumbersome bureaucracy lacking in innovation and proper judgment, along with a stagnating economy, soon caused the firm's market share and revenues to shrink. Characterized by a corporate culture that was risk-aversive, in combination with marketing and acquisition blunders that developed the wrong product or acquired the wrong business at the wrong time (e.g., moving away from packaged consumer goods to recreational equipment), Johnson Wax soon lost its luster. A former 12 percent annual sales growth plummeted to 0 percent annual sales growth, and annual earnings of $60 million in 1980 were the same in 1984.

With the entrance of new blood in the person of S. C. Johnson, III, son of chairman and CEO, S. C. Johnson, II, the company has begun to turn its fortunes around. The company culture is now characterized as aggressive. The most apparent change with this new attitude is Johnson's entrance into the venture capital business, whereby funds are invested in such diverse growth industries as fast foods, drugs, and voice mail. Rather than take the entire risk upon itself, Johnson has raised additional investment funds from other partner institutions and individuals. Concerning partnerships, Johnson has entered the lucrative personal care and over-the-counter drug markets through its licensing agreement with Sweden's Halsa. Johnson will market and sell Halsa products such as botanical conditioners and shampoos. This decision, made in 1985, was based on a Johnson in-house study conducted in 1977 that determined that personal care, particularly skin care, would be the next big opportunity for the company. Hence, the later licensing agreement with Halsa. Because past company success was attributed to new product development and marketing, the firm has recently launched three new home-consumer products and is test marketing twelve others. Moreover, after thorough market testing and the use of promotional techniques, Johnson is reintroducing products that previously had "bombed."

Sources: "Trying to Bring Out the Old Shine at Johnson Wax," *Business Week* (August 13, 1984), 138–145; L. Freeman, "S. C. Johnson Shines with New Products," *Advertising Age* (June 10, 1985), 4; L. Freeman, "Johnson Hopes to Clean Up with Aveeno," *Advertising Age* (November 11, 1985), 41.

To ensure that these new endeavors are successful, Johnson has reduced its work force and modified its management structure. Taking advantage of early retirement programs, about 3,500 employees have left the company. A matrix organization structure has been introduced to motivate managers who traditionally have been preoccupied with their own particular function, for example, marketing, manufacturing, finance, and so on. The firm is now organized along enterprise units—personal care, home care, chemicals, and insecticides. Within each enterprise unit are individual representatives responsible for marketing, finance, research, and manufacturing.

The research and development function has been bolstered at Johnson through a 40 percent increase in its budget, and a new chief scientific officer now controls subordinates who previously reported to the all-powerful marketing managers. But Johnson will not enter new markets without first having a basic mastery of applicable technologies. In this regard, Johnson has maintained its preeminence in monomer and polymer film coating techniques.

The need to respond faster to tougher competition and to take advantage of environmental opportunities has caused S. C. Johnson and Son, Inc. to face outward toward a long-term, successful future.

QUESTIONS FOR DISCUSSION

1. How do changes in the external environment, more specifically, in the area of competition, spur a company such as Johnson to action?
2. How could a large successful company such as Johnson stagnate in the late 1970s and early 1980s?
3. Discuss the issues of aggressiveness and passiveness as they relate to an organization's approach and performance. Is it ever proper to be passive? Explain your answer.

2

Organizations as Systems

<table>
<tr><td colspan="2" style="text-align:center">K   E   Y</td></tr>
<tr><td colspan="2" style="text-align:center">C O N C E P T S</td></tr>
</table>

Systems
Interdependency
Holism
Synergism
Subsystems
Open systems
Closed systems
Entropy
Negative entropy
Functionalism
Static systems
Dynamic systems
Abstract systems
Concrete systems
State-maintaining systems
Goal-seeking systems
Multigoal-seeking and
purposive systems
Purposeful systems
Equifinality
Cybernetic system
Servo-mechanisms
Input–output analysis
Transformation process
Feedback
Bounded rationality
Micro–intermediate–macro
environments
Environmental linkages
Alternative models of
organizations
General systems approach

Staying at the Cornhusker

The Cornhusker Hotel in Lincoln, Nebraska, is a very successful organization because it delivers a superior product (hotel service) to a market clamoring for more. All aspects of the hotel's operations are tied together into a finely tuned and interdependent system that provides guests with such high-quality service that *Lodging* magazine recently featured the hotel as its cover story.

Much of the credit for the hotel's success goes to hotel manager Dave Green, who learned about hotel operations as a young man by doing a little bit of everything—food and beverage control, marketing, personnel training, conventions, and even housekeeping. Green was contacted by the First National Bank of Lincoln in 1978 after it had bought the recently closed "old" Cornhusker. The bank wanted Green to conduct a feasibility study to assess the plausibility of a hotel project on the site—that is, should the hotel be renovated or razed and rebuilt?

Green first sought inputs from those who suffered the most from the hotel's demise—the Chamber of Commerce, the Convention Bureau, bankers, merchants, and state government. Green discovered there was an incredible amount of community support for reopening the hotel, and that the potential for hotel business on the site would be comprised of (1) 50 to 60 percent conventions, (2) 30 to 35 percent corporate and transient, (3) 6 to 7 percent state government and education, and (4) 3 to 4 percent tourists.

In conjunction with the city of Lincoln and private developers, Green came up with an urban development concept. The city would build a 400-stall parking garage, a convention center with 11,500 square feet, and a four-story atrium, architecturally stun-

Source: Jim Pearson, "Resurrection of a Legend," *Lodging* 9, no. 10 (July 1984): 37–44.

ning, as a passageway between the various buildings. Private funds, in turn, would resurrect the old Cornhusker into a ten-story, 304-room hotel, with 206,000 square feet, and an office building (joined to the hotel by the atrium), seven stories high with 140,000 square feet. The resulting renovation and building project cost $41 million and proved to be the biggest project in Lincoln since the opening of the state capitol building.

The completed project is a stunning accomplishment, and demonstrates how the successful organization is run as an open system, which, in turn, is comprised of numerous interrelated subsystems.

The most elaborate subsystem of the Cornhusker system is comprised of the hotel's restaurants. Tom Rhoubin, director of food and beverages and catering, learned his craft by experience as a waiter, maitre d', bartender, banquet manager, houseman, restaurant manager, front-office manager, hotel general manager, and director of sales.

Among the hotel's restaurants and banquet rooms, the most outstanding is the Renaissance Room, a large party/banquet room that seats 137 people. There are also four smaller party rooms that lead directly from the Renaissance. These smaller rooms are popular for social and business functions, both for noon and evenings.

Making the restaurants profitable is partially a result of the efforts of the staff, who have made the entire food service and restaurant process more efficient by learning to minimize waste. They gauge preparation needs by reviewing previous requisitions versus leftovers.

The Cornhusker offers unique buffets that are special favorites, not only for hotel guests, but for the local population as well. Friday night is seafood buffet night. Rhoubin came up with the idea after noting that there were no seafood buffets advertised in the local papers. Wednesday night is international buffet night, featuring dishes from five countries on a revolving basis. Sunday is famous for its brunches. These special buffets are so popular that they take place in the Renaissance Room where there is enough space, although the hotel has five other restaurants located in its facility. Rhoubin and the hotel management plan to open a dinner theater in an adjoining building to boost weekend business and to broaden the family market.

Concomitant with the restaurant subsystem is the food preparation subsystem. Head chef Marcel Bonetti orders his food strictly by specifications to ensure quality, and different items are ordered regularly from different parts of the country—fresh beef twice a week from Chicago, fresh seafood weekly from Boston. Bonetti's rules are, "Know your purchasing, and rule no. 2 is, know your receiving. In brief, specify what you want and get what you order." Rule no. 3 is recipe cooking. Bonetti supervises four kitchens, for which he supplies recipe manuals with written instructions for quantity, ingredients, method, timing, temperature, and yield.

When Green's feasibility study determined that 60 to 70 percent of the hotel's business would be conventions, he knew that it was imperative to set up a convention subsystem that would not only attract this type of business, but ensure repeat business. Jeanne Harvey, the Cornhusker's convention sales manager, worked at the old Cornhusker and knew the accounts. She reviewed a list of 700 state associations in Nebraska that held conventions attended by at least 150 people, and within months, she had contacted 293 prospects, set up alphabetical files, color-coded entries to indicate whether they were regional, state, university-related, or government-related. The result—the Cornhusker booked more than $6 million worth of convention business during its first year of operations.

Two important features enhance the Cornhusker's attractiveness as a convention center. First, the hotel and its immediate surroundings are like a "city under one roof." No matter how brutal the weather, visitors can move by skywalks anywhere within a five-block radius to shops, parking areas, office buildings, and restaurants. Second, the convention staff sets up meeting and function rooms the night before, which is a great improvement over having a meeting planner arrive at an unprepared function room at 9:00 A.M.

Housekeeping is another essential function in the Cornhusker system. The housekeeping staff consists of seventeen maids, three inspectresses, one inspector, one laundry supervisor, eight laundry workers, four janitors, two housemen, and six night workers. They all work together to provide the lodging industry's most priceless product—clean rooms. All personnel are first trained to clean rooms. This subsystem works so efficiently that if the hotel has to check out 200 people and check in another 200 within an hour, the housekeeping staff can handle it.

The reception a hotel guest receives creates a strong first impression. The Cornhusker pays special attention to this particular aspect of its overall system, and four doormen, three chauffeurs, six bellmen, eight desk personnel, and four reservations personnel are on hand to serve incoming guests. Indeed, the chauffeurs are perhaps the greatest symbol of the quality of this particular operation. They offer their services, at no charge, to and from the airport as well as to all corporate headquarters in the Lincoln area.

The resurrection and current operation of the Cornhusker provide an excellent example of how a complex organization is, in reality, an open system in which various parts are combined and interact in a way that achieves a goal in the most effective and efficient manner.

The Cornhusker Hotel, like any organization, is an example of an organization operating as a system. The parts work *together*. The restaurant complements the lodging. Banquets and conventions complement lodging and restaurants. Service, style, and decor blend into a functioning whole.

Not all organizations illustrate the smooth-running system idea as exemplified by the Cornhusker. But they should. Organizations are made up of interrelated parts that must work together for maximum effectiveness. Production, marketing, personnel, and accounting all must complement and support each other. Interrelated product lines must, in fact, interrelate. Departments that need to work together must interact smoothly. In short, the right hand needs to know what the left hand is doing. The systems view helps us to understand the issue of coordination.

CHAPTER PLAN

The material in this chapter is aimed at explaining how organizations function as systems. We discuss the concepts of the general systems approach and look at the organization as a totally open system. We also examine the advantages and disadvantages of studying organizations using a systems approach and consider some elements to take into account when designing the organization from a systems perspective. We next briefly examine some alternative approaches to the systems concept. Finally, we relate organization theory to the general systems approach.

In our study of organizations we are taking a systems view.* The major reason for adopting a systems view is that it facilitates the development of an overall framework that integrates the various facets involved in understanding organizations. The systems approach allows us to better consider the major forces and variables, both in the external environment and in the organization, that have a major bearing on how and why organizations act as they do. It allows us to establish an integrating framework to identify these factors and to determine where and how they impact organizations.

This chapter introduces the systems approach. Major concepts are defined and their applications are made to organizations as systems. Our intent is to use the systems approach not only to describe how organizations operate but also to prescribe how they should operate. Each of the following sections examines various components of the operation of organization systems.

*Although we are adopting a systems perspective to examine organizations, we do not mean to imply that every aspect of an organization or of our theory of organizations will be examined from a systems perspective. Rather, the systems perspective enables us to develop an overall model of organizations.

DEFINITION OF CONCEPTS IN THE GENERAL SYSTEMS APPROACH

Because the application of the systems approach to the field of management evolved from the areas of engineering, operations analysis, production management, and computers, many students believe that the approach requires using mathematical equations, sophisticated quantitative methods, and computer technology. Although the systems approach can be, and often is, expressed using mathematical notation, it need not be expressed in those terms. In this book we use some terminology from computer science and we use some diagrams and flow charts. However, we will not use mathematical notation. While the quantification and mathematical expression of relationships in organization theory is a worthwhile pursuit, this application of the systems approach is better left to advanced graduate courses in organization theory.

Systems

Most individuals are familiar with the word *system* and use it in everyday language. We speak of heating systems, communication systems, economic systems, transportation systems, plumbing systems, and electrical systems. We even talk of cultural and social systems. The word *system* is used because it conveys the idea that these things are made up of parts and that the parts somehow interact with each other for some purpose or reason. The definition we will use for *system* conveys this same idea. A system is an organized or complex whole—an assemblage or combination of things or parts performing as a complex or unitary whole.[1]

This definition implies several ideas. First is the concept of *interdependency*. The parts that make up a system are interdependent. If a change occurs in one part or set of parts, it affects all other parts of the system. This effect on each part in the system may be direct or indirect. For example, in a telephone system the quality of the transmission cables will directly affect the efficiency of the switching equipment and thus the overall performance of the system. However, repainting the maintenance vehicles will have little direct, immediate effect on the operation of the overall system. Thus, the change in a particular part or set of parts of the system will have a direct or indirect effect on the system, depending on the importance, role, and function of the part.

A second implication of the definition of a system is the concept of *holism*. This means that the system should be considered as a functioning whole. Changes in parts of the system and in the functioning of elements of the system should be considered from the standpoint of the system's overall performance. In the telephone example, any changes in the quality of transmission mechanisms not only directly affect the switching mechanisms but also have a direct effect on the total performance of the system. This concept of holism requires one to consider the performance of all aspects of the system when introducing change into one component of the system. For example, we would not be interested in developing a video transmitting and receiving device for telephones unless we had the switching system to handle such transmissions. Nor would we create such a video service for home use if the cost of the service were substantially greater than present telephone service. Finally, we would not even be interested in such a service unless customers, an integral part of the system, desired it. All parts of the system must be considered.

A third concept implied by the definition is *synergism*. This refers to the interactive effect of the parts of the system working together. The actual interaction of the parts creates an effect greater than the effect of the parts acting separately. A football team is synergistic in that as a team, members can accomplish more on the field than they can as individuals. The key concept is that as each part of the system performs its role, it enhances the performance of other parts and hence the total performance of the system. In fact, this is usually why the parts are brought together in the first place.

As we saw in our introductory case, the Cornhusker Hotel is a combination of interdependent units. Lodging, housekeeping, food service, banquets, and so on all fit together to make up the Cornhusker experience. Should one of these parts malfunction, it is quite probable that guests' perceptions of the entire Cornhusker system would be affected; thus, all units of the hotel depend on each other to make up a functioning whole. Moreover, the Cornhusker experience is more than the sum of its different operations. Guest satisfaction is a result of synergism, the interactive effect resulting from the smooth interaction of all hotel functions.

Subsystems

Closely related to the concept of holism is the analysis of subsystems within a system. *Subsystems* are a group of functioning elements within a larger system. They are systems within larger systems. In our telephone example, the customer billing system is a subsystem of the ABC Telephone Company accounting system. The accounting system is a subsystem of the telephone system. The ABC Telephone Company is a subsystem of the entire telephone system in the United States. The telephone system is a subsystem of the nationwide telecommunications system.

The determination of subsystems depends on the desired level of abstraction at a given time for a desired type of analysis. If we are concerned with the overall functioning of the telecommunications system in the

United States, we would be concerned not only with the functioning of the telephone system but also with the functioning of this system as it relates to the functioning of radio and television broadcasting, telegraph, and teletype systems.

On the other hand, if we are attempting to improve the accounting system of the ABC Telephone Company, we would be concerned with the information flows, financial statements, billing system, and use of an electronic data system within the accounting system. The accounting system would be the system and the other facets would constitute subsystems. Determining what is considered the system and what are considered the subsystems depends on the purpose of the analysis.

These relationships can be summarized for our telephone example as shown in Figure 2.1. Of course, this figure could be carried to the extreme in either direction. It could be extended upward to the business system, economic system, cultural system, and, after several more levels of abstraction, to the universe. It could also be extended downward to points of further specificity until we got to the level of atoms and their parts. In a technical sense, all systems are subsystems of the universe, and all systems can be carried to the level of specificity of the atom. Although these levels of abstraction and specificity are certainly necessary for some scientists, such as physicists and chemists, we in management normally are not interested in either of these two extremes of any system. Basically, we are interested in examining organizations as systems. For some purposes, we will view them as subsystems of a larger system such as an industry group. For other purposes, we will view their components—production, marketing, and so on—as subsystems of the organization.

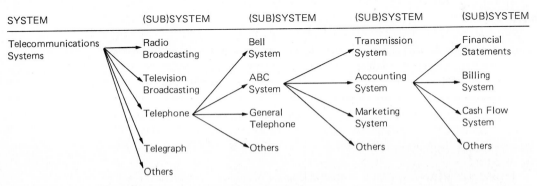

SYSTEM	(SUB)SYSTEM	(SUB)SYSTEM	(SUB)SYSTEM	(SUB)SYSTEM
Telecommunications Systems	Radio Broadcasting	Bell System	Transmission System	Financial Statements
	Television Broadcasting	ABC System	Accounting System	Billing System
	Telephone	General Telephone	Marketing System	Cash Flow System
	Telegraph	Others	Others	Others
	Others			

FIGURE 2.1

An Example of Systems and Subsystems for the Telecommunications Industry

Open–Closed Systems

The concept of subsystem analysis leads us to consider *open* and *closed* systems. An open system is a system that interacts with its environment, usually a larger system. A closed system does not interact with its environment. All biological and social systems are open systems. The environment not only affects but is affected by the system. However, at any point at a given level of analysis, a system may be considered closed even though it does, over time, interact with its environment. This may happen, for example, when a system attempts to temporarily isolate or insulate itself from its immediate environment.

The railway industry in the late 1960s had approached a closed system with regard to passenger service—an important part of its immediate environment. It was difficult for potential passengers to make reservations; there was little advertising by railroads for passenger service; passenger trains were eliminated from runs; new cars were not ordered; old ones were not remodeled; and passenger train stations were closed. Officials of the railroads apparently believed people would rather drive, fly, or ride the bus. They also believed that by concentrating on freight service they could maximize their profit.

However, this changed when Congress passed a bill creating Amtrak. The fuel shortage also affected the actions of the railroads. Now they have a toll-free number for passenger reservations; they are advertising; new trains and schedules have been added; new cars have been purchased; old ones remodeled; and train stations have been remodeled and new ones built. The system is now interacting more with its environment. In short, railroads now operate more as an open system with regard to passenger service. Thus, for analytical purposes, it is appropriate to view the open–closed systems concept as a continuum rather than a dichotomy.

Systems that are closed begin to suffer *entropy* at some point; that is, they expend more energy than they are able to replace from the outside. Eventually such systems deteriorate and die. It is for this reason that all biological systems are open systems. It is a matter of survival. Organizations must also be open for the same reason. In fact, by remaining open the organization tries to achieve *negative entropy*—the ability to take in at least as much energy as is expended. This keeps the system from deteriorating.

INTELSAT, a 110-member commercial cooperative that owns and operates a global communications satellite system, provides an excellent example of an organization that faced entropy, and, fortunately for it, turned its fortunes around in order to achieve negative entropy.

Before 1983, the organization had conducted no external analyses of trends and changes in the level of use of its satellite systems. By 1984, INTELSAT began to experience entropy, for example, severe revenue shortfalls and communications traffic backup. This occurred as a result of competing technology and changes in U. S. government policy concerning INTELSAT's "monopoly." However, by the fall of 1986, the organization had redirected its efforts so that, as an organizational system, it once again achieved negative entropy—sufficient revenues and well-managed communications traffic. This turnaround was accomplished by implementing changes that enabled INTELSAT's management to better appreciate and prepare for external changes that affected their system. These changes included internal restructuring, introducing new technology, and implementing more aggressive marketing strategies. In other words, the organization became an open system, interacting with its external environment.[2]

Functionalism

Functionalism attempts to look at social systems in terms of structures, processes, and functions in order to understand the relationship between these components. It focuses on the question, How does the system work or function? It differs from a pure systems approach in that it attempts to *explain* rather than simply *describe* the operation of a system. It is part of a modern systems philosophy in management, however, in that we not only want to describe the operation of a system but we also want to analyze it, explain why it works as it does, and learn what can be done to control its operation.

A useful concept of functionalism is the *functional–dysfunctional* continuum. When a part or subsystem of the system efficiently aids the system in its overall operation, it is termed *functional*. When a part or subsystem of the system hinders the overall operation of the system, this part or subsystem is termed *dysfunctional*. This concept is useful because it enables judgments to be made about the efficiency and effectiveness of subsystems. It enables us to relate a given change in a part of the system to the overall operation of the system.

For example, say that salespeople in a business organization wish to increase the number of products sold. To do this, they may secure more orders than can be produced in a given time period with the firm's physical and human resources. They may also extend credit very liberally, thus increasing the possibility of poor credit risks. Thus, the salespeople's desire to maximize sales may be dysfunctional to the organization's goal of maximizing profit. To meet the higher number of orders, marginal obsolete equipment may need to be put back into use; the work force may need to work overtime; and product quality may suffer. A liberal credit policy may significantly increase the bad-debt loss experienced by the firm. Thus, these increasing costs may be significantly greater than the extra revenue generated by the higher sales. Profit would actually be less at the higher level of sales than at the previous level.

Static and Dynamic Systems

Systems can be either static or dynamic. A *static* system is one in which no changes take place, while a *dynamic* system is one whose states change over time.[3] A table is an example of a static system since it consists of four legs, top, glue, screws, and so on, and it changes very little over time. Most social and biological systems are dynamic because they change over time. A university is a dynamic system since new students enter, others graduate or drop out, faculty and staff come and go, courses and methods of teaching change, and the physical plant changes.

Again, as with other systems concepts, this should not be viewed as a dichotomy but rather as a continuum. For a given time interval at a given level of analysis, a system may be considered rather static. However, over a longer period of time at another level of analysis, it may be dynamic. In the table analysis, over a long time period, say ten years, the table is dynamic in that the varnish wears and cracks, the glue becomes loose causing the legs to wobble, and the color changes as it is exposed to the elements.

Abstract and Concrete Systems

An *abstract* system is composed of ideas or concepts. A *concrete* system is composed of physical components. A mathematical formula is an abstract system. A particular manufacturing plant with its production process is a concrete system. Most social and biological systems are composed of both concrete and abstract elements. For example, a business organization is composed of physical and material resources as well as a philosophy, ideas, objectives, and operational policies.

Behavioral Classification of Systems[*]

Systems can be classified into one of four behavioral categories, depending on how they function. These are as follows:

1. State-maintaining
2. Goal-seeking
3. Multigoal-seeking and purposive
4. Purposeful

[*]Most of the material in this section has been developed from Ackoff, "Systems Concept," 665–667.

A *state-maintaining* system reacts in a *specific* way to a given internal or external event to produce the *same* internal or external state (outcome). It only reacts to changes. A homeheating unit with a thermostat is a state-maintaining system. A department-store sprinkler system that reacts to heat or smoke from a fire is another example. The key element is that it reacts to change to provide a previously determined outcome or steady state.

A *goal-seeking* system can react differently to a given internal or external event to produce a different internal or external state (outcome). Such a system can choose its behavior, unlike the state-maintaining system. It seeks a goal or given end-state. Systems with automatic pilots are goal seeking: Automatic pilots make a range of choices that keep a plane on course at various speeds and altitudes.

Multigoal-seeking and purposive systems seek different goals in at least two different external or internal states. However, these different goals have a common property. Production of that common property is the system's purpose. Even though the goal is determined by the initiating event, the system chooses the means by which to pursue its goals. Many computer programs are multigoal-seeking and purposive. For example, a computer programmed to bill customers and pay bills of suppliers is multigoal-seeking in that it does what it does because of an instruction from an external source. It is purposive because the billing process (the acquisition or disbursement of funds) is a common property of the different goals which it seeks.

A *purposeful* system can produce the same outcome in different ways and can produce different outcomes in the same way. It can change its goals under constant conditions, and it selects goals as well as the means to achieve them. A human being is a purposeful system, as is a family, fraternity, and most other social groups. Purposeful systems display a will and can make complex decisions. Systems that can produce the same output in different ways have the quality of *equifinality*—the ability to achieve the same end using different means.

In each of these four types of systems, the communication and control system that operates to maintain a steady state or to bring system performance back on line is a *cybernetic system*. This system depends on information provided through a feedback mechanism in order to effect a corrective change in total system performance. A quality-control operation in a production-line operation is a cybernetic system, and so is a performance appraisal interview.

Cybernetic systems that rely on an outside device for self-correction use *servo-mechanisms*. A servo-mechanism is an outside device or system that magnifies a force to effect system correction. It is not changed as it effects change in the system. It acts as a stabilizing mechanism. The clutch, which engages and disengages the air conditioner on a car, is a servo-mechanism. So is a marriage counselor or minister who is asked to help solve marital problems in order to effect change in a marital relationship.

With the introduction of new technology, cybernetic systems have become very sophisticated in regulating the physical environment of office buildings. Cybernetically controlled buildings, called "smart" buildings, provide for small-zone heating/air conditioning and lighting. At Honeywell Corporation's headquarters, an employee who comes in after hours uses an access card that not only opens the door, but alerts the elevator to stop on a particular floor, and automatically turns on the individual's office lights, phone, and air conditioning/heating. Buildings in other organizations now have motion-detecting lights that automatically turn on and off when an individual enters or exits a room, thereby replacing the light switch.[4]

Input–Output Analysis

As we have indicated, most biological and social systems are open systems. Because an open system interacts with its environment, it is often useful to visualize this system as being affected by (taking or receiving from) and affecting (contributing or giving to) its environment or other systems and subsystems. Using input–output analysis, we attempt to explain a system's relationship with its environment as well as to examine its internal operation.

Input–output analysis involves examining a flow of materials, ideas, concepts, money, people, and so on from beginning to end through a system. It has six facets:

1. Determination of inputs
2. Determination of sources of inputs
3. Determination of the transformation process
4. Determination of outputs
5. Determination of users of outputs
6. Determination of the feedback process

A commonly used input–output diagram appears in Figure 2.2. Reading this figure from left to right, we begin with *sources* of inputs. These sources exist in the environment. They may be outputs of other systems or outputs of a subsystem of the same system. The several arrows indicate that the sources for inputs are often multiple and varied.

The *inputs* are the major and minor resources coming into the system. They are the essential building blocks of the system, what the system must have to operate. The *transformation* process of a system is the process that works on the inputs. It changes the inputs, usually, by adding value to them. It does this to produce *outputs*, or the end results of the

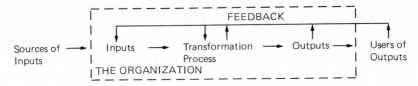

FIGURE 2.2

An Input–Output Diagram of an Open System

system. These outputs are then used by the environment or by other systems or subsystems.

The operation of the transformation process, as well as its results (outputs), provides *feedback* for the system so that changes may be made in inputs and/or the transformation process in order to change outputs. Feedback also can be generated from the users of the outputs (such as customers) and other external sources, or it can be generated by an internal source. An example of an internal source of feedback is a quality-control operation that inspects finished goods before they are shipped to customers. Feedback is provided to the system, and it may change the inputs and/or transformation process of the system.

THE ORGANIZATION AS A SYSTEM

An organization is an open, dynamic, multigoal-seeking, purposeful system that has elements of concreteness and abstraction. It consists of resources that are transformed into outputs for users. All organizations fit this description whether they are public or private, profit or nonprofit, business or government, socialist or capitalist, small or large, efficient or inefficient, or weak or powerful. They transform inputs into outputs for users as shown in Figure 2.3. The Cornhusker Hotel, which we described at the beginning of the chapter, is an excellent example of the organization as a system. Inputs such as food, equipment, supplies, and so on are transformed into comfortable rooms, outstanding restaurants, cleanliness, and so forth. In turn, the output is a satisfied guest, who either returns to the hotel at some future date or recommends it to friends.

Organizations make this transformation within a particular outside environment. This environment is a source of opportunities and constraints for particular organizations. They are affected by this environment, and they also try to affect it. They receive their inputs from this environment, and their outputs are used by people or other systems in the environment. What one organization sees as a constraint in the envi-

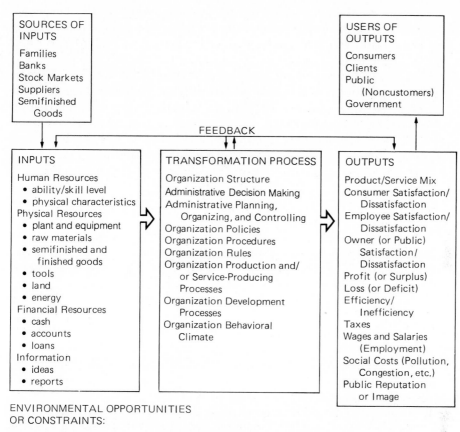

FIGURE 2.3

The Organization as an Open System

ronment, another might see as an opportunity. For example, a paper mill might see the Environmental Pollution Control Act of 1970 as a severe constraint since much money must be invested in pollution-control equipment, money that could be spent on upgrading machinery or in other areas. However, a firm manufacturing pollution-control equipment would see this act as a major opportunity. The legal structure, culture, state of human skills and education, political system, economic system, state of technology, time, demographic factors, climate and natural resources, and the state of multinational relations can all be considered environmental opportunities and constraints. Of course, an organization should try to take advantage of its environmental opportunities while minimizing the effects of environmental constraints.

An organization's inputs consist of four essential resources: human, physical, financial, and informational. Within each category, there are several types of resources. For example, human resources include people with varying interests, abilities, skills, aspirations, and physical characteristics (e.g., sex, build, strength, color of hair, and so on). Physical resources include an organization's plant, office buildings, land, equipment, tools, raw materials, semifinished goods, finished goods, and energy sources. Financial resources include cash, accounts, credits, budgets, and so on that an organization uses in the purchase and utilization of resources. Informational resources consist of data, ideas, reports, and so on that are generated internally or externally and that inform the organization as to its inputs, transformation process, and outputs. It is a key resource in that its quality tells us much about the state and utilization of other resources.

Perhaps the most important resource that an organization has is its people, or human resource. It is through working with people that all other resources are generated and utilized. Physical and financial resources are obtained and used through dealing and bargaining with people. People generate data and analyze them to provide information. Human resources would probably be the most difficult resources to replace should an organization lose all its resources. The proper mix of skills, attitudes, abilities, and aspiration levels needed by an organization in its human resources does not come easily and is often not purchasable in the marketplace at the desired price. The tremendous investment that organizations make in training, developing, and orienting their human resources is not reflected in the various financial statements used to make decisions. This condition needs to be corrected if the organization's resources are to be accurately depicted.

An organization's resources come from many sources. Families produce children who are educated in schools and join the labor market. People immigrate from other countries. Individuals move from one part of the country to another, from one industry to another, and from one skill or occupation to another. Banks, bond markets, and buyers of stock provide financial resources for the organization, as do customer sales. Suppliers provide raw materials, equipment, and semifinished and finished goods as well as fuel or energy to operate the transformation process.

Transformation, the process whereby the organization adds value to the inputs, involves the manufacturing or service-producing process of the organization. It also includes the way the organization structures itself; the policy, procedures, and rules it develops to run its day-to-day operations; the methods and quality of its decision-making process in allocating and using resources; and the overall planning, organizing, and controlling skills of its managers. It includes the behavioral climate of the organization. The behavioral climate is the atmosphere of the organization as it affects motivation, commitment, morale, and productivity. Organization development programs and processes are the organization's renewal efforts for improving its personnel, structure, policies, and procedures.

The end result of the transformation process is the organization's outputs. Most of us think of a product or service as the only organization output, but organizations produce much more than these. Wages and salaries are produced for employees. A profit or a loss is produced for owners. Employee, customer, and public (noncustomer) satisfaction or dissatisfaction are produced. Taxes are produced for government units. Also, social costs in the form of pollution, congestion, and racial and sexual discrimination are often outputs of organizations. Another output hoped for is efficiency and high productivity, but inefficiency and low productivity may also result.

These outputs are used by customers, in the case of business organizations, and by clients, in the case of government and other public organizations. An organization's nonbuying public is also a user of some of an organization's output. For example, one may not own an automobile, but one still breathes the polluted air an automobile produces. Also, a person consumes products and services transported by cars and trucks. Government not only buys organization products and services, it also receives tax payments generated by the organization's operations. Organizations buy the output of other organizations. Thus, we see that organizations actively interact with their environment in a dynamic manner. They obtain resources (inputs) from the environment and add value to these resources (transformation) to produce products and services (outputs) that are used by people in the environment.

ADVANTAGES AND DISADVANTAGES OF A SYSTEMS APPROACH

Even though we use the systems approach in our analysis of organizations, it is not without its disadvantages. Often these disadvantages, once recognized, can be at least partially overcome. Also, we believe that the advantages of the approach clearly outweigh its disadvantages, and for that reason we use it as an analytical tool.

Advantages of a Systems Approach

One major advantage of a systems approach is that its holism enables one to consider an organization as a whole. The elements of the organization are clearly specified, and changes in one element can be traced through the system to determine their effect on system performance and output. Subsystem interface is considered as it interacts with the broader system. Organizational interface with its environment is explicitly considered. The flow of energy and resources through the input–transformation–output process is clearly depicted. The sources of inputs and users of outputs are specified. The role of feedback in the system is given the importance it deserves. Thus, predicted consequences of changes made to an input or to the transformation process can be stated more clearly in terms of how these consequences affect other inputs, other parts of the transformation process, outputs, users of outputs, and the quality and type of feedback.

The systems approach also allows the integration of what initially may seem to be diverse concepts, ideas, or elements. Concepts or elements are synthesized into a system. A framework is provided in which there is a place for every aspect of an organization. The pieces of the organization puzzle can be put together.

The systems approach also allows for model building, which makes graphic presentation of ideas easier. By focusing on flows and interrelationships of elements, we can develop models that can be depicted as a flow diagram or as a set of equations. Variables are specified, and the relationships among them are made explicit. Because model building is the first step to empirical research, hypothesis generation and testing are facilitated.

The approach also allows for quantification of relationships between elements. The advantage of quantification is the preciseness that is required in stating relationships. No longer do we rely on words that have many meanings. Mathematical formulas reduce the semantic barrier in explaining relationships among organization elements.

Disadvantages of a Systems Approach

Most of the disadvantages of adopting a systems framework as an analytical tool need not exist. However, they often do exist because of misunderstanding or misapplication of the approach. Users of this approach need to know the pitfalls in its application and how they might be avoided.

There is a tendency for some students and practitioners who apply the systems approach to advocate a more centralized administrative structure in organizations. This tendency toward centralization probably results from the holistic aspect of the systems approach. Viewing the organization as a whole may tempt some to concentrate decision-making power at the top of the organization, delegating little power below the top level. Because of the possible adverse consequences of centralization (which are more fully discussed in subsequent chapters), centralization should not be blindly adopted by an organization just because it is using a systems approach.

The systems approach can also oversimplify organization relationships. Both intraorganization relationships (among elements within an organization) and interorganization relationships (between the organization and its environment) may be oversimplified. The systems approach relies quite heavily on conceptual and analytical models. However, the human mind may not be able to express adequately all the relationships among elements through modeling. Most models or organizations, therefore, tend to oversimplify reality. Relying exclusively on these models at the expense of managerial judgment, experience, and other information can have dysfunctional consequences. Models developed from a systems philosophy should be considered tools for understanding a complex reality rather than as total representations of reality.

The shortcomings of models are particularly severe with an open system. Thompson points out that in closed systems, knowledge of cause-and-effect relationships may be complete. Results for every possible combination of variables can be known from experience or can be calculated. However, with the open system, actions often have multiple causes and effects that go in different directions at different times. Effects within the system are affected by actions outside it, and it can be difficult to trace specific effects to specific causes.[5]

Simon suggests the notion of *bounded rationality* to deal with this uncertainty. We assume that organizations are rational entities; that is, they attempt to efficiently use inputs (resources) to maximize production of outputs. Yet in open systems it is difficult to achieve perfect rationality; there are simply too many unknowns. The notion of bounded rationality suggests that limits must be placed on the way an organization defines a situation—at some point the organization must go ahead with a decision without having all the information it desires.[6] Basically, bounded rationality means that organizations are generally required to make decisions without complete information; hence, they make decisions with the best information available.

Many people find the systems approach too abstract and difficult to apply. The cause of this problem is often the manner in which the systems approach is studied and applied. As we indicated previously in this chapter, some people believe the systems approach is the same as the management science or computer science approach, though this is not the case. Yet, when a systems approach is presented, it may use many models, quantifications, and abstractions that tend to be too difficult for readers not skilled in using mathematical notation. The key to overcoming this disadvantage is to resist the temptation to rely excessively on model building and quantification in studying and applying the systems approach.

Finally, the use of quantitative methods with a systems approach can present the illusion of finiteness. Very few relationships in the social sciences, including the study of organizations, can be stated with precision. Human beings and social interrelationships are so complex that we often do not specify all relevant variables and their cause-and-effect relationships, let alone determine their magnitudes. Therefore, in applying the systems approach, we must caution against relying on quantitative tools to the exclusion of basic description. Given these pitfalls, however, the systems approach is a valuable analytical guide to the study of organizations.

CONSIDERATIONS IN SYSTEM DESIGN

What are the concerns of managers when designing organizations from a systems perspective? System design in organizations must account for managerial philosophy, open–closed systems perspectives, system effectiveness, system change and adaptation, and system interface with other systems. We discuss each of these topics in depth in various other sections of this book. At this point, however, these topics are introduced to provide a clearer explanation of the systems concept.

Managerial Philosophy

All managers have a managerial philosophy. It may be explicit or implicit, clearly formed or vague, but it exists. It is a basic set of values that provides a general guide or framework for managerial behavior. This philosophy serves as a foundation for organization design. Miles has identified three theories of management that serve as the basis for a management philosophy.[7] The traditional model or theory is similar to the Classical School approach discussed previously. The human relations theory is similar to the Behavioral School. The third, human resources theory, emphasizes the maximization of human resource performance within a system perspective.

Each of these philosophies affects organization design considerations. For example, the traditional philosophy would emphasize many layers of management, extreme specialization of function, and formalized policies and procedures. If the human relations philosophy were used in the organization, the organization would be designed to maximize the formation of effective interpersonal relations in the organization. The work group would be the central focus around which the organization would structure itself. If the human resources philosophy were predominant, the organization would design itself to maximize human resource performance. Open communication, minimum status differentials, and flexible policy would prevail.

Environmental Interface

A second design consideration is the establishment of linkages between the organization and its environment that will maintain the degree of openness needed between the organization and its environment. The organization must decide which mechanisms and processes it will use to interface with its environment and the extent to which this interface shall function. Interface means the way the organization meets and interacts with its environment. For example, the organization must decide such practical issues as:

1. Should most of the promotion be from within the organization? If a strong promotion-from-within policy is followed, it would indicate a degree of closedness.
2. From what labor pools should the organization recruit and how should recruiting be done? For example, should the organization use employment agencies or its own recruiters? Recruitment from wide geographic areas would indicate openness.
3. Should financing of future growth be primarily from retained earnings, stock and bond issues, or from long-term bank loans? Financing from retained earnings would reduce dependency on outside sources and, hence, increase closedness.
4. Should the organization employ sales agents and brokers or its own salespeople? Using an internal sales force exclusively would indicate closedness.
5. Who should provide the organization with information on customer or client needs and satisfaction, and how shall it be provided? If outside market research consultants are used, a degree of openness would be indicated.
6. How shall the organization interact with government regulatory agencies? If a conscious effort to ignore or subvert the law is made, a certain degree of closedness would be indicated.

The first decision the organization must make before it answers questions like these is to what extent it wants and needs to interact with its environment. All organizations are open systems in the long run, although for various reasons they may act as if they are semiclosed systems in the short run. There are reasons inherent in the environment, technology employed, or economic conditions that will cause an organization to review

ıd evaluate where it will operate on the open–closed system
ontinuum.

System Effectiveness

Organizations should be designed to enhance their overall effectiveness
in meeting their mission and objectives. Moreover, the design should enhance the accuracy of measurement of organizational performance. Any
organization must be concerned with its effectiveness for long-term survival. If an organization ceases to provide benefits for its customers or clients, it will cease to exist, although this cessation may not occur for
several years. Measures of effectiveness are the keys to the growth and
survival of an organization and so deserve explicit consideration when organizations are designed.

System Change and Adaptation

All organizations change over time, some more slowly than others. All organizations eventually adapt to their environment or they cease to exist.
The ease with which an organization can change to meet environmental
challenges is a crucial factor to consider in designing the organization.
Organizations can be designed with effective environmental sensors,
such as salespeople, personnel recruiters, and market researchers, that
provide a relatively penetrable boundary between the decision-making
centers of the organization and its environment. In today's dynamic environment, change and adaptation must be critical concerns in organization design.

Interface with Other Systems

Closely associated with open–closed system change and adaptation
considerations is the system–system interface networks that organizations can explicitly establish with cooperating and competing systems
in the environment. Mechanisms need to be established that specifically integrate organization subsystems with subsystem components
in the environment.

A means for acquiring resources from the environment (e.g., people, money, and land) needs to be established. The resources may need
to be modified once obtained. For example, personnel often require
training. However, the quality of the resource when acquired is important to the organization.

Mechanisms to distribute the value produced by the organization
also need to be established. For example, dealers in the automotive industry serve as an interface between the manufacturer and the customer. The

services to the environment. Banks provide financial resources; employment agencies assist in locating human resources; distributors, brokers, and agents provide the resources to bring the products and services to the customer; and advertising and public relations agencies communicate organization, product, and service characteristics to customers.

Some units within the organization also play a linking role. While not officially in the intermediate environment, the function they perform is a linking function. They have the same function as that performed by units in the linking environment. For example, company recruiters who visit colleges and universities provide human resources to the organization. Corporate staff lawyers interact with other companies and the government as do law firms hired by the company. A firm's advertising department may perform the same functions as an ad agency.

The Macro Environment (The External Environment)

We can broadly classify the organization's macro environment into seven major systems: (1) the cultural system; (2) the political system; (3) the economic system; (4) competition; (5) technology; (6) the human resources skill/educational mix; and (7) customer/client groups. Within each of these systems are the specific groups and subsystems with which an organization must interact. We briefly discuss each of these environmental components here and deal with them in more depth in Chapter 3.

CULTURE. The cultural system of a society is the society's basic beliefs, attitudes, and role definitions and interactions. It is the vehicle by which a society is created and propagated through time. It enables a society " . . . to pass the accumulated learning of the species from generation to generation, and to continue to make the accumulations of learning. . . ."[10] Each generation does not need to experience the past to learn from it. It can take the accumulated knowledge and build on it.

Specific institutions in the cultural system include the family, the religious system, and the education system. These institutions transmit the culture from one generation to the next. However, not only do they transmit, they redefine and build upon cultural values, norms, and role patterns. In recent years, youth in particular has played a major role in examining and redefining cultural values, norms, and role patterns.

POLITICAL SYSTEM. The political system is the way in which a society governs itself. It includes various governmental units at all levels of government from international to local. It also includes political processes used to elect or appoint people to various offices. Formation of parties, nomination procedures, election procedures, and appointing procedures are all systems used in the governing process.

The way in which a political system operates has a major impact upon

dealer uses manufacturing subsystem outputs to sell to customers, as described in Figure 2.4. Consideration in system design would involve the amount of autonomy dealers should have, how they should be selected and evaluated, how inputs (cars) should be provided to them (terms and conditions of sale or consignment), how the dealer should provide communication back to the manufacturer, and what relationship the dealer should establish with customers. Thus, the interface system is composed of the transportation, information, and finance systems designed to link the manufacturer with the dealer.

In designing the system interface network, managers must consider the following:

1. With what environmental components must they maximize interaction?
2. With what environmental components do they wish not to interact?
3. With what environmental components do they wish to be neutral in terms of interaction?

Those environmental systems critical to the organization's mission and objectives should have effective system interface networks. Those environmental systems that hinder the mission accomplishment should be effectively screened from the organization by the interface network.

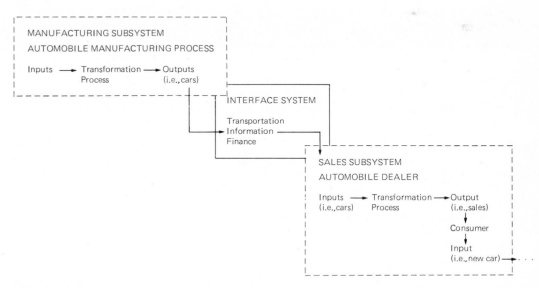

FIGURE 2.4

System–System Interface in the Automotive Industry

Finally, those environmental systems having no bearing on mission accomplishment should have no effect on system interface design.

MICRO–INTERMEDIATE–MACRO ENVIRONMENTS

A good way to conceptualize the interaction of an organization with its environment is to use the micro–intermediate–macro environmental distinctions.[8] The micro environment is the organization itself. It includes the mission, people, objectives, resources, policies, procedures, product/service production process, and product/service produced. The intermediate environment is those systems that span the boundaries between the organization and its general or macro environment. The automobile dealer mentioned above, for example, would be in the intermediate environment. The macro environment is the general environment within which the organization works. Figure 2.5 depicts the interaction of these three environments.

The Micro Environment

The micro environment (the organization itself) can be visualized as being made up of three major subsystems: (1) the goal and work system, including technology; (2) the structure, communication, authority, and

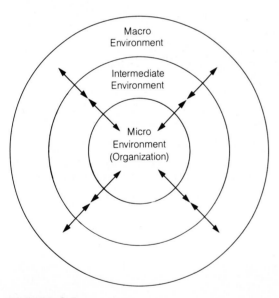

FIGURE 2.5

The Organization's Micro–Intermediate–Macro Environmental Interface

power systems (internal linking systems); and (3) the human factors system.[9] These three systems are the major systems in the organization operating to produce the outputs of the organization. Each of these system with the exception of the human factors system, is discussed in grea detail in later chapters; however, a brief discussion of each system follows. The human factors system, while treated below briefly, is not cussed in greater detail in the book because this subject is m appropriate for a book dealing with organizational behavior.

The goal and work system of the organization is made up of the mary mission, the specific objectives, and the types of work (includ the technology involved) undertaken to accomplish the mission and jectives of the organization. These factors serve as the basis for all orga zation activity. Without the mission, objectives, and work subsyste there would be little need for the other organization systems. The te nology used is the state of the art and science employed to carry out ganization work. Chapter 12 discusses this system in more detail.

The power and authority system is concerned with the way the org ization allocates decision-making authority throughout the organ tion. Such concepts as organization design, delegation, and control primary considerations here. These systems—communication, po authority, and structure—are linking systems that operate to ensure the work required to produce organization objectives is carried out ciently and effectively.

The human factors system is the network of interpersonal relat ships and behavior patterns within the organization. Both formal and formal relationships are part of the human factors system. Such conc as role behavior, motivation, perception, reference groups, and lea ship are all components of the human factors system.

The Intermediate Environment

The intermediate environment links the organization and its macro e ronment. The intermediate environment is made up of *linking* syst that facilitate interface between the micro and macro environments. made up of the following components (among others):

1. Suppliers/distributors
2. Advertising/public relations agencies
3. Brokers/agents
4. Employment agencies
5. Service units, for example, law firms, lending institutions, an surance agencies

Each unit in the intermediate environment facilitates the acquis of resources from the environment or the distribution of product organizations today in the United States. Not only do government agencies specifically regulate much behavior of organizations by pollution control, equal employment opportunity and antitrust laws, and so on, but the political system also sets the foundation by which the influence process occurs in a society. For example, a representative democracy such as the United States relies quite heavily on lobbying procedures and the mobilization of opinion for the passage or defeat of specific pieces of legislation. This same process often carries over to the way a specific organization is run. Individuals in the organization may mobilize and lobby with other groups of individuals for the development and implementation of policies. A union essentially conforms to our democratic political processes in that it is elected by a majority of workers to serve as a bargaining agent with management in order to implement or change policies dealing with wages, hours, and other terms and conditions of employment. Thus, the values that give rise to various political institutions and the processes by which they operate greatly affect similar influence and governing processes within organizations.

Another major aspect of the political system today for many organizations is the effect of the state of international relations on an organization. Many organizations depend on raw materials or finished goods shipped from other countries, or sell their finished products to customers in other countries. Some have manufacturing plants in other countries. Tariffs affect many organizations. The increasing international dependency of domestic firms has added this dimension of the macro environment to the concerns of many organizations. Even universities and state governments are affected: Many universities have overseas branches, and most state governments are eager to acquire direct foreign investment in their state. The very large ebb and flow of dollars spent on petroleum affects banking on an international scale. Few organizations today can ignore the state of international relations.

ECONOMIC SYSTEM. The economic system of a society is the way in which a society creates and distributes wealth. It is the system that allocates scarce resources to competing individuals and groups. In U.S. society, the economic system includes the operation of a mixed free-enterprise system consisting of a free market, private ownership of property, and some government regulation and control. Thus, we have large and small private corporations, partnerships, and sole proprietorships. We have government fiscal and monetary processes to stimulate or restrict the demand for goods and services. We have government ownership of some corporations, for example, the Tennessee Valley Authority. We have government regulation of business practices, for example, equal employment opportunity, regulation of advertising, and antitrust laws. We have markets that are monopolistic (utilities), oligopolistic (automobiles and steel), and competitive (agriculture). All these factors make up the economic system in the United States.

A major part of the economic system for organizations is the availability of resources for the organization. Also included is the climate within which the organization exists. The *climate* and *natural resources* of the geographic area in which the organization operates affect the type and use of many of its physical resources. The availability of resources (including energy) is defined and alternative routes are sought for those resources not readily available. This availability affects how an organization operates. For example, the lack of sufficient domestic petroleum reserves has had a major impact on the U.S. automobile industry by changing not only the products it offers but also the way auto manufacturers are designed. They must now be more concerned with foreign competition, for example.

COMPETITION. Most organizations, even many government agencies and private associations, compete with other organizations that provide similar products or services. Think of how many restaurants exist in even a small- to medium-sized town. Even governmental units, such as a state university, compete for good students and legislative funding. This competitive environment greatly affects the strategies an organization adopts in serving the customer or client. Actions are taken to differentiate the product or service in terms of price, quality, or other factors to convince the customer to purchase from the particular organization.

TECHNOLOGY. As we briefly discussed in Chapter 1, technology is the art and science of production and distribution employed by the organization. Because of its profound impact on organizations, we give further attention to this component in Chapter 12.

THE HUMAN RESOURCES SKILL/EDUCATIONAL MIX. The macro environment provides a labor pool, in the broadest sense of the term, for the organization from which to draw for employees at all levels. This labor pool is characterized by a particular skill and educational mix. This mix is critical in determining the types of jobs and technology the organization uses. For example, developing countries have difficulties using and maintaining sophisticated farm machinery provided by the United States because the skills and education of farmers and support services (e.g., implement dealers) are not consistent with that required by the equipment. Sturdy metal plows and other well-made nonpowered equipment may be more suited to the skills and educational level of the people who use them in some developing countries.

CONSUMER/CLIENT GROUPS (THE MARKET). The macro environment is the source of an organization's market. From the broad populace, people are targeted by the organization as potential consumers or clients for delivery of goods and services; the organization defines those whom it will try to serve.

Another consideration in examining both the human resources skill mix and customer/client group is the *demographic characteristics* of a society that affect organizations. Demographics is concerned with the study of population characteristics of a given group or society. This study includes information on birth and death rates, income levels, family make-up, geographic and occupational mobility, and so on. In the United States most of this information is gathered and analyzed by the Bureau of the Census and is readily made available to organizations desiring it. For example, information on birth rates would be valuable to manufacturers of baby-related items.

Thus, the organization exists within a macro and intermediate environment. Each of these environmental systems is made up of subsystems that interact directly or indirectly with the organization. Figure 2.6 summarizes this expanded concept.

Environmental Linkages

All organizations are linked to the macro environment whether or not they interact through a fully developed intermediate environment. Some organizations incorporate aspects of the intermediate environment. A business firm's board of directors may include bankers and major suppliers. Through vertical integration, an organization may own its own suppliers and dealers. It may have its own legal, personnel recruiting, and advertising staffs. Whether it performs these functions itself or uses intermediaries, it is developing and using linkages that give the organization its life line to the environment.

Organizations that adopt a closed-system philosophy and attempt to totally sever ties with their environment will eventually cease to exist. They will atrophy because of their inability to bring in new resources from the environment. In addition, their inability to effectively provide goods and services to the environment will ultimately result in their demise since they will no longer be satisfying a need in society. Of course, organizations realize a closed-system philosophy will lead to their ultimate demise and few, if any, have ever attempted to adopt such a philosophy. More commonly, the organization uses the intermediate environment as a barrier or screen to make it more difficult for certain aspects of the macro environment to impinge on the operation of the organization. Since organizations depend on the macro environment for resources and markets for outputs produced, building too great a buffering or blocking system will reduce resource and product market options. Often this un-

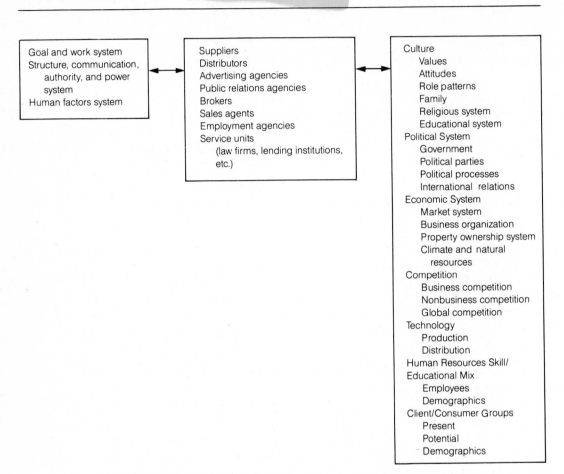

FIGURE 2.6

Components of the Organization's Micro, Intermediate, and Macro Environments

necessary buffering structure occurs because an organization does not adequately understand, and therefore cannot cope with, its environment. In effect, it begins to act as a closed system, at least in the short run, and begins to suffer the consequences of this short-run philosophy.

ALTERNATIVE APPROACHES

Traditionally, organizations have been studied from several different perspectives. Each of these alone does not fully explain the operation of a given organization. However, when taken in combination or when studied with systems analysis, they may be very useful in explaining how organizations operate. We will focus on six main approaches: (1) the mechanistic or bureaucratic model, (2) the human relations or group behavior model, (3) the individual behavior model, (4) the technological model, (5) the economic model, and (6) the power model.[11] Each of these models has its roots in one of the three schools of organization theory discussed in Chapter 1.

Mechanistic or Bureaucratic Model

This model focuses on the formal operations of organizations. It developed from the Classical School of organization theory. Such subjects as principles of specialization, hierarchical arrangements, delegation of authority and responsibility, structure, and efficiency are usually examined within a closed or semiclosed framework. The model is also known as the traditional model or structural model. It emphasizes the predictability and stability of organization operations and gives little consideration, if any, to the environment within which the organization operates.

People within the organization are viewed as programmable. Little attention is given to individual differences in the areas of needs, wants, or levels of aspiration. Efficient managers using effective techniques can cause people to behave in a certain way. The psychological behaviorists, such as B. F. Skinner, follow this approach in their study of human behavior. Using proper rewards and penalties under a stimulus–response framework, individual behavior becomes a mechanistic series of predictable response patterns.

Human Relations or Group Model

As a result of the Hawthorne studies in industry and work by Kurt Lewin and other psychologists, a model developed that explains organization operations on the basis of group intra- and interaction processes within the organization. Social rewards and satisfaction derived from interpersonal actions are used to explain why people work, how hard they work, and how effective they are. The informal or *de facto* operations of the organization are examined in detail and are used to explain organization operations. Little consideration is given to the formal or *de jure* organization.

Individual Behavior Model

A perspective that evolved from the human relations model emphasizes individual behavior within the group and organization. Writers such as Maslow and Herzberg carefully examined individual perception and motivation within the organization and explained organizational operation occurring as a result of the response of individuals to satisfy needs. Such factors as individual personality and traits were stressed.

The Technological Model

The technological model focuses on the technology employed by the organization to explain how an organization develops and operates. The guiding principle of this model is that organizations structure themselves around the existing technology in their particular field. For example, the structure and operation of an automobile company can be explained to a great extent by the technology involved in mass assembly-line production processes. This model emphasizes the way an organization internalizes a major segment in its macro environment.

The Economic Model

The economic rationality of a firm's decisions serves as the foundation for this model. This model was originally developed to explain the decision processes of business organizations and the maximization of a firm's economic gain in using scarce resources. All decisions are economic decisions. The way a firm operates in the marketplace is determined by its desire to maximize profits. The model has great applicability to business firms but also can explain behavior of nonprofit organizations, particularly those which experience periodic budget reductions.

The Power Model

All organizations have some degree of power in their environment and have internal power relationships and structure. The power model focuses on organizations as social systems in which power differentials determine a major part of what occurs. Resource allocation, decision making, and overall organization performance are explained from the perspective of the power relationships generated internally and externally. Power is viewed as the ability of the organization to exercise influence over its members and its environment. In turn, the operation of the organization is viewed as a series of power struggles.

ORGANIZATION THEORY AND THE GENERAL SYSTEMS APPROACH

The general systems approach can be used to organize the concepts we will be examining in our study of organizations. Figure 2.7 indicates how

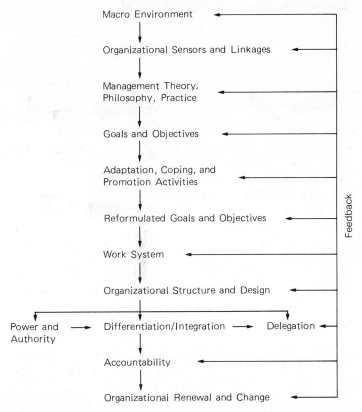

FIGURE 2.7

The Organization's Integrative Mechanisms in Response to Environmental Opportunities and Constraints

an organization conceptually arises and responds to the needs of its environment. Each block in this figure is more fully explored in later chapters.

The environment is the basis for all organization action. Organizations exist to satisfy some need in the environment. Organizations may try to amplify these needs through advertising should the needs wane or change. They will also argue that their product or service is best for satisfying a need: for example, "Buy a Seville and get more than transportation." It is doubtful that organizations can actually create needs that do not exist, but they may amplify, redirect, and interpret environmental needs.

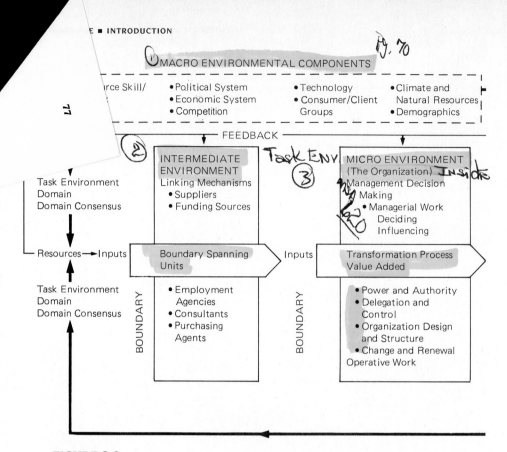

pg. 70

FIGURE 2.8

A Framework for Studying and Analyzing Organization Theory Using the Systems Approach

Source: Adapted from William A. Shrode, unpublished manuscript, Florida State University, 1980.

Society ultimately sanctions all organizations. The organization sensors and linkages in the intermediate environment interpret the macro environment and environment needs for management. Management devises goals and objectives to satisfy perceived environmental needs. Management also changes these through various adaptation, coping, and promotion mechanisms, and determines modified goals and objectives that will satisfy changing needs of the environment. Additionally, through advertising and promotion, management tries to influence the ways people in the environment satisfy a need.

Through the organization's work system, organization effort is directed toward achieving the objectives. The organization is designed to

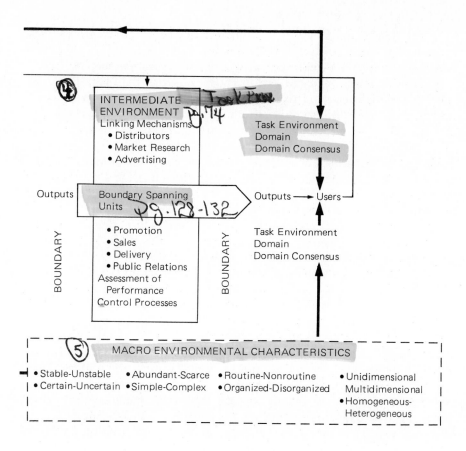

facilitate this work system. Design considerations involve resolving such issues as power and authority relationships, functional differentiation, and delegation of decision making throughout the organization. Of course, once this differentiation and delegation have occurred, the organization must integrate activity and effort to ensure that it is directed toward the objectives originally established. The appropriateness of these objectives, as well as how efficiently and effectively they are achieved, serves as the basis of the organization's accountability to society. The final step in the process is the renewal and change process whereby the organization renews its internal processes to better meet the needs of the environment.

An Integrating Model for Analysis

We conclude this chapter by presenting a model (Figure 2.8) that provides a framework for studying and analyzing organization theory. In this model we have integrated basic concepts of input–output analysis with the concepts of organization theory discussed in this book. Although not all aspects of this model have yet been explained, each aspect will be thoroughly discussed in the remaining chapters. The purpose of this model is to provide an overview of organization theory from an open-systems perspective. It will be helpful to refer to this model while studying the remaining chapters to see where the pieces fit into the total picture. The general systems approach provides us with a useful model to study a complex phenomenon—organizations. While the systems approach is but one way to study organizations, we believe it has certain advantages. Conceptualizing an organization as a system of inputs, transformation processes, and outputs allows one to take a holistic approach to the study of organizations. Alternative methods do not have this advantage since they tend to explain organizations in terms of a single predominant factor, whether it be power, bureaucracy, interpersonal interaction, or technology. The systems approach allows us to integrate these various approaches.

In addition, by using the systems approach, we are better able to explain how an organization interacts with its total environmental complex. Today's organization faces increasingly complex and rapidly changing environments. Its ability to cope with these environments is a major determinant of its success. Using the micro–intermediate–macro approach, the relationship between the organization and its environments becomes a series of interchange processes. Resources are obtained from the macro environment, worked on in the organization, and returned to the macro environment in a different form with increased value. This value added by the organization justifies the organization's existence. If the organization efficiently adds the proper amount of value to acquired resources and if the products or services are deemed acceptable by society, the organization will continue to be a viable entity.

The remainder of this book examines in detail many of the concepts introduced in this chapter. The organization's ability to meet the challenges of its environmental complex through renewal and change serves as the final section of the book and is the ultimate challenge of the organization.

SUMMARY

The general systems approach provides us with a useful model to study a very complex phenomenon—organizations. While the systems approach

is but one way to study organizations, we believe it has certai⎯
that make it preferable to alternative methods. Conceptual⎯
ganization as a system of inputs, transformation processes, ⎯
allows us to take a holistic approach to the study of organizat⎯
native methods do not have this advantage since they tend to⎯
ganizations in terms of a single predominant factor, whether i⎯
bureaucracy, interpersonal interaction, or technology. The sy⎯
proach allows us to integrate these various approaches.

In addition, by using the systems approach, we are better a⎯
plain how an organization interacts with its total environmer⎯
plex. Today's organization faces increasingly complex and rapidly
changing environments. Its ability to cope with these environments is a
major determinant of its success. Using the micro–intermediate–macro
approach, the relationship between the organization and its environments becomes a series of interchange processes. Resources are obtained from the macro environment, worked on in the organization, and
returned to the macro environment in a different form and, hopefully,
with increased value. This value added by the organization justifies the
organization's existence. If the organization efficiently adds the proper
amount of value to acquired resources and if the products/services are
deemed acceptable by society, the organization will continue to be a viable entity through time.

The remainder of this book examines in detail many of the concepts that have been introduced in this chapter. The remaining chapter
in this part will carefully examine the organization's external (macro)
environment, while the chapters in Part Two will demonstrate how the
organization links up to both its intermediate and macro environments. Part Three examines the inner workings of the organization's
micro environment (the organization itself), and the chapters in Part
Four will show some of the dynamics involved as we continue to study
organizations as systems.

QUESTIONS FOR REVIEW AND DISCUSSION

1. What is the systems approach? How can it be used to study organizations?
2. Define holism, synergism, interdependency, and subsystems.
3. What is the functional–dysfunctional continuum and of what use is it in studying organizations?
4. Are there any closed systems? Are all biological and social systems open? If so, then why consider the closed-system concept when studying organizations?

5. What are four behavioral classes of systems? In what class do organizations belong? Why?

6. Using input–output analysis, explain how your university or college operates.

7. What are the advantages and disadvantages of a systems approach to studying organizations? How can these disadvantages be overcome?

8. What major factors should be considered from a managerial standpoint when using a systems approach to design and examine organizations?

9. Explain the macro–intermediate–micro environmental interface.

10. What are six other approaches to studying organizations besides the systems approach?

11. Explain this statement: "Organizations can insulate themselves from sources of uncertainty in the environment without being closed systems, or indeed suffering the consequences of totally closed systems." Do you agree with it?

12. Do organizations create environmental needs?

ENDNOTES

1. Fremont E. Kast and James E. Rosenzweig, *Organization and Management: A Systems Approach* (New York: McGraw-Hill, 1970), 110.

2. Richard R. Colino, "Turnaround Strategies for an International Organization," *The Journal of Business Strategy* 7, no. 2 (Fall 1986): 52–61.

3. Russell Ackoff, "Toward a System of Systems Concept," *Management Science* (July 1971): 665.

4. Megan J. Paznik, "Intelligent Buildings Get Smart Enough to Save You a Bundle," *Administrative Management* 48, no. 1 (January 1987): 25–33.

5. James D. Thompson, *Organizations in Action* (New York: McGraw-Hill, 1967), 85.

6. Herbert A. Simon, *Models of Man: Social and Rational* (New York: John Wiley & Sons, 1957).

7. Raymond E. Miles, *Theories of Management: Implications for Organizational Behavior and Development* (New York: McGraw-Hill, 1975), 31–49.

8. B. J. Hodge and H. J. Johnson, *Management and Organizational Behavior* (New York: John Wiley & Sons, 1970), 65–170.

9. Ibid., 119.

10. Alfred Kuhn, *The Study of Society* (Homewood, Ill.: Richard D. Irwin and the Dorsey Press, 1963), 205.

11. Richard H. Hall, *Organizations: Structure and Process* (Englewood Cliffs, N.J.: Prentice-Hall, 1972), 27–35.

ANNOTATED BIBLIOGRAPHY

Abert, Steven L. "Archetypal Social Systems Analysis: A Reply to Mitroff." *Academy of Management Review* 9, no. 4 (October 1984): 757–762.

Examination of Mitroff's archetypal social system analysis (ASA) reveals its hierarchical vision of a single reality and several of its key constructs to be inconsistent with archetypal psychology's dualistic vision of reality. Alternative views of these issues, more consistent with mainstream depth psychology, are offered. Analysis of a dyadic social system develops the concept of an organizational psyche. Mitroff's applications of ASA are then reexamined to illustrate the greater significance of the current view.

Ackoff, R. L. "Toward a System of Systems Concepts." *Management Science* (July 1971): 661–671.

Ackoff fills an important gap by attempting to organize the varied terminology and concepts used in systems discussion. The central focus of the exposition is the consideration of an organization as a system.

Daft, Richard L., and Weick, Karl E. "Toward a Model of Organizations as Interpretation Systems." *Academy of Management Review* 9, no. 2 (April 1984): 284–295.

A comparative model of organizations as interpretation systems is proposed. The model describes four interpretation modes: enacting, discovering, undirected viewing, and conditioned viewing. Each mode is determined by (1) management's beliefs about the environment, and (2) organizational intrusiveness. Interpretation modes are hypothesized to be associated with organizational differences in environmental scanning, equivocality reduction, strategy, and decision making.

Forrester, J. W. *Principles of Systems.* Cambridge, Mass.: Wright-Allen, 1968.

This book is a technical approach to the operation of systems. In particular, quantitative attention is given to feedback dynamics, system structure, and the modeling and simulation of systems.

Mantell, L. H. "Systems Approach and Good Management." *Business Horizons* (October 1972): 43–51.

Mantell argues that managers have difficulty applying the systems approach because system-wide objectives are not clear and because reward systems are not oriented toward optimizing total system performance.

Markus, M. Lynn. *An Organizational Angle on Systems.* Marshfield, Mass.: Pitman, 1984.

This text offers a clear-cut base for identifying, explaining, predicting, and controlling the impacts of systems on people and organizations. The author argues that poor results of systems interpretations lie not in the technology of the systems, nor in the people or organizations that use them, but in the interaction between the specific design features of systems and the organization's environment.

Miller, E. J., and Rice, A. K. *Systems of Organization.* London: Tavistock Institute, 1967.

The authors develop a conceptual systems approach to the organization and its people, giving detailed attention to boundary dynamics. Principles and propositions are illustrated with analyses of modern organizations in varied industries.

Mitroff, Ian I. "Archetypal Social Systems Analysis: On the Deeper Structure of Human Systems." *Academy of Management Review* 8, no. 3 (July 1983): 387–397.

This paper extends the concept and method of stakeholder analysis, showing that deeper symbolic aspects of human systems can be understood in terms of a special set of stakeholder entities known as archetypes. Archetypes are the most basic symbolic images that the human mind is capable of having and experiencing. Archetypes and their associated properties are radically different from the kinds of stakeholders that are discussed in a typical analysis of social systems.

Shell, R. L., and Stelzer, D. F. "Systems Analysis: Aid to Decision Making." *Business Horizons* (December 1971): 67–72.

The authors explain the necessity of and approach to the application of systems theory to decision making. An iterative model of the systems approach is presented and explained.

Thimm, A. L. "General Systems Theory: A Tool for Social Analysis." *Journal of Systems Management* (October 1970): 16–21.

The article describes and illustrates the use of systems theory in analyzing complex social problems. Specifically, analysis of urban transportation systems is discussed with emphasis on positive feedback.

Vaill, Peter B. "The Purposing of High Performance Systems." *Organizational Dynamics* 11, no. 2 (Autumn 1982): 23–29.

The author has found that high-performing systems have unique characteristics and that their leaders share certain commitments—discoveries that are certain to have profound implications for other organizations and their leaders.

ADDITIONAL REFERENCES

Adam, Everett E., Jr. "Towards a Typology of Production and Operations Management Systems." *Academy of Management Review* 8, no. 3 (July 1983): 365–375.

Beer, Michael. *Organization Change and Development: A Systems View.* Santa Monica, Calif.: Goodyear, 1980.

Beyer, Janice M., and Scott, W. Richard. "Organizations: Rational, Natural, and Open Systems." *Administrative Science Quarterly* 29, no. 1 (March 1984): 134–137.

Cleland, David I., and King, William R. *Management: A Systems Approach.* New York: McGraw-Hill, 1972.

Cleland, David I., and King, William R. *Systems Analysis and Project Management.* 2d ed. New York: McGraw-Hill, 1975.

Couger, J. Daniel, and Knapp, Robert W. *System Analysis Techniques.* New York: John Wiley & Sons, 1976.

Dove, G. A. "Objectives, Strategies and Tactics in a System." *Conference Board Record* (August 1970): 52–56.

Johnson, Richard A.; Kast, Fremont E.; and Rosenzweig, James E. *The Theory and Management of Systems*. 3d ed. New York: McGraw-Hill, 1973.

Katz, Daniel, and Kahn, Robert L. *The Social Psychology of Organizations*. 2d ed. New York: John Wiley & Sons, 1978.

King, William R. "The Systems Concept in Management." *Journal of Industrial Engineering* (May 1967): 320–323.

Markus, M. Lynne. *Systems in Organizations: Bugs and Features*. Boston: Pitman, 1984.

Neuschel, Richard F. *Management Systems for Profit and Growth*. New York: McGraw-Hill, 1976.

Petit, T. A. "Systems Approach to Management Theory." *Journal of Systems Management* (October 1970): 16–21.

Pondy, Louis R., and Mitroff, Ian I. "Beyond Open Systems Models of Organizations." In *Research in Organizational Behavior*, edited by Barry M. Staw. Greenwood, Conn.: JAI Press, 1978.

Ross, Joel E. *Modern Management and Information Systems*. Reston, Va.: Reston, 1976.

Sayles, Leonard R., and Chandler, Margaret K. *Managing Large Systems: Organizations for the Future*. New York: Harper & Row, 1971.

Swinth, Robert. *Organizational Systems for Management: Designing, Planning, and Implementation*. Columbus, Ohio: Grid, 1974.

Wilson, Brian. *Systems: Concepts, Methodologies, and Applications*. New York: Wiley, 1984.

<table>
<tr><td>C</td><td>A</td><td>S</td><td>E</td></tr>
</table>

What's Good for Toyota Is Good for the Country

During the 1950s, when it seemed that the U. S. auto industry, particularly General Motors, would always remain on top, GM Chairman Charles Wilson said to reporters, "What's good for General Motors is good for the country." Thirty years later, 25 percent of all autos sold in the United States are foreign, and of this percentage, Toyota sells more automobiles than any other foreign manufacturer. At present, Toyota Motor Company is only half the size of Ford and one-third the size of GM. But that will change if Toyota has its way. The Japanese automaker has targeted GM as its ultimate victim in the auto manufacturing wars, and that's why Toyota has decided to locate a large manufacturing plant in the United States.

Toyota's plan is called "Global 10," a sobriquet the company uses to signal its intent to capture 10 percent of the world market. But in November, 1985, Toyota upped its target to 12 percent, and if it accomplishes this goal, while whittling down GM's 19.9 percent of the world market, the Japanese organization firmly

Sources: Larry Armstrong, Leslie Helm, James B. Trecce, William J. Hampton, Maralyn Enid, Richard Brandt, and William J. Holstein, "Toyota's Fast Lane: It Wants to Overtake GM—and Building its Cars in the U. S. Is a First Step," *Business Week* (November 4, 1985): 42–44; John Y. Lee, "The Quiet Revolution in Inventory Management," *FE* (December 1985), 37–40; B. Berger and G. Lundstrom, "Two Japanese Automakers Plan Assault on U.S.," *Automotive News* (March 24, 1986), 1.

believes that it will replace the U. S. giant as the world's number-one automaker.

Toyota first put its foot in the door by forming a joint venture with GM called the New United Motor Manufacturing, Inc. (NUMMI), and both organizations joined forces to build a new plant in California. However, this collaborative effort is just one calculated step in Toyota's plan to overtake GM by first experimenting with and fine-tuning its "just-in-time" production system in North America.

The essence of this system is to have the component parts of automobiles delivered to the assembly line as needed in the manufacturing process. This is opposed to the standard American practice of ordering large lots that are stored in warehouses for future use, or, alternatively, exhausting supplies, sometimes before new inventories are delivered. In Japan, the heart of the system is "Toyota City," where a dense concentration of Toyota-owned factories and nearby suppliers ensure that parts are delivered no more than a few hours before they are needed. In short, the supply and inventory system is driven by the speed of the production line, *not* vice versa.

The Toyota production system is based on five interconnected subsystems: activities and morale of the work force, set-up time and standardized operations, production smoothing and shortened lead times, inventory flow, and quality control.

Activities affect the morale of the work force. Assembly-line activities at Toyota are divided between manual and machine operations. Improvements to manual operations include the elimination of time spent waiting for a process to finish (before another can begin) and the elimination of having to move work-in-process inventory from one machine to another. After all manual operations are accomplished in the most efficient and effective manner, machine improvements are made. Toyota has a policy of introducing new machines only when a strong need exists—the company will not simply automate a manual function because it is easy to do so. Hence, work force morale is maintained. In addition, Toyota assembly-line workers are cross-trained in multiple assembly-line operations.

Set-up time is reduced and work standardized in several ways. For some operations, workers are able to set up their changes while the machinery is still running. In other situations, set-up time has been eliminated completely because of uniform product design. Because Toyota has predetermined the time necessary to complete each assembly cycle, manual operations are easy to refine and standardize. Should a worker be unable to complete his or her task in the necessary time, a supervisor or other worker will come to his or her aid and the cycle will be accomplished during the prescribed time period. Finally, because the Toyota assembly line is designed so that the product moves from one worker's cycle to another without having to stockpile inventory between operations, the smooth flow is constantly maintained.

Production smoothing is maintained because it is based on projected and actual orders. The orders for production are transmitted for different models well ahead of the actual assembly operations; thus the line runs smoothly without interruption. Because Toyota workers are multiskilled, production remains balanced, and the waiting time between different processes has been nearly eliminated.

Inventory control is the fourth sub-

system of the Toyota production system. Little or no inventory is kept on the assembly line (except what is needed for the shift work in progress). Suppliers make deliveries at the time necessary to meet the production schedule. Toyota develops a monthly production plan and distributes it to its suppliers at the midpoint of the preceding month.

Quality control and the automatic detection of defects are an integral part of the production system at Toyota. If any part is defective at any point, the problem is corrected at that point. Moreover, the cause of the defect is determined to prevent its recurrence. Quality control is enhanced by having a stock of parts just large enough for daily use. In addition, a close relationship exists between Toyota and its suppliers, particularly concerning the quality of parts.

Other subsystems in the Toyota scheme include 300 parts suppliers that are located near Toyota City. The paternalism aspect of Toyota's management style has its counterpart with suppliers as well. These suppliers are required to open their books to their key customer, and Toyota sets the price. In addition, if a supplier cuts costs, it is expected to pass along the additional savings. Toyota's main suppliers, in turn, subcontract work to 5,000 second-tier suppliers who, also in turn, subcontract work to 20,000 third- and fourth-tier suppliers.

Toyota has advanced this system one step further in Japan. It is bringing dealers into the just-in-time concept, in effect building a new auto only when a customer is ready to buy one.

Some business analysts predict that Toyota will have problems instituting this type of system in America; however, Toyota isn't listening to them, although it has had to make modifications. For example, at the Fremont, California, NUMMI plant, suppliers aren't close by. Nevertheless, NUMMI informs about fifty Midwest suppliers what parts will be needed. They are then delivered to an amalgamation point in Chicago for immediate shipment to the NUMMI plant by rail.

As we pointed out previously, quality is an important component of the Toyota system. When windshields delivered to the NUMMI plant were considered not up to standard, the just-in-time production system was actually shut down, because Toyota will not sell defective cars. In Japan, workers are encouraged to provide inputs into the system, and employees have come up with over 10 million suggestions for quality improvement and cost-cutting since 1951.

Reducing costs to gain a competitive edge is another major cornerstone of Toyota's operations. In the United States, Toyota will employ a younger work force (thereby accruing minimal pension costs), and has decided to locate its new plant in Kentucky, a state where labor unions are not particularly strong. More-

over, the company will have easy access to the world's lowest cost source of major components, its plants in Toyota City. But that is not all—Nippondenso, an electronics company, 22.2 percent of which is owned by Toyota, has set up a factory in Michigan to service the NUMMI plant, and many more loyal suppliers are expected to set up shop in Kentucky near the new Toyota facility.

As you have already read, the actual production process is finely geared to reducing costs and maximizing efficiency. For example, hoses on painting machines have been shortened to reduce waste when colors are changed. Flexibility is another important aspect that Toyota has perfected in its system—its production lines are so designed that they can switch, in minutes, from four-cylinder engine production to six-cylinder engine production and vice versa.

If Toyota is successful in introducing its system of operations in the United States, then it feels certain it will produce and sell enough high-quality, low-priced cars to reach its goal, that is, replacing GM as the world's number-one automaker.

QUESTIONS FOR DISCUSSION

1. How does the just-in-time concept exemplify the systems approach?
2. How does the fact that Toyota will shut down the assembly line rather than sell defective cars reinforce Toyota's view of the company as a system?
3. Do you believe that Toyota will be successful in introducing its system of operations in the United States? Why or why not?
4. What factors in the macro environ-

ment are important for Toyota's success in the United States?
5. Enumerate other approaches to management (other than systems) that Toyota could use to meet its Global 10 objective.
6. Do you believe that it is possible to form a joint venture (such as NUMMI) without using a systems approach? Why or why not?

3

Macro-Environmental Components

More Than Apples and Oranges

South Florida nursery owners have recently discovered a wide variety of exotic fruits that might very well help offset the damage done to Florida's agricultural economy by unusually cold weather, citrus canker, the fruit fly, and low prices caused by strong competition.

The talk of the 1984 Produce Marketing Association convention, held in Washington, D.C., was the carambola, an exotic fruit grown by the Dade County (Florida) Fruit and Citrus Park organization. Besides being a versatile fruit (it can be eaten plain, used as a garnish, made into preserves, and so on), the carambola is also a health nut's dream, high in vitamin C and low in calories and sodium.

Dade County Fruit and Citrus's carambola was representative of Florida's efforts to stimulate the public appetite for exotic fruits that are much different from the oranges, grapefruit, and winter vegetables that the state is famous for. Other exotica, such as the atemaya, black sapote, and sugar apple are presently being grown and marketed by Florida nurseries, food shops, and food chains. In fact, one exotic legume, the winged bean, has more protein than a soybean, is edible in its entire form (leaves, stems, seeds, and flowers), and is being cited as a possible answer to food shortages in underdeveloped countries.

Health nuts and fruit fanciers are not the only Florida residents attracted to these new fruits. Southeast Asian and Latin American immigrants, many of whom live in south Florida, are hungry for fruits they ate in their native lands, and in some instances, the demand far exceeds the supply, even though supermarket giants such as Publix and Safeway now stock these delectable fruits.

Present revenues from the cultivation and sale of fruity exotica now account for $40 million annually for the Florida economy, and that figure is expected to double by 1990. According to the Dade-Broward Agricultural Stabilization and Extension Service (a state of Florida agency), these crops now cover over 11,000 acres of south Florida farmland. Moreover, agriculturists and farm economists alike hope that these new fruits can make up for the financial losses incurred by south Florida nurseries as a result of avocado competition from California. Talented, commercially oriented horticulturists and nursery owners might very well put Florida back on top as an agricultural state.

Federal and state agencies believe in the future of these crops, and both the U. S. Department of Agriculture and the University of Florida Research Station in Homestead have begun research on developing stronger and hardier exotic fruit crops.

However, as Florida nursery organizations and government agencies work on producing better exotic fruit crops, they are also laying the basis for greater competition in this specialized field. Exotic fruits are rarely imported into the mainland United States because the fumigation process causes them to disintegrate. But new technology is greatly improving preservation and handling methods, and it is expected that Hawaii and Central America will soon start competing with south Florida in this area.

Source: Annetta Miller, "Exotic Fruits Are Taking a Slice out of Traditional Markets," *Florida Trend* 28, no. 1 (January 1985): 63–68.

As the preceding article illustrates, the various components of an organization's external environment have a direct and all-powerful impact on the organization. South Florida's nurseries and associated organizations, through their experimentation and marketing of exotic fruits, are reacting to a combination of environmental forces: the culture of south Florida's residents, both native-born and recent immigrants; the political system as evidenced by the actions of both state and federal agencies; conditions in the state's agricultural economy; new technological advances that aid in the cultivation of exotic fruits; actual and potential competition from other states and foreign countries; the quality and availability of special horticultural skills in the labor force; and consumer demand for the products.

As you read the chapter, you will gain a greater understanding of the nature of these environmental forces and realize that no successful organization can exist independent of them.

The macro environment surrounds the organization and is composed of those forces that make it possible for a successful organization to convert inputs into outputs. It is made up of seven components: culture, the political system, the economic system, technology, competition, the skill mix of the population, and customer/client groups. The organization must deal with the combination of these forces and factors if it is to continue over time.

All organizations exist within an envelope of factors and forces that affect their operations. This envelope is the source of inputs in the form of resources and information as well as the source of demand for outputs in the form of consumer wants and needs.

For the purpose of the present discussion this envelope is called the *macro environment*, a term chosen for convenience as well as for its descriptive nature. The word *macro* means large, whole, or global, and so can be used to describe the aggregate of factors that surround the organization. Among the major components of the macro environment are culture, political system, economic system, competition, technology, skill mix, and consumer/client groups, as we see in Figure 3.1.

This chapter examines the nature of the macro environment and its components in some detail in order to explain their role in organization life.

THE NATURE OF THE MACRO ENVIRONMENT

The macro environment is bounded by geography. The laws, customs, and societal values of the citizens of an area have a major impact on how an organization is put together, what it produces, the technology and people it employs, and the type of consumer it serves.

All organizations operating in the United States are affected by certain laws and customs that are somewhat different from those of Canada, for example. At the same time that societal values can be viewed at the national level and their effect on all organizations in the United States can

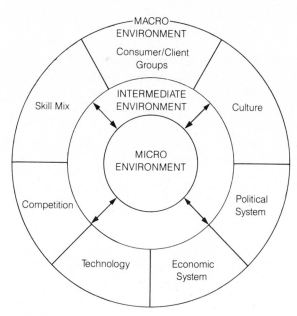

FIGURE 3.1

The Organization's Macro Environmental Components (outer circle)

be traced, there are state, regional, and local laws and customs that affect how an organization in a particular state might operate differently from one in another.

A good example of how an organization is affected by both national and local conditions can be seen in the case of the Haitian and Cuban refugees in the state of Florida. Firms operating in the greater Miami area were faced suddenly with a series of political, economic, and cultural issues that probably did not affect firms operating in Denver, for example. Firms located in Miami cannot ignore this pervasive problem. These forces, in the form of the refugee problem, affect how firms live.

An example can be seen when one considers the assumptions that managers make about the future availability of fuel for automobiles. Predictions from experts tell us that the U.S. economy must seek some alternative to fossil fuels in the near future. If these predictions are correct, some drastic design changes will have to be made in the engines of future models of automobiles. Consequently, it is imperative for managers to follow closely the state of the supply of fossil fuels as well as stay informed of the development of alternative fuels.

A LOOK AT THE MACRO ENVIRONMENT

The modern organization is shaped by the components in its macro environment—from its purpose, to the technology it employs, to the definition of its success. Simply stated, this means that no organization today can ignore the total environment within which it exists.

The message for organization managers is clear: They have little choice but to devise some effective means for coping with the forces and events that are likely to have an important part in shaping the future of their organizations. The message for organization theory is similarly clear: A contemporary view of organizations must assume that they are open systems interacting with their environment.[1] This means that the view of organizations that holds environmental forces as givens or as constants is not appropriate for understanding how and why organizations behave as they do.

An organization out of touch with its environment would soon use up all its resources, rely on dated information for decision making, and lose contact with consumer wants and needs. Consequently, in the long run such an organization would eventually die. This is true even though in the short run the organization might enjoy a measure of success. To survive over time, however, today's organization must interact successfully with its macro environment.

Although there are perhaps other classification schemes that could be employed, we believe that for our purposes this environment can be analyzed by investigating culture, political forces, economic forces, competition, technology, skill mix, and consumer/client groups.[2] In discussing these forces, we will also pay attention to their legal and ecological aspects, considering the effect they can have on the organization.

The macro-environmental components discussed below are not arranged in any particular order; their place in the discussion is not intended to assign them any order of importance. Instead, they are treated as discrete components for discussion purposes although it is evident that in practice their importance and effects may be interwoven. Table 3.1 summarizes our discussion of the macro environment.

Culture

Every society develops its own culture over time, and this culture determines in large measure how its members behave and interact with each other.[*] Included in culture are such components as values, norms, arti-

---

[*]Because of culture's unique part in organization life, a separate chapter (13) is devoted to its composition and role in organization theory. The following discussion is intended to be simply an overview of this component.

TABLE 3.1

Macro-Environmental Subcomponents

Major Component	Subcomponent
Culture	Societal values, norms, beliefs, artifacts, a behavior patterns, institutions
Political system	National, state, and local laws, regulation ordinances, government services, political parties and processes
Economic system	Resource availability and means of allocation, market structure, pricing mechanisms, economic regulations
Competition	Domestic competition, global competition, nonbusiness competition, substitutability, competitive information processing
Technology	Techniques and science of production and distribution, machinery/automation, work flows and processing, state of industrial development
Skill mix	Labor availability by skill and geographic area, mobility, training and development, unionization
Consumer/client groups	Buying power, expectations (time, place, quality, quantity, price), need, wants, perceptions

facts, and accepted behavior patterns. Since society is really a collection of organizations and institutions, it is affected considerably by cultural forces in the macro environment.

Culture affects the way organizations operate. The societal values held by consumers, for instance, are determined to a great degree by the values society at large holds important. To the extent that society's values change, the organization must adjust its methods of operation. The case of pollution and its place in the manufacturing and distribution processes in this country provides a classic case in point. Once society decided there must be a reduction in the amount of pollution that was tolerable, manufacturers began to make changes in the techniques, processes, and materials that went into their products.

Likewise, dress codes have changed rather drastically in recent years, due partly at least to changing cultural values. These values and standards (or norms) have been infused into today's organizations at a fantastic rate with the result that, once again, the organization has had to adjust or face lawsuits, protests, or even failure.

Societal norms are those standards that mold the behavior, attitudes, and values of those members who constitute a society.[3] Norms come from laws, customs, religious teachings, and common practice. They are standards because members of society take them into account in their decisions and behavior. In other words, one can say that behavior and attitude actually reflect the prevailing norms within a society or organization. Dress, speech, what is considered to be in good taste, and the general understanding of what is right and wrong are all affected by societal norms. We can see evidence of dramatic change in almost all of these areas if we examine the last two decades or so in the United States.

Environmental scanning conducted by the American Council of Life Insurance Trend Analysis Program indicates a renewed interest in evangelical religion.[4] John Naisbitt also notes that the future will see a tremendous growth in religious revitalization as Americans search for structure in their lives during a period of turbulent change.[5] The practical effects of this cultural variable in the macro environment are evidenced by the 1,300 radio stations and dozens of television stations that devote all or part of their time to religion. In addition, he notes, evangelical publishers now account for one-third of total U.S. domestic book sales. Therefore, for the publishing or telecommunications industries the revitalization of religion in America would be an important variable to consider in formulating long-range strategies and plans.

Likewise, as we saw in our introductory case, one of the characteristics of modern American culture is the desire for health and physical fitness, which in turn has fueled the consumer demand for Florida's exotic fruits. This, among other reasons, explains the success experienced by Florida exotic-fruit growers.

Thus, culture is largely responsible for an organization's success. If an organization's management is aware of and accounts for culture in its decisions, it is possible to produce those goods and services that consumers deem desirable. Its production and marketing practices must be in tune with its culture; indeed, literally every facet of the organization must be geared to those values, norms, and behavior patterns that its macro-cultural components demand.

This is not to say, however, that the organization has no influence on culture. On the contrary, almost every institution in a society is capable of transfusing some of its values, norms, and behavior patterns into its macro environment. Take the case of schools and churches, for example. These two institutions are responsible to a great extent for the kinds of behavior and values that make up society's culture.[6] At the same time they can be properly labeled exporters of culture, however, it is important to note that they must be aware of changing cultural patterns in the outside world so they can adjust to them. Schools and churches alike in recent years have drastically changed their programs in response to cultural change.

These examples illustrate that the cultural component of the macro environment is a powerful force to be reckoned with by managers of all types of organizations. For this and other reasons, it is important to include culture as a part of the organization's macro environment to be studied and dealt with by management in every phase of its decision-making activities.

Political System

All organizations are affected to some degree by the political system in their macro environment. The political system, that is, government and political processes, is an important variable in managerial decision making in virtually all aspects of activity. To exist, organizations must comply with certain legal procedures to begin operation; they must observe applicable laws in the conduct of everyday affairs; and they must comply with laws when ceasing operation.

For our purposes here, the political system is important to organization theory because it is the source of these laws and regulations. The political system includes national, state, and local laws, regulations, and ordinances that affect the organization. Likewise, those goods and services that are available to managers from these government agencies are properly included in the political system.

Today, as never before, managers need to become familiar with applicable laws because every facet of their operations is affected by legal considerations. In the United States in the personnel area, for example, there are laws regulating wages, hiring practices, benefits, and retirement. Buildings must meet fire code and Occupational Safety and Health Act (OSHA) requirements as well as have provisions for access by the handicapped.

On the other hand, governments at all levels offer a rich variety of services to organizations. These range from providing public utilities, to advising on income tax questions, to subsidies, to books and pamphlets on topical matters, to police and fire protection. When one thinks of the government sector, one might be likely to think of its negative connotation and red tape. Although there is an element of restriction on organizations originating from the political sector, it is by no means dominant. As a matter of fact, one might think of the net influence of the political system as positive in spite of some prohibitions. Consider the results if there were no fire and police protection, no assistance in preventing unfair competition, and no uniformity of chartering businesses. Chaos would certainly rule.

Moreover, businesses and other organizations must adapt to recent trends indicating that national political power is shifting from the federal government to the states. Naisbitt notes that during the past two decades, the states have become "structurally and procedurally stronger, more accountable, assertive, and perform a major intergovernmental management role."[7] A recent example would be the fact that the states of Alabama, Nevada, Texas, and Arizona have neutralized the Food and Drug Administration's authority by legalizing the controversial drug laetrile. In Missouri, the governor asked the State Department of Natural Resources to deny the federal government a permit to dump nuclear wastes into the Mississippi River. The states are not only resisting the authority of the national government but in fact have taken the initiative in passing laws relating to myriad activities such as environmental cleanup programs and taxes. In terms of sheer volume of activity, Naisbitt notes, the states passed an average 1,000 laws apiece from 1980 to 1982 while Congress passed only 500. Moreover, Naisbitt reports, this trend is continuing down to the municipality and citizens-group level. In the future, organizations might find themselves being much more affected by state and local political actions than by the federal government.

The contemporary organization manager must also consider other countries' political structures and inner workings. There is hardly an organization one can think of today that is not affected by the Middle East crisis, grain shortages in the Soviet Union, or international terrorism. Indeed, some large multinational organizations have created separate departments to deal with the problem of terrorism. New organizations have been created, in both the public and private domains, to protect both individuals and other organizations from violent acts.

Communication and transportation have made the world a much smaller place in which to live. This means that organization theory should provide in the macro environment a place for international relations and international government superstructures such as the United Nations, the North Atlantic Treaty Organization, or the European Economic community. These superstructures represent a combination of political, cultural, and social forces even though they are basically political in nature.

Management, then, has a responsibility to become thoroughly familiar with the political system and to adjust to it. At the same time, however, there is also an opportunity to attempt to influence the political system in a manner that will benefit the organization. This is well evidenced by actions taken by Harris Corporation, TRW, and Morton Thiokol, major defense contractors, to derail federal legislation aimed at curbing defense fraud. These organizations, led by Harris, managed to persuade key U. S. senators to put holds on pending bills that would make it easier for the federal government to prosecute those who fleece the government. As a result, these bills have languished in limbo between committee action and the Senate floor. Analysts say these organizations have managed to influence lawmakers by contributing to various political action committees (PACs).[8] The political system, then, is a vital force in the macro environment and one with which management must deal effectively if the organization is to be successful.

The following section deals with the economic system, the companion part of the political system. In reality, these two systems are practically inseparable, because actions taken in one generally will have some impact on the other. They are treated as individual systems here for discussion purposes only.

Economic System

Organizations exist within some form of economic system that exerts a tremendous influence on how they behave. There are, of course, many forms of economic order, ranging from the mixed private-enterprise system of the United States to partially or completely controlled economies of certain European and Asian nations. Regardless of their form, however, all economic systems are concerned with resource allocation and the distribution of goods and services.

In the United States our form of economy is basically one of private enterprise, which means that decisions about what and how much to produce are left to the discretion of owners and managers. In controlled economies, such decisions are the responsibility of some government agency. There is, of course, no economy today that is completely free from government influence, nor is this condition necessarily undesirable.

Among the functions of the economic order is to provide some means of resource allocation.* In private enterprise this function is basically performed by the price mechanism. This simply means that demand for and supply of goods and services interact to set market prices. However, in the case of regulated utilities, for instance, government agencies such as public service commissions determine the rates that may be charged by utility companies. Rates are set at the level that will allow a fair return on investments made by the companies. This form of regulated monopoly is considered, on balance, preferable to unchecked competition because of efficiency reasons. Imagine the problems, for instance, with open competition for utility services within a single municipality. Think of the confusion that would result with different electrical lines, billings, sewage systems, and so on for homes and businesses.

Recent events on the energy scene have pointed out how fragile a given economy can be. Consider, for a moment, what the sudden and dramatic increases in the price of petroleum did to the American economy during the 1970s. Because petroleum is such a basic part of our economic

---

*Detailed elaborations of how the resource-allocation process functions can be found in any basic economics text.

system, virtually every good and service was affected by these price increases. At the same time, and probably as a direct result of these increases, managers in every kind of organization have begun to devote attention to conservation methods as well as to seeking alternative sources of energy.

Conversely, the sharp drop in oil prices in 1986 and 1987 has had a dramatic impact on organizations. Burlington Northern Company, a rail and energy company, lost $785 million in the second quarter of 1986, and Standard Oil is shedding oil leases, downgrading oil properties, selling industrial businesses, and laying off thousands of employees. This, in turn, has caused a ripple effect—for example, profits were down 40 percent at the Golden Nugget in Las Vegas because southwesterners, living in a region whose economic base is oil drilling and exploration, decided to stay home.[9] In early 1987, the states of Texas, Oklahoma, and Louisiana began undergoing a virtual depression—office plazas and condominiums stand vacant in Houston; supermarkets have closed in Tulsa; and the city of New Orleans is being especially nice to Mardi Gras visitors in order to make up for some of its lost revenues as off-shore drilling operations come to a halt in the Gulf of Mexico. Surely, energy will continue to be a major concern in the economic component of the macro environment.

There are also political implications to the presence and use of natural resources. For example, the United States consumes far more than its per capita share of natural resources. It has been blessed with a rich variety of resources and, as emerging nations enter the contemporary world scene, there are doubtless concerns about our resource base and how we use it (as well as theirs). There is also some question about our "right" to the foreign oil supply. Such a question has economic as well as political dimensions and demands an answer from today's manager.

One final aspect of the economic order is changing demographic variables such as age, sex, and education. Obviously, as these variables change and a nation such as the United States begins to get older, undergo a sex-ratio change, and encourages its citizens to become better educated, it witnesses changes in consumer tastes as well as changes in the aggregate demand for goods and services. The drive in the 1970s and 1980s toward sexual equality has had dramatic effects on our economy.

The last decade brought about other major shifts in demographic variables. One of the largest has been the shift of population to the "Sunbelt" states. This shift has brought considerable ripples to the political power bases. As companies move national headquarters and personnel into this area, political alliances and strengths must change.

Medical treatments have prolonged life expectancy, which, in turn, has placed unprecedented demands on Social Security, medical facilities, and even changed the balance of support for changes in the income tax laws.

These examples show that an economic order must be viewed as a combination of forces and factors that has to do with the way an organization acquires its resources and produces and distributes its products or services. Moreover, the economy in which business organizations function is becoming more global and less national. For example, we may drive to work in Japanese cars, work in buildings made from Korean steel, and wear Brazilian-made shoes, while West German businesses use American-manufactured computers and Soviet citizens eat bread made from American wheat. In fact, according to environmental scanners, not only is our economy becoming more interrelated with the economies of the rest of the world, but the base of the economy is dramatically changing from a resource-abundant, capital-intensive, heavy-industry base to one of information sharing and high technology. Some authors, such as Botkin, Dimancescu, and State, maintain that we must shift our thinking from a domestic economy based on abundant physical resources to a global economy based on information and knowledge-based resources.[10] In addition, such a reorientation further requires that new emphasis be placed on technical education and research. If this is true, then American industry and government must create a new partnership to ensure that we have the human, technical, and political resources necessary to remain competitive within a global economic environment.

Because of the role the economy plays in the daily life of their organizations, managers owe it to their organizations to become familiar with how the economy operates and how it affects them. Ignorance of economics will surely bring about the caliber of decisions that will lead to disaster sooner or later.

Technology

Another important force in the macro environment is the state of technology—the art and science of production and distribution. Every organization employs technology to some extent, whether it is a small social club that uses a typewriter to send out notices of monthly meetings or a complex industrial plant that relies on robots, rather than people, to run its assembly line.*

The United States has perhaps the most advanced state of technology in the world. Its economic progress is due in large measure to the ability to develop and use technology in both the labor and materials areas. It would be difficult to imagine building our modern skyscrapers without

---

*Because of its vital importance to understanding organization theory, technology is treated in depth in Chapter 12. This section merely serves to place technology into the macro environment.

the aid of a variety of machines and equipment. Likewise, the success rate in hospitals would certainly be reduced in the absence of the medical technology that has enabled doctors to detect and cure disease at an unprecedented rate. Diagnostic procedures themselves have been vastly improved by a host of technological breakthroughs.

To be able to compete successfully, organizations must have access to modern technology. How would a carpenter using hand tools fare against one who uses power equipment? How could a grocery store that relied on old-fashioned cash registers and bookkeeping methods hold its own against a chain store that used computers for inventory control and for financial record keeping? These are just two examples illustrating that today's managers must give considerable attention to technology in deciding to form organizations, what products or services they will make and distribute, and what processes to employ in daily operations.

It should be noted that there is an economic side to technology decisions. For instance, one deterrent to the establishment of a steel mill or an automobile assembly plant would doubtless be the enormous amounts of capital required to obtain the technology needed in the production processes. This condition regulates the entry of organizations into this industry, and thus it is incumbent on government as well as on the industry itself to police activities to ensure a reasonable level of competition.

An organization's success is measured by its ability to adjust to and to employ technological innovations.* For example, let's examine the case of N.V. Phillips, the Dutch manufacturer of consumer electronics. In 1972, Phillips produced the first practical VCR—three years before the Japanese entered the market. However, Phillips failed to capture the VCR market because of its creaky and conservative methods for bringing high-tech products to market. On the other hand, Japanese firms such as Honda, Fuji, Canon, and NEC, *use* high technology to introduce high technology to the marketplace. These Japanese firms pick a multidisciplinary team that stays with a product from start to finish. The baton of responsibility passes from product planners to designers, to manufacturers, and then to marketers. This does not occur in a relay fashion; rather, the "ball" is passed back and forth in rugby fashion as the whole team moves downfield toward the goal. Moreover, throughout this approach, team members depend on computer systems for designing, simulating, and analyzing products.[11]

It has been said that the Industrial Revolution began in England rather than in France for the simple reason that the English were willing to accept mass-produced products while the French were not. The United

---

*Refer to Joan Woodward, *Industrial Organizations: Theory and Practice* (London: Oxford University Press, 1965), 68–80 for a treatment of the relationship between technology and success.

States economy has witnessed a massive technological revolution in its history. This revolution has brought new products and production techniques to the market that have enabled succeeding generations of organizations to profit from them.

Among their responsibilities, then, organizations today must count the obligation to maintain a spirit of creativity and ingenuity among members so that continued progress on the technological front can be made. The ever-growing shortages of resources of all types are but one indication of the seriousness of this obligation. No theory of organization would be complete that did not include technology and its effect on the organization as a vital component of the macro environment.

Competition

Competition affects virtually every aspect of our lives—from the very beginning, we vie for attention, food, and so on in an effort to satisfy our whole range of needs. Indeed, this spirit of competition is at the heart of most of our modern institutions. One would be hard put to think of an institution that is not somehow affected by others in its environment. For example, universities and colleges compete for students and faculty when they recruit; employers try to attract the best possible talent to join a particular organization in preference to another; and, on the social level, fraternities and sororities hold "rush" in order to gain members. Because of its pervasiveness, competition must be counted as part of the macro environment.

Competition today is truly an international phenomenon. This fact places sharp focus on the competitive environment. Trade deficits, embargos, and the balance of payments are not only everyday topics in leading business publications, they are powerful forces to be reckoned with by the organization. A coal strike in Britain is felt in the U. S. economy. A large grain harvest in the United States can bring more foreign goods into this country.

As technology becomes more generally available, there will doubtless be competition in space. Ariane, the European space consortium, is already competing with NASA in the satellite launching business. Can competition between space stations be far away?

The global marketplace accounts for a major part of the competitive environment of the organization. Understanding the structure, culture, and objectives of foreign competition is simply a must for today's student of organizations.

In order to appreciate and to cope with its competition, the organization must constantly scan its environment. For instance, all members of the soft-drink industry watched very carefully the effects the introduction of "new" Coke had on the market. The same is true for the return of the "old" or Classic Coke. The auto, electronics, and computer industries, among others, keep watchful eyes on foreign competition, especially from Japan.

This competition affects the organization in a variety of ways. Pricing policies and practices, for example, are a function of "what the competition is doing." Consider, for example, that the price of Pepsi, Seven-Up, and Coke are all very similar, and the introduction of a new product by one seems always to invite retaliation by the others.

Let's examine briefly what organizations scan for in their competitive market environment. William F. Glueck developed an excellent composite of the forces and factors.[12] Among these factors are changes in population, age shifts in the population, income distribution of the population, and product/service life cycles. Additionally, organizations must be aware of other forces in their competitive environments. What is the ease of entry into and exit from the relevant market? Will an exit cause a given firm to gain a larger share of the market or subject it to monopolistic practices charges?

Then, of course, is the question of substitutability. The availability and quality of less costly substitutes for a firm's products or services, and how competitive the substitute industry is, will determine how viable the substitute is. For example, sugar companies must be concerned with such products as fructose, aspartame, and corn syrup.

Major strategic moves by other firms in the market obviously affect how a company behaves. New products, services, or guarantees brought out by one firm will definitely affect decisions in others. These and other factors and forces must be accounted for when an organization scans and evaluates its macro environment.

It is important to take a systems approach to analyzing the competitive environment. As we argued in Chapter 2, the systems approach provides an excellent conceptual framework for understanding. This approach to analyzing the competitive environment is the subject of an incisive article by Bruce Henderson.[13] The article presents some twenty-one principles that, taken together, give the reader a sense of wholeness, yet separateness, about the competitive environment system. These principles help us understand how and why organizations behave as they do. Although it is impractical to discuss all twenty-one principles, six key ones do merit mention and enhance the environmental and systems aspects of this text: (1) All competitors who persist and survive have a unique advantage over others; (2) the more similar competitors are to each other, the more severe their competition; (3) competitors must each have an advantage and each must match different environmental factors to survive. Thus, there is a point or series of points along an imaginary continuum where the advantage shifts from one competitor to another. The point(s) of no relative advantage defines the competitive segment boundary; (4) competitors that exist must be in equilibrium with each other; (5) changes in the environment change the factor weighting of environmental characteristics and, therefore, shift the boundaries of the competitive segment and disrupt this equilibrium; and (6) the total competitive environment consists of a web of interfacing competitors, all of which are uniquely advantaged, constrained by their competition, and in dynamic equilibrium with those with which they interface.

The work of Michael E. Porter sheds greater light on the competition component of the macro environment and how organizations can react to, and perhaps even control it. Basically, Porter outlines three strategies that organizations can use to jockey for position along the continuum discussed above.[14]

First, Porter argues that organizations can seek *overall cost leadership* in their industry. This is accomplished by such measures as overhead control, avoiding marginal customer groups, and minimizing costs in such areas as service, sales, research and development, and so on. By maintaining a low-cost position in an industry, an organization can earn profits during times of heavy competition.

A *differentiation strategy* involves the creation of a product or service that is perceived throughout the industry as being unique, and is accomplished through brand image, features, a dealership network, and so on. The purpose of differentiation is to create brand loyalty among customers, such as that exhibited by those individuals who have the ability and desire to buy Porsche ("there is no substitute") automobiles.

Finally, an organization can use a *focus strategy* to concentrate its efforts on a particular buyer group, geographic market, or product-line segment. For example, Johnson Products successfully used a focus strategy, and thus beat its competition, by manufacturing and selling hair care and cosmetics products for black consumers.

Although we will discuss the concepts of strategy in greater detail in Chapter 7, we point out Porter's work here to show how important it is for an organization to have the capabilities to outperform other organizations in order to survive and prosper within the macro environment.

The competitive component of the macro environment must be accounted for in any analysis of organizations today. It will also doubtless be a more powerful force with which to reckon in the future.

Skill Mix

Another facet of the macro environment that deserves some attention is the skill mix available to the organization. The nature of the organization will determine to a large extent the kinds and amounts of abilities that it must have in its work force. Labor-intensive industries, those that rely heavily on labor vis-à-vis machines and equipment, must be especially sensitive to this factor.

One of the major factors in deciding the location of an industrial plant, for example, is the skill available in the local labor market. Westinghouse Corporation chose to locate its new plant for assembling military radar at College Station, Texas, among other reasons, because of the reservoir of engineering and scientific talent available from nearby Texas A & M University. Fruit and vegetable farmers in many sections of the United States must depend on itinerant labor to gather crops. One reason heavy manufacturing has moved out of the New England states to the extent it has is the availability of relatively cheap, trainable, and nonunionized labor in other parts of the country.

To import necessary skills is expensive, as are the costs required to conduct training programs. It is much more efficient to employ already capable personnel. The presence of labor unions also must be taken into account because these organizations represent a potent factor in the labor markets of the country.

Organizations that require skilled labor generally have a larger geographic market from which to draw their employees than do those that employ unskilled labor. Often organizations use personnel recruitment firms that specialize in finding certain kinds of talent. Even though this method of contracting for personnel searches is expensive, it is often cheaper than attempting to hire staff specialists in a very competitive field.

Two crucial variables affecting the skill-mix component of the macro environment are women in the work force and the current shortage of scientists, engineers, and information specialists, the lifeblood of the new high-technology companies that are the emerging dominant force in the American and world economies. Regarding the former, Naisbitt noted in 1982 that women made up 40 percent of the work force, were entering positions formerly occupied exclusively by men, and that, by 1990, women getting professional degrees will be eight times the number of women getting these degrees in the 1960s.[15] These changes in the skill-mix component not only affect an organization's management of its human resources, but have a tremendous impact on other macro-environmental components as well. Certainly, however, organizations will have to acknowledge the fact that women are not only entering the work force in larger numbers, but are taking over new positions as well. Therefore, personnel departments in large companies will be faced with formulating new policies regarding such items as maternity leave, part-time employment options, and pay differentials.

Regarding the latter trend, many authors cite the challenge facing American industry and education concerning the necessary skills and education needed by a high-technology, information-based economy. It will be essential for future American educational institutions and business organizations to develop curricula geared toward providing required skills.

Consumer/Client Groups

Organizations process various inputs into some output in the form of goods and services. In essence, the organization is concerned with converting resources into some form that is acceptable to consumers and ensuring that this form is available at the desired time, place, price, and quantity.

All of this means that management must carefully analyze the marketplace to define the group of people that it will seek to serve.* All too often managers have opened various shops and factories, without the advantage of a thorough market analysis, only to find that this was a disastrous course of action. Many fast-food stores, for example, have failed for just this reason. The prudent manager will insist on adequate information about potential consumer tastes and desires prior to opening a business or introducing a new product or eliminating an old one.

It is imperative to identify the final consumer of a product or service if intelligent decisions are to be made. For example, one must not lose sight of the fact that it is, after all, dogs that consume dog food. Dog owners, of course, are the purchasers of dog food and presumably can represent their animals in purchasing decisions. Whether this is true, of course, depends on whether their dogs will eat the dog food. The point is that it is the dog that must finally approve the product.

Once consumers are identified and decisions made about the nature of the product or service that will satisfy their wants and needs, the organization is in a position to define the production and marketing processes necessary to meet these wants and needs. Basically, what the organization knows at this point is the nature of the needs and wants. The aim of the organization, then, is to produce and distribute a product or service to that consumer group.

For example, in recent years, entertainment organizations have discovered the popularity of sheds, or outdoor amphitheaters, in a country-like setting near major metropolitan areas. These include the 105-acre Great Woods Center for the Performing Arts near Boston, the Starwood Amphitheater near Nashville, and the Blossom Music Center near Cleveland. In all these instances, there existed a hitherto untapped consumer demand for concerts and music festivals in a bucolic setting by urban dwellers. In short, these organizations are successful because they

---

*This notion is subsumed under the concept of "organizational domain." For a discussion see Sol Levine and Paul E. White, "Exchange as a Conceptual Framework for the Study of Interorganizational Relationships," *Administrative Science Quarterly* (March 1961): 583–601.

are providing a particular service (outdoor music) to a specific group of consumers (urban music lovers).

One of the more noticeable trends in the macro environment during the past two decades has been the rise in consumerism and consumer groups. Consumer activity in both the political and economic arenas has resulted in the necessity of organizations seriously considering and weighing consumer desires. In the future, according to Naisbitt, business organizations will have to do more than perform market surveys to satisfy this group: It will become necessary for companies to actively include consumers in the corporate decision-making process. A 1977 study indicated that corporations have only ten years or less to include consumers in their decision-making process—or face a new strain of militant consumer action.[16] However, as stark evidence of the turbulent nature of the macro environment, this dramatic prediction has not proven to be accurate. As a matter of fact, there is mounting evidence that the consumer movement itself is moribund some ten years later.

In spite of this slowdown in consumer militancy, organizations must nevertheless continue to be aware of consumers in order to be in a position to acquire value from them in return for satisfying their needs and wants. Imagine the consequences to a university, for example, if its administration had no knowledge of who the consumers of its output were. Many universities, incidentally, have struggled and are continuing to struggle with this thorny issue. Some might decide that the present student body is the basic group to attempt to satisfy; others might favor the alumni; others might opt for the governing board; while still others might argue that it is those firms that employ the graduates that should be counted as the consumer group.

Taken together, culture, political forces, the economic system, competition, technology, skill mix, and consumer/client groups make up an organization's macro environment. It surrounds the organization much like an envelope and serves as a source of inputs and a receiver of outputs. This envelope is not static but rather quite dynamic today. This means that the organization must be viewed as interacting with its environment in an open-system manner.*

ENVIRONMENTAL CHARACTERISTICS

From the writings of Ludwig von Bertalanffy has come the notion that organizations are open systems, interacting with their environments.[17] The interactions can take place in a calm, placid setting or they might occur in a turbulent atmosphere where change tends to be rapid and discontinu-

---

*The open-systems concept was discussed in some detail in Chapter 2.

ous. Turbulence in the environment is often transmitted in much the same manner as turbulence in the weather.

In a storm, ships at sea batten down the hatches and prepare for the shock of bad weather. Every ship has a plan for dealing with foul weather. These plans cover every detail of the ship's operation from caring for the cargo to protecting the ship's structure and crew.

Organizations are also called upon to "batten down the hatches" in times of environmental turbulence. For instance, during periods of economic recession, it is often necessary to curtail operations. This calls for a plan of action, including a list of priorities, that can be likened to the ship's plan for surviving a storm at sea.

In calm seas, ships can be more lax and employ methods that might not be so stringent in their demands on the ship or its crew. The same can be said for organizations enjoying a relatively calm environment. Yesterday's plans are acceptable; tried-and-proven methods will suffice; and seat-of-the pants management methods will produce acceptable results. In other words, even the marginal firm can often survive in good economic times. Just as the ship's environmental turbulence causes it to employ effective plans or sink, so is it true that organizations must devise and implement plans for dealing with turbulence in their environments or succumb to its effects.

The trend in environmental conditions in the United States in the last fifty years or so has definitely been toward increased environmental turbulence. Alvin Toffler's classic, *Future Shock*, stands witness to the unprecedented change with its all-encompassing impact on virtually every institution in society.

If we have learned anything from the type of turbulence that Toffler discusses, it is that management has a new and challenging responsibility—to monitor environmental conditions and to develop and implement an effective plan for dealing with them. The organization of today that cannot adjust to change efficiently cannot survive over the long run. The trend appears to be continuing unchecked— adaptation to turbulence is the normal mode today and will be even more the case in the future.

In addition to environmental turbulence, organizations must also recognize the receptivity characteristic of the macro environment. *Receptivity* refers to the degree to which the organization's outputs are welcomed or received by the macro environment. For example, the U. S. economy is characterized by frequent fads that are quite popular for a short time and then fade from the scene. In 1982, after the movie *Urban Cowboy*, western-clothing stores mushroomed. However, by 1987, many of these stores had closed as the American public turned its attention to other fashion fads. This example indicates that organizations must be continually sensitive to the receptivity factor in their environment or they will no longer be able to survive.

A review of the history of the macro environment in the United States shows a distinctive shift away from rather simple environments that are characterized by few choices and a relative lack of interorganizational relationships. Today, we see a highly complex macro environment that presents very complex choices and a tremendous number of interorganizational relationships. As we saw in our introductory case, exotic fruit growers in south Florida must decide on which fruits to grow, how to develop them, where and how they should be marketed, how to compete with foreign fruit growers, and so on. In addition, fruit growers must interact with supermarket chains, various state and federal government agencies, and agricultural associations.

SUMMARY

All organizations exist in a network of systems called the macro environment. This network, composed of culture, political forces, economic forces, technology, competition, skill mix, and consumer/client groups, brings resources and other inputs to the organization for processing. Once the organization has built its product or defined its service, it must distribute it to consumer/client groups who have wants and needs that they attempt to satisfy through the consumption of such products and services.

Culture, composed of values, norms, artifacts, and accepted behavior patterns, affects the way the organization is formed and how it operates once in existence. Indeed, one must recognize that all decisions made in an organization are culture-bound, a reflection of all these components of culture.

Political forces are classified as the form and role of government in a society. The source of law and other regulations that restrict or at least affect the organization, the political system also is the source of services for the organization. These services range from fire and police protection to the provision of recreational areas. Organizations, needless to say, are tremendously affected by the political system of the macro environment from both a national and an international point of view.

The political system is coupled with the economic system. The type of economy a society has can range from private enterprise to planned economy. Whatever its form, the economic system is concerned with the allocation of scarce resources and the provision of some form of distribution. Climate, natural resources, and changing demographic variables all affect how the economic system operates.

The macro environment is also the source of technology—the machines, techniques, and methods required for production and distribution. The advanced state of technology in the United States is no doubt largely responsible for its high standard of living. It is also the result of the type of culture the United States has that will accept and nurture an advancing state of technology.

Competition pertains to organizations in a given environment that offer the same or similar products and/or services, and it exists both nationally and internationally. The student of organization theory should realize that the competitive component of the macro environment affects all types of organizations—public, private, profit, and nonprofit.

Skill mix in the labor force is likewise an important facet of an organization's macro environment. All organizations depend to some extent on a supply of labor that possesses the skill and ability to perform the work necessary to attain objectives. Consequently, labor market conditions and skill mixes are crucial to success.

The consumers are the ultimate arbiters of the organization's success, for it is they who make the critical choices to consume or not to consume an organization's output. Without the income (in whatever form) that results from this consumption, the organization is doomed to a relatively short life.

This macro environment is in a state of turbulence today, which means that managers must be more aware of and sensitive to the total environment of their organization in order to develop and implement plans for successfully coping with it. Otherwise, there is little chance for success, for no longer will yesterday's methods based on a placid environment serve in today's turbulent outside world.

QUESTIONS FOR REVIEW AND DISCUSSION

1. Describe fully the macro environment and explain why it is important for managers to be knowledgeable about it.
2. Why is it important to view organizations as open systems interacting with their environment?
3. What should a management group consider when deciding on the proper mix of technology and personnel skills?
4. Explain the role of the economic system in the decision-making activities in today's organization.
5. What part does an organization's culture play in the daily lives of its members?
6. What advice would you give a management that is seeking to identify its basic consumer client group?
7. How does the shift from a static to a dynamic environment affect an organization?

8. Explain why it is so important for an organization to actively seek information about other organizations offering similar products/services.

ENDNOTES

1. Raymond Forbes, "Organizational Success," *Journal of Systems Management* 25 (June 1974): 38–39.

2. This classification scheme is based in part on the scheme discussed in Billy J. Hodge and Herbert J. Johnson, *Management and Organizational Behavior* (New York: John Wiley & Sons, 1970), Chapter 4.

3. W. Jack Duncan, *Organizational Behavior* (Boston: Houghton Mifflin, 1978), 177–182, has a good presentation of norms.

4. *The Uncertain Future: TAP 20* (Washington, D.C.: American Council of Life Insurance, 1981), 16.

5. John Naisbitt, *Megatrends: Ten New Directions for Transforming Our Lives* (New York: Warner, 1982), 239.

6. Daniel Katz and Robert Kahn, *The Social Psychology of Organizations* (New York: John Wiley & Sons, 1966), 111–115.

7. Naisbitt, *Megatrends*, 104.

8. Paula Dwyer, "How Corporate Lobbying Stalled Two Defense-Fraud Bills," *Business Week* (July 7, 1986), 48–49.

9. Laure Baum, "Business Is Biting the Bullet," *Business Week* (August 18, 1986), 104.

10. James Botkin, Dan Dimancescu, and Ray State, *Ideas from Global Stakes: The Future of High Technology in America* (Cambridge, Mass.: Ballinger, 1982).

11. Bro Uttal, "Speeding New Ideas to Market," *Fortune* (March 2, 1987), 62–66.

12. William F. Glueck, *Business Policy and Strategic Management* (New York: McGraw-Hill, 1980), 96–99.

13. Bruce D. Henderson, "The Anatomy of Competition," *The Journal of Marketing* 47 (Spring 1983): 7–9.

14. Michael E. Porter, *Competitive Strategies* (New York: The Free Press, 1980), 36–46.

15. Naisbitt, *Megatrends*, 234–237.

16. Ibid., 177.

17. Ludwig von Bertalanffy, *General Systems Theory* (New York: George Braziller, 1968).

ANNOTATED BIBLIOGRAPHY

Bourgeous, L. J., III. "Strategy and Environment: A Conceptual Integration." *Academy of Management Review* 5, no. 1 (January 1980): 25–39.
This article states that an elaboration of the concepts and strategy of environment can be achieved by categorizing environment into its objective and perceived states, and by subdividing strategy according to content (outcomes) or

process. The concepts of strategy and environment are integrated in that primary strategy concerns opportunities in the general environment, and secondary strategy involves navigating within the task environment.

Bowman, James S. "Business and Environment: Corporate Attitudes, Actions in Energy-Rich States." *MSU Business Topics* (Winter 1977): 37–49.
Whereas previous business attitudes and actions have meant resistance to or avoidance of environmental consideration in conducting operations, this study presents evidence that business and industry now are displaying a willingness to be concerned about and to deal with environmental problems.

DeGreene, Kenyon B. "Organizational Best Fit: Survival, Change, and Adaptation." *Organization and Administrative Sciences* 8 (Spring 1977): 117–133.
This conceptual article takes a systems approach to the reactions of organizations to environmental turbulence. The author concludes that survival of an organization depends on an organizational design that integrates internal interactions and environmental interactions. This process will require improved environmental perception and understanding.

Emery, F. E., and Trist, E. L. "The Causal Texture of Organizational Environments." *Human Relations* 18 (February 1965): 21–31.
This article is a classic in the field. Its main contribution is a discussion of connectedness in the environment and a typology of "causal textures" or contexts in which organizations exist. In particular, the idea of a "turbulent" environment gained widespread use after this article appeared.

Greer, Charles R., and Downey, H. K. "Industrial Compliance with Social Legislation: Investigations of Decision Rationales." *Academy of Management Review* 7, no. 3 (July 1982): 488–498.
The author presents a model of compliance behavior and a research paradigm for testing the model's validity in organizational settings. The author seeks to determine whether compliance decisions are based on normative or calculative criteria, and whether such rationales are individual or organizational in design.

Kimberly, John R. "Environmental Constraints and Organizational Structure." *Administrative Science Quarterly* 20 (March 1975): 1–8.
Environmental constraints affect organization structure. Specifically, social structure affects organization structure. Also, the external control of resources was found to be a major constraint on an organization. The structure adapts to this constraint so as to become visible to and to influence those that control essential resources.

Lawrence, Paul R., and Lorsch, Jay W. *Organization and Environment.* Homewood, Ill.: Richard D. Irwin, 1969.
An excellent and well-known work that concentrates on the management of differentiation and integration in response to environmental change. Particularly useful chapters address environmental demands, organizational states, and practical application.

McCann, Joseph E., and Selsky, John. "Hyperturbulence and the Emergence of Type 5 Environments." *Academy of Management Review* 9, no. 3 (July 1984): 460–470.
This paper explores what happens when complexity and change exceed the collective adaptive capacity of members populating an environment—a con-

dition called *hyperturbulence*. The prospect of hyperturbulence generates an adaptive response by members called *partitioning*, which attempts to allocate and protect scarce capacity. Two types of domains emerge within the environment: the social enclave and the social vortex. Both domains are described, examples of each given, and implications for future research noted.

Meyer, Alan A. "Adapting to Environmental Jolts." *Administrative Science Quarterly* 27, no. 4 (December 1982): 515–537.

This paper examines organizational adaptations to environmental "jolts"—a sudden and unprecedented event (in this case, a doctors' strike) that created a natural experiment in a group of hospitals. Although adaptations were diverse and appeared anomalous, they are elucidated by considering the hospitals' antecedent strategies, structures, ideologies, and stockpiles of slack resources. Although abrupt changes in environments are commonly thought to jeopardize organizations, environmental jolts are found to be ambiguous events that offer propitious opportunities for organizational learning, drama, and change.

Miles, Raymond E.; Snow, Charles C.; and Pfeffer, Jeffrey. "Organization and Environment: Concepts and Issues." *Industrial Relations* 13 (October 1974): 244–264.

Organizations adjust strategies, technologies, structures, and processes to cope with changing environments. Such coping adjustments depend to a great extent on managerial perceptions. The concern of this work is the *process* by which adjustment takes place.

Terreberry, Shirley. "The Evaluation of Organizational Environments." *Administrative Science Quarterly* 12 (March 1968): 590–613.

This work, an elaboration of the Emery and Trist article, contends that environments themselves evolve. Major attention is directed toward two hypotheses: (1) organizational change is increasingly externally induced, and (2) organizational adaptation is a function of ability to learn and to perform according to changes in the environment.

ADDITIONAL REFERENCES

Adams, J. Stacy. "Interorganization Processes and Organization Boundary Activities." In *Research in Organizational Behavior* 2, edited by Barry M. Staw and L. L. Cummings, 328–332. Greenwich, Conn.: JAI Press, 1980.

Agee, M. "Futurism: A Lesson from the Private Sector." *Business Horizons*, June 1978.

Anderson, D.; Hellriegel, D.; and Slocum, J. W. "Managerial Response to Environmental Hazard." Paper presented at the National Academy of Management Meeting, 1974.

Boulding, Kenneth E.; Kammen, Michael; and Lipset, Seymour. *The Hammond Lectures No. 1, From Abundance to Scarcity, Implications for the American Tradition.* Columbus: Ohio State University Press, 1978.

Child, J. "Organization Structure, Environment, and Performance—The Roles of Strategic Choice." *Sociology* 6 (1972): 1–22.

DeGreene, V. B. *The Adaptive Organization*. New York: John Wiley & Sons, 1982.

Dickson, Douglas N., ed. *Business and Its Publics*. Cambridge, Mass.: HBR Executive Book Series, 1984.

Dill, W. R. "Environment as an Influence on Managerial Autonomy." *Administrative Science Quarterly* 2 (1958): 409–443.

Galbraith, J. *Designing Complex Organizations*. Reading, Mass.: Addison-Wesley, 1973.

Green, Mark; Marlin, Alice Teffer; Kambler, Victor; and Bernstein, Jules. "The Case for a Corporate Democracy Act." *Business Horizons*, Summer 1980.

Hine, Virginia. "The Basic Paradigm of a Future Socio-cultural System." *World Issues*, April–May 1977.

Kast, Fremont E., and Rosenzweig, James E. *Organization and Management: A Systems and Contingency Approach*. 3d ed. New York: McGraw-Hill, 1979.

Kilman, Ralph H. "An Organic-Adaptive Organization: The MAPS Method." *Personnel* 51 (May–June 1974): 35–47.

Kimberly, John R. "Environmental Constraints and Organizational Structure." *Administrative Science Quarterly* 20 (March 1975): 1–8.

Kraus, William A. *Collaboration in Organizations: Alternatives to Hierarchy*. New York: Human Sciences Press, 1980.

MacNulty, C. A. R. "Scenario Development for Corporate Planning." *Futures*, April 1977.

Marcus, Alfred A. *The Adversary Economy: Business Responses to Changing Government Requirements*. Westport, Conn.: Quorum Books, 1984.

Meyer, John W., and Scott, W. Richard. *Organizational Environments: Ritual and Rationality*. Beverly Hills, Calif.: Sage, 1983.

Miles, Robert H. *Macro Organizational Behavior*. Santa Monica, Calif.: Goodyear, 1980.

Newgren, Kenneth E., and Carroll, Archie B. "Social Forecasting in U.S. Corporations—A Survey." *Long Range Planning*, August 1979.

Preble, J. F. "Corporate Use of Environmental Scanning." *University of Michigan Business Review*, September 1978.

Segal, M. "Organization and Environment: A Typology of Adaptability and Structure." *Public Administration Review* (May–June 1974): 212–220.

Terry, P. T. "Mechanisms for Environmental Scanning." *Long Range Planning*, June 1977.

Thomas, P. "Environmental Analysis for Corporate Planning." *Business Horizons*, October 1974.

Turkovich, R. "A Core Typology of Organizational Environments." *Administrative Science Quarterly* (September 1974): 380–394.

Whetten, David A., and Aldrich, Howard. "Organization Set Size and Diversity: People Processing Organizations and Their Environments." *Administration and Society II*, 1979, 251–281.

Woodward, S. N. "The Myth of Turbulence." *Futures* 14, no. 4 (1982): 266–279.

```
┌─────────────────────────────────────┐
│                                     │
│   C       A       S       E         │
│                                     │
└─────────────────────────────────────┘
```

Harvard, Columbia, and George Mason

It was only twenty-eight years ago when cows grazed on the northern Virginia land where George Mason University (GMU) now stands. From its very humble beginnings (seventeen students as an extension campus of the University of Virginia), GMU is now rapidly being recognized as one of the nation's top schools in economics and high technology (so says *The Wall Street Journal*).

Located in Fairfax County just outside of Washington, D.C., the university has created a niche for itself in the world of higher education, despite a shrinking college-age population and federal education cutbacks. At present, 11 percent of the school's 16,500 students are from out-of-state, and the average student SAT score at GMU is significantly higher than the nation's average. The current $24 million worth of construction will be accompanied by an additional 1 million square feet of building space within the next twenty years.

GMU's remarkable growth has occurred partially as a result of its physical proximity to Washington, D.C. By taking advantage of the nation's conservative political and economic moods, in addition to a rapidly expanding high-tech/information-systems economy, GMU has developed unparalleled resources in

Source: David Shribman, "University in Virginia Creates a Niche, Aims to Reach Top Ranks," *The Wall Street Journal* (September 25, 1985), 1, 13.

economics and technology. Its economics faculty is comprised of the leading conservative thinkers in the nation. As stated by Phillip Trudeau, vice-president of the Heritage Foundation, "If you're sitting around Washington looking for new conservative ideas, you look to George Mason."

Much of the university's recent success can be traced to the efforts of President George W. Johnson, who left his position at Temple University in 1978 to become GMU president. He "sensed an opportunity right away.... This was a frontier, but a sophisticated frontier. There were a million and a half of the most highly educated people in the world, with nothing to rally around but the Redskins. There was a perfect opening for a university." Not only was Fairfax County an excellent location for the university because of its proximity to Washington, but, moreover, the county's economic base, in and of itself, is particularly strong. More than 800 companies, many in high-tech, call Fairfax County home, and the number of jobs has jumped from 115,000 to over 230,000 since 1975.

Getting world-renowned faculty in economics and high-tech was one of President Johnson's first priorities when he took over the university's leadership. When Professors James Buchanan and Gordon Tulock, the fathers of the populist free-market school of economics, became disenchanted with their positions at Virginia Tech, they sensed a new aggressiveness and sense of commitment at GMU and relocated their study center there. This center now studies such problems as analyzing the federal budget deficit and its effects, limiting taxes and the role of government in economic life, and examining the effects of a Constitutional amendment requiring a balanced federal budget. In the high-tech area, Dr. Andrew Sage, former chairman of the department of electrical engineering at the University of Virginia, was paid $108,780 to leave Charlottesville and move to Fairfax.

The university's niche in the area of high technology is on an equal footing with its niche in economics. In 1982, GMU examined ads in *The Washington Post* and determined that the capital area's job needs were concentrated in electronics, information systems, and systems engineering. By being able to attract large gifts and grants from area businesses and foundations, the university attracted high-priced faculty to its School of Information Technology and Engineering, the nation's only engineering school rooted in information sciences rather than the physical sciences.

These niches have been expanded and strengthened by the University's filling its board of trustees with executives from such national firms as Arthur Andersen and Company, Dynalectron Corporation, TRW, Xerox, AT&T, Mobil, and Comsat Telesystems. Such ties with business have also attracted a tremendous amount of money. For example, four years ago, GMU had an endowment of less than $1 million and no endowed professorships. By September 1985, there was an endowment of $20 million and twenty-nine endowed chairs.

A very few years ago, GMU's competitors in the arena of higher education were its sister schools—Virginia Commonwealth University and Old Dominion University. Now, the school sees its main competition coming from such academic notables as Georgetown and the University of Virginia. In fact, GMU is listed with Harvard, Columbia, Chicago, UCLA, and MIT as having the majority of the economists cited in a recent book, *Great Economists Since Keynes.*

GMU is also finding itself another niche to fill in northern Virginia—high-caliber basketball. Fourteen years ago, the university's basketball schedule included the Philadelphia College of Pharmacy and Science (GMU lost). For the 1985–1986 season, the schedule includes such powerhouses as Georgetown, which will play the GMU Patriots in the latter's new, $16 million, 10,000-seat arena.

QUESTIONS FOR DISCUSSION

1. Speculate on the causes for GMU's phenomenal success.
2. Can GMU deliberately and successfully select its competition? If so, how would you propose this be done? If not, why not?
3. What effect do you think the nation's conservative political and economic mood has had on GMU's success? Speculate on the consequences of a move toward more liberal trends.
4. How do you think the cultural opportunities in and around Washington, D.C. affect and are affected by the presence of GMU?
5. Do you think that the educational technology and areas of specialization chosen by GMU could be a function of the available faculty/student skills and expectations?

PART TWO

The Organization's Linkage Systems

How do organizations cope with their environments? This question is the focus for the second part of the book. The macro environment serves as the organization's envelope; it is the source for organization resources and the depository for organization outputs. The organization takes from the environment, adds value to what it takes, and gives back more than it receives. When doing this the organization faces a series of dynamic environmental opportunities and constraints that affect its operations.

Within its environmental complex, the organization must establish some linkage or channel to bring in the necessary resources, to process these resources into the finished product or service and, in turn, to distribute this product or service to customers in the environment. Changes in this environment cause the organization to be ever wary in order to keep untoward circumstances from disrupting normal activities. The organization's external linkages provide this monitoring function.

When an organization interfaces with its environment, it simply adapts to environmental pressures and influences. This adaptation does not always mean that the organization must be reactive to these pressures and influences. Indeed, a popular strategy for dealing with the environment is for the organization to be proactive—for the organization itself to initiate action to deal with these forces.

As an example of such a strategy, a textile company might lobby the federal government in order to have favorable legislation passed. This strategy contrasts with one by which the company simply adjusts to legislation drawn by others without its input.

Today's organization faces a generally turbulent environment, one that is highly dynamic, so it becomes the task of the organization to monitor this environment and take the action necessary to stay in harmony with it. Part Two of this book deals with the dynamic interrelationship between the organization and the macro environment. Chapter 4 describes the various linkage networks and other mechanisms that the organization utilizes for coping with its environment. Chapter 5 examines in detail how information gleaned from the macro environment is processed for decision-making purposes. Chapter 6 contains material showing how organizations must be aware of, and adjust to, other organizations in their environment.

The chapters in this part describe the concepts and processes that facilitate an understanding of organizational/environmental linkages.

4

The Organization's External Linkages

If the Shoe Fits

When world-class athletes or sports officials visit Herzogenaurach, Germany, they do two things. First, they visit a one-room museum devoted to the history of sneakers. Second, should they stay overnight, they stay at the Sports Hotel. Although it contains only thirty-two rooms, the hotel boasts an indoor swimming pool, tennis courts, a soccer field, saunas, coaches for a wide variety of athletic endeavors, and a magnificent chef who prepares fine cuisine. The best part of all is the tab—there isn't one, at least for the guests. That's because the bill is paid by the Addidas Company, the hotel's owner and German sports equipment manufacturer. The simple purpose of this hospitality is to maximize exposure of the Addidas logo by making all who wear Addidas products with the logo into walking, running, vaulting, and kicking billboards.

The Sports Hotel in Germany is just one example of Addidas's Chairman Horst Dassler's deep involvement in amateur sports. His philosophy of business is to make friends and then deals. Besides the business aspect, Dassler also dabbles in the politics of international sports, and his opinion carries tremendous weight when sports officials make such decisions as where the 1992 Olympics will be held. And although Addidas's past focus has primarily been directed at amateur sports, Dassler has been paying more attention to the professional sports environment, as exemplified by his firm's payment of $1 million to Patrick Ewing of the New York Knicks for wearing Addidas shoes.

Most people think of lobbying as political activity taking place in the halls of the Capitol in Washington, D.C., but Dassler has taken the practice to new dimensions with

sports. An Addidas dinner or reception is commonplace at any International Olympic Committee (IOC) meeting, and Dassler can usually be found at these, mingling with the delegates.

Dassler considers this lobbying necessary in light of the IOC's decision, made after the 1968 Olympic Games, that required a country's Olympic committee, not individual athletes, to choose what shoes and uniforms would be worn. The result—89 percent of the countries attending the 1984 Los Angeles Olympic Games wore Addidas products. More recently, in 1985, Addidas gave out over $30 million in cash and equipment to Olympic teams. The company's support for the U. S. Olympic boxing team included uniforms, advertisements in programs, and even towels for the competition.

The Addidas chairman doesn't just talk and listen to sports officials and athletes, however. Acknowledging the fact that 80 percent of his company's products are worn by "civilians," Dassler has embarked on a new $22 million advertising campaign aimed at the leisure market.

Dassler manages to absorb a tremendous amount of information affecting his business by controlling a small army of his company's representatives who are stationed in over 160 countries where Addidas does business. These representatives are officially responsible for keeping the chairman informed of any and all information dealing with sports politics. In addition, Dassler employs Hassine Hamoudi, a former colonel in the Tunisian army, who has tremendous influence with sports executives in Arab countries and French-speaking North Africa. More important, Addidas representatives have seats on many important Olympic advisory committees (e.g., Hamoudi is a member of the IOC Press Commission). Thomas Bach, recently hired by Addidas, is a former Olympic fencer who is also a member of the IOC Athletes' Advisory Committee. Attor-

Source: Bill Abrams, "Sports Boss: Addidas Makes Friends, Then Strikes Deals that Move Sneakers," *The Wall Street Journal* (January 23, 1986), 1, 15.

ney Richard Pound is one of Canada's two IOC delegates, sits on the IOC executive board, and just happens to be an Addidas lawyer as well. Dassler claims that his connections enable his company to bridge the political and cultural differences between East and West as well as those between developed and underdeveloped countries.

And as an afterthought to helping bridge these international differences through his connections, the IOC Congress, meeting in 1985, awarded all marketing rights for the 1988 Olympic Games to the ISL Marketing Company. Incidentally, the majority of ISL stock is held by Dassler and members of his family.

Mr. Dassler certainly realizes the need to maintain effective linkages to key elements of Addidas's outside environment. He believes this is such an important function that, as CEO, he is willing to spend considerable time and effort building and maintaining these linkages. In other words, as we describe in this chapter, he plays a *boundary-spanning* role for the organization in addition to carrying out his internal administrative duties.

Of course, Addidas maintains other units in the organization that span the organization's boundary to develop and maintain linkages. Marketing, purchasing, legal, and other units maintain vital linkages to Addidas's environment.

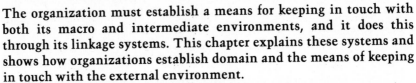

CHAPTER PLAN

The organization must establish a means for keeping in touch with both its macro and intermediate environments, and it does this through its linkage systems. This chapter explains these systems and shows how organizations establish domain and the means of keeping in touch with the external environment.

Boundary-spanning linkage systems provide sensors to monitor the events occurring in the external environment. These sensors, after gathering environmental information, relate it to the decision-authority centers that exist within the organization so that proper decisions and strategies can be adopted to keep the organization vibrant.

Organizations know their environment through linkage networks. Linkage networks are systems established between the organization and the macro environment that link the organization to the macro environment. These systems are also called interface networks, boundary-spanning units, or intermediate environments. The function of these systems is to serve as conduits for sources of inputs to the organization and as conduits for the distribution of products or services produced by the organization, as we see in Figure 4.1.

In this chapter we examine the components and functioning of the organization's linkage network. We look at the various kinds of boundary-spanning networks that organizations employ to know and use their environment to the best advantage. Various strategies organizations use in sensing their environment are also explored. Finally, the way the macro environment affects the internal design and operations of the organization is examined.

For many managers, the environment is an abstract, hard-to-deal-with concept. Managers know their environment in terms of specifics. They know their suppliers, competitors, distributors, customers, specific government regulatory agencies, and so on. But they do not know their environment in the global sense. There is simply too much to know; consequently, managers suffer from information overload.

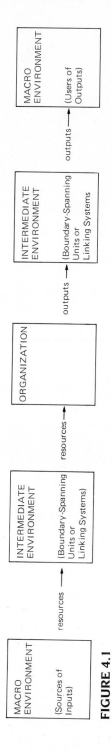

FIGURE 4.1

The Organization's Intermediate Environment as a Conduit for Inputs and Outputs

Therefore, organizations scope, or limit, their environment. They make decisions about which parts of the environment they plan to link up to and monitor, and which ones they plan to ignore, at least for the time being. In scoping the environment, the risk of ignoring some important aspect is always present. How many managers were really prepared for the OPEC-led oil shock of 1973? How many knew that over 50 percent of U.S. oil was imported? Few monitored that aspect of their environment very carefully.

TASK ENVIRONMENT AND DOMAIN CONSENSUS

Organizations establish a *domain* in the environment. This domain consists of organizational claims in terms of (1) range of products offered, (2) population served, and (3) services rendered.[1] Organizations also have a *task environment*, which consists of those components of the environment that are relevant or potentially relevant for goal setting and attainment.[2] This environment is composed of (1) customers, (2) suppliers of equipment, materials, labor, capital, and work space, (3) competitors for both markets and resources, and (4) regulatory groups, including government agencies, unions, and interfirm associations.

Individuals in the task environment as well as top management and owners (if it is a business organization) share the responsibility for determining *domain consensus*. Domain consensus is concerned with defining "a set of expectations both for members of an organization and for others with whom they interact, about what the organization will and will not do. It provides . . . an image of the organization's role in a larger system."[3] Figure 4.2 shows how the environment is narrowed using the concepts of task environment, domain, and domain consensus.

The failure of an organization to accurately determine and operate within its domain can lead to organizational dysfunction. For example, Stop and Shop Companies, a small New England supermarket chain known for providing good values and low prices to its customers, diversified in the early 1970s by acquiring Bradlee Stores, also known for good values and low prices. However, Stop and Shop's chairman, A. V. Goldberg, had "visions of grandeur." In attempting to upgrade Bradlee's image and gain a share of the upscale department store market, Goldberg unloaded his low-priced items, stocked the shelves with higher-quality (and higher-priced) goods, and went on an acquisition rampage by purchasing eighteen Jefferson Ward Stores in addition to Almy's, a nineteen-store department store chain. But this was not what Bradlee's customers wanted—profits nosedived 64 percent in fiscal year 1986 for Bradlee Stores, and earnings for the Stop and Shop Companies fell by almost 50 percent for the same period. This occurred because the organization did

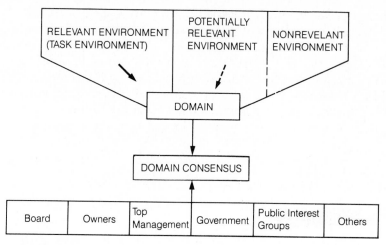

FIGURE 4.2

Scoping the Outside Environment

not accurately determine its domain, particularly the task environment components of customers, product lines, and competition. In short, there was no domain consensus as to what Stop and Shop and Bradlee, in particular, were to be. Goldberg recognizes his error of trying to move upmarket and make Bradlee Stores high-priced department stores when all the customer really wanted was good value.[4]

THE ORGANIZATION'S BOUNDARIES

Where does the organization end and the environment begin? One way to approach this question is to identify the core technology of an organization. The *core technology* of an organization is the system the organization employs for the production of its primary utility. For an automobile manufacturer, it is the assembly line. For a university, it is the classroom, library, and laboratory. For a state welfare department, it is the process of certifying those eligible for welfare and seeing that they receive their checks on time.

Thompson maintains that rational organizations seek to seal off, or at least protect, their core technologies from environmental influences.[5] They do this by using input and output components that seek to smooth input and output volumes. Airlines may offer reduced fares on light days or in slow seasons. Telephone companies may offer reduced rates in the evening. Inventory-control units of organizations may attempt to smooth the materials-ordering process. In each of these cases, actions are being taken to reduce the fluctuation in the flow of inputs to the technical core and in the outputs from the technical core.

Thus, the boundary of the organization might be thought of as those units of the organization that surround the technical core and moderate the flow of inputs to the core and outputs from the core. Company recruiters on college campuses are members of the organization boundary because they are concerned with moderating inputs by recruiting and selecting new employees. Salespeople employed by a company are also members of the boundary, but they are concerned with monitoring output by selling and perhaps distributing the product or service.

Boundary-Spanning Units

Boundary-spanning units are those units whose primary purpose is to adjust the organization to the constraints and contingencies found in the environment that are not controlled by the organization.[6] A law firm that the organization retains for handling government suits is a boundary-spanning unit, as is an employment agency or an advertising agency. These units exist to tie the organization to its environment by spanning the organization's boundaries.

A boundary-spanning unit can be either within the organization or within the intermediate environment. If the boundary-spanning unit such as an employment agency exists within the intermediate environment, then the organization must have a unit or position to link with it. For example, the personnel department may be designated as the unit to work with employment agencies. Some might argue that the personnel department in this case is the boundary-spanning unit. It is, in that it spans the boundary of the organization with a unit in the outside environment. But the employment agency in the intermediate environment is playing the true role of adjusting the organization to the constraints and contingencies found in the macro environment. However, not all boundary-spanning units are located in the intermediate environment. Some units within the organization function as boundary-spanning units. An organization may have its own internal cadre of lawyers. It may have its own recruiters. It may be vertically integrated and own its sources of raw materials as well as the transportation system needed to deliver the raw materials to the organization. It may also own the system used to serve the customer or client. However, even though these units are part of the organization, they are boundary-spanning units because they perform boundary-spanning functions. Figure 4.3 depicts some examples of common boundary-spanning units for a large corporation. This figure presents in detail some of the elements in the macro, intermediate, and micro environments.

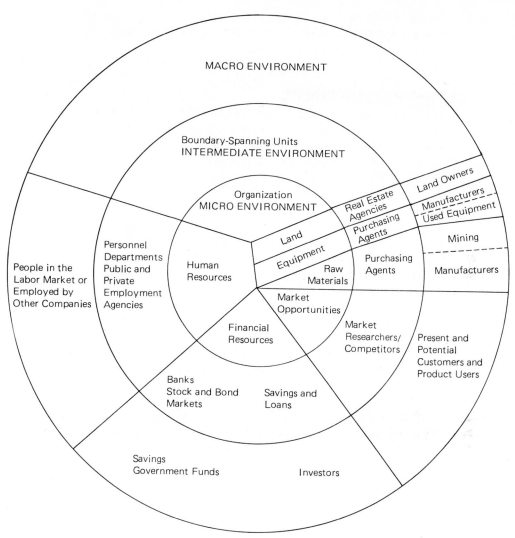

FIGURE 4.3

Some Common Boundary-Spanning Units for a Large Corporation

What causes an organization to internalize its own boundary-spanning units? Two factors have a major bearing: economies of scale and reduction of uncertainty by obtaining greater control. An organization may find it cheaper to have its own recruiters, legal staff, and advertising department if it can spread the costs of these units over a large number of transactions. Also, an organization might find that it can reduce the uncertainty involved in securing inputs or distributing outputs if it owns sources of inputs and transportation.

Boundary-Spanning Roles

Sometimes a person who is not in a boundary-spanning unit will play the *role* of a boundary spanner. For example, the chief executive officer of a major corporation may spend more time and effort dealing with stockholders, major suppliers and customers, or federal agencies than in managing the day-to-day operations of the company. A university president may spend more time on the road giving speeches to alumni or dealing with prospective donors than in the office. A business school dean may be more concerned with interacting with the business community and various state and federal agencies than in managing the internal affairs of the school. Dassler, in the Addidas article in the beginning of this chapter, is an example of a CEO who plays a boundary-spanning role.

Indeed, one of the characteristics of American industry in the 1980s is the boundary-spanning role played by American executives, particularly vis-à-vis the political component of the macro environment. Remember that Lee Iacocca worked with the federal government in 1980 in order to obtain federally backed loans for Chrysler. Other examples include J. Peter Grace, head of W. R. Grace and Company, who headed the President's Commission on Cost-Cutting in Government; Robert Beck, the head of Prudential, who is especially influential with the Senate finance committee; and Stephen Levy, chairman of Bolt, Barenek, and Newman, a Massachusetts high-tech company, who has great influence with his congressional friends concerning foreign trade issues.

When a non-boundary-spanning unit plays the role of a boundary spanner, this is often done because of the prestige and status carried by the position the person occupies. A university's president, for example, may be more effective in raising funds for the university than its director of development. There is nothing wrong with a non-boundary-spanning unit playing the role of a boundary spanner, provided that someone in the office is given the job of running the organization or unit when the person is gone. If this does not happen, important decisions and day-to-day administrative work will not get done. A university president may have an executive vice president who actually runs the university. A business school dean may have an associate dean for administrative affairs to run the internal aspects of the business school. The point is, unless the person playing the role of boundary spanner explicitly delegates duties to make decisions in the office, the management work of the individual will not be accomplished while the boundary-spanning work is being carried out.

Mintzberg explicitly recognizes this boundary-spanning role of many top managers. Among the ten roles he identified that managers perform are the roles of "liaison" and "figurehead." The role of liaison "deals with the significant web of relationships that the manager maintains with numerous individuals and groups outside the organization that he leads."[7] Again, think of the Addidas case at the beginning of this chapter and all the various boundary-spanning roles played by its CEO, Horst Dassler. The figurehead role rests on the fact that the manager is a symbol and thus is required to perform a number of duties including that of representing the organization to outsiders. A manager must be careful that performing these roles does not seriously conflict with other roles of a more internal nature, such as leader, disturbance handler, and resource allocator.

Boundary Spanning and Environmental Scanning

Some organizations establish a specific unit to scan or read and interpret the environment on a regular basis. Often this environmental scanning unit is located in a long-range planning, forecasting, or research and development department. General Electric, for example, has a unit devoted to scanning and long-range forecasting.

Environmental scanning differs to some extent from boundary spanning. *Environmental scanning* is a particular type of boundary spanning concerned with assessing and projecting change in various macroenvironmental components in the short or long term.[8] For example, the organization may examine changes in demographics, competition, technology, and customer needs and wants and project these over five-, ten-, and twenty-year time periods. The idea behind this examination is that the organization may need to begin developing new products, services, and markets today to take advantage of the forecasted trends. Although boundary-spanning units and people in boundary-spanning roles can help gather information useful for scanning and forecasting, it is helpful to establish a unit in the organization that is responsible for interpreting and analyzing these trends for planning and decision-making purposes. This is particularly so for organizations that live in changing and uncertain environments. The better these organizations scan, forecast, and plan for change, the higher the quality of decision making and the easier it will be for them to cope with environmental change.

Permeability, Resilience, and Maintenance of Organization Boundaries

Using the concepts of boundary-spanning units, domain consensus, and the task environment, we can begin to examine more specific characteristics of organization boundaries. In particular, we are interested in the permeability, resilience, and maintenance of organization boundaries.

PERMEABILITY. To what extent do boundary-spanning units facilitate the flow of information and resources between the organization and the macro environment? As we mentioned earlier, the main function of boundary-spanning units is to serve as lifelines between the organization and its environment. In particular, they serve as enhancers of the technical core of the organization. If an organization has staked out its domain and identified its task environment, then it is up to the boundary-spanning units to focus specifically on those environmental units in the organization's domain and task environment, and not on the environmental sectors outside its domain.

Thus, we see a measure of permeability—the ability of an organization's boundary to screen information and selectively allow it to enter the organization. Are significant resources and information from the organization's domain and task environment efficiently processed by the boundary-spanning units? Are peripheral resources and information outside the domain efficiently dealt with by the boundary-spanning units so that there is little interference with the technical core? In other words, boundary-spanning units need to be relatively permeable with regard to significant sectors of the macro environment, and yet they must screen or buffer other environmental sectors not significant for the organization. They do this by evaluating sections of the environment in relation to their effect on the task environment and the organization's technical core. Unless this happens, the technical core of the organization will be overwhelmed by information overload with which it might be unable to cope. It will have difficulty determining what is important, what is unimportant, and what is functional rather than dysfunctional for organizational operation.

Let us look at some examples. A small, Lutheran-supported, liberal arts college located in a small midwestern town needs to create boundary-spanning units that will effectively attract students who want to major in areas of study offered by the college. The boundary-spanning units ought not to focus on students who wish to obtain an M.B.A. degree or a Doctor of Veterinary Medicine degree, since these are not offered. Similarly, the boundary-spanning units must be in tune with the wishes of the sponsoring Lutheran organization more so than the wishes of Jesuit Catholics.

Let us take the example of a real-life organization. Waste Management is one of the nation's largest domestic and industrial waste handling organizations. This company, because of the nature of its business, is very sensitive to environmental critics, both within and outside of government agencies. Therefore, they have established official boundary-spanning positions to provide two-way communication between the organization and both governmental and private environmental protection groups. For example, there are ten environmental compliance officers constantly in the field to monitor the sites of its subsidiary, Chem

Waste, on a regular basis. Likewise, Waste Management has dramatically expanded its government liaison and lobbying efforts with the federal Environmental Protection Agency (EPA). In addition, two prominent environmentalists, James T. Banks and William Brown, have joined Waste Management to establish a dialogue with critics.[9]

In short, Waste Management understands its task environment, recognizes the fact that government agencies, communities, and critics are part of that environment, and, thus, has created specific boundary-spanning positions to deal with them. Moreover, these boundary-spanning positions are selectively permeable in that they seek out and interact only with those specific parts of the task environment that are of paramount importance to Waste Management's operations. For example, environmentalists Banks and Brown would not report information about homeowners' dissatisfaction with municipal garbage collection to Waste Management executives.

RESILIENCE. This leads us to the concept of resilience. Suppose the small liberal arts college from our example above decided to change its mission or primary purpose in response to changes in its task environment. The kinds of information and resources processed by the boundary-spanning units would also change. The resilience of boundary-spanning units refers to the degree to which they respond to changes in the mission and goals of the organization. Can the units now seek out and process new types of information? Can different resources be located and brought to the organization? If the small liberal arts college decides to offer an M.B.A., can the boundary-spanning unit, for example, the admissions office or high-school recruiters, now recruit individuals with that interest, or will new boundary-spanning units need to be created?

In our Waste Management example, we noted that the company's boundary-spanning units are primarily interested in interacting with government agencies, communities, and critics. This is because all three significantly affect Waste Management's land-based operations. However, should Waste Management change its goals or operations, then the actions of the boundary-spanning units would have to change to reflect this. For example, the company is currently speculating on operating an off-shore incinerator ship for toxic wastes instead of using land-based toxic waste dumps. The information and interactions needed for this new venture are significantly different from those needed for land-based operations; that is, Waste Management's boundary-spanners need to interact more with the EPA for this purpose than with state or community groups. Also, critics of Waste Management's operations in midwestern communities would probably not provide valuable information regarding the operation of an ocean-based incinerator ship; rather, the organization's boundary-spanners would need to obtain information from coastal residents, marine biologists, oceanographers, and so on.

Notice that the concept of resilience depends to a great extent on the interface between organization mission and goals and the perceived environmental opportunity. If the environmental opportunity changes, and this change is consistent with top management values and philosophy, then the organization mission and goal structure should change to take advantage of the new environmental opportunity. This, then, causes a change in the function of the boundary-spanning unit. Therefore, the boundary-spanning unit has brought in information that can cause a reevaluation and change in mission.

But how does an organization know of a new environmental opportunity if the boundary-spanning units are concerned only with satisfying the organization's present domain and task environment? We have stated that boundary-spanning units need to focus on those aspects of the environment that are relevant to the organization. If this is done, how are opportunities outside of the present scope of the organization's operations identified? Organizations need to set up a means to monitor and maintain boundary units.

BOUNDARY MAINTENANCE. Boundary-spanning units need to be managed just as other units of the organization need to be managed. Managing boundary-spanning units helps ensure their permeability and resilience. Also, and just as important, adequate management of boundary-spanning units will help assure not only that the organization is in sufficient contact with its environment but that it is also receiving information on *potential* task environments. In other words, one function of boundary-spanning units is to differentiate relevant from nonrelevant information and to classify some currently nonrelevant information as *potentially relevant*, based on the probability that the mission can change.

For example, suppose the engineering staff of an automobile engine parts manufacturer, through scanning, learns of a new development in jet engines that creates a need for a new engine part similar to a part now being manufactured by the company. This information needs to be communicated to top management, and a decision needs to be made as to whether the company should produce this jet engine part. In making this decision, top management will decide whether manufacturing this part is within the present scope of the organization's mission and goals. If it is, it may then decide to make the part if it can be manufactured profitably. If it is not within present mission and goals, then top management must decide if the perceived market opportunity has enough profit potential and is within the scope of managerial values and philosophy so that the mission and goals of the organization should be changed to accommodate the manufacture of the jet engine part. If they decide in the affirmative, then the mission and goals of the organization might well be changed to take advantage of the market opportunity.

Notice several things from this example. First, the boundary-spanning unit must be managed so as to communicate this important market opportunity to a place in the organization where authority exists to act on the information. This linkage to a *decision-authority center* is critical for effective boundary management and is discussed further in the next section of the chapter. Second, criteria the decision authority can use in making a decision must exist. In our example, the criteria were potential profitability and consistency with top management values and philosophy. For a nonprofit organization such as the small liberal arts college, criteria used to judge whether to add a new degree program might include the necessity of increasing enrollments as well as the consistency of the market opportunity with the philosophy and values of the college's board of trustees.

Finally, a boundary-spanning unit (or a portion of one) needs to be given a specific charge to monitor developments outside the present organizational domain and task environment. In the engine parts case, we indicated that some engineers learned of new developments in jet engine manufacture that presented an opportunity for the organization. Perhaps they learned of this through contacts in a professional or trade association, or through reading professional and technical journals. This same information could have also come from a product research and development group or from a market research group in the organization had they been given such a charge. The point is, some unit in the organization must be given the specific task of monitoring developments outside the present organizational domain that have potential for the organization if the organization is to remain viable. Thus, this unit is responsible for scanning.

We can diagram this process as shown in Figure 4.4. The permeability of the boundary-spanning units determines the extent to which they are adequately monitoring the task and potential task environments and screening out information from the nonrelevant environment. Information received is processed by the units in terms of its consistency with decision criteria such as profitability, growth, goals, and mission. If the information is found to have present or potential benefit for the organization, it is passed on for processing to the appropriate decision-authority center in top, middle, or lower management. The decision center then decides whether to incorporate the information into the technical core. The degree to which the boundary-spanning units can adjust to changes in the need for information coming from monitoring of the task and potential task environments determines boundary-unit resiliency.

136

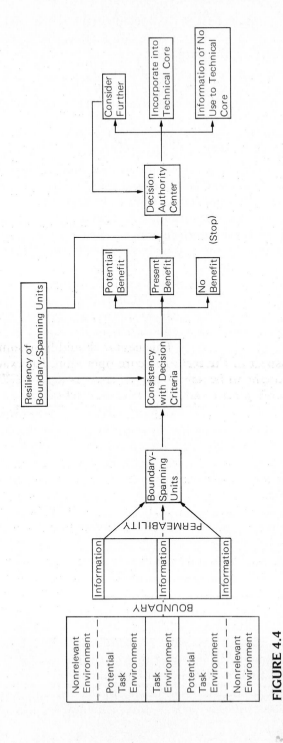

FIGURE 4.4
Boundary-Spanning Unit Permeability, Resiliency, and Their Influence on Technical Core

The role of the boundary-spanning unit in serving as a linking mechanism to a decision center (as indicated in Figure 4.4) is extremely important. Consequently, in the next section we expand on this concept and its relationship to boundary-unit management and authority.

BOUNDARY-SPANNING LINKAGE: SENSORS AND DECISION-AUTHORITY CENTERS

As we have indicated, boundary-spanning units link the organization to its environment. As depicted in Figure 4.4, this linkage occurs specifically between the task and potential task environments and a decision-authority center in the organization. We need to explore further two aspects in this linkage: (1) the interface of the boundary-spanning units with the decision-authority centers in the organization, and (2) the establishment and use of devices to "sense" the environment.

Linkage to Decision-Authority Centers

Each boundary-spanning unit should be directly linked to a decision-authority center in the organization. This center should have some authority over some aspect of the technical core operation. For example, market researchers ought to be able to input new customer needs and wants to product development and production specialists. Buyers and purchasing agents must be able to have input into the decision-making process of inventory control specialists. Personnel recruiters must be able to influence the human resource development process used by managers in the technical core.

Although the process of linking the boundary-spanning unit to the decision-authority center may seem simple, it often does not work as neatly as described. Decision-authority centers tend to isolate themselves by establishing staff groups and subordinate layers of management to screen information. The purpose of these groups is to process information for the decision center so as to avoid information overload. When information gathered by the boundary-spanning unit is fed to the decision authority, it is often filtered and distorted, or it may be inaccurate or received too late.

For example, suppose personnel recruiters find it increasingly difficult to recruit an occupational group, such as industrial engineers. In a typical organization this information may pass through several layers of management and staff groups before it reaches a decision authority where some action can be taken. The communication flow could look something like that shown by the solid lines in Figure 4.5. Obviously, by the time the information is received by engineering unit supervisors so

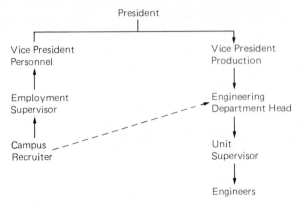

FIGURE 4.5

**Two Forms of Boundary-Spanning Linkage Between
Recruiters and Engineering Staff**

that work loads could be adjusted or, in extreme cases, so that paraprofessional engineering technician jobs could be created, the information could be severely distorted or a crisis in work output could occur. One solution would be to allow the recruiters to communicate directly to the engineering department, as indicated by the dashed line in Figure 4.5. Even though this violates the formal lines of managerial authority and communication in the organization, it would allow the information to get to the decision center more quickly and accurately.

This may not solve the problem, however, for the decision authorities in the engineering department may have surrounded themselves with staff and administrative assistants who are used as screening devices. While the original intention of setting up these staff and assistant positions may have been to relieve the work load of the people in the decision center, the practical result is to insulate the heads of the decision centers from inputs from other areas of the organization—particularly the boundary-spanning units.

So how does the boundary-spanning unit pass on necessary information to decision-authority centers? The answer rests in the nature of the management of the boundary-spanning linkage system. Too often managers in organizations view the organization as a set of separate systems instead of subsystems of the total organizational system. Thus, the points at which these systems interface are critical for effective overall system operation. This is particularly true for the boundary-spanning units found in organizations. Usually these boundary-spanning units are within organizational subsystems: Personnel recruiters are in the personnel subsystem; market researchers are in the marketing subsystem; salespeople are in the sales or marketing subsystem; public relations is often in the marketing subsystem; and purchasing is in the logistics or production subsystem. All these boundary-spanning units are linked to an organizational subsystem. Thus, the critical question is how do these boundary-spanning units get information through their own subsystem to other decision-authority centers?

One method now being increasingly advocated by managers is the establishment of a *management information system* (MIS). An MIS is an integrated system of information produced by various organizational subsystems. The key is that the total information flow is coordinated as a total system. This ensures maximum system interface and the passage of needed information from boundary-spanning units to decision centers.

Although we discuss the MIS in more depth in Chapter 5 and examine technology in Chapter 12, we should point out here how high-tech MISs allow information to pass directly from the environment to the decision-authority centers in an organization. With the aid of computers, managers in decision-authority centers are now capable of acting as their own boundary-spanners. Irwin Sitkin, vice president for Corporate Administration at Aetna Life and Casualty, now views his organization as "one great big information processing business. . . . The game has become 'Get the right information to the right guy at the right time to make the right decision.'"[10]

The "game," played by most large organizations with high-tech information processing capabilities, is mostly aimed at getting and using information from the customer/client component of the macro and task environments. For example, Merrill Lynch's Cash Management Account automatically combines information on a customer's checking, savings, credit cards, and securities accounts into one computerized monthly statement and sweeps idle funds into interest-bearing money market funds. American Hospital Supply Corporation (AHS) managers keep close tabs on that organization's customers and suppliers through its computer links. Hospitals, themselves, can enter orders directly through AHS terminals. This, in turn, often locks out competitors who do not have direct pipelines to their hospital customers. Certainly, a well-integrated, high-tech MIS has become an indispensable attribute of a successful linkage system between the organization and its environment.[11]

Another means of enhancing linkage is through a type of project management where the significant subsystem components for a given project are brought together temporarily in order to complete the project. For example, in an aircraft manufacturing company, individuals from design, fabrication, assembly, and testing might be brought together for a brief period to work on the development of a particular aircraft. We discuss project management in greater detail in Chapter 10.

A final method of enhancing system linkage is through task forces and committees that periodically bring together people from different organizational subsystems to discuss mutual issues. For instance, in the above example of a personnel recruiter, perhaps if the personnel recruiters met periodically with managers in various other subsystem units (e.g., engineers, accountants, and salespeople), they would be in a better position to communicate the labor market situation for various occupations needed by these subsystems.

A Taxonomy of Linkages

What kinds of linkage systems do organizations actually use? We can place the linkage systems organizations employ into four primary classes based on the type of environmental interface strategy the organization has adopted. These classes are (1) imperviousness—the withdrawal model, (2) selective imperviousness, (3) adaptation, and (4) action-adaptation.[12]

IMPERVIOUSNESS: THE WITHDRAWAL MODEL. Organizations that adopt this linkage strategy actually try to seal themselves off from their environment: They withdraw. The key issue as they see it under this strategy is to develop means to keep the environment from interfering with their operations.

Of course, we know that if the withdrawal model were carried to the extreme, the organization would soon die. How would it get its resources? How would it distribute the goods and services it produced? It would soon atrophy and die because it would use more resources than it received from the environment. Most organizations attempt to achieve *negative entropy*; that is, they attempt to create more resources than they actually use. Instead of one unit of resource plus one unit of resource equalling two units of output, it actually equals two plus a fraction more.

The many leveraged buyouts that characterized the mid-1980s are good examples of conditions in which organizations have been able to acquire and/or control relatively large amounts of resources though expending relatively small amounts of resources. (Leveraged buyouts are discussed further in Chapter 6.) Note, however, that negative entropy is impossible to achieve if an organization strictly adheres to the withdrawal model.

Few organizations actually adopt this mode as a long-term linkage strategy. However, some organizations act as if they are in the withdrawal model, at least in the short run. They isolate themselves or some of their operations from their environment for periods of time. Railway passenger service in the late 1950s and the 1960s acted as if it was a closed system under the withdrawal model, as we explained in Chapter 2. Passengers had a difficult time making reservations. Rolling stock and track were not maintained or modernized and passenger stations were closed. Amtrak is an effort to overcome this strategy.

The Goldman Sachs organization, a New York investment banking firm, is somewhat of an anomaly in its industry because it comes very close to practicing an imperviousness strategy. Rarely are outsiders brought into the organization; rather, employees are hired directly from college and usually stay with Goldman Sachs and a particular department for their entire careers. Goldman Sachs also prefers to ignore a major component of its task environment, its competitors, and, moreover, is very choosy about which clients it will serve. Surprisingly, Goldman Sachs does maintain negative entropy—it is one of the most successful investment banking firms in the nation. We will further discuss this particular organization in Chapter 13.

Universities, at one time, acted as if they were under the withdrawal model. Professors did little consulting. Theoretical developments that had little immediate application were prized. Students were viewed as receivers of knowledge to be dispensed as the university saw fit. Most universities today, of course, are trying to or have overcome this "ivory tower" image.

SELECTIVE IMPERVIOUSNESS. This is probably a more commonly used model than the withdrawal model. Here the organization is quite selective about the linkage systems it sets up. Only key parts of the task environment (those that have an immediate effect on the technical core operations) are allowed to penetrate the organization, and these parts may only penetrate when there is vital information or resources to be provided. There is little concern for the remainder of the task environment and almost none for the potential task environment.

Under this strategy, boundary-spanning units primarily function as screening and blocking devices to buffer and insulate the organization. They play a minor role in information and resource transmission to the decision-authority centers in the organization. Their effectiveness is judged on the basis of how well they protect the organization's technical core from environmental changes.

Many large organizations with a technical core based on a history of stability in the environment adopt this strategy. Once again, universities fit this model, as do railway passenger services. But other organizations do, too. The military initially resisted changing long-established procedures and structures when faced with a call for change from both inside and outside the organization. Business machine companies in the late 1940s and 1950s resisted a call for changes in product and service markets, which allowed two upstarts, IBM and Xerox, to capitalize on market opportunities. These two companies rapidly and successfully introduced a wide variety of office products that revolutionized the office

workplace. Their copy machines and typewriters have evolved into sophisticated word processors and personal computers that are being
widely used today. Selective imperviousness can be a dangerous strategy
for an organization because it effectively screens out market opportunities in the potential task environment.

The case of Nissan Motor Company demonstrates some of the dangers involved with selective imperviousness. Nissan basically maintains
boundary contacts with its customers through its dealerships. However,
unlike its major competitor, Toyota, which sells its cars through rich, independent dealers, Nissan has equity in half its dealerships. Toyota's
dealers tend to be more aggressive and profit-driven; thus, they transmit
vitally important consumer information from the environment to decision makers at corporate headquarters in Japan. Nissan dealers, on the
other hand, tend to listen more to the manufacturer than to the market. In
1987, analysts predicted a 5 percent sales decline for Nissan car and truck
sales, a decline caused because Nissan's linkages do not bring in enough
accurate information about what customers are thinking.[13]

ADAPTATION. Under this strategy the linking systems adapt the organization to the environment. The organization actually changes itself to adapt
to the contingencies in the environment. In fact, Leavitt, Dill, and Eyring
subtitle this strategy "the organizational chameleon."[14] We have indicated that organizations should adapt to their environments. But there is
a danger to the wholesale implementation of this strategy: Because most
organizational environments are constantly changing, the organization
constantly changes. There is a danger of too little stability within the organization. The organization hops from one opportunity to another or
tries to be all things to all people. Obviously, the wholesale adoption of
this strategy can have serious dysfunctional consequences for the organization since stability, unity of purpose, and efficient use of resources become difficult to achieve. Some office machine and electronic companies
faced this problem as they tried to become computer manufacturers in
the late 1960s in order to compete with IBM. They found that they could
not adapt and soon liquidated their computer operations.

However, one company that so far has managed to use a successful adaptation strategy is Bell and Howell, the one-time manufacturer of home
movie cameras. The competition component of both the macro and task
environments, that is, Japanese competition, forced Bell and Howell out
of the movie camera business in the late 1970s. The company adapted to
this environmental situation by entering the booming video duplication
business. In fact, Bell and Howell is the number one duplicator of home
entertainment video cassettes in the United States.[15]

ACTION-ADAPTATION. This leads us to our fourth model. Under this strategy the organization is not merely a passive chameleon adapting to the environment; it also becomes a change agent in the environment. Not only does it adapt to significant existing environmental opportunities, it also attempts to create opportunities. This strategy differs from mere adaptation in that the organization attempts to structure or influence its environment in ways that are favorable to the organization. Advertising reflects an action-adaptation strategy. The organization attempts to convince customers/clients that the organization's product/service is needed and is better than competing products and services. Market research that seeks to discern trends in customer/client needs and wants that could be satisfied by new products is also action-adaptation. Purchasing agents who bargain for specific resources under contract sales conditions that are favorable to the organization also are following an action-adaptation strategy.

We can see an action-adaptation strategy at work at Apple Computers as that organization, famous for its home personal computers, attempts to manufacture and market business PCs that will compete directly with IBM by being able to hook up to the latter's mainframes. Should Apple's action-adaptation strategy prove successful, then Apple can become a viable competitor with IBM in the business PC market, long-dominated by IBM.

This strategy is probably the most common one for organizations. However, it, too, is not without its dangers. A very powerful organization, such as a monopoly, or a group of organizations under oligopolistic conditions, can exercise an inordinate amount of power over its environment. The United States has always believed in a system of checks and balances, both in the economic and political realms. It has established economic (competition) and political systems (branches of government) to maintain this system of checks and balances. In the same way, organizations that can control their task environments have the potential of shaping the environment in accordance with the organizations' wishes.

Galbraith addresses this phenomenon when he speaks of technocrats who engage in planning in our large corporations.[16] He argues that many large organizations have such a sophisticated planning process that they, in effect, are able to control their environments. Rather than adapting to the environment, they create environmental conditions. There is little in the way of checks and balances, in his opinion, in the market or political systems to control these organizations. He also maintains that this process will probably not change unless pressure comes from outside the organization because of the organization's tremendous concern for reducing or eliminating uncertainty in its environment.

Although Galbraith's thesis may hold true for some organizations, it does not apply to all of them. We can see that an unregulated monopoly or oligopoly certainly can exercise a great deal of power in society. Of course, this is why we have government agencies whose job it is to regulate monopolies and to enforce antitrust and other types of legislation. Yet the action-adaptation strategy is probably the most appropriate for organizations and for society, provided that a system of economic and political checks and balances works effectively to discourage the concentration and abuse of power.

Organizational Sensors

From strategy considerations in linkages, particularly as they relate to decision-authority centers, it is appropriate to move to the linkage of the boundary-spanning unit to the environment. This linkage is accomplished through *sensors*. Sensors are the points of contact of the boundary-spanning unit with the environment. Sensors keep the organization in tune with its environment; they determine the level of the organization's sensitivity to environmental changes.

SENSORS AND THE BOUNDARY NETWORK. Typically, each boundary-spanning unit in the organization has several sensing units and processes. The personnel department may have interviewers, personnel researchers, industrial relations specialists, and training and development specialists, all of whom come in contact with the organization's human resource task environment. The marketing department (a boundary-spanning unit) may have market researchers, salespeople, distribution specialists, and advertising people who all come in contact with the task environment. These sensors are the environmental "plugs" of the boundary-spanning units, as shown in Figure 4.6, and they make up the boundary network for the organization.

The type, sensitivity, and number of an organization's sensors will depend heavily on the organizational linkage strategy. Organizations under the imperviousness model will have few, relatively insensitive sensors. Their job will be to serve as barriers to buffer the boundary-spanning unit. At the other extreme, an organization that has wholeheartedly implemented the adaptation strategy will have many supersensitive sensors whose job it is to rapidly transmit information through the boundary-spanning units to the decision-authority centers. Thus, the permeability and resiliency of the organization's boundary depend heavily on the role given to the sensors.

The sensors have an additional effect on the organization's boundary—supersensitive sensors cause the boundary to change rapidly as different task environments are identified and responses implemented. The boundary here is rather fluid, much like the wave action on a beach, which changes as atmospheric and other conditions change. Sensors under the imperviousness model tend to form a rather rigid organiza-

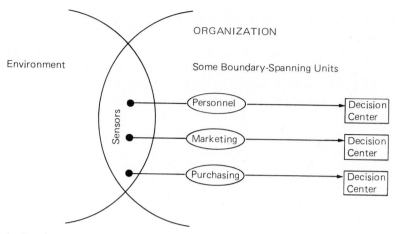

FIGURE 4.6

Sensors Are the Boundary-Spanning Units' Environmental Plugs

tional boundary that changes very little in the face of environmental changes.

DEVELOPING EFFECTIVE SENSORS. The determination of the sensors' effectiveness depends on the boundary-spanning strategy of the organization. Under the imperviousness model, an effective sensor is one that screens out most of the task environment. It must be able to deal with environmental forces and neutralize or deflect them. This type of sensor would need to be the seat of considerable authority that could take immediate action without having to clear proposals with boundary-spanning units or decision-authority centers. Consequently, there would need to be considerable authority delegated to these sensor units so that they could act quickly.

Sensors under the adaptation strategy are effective when they rapidly communicate environmental conditions through the boundary-spanning unit to the appropriate decision-authority units. Consequently, there must be clear channels of communication to the delegated sensor authority. Facilitating mechanisms such as MISs, committees, task forces, and project management arrangements also need to exist, with the authority for activating these systems resting primarily with the sensor units.

Sensor units under the action-adaptation strategy are effective when they can influence the environment. Consequently, their personnel need to have the authority to speak for the organization and to represent the organization in its environment. They need to be well linked to the organization's decision-authority center so they can receive pertinent information that can then be used to influence the environment. Of course, they also need to be able to influence the decision-authority center when appropriate.

Indeed, the development and use of effective sensors is at the heart of the Apple Computer action-adaptation strategy discussed above. While the Apple organization formally relied on 300 independent manufacturers representatives scattered around the United States to sell its products, in 1984 the company replaced these with 350 field sales personnel. After intensive training with the firm's new business PC, the sales personnel were placed in the field, where they maintain a vital linkage between the corporate headquarters and the 2,200 independent dealers who sell Apple products in addition to those firms already using Apple business PCs. Moreover, the sales personnel are closely monitored and directed by William V. Campbell, Apple's executive vice president for sales, marketing, and distribution.[17]

Another technique for maximizing sensor use, regardless of the boundary network interface strategy employed, is to practice *organizational parallelism*. The organization often deals with its task environment through other organizations in that environment. These organizations have sensors. Organizational parallelism refers to the strategy of matching the status of organizational sensors with the status of other organizational sensors in the environment. For example, a corporation purchasing agent in an organization is concerned with obtaining raw materials for the organization to use. The purchasing agent deals with other organizations that offer these materials and products. Normally, he or she will deal with the sales force in these organizations and not with other units of the supplying organization. However, perhaps on significantly large purchases, the head of the purchasing department or, indeed, a vice president or president of the corporation will need to deal with the supplier. Under organizational parallelism this person should deal with the head of the sales department or a vice president or president of the supplier—in other words, with units of the supplier that correspond in status and authority.

Another example of organizational parallelism can be seen in the case of state visits. Protocol dictates that when a head of state visits with a foreign government, he or she is greeted by an appropriate counterpart in that government. For example, the head of a major country, such as the USSR, would be greeted by our president, or at least the vice president. The head of a smaller country, however, such as Togo, might be greeted by the assistant secretary of state for African affairs. Organizational parallelism attempts to assure that the status and authority levels of interfacing units of organizations are on relatively equal footing, with the aim of assuring the best bargaining position for the organization. Figure 4.7 depicts the organizational parallelism strategy.

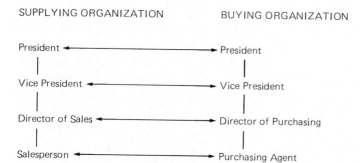

FIGURE 4.7

Organizational Parallelism in a Purchasing Decision

PROBLEMS WITH SENSOR USE. Certain problems can easily develop with sensors that require management attention to prevent or correct. First, sensors can become *desensitized*. They become so used to environmental stimuli that the stimuli begin to have little effect on them. This happens often in sensor-type jobs. The new caseworker in the vocational rehabilitation department may initially be eager and willing to help solve clients' problems, even to the point of working overtime without pay; there seems to be so much to do and so many people to help. However, as the months go by, the caseworker may become less enthusiastic and more defensive while dealing with clients. An impersonal attitude may develop. Finally, the caseworker may become uninterested. Another example is the new college professor, eager to spend many hours counseling and advising students. Soon, other demands are placed on his or her time, and all of the students seem to have the same recurring problems. Enthusiasm drops and impersonal attitudes develop.

How do organizations maintain sensor sensitivity? Many techniques are used. Salespeople are given periodic pep talks at motivation seminars. Limits are placed on the time a person spends in a sensor position, so new people are constantly flowing to the positions. Periodic training and development programs are conducted to improve the skills and proficiencies of people in sensor positions. Greater management monitoring of sensor performance is also useful.

Another problem that can develop with sensors is *sensor misplacement*. The sensors can be interacting with inappropriate parts of the task environment while ignoring the appropriate parts. This condition is known as sensor misplacement. A state university facing declining funding allocations from the state legislature has to be sure that its sensors are investigating alternative funding sources such as foundations, alumni, businesses, and the federal government, and it may need to reduce sensor interaction with the state legislature. A large consumer products company, such as Procter and Gamble, not only needs to monitor developments in its present market but also developments in competitors' markets and potential product markets. The concept of resiliency discussed earlier is important for overcoming sensor misplacement.

A third problem with sensor use is *sensor isolation*. Under adaptation or action-adaptation strategies, sensors need to create permeable boundaries, as discussed earlier. If sensors are always bearers of bad news, they can soon be cut off from decision-authority centers, thus losing boundary-spanning permeability. If information provided is inaccurate or delivered too late for appropriate action, the organization may establish informal or de facto sensors to short-circuit the boundary-spanning system. This is practiced when the university president meets directly with students or when the corporation president randomly interviews the corporation's customers. At the extreme, industrial espionage may be undertaken.

Finally, sensors sometimes *distort* and *filter* information based on the unique background and personal characteristics of the sensor. For example, the training provided a sensor will influence how information is processed. A person well trained in computers and their use will perceive and interpret information from computer companies differently than one not as well trained in computer concepts. Also, the reward system and goals of the organization will affect how sensors provide information. If a person is always penalized or ignored when he or she provides news the organization views as discomforting, the sensor likely will filter out this news in the future.

These problems can be prevented by appropriate managerial action. The point is that management should devote as much time, effort, and expertise to maintaining sensor and boundary-spanning effectiveness as is devoted to maintaining the internal processes of the organization. Sensors are not of secondary importance to the organization.

We can see the results of sensor mismanagement in the case of Sperry Corporation, the computer manufacturer. Until quite recently, Sperry's sensors were engineers and technocrats who concentrated their activities solely on the technological aspects of the task and macro environments. Thus, Sperry became isolated from its customers and competitors. What Sperry needed to do, and now has done, is to place greater emphasis on the boundary-spanning and sensing responsibilities of its marketing professionals. Because Sperry has now done this, it is no longer a "closed-door" company and has become quite successful as an aggressive seller of other companies' equipment.

Organizational Learning and Sensor Input

It is probable that organizations learn from decisions made based on sensor input. In other words, decisions at one date are affected by the results of decisions made at an earlier date. Sensor input used in making the earlier decision is evaluated and adjusted as it is used in making later decisions. For example, if a plant-location decision failed to consider the availability of a particularly critical skill in the local labor market, such information will be obtained from sensors for future decisions—the firm has learned from information provided (or not provided) by sensors in an earlier time period. Carter[18] suggests a variety of factors that influence this process, including the number of management levels involved in the decision, the amount of bargaining that goes on between project proponents and the managers who have the authority to make the decision, and the amount of uncertainty in the environment.

THE INTERFACE NETWORK, ORGANIZATION DESIGN, STRATEGY, AND TECHNOLOGY

In the final section of this chapter, we will briefly summarize the effects that the environment has on organization design and processes, strategy, and technology. We will look at design, processes, strategy, and technology in greater depth in Part Three. However, it is important to note here that an organization's environment has a major impact on how it designs itself internally, how it develops and implements strategy, and, finally, how it utilizes, and, in turn, is affected by technology.

Homogeneity and Stability in the Environment

Two key variables in the task environment have a great impact on structure. The two variables exist on two continua. The first is the degree of homogeneity or heterogeneity found in the environment. Are people who are served by the organization similar or very different? Are the sources of supply for raw materials similar or substantially different? Are sources of supply for human resources homogeneous or heterogeneous?

The second continuum is the degree of environmental stability. The stability issue is further defined as to the degree of certainty of the range of variation found in the environment. For example, an organization may face an unstable environment but, if there is a pattern to the instability, the organization may be able to predict or know the range of variation. On the other hand, an organization facing an unstable environment that follows no pattern will have difficulty predicting or knowing the ranges of

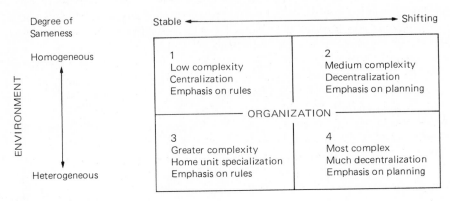

FIGURE 4.8

An Organization's Environment and Its Effect on Complexity, Rule Making, Planning, and Decentralization

variation it faces. The key for the organization with respect to stability is knowing the degree of uncertainty.

Influence on Structure and Process

These environmental influences affect three major aspects of organization design: (1) the degree of organization complexity, (2) the emphasis on rule making and planning, and (3) the amount of decentralization. We can depict these relationships in a matrix as shown in Figure 4.8.* Organizations facing a stable task environment that is also homogeneous will tend to be uncomplicated and centralized, and will tend to emphasize rules for action (box 1). Because the environment is known and predictable, accurate rules can be developed to guide organizational action. There is little need for complexity (vertical and horizontal differentiation) because many specialized units do not need to be established to deal with different aspects of the task environment.

An organization facing a homogeneous but shifting task environment, however, must develop ways to handle this instability (box 2). It does this by decentralizing more authority at lower levels so that it can more easily respond to environmental changes as they occur. It also estab-

---

*This figure and the discussion that follows were developed from Thompson, *Organizations*, 70–73.

lishes planning units whose job is to attempt to predict and thus know this change.

In box 3 of Figure 4.8, the organization faces a stable but much differentiated task environment. Here we see greater complexity as the organization becomes even more vertically and horizontally differentiated in order to handle many environmental components. Rules can still be developed since the environment is known, but since the environment is so diverse, many organizational units must be established to apply them.

In box 4 we have an organization facing an environment that is neither stable nor homogeneous. Such a dynamic, heterogeneous environment presents the greatest challenge to the organization. Few rules can be made, so the emphasis rests heavily on planning. The organization becomes extremely complex as it differentiates itself to handle so many different and shifting environmental components.

We can summarize these relationships with two general principles:

1. The more homogeneous and stable the task environment, the less the need for organizational complexity and the greater the use of rule making.
2. The more heterogeneous and shifting the task environment, the greater the organizational complexity, planning, and decentralization.

In Chapter 10 we will expand on these two basic principles in describing the various internal organizational arrangements that are actually used. The concepts of bureaucracy, line-staff arrangements, and matrix and project management are explored as they relate to efforts of organizations to ensure rational internal operations in the face of environmental opportunities and constraints.

Influence on Strategy

As we have pointed out through numerous real-life examples in this chapter, organizations use inputs from boundary-spanning units and sensors in order to develop proper strategy. Strategy is the comprehensive and unified plan the organization undertakes to accomplish the organization's mission, sustain long-term viability, and enhance the value of its products and services. It is practically impossible for an organization to develop a successful strategy unless it is cognizant of both opportunities and threats presented by the environment. These opportunities and threats are brought to the attention of organizational decision makers through its linkage systems, that is, boundary-spanning units and sensors. Should these linkage systems not provide the right environmental information, then the organization will be unable to devise a successful strategy.

Influence on Technology

Perhaps no other component of the macro environment has had such a profound impact on organizations as has technology. Indeed, as we discussed earlier in this chapter, high-tech, well-integrated MISs have revolutionized the way environmental information is passed on to the organization's decision-authority centers. Technological information is one of the most important types of information that the organization seeks from its environmental linkage systems. Apple Computers seeks the right technology so it can tie in its business PCs with IBM mainframes, while Waste Management must develop and use a safe and efficient technology for disposing of toxic wastes, thus pleasing customers, a wide variety of government agencies, communities, and critics. Most important, and we will discuss this further in Chapter 12, technology not only exerts major influence on organizations, but on society and even entire nations as well.

SUMMARY

Organizations are linked to their environment through an interface network. This network consists of boundary-spanning units that transcend organizational boundaries and that receive resources from the environment and place outputs into the environment. These boundary-spanning units have sensors, which are mechanisms or people that monitor the environment for the boundary-spanning units. Internally, boundary-spanning units are linked to decision-authority centers in the organization that influence the operation of the organization's core technology.

The actual operation of the linkage between sensors and decision-authority centers depends on the strategy the organization follows in dealing with its environment. Sensors serve as environmental blocking and screening devices for the organization under the imperviousness strategy. Under the selective imperviousness strategy, selected aspects of the task environment are brought to the attention of the decision-authority centers while the remainder of the task environment and potential task environment is screened out. The organization changes with the times under the adaptation strategy. It becomes a follower of environmental changes and attempts to adapt to these changes. Under the action-adaptation model, the organization attempts to influence its environment in order to create favorable conditions.

The environment has a direct effect on the structure and processes of the organization. Organizations facing stable, homogeneous environments tend to emphasize rule making and tend not to be very complex.

Organizations facing shifting, heterogeneous environments tend to be complex in design and to emphasize planning and decentralization in an effort to cope with their environments. The environment is also the source of those threats and/or opportunities that are the basis for the organization's strategy. In addition, technology is one of the most important environmental components for which the organization seeks information through its linkage systems.

QUESTIONS FOR REVIEW AND DISCUSSION

1. What is the organization's interface network?
2. What is an organization's boundary? Where does an organization end and the larger society begin?
3. What are boundary-spanning units? How do they differ from people in boundary-spanning roles?
4. What is meant by the terms *task environment* and *domain consensus*?
5. Explain the characteristics of permeability and resiliency of organizational boundaries.
6. What is meant by the term *boundary maintenance*?
7. What is a decision-authority center and what role does it play in boundary maintenance?
8. Explain the four types of boundary linkage strategies discussed in the text, and give an example of each.
9. Must organizations be powerful to use the action-adaptation strategy?
10. What are organizational sensors and how can effective ones be developed?
11. What is meant by the term *organizational parallelism*?
12. What is the relationship between an organization's environment and its effect on internal centralization, complexity, and rule making?
13. Should an organization completely change its mission and purpose in view of dramatic changes in its task environment? (For example, should a small, Lutheran, liberal arts college begin offering weekend M.B.A. programs if student enrollments fall off to such an extent that the very survival of the school is at stake?)
14. How can a boundary-spanning unit have the function of insulating the organization from outside influence? Is this not just the opposite of a spanning function?

ENDNOTES

1. Sol Levine and Paul E. White, "Exchange as a Conceptual Framework for the Study of Interorganizational Relationships," *Administrative Science Quarterly* 5 (March 1961): 583–701.

2. William R. Dill, "Environment as an Influence on Managerial Autonomy," *Administrative Science Quarterly* 2 (March 1958): 409–443.

3. James Thompson, *Organizations in Action* (New York: McGraw-Hill, 1967), 29.

4. Howard Gold, "Learning the Hard Way," *Forbes* (May 19, 1986), 40–41.

5. Thompson, *Organizations in Action*, 18–21.

6. Ibid., 66–67.

7. Henry Mintzberg, *The Nature of Managerial Work* (Englewood Cliffs, N.J.: Prentice-Hall, 1980), 63.

8. Liam Fahey and William R. King, "Environmental Scanning for Corporate Planning," *Business Horizons* (August 1977): 63.

9. Kenneth Dreyfack and Richard Hoppe, "Waste Management's Image Is Still Less Than Pristine," *Business Week* (September 9, 1985), 79–80.

10. Catherine L. Harris, "Information Power: How Companies Are Using New Technologies to Gain a Competitive Edge," *Business Week* (October 14, 1985), 111.

11. Ibid., 112–113.

12. Harold J. Leavitt, William R. Dill, and Henry B. Eyring, *The Organizational World* (New York: Harcourt, Brace, Jovanovich, 1973), 306–310.

13. Andrew Tanzer and Marc Beauchamp, "Confession Time at Nissan," *Forbes* (November 3, 1986), 48–49.

14. Leavitt, Dill, and Eyring, *The Organizational World*, 308.

15. Eleanor J. Tracy, "Bell and Howell Gets Back into Home Movies," *Fortune* (June 17, 1985), 26.

16. John K. Galbraith, *The New Industrial State* (Boston: Houghton Mifflin, 1967), 57–59.

17. Felix Kessler, "Apple's Pitch to the Fortune 500," *Fortune* (April 15, 1985), 53–56.

18. Eugene C. Carter, "The Behavioral Theory of the Firm and Top-Level Corporate Decisions," *Administrative Science Quarterly* 16 (December 1971): 413–428; and Richard M. Cyert and James G. March, *A Behavioral Theory of the Firm* (Englewood Cliffs, N.J.: Prentice-Hall, 1963).

ANNOTATED BIBLIOGRAPHY

Aldrich, Howard. "Organizational Boundaries and Interorganizational Conflict." *Human Relations* 24 (August 1971): 279–294.
   Organizations are considered boundary-maintaining systems. Within this context, interorganizational conflict and power and authority are discussed and related to various organizational processes.
Aplin, John C., and Hegarty, W. Harvey. "Political Influence: Strategies Employed

by Organizations to Impact Legislation in Business and Economic Matters." *Academy of Management Journal* 23, no. 3 (September 1980): 438–450.

This study examines strategies that business lobbyists, consumer groups, unions, and federal agencies employ to shape federal legislation. Major sectors adopt different strategy sets that have varying impacts on the legislative process.

Burns, T., and Stalker, G. M. *The Management of Innovation.* London: Tavistock, 1961.

This early research-based book concentrates on the managerial problems involved in handling people working on innovative technology and the application of that technology. Enlightening points are made about the design of organizational work roles in change situations.

Emery, Fred, and Trist, C. L. "The Causal Texture of Organizational Environments." *Human Relations* 18 (February 1965): 21–32.

This is a classic conceptual article relating the study of organizational change to the type of "texture" of environment faced by an organization. A typology of environments is presented and explained.

Engelow, Jack L., and Lenz, R. T. "Whatever Happened to Environmental Analysis?" *Long Range Planning* 18, no. 2 (1985): 93–106.

This article discusses a longitudinal study of firms selected for their expertise in environmental analysis. It is primarily designed to test two general propositions: the first, that environmental analysis is increasing in importance over time — both within and between firms; and the second, that environmental analysis is most viable as a separate, free-standing function within the organization.

Ford, Jeffrey D., and Schellenberg, Deborah A. "Conceptual Issues of Linkage in the Assessment of Organizational Performance." *Academy of Management Review* 7, no. 1 (January 1982): 49–58.

Current perspectives on the assessment of organizational performance assume that organizations exhibit a oneness of structure and that linkages among organizations are rational. This paper examines the validity of these assumptions and their implications for assessing organizational performance.

Gladstein, Deborah, and Caldwell, David. "Boundary Management in New Product Teams." In *Academy of Management Proceedings '85*, edited by Richard B. Robinson, Jr. and John A. Pearce II, 161–165. San Diego, Calif.: Academy of Management, 1985.

To groups that must engage in exchange relationships, boundary management is proposed to be a critical predictor of performance. Propositions linking boundary roles to team performance at different phases of new product development are presented. These imply a need to change existing performance models to account for the dynamic and interdependent nature of groups.

Leifer, Richard, and Delbecq, André. "Organizational/Environmental Interchange: A Model of Boundary Spanning Activity." *Academy of Management Review* 3 (January 1978): 40–49.

A theoretical framework for analyzing determinants and functions of activity at the boundaries of organizations is developed. A model of the organization/environmental information interchange process suggests relationships between organizational, environmental, and individual aspects of boundary activity.

Leifer, Richard, and Huber, George P. "Relations among Perceived Environmental Uncertainty, Organization Structure, and Boundary Spanning Behavior." *Administrative Science Quarterly* 22 (June 1977): 235–247.

This study shows that perceived environmental uncertainty does not influence the relationship of boundary spanning to structure, but structure reduces the relationship of perceived uncertainty to boundary spanning to zero, and boundary spanning reduces the relationship between structure and environmental uncertainty to zero. Boundary-spanning activity is conceived of as an intervening variable between organization structure and perceived environmental uncertainty.

Milliken, Frances J. "Three Types of Perceived Uncertainty about the Environment: State, Effect, and Response Uncertainty." *Academy of Management Review* 12, no. 1 (January 1987): 133–143.

The literature on environmental uncertainty is briefly reviewed to illustrate problems and inconsistencies in conceptualizing and measuring the construct. Three types of perceived uncertainty about the environment are described and their implications for the behavior of an organization's administrators are discussed.

Smircich, Linda, and Stubbart, Charles. "Strategic Management in an Enacted World." *Academy of Management Review* 10, no. 4 (October 1985): 724–736.

There is a debate within strategic management about organizational environments—are they objective, perceived, or both? Still another view of environments, derived from an interpretive world view, claims that environments are enacted. This paper explores three major implications of the enacted environment concept for strategic management theory and practice: abandoning the prescription that organizations should adapt to their environments; rethinking constraints, threats, and opportunities; and considering the primary role of strategic managers to be the management of meaning.

Terreberry, Shirley. "The Evolution of Organizational Environments." *Administrative Science Quarterly* 12 (March 1968): 590–613.

Terreberry's work is an elaboration of that of Emery and Trist on organizational environments. Specifically, support is expressed for the hypotheses that (1) externally induced change is becoming prevalent, and (2) organizational adaptability is a function of response to environmental change.

Tushman, Michael L. "Special Boundary Roles in the Innovation Process." *Administrative Science Quarterly* 22 (December 1977): 587–605.

The research described focuses on one important aspect of the innovation process: the need for the innovating system to gather information from and transmit information to several external information areas. Special boundary roles evolve in the organization's communication network to fulfill the essential function of linking the organization's internal network to external sources of information.

Wall, J. A., Jr., and Adams, J. Stacy. "Some Variables Affecting a Constituent's Evaluation of and Behavior Toward a Boundary Role Occupant." *Organizational Behavior and Human Performance* 11 (1974): 390–408.

Two factors were found to be important in responding to boundary occupants: (1) the effectiveness of an organization's outputting function and (2) the boundary occupant's obedience to the organizational constituent.

Weick, Karl E. *The Social Psychology of Organizing.* Reading, Mass.: Addison-Wesley, 1969.

This excellent book focuses on the behavioral phenomena, problems, and processes involved in organizing for coordinated activity.

ADDITIONAL REFERENCES

Adams, J. Stacy. "The Structure and Dynamics of Behavior in Organizational Boundary Roles." In *Handbook of Industrial and Organizational Psychology,* edited by Marvin D. Dunnette. Chicago: Rand McNally, 1976.

Aldrich, Howard. "Visionaries and Villains: The Politics of Designing Interorganizational Relations." *Organization and Administrative Sciences* 8 (Spring 1977): 23–29.

Aldrich, Howard, and Herker, Diane. "Boundary Spanning Roles and Organization Structure." *Academy of Management Review* 2 (1977): 217–230.

Brown, W. B., and Schwab, R. C. "Boundary-Spanning Activities in Electronic Firms." *IEEE Transactions on Engineering Management* 31 (August 1984): 105–111.

Dailey, Robert C. "Group, Task, and Personality Correlates of Boundary-Spanning Activities." *Human Relations* 32 (April 1979): 273–285.

Dess, Gregory D., and Donald W. Beard. "Objective Measurement of Organizational Environments." In *Academy of Management Proceedings '82,* edited by Kae H. Chung, 245–249. New York: Academy of Management, 1982.

El Sawy, Omar A. "Understanding the Process by which Chief Executives Identify Strategic Threats and Opportunities." In *Academy of Management Proceedings '84,* edited by John A. Pearce II and Richard B. Robinson, Jr., 37–41. Boston: Academy of Management, 1984.

Gillespie, David F., and Mileti, Dennis S. "Action and Contingency Postulates in Organization-Environment Relations." *Human Relations* 32 (March 1979): 261–271.

Jemison, D. B. "The Importance of Boundary-Spanning Roles in Strategic Decision-Making." *Journal of Management Studies* 21 (April 1984): 131–152.

Keller, Robert T.; Szilagyi, Andrew D., Jr.; and Holland, Winford E. "Boundary-Spanning Activity and Employee Reactions: An Empirical Study." *Human Relations* 29 (1976): 699–710.

Keller, Robert T., and Holland, Winford E. "Boundary-Spanning Activity and Research and Development Management: A Comparative Study." *IEEE Transactions on Engineering Management* EM-22 (November 1975): 130–133.

Keller, Robert T., and Holland, Winford E. "Boundary-Spanning Roles in a Research and Development Organization: An Empirical Investigation." *Academy of Management Journal* 18 (June 1975): 388–393.

Kochan, Thomas A. "Determinants of the Power of Boundary Units in an Interorganizational Bargaining Relation." *Administrative Science Quarterly* 20 (September 1975): 434–452.

Kuhn, Alfred. "Boundaries, Kinds of Systems, and Kinds of Interactions." *Organization and Administrative Sciences* 6 (Spring 1975): 39–46.

Lawrence, Paul R., and Lorsch, Jay W. *Organization and Environment: Managing Differentiation and Integration.* Cambridge, Mass.: Harvard University, 1967.

Litwak, Eugene, and Hylton, Lydia. "Interorganizational Analysis." *Administrative Science Quarterly* 6 (March 1962): 395–420.

Milburn, Thomas W. "Boundaries and Their Determinants: A Comment." *Organization and Administrative Sciences* 6 (Spring 1975): 53–54.

Parson, Talcott. *Structure and Process in Modern Societies.* New York: Free Press of Glencoe, 1960.

Pennings, Johannes M. "The Relevance of the Structural-Contingency Model for Organizational Effectiveness." *Administrative Science Quarterly* 20 (September 1975): 383–410.

Perry, James L., and Angle, Harold L. "The Politics of Organizational Boundary Roles in Collective Bargaining." *Academy of Management Review* 4 (1979): 487–495.

Pfeffer, Jeffrey. "Size, Composition and Function of Hospital Boards of Directors: A Study of Organization-Environment Linkages." *Administrative Science Quarterly* 18 (September 1973): 349–364.

Provan, Keith. "The Federation as an Interorganizational Linkage Network." *Academy of Management Review* 8, no. 1 (January 1983): 79–89.

Sabatier, Paul. "The Acquisition and Utilization of Technical Information by Administrative Agencies." *Administrative Science Quarterly* 23 (September 1978): 396–417.

Selznick, Philip. *TVA and the Grass Roots.* Berkeley: University of California Press, 1949.

Snyder, Neil H., and Glueck, William F. "Can Environmental Volatility Be Measured Objectively?" *Academy of Management Journal* 25 (March 1982): 185–192.

Tung, Rosalie L. "Dimensions of Organizational Environments: An Exploratory Study of Their Impact on Organization Structure." *Academy of Management Journal* 22 (December 1979): 672–693.

C	A	S	E

Getting the Word—In and Out

Within hours after the Union Carbide Plant in Bhopal, India, leaked poison gas into the nearby community in 1985, Robert A. Roland, president of the Chemical Manufacturers Association (CMA), a national trade organization, was in touch with Union Carbide representatives to get as much information as possible so that the CMA could make an appropriate and timely public response. What soon became apparent was that the aftershock of the tragedy would not only affect Union Carbide, but the entire U.S. chemical manufacturing industry as well. Therefore, the CMA found itself in the role of communicator to the general public. CMA's main immediate objective was to try to counteract the negative effect of adverse news coverage by pointing out the positive overall safety record of the industry.

Until the early 1980s, individual chemical manufacturers and the CMA worked hard to keep a low profile. By its very nature, the chemical manufacturing industry faces an uphill battle in projecting a positive image to the public. However, under the leadership of CMA's vice president for communications, Jon Holtzman, the organization has become more available and open to the press and general public. When the Bhopal disaster occurred, this new philosophy of openness and accessibility, backed by a superior staff and other re-

Source: Susan M. Bistline, "Trial by Fire," Association Management (June 1985): 70–77.

sources, allowed the CMA to preclude many of the negative consequences that would otherwise have occurred for the industry.

Dr. Geraldine Cox, a vice president and technical director for the CMA, was specially chosen to speak for the organization as well as for the chemical manufacturing industry. She was selected as the spokesperson because she is comfortable in front of cameras, articulate, and a trained scientist. Moreover, her normal CMA duties included responsibility for the organization's regulatory affairs division, which constantly interacts with government agencies and association members. Thus, Cox was a natural to act in the role of the boundary-spanner, that is, that individual, or organizational subunit, that forms a two-way linkage between the organization's decision centers and the various environmental segments.

CMA's Washington office, where Cox is headquartered, has both the technical equipment and staff to facilitate her mission. A sophisticated videotaping system permits association members, speaking on a variety of issues, to be viewed almost instantaneously. Thus, the CMA makes its own tape of its representatives' responses to an issue and then distributes copies to the major networks as well as local TV stations. In fact, during the immediate aftermath of the Bhopal tragedy, Dr. Cox appeared on such shows as "Nightline," "The Today Show," "Good Morning America," and on a CNN news program. She also participated in interviews for local TV stations through CMA's own live satellite broadcasts. By being in constant contact with Union Carbide representatives and the news media, CMA was able to provide the public with a means to ask questions and obtain responses. In fact, the CMA was complimented by the trade magazine *Chemical Manufacturing*, which stated that the timing of CMA's response to the Bhopal disaster was "about as fast as possible," given the delay in getting information from India.

Once the immediate shock of Bhopal had passed and CMA had been able to make a timely public response to the crisis, the next challenge facing the organization was to analyze the long-term effects that such an incident would have on the chemical manufacturing industry in the United States. Dr. Cox was put in charge of a special CMA group whose goal was to consider all the possible ramifications of the disaster on the industry as well as the CMA itself. Questions to be asked and answered by the group included: What does the general public want to know? What are other communities concerned about?

After determining multiple responses to these questions, the information was loaded into a computer, with each piece of information coded to match an issue area. The result was a thick printout outlining the effects of Bhopal on all issues concerning the CMA and its various member organizations.

Note that the Bhopal disaster magnified rather than initiated CMA's response mechanisms. As a matter of organizational policy and procedure, CMA has consistently maintained a tracking system on approximately 200 issues affecting the chemical manufacturing industry. Called "matrix management," this system divides issues into twelve categories—transportation, communications, manufacturing, and so on. Each issue is assigned a team comprised of representatives from CMA departments such as government relations, technical, and communications. The teams meet regularly, noting changes or movements in their particular areas. Once an issue has been analyzed and put on active status, the important points for the analysis are handed over to an issues team and committee for planning purposes. The CMA considers an issue active when it is at the stage when Congress will hear testimony and advocacy hearings begin to take place. The issues team is comprised of both CMA staff and industry representatives.

Concerning Bhopal, a specific issues team, after studying preliminary information gathered by the Cox group, called for two initiatives on the part of the CMA and its members: (1) a community awareness and emergency response program, and (2) a national chemical response and information center. The CMA and its members are also considering a tougher Toxic Substances Control Act, stricter enforcement of OSHA regulations, and tighter control of certain chemicals under the Clean Air Act.

The CMA response to Bhopal was not a hit-or-miss operation. Rather, CMA is organized so that it has a continuing program of maintaining contact with its various environmental segments to ensure that the chemical industry is equipped to handle unplanned events of tremendous magnitude.

QUESTIONS FOR DISCUSSION

1. Did Union Carbide effectively use its linkage system in dealing with the poison gas leak? Cite some evidence to support your position.
2. Do you think that a large company such as Union Carbide can adopt a strategy of imperviousness? Why or why not?
3. Under what circumstances would an organization, such as Union Carbide, choose each of the four kinds of linkage systems (imperviousness, selective imperviousness, adaptation, and action-adaptation)? Can you name an organization that has adopted each kind?
4. What is required of a trade association, such as the CMA, to play an effective linkage role?

MultiNational - Global Range w/ one big Hdqtrs.

MultiDomestic

5

Information Processing and Organizational Choices

CHAPTER PLAN

As discussed in Chapter 4, the organization must develop a linkage system to keep it in tune with its external environment. Following the establishment of such systems, the organization is in the posture of gathering and processing information in order to make proper organizational choices. This chapter examines the value of such information and describes its characteristics.

In this chapter we describe the information process from a generic point of view. We briefly describe the management of the information process and show how information is related to decision making. This chapter complements Chapter 4 in that it describes how organizations process the information received from their linkage networks in order to make proper organizational choices.

Organizations are great information processors. They gather, analyze, synthesize, and interpret information from their environment for their own uses and for return to the environment. They use this information to make choices or decisions about what the organization will and will not do and how it will do it. In short, information and the knowledge it represents are the lifeblood of the organization. No organization can exist for long if it does not have valid and reliable information on which to base its decisions and operations. Using our systems approach, we can depict the information flow through the organization as seen in Figure 5.1.

THE VALUE OF INFORMATION

Information is valuable to the organization only if it is useful in decision making and operations. The more useful the information, the more valuable it is. General Motors is certainly more interested in consumer auto preferences than it is in consumer satisfaction with toothpaste. As we saw in our introductory case, the Bank of America designed its new information system specifically to capture that customer information it regards most valuable for successful banking operations.

There are five primary characteristics of information that make it val-

You Can Bank on It

Banking is big business, and one of America's biggest banks, the Bank of America, has big plans to completely update and modernize its computer-based information services. In fact, during 1984 and 1985, the company increased its computer equipment and facilities expenditures by 25 percent, from $587 million to $733 million. This figure includes a $200 million prototype computer-based information system for the bank's international operations. This system will allow corporate lending officers to pull up on electronic file a customer's current account balances, outstanding loans, foreign exchange positions, and other financial data anywhere in Europe. This information, in turn, allows bank officers to determine which of the bank's products and services it should push as well as to provide complete information with which to assess a customer's creditworthiness. The Bank of America has other plans to spend over $5 billion for new technologies as well as for the maintenance of its older systems.

These innovations are just a few examples of the steps taken by Samuel Armacost, president of the Bank of America, to enact his organization's new strategy for "capturing the customer to sell him other products." For large banks, the necessity of developing and implementing such strategies came as a result of bank deregulation in the late 1970s and early 1980s. This deregulation allowed such marketeers as Sears, Roebuck and Merrill-Lynch to offer banking services and steer customers away from traditional banking institutions.

Prior to the launching of Armacost's new

Sources: "Rising Network Costs Make Bank of America Consider Global Voice/Data Network," *Data Communications* (October 1984): 87–88; C. Howe, "Wiring the Globe," *Datamation* (October 1, 1984): 5; Jonathan P. Levine, "Bank of America Rushes into the Information Age," *Business Week* (April 15, 1985), 110–112.

strategy, it was impossible for the Bank of America to pull together complete customer profiles. Moreover, the bank's central management treated its huge network of 950 U.S. branches and international operating units as independent businesses; thus, different reporting methods and incompatible computer systems were used. The Bank of America became less competitive and lost much of its market share, particularly to its main competitor, Citibank. Indeed, until the end of 1984, the Bank of America had forty different communication networks that it used for different purposes. For example, there was a network for branches' teller terminals; a separate network for automated teller operations; a network for U.S. commercial operations; a network for Asian operations; and so on.

This type of system dysfunction and competitive loss is best exemplified by the fact that, prior to 1985, the Bank of America had no way of knowing whether its 250,000 annual mortgagees either had bought or had need of other banking services. Now, every time a Bank of America branch approves a mortgage loan, a new loan-processing computer system will automatically generate a complete report about the buyer to the branch office closest to the mortgaged property.

Armacost's right-hand man, responsible for these new innovations, is Max Hopper, formerly of American Airlines. He developed American's SABRE reservation system, a highly competitive "weapon" that allows the airline to keep track of its most frequent flyers, businesspeople, who are not generally sensitive to price and are, moreover, regarded as the "elite" customers. SABRE has the capability to tell if frequent flyers stop flying regularly, thus allowing American to send personal letters asking them why.

Commenting on Hopper's appointment, Russell J. Harrison, Jr., senior vice president

for strategic technology management at the Bank of America, stated, "This is the first time that the Bank of America has treated information as a corporate resource." It was Hopper who came up with the idea that the Bank of America should strive to develop and use *one* single network to handle both voice and data communications. By the end of 1984, Hopper had developed realistic plans to reduce Bank of America's forty-plus systems to four. Two of these systems, previously described in this case, were already functional by the spring of 1985. As new technology becomes available, Hopper and his colleagues believe that their goal of developing a single system for Bank of America will become attainable.

New information technologies are a must for the Bank of America. With its sheer size, combined with the right information-processing technology, it has the capability

of creating unmatched economi[...]
The bank has over 4 million cust[...]
processes more financial transa[...]
day than any other banking ins[...]
the world—14 million. To match[...]
tial, the Bank of America had to [...]
battleship" in order to compete i[...]
trolled by "nuclear subs and l[...]
fighter aircraft."

Using information more strate[...]
important not only for the Bank[...]
ica, but for all organizations. De[...]
a system of information in order[...]
capture and serve a custome[...]
Bank of America is doing, is but[...]
organizations are better utilizi[...]
mation resources.

FIGURE 5.1

Information Flows from and to the Environment

uable to the organization: *relevance, quality, quantity, timeliness,* and *accessibility.* Let's look at each of these.

Relevance of Information

The more relevant the information to the core technology of the organization, the more valuable it is.[1] Two of the key information challenges faced by the organization are deciding what environmental information is relevant and to whom in the organization the information is relevant. By using the concepts of domain and task environment, the organization decides which aspects of the environment are relevant for scanning purposes. A decision is made on sensor placement and function in order to avoid both information overload and tracking inappropriate aspects of the environment.

In addition, linking sensors to proper decision-authority centers will ensure that environmental information is provided to the decision center where action can be taken, as shown in Figure 5.2. For example, the personnel unit needs to know labor market availability figures, and the purchasing manager needs to know raw material prices, not vice versa.

The most relevant information the organization needs is that information needed to make the strategic decisions in the organization. Strategic decisions are those major decisions that affect the long-term direction of the organization. Decisions to build a new plant, develop a new product, or enter a new market with an existing product are examples of strategic decisions.

Strategic decisions made without the proper information can often lead to organizational disaster. For example, People Express Airlines became famous in the early 1980s for its rapid expansion and no-frills service. People made the strategic decision to increase both its arrivals and departures at Denver's Stapleton Airport without first obtaining information vitally important and relevant to that decision. First, Stapleton was physically set up to handle heavy traffic from only two major domestic carriers (that were already well entrenched within Stapleton). There

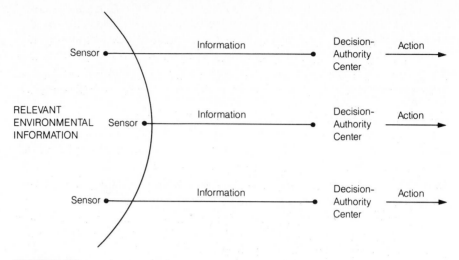

FIGURE 5.2

Information Links the Environment with the Decision-Authority Center

simply were not enough facilities and space to handle a third domestic carrier efficiently and effectively. Second, there were no plans by the city of Denver to expand Stapleton; rather, long-range plans call for a new airport miles away. Nevertheless, People expanded its flight service into and out of Stapleton without heeding these two important pieces of relevant information. This, among other reasons, eventually resulted in People's becoming a takeover target for Frank Lorenzo and his Texas Air conglomerate in 1986.

Quality of Information

The quality of information refers to its accuracy. Does the information accurately represent reality? The more accurate the information, the higher its quality and the more confident organizations can be when using it to make decisions.[2] The cost of information generally increases as the quality desired becomes higher. However, this cost must be balanced against the cost of having and acting on erroneous information. If Chrysler Corporation believed the market wanted sporty, high-performance cars and designed cars to meet this objective, a grave mistake would be made if, in reality, the market wanted large, luxury sedans.

TYPE I AND TYPE II ERRORS. There are two essential types of errors that can be committed with information quality. The first, *Type I error*, occurs when the organization accepts as *true* a piece of information that is actually *false* (e.g., believing that people want to buy expensive home computers when they do not). A *Type II error* occurs when the organization accepts as *false* something that is actually *true* (e.g., believing that the purchase of home video recorders has peaked, thus leaving the market, only to realize two years later that sales continue to increase). In both cases, organizations act on information and make poor decisions. "Unk-unks," "unknown-unknowns," should also be avoided. With an unk-unk, the organization does not know something, but does not realize that it *should* know it. A known-unknown, on the other hand, reflects that even though the organization does not know something, at least it realizes it should know it.

This concept came from the early days of the space program. Envision this: A rocket is sitting on the launch pad. The countdown begins. The button is pushed. A powerful explosion immediately occurs and the rocket disintegrates in a ball of fire on the pad. The engineers and scientists are puzzled as to what happened. As they read through their data printouts and examine the wreckage, they realize that the fuel pressure in a second stage secondary fuel line became excessive, causing the line to break and the whole rocket to explode. They did not measure this pressure at the time of launch because they did not believe it to be important.

However, prior to the launching of a similar rocket, they install a sensor to measure the pressure on the secondary fuel line. As the countdown proceeds, they are reading their telemetry and they notice that they are not receiving a readout from the secondary fuel line. They then make a very important decision—they do *not* push the button for launch.

Now in both cases—the first one, in which the rocket exploded, and the second one, in which the launch was aborted—the engineers did not know the pressure in the secondary fuel line. But in the second case, they realized it was an important fact so they did not push the button. They had turned an unknown-unknown into a known-unknown, which resulted in their taking an entirely different course of action.

Quantity of Information

Organizations walk a tightrope with respect to quantity of information. Enough information is needed in order to make an informed decision, but too much information causes information overload. When information overload occurs, decision-authority centers often ignore *all* the information provided. They reason, "Who has time to wade through that thick report and find the information I need in my job?"

Consequently, organizations must constantly monitor the linkage between sensors and decision-authority centers to ensure that the right quantity of information is provided. There is a tendency today to provide too much information, most of it irrelevant. The computer is a wonderful machine for generating printout after printout. Without careful monitoring, organizations can drown in a sea of computer printouts.

ASSUMPTIONS. Some organizations are slow to make decisions because they think they need more information. In effect, they study an issue to death. Organizations never have perfect and complete information. Even if good historical data describing an issue or problem are available, the future cannot be predicted with complete accuracy. Therefore, organizations must make assumptions about pieces of information they know they need but do not have. They must fill in the gaps, as shown in Figure 5.3.

These assumptions must be reasonable. That is, they must be based on the information available. For example, if an organization decides to introduce a new product related to fitness, such as a home exercise machine, assumptions about the future of the fitness trend, health, home exercise, and so on should be based on what it knows is occurring now and what it can reasonably project for the future.

Organizations also must know about information they need to make assumptions about. There are two key issues involved here. First, they must realize their known-unknowns. (No assumptions will be made about unk-unks because the organization does not know it needs the information.) For example, if the primary factor that determines the success of walk-in emergency facilities is future population density average over either age or income, then when a health-care organization is making

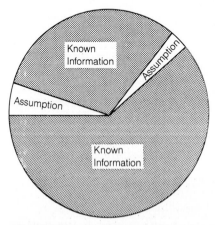

FIGURE 5.3

Assumptions Fill in the Information Gaps

an expansion decision, it will need to make an assumption about future population density. It will do this only if it knows population density is the key factor. Ignoring population density and making assumptions about future age or income patterns would be incorrect in this case.

Second, the cost of information increases geometrically as the organization tries to gather more information about a particular issue, as shown in Figure 5.4. This occurs because the organization usually has some information about an issue readily available in regular reports or on file. However, as the need for more information on the subject expands, the organization may need to begin generating new reports and gathering new data. It may be able to use secondary data sources, such as census data on markets, or it may need to conduct a special market survey, which is quite expensive. The organization must always balance the cost of this new additional information with its benefit.

Timeliness of Information

There is a time value to information. Knowing after the fact that a given stock has doubled in value is not as useful as knowing this piece of information prior to its actually doubling in value. Most information the organization uses is historical. Data are collected on customer buying patterns, inventory turnover, sales, assets, and so on, and these data reflect what *has* occurred. Accounting data are all historical. The useful-

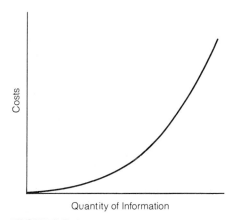

Costs

Quantity of Information

FIGURE 5.4

Information-Gathering Costs Increase Geometrically

ness of these data increases the more recent they are. A company is more interested in quarterly sales reports for the past year than in reports from two years ago.[3] In our introductory case, notice how quickly the Bank of America is able to transmit information about a property buyer to its branch office nearest to the mortgaged property once the mortgage has been finally approved at the headquarters.

Historical data can be used to project future trends. Through trend line analysis and other forecasting techniques, organizations attempt to project historical data into the future. This is fine as long as the conditions that shaped the historical data are similar to those that will shape future data. Forecasters were predicting oil prices would rise to $50 to $55 per barrel in the early 1980s, only to see the price drop below $20 per barrel in 1986. The assumptions about world oil usage, oil supply, and the power of OPEC were all flawed.

The key factor in timeliness is the need to obtain information soon enough to take or not to take action. In 1986, had the crew of the space shuttle Challenger known of the fuel leak in the right solid rocket booster during lift-off, they might have been able to jetison the craft from its rockets and fuel tank and escape the horrible explosion that occurred. Had Eastern Airlines known about the effects of deregulation in the airline industry prior to their occurring, they might have been able to institute a cost-cutting program much earlier, thereby reducing fares to compete more effectively, rather than to teeter on the verge of bankruptcy as it did in 1986.

No one ever knows the future with certainty, and hindsight is always illuminating. We can all be Monday morning quarterbacks. Organizations should learn from their mistakes and try to obtain information in such a way that they do not repeat the same mistakes in the future. If it takes several hours for the results of a quality-control check to get to the production superintendent, a whole production run may need to be stopped if poor quality greatly exceeds tolerance levels. If a company continues to push a computer product that has become obsolete because it is unaware that a competitor has introduced a markedly better and less expensive product, much sales effort, time, and money that could be better spent elsewhere will be wasted. If an organization doesn't have the proper information to develop a new product to meet or beat the competition, it might find itself out of business.

ACCESSIBILITY. In order for information to be valuable to the organization's decision makers, it must be accessible. In other words, it must be available and relatively easy to obtain. Research conducted by O'Reilly indicated that the accessibility of information, rather than its quality, might be a more important determinant of a manager's preference for information sources.[4]

Ideally, managers would select information from those sources perceived to offer the highest value (i.e., relevancy, accuracy, quantity, and timeliness). However, in practice, the less qualified, more easily accessible information sources might be used more frequently by managers. Indeed, the managers studied by O'Reilly indicated that they chose information sources because of their accessibility even though the information obtained from such sources might be of inferior quality than that obtained from less accessible sources.

O'Reilly stated that managers choose information based on accessibility for several reasons. First, managers incur both social and economic costs in searching for valuable information that might not be readily available. Because of organizational pressures on managers to produce results, the more accessible sources of information are likely to be used. Second, the structure of the organization can restrict access to higher-quality, more valued information sources. Think of a situation in which an organization's marketing managers need technical information that is only readily available to the firm's production managers. Third, organizational incentive systems can reward members for seeking information from a particular source while punishing them for seeking information from other sources. For example, in O'Reilly's study of information sources in a social welfare agency, social welfare workers were expressly forbidden to rely on certain types of information provided by clients. Finally, information in organizations is often incomplete, vague, and subject to various interpretations; therefore, managers may come to rely on those sources used over a period of time that are considered both trustworthy and readily accessible. For example, coworkers can be considered by some managers to be very trustworthy and accessible sources of information. Thus, the student of organization theory should be aware that accessibility is a key factor in determining information value, even to the point where it might outweigh other factors, particularly relevance and quality.

The concepts of relevance, quality, quantity, timeliness, and accessibility of information all give information value. Organizations should manage their information in a way that enhances these attributes, at the same time realizing the costs associated with doing so. The next section discusses how this can be accomplished.

SYSTEMS FOR MANAGING INFORMATION

Information consists of a series of both flows and stocks, as shown in Figure 5.5. Information moves between the organization and its environment, and within the organization as well. It also moves from one unit to the next within the organization.[5] However, information is also stored in

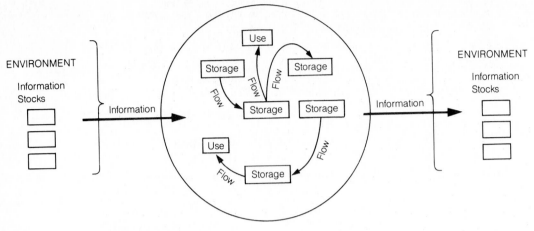

FIGURE 5.5

Stocks and Flows of Information

the environment and organization for later use. The system of gathering, reporting, analyzing, accepting, storing, retrieving, and using information in the organization is the *information system*. This system must be managed by the organization just as its production, marketing, or accounting systems must be managed.[6] Let's briefly look at the information process and then at some ways in which organizations manage it.

The Information Process

The information process is shown in Figure 5.6.

GATHERING INFORMATION. Gathering involves obtaining necessary information from both outside and inside the organization. This information may come from *primary* data sources such as personal interviews or conversations, observation, or mailed questionnaires, or it may come from *secondary* sources such as census data, industry reports, or reports generated by the organization for other purposes. (For example, the personnel manager may interpret various productivity figures generated by the production department in designing a new training program.)

The issues of *validity* and *reliability* are key factors when information is gathered. Because information is sometimes gathered through questionnaires, tests, or interviews, the validity and reliability of information-gathering devices becomes critical.

Suppose, for example, that the organization tests its job applicants for manual dexterity. The test would need to have high levels of validity and reliability if it were to be truly useful to the organization in screening ap-

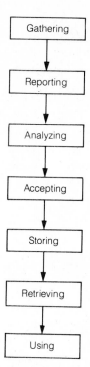

FIGURE 5.6

The Information Process

plicants. Let's assume that manual dexterity is, indeed, a job requirement. The test would be *valid* if it actually measured what it claims to measure. In this case, the test would need to measure the applicant's ability and skill in using hands and fingers to do a manual task of some sort. The test would be *reliable* if it produced consistent measurements over time, that is, if applicants were retested the following day or several days thereafter, the same results would be obtained. Whenever gathering information using some measuring device such as a questionnaire or test, be very concerned with assessing the validity and reliability of the device or instrument.

Let's revisit the issue of test relevance. If the job in the above example does not require manual dexterity, then testing for it obtains an irrelevant piece of information about the job applicant. If this information is used in selecting and hiring decisions, the quality of the decisions will be severely affected. A random drawing might as well be used. This situation unfortunately exemplifies an all-too-common situation in information-gathering in organizations—information is gathered for one purpose, but is used for a different, inappropriate purpose. For example, some organizations will gather information on employee ages in order to plan retirement programs, only to use the information to discriminate against older employees. Such discrimination is illegal.

The purpose of gathering information should be clearly spelled out and understood by all involved. Checks should be made periodically to ensure that the information is being gathered for the purposes intended.

REPORTING. Making sure that the information is reported or communicated to the right person or unit is extremely important. For environmental information, this means it must eventually be received by the decision-authority center. For internally generated information, it means that the information is sent to a unit or person for decision and operations purposes.

The problem here, of course, involves information coordination. Organizations must address the question of how to get information to proper units fast enough so that "the right hand knows what the left hand is doing." Information reporting is critical for coordination.

Again, refer to the introductory case at the beginning of the chapter. An international lending officer at the Bank of America in the United States can, via computer, immediately pull up information on a foreign customer in Europe concerning the latter's current account balances, outstanding loans, foreign exchange positions, and practically any other type of foreign financial information deemed necessary for processing an international loan.

If the production unit implements a new process requiring a different skill, the personnel unit will need to know this in order to design a training program and to begin using that skill as a criterion in the selection process. If marketing undertakes a heavy sales and promotional campaign, production will need to know this in advance so that it can produce enough product in order to avoid extended delivery delays; purchasing will need to order enough raw materials and semifinished goods; personnel may need to hire more people; and so on. The point is, very often a decision in one unit of an organization affects many others, and this information must be reported to or communicated to these other units.

ANALYZING. This step answers the question, "What does the information mean?" Often, staff groups in an organization are responsible for performing detailed analyses of information for line managers. The key issue of analysis is to balance the need for it with any bias that may occur. Any time information is analyzed, there is a potential for bias. The person who analyzes the information may interpret it in such a way that personal bias intentionally or unintentionally enters the analysis. Important points may be omitted and minor points emphasized. Politicians often claim to be "quoted out of context" by the news media.

The problem of bias is exacerbated if the information is analyzed at each stage as it passes through the organization. Each time it is analyzed, it is reinterpreted. One ends up with a message at the end much like one receives at the end of the line when children play telephone-pass-it-on.

Therefore, the organization needs to provide guidelines for those analyzing information. Sometimes standard reporting forms, such as those frequently used for sales, production, or budget reports, help. In addition, people may be required to include original data as appendices. Care must also be taken to ensure the information is not needlessly transferred to a unit for analysis when additional analysis is not that useful.

ACCEPTING. Information is useless unless it is accepted by those to whom it is sent. Just because it is sent to an organizational unit does not mean it is received and accepted. There needs to be a follow-up of some sort (e.g., a phone call, return initial sheet, and so on) to indicate something was received.

Acceptance does not mean agreement. Acceptance means that the unit has received the information and should have read it. The individuals in the unit may or may not agree with the information.

STORING. Sometimes the information can be acted on immediately, but often it is stored. This may simply mean placing it in a pile on some executive's desk, or it may mean storing it in a file or on computer disk or tape. The key factors in storing are cost, timeliness, and access. Any time an organization stores information, it costs something. Not only are personnel costs involved with the actual storage procedure, but there are also equipment costs (e.g., computer, filing cabinet) and access costs, the costs of not having the information readily available. It will cost something not to have the data when needed and to retrieve them. Of course, the computer has substantially reduced the need for storage space and thus its cost.

RETRIEVING. How accessible is the information? Again, computers have made information much more accessible than ever before. On-line capability allows executives to retrieve information from desktop terminals or personal computers. This has greatly expanded managers' access to information. Although this is generally viewed as good, it can cause problems if managers retrieve data and information out of their job area and attempt to tell others how to run their operations.[7]

The retrieval decision is actually made at the time the information is stored. At that point the ease and time of retrieval should be considered as factors in information storage. Information would not be stored in boxes in some faraway warehouse if the organization expected to retrieve it soon.

USING. Information should be gathered only if it is to be used. Too often, organizations gather information because it was determined by someone that "It would be nice to have—you never know what might come up." This contributes to irrelevant information and information overload. There should be a purpose and a goal for every piece of information. In other words, the expected use of the information should be clearly formulated *before* it is gathered.

This characteristic of information is called *user-based*. The users of the information should have the most significant say-so as to what information is to be gathered and how it is to be reported. Although this seems obvious to many people, it has not often occurred in the past. Rather, the person or unit gathering the information or the unit analyzing and storing it (e.g., the computer unit) often would determine the quality, form, and purpose of the information. The end user would have little say-so.

Frequently, this situation is particularly bad with budgetary information. Managers in an organization that the authors have worked with receive computer printouts of budgetary expenditures that are difficult to read and interpret. These printouts usually arrive several weeks late as well. When both the budget staff and computer people were asked for a different form depicting the information in a different way on a more frequent basis, the response was "the system was not set up to do that." Consequently, no changes were made, and the managers continue to keep their budgets using pen and paper while the computer printouts end up unused in a filing cabinet.

An *information audit* is a useful tool for determining if and how information is actually being used. An information audit reviews reports, memos, printouts, and so on to determine how they are generated, where they go, and how they are used. The goal is to streamline information flow and reporting procedures as well as to ensure that information being collected is being used as intended. It also attempts to determine if there are information needs not being satisfied and whether it would be cost effective to satisfy them.

Audits can be conducted by interviewing managers, using questionnaires, or through an *operations analysis*. An operations analysis involves examining the organization's operations and *flowcharting* the information flow. Operations analysis is the application of the systems concept, using input, throughput, and output analysis to the organization's information flow as shown in Figure 5.7. Three examples are shown in Figure 5.7: customer, vendor, and job applicant information. The notation below each arrow shows the report generated, and the unit at the end of each arrow shows where the report is sent. Of course, an actual information audit using an operations analysis would be much more complex than the example shown in Figure 5.7.

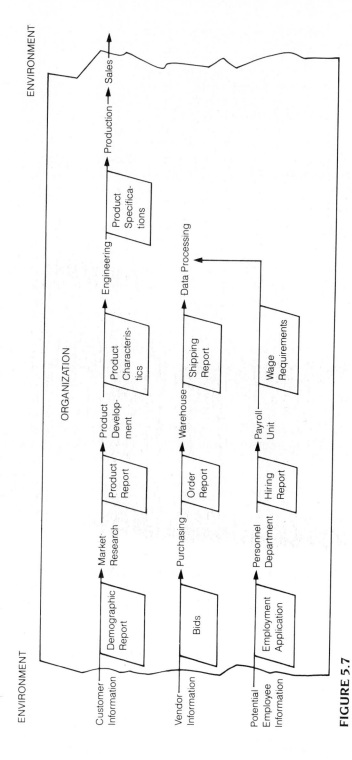

FIGURE 5.7
Simplified Operations Analysis to Track Information Flow

The operations analysis is concerned with answering these questions:

1. Where does the information originate?
2. What reports are generated?
3. Where do they go?
4. How are they used?
5. Can the system be simplified?

Some organizations call this process a *systems analysis* or a *paper-trail analysis*. However, the objective is the same—to depict the information flows and determine how they can be streamlined.

MANAGING THE INFORMATION PROCESS

The organization should be concerned with managing information just as it manages its other resources—people, money, materials, plant, and so on. To do this, organizations must design a *management information system* (MIS). An MIS is a formalized system of making available to management timely, accurate, and relevant information for decision making.[8] It implies that the organization has established a formal system to ensure that the right information is available at the right time for the right managers so they can make the best possible decisions.

An organization has basically two options in managing information: It can either increase information-processing capacity or it can decrease it. Computer information systems are popular because they increase capacity in an organization. Because organizations face ever-increasing requirements for information, not only from the macro environment but from the micro (i.e., internal) environment as well, computers have become not only popular, but essential for information-management purposes.

Characteristics of an Effective MIS

An effective MIS has several characteristics. First, the information should be *user-based*. It should fulfill the needs of the user for effective decision making. Second, it should be *timely, accurate,* and *relevant*. Third, it should be *tied to a computer* for ease of analysis, storage, and access. Fourth, it should be *cost effective*. The process, as well as the information carried, should justify itself in terms of benefits. Fifth, the MIS should be a *system of systems*.* The accounting system, marketing information sys-

---

*See Larry E. Long, *A Manager's Guide to Computers and Information Systems* (Englewood Cliffs, N.J.: Prentice-Hall, 1983), 42–56, for a detailed examination of the relationship between management, computers, and information systems.

tem, inventory control system, and so on should be viewed as a total system of information to be integrated and coordinated in order to minimize overlaps, duplicate reports, and separate systems for data gathering. Finally, the system should be *managed*. An organizational unit should be vested with the authority to manage the system and to act in a staff support capacity to line managers.

One of the main challenges facing an MIS department and its managers is to ensure that the information it provides truly benefits the entire organization, that is, that the information has value to both the organization as a whole and to various subunits within the organization. At Rayovac Corporation in Wisconsin, an Information Policy Board (IPB) comprised of representatives from each functional area within the organization was set up to provide overall direction to Rayovac's MIS department in the areas of policy, project priorities, the monitoring of progress, and the provision of clear communication channels between the MIS department and other areas. IPB members survey their individual areas for proposed projects, with the emphasis on bringing forward only those projects that have either a high payback for a particular subunit or organization-wide support.[9]

The Evolution of MIS

Organizations have always had a system for managing information even if it was simply a set of books, staff meetings, or occasional memos and reports. The difference in today's systems is that they have been substantially affected by the computer and are much more sophisticated. As organizations became larger and more complex, data needs increased greatly. Computers helped handle these needs. This led to the first step in the development of current information systems found in organizations—the development of electronic data processing (EDP) departments. The evolution of the information system is shown in Figure 5.8. Electronic data processing, the use of computers to handle information, led many organizations to first formalize and systematize their information system. EDP departments were established and EDP directors were appointed. Unfortunately, these individuals were often computer technicians and knew little about management or the decision-making needs of managers. Consequently, many of the early systems were not user-based, but rather were designed to satisfy the needs of the EDP department.

Because these early systems were used primarily in accounting, billing, and payroll, the EDP department's function was to gather and process data rather than provide timely information to managers for decision-making purposes. However, the standardized reports and procedures developed, in addition to the systems concept, would serve as

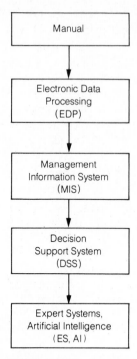

FIGURE 5.8

The Evolution of Information Systems

the basis for the next phase of MIS development—the development of MIS departments.

MIS. The growth of EDP departments caused managers to look at their information needs more systematically. Managers realized that computers were useful for more than the routine processing of masses of standardized data needed for payroll, billing, or accounting purposes. They realized that the computer was also useful for storing and manipulating data for decision making. Consequently, MIS departments were formed and MIS directors, whose job it was to coordinate the management of the organization's information flow in a systematic manner, were appointed.

DSS. The third phase of growth in information management was the development of *decision support systems* (DSS). A DSS is an interactive computer system that can easily be used by noncomputer specialists to assist them in making decisions. It is an easy-to-use system for desktop terminals or personal computers that requires little computer expertise.

Information is available on a *real-time* basis, that is, there is no need to wait "until we get that report from EDP" before going ahead with the decision.[10] For example, suppose an organization is considering new transportation routes and methods for its product. Factors that must be weighed include the current delivery routes, schedules, and costs. Rather than preparing a request for this information and forwarding it to the EDP department, the information can be called up via a desktop terminal hooked to the organization's computer. Data can be read off the screen, and a hard copy can be generated. This is much faster than the old method, and its ease and speed encourage managers to use the computer for decision making much more than was the case when a specifically generated computer report had to be ordered by the manager. In the case at the end of this chapter, you will learn how Wausau Insurance Company developed an outstanding DSS that allows its managers to select, analyze, and project information without having to request reports from subordinates.

DIFFERENCES BETWEEN DSS AND MIS. There are some similarities between the MIS and DSS concepts—both are computer based and designed to supply information to managers. But there are some key differences. First, a DSS allows information *manipulation*, not just data storage and retrieval. Managers can call up information when they need it and analyze it in order to get the information they need for a particular decision. A second key difference is that a DSS allows managers to make nonroutine decisions in unstructured situations. An MIS, on the other hand, emphasizes routine, structured decisions. For example, analyzing a monthly quality control report would be a typical MIS function, but using quality control information to change training requirements would be an issue for the DSS. Interorganization conflict can be reduced with a DSS more than with an MIS. Because managers can access and manipulate data directly, they do not depend so much on the EDP/MIS unit for assistance. The clash of orientations and backgrounds between managers and technically trained computer people is reduced because they need not interact as much. Finally, the DSS may obviate the need for a separate EDP/MIS department. The proliferation of microcomputers, diverse and user-friendly software programs, and fourth-generation programming languages may reduce the need for a large number of technically trained EDP specialists in the organization.

EXPERT SYSTEMS. The next stage of information growth involves *expert systems*. These are knowledge-based systems that allow users to solve problems and to actually learn from the process. These systems may also be called *artificial intelligence* because the computer acts as if it were thinking through a problem or an issue. Although this area is still new, it may eventually replace the DSS concept as the key tool for improving decision making.[11]

Expert systems work by guiding users through problems by asking them a structured set of questions about the issue. The computer then draws conclusions based on the answers it has been given. Its problem-solving abilities are guided by a set of programmed rules modeled on the actual reasoning of human experts in the field. A human expert has specialized knowledge that is used to solve problems. This knowledge is constantly being updated through new learning and experience. The computer is actually programmed to play the role of a human expert, capable of continued learning.

At Allstate Insurance Company, an expert system designed by Vision Systems is used to determine the amount of money to pay a patient covered by Allstate's workers' compensation policy. The system takes information from a list of 3000 rules and regulations (in addition to a multitude of other variables) and makes the payment decision. This expert system has already saved Allstate millions of dollars by cutting the number of employees and the amount of time needed to make such calculations.[12]

Although expert systems are not widely used, Winston and Pendergast suggest that artificial intelligence and expert systems could be the most exciting scientific and commercial development of this century.[13] Computers that actually think and learn certainly would be a major aid in managerial decision making and organizational information processing. Researchers are now working on the development of "neural" computers that will actually be able to mimic the human brain's vast web of interconnected neurons. This is a quantum leap from expert systems, which are programmed to solve special problems within the parameters set by the designer. The neural computer, like the human brain, will be capable of creating rational and organized thought patterns on its own.

Expert systems are being used in some areas. Besides the Allstate example above, they are used to solve problems of resource allocation, such as portfolio management and capital budgeting. They are also used to diagnose problems with accounts receivable reports, financial statements, and other reports and to schedule and assign tasks such as personnel shifts in hospitals or timetables for delivery trucks. Finally, they can be used to actually manage information and data files. Schlumberger, an oil-equipment company, uses an expert system to evaluate potential oil sites. The system interprets a much larger set of information than can be handled by human experts.

Expert systems appear to be the next revolution in information management. The implications of this revolution are now only being speculated on. Full adoption of expert systems will change completely the way computers are used to manage an organization's information system.

INFORMATION NEEDS FOR DECISION MAKING

The first requirement for an information system is to aid managerial decision making. Managers have different information needs, depending on the level of their jobs and functional requirements. First-line production supervisors need different types of information than do vice presidents for marketing. An information system should provide managers at any level in any functional area of specialty with the kind of information needed to make good decisions. The quality of a decision will be enhanced by the quality, quantity, timeliness, and relevance of information available on which to base the decision. Consequently, an organization needs to design its system to satisfy the needs of managers on all levels.

Work by Gorry and Scott Morton shows how the need for information differs from one management level to the next.[14] A summary of their analysis is shown in Table 5.1. First-line supervisors tend to need accurate, current, detailed information that they can access frequently in order to stay on top of operations, primarily for control purposes. At the other extreme, top-level managers need a wide scope of information, largely external, infrequently accessed, that deals with the future for strategic planning and decision-making purposes. Middle management falls between the two extremes on each dimension.

More recent research conducted by Specht indicates that top-level managers do need information that is both current and accurate, particularly for strategic decision-making purposes.[15] This is opposed to earlier research by Gorry and Scott Morton that indicated that top-level managers utilize information that is fairly old and relatively inaccurate. Moreover, Specht found that top-level managers who are involved with

TABLE 5.1

Information Needs at Different Management Levels

Information Characteristics	First-line Management	Middle Management	Top Management
Source	Internal	Both	External
Scope	Well defined, narrow	Middle	Very wide
Level of aggregation	Detailed	Middle	Aggregate
Time horizon	Historical	Current	Future
Currency	Very current	Middle	Fairly old
Accuracy	High	Middle	Low
Frequency of use	Very frequent	Middle	Infrequent

Source: Adapted from G. A. Gorry and M. S. Scott Morton, "A Framework for Management Information Systems," *Sloan Management Review* 13, no. 1 (Fall 1971): 59, by permission of the publisher. Copyright © 1971 by the Sloan Management Review Association. All rights reserved.

strategic decision making and who perceive their jobs as being complex need manipulated information, that is, information that has been "crunched" into graphics and statistical tables.

The reasons for the changing information needs and practices of top-level managers can be partially explained by the introduction of the computer into the organizational world. Specht's study pertained directly to organization members' use of computer-based information systems (CBISs) that are now common in all types of organizations. Therefore, information that is both current and accurate is now more readily available to an organization's executives.

Other recent research conducted by Daft and Lengel also helps explain the changing information needs and practices of top-level managers.[16] As the organization's external environment becomes more unanalyzable and uncertain, then top-level managers, in order to develop the proper long-term strategy, need both richer and larger quantities of information. *Rich* information is that which helps clarify ambiguous situations, and increasing quantities of information help reduce uncertainty about the environment. Although more research is needed in this area (the Specht study pertained only to one public-service organization, and the Daft and Lengel work is theoretical), there is now some evidence, both empirical and theoretical, suggesting that top-level managers' information needs are becoming more specific, detailed, timely, and quantitative.

Another way of examining information needs relates to function. Those concerned with the operation of the technical core, the internal operations, need data generated internally by the organization about its own operations. Production supervisors need production and quality control reports. Those dealing at the boundaries of the organization, such as purchasing agents and personnel recruiters, need primarily external information. However, external positions also need some internal information. For example, a personnel recruiter needs to know the job characteristics of the job for which he or she is recruiting.

In addition, units within the organization must have information about other organizational units with which they interface. Production and the warehouse must communicate. Production needs to keep personnel informed of employment needs. Personnel needs to communicate with production about applicants. Communication must also occur up and down the chain of command within the organization's structure. Top management directives must ultimately be carried out by operative workers. Conversely, there must be bottom-to-top communication so that top management is aware of the needs, productivity, and satisfaction of operative employees.

This up-and-down and crosswise communication within the organization, as well as organizational and environmental communication, does not occur automatically. The process must be managed to ensure that it occurs in a systematic and coordinated manner. A properly structured and functioning MIS/DSS is essential to achieve an effective information system.

SUMMARY

Information is the lifeblood of the organization. It links the organization to its environment, and it is the oil that lubricates the internal operations. Consequently, information must be managed just as any other valuable resource is managed.

Information systems have evolved from manual systems through electronic data processing (EDP), management information systems (MIS), decision support systems (DSS), to expert systems using artificial intelligence (at least in some organizations).

Regardless of the stage of information evolution of a particular organization, the information process remains basically the same. Information is gathered, reported, analyzed, accepted, stored, retrieved, and used. The value of information is determined by its quality, quantity, timeliness, accessibility, and relevance.

The system of information management must ensure that the right quantity, quality, timeliness, and relevance of internal and external information is provided to decision-authority centers. An information audit is critical for determining what information is being gathered and reported and for how it is actually being used.

QUESTIONS FOR REVIEW AND DISCUSSION

1. Why is information important for an organization?
2. Why does information overload occur? How can it be reduced or prevented?
3. What are the steps in the information process?
4. What are the steps in the evolution of information processing on management?
5. What are the differences between an MIS and a DSS?
6. What are expert systems and artificial intelligence? How do they differ from a DSS?
7. In what ways do you think expert systems will revolutionize information management in organizations?

8. What is an information audit? Why is it important?
9. How do the concepts of domain and task environment affect information handling decisions?
10. Why is the value of information ultimately judged on the basis of its impact on managerial decision making?

ENDNOTES

1. James O. Hicks, Jr., *Management Information Systems: A User Perspective* (St. Paul, Minn.: West, 1984), 12.

2. John G. Burch, Jr. and Felex R. Strater, *Information Systems: Theory and Practice*, 2d ed. (New York: John Wiley & Sons, 1979), 16–17.

3. Hicks, *Management Information Systems.*

4. Charles A. O'Reilly III, "Variations in Decision-Makers' Use of Information Sources: The Impact of Quality and Accessibility of Information," *Academy of Management Journal* 25, no. 4 (December 1982): 756–771.

5. Don Matthews, *The Design of Management Information Systems* (New York: Pettrocelli/Charter, 1976), 42–49.

6. Henry C. Lucas, Jr., *Information Systems: Concepts for Management* (New York: McGraw-Hill, 1967), 7–13.

7. Peter F. Drucker, "Playing in the Information-Based Orchestra," *The Wall Street Journal* (June 4, 1985), 32.

8. James A. E. Stoner and Charles Wankel, *Management*, 3d ed. (Englewood Cliffs, N.J.: Prentice-Hall, 1986), 622.

9. John P. Murray, "Developing an Information Center at Rayovac," *Data Management* (January 1983): 20–25.

10. Steven Alter, "A Taxonomy of Decision Support Systems," *Sloan Management Review* 19, no. 1 (Fall 1977): 39–59.

11. Robert W. Blanning, "Knowledge Acquisition and System Validation in Expert Systems for Management," *Human Systems Management* 4, no. 4 (Autumn 1984): 280–285.

12. David E. Whiteside, "Artificial Intelligence Finally Hits the Desk Top," *Business Week* (June 9, 1986), 68.

13. Patrick H. Winston and Karen A. Pendergast, eds., *The AI Business: The Commercial Uses of Artificial Intelligence* (Cambridge, Mass.: MIT Press, 1985), preface.

14. G. Anthony Gorry and Michael Scott Morton, "A Framework for Management Information Systems," *Sloan Management Review* 13, no. 1 (Fall 1971): 59.

15. Pamela H. Specht, "Job Characteristics as Indicants of CBIS Data Requirements," *MIS Quarterly* 10, no. 3 (September 1986): 271–286.

16. Richard L. Daft and Robert H. Lengel, "Organizational Information Requirements, Media Richness, and Structural Design," *Management Science* 32, no. 5 (May 1986): 554–571.

ANNOTATED BIBLIOGRAPHY

Alter, Steven. *Decision Support Systems: Current Practices and Continuing Challenges.* Reading, Mass.: Addison-Wesley, 1980.

This book is based on a large-scale study concerning the development and operation of decision support systems in organizations. The study revealed a diversity of types of decision support systems and a wide range of usage and development patterns. The book is primarily empirical and is strongly oriented toward decision support system implementation rather than technology. The case studies provide the reader with a context and intuitive feeling for how decision support systems operate in organizations.

Bennett, John L., ed. *Building Decision Support Systems.* Reading, Mass.: Addison-Wesley, 1982.

This text takes stock of where we stand in terms of clear, articulate principles for the design and development of decision support systems. An important feature of the book is that the authors of the articles have worked in the decision support system field since its inception. The outcome of the various authors' experiences has been distinctive techniques for decision support system development.

Cheney, Paul H., and Dickson, Gary W. "Organizational Characteristics and Information Systems." *Academy of Management Journal* 25, no. 1 (March 1982): 170–184.

The impact of the introduction of a computer-based information system on the system users' level of information, satisfaction, and job satisfaction was investigated. Both types of satisfaction increased after the new systems were introduced. In addition, it was found that those information system departments that were well managed tended to produce a greater degree of satisfaction among their system users.

Daft, Richard L., and Weick, Karl E. "Toward a Model of Organizations as Interpretation Systems." *Academy of Management Review* 9, no. 2 (April 1984): 284–295.

A comparative model of organizations as interpretation systems is proposed. The model describes four interpretation modes: enacting, discovering, undirected viewing, and conditioned viewing. Each mode is determined by management's beliefs about the environment and organizational intrusiveness. Interpretation modes are hypothesized to be associated with organizational differences in environmental scanning, equivocality reduction, strategy, and decision making.

Diebold, John. *Business in the Age of Information.* New York: AMACOM, 1985.

As computer technology rapidly advances, it renders our current business concerns almost obsolete as quickly as we can cope with them. Issues such as competitive strategies, staffing, organization, accounting, and technological change raise troubling questions for those who manage information systems. The author also discusses national policies relating to information technology in the areas of international trade, privacy, copyright, and antitrust regulation.

Dinerstein, Nelson T. *Winning the Information Systems Game: A Manager's Guide to Survival.* Homewood, Ill.: Dow Jones-Irwin, 1985.

Movement to an upper-management position does not just come from a manager doing the job well, but by demonstrating that one has the ability to innovate and solve unusual problems. This book explains how managers can use their organization's information system in innovative ways to reduce the amount of time spent doing their jobs. The book explains the fundamentals of information systems and how managers can create their own private information system in a cost-effective manner.

Ewusi-Mensah, Kweku. "Information Systems for Planning." *Long-Range Planning* 17, no. 5 (October 1984): 111–117.

This paper presents a view of planning as an attempt to create a desired or preferred future. Three different modes of planning in three different environments are discussed. The framework is used to examine the role of information systems to meet the planning information needs of the different environments.

Federico, Pat-Anthony. *Management Information Systems and Organizational Behavior.* 2d ed. New York: Praeger, 1985.

The relevant professional literature concerning the impact of management information systems on managerial and organizational behavior is reviewed, integrated, and evaluated. The text identifies the alleged and actual effect of these systems on different managerial functions and management levels; organizational structure, problems, and information processing; and executive and organizational decision making.

Fisher, Royal P. *Information Systems Security.* Englewood Cliffs, N.J.: Prentice-Hall, 1984.

This book was written to present a simple, effective, complete, and structured approach for the design of data security in computerized systems. It provides guidance as to where attention should be focused before resources are committed to such an endeavor; that is, what cost-effective actions may be taken immediately to secure information systems to an acceptable level of risk?

Horton, Forest W., Jr. *Information Resources Management.* Englewood Cliffs, N.J.: Prentice-Hall, 1985.

This text is a primer on how to harness information assets and resources in three major work contexts: the office, the factory, and the laboratory. There are similarities in the way that information needs are planned, managed, and controlled in all three cases. These three work contexts are discussed because most large organizations (e.g., multinational corporations, associations, hospitals, government agencies) must deal with them.

House, William C. *Decision Support Systems: A Data-Based, Model-Oriented, User-Developed Discipline.* New York: Petrocelli, 1983.

Many of the highly touted management information systems of the 1970s failed, largely because they overemphasized machine efficiency, accounting-oriented transaction processing, and fixed-format report generation. Decision support systems appear to have a better chance for successful implementation because they emphasize human effectiveness more than machine efficiency, provide flexible responses to queries about less-structured, but higher payoff problem environments, and encourage user involvement in system development.

Knight, Kenneth E., and McDaniel, R. J., Jr. *Organizations: An Information Systems Perspective*. Belmont, Calif.: Learning Press, 1979.

This book attempts to construct a framework for organization theory based on information and systems concepts as they are applied to organizations. The authors use a system-information approach to describe the flow of information and its transformation by organizational systems. In explaining this perspective of organization theory, the authors explain organizations in terms of information flows, information transactions, and systems analysis.

Kroeber, Donald W. *Management Information Systems: A Handbook for Modern Managers*. New York: The Free Press, 1982.

This is a practical guide to management information systems. The text covers such topics as the concept of system, computer hardware and software, data processing, and decision making. It is the author's point of view that management information systems exist to serve managers and that the most important thing that managers do is to make decisions.

Lundeberg, Mats; Goldkuhl, Göron; and Nillson, Anders. *Information Systems Development: A Systematic Approach*. Englewood Cliffs, N.J.: Prentice-Hall, 1981.

This book describes information systems development with special emphasis on analysis and design of information systems. Information systems development consists of analysis, design, and realization (building) of the system. The text gives an overview of information system development as well as separate descriptions of each of the four areas of analysis and design of information systems: activity studies, information analysis, data system design, and equipment adaptation.

McFarlan, F. Warren, and McKenney, James L. "The Information Archipelago—Governing the New World." *Harvard Business Review* 83, no. 4 (July–August 1983): 91–99.

In dealing with new information technologies, top executives must decide how much control they want to give to users and how much they think should remain with the central information hub. As companies deal more and more with computers, telecommunications, and word processors, they will need to develop policies to integrate these formerly separate technologies. Indeed, modern organizations are challenged by the complex task of encouraging innovations while simultaneously maintaining control and efficiency.

March, James G., and Riger Weissenger-Baylon, eds. *Ambiguity and Command: Organizational Perspectives on Military Decision Making*. Marshfield, Mass.: Pitman, 1986.

This collection of original chapters written for this volume shows that decision making is not as well organized and rational as many theories suggest, particularly when made under extreme pressure, as in a military context. "Garbage can" models of information processing and decision making are shown to be an effective approach to the ambiguous, disorderly side of decision making. Instead of relying on consequential order to form linkages, their models focus on temporal order, that is, the elements of a problem are assumed to be connected only by the virtue of their simultaneity.

Meltzer, Morton F. *Information: The Ultimate Management Resource.* New York: AMACOM, 1981.

This book looks at managers in a new work environment—an information milieu—and addresses the real-world problems that have accompanied the new environment's arrival. The emergence of information resource managers will make a major impact on how society develops economically, politically, and socially in the years to come. Managers and government executives must reassess their own roles and decide in which direction their organizations will move in light of the recent developments in knowledge and information processing.

Rocker, John F., and Creszenzi, Adam D. "Engaging Top Management in Information Technology." *Sloan Management Review* 25, no. 4 (Summer 1984): 3–16.

Through a case study of a steel service industry, the authors outline the various steps involved in capturing senior executives' attention and expanding their awareness of the many potential benefits of information technology. Once a company commits itself to the process of information technology, the rewards will be self-evident: management will improve its delivery of products and services as well as the effectiveness and productivity of organizational processes.

ADDITIONAL REFERENCES

Attewell, Paul, and Rule, James. "Computing and Organizations: What We Know and What We Don't Know." *Communications of the ACM* 27, no. 12 (December 1984): 1184–1192.

Barnett, Arnold. "Preparing Management for MIS." *Journal of Systems Management* (January 1972): 4–43.

Benton, F. Warren. *Execucom: Maximum Management with the New Computers.* New York: John Wiley & Sons, 1982.

Borberly, J. "Information Management: What's in Store for the Professional and the Information Center." *Online* 8 (May 1984): 13–23.

Bringberg, H. R. "Effective Management of Information: How to Meet the Needs of All Users." *Management Review* 73 (February 1984): 8–13.

Carter, John C., and Silverman, Fred N. "MIS Development Procedures." *Journal of Systems Management* 31, no. 1 (January 1980): 15–21.

Dascher, Paul E., and Harmon, W. Ken. "The Dark Side of Small Business Computers." *Management Accounting* 65, no. 11 (May 1984): 62–67.

Demski, Joel S. *Information Analysis.* 2d ed. Reading, Mass.: Addison-Wesley, 1980.

Gardner, Laura. "Now the Hard Part: Getting Customers on Line." *Venture* 7, no. 9 (July 1985): 70.

Goldhaber, Gerald. *Information Strategies: New Pathways to Management Productivity.* Norwood, N.J.: ABLEX, 1984.

Grindlay, A. "Sizing Up Your MIS Department: 10 Critical Measures." *Business Quarterly* 49 (Spring 1984): 87–90.

Hicks, James O. *Management Information Systems: A User Perspective*. St. Paul, Minn.: West, 1984.

Hurtobise, Rolland A. *Managing Information Systems: Concepts and Tools*. West Hartford, Conn.: Kurarian Press, 1984.

Ives, Blake, and Olson, Margarethe H. "User Involvement and MIS Success: A Review of Research." *Management Science* 30, no. 5 (May 1984): 586–603.

Katzan, Harry, Jr. *Management Support Systems: A Pragmatic Approach*. New York: Van Nostrand Reinhold, 1984.

Lesin, Eric S. "Mergers and Acquisitions: Consolidation Key to Computer Compatibility." *The Journal of Corporate Computing* 3, no. 2 (March–April, 1986): 22–24.

Lucas, Henry C., Jr. *Information Systems Concepts for Management*. 2d ed. New York: McGraw-Hill, 1982.

Miller, V. E. "Decision-Oriented Information." *Datamation* 30 (January 1984): 159–162.

Mockler, Robert J. *The Management Control Process*. Englewood Cliffs, N.J.: Prentice-Hall, 1972.

Murdick, Robert G. "MIS Development Procedures." *Journal of Systems Management* 21, no. 12 (December 1970): 22–26.

Murray, John P. *Managing Information Systems as a Corporate Resource*. Homewood, Ill.: Dow Jones-Irwin, 1984.

Notowidigdo, M. H. "Information Systems: Weapons to Gain the Competitive Edge." *Financial Executive* 52 (February 1984): 20–25.

Reimann, Bernard C., and Warren, Allan D. "User-Oriented Criteria for the Selection of DSS Software." *Communications of the ACM* 28, no. 2 (February 1985): 166–179.

Sage, Andrew P.; Galing, Bernard; and Langomasi, Adolpho. "The Methodologies for Determination of Information Requirement for Decision Support Systems." *Large Scale Systems* 5, no. 2 (October 1983): 158–170.

Stine, G. Harry. *The Untold Story of the Computer Revolution*. New York: Arbor House, 1985.

Wood, Donald R. "The Personal Computer: How It Can Increase Management Productivity." *Financial Executive* 52, no. 2 (February 1984): 15–20.

```
┌──────────────────────────────┐
│                              │
│  C      A      S      E      │
│                              │
└──────────────────────────────┘
```

Insurance Benefits

Managerial decision making at Wausau Insurance Company is greatly enhanced by using a computer-based decision support system (DSS) that effectively meets the information needs of this large and complex insurance organization. As more and more senior managers in the Wausau organization become exposed to the system's potential, they become more confident about the kinds of information it can deliver for their individual decision-making needs.

The Wausau DSS is comprised of three subsystems. The first, an enhanced IBM Trend system, provides for the presentation of data at the "read-only" level with tabular reporting format. Besides the usual in-house data, Wausau's system also includes a large volume of public data on the firm's competitors and the insurance industry in general. The second subsystem, an expansion of the IBM Trend, has the capabilities of graphic presentations that can help determine stability, volatility, changes, and aberrations in Wausau operations. In addition, this second subsystem can also adjust data on a seasonal basis and is thus extraordinarily useful for monitoring performance. The third subsystem, available on-line from Data Resources, provides quantitative analysis tools at a manager's fingertips for shaping data. The most

Source: Gerald D. Viste, "Making Decisions Are a Snap, Because of DSS, at Wausau Insurance," Data Management (June 1984): 22–24.

exciting uses for this third subsystem are modeling and forecasting — asking "what if?" — and then extrapolating and projecting trends to examine the probable results of different courses of action.

The implementation of this advanced DSS at Wausau did not come about by accident. As early as 1956, Wausau began to harness the newly emerging computer and communications technologies to enhance its information system. Moreover, Wausau executives recognized the fact that any information system, to be successful, must be coordinated with and supportive of the management planning and control system. The computer terminal on a manager's desk is not a decision-making system; rather, it is an aid for decision making.

Thus, when Wausau's information and computer specialists designed the current DSS, they consulted with the firm's actuaries, market analysts, and financial analysts for inputs regarding the tools and methods most needed for the optimal use of the system. Likewise, a common thread throughout the development of the system was the proper definition of objectives related to management responsibilities. It was clear to Wausau executives that for a DSS to be truly valuable to the organization, senior managers would have to participate in its design and implementation throughout all phases.

The melding of managerial expertise and perspective with powerful computer technology and quantitative methodologies has significantly expanded the value of Wausau's information system and made it a true decision support system. Managers find value in being able to select, analyze, organize, and project information directly without having to request reports through subordinates. Direct executive access to the computer allows senior managers to bring their unique knowledge, expertise, and perspective to deal with the problem at hand.

Now that the system's potential and value have been proven by its use with Wausau executives, plans are now being formulated to implement its use with middle managers. As the system further evolves and expands, middle managers will find themselves with new roles and challenges. They will find themselves less as the middle person in the information process and will become managers in a more complete sense.

QUESTIONS FOR DISCUSSION

1. Why should an information system be "coordinated with and supportive of the management planning and control system" as designed by Wausau?
2. Why did Wausau deem it desirable to have senior managers involved in the design and implementation of the decision support system?
3. Why did Wausau believe it important to "meld managerial experience and perspective with powerful quantitative methodologies" in the design of its DSS?
4. What factors enhance managerial use of the DSS at Wausau?

6

Interorganizational Relationships

Building Blocks

Lincoln Property Company, a residential developer with corporate headquarters in Dallas, has ongoing development activities throughout the United States, the Middle East, and Western Europe.

During the past several years, they have placed significant emphasis on the successful development of quality commercial properties. More than 56 million square feet of commercial space have been completed by Lincoln in the past twelve years, with an aggregate development cost of over $7.5 billion.

The company is comprised of a series of partnerships that are organized within five geographic regions. The hands-on administration of each development is performed by operating partners who are experienced in and based near the markets in which the projects are located.

Lincoln Property Company is an investment developer structured on the principle of ownership by partners. Because each partner stands to benefit from a project's success, high commitment to excellence is found at every stage of the development process. The partnership/team concept and commitment to quality have produced consistent results—projects that few match in integrity of design and execution.

Operating partners keep firm control of on-site development, marketing, leasing, and management activities. However, comprehensive centralized administrative services are provided by the Dallas headquarters. The administrative services division, with the aid of computerized systems, provides budget development, cash management and cost control data, and operations analysis for the 400 closely related companies that combine to form Lincoln.

Source: *Proposal for the Tallahassee-Leon County Civic Center Area Mixed-Use Project* (Tampa, Fla.: Lincoln Property Company, April 23, 1986).

Lincoln is recognized as one of the strongest joint-venture organizations in the development business. Institutions and equity partners appreciate the conservative approach Lincoln takes to financial control. Indeed, such institutions as Metropolitan Life Insurance Company, Aetna Life Insurance Company, and Shearson Real Estate Corporation have participated in joint ventures with Lincoln over a number of years.

These and other partners have contributed more than $1 billion since 1972 for various projects. The majority of these partners have participated in more than one venture with Lincoln and continue to invest equity funds year after year. In eighteen years of development experience, Lincoln has returned profit to its investors on every project.

The organizational structure—regional partner/operating partner—has resulted in a particularly effective approval process. The validity of each project is confirmed long before development commitments are made. For example, Lincoln Property Company CSE is a subsidiary in Dallas under the direction of regional partner Bill Duvall. He administers, reviews, coordinates, and controls the development of office, industrial, and retail facilities with the operating partners, who are experienced in each type of development. They, in turn, direct project construction and marketing management. Concomitant with this process, the corporate Administrative Services Division serves as a centralized data bank so that regional operations share and benefit from each other's experiences.

Operating partners locate the best available development opportunity in target geographic markets, perform a thorough market analysis, and initiate a development scheme that responds to market demand. The plan is presented to the regional partner who consults with the regional office staff specialists to pinpoint possible improvements to the preliminary development scheme. When the operating and regional partners are convinced of a project's merit, it is presented to Lincoln CEO Mack Pogue for final review and predevelopment analysis.

Historically, this system of checks and balances is also applied through the development, marketing, leasing, and management phases, and has achieved exceptional results. The regional headquarters provides a vast resource of professional staff consultants to each operating partner. Project status is regularly reviewed by tax, construction, legal, and accounting experts to ensure progress on all development projects.

Lincoln Property Company's joint-venture operations provide an excellent example of how separate organizations can work together to accomplish a common objective. In this chapter, we will analyze some of the myriad interorganizational relationships that exist as organizations adjust to each other, either voluntarily or involuntarily, to better cope with the macro environment or even to change this environment to the organizations' mutual advantage.

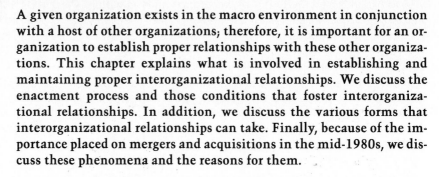

CHAPTER PLAN

A given organization exists in the macro environment in conjunction with a host of other organizations; therefore, it is important for an organization to establish proper relationships with these other organizations. This chapter explains what is involved in establishing and maintaining proper interorganizational relationships. We discuss the enactment process and those conditions that foster interorganizational relationships. In addition, we discuss the various forms that interorganizational relationships can take. Finally, because of the importance placed on mergers and acquisitions in the mid-1980s, we discuss these phenomena and the reasons for them.

The macro environment presents many uncertainties for an organization. We saw in Chapter 3 that suppliers may not deliver on time and that the organization may need to resort to buffering or rationing resources. Customers are fickle, and the organization attempts to maintain good customer relations. Government laws and regulations are always changing and present continuing challenges for organizations. There are uncertainties in resource markets, including labor, and the organization must try to anticipate and deal with them.

In Chapter 4 we saw that organizations design systems to link with their macro environment. Using the intermediate environment, boundary-spanning systems, and various linkage strategies, organizations seek to maintain their lifeline with their outside environment. Chapter 5 showed how important the role of information processing was in maintaining viability with the environment.

In this chapter, we review the use of interorganizational relationships as a means of dealing with the macro environment. An organization may form a relationship with other organizations to reduce uncertainty and thus gain greater control over the aspects of the macro environment that are critical for the organization's survival.

In this chapter, in other words, we will examine one commonly used technique in dealing and linking with the organization's outside environment. This technique involves designing a system of interorganizational arrangements. Organizations form agreements with one another to better cope with the outside environment. These agreements vary in type, form, and purpose. They present advantages and disadvantages for each participating organization.

The use of interorganizational arrangements is a rather new field of study in organization theory. It shows that we must be concerned with groupings of organizations rather than focusing on an individual organization as the highest unit of analysis. By understanding how and why organizations interact with one another for mutual benefit, we are in a better position to explain why organizations behave as they do.

THE ENACTMENT PROCESS

Not all aspects of the macro environment are of immediate and important concern for the organization. We saw in Chapter 4 that the organization does not deal with the entire macro environment. Using the concepts of task environment, domain, and domain consensus, the organization focuses on key aspects of the macro environment that are important for it for linking purposes. Key intermediaries in the intermediate environment and sensors (and their attendant boundary-spanning units) are used to plug the organization into the critical parts of the environment.

This process of scanning, scoping, and narrowing the macro environment to its pertinent parts for the organization is the critical element in what Weick calls the *enacted environment*.[1] The organization creates the environment to which it adapts as a system; it does not react to the environment. The difference between creating the environment and reacting to it is a fine but important difference. In effect, the managers in the organization state, "this is our environment, given what we are trying to accomplish. We will be concerned with these aspects and will ignore, at least temporarily, other aspects of the environment." Organizations thus give meaning to the environment based on what they determine to be important for their proper functioning.

An enacted environment implies a *proactive* approach in dealing with the environment: The organization takes an active and aggressive role in actually defining its environment. On the other hand, a *reactive* approach implies that the organization is not aggressive but merely reacts to its environment. It does not define its environment but instead lets important factors in the environment define the environment for the organization.

For example, General Motors took a proactive position in dealing with Congress on passive collision restraints (air bags) and other safety measures that were to be mandated by law. GM said, in effect, "We do not see the development and manufacture of air bags as an appropriate part of our environment and we do not wish to expend the resources for these items." If GM had been reactive instead of proactive, it would have gone along with the environmental demand from the government for the safety equipment. As it turns out, the air-bag legislation was rescinded. An important part of the outside environment was identified and dealt with by GM. Legislation that GM saw as adverse to its long-term interest and profitability was defeated.

What is important for the proper functioning of an organization in the environment are those aspects that are critical for its survival and growth. It is these aspects that the organization is most concerned about in terms of reducing uncertainty and increasing control. The rational organization (using Thompson's terminology) reasons that it is not necessary to expend resources and energy dealing with other aspects of the environment that have little effect on the survival and growth of the organization. Although these other aspects may have a tangential effect, it is not an important one.

Of course, as we saw in Chapters 4 and 5, an organization may misread its outside environment and ignore some aspects that are very important. Consider the small manufacturer that ignores occupational safety laws because it does not believe it will ever be inspected, only to find a team of OSHA inspectors at the front door some Monday morning. Or consider the organization that paid little attention to its fuel oil supplier only to be hit with major cutbacks in 1973 and 1979 when oil was tight as the supplier devoted attention to "loyal customers" instead. The organization must ensure that the enactment process is rational and effective, resulting in an environment containing the critical factors with which the organization must deal.

CONDITIONS THAT FOSTER INTERORGANIZATIONAL RELATIONSHIPS

In attempting to deal with these critical factors in the enacted environment, the organization will do all it can to reduce the dependencies these factors present to it. It does this by reducing the uncertainty presented by these factors and by attempting to gain control over them to the extent possible. One major means to that end is to link with other organizations. For example, an organization may develop a formal relationship with a supplier that guarantees delivery even in times of shortage. An organization may place a law firm on retainer to guarantee access to the firm's legal services over others who might ask for them. An organization may integrate vertically by buying its suppliers and even the sources of supply, as has happened in both the steel and oil industries. In each case an interorganizational relationship is developed in order to reduce uncertainty and gain control over key aspects of the enacted environment. Interorganizational relationships result in organizational interdependency. Litwak and Hylton consider two or more organizations interdependent if they take each other into account in pursuing individual goals.[2] What causes them to form these relationships? Figure 6.1 shows some of the reasons.

Cost-Benefit (Inducement-Contribution)

The first reason is increased benefits relative to costs for the organization. The organization will form these linkages with other organizations when it believes it has more to gain by doing it than by not doing it. Each interorganizational relationship costs the organization something. It may have to commit resources—people, money, facilities. It may give up some autonomy in order to be part of a larger team. But an organization will do these things if it judges that the benefits outweigh the costs. This cost-benefit relationship rests on the *inducement-contribution* concept developed by Homans as to why people join an organization.[3] Organizations join with other organizations when the inducements—the rewards and returns (benefits)—outweigh the costs—contributions that must be made in order to be part of a larger whole.

We can see the inducement-contribution concept at work in the case of Warner Amex Cable Communications, the result of an alliance formed between American Express Company (AmEx) and Warner Communications. Warner had what AmEx wanted: a headstart in the cable TV business and the technology necessary for at-home banking. AmEx had what Warner needed: cash to expand cable TV into city markets.[4]

While joining other organizations can reduce environmental dependencies for the firm, it creates interdependencies among organizations. In order to maintain a relationship, each organization must be somewhat sensitive to the needs of the other. In a family, dependencies among family members arise in order for the family to stay together as a unit. There must be some give and take among family members. Just like a family,

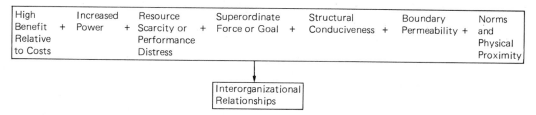

FIGURE 6.1

Conditions That Foster Interorganizational Relationships

organizations will put up with these interdependencies if they feel the costs of doing so are less than the benefits gained. The principal benefit gained is reduced environmental dependency.

Indeed, Warner Amex Cable Communications came to an end in February 1986, when AmEx sold its stake to partner Warner for $450 million. Each partner was insensitive to the needs of the other; there was little give and take; and, moreover, the environmental uncertainty that was supposed to be reduced by this partnership actually increased as demand for cable TV declined while costs simultaneously increased. Warner Amex CEO Drew Lewis summed up this gone-awry alliance: "You had two companies with diverse views on almost everything that came up, and we had people all over us from both companies trying to call every shot."[5]

Interorganizational dependence can create problems because the greater the level of system connectedness, the more uncertain and unstable becomes the environment for a given organization. Thus, the very problem the organization is trying to avoid becomes exacerbated. Simon has argued that *loosely coupled systems* are more likely to survive than tightly coupled ones.[6] In a tightly coupled system, any disturbance entering the system at any point would rapidly affect every element; but in a loosely coupled system, disturbances would have a greater chance of being localized, thus the system would be more stable and certain.

However, a tightly coupled system is likely to have a greater chance of survival when facing other systems. As the old saying goes, "In unity there is strength." Thus, a group of organizations acting together may be able to achieve more in the environment than a group of autonomous, independent organizations. This, of course, is what the organization tries to achieve by forming interdependencies in dealing with the environment.

Power

The second critical variable is power. An organization will join other organizations when it can achieve more power in the environment than when it acts alone. Galbraith recognized this several years ago in his theory of *countervailing power*.[7] This theory states that as certain organizations or institutions become powerful in the environment, other organizations will coalesce to build a competing power base to, in effect, try to countervail the power of the first group. This results in a balance of power among various organizations that have an interest in a similar enacted environment. For example, Sears, Roebuck formed as a major retail chain so that it would have more buying power in dealing with major manufacturers. True-Value hardware stores are an affiliation of locally owned stores that formed into a unit to deal with manufacturers of hardware goods.

Unions formed to give workers more power in dealing with large employers.

We can diagram the theory of countervailing power as shown in Figure 6.2. Organizations coalesce into competing power groups to deal with a large organization or institution in the enactment environment. This theory of countervailing power, and the resulting balance of power, has actually been around for some time. The founders of the United States had this in mind when writing the Constitution with its system of checks and balances among the two legislative houses in Congress, the executive branch, and the judicial branch. Also, the states were given certain powers as a check on the federal government. This was a reaction to the overbearing power of the English monarchy. The founders worked to avoid this high concentration of power in any one governmental unit.

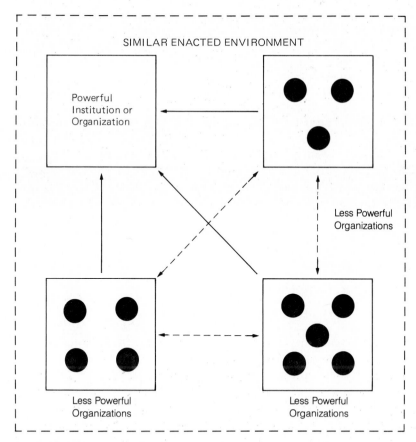

FIGURE 6.2
The Theory of Countervailing Power

Resource Scarcity or Performance Distress

Schermerhorn summarizes research indicating that when organizations have difficulty obtaining resources or achieving their purpose and goals, they are likely to seek interorganizational relationships.[8] This is a way to both increase power and share scarce resources. It is also a way a weaker organization tries to survive by aligning itself with a stronger organization. We see this last phenomenon in the area of credit unions, for example, where smaller credit unions that are having financial difficulties seek to merge with larger credit unions that have access to greater financial resources.

Likewise, we can see this phenomenon occurring during the mid and late 1980s in the U.S. microchip industry as small manufacturers, in order to survive, form alliances with larger ones. In 1985, sales of integrated circuits, comprised of microchips, plunged 19 percent, resulting in losses of more than $500 million for the industry. Thus, we see a small microchip company such as Synertek being picked up by AT&T. Though subsumed by the larger organization, Synertek will probably be able to survive as a subsidiary because AT&T provides a ready outlet for the microchips it manufactures.[9]

Pfeffer and Salancik use a *resource dependence* perspective to help explain why interorganizational relationships form.[10] The more critical the resources in the environment furnished to the organization, the more the organization wishes to control these resources. To the extent that other organizations control their critical resources, they have power over the organization. Organizations, therefore, try to form relationships with their outside organizations in order to reduce that outside control, such as when a plant tries to buy or form an arrangement with a fuel supplier. Another example is retailers that are given exclusive dealerships for certain products, such as fast-food franchises in an area.

Reaction to Superordinate Goal or Outside Force

When faced with an outside threat or with the need to coalesce around a major outside goal, organizations are likely to form interorganizational relationships. We saw this in the United States after the Japanese attack on Pearl Harbor. The political divisions in the society caused by problems of the Depression and internal economic distress fell greatly in importance as disagreeing groups rallied around winning the war and against the common enemy. In effect, organizations sometimes unite to fight a common enemy or seek a mutual goal. Completing the Alaskan oil pipeline in the face of OPEC actions caused several oil companies to pool resources and efforts to get the job done quickly. The main reason why U.S. microchip manufacturers are joining into a vast array of alliances is because of the threat from Japanese competition. As the Japanese flood the United States and world markets with their microchips, overcapacity is soon reached, with resultant lower prices for this particular product. Therefore, U.S. chipmakers form strategic alliances in order to exchange high technology and achieve economies of scale that will, hopefully, enable them to meet the Japanese threat.

Structural Conduciveness of the Environment

The structure of society may permit and even encourage organizations to form interorganizational relationships. Smelser calls this *structural conduciveness* and uses it to explain how social movements form in a society.[11] For example, law, custom and tradition, and institutional economic conditions might be favorable to forming interorganizational relationships in one society but not in another. It is easier for European manufacturers to form a cartel than it is for U.S. firms; such an arrangement in the United States would violate antitrust laws. In this country, emphasis is placed on competitive markets. Actions that reduce competition by placing economic power in the hands of a few firms are generally resisted by the government. However, in other societies, such as the Soviet Union, the maintenance of competition is not a goal, and one finds industries dominated by a very few, large, state-owned firms. Thus, one must look to the structural conduciveness of a society to determine whether interorganizational relationships are likely to form. Generally, in the United States the structural conduciveness does allow interorganizational relationships, provided that competition in markets is not reduced unduly.

Following the large number of hostile takeovers that occurred in the United States during the early and mid-1980s, certain members of the U.S. Congress took action to strengthen the powers of both the Federal Reserve Board and the Securities and Exchange Commission regarding the rules for such takeovers. However, although a variety of legislation was introduced to curb "junk-bond financing" and strengthen the Williams Act of 1968 (which ensures that stockholders aren't "snookered" into selling their stock too cheaply because of inadequate disclosure or pressure tactics), no final action was taken by Congress on these matters during 1986. Therefore, at the time of this writing in early 1987, Congress's inaction in this area seems to have strengthened this particular aspect of structural conduciveness for interorganizational relationships.

Taking a different approach to environmental structure, Pfeffer and Salancik describe three essential structural characteristics that also should be examined in the environment. These are *concentration, munificence,* and *interconnectedness.*[12] Concentration refers to the extent to which power and authority are dispersed in the environment. Munificence refers to excessive amounts of critical resources. Interconnectedness is the number and pattern of linkages or connections among organizations. Environments with low levels of concentration, low levels of critical resources (lack of munificence), and high levels of interconnectedness foster high levels of interdependence among organizations. This, in turn, can lead to conflict and uncertainty that, in turn, can lead to interorganizational relationships to reduce the conflict and uncertainty. We see these relationships in Figure 6.3.

An example of this situation will be helpful. In the financial industry, there traditionally have been low levels of concentration since there are many banks in any given region or state, with no one bank having a large proportion of the market on a regional or state basis. However, during the 1970s and early 1980s, money generated by the Federal Reserve System became very scarce as the Fed reined in the money supply to reduce inflation. This fostered a high level of interconnectedness among banks as they tried to develop ways to acquire more money. Actions of one bank would affect others as they set loan rates, for instance. In fact, during this time the prime lending rate fluctuated greatly as banks tried to generate profitable loans.

This interconnectedness led to interdependence among banks; the actions of one bank affected others. If one bank dropped its prime rate,

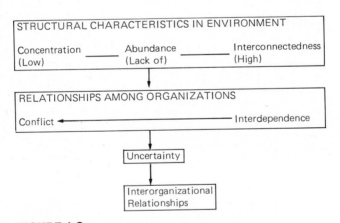

FIGURE 6.3

Structural Characteristics and Interorganizational Relationships

Source: Adapted from Jeffrey Pfeffer and Gerald R. Salancik, *The External Control of Organizations* (New York: Harper & Row, 1978), 68.

others would likely follow. This interdependence led to conflict. Conflict means uncertainty. In order to reduce uncertainty, formal interorganizational relationships were formed. Bank holding companies became popular, and many banks merged with other banks.

At the other extreme, we are likely not to see many interorganizational relationships, according to Pfeffer and Salancik, when the opposite conditions exist in the environment. In other words, where there is high concentration (few firms), munificence (large supply of critical resources), and low interconnectedness, there is likely to be low interdependence, conflict, and uncertainty, and thus little chance for interorganizational relationships to form.

The domestic steel industry is an example. Here a few firms dominate the market. Supplies of coal and iron are plentiful. There is low interconnectedness among the firms. Thus, there is little interdependence and resultant conflict. Little uncertainty is produced. The chance of interorganizational relationships among steel firms is low.*

The model Pfeffer and Salancik present can be of assistance in examining the growth of a particular industry. For example, as an industry begins, it is usually dominated by one or two firms. Soon thereafter, however, many competitors enter the market. After a time, these competitors merge or otherwise fall out of the market and the industry is dominated by a few powerful firms. We have seen this in the automobile, steel, rubber, computer, and copying industries, among many others.

More recently, because of deregulation in the airline industry, we this phenomenon occurring quite frequently between airlines. For example, Texas Air has acquired Eastern Airlines; People Express, before it was acquired by Texas Air, acquired Frontier Airlines; and the merger between Northwest and Republic has made the two Minneapolis-based carriers the fourth-largest carrier in the United States. One analyst predicts that within ten years, because of these acquisitions and mergers, the United States will be served by only six giant carriers.[13] We further discuss the interorganizational relationships between airlines in the Pan Am–United case at the end of this chapter.

Boundary Permeability

Schermerhorn summarizes research showing that the more permeable the organization's boundary, the more likely interorganizational relationships will form.[14] The idea here is that organizations that try to seal themselves off from their environments will not be interested in linking up with other or-

---

*This is not to say that there may not be cooperative efforts on pricing activities. For example, in the steel industry it is not uncommon to see price leadership behavior. One steel firm often will establish a price that other firms soon adopt. An explanation for this phenomenon is found in oligopoly theory in economics.

ganizations for mutual benefit. In fact, they will often resist overtures from other organizations as outside interference in internal operations and may seek to protect their technical core more vigorously.

Organizational Goals

As Schermerhorn points out, if two or more organizations see a mutual purpose or goal, and they are not jealous over organizational domains, they are more likely to cooperate. If two or more organizations are trying to accomplish essentially the same thing, and they are not in direct competition with one another in the same domain so that one wins at the other's expense, they are likely to form an alliance.[15]

As we saw in our introductory case to this chapter, a variety of organizations often work together on a partnership basis for very large construction projects. This occurs because they all have basically the same goals and mutuality of interests. Lincoln Property Company works with a host of other organizations, such as architectural firms, engineering firms, construction companies, and so on, on its major construction projects. We can also see this mutuality of goals among smaller colleges in recruiting graduate students from different parts of the country. They hold periodic recruiting conferences in major cities to reach potential graduate students. Also in the construction industry, one firm may help out another on a bid if the first firm decides not to bid on the project. The first firm, then, expects assistance in a later project on which the second firm decides not to bid. This arrangement can border on illegality if it becomes too formal an arrangement among too many firms, especially if its leads to rigging of bids. In the early 1980s, for example, federal indictments were filed against fifty-seven corporations and eighty of their officers in Tennessee, Virginia, North Carolina, South Carolina, Georgia, Mississippi, and Kansas for rigging contracts on highway paving jobs.[16]

Opportunities to Cooperate

If the prevailing norms of the organization and its external environment support interorganizational activity, it is more likely to happen. Also, if the physical opportunity for interorganizational cooperation exists, it is more likely to happen. In other words, if interorganizational cooperation has been common practice in the past, and if it is fairly easy to do physically, it will more likely occur.[17]

We see this in the highway-paving example above. A veteran road builder in Tennessee is quoted as saying, "setting up asphalt contracts, or bid rigging, was a way of life here for at least thirty years. People did business the way their fathers did." In addition, the bids would be let about ten times a year, and the day before a letting, "the hotel where the bids were to be submitted was jammed with contractors and salesmen peddling asphalt, stone and steel."[18] Rigging and arranging went on until morning, until contractors agreed who would and who would not bid on various contracts and what price would be charged. Thus, physical proximity of the contractors before the letting made it easier for them to form interorganizational relationships.

FORMS OF INTERORGANIZATIONAL COOPERATION

How do organizations cooperate with one another? What forms does this cooperation take? In this section we highlight the major forms these arrangements commonly take today.

Contexts for Interorganizational Arrangements

Warren identifies four separate contexts in which interorganizational dependencies occur.[19] The four are points along a continuum, as shown in Figure 6.4. In the *social choice* context, there is little, if any, organizational cooperation. Organizations act autonomously without much regard for any common goals or transcending values, and interdependencies result inadvertently, almost by accident. There is no planned interorganizational cooperation. In fact, much interaction that does occur is competitive. For example, one firm may consider a competitor's advertising campaign before it designs its own. A firm will attempt to gauge competing employers' benefit packages when designing its own. In this context, organizations are aware of what others are doing and consider the actions of competitors when planning their own actions. To that extent there is some interdependency.

In the second context, *coalitional*, deliberate and cooperative interdependencies occur. Here, the relationship is issue-specific: Participating organizations interact only with regard to a specific issue or a small range

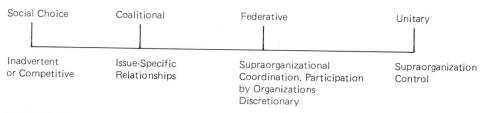

FIGURE 6.4

Contexts (Types) for Organizational Dependencies

of issues, and retain their autonomy in all other areas. For example, a group of organizations may act through membership in a local chamber of commerce to attract new industry to an area. A group of organizations may form a trade association or political action group to lobby and influence legislation. A group of colleges may hold regional meetings to recruit new students. Much effort that occurs in trade associations, lobbying efforts, and other loose groupings of organizations is of the coalitional type.

The third context for cooperation is called *federative*. A supraorganization authority structure controls and monitors interdependent activities of the federated organizations. The cooperating units retain some autonomy, and the extent of participation by each organization is somewhat discretionary. A large conglomerate such as Beatrice, with independent and autonomous, wholly owned subsidiaries, is of this type. The AFL-CIO union is also of this type since a member union may withdraw from this federation if it chooses, as the United Auto Workers and the Teamsters have done. Some would argue that the United States is also such a federation, but this is certainly debatable.

The fourth context that Warren identifies is the *unitary* context. Here, the supraorganization exercises authority over and actually governs the interdependencies among the organizations under its control. A large corporation, such as General Motors, with operating divisions is an example of this form. A state university system in which all campuses operate under the auspices of a board of regents that exercises policy and control over individual university action also fits this model.

It is important to realize that these contexts exist on a continuum. There can be shadings in an individual case, and it might not always be easy to type a particular relationship. For example, where would the National Collegiate Athletic Association be classified? Membership is voluntary and issue-specific (athletics) for organizations but, for the member, there are very specific and detailed rules that govern recruiting, scheduling, television appearances, coaching staffs, and other important factors affecting athletic competition of schools. Where would the National Football League be classified? The club owners maintain much freedom, even as to franchise location, but there are many rules that govern league and team operations.

Vertical Integration

We now move to a discussion of more specific forms of interorganizational cooperation. The first is *vertical integration*, which occurs when an organization buys or otherwise takes control of its suppliers or dealers, as shown in Figure 6.5. The organization is, in effect, incorporating its intermediate environment by taking control of its inputs and out-

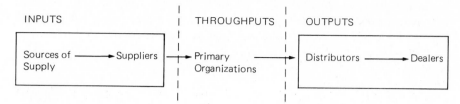

FIGURE 6.5
Vertical Integration

put processors. In some industries, vertical integration reaches throughout the entire chain of manufacturing or processing. For example, large steel firms own not only the supplier that provides coal and iron ore, but often the mines and the railroads, ships, and barges that transport the ore and coal to the steel mills. Giant Supermarkets, which we will discuss in Chapter 7 dealing with strategy, practices vertical integration that is unparalleled in the supermarket industry. It not only produces and distributes many of the grocery products found on its shelves, but also has its own construction company to build new stores, its own fleet of delivery trucks, and even its own computer software development operations to manage its information.

As shown in Figure 6.6, vertically integrated oil firms own the crude oil fields; the drilling rigs; pipelines to refineries; storage tanks for crude refineries; storage tanks for distillates; pipelines, ships, trucks, and rail cars used to ship distillates to regional storage sites; trucks to ship to dealers; and dealerships that deliver the product to customers. This extensive vertical integration was done both to achieve economies of scale and to reduce dependencies. Not all oil companies are so vertically integrated. For example, both Ashland and Clark Oil suffered financially during the oil glut of 1981 because refining and distribution were costly and uneconomical at the lower consumption levels of that period. Those oil firms that owned exploration and production suffered much less.[20]

Vertical integration is likely where the organization is concerned with reducing the uncertainties associated with fickle suppliers and distribution systems. Usually, organizations are not prohibited from integrating vertically unless it can be shown that the act has reduced competition. For example, during the middle and late 1970s, Congress held hearings on *divestiture,* which was an attempt to get the oil companies to give up their refineries, their dealers, or both. The argument used was that vertical integration gave the oil companies too much economic power, which could lead to market abuses and a reduction of competition.

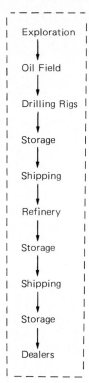

FIGURE 6.6
A Vertically Integrated Oil Firm

Horizontal Integration

Horizontal integration *can* get organizations in trouble with either the antitrust division of the Justice Department or the Federal Trade Commission that is responsible for administering the law. The key laws involved are the Sherman Antitrust Act of 1890, the Clayton Act of 1914, and the Seller-Kefauver Anti Merger Act of 1950.

There are two types of horizontal integration. The first type occurs when a firm obtains another firm in the same industry. For example, Saatchi and Saatchi Company, a London-based advertising organization, is striving to become the world's largest advertising company. And it is reaching this goal, partially through its acquisition in May 1986 of Ted Bates Worldwide, the third-largest advertising firm in the United States, for $450 million.[21] Note, however, that some forms of horizontal integration could be ruled illegal in federal court if it is shown that such a merger or acquisition reduced competition or had the capability to do so.

In the second type of horizontal integration, the organization acquires a firm in a noncompeting industry. This is called *conglomerate merger* or *diversification*, since the organization diversifies its operations into other product markets. This can be declared illegal if such action indicates an inordinate amount of power for the organization, with the potential to reduce competition. Legal action on conglomerate mergers is much less frequent than legal action on mergers in the same industry since there is less likelihood that competition is reduced. For example, Mobil was defeated in its attempt to take over Marathon Oil partially because of this reason, although U.S. Steel was able to successfully complete the takeover. One factor was that U.S. Steel was not in the oil business. Since the mid-1960s, conglomerate mergers have been very common, and there are many examples of very large firms that operate in a variety of industries. For example, Beatrice owns a variety of food and nonfood companies and several other owned subsidiaries in other industries. LTV has steel, meat, aerospace, and electronics firms, and subsidiaries in other industries.

Organizations merge with other organizations in the same industry in order to gain power in the industry and thus to reduce the dependencies created by competition, which is why the government is so quick to scrutinize these mergers. The conglomerate merger is undertaken for a different reason, however. Here the attempt is to reduce risk and uncertainty by investing in different industries. Thus, a firm may own subsidiaries in the steel, food, and recreational industries, hoping to spread the risk of loss during an economic downturn. The thinking here is that perhaps one or two areas will be profitable even in a downturn. Indeed, Beverly F. Dolan, chairman and president of Textron, one of the nation's largest conglomerates, stated, "I like the conglomerate form of business because we can change our bets around. We can change our businesses rather swiftly."[22]

Some conglomerate mergers are undertaken to counterbalance the variable sales of seasonal or cyclical industries. For example, a firm might have subsidiaries in the pleasure boat (high summer sales) and toy (high winter sales) industries. Or a firm may have subsidiaries in industries relating to housing construction, such as furniture or appliances, that vary directly with the business cycle, and other subsidiaries in industries (such as movie production) that vary inversely with the business cycle. Movie attendance generally increases during recessionary periods as people look for less costly ways to spend leisure time.

Coalitions

Sometimes organizations form an interorganizational relationship for a specific purpose or project, as Warner explains in describing the coalitional context. One common form is the *joint venture*, where two or more firms pool resources and spread the risk for a major project. This is common in the oil industry because of the high costs and risks associated with exploration and drilling for oil. For example, the development of the North Slope in Alaska and the building of the Alaskan pipeline were done by a consortium of oil companies called Alyeska. The pipeline itself cost $8 billion. Also, remember in our introductory case how Lincoln Property Company forms joint ventures with a host of other organizations to accomplish specific construction projects. Although many of the organizations comprising such a joint venture stay with Lincoln on a more or less permanent basis, some of the organizations break off the relationship as soon as the project is completed.

Pfeffer and Nowak found that joint ventures also tended to form as a means to manage interorganizational dependence.[23] Using Federal Trade Commission data on joint ventures during 1960 to 1971, they found that in industries with high industrial concentration ratios (few producers in the market), most of the mergers occurred in purchase transactions. Here, the few producers joined together to mediate the uncertainties in purchasing critical raw materials and semifinished goods. Where industrial concentration was moderate, sales transactions were the reasons for most joint venture agreements as the firms tried to manage their dependency on customer buying behavior.

Coalitions tend to be somewhat temporary. When the project is completed or when its purpose is accomplished, the coalition may disband until another project comes along that is of common interest to the parties. We are likely to see more of this form, especially in heavy industry and energy, as major projects involved with reindustrialization and energy development are undertaken in the 1980s.

Interlocking Directorates

Despite federal regulations designed to discourage this practice, the use of interlocking directorates is standard procedure for the largest firms in the United States, according to Pennings.[24] Interlocking directorates form when one or more individuals serve on two or more boards of directors. This is done for two reasons: (1) to facilitate interorganizational communication and coordination and (2) to increase organizational effectiveness. Pennings analyzed the boards of 800 of the largest corporations in the United States and found that interlocking directors often included an organization's suppliers, major customers, financers, and even, in some cases, competitors. Interlocking among competing firms is relatively rare, but it does happen. It is usually closely scrutinized by the antitrust division of the Justice Department for possible legal violations.

Interlocking directorates are most common in financial organizations such as commercial banks, investment banks, and insurance companies, according to Pennings. Interlocking is most pronounced in markets approaching monopoly conditions. Presumably, under these conditions there is a need for interlocking to maintain dominant market power. Pennings also found that the resource-dependency theory as a reason for interlocking was not supported by his data. Financial institutions actually resisted interlocking with firms with a high need for capital. But he also found that firms with extensive financial interlocks enjoy lower interest rates than similar firms without such locks. Well-interlocked firms have somewhat higher rates of sales, profitability, and growth, and these benefits are primarily due to connections with large financial institutions. He concludes that financial institutions are attracted to high-performance firms and that they may supply capital at lower rates of interest in exchange for representation, and thus influence, on the boards of such firms.

Reciprocity

Some interorganizational relationships consist of *reciprocal agreements* among organizations. One firm agrees to do something for another if the second firm agrees to do something for the first. This quid-pro-quo relationship frequently exists between a firm and its suppliers. For example, a firm may agree to purchase a key raw material, such as coal, from only one supplier for a specified period of time, provided that the supplier guarantees delivery dates and quantity even during periods of shortages. A very large reciprocal agreement exists between General Motors and Fanuc of Japan whereby 90 percent of the latter's robots are bought by GM for its assembly plant operations.

If such an agreement exists between a manufacturer and a wholesaler or a retailer it could violate provisions of the Robinson-Patman Act, which outlaws tie-in agreements that tend to reduce the scope of competition. For example, if a retailer agrees not to carry a product from its supplier's competition, it could violate Robinson-Patman. If a manufacturer requires a retailer to carry its other product lines in addition to the one the retailer wants, it could be in violation of Robinson-Patman.

Because of possible legal issues, many reciprocal agreements are informal and unwritten. They are common understandings that exist. This does not necessarily exempt organizations from legal action, but it can make illegal reciprocal agreements difficult to prove in court.

One form of reciprocity that is becoming more popular, particularly in nonbusiness forms of organization, is the *resource-exchange network*.[25] Such networks are informal associations wherein private citizens and representatives of various organizations join together voluntarily to exchange knowledge, services, personnel, and other resources to fill human service needs in their communities. The exchanges are made barter-style, with network members trading available resources among themselves without relying on outside funding or agency support.

The resource-exchange network is becoming more popular with schools, colleges, welfare agencies, hospitals, and counseling services even though it is not yet widespread. Sarason and Lorentz show how these networks have been used effectively in programs of adult education and skill training, assistance for the handicapped and persons with chronic disease, and medical and support services (such as transportation, legal assistance, and nutritional counseling) for the elderly.

Whether such networks will become common among industrial firms is debatable. Such programs are developed among social service agencies to provide better coordination among the varied services offered to a particular client group in a local area. Many programs offered to these groups are provided in an uncoordinated manner, and the client becomes lost in a bureaucratic maze while being shuffled from one office to another. This tendency, coupled with a scarcity of resources to begin with, is very inefficient and ineffective. Whether industry needs such an arrangement is unknown, although it could be argued that something similar to resource-exchange networks will be needed in the reindustrialization process in the United States, especially in the energy industry. Such an arrangement might provide a better means of coordinating the vast effort needed to reindustrialize sections of the country, such as the depressed Rust Belt.

Social Interlocking

The final form of interorganizational relationship discussed here is *social interlocking*. These are the informal relationships that organizations form with one another and that arise primarily from the social interactions of its key managers. These interlockings arise on the golf course, at exclusive clubs and resorts, in upper-class neighborhoods, and through volunteer work in civic, political, and charitable organizations. The importance of these relationships is that they provide *contacts*. For example, relationships form between two organizations because the two chief executive officers (CEOs) are members of the same country club and get to know and like each other. This is not a sufficient condition for an interorganizational relationship; each organization must also have something the other needs. But the club brings the two CEOs together, and this proximity, plus the personal knowledge and friendship of the CEOs, produces conditions ripe for interlockings.

Certainly the use of personal contacts can be overemphasized as the basis for interorganizational relationship; yet many key organization executives travel in a limited circle of exclusive clubs and resorts and expensive neighborhoods. Access to clubs sometimes is a prerequisite for access to the organization's key decision makers.

Table 6.1 summarizes the various forms of interorganizational cooperation discussed here.

Mergers and Acquisitions

Mergers and acquisitions occur when two or more organizations become one, and they are typical forms of interorganizational relationships. In a *merger*, two organizations merge to become a third organization. For example, the Owens Glass Company merged with the Illinois Glass Company to become Owens-Illinois (O-I), Inc. In an *acquisition*, one organization acquires another organization. The acquiring company is considered the parent company, and the acquired company is considered a subsidiary. The acquired company may be allowed to keep its original name, as is the case with United Technology (the parent company) and its acquisition of Otis Elevator, or Allied's acquisition of Bendix. Or, the acquired company may give up its name and simply become part of the acquired company as did Southeastern Telephone Company when it was acquired by Central Telephone and Utilities Company (Centel).

When an organization acquires or merges with a supplier or distribu-

TABLE 6.1

Summary of Interorganizational Cooperation

Type	Definition	Example
Vertical integration	Absorbing suppliers, distributors, and others in the intermediate environment	Integrated oil firm Integrated steel firm
Horizontal integration	Mergers with competition, conglomerate mergers with firms in different industries	LTV, Beatrice
Coalitions	Joint ventures, joint lobbying efforts	Alyeska, trade association (e.g., Iron and Steel Institute)
Interlocking directorates	Membership on two or more boards of directors	General Motors, nationwide insurance group
Reciprocity	Quid pro quo exchange sometimes in resource-exchange network context	Agreements with suppliers or distributors, social service to aged
Social interlocking	Social interactions of key managers of different organizations	Cliques

tor, it is called a *vertical* merger or acquisition. When a competitor is merged with or acquired, it is considered a *horizontal* merger. When a company outside of the same industry is acquired or merged with, it is considered to be a *diversified* merger or acquisition. For example, R.J. Reynolds' major lines include Nabisco Brands (packaged food), Kentucky Fried Chicken, Heublein (packaged liquors), and Reynolds Tobacco. A *conglomerate* is a large company of diversified, horizontally and vertically acquired subsidiaries.

REASONS FOR ACQUISITIONS AND MERGERS. There are many reasons why companies merge or acquire other companies. These are derivatives of the reasons listed in Figure 6.1. Some of the reasons are:

To enhance power and competitive status in the market

To enhance profitability

To take advantage of a relaxed federal stand toward mergers and acquisitions that exists during the Reagan administration

To carry out a federal request in the banking, savings and loan, and credit union industry where financially ailing institutions are encouraged to merge with healthy institutions

To capitalize on an undervalued stock price as in a hostile takeover or leveraged buyout

Historically, increased merger activity has occurred periodically in the United States. For example, during the 1880s and 1890s, there were many mergers that led to many abuses of power through monopolistic practices. This, in turn, led to a reaction on the part of the federal government, resulting in the passage of the Sherman Antitrust Act in 1890, the Clayton Act in 1914, and the Federal Trade Commission Act in 1914. These acts attempted to make it more difficult for companies to merge, dominate the marketplace, and thereby reduce competition. During the 1920s, a growing economy sparked another surge of mergers, which ended with the Great Depression of the 1930s.

During the 1960s, there was an upsurge in merger activity, leading to the formation of such giants as Ling-Temco-Vaught (LTV). And in the 1980s, once again many mergers and acquisitions are taking place, primarily because of three reasons: (1) the relaxed posture of the Reagan administration toward mergers and acquisitions, (2) the necessity of meeting the challenges of competitive survival in what was once a protected and regulated industry (e.g., airlines, trucking, telecommunications, and shipping), and (3) the taking advantage of undervalued stock prices in the market. In 1984 alone there were 2,543 mergers and acquisitions in the United States.[26] Some of the more famous mergers widely covered by the news media are shown in Table 6.2

TABLE 6.2

Some Large Mergers of the Mid-1980s

Year	Acquisition
1984	General Motors's acquisition of Electronic Data Systems
1984	Beatrice's acquisition of Esmark
1985	General Motors's acquisition of Hughes Aircraft
1985	Phillip Morris's acquisition of General Foods
1985	Inter North's acquisition of Houston Natural Gas
1985	Chevron's acquisition of Gulf Oil*
1985	Capital Cities' acquisition of American Broadcasting Corporation
1985	People Express Airline's acquisition of Frontier Airlines
1986	Texas Air's acquisition of People Express Airline
1986	Texas Air's acquisition of Eastern Airlines
1986	BCI's acquisition of Beatrice
1986	USX's acquisition of Texas Gas and Oil
1986	General Electric's acquisition of RCA
1986	Turner Broadcasting's acquisition of MGM/UA
1986	GAF's acquisition of Union Carbide
1986	British Petroleum's acquisition of Standard Oil
1986	Procter and Gamble's acquisition of Richardson-Vicks
1986	Pantry Pride's acquisition of Revlon

*At $13.3 billion, this is the largest merger as of January 1, 1986.

Space does not permit us to explain the legal, economic, political, and financial forces affecting mergers and acquisitions. The reader is referred to several works on the subject listed in the bibliography at the end of the chapter. However, we do summarize in Table 6.3 some of the colorful terminology found in the merger and acquisition field. Much of the attention and terminology is caused by the conflict caused by hostile takeovers.

Indications are that as long as the forces that push companies toward mergers and acquisitions continue to exist, corporations will view this as a viable alternative for meeting the competition and increasing profitability.

SUMMARY

The macro environment presents many uncertainties for organizations. Organizations wish to reduce these uncertainties, and they often do this by gaining some control over aspects of the macro environment that are of key importance to them. The organization deals with its enacted environment—that part of the environment that the organization creates and that contains the most important elements for it.

TABLE 6.3

Merger and Acquisition Terminology

Term	Description
Leveraged buyout	Acquisition of a company with very little money down and a large amount of debt financed by a lending institution, the debt to be paid back from earnings of the acquired company.
Hostile takeover	When a company is acquired against its will.
Greenmail	The buying back of the stock involved in a hostile takeover, often at a premium price not offered to all shareholders, to reacquire control.
Golden parachute	A large salary benefit in the form of severance or termination pay given to top executives of the acquired company by the acquiring company, should the acquiring company eventually decide to terminate them.
Poison pill	Taking a large load of debt or some other obligation by a company to make it less attractive in a hostile takeover bid.
Arbitrage	Taking advantage of differing interest rates by borrowing money at a lower rate and investing it at a higher rate of return (e.g., investing in a company).
Shark repellants	Actions to strengthen management's control to avoid a hostile takeover. One example is to allow management to issue new classes of stock with greater voting rights than those held by other shareholders.
Junk bonds	Low-rated or unrated corporate debt in the form of bonds to finance mergers and acquisitions. Although very risky, these bonds have the potential to produce very high yields.
White knight	A friendly company summoned by a company that is the target of a hostile takeover, in hopes of having the friendly company beat out the hostile company in the takeover.
Pac-man	The target company in a hostile takeover takes the offensive and becomes the acquirer of the previously acquiring company.

There are certain conditions that foster interorganizational relationships. First, since organizations have to give up something to form an interorganizational relationship, the projected benefits must outweigh the projected costs. Environmental dependencies are both created and reduced by interorganizational relationships. Organizations also form relationships to gain power in the environment. Galbraith's theory of countervailing power tells us that organizations will form into blocks of power to compete with other large power centers in the environment.

Resource scarcity or performance distress that affects the organization is another factor that can lead to interorganizational cooperation as the organization tries to acquire more resources or to improve performance. A superordinate force or goal will also cause organizations to coalesce. Environmental structural conduciveness in the form of the structure of society, scarcity or munificence, concentration, and interconnectedness all can enhance organizational cooperation. The permeability of organizational boundaries also affects the degree to which organizations cooperate with each other. Finally, organizational norms and physical proximity affect the degree of interorganizational relationships.

Interorganizational relationships occur in four environmental contexts: social choice, coalitional, federative, and unitary. The types of relationships that occur in these environments include horizontal integration, vertical integration, coalitions, interlocking directorates, reciprocity, and social interlocking.

Mergers and acquisitions are formal expressions of the unitary form of interorganizational relationships. They occur on both friendly and hostile terms, and are common forms of interorganizational relationships during the 1980s.

QUESTIONS FOR REVIEW AND DISCUSSION

1. What is an organization's enacted environment and how is it related to the concepts of task environment, domain, and domain consensus?
2. Why do organizations form interorganizational relationships, and what factors encourage them?
3. Explain Galbraith's theory of countervailing power. Give some examples of this theory.
4. What are the four environmental contexts for interorganizational relationships?
5. What are some forms of interorganizational relationships? Under what conditions might each form occur?
6. Do you think that the resource-exchange network idea now found in some nonbusiness organizations is ever likely to be adopted by business organizations? Why or why not?
7. Is it appropriate that some interorganizational relationships are formed through social interlocking. What are the dangers of this approach?
8. Even though competition is reduced, should horizontal mergers

be permitted in depressed industries such as auto or steel in order to ensure their continued viability in the United States?

9. Is there a difference between relationships formed among only domestic organizations compared to those formed between domestic and foreign corporations? Explain your answer.

10. Should U.S. corporations be permitted to form a cartel when dealing with cartels of other countries (such as OPEC or those found in Western Europe) in international markets? What are the implications of your answer?

11. Should hostile takeovers be prohibited or regulated more closely by Congress?

ENDNOTES

1. Karl E. Weick, *The Social Psychology of Organizing* (Reading, Mass.: Addison-Wesley, 1969).

2. E. Litwak and L. Hylton, "Interorganizational Analysis: A Hypothesis on Coordinating Agencies," *Administrative Science Quarterly* 6 (1962): 395–420.

3. George Homans, *The Human Group* (New York: Harcourt Brace, 1950); and Chester I. Barnard, *The Functions of the Executive* (Cambridge, Mass.: Harvard University Press, 1938).

4. Johnathan B. Levine and J. A. Byrne, "Corporate Odd Couples," *Business Week* (July 21, 1986), 101.

5. Ibid., 102.

6. H. A. Simon, *The Sciences of the Artificial* (Boston: MIT Press, 1969). Also see Karl E. Weick, "Educational Organizations as Loosely Coupled Systems," *Administrative Science Quarterly* (March 1976): 1–11, 19.

7. John Kenneth Galbraith, *The New Industrial State* (Boston: Houghton Mifflin, 1967).

8. John Schermerhorn, "Determinants of Interorganizational Cooperation," *Academy of Management Journal* 18 (December 1975): 846–856.

9. Bro Uttal, "Who Will Survive the Microchip Shakeout?" *Fortune* (January 6, 1986), 82.

10. Jeffrey Pfeffer and Gerald R. Salancik, *The External Control of Organizations: A Resource Dependence Perspective* (New York: Harper & Row, 1978), 258–260.

11. Neil J. Smelser, *Theory of Collective Behavior* (New York: The Free Press, 1962).

12. Pfeffer and Salancik, *External Control of Organizations*, 68.

13. Kenneth Labich, "Why Bigger Is Better in the Airline Wars," *Fortune* (March 31, 1986), 52–55.

14. Schermerhorn, "Determinants of Interorganizational Cooperation," 850–851.

15. Ibid., 851.

16. Robert E. Taylor, "Paving Firms Accused of Rigging Road Bids on South-east Projects," *The Wall Street Journal* (May 29, 1981), 1.

17. Schermerhorn, "Determinants of Interorganizational Cooperation," 851–852.

18. Taylor, "Paving Firms Accused," 1.

19. R. Warren, "The Interorganizational Field as a Focus for Investigation," *Administrative Science Quarterly* 12 (1967): 396–419.

20. Paul Ingrassia and Ralph E. Winter, "Operations Sag at Ashland and Clark Oil After Moves to Concentrate on Refineries," *The Wall Street Journal* (June 4, 1981), 29.

21. "Saatchi and Saatchi Reached Top of Ad World in 16 Years," *The Tallahassee Democrat* (May 14, 1986), 9D.

22. David Wessel, "Textron Is in an Acquiring Mood Again," *The Wall Street Journal* (January 13, 1987), 6.

23. Jeffrey Pfeffer and Phillip Nowak, "Joint Ventures and Interorganizational Interdependence," *Administrative Science Quarterly* 21 (September 1976): 398–418.

24. Johannes M. Pennings, *Interlocking Directorates* (San Francisco: Jossey-Bass, 1980).

25. Seyman B. Sarason and Elizabeth Lorentz, *The Challenge of the Resource Exchange Network: From Concept to Action* (San Francisco: Jossey-Bass, 1979).

26. Clemens P. Work and Jack Seamonds, "What Are Mergers Doing to America?" *U.S. News and World Report* (July 22, 1985), 50.

ANNOTATED BIBLIOGRAPHY

Blake, Robert, and Mouton, Jane S. "How to Achieve the Integration on the Human Side of the Merger." *Organizational Dynamics* 13, no. 3 (Winter 1985): 41–56.

The model discussed in this article is designed to maximize success in merging two independent organizations. Taking into account each company's cultures, histories, traditions, policies, and practices, the model uses open communication, participative problem solving, and collaborative reorganization to maximize the likelihood of success.

Emerson, R. E. "Power-Dependence Relations." *American Sociological Review* 27 (1962): 31–41.

This classic sociological work sets forth the theory of power dependence of organizations and institutions on one another and on critical factors in the environment.

Fottler, Myron D.; Schermerhorn, John R., Jr.; Wong, John; and Money, William H. "Multi-Institutional Arrangements in Health Care: Review, Analysis and a Proposal for Future Research." *Academy of Management Review* 7 (January 1982): 67–79.

Multi-institutional arrangements in the health-care industry have grown rapidly since 1970. This paper provides a literature review and a research proposal concerning the managerial aspects of this phenomenon.

Galbraith, John Kenneth. *The New Industrial State*. Boston: Houghton Mifflin, 1967.

This classic work is where Galbraith sets forth his theory of countervailing power and its implications for an industrialized society. It examines the role of business, government, unions, and other major institutions of an industrialized society.

Harrigan, Kathryn R. "Formulating Vertical Integration Strategies." *Academy of Management Review* 9, no. 4 (December 1984): 638–652.

A framework is proposed that develops the dimensions of vertical integration strategies and proposes key factors that might augment their uses within various scenarios. These represent new hypotheses and conjectures about make-or-buy decisions that require empirical testing. If the framework is valid, strategists could formulate better hybrid vertical integration strategies by recognizing the hypothesized effects of these forces on the industries that might be linked.

Jemison, David B., and Sitkin, Sim B. "Corporate Acquisitions: A Process Perspective." *Academy of Management Review* 11, no. 1 (March 1986): 145–163.

Historically, acquisition scholars and practitioners have adopted a choice perspective, which portrays the corporate executive analyzing acquisition opportunities as a rational decision maker. This article suggests that the choice perspective be supplemented with a process perspective that recognizes the acquisition process itself as a potentially important determinant of activities and outcomes.

Litwak, E., and Hylton, L. "Interorganizational Analysis: A Hypothesis on Coordinating Agencies." *Administrative Science Quarterly* 6 (1962): 395–420.

The article deals with the confusion of terms dealing with interorganizational relationships and postulates that the lowest common denominator is organizational interdependency. Two or more organizations are viewed as being interdependent if they take each other into account when pursuing individual goals.

Millstein, Ira M., and Katsh, Salem M. *The Limits of Corporate Power: Existing Constraints on the Exercise of Corporate Discretion*. New York: Macmillan, 1981.

The book explains eight major factors that limit corporate power and the ability to form interorganizational relationships. These factors are general state and federal regulations, economic and market constraints, the federal tax system, social values, specific regulations in labor relations, equal opportunity, politics, and energy.

Morris, Betsy, and Johnson, Robert. "How Beatrice Adjusts to Latest Takeover, This Time of Itself." *The Wall Street Journal* (December 5, 1985): 1, 24.

This article examines some of the negative consequences that an organization can experience as a result of a series of takeovers, the final one being its own takeover. In 1984 and 1985, Beatrice was involved in a number of takeovers, both hostile and friendly; however, on November 14, 1985, the Beatrice organization itself was taken over by Kohlberg Davis. This has resulted in a number of negative consequences for the Beatrice organization, including worker stress, delayed decision making, and general operational inefficiency.

Pennings, Johannes M. *Interlocking Directorates*. San Francisco: Jossey-Bass, 1980.

The book explains the origins and consequences of connections among organizations' boards of directors. The results of a study of 800 of the largest American corporations are reported.

Pfeffer, Jeffrey, and Salancik, Gerald R. *The External Control of Organizations: A Resource Dependence Perspective*. New York: Harper & Row, 1978.

Pfeffer and Salancik use resource dependency to provide a comprehensive explanation of why organizations form interorganizational relationships. They explain much organizational and managerial action as a result of trying to reduce dependency on factors in the outside environment.

Sarason, Seymour B., and Lorentz, Elizabeth. *The Challenge of the Resource Exchange Network: From Concept to Action*. San Francisco: Jossey-Bass, 1979.

The book sets forth the use of resource exchange networks in nonbusiness organizations such as schools, colleges, welfare agencies, hospitals, and counseling services. Detailed examination of examples of programs in adult education and training, assistance for the handicapped, and medical and support services for the elderly is provided.

Schermerhorn, John R., Jr. "Determinants of Interorganizational Cooperation." *Academy of Management Journal* 18 (December 1975): 846–856.

This article summarizes research conducted on interorganizational cooperation and environmental dependencies. It develops ten propositions that relate key variables to one another to explain why interorganizational cooperation is likely to form.

Tushman, Michael L., and Scanlan, Thomas J. "Boundary Spanning Individuals: Their Role in Information Transfer and Their Antecedents." *Academy of Management Journal* 24, no. 2 (June 1981): 289–303.

This is an investigation of alternative mechanisms by which information is imported into organizations that indicates that information boundary spanning is accomplished only by those individuals who are well connected internally and externally. These key individuals are nominated as technically competent in their unit and have the personal characteristics to effectively link their unit to external areas.

Warren, R. "The Interorganizational Field as a Focus for Investigation." *Administrative Science Quarterly* 12 (1967): 396–419.

This article sets forth four environmental contexts in which interdependencies occur: social choice, coalitional, federative, and unitary.

ADDITIONAL REFERENCES

Aldrich, H. "An Organization-Environment Perspective on Cooperation and Conflict Between Organizations in the Manpower Training System." In *Conflict and Power in Complex Organizations: An Inter-Institutional Perspective*, edited by A. R. Negandi, 11–38. Kent, Ohio: Comparative Administration Research Institute, Kent State University, 1972.

Baker, F., and O'Brien, G. "Intersystems Relations and Coordination of Human Service Organizations." *American Journal of Public Health* 61 (1971): 130–137.

Baty, G.; Evan, W.; and Rothermel, T. "Personal Flows as Interorganizational Relations." *Administrative Science Quarterly* 16 (1971): 430–434.

Beresford, D. R., and Neary, R. D. "Making a Merger Work: Financial Management Issues." *FE* 1 (October 1985): 1, 9–10.

Black, B., and Kase, H. "Interagency Cooperation in Rehabilitation and Mental Health." *Social Service Review* 57 (1963): 26–32.

Braito, R. S.; Paulson, S.; and Klonglon, G. "Domain Consensus: A Key Variable in Interorganizational Analysis." In *Complex Organizations and Their Environments*, edited by M. Brinkerhoff and P. Kunz, 176–199. Dubuque, Iowa: William C. Brown, 1972.

Chandler, Alfred D., Jr.; Bruchey, Stuart; and Galambos, Louis. *The Changing Economic Order.* New York: Harcourt, Brace & World, 1968.

DeAngelo, Harry, and Rice, Edward M. "Antitakeover Charter Amendments and Stockholder Wealth." *Journal of Financial Economics* 11 (April 1983): 329–360.

Domoff, G. William. *The Higher Circles.* New York: Random House, 1970.

Domoff, G. William. *Who Rules America?* Englewood Cliffs, N.J.: Prentice-Hall, 1967.

Elkins, Arthur, and Callaghan, Dennis W. *A Managerial Odyssey: Problems in Business and Its Environment.* 3d ed. Reading, Mass.: Addison-Wesley, 1981.

Evan, W. "Toward a Theory of Interorganizational Relations." *Management Science* 11 (1965): 217–230.

Fogg, J. G. "Takeovers: Last Chance for Self-Restraint." *Harvard Business Review* 63 (November–December 1985): 30–32.

Goldberg, Walter H. *Mergers: Motives, Models, Methods.* New York: Nichols, 1983.

Gueztkow, H. "Relations Among Organizations." In *Studies on Behavior in Organizations*, edited by R. Bowers, 13–44. Athens, Ga.: University of Georgia Press, 1966.

Hall, R.; Clark, J.; Giordano, P.; Johnson, P.; and Van Roekel, M. "Interorganizational Relationships." Paper presented at the 8th World Conference of Sociology, International Sociological Association, 1974.

Levine, S., and White, P. "Exchange as a Conceptual Framework for the Study of Interorganizational Relationships." *Administrative Science Quarterly* 5 (1961): 583–601.

Levine, S.; White, P.; and Paul, B. "Community Interorganizational Problems in Providing Medical Care and Social Services." *American Journal of Public Health* 53 (1963): 1183–1195.

Linn, Scott C., and McConnell, John J. "An Empirical Investigation of the Impact of 'Antitakeover' Amendments on Common Stock Prices." *Journal of Financial Economics* 11 (April 1983): 361–399.

Litwak, E., and Rothman, J. "Toward the Theory and Practice of Coordination Between Formal Organizations." In *Organizations and Clients*, edited by W. Rosengren and M. Lefton, 137–186. Columbus, Ohio: Charles E. Merrill, 1970.

Marrett, C. "On the Specification of Interorganizational Dimensions." *Sociology and Social Research* 56 (1971): 83–97.

Melcher, A., and Adamek, R. "Interorganizational Models: A Critical Evaluation." In *Organization Theory in an Interorganizational Perspective,* edited by A. R. Negandhi, 1–18. Kent, Ohio: The Comparative Administration Research Institute, Kent State University, 1971.

Mills, C. Wright. *The Power Elite.* New York: Oxford University Press, 1969.

Provan, Keith G. "Interorganizational Linkages and Influence over Decision Making." *Academy of Management Journal* 25 (June 1982): 443–451.

Reed, Richard, and Luffman, George A. "Diversification: The Growing Confusion." *Strategic Management Journal* 7 (July 1984): 29–35.

Reid, W. "Interagency Coordination in Delinquency Prevention and Control." *Social Service Review* 38 (1964): 418–428.

Reid, W. "Interorganizational Coordination: A Review and Critique of Current Theory." In *Interorganizational Research in Health: Conference Proceedings,* edited by P. White and G. Vlasak, 84–101. Washington, D.C.: U.S. Government Printing Office, 1972, #0-421-532.

Schoorman, F. David; Bazerman, Max H.; and Atkin, Robert S. "Interlocking Directorates: A Strategy for Reducing Environmental Uncertainty." *Academy of Management Review* 6 (April 1981): 243–252.

Starkweather, D. "Beyond the Semantics of Multi-hospital Aggregations." *Health Services Research* 7 (1972): 58–61.

Thompson, J., and McEwen, W. "Organizational Goals and Environment: Goal-setting as an Interaction Process." *American Sociological Review* 23 (1958): 23–31.

Turk, H. "Comparative Urban Structure from an Interorganizational Perspective." *Administrative Science Quarterly* 18 (1973): 37–55.

Van de Ven, A., and Koenig, R., Jr. "Pair-Wise Inter-Agency Relationships: Theory and Preliminary Findings." Unpublished paper, Graduate School of Business Administration, Kent State University, 1975.

Walton, R. "Interorganizational Decision Making and Identity Conflict." In *Interorganizational Decision Making,* edited by M. Tuite, R. Chisolm and M. Radnor, 9–19. Chicago: Aldine, 1972.

Warren, R. "The Concerting of Decisions as a Variable in Organizational Interaction." In *Interorganizational Decision Making,* edited by M. Tuite, R. Chisolm, and M. Radnor, 20–32. Chicago: Aldine, 1972.

```
┌─────────────────────────────────────┐
│  C        A        S        E        │
└─────────────────────────────────────┘
```

Pan-United

Pan American Airways was truly a trail-blazer in the early days of commercial aviaation and was perhaps best known for its Asian-Pacific routes. But in May 1985, Pan Am struck a deal with United Airlines to sell those routes for $750 million.

This deal came about as a direct result of the airline deregulation that was begun by the Carter administration in the 1970s. "This is a direct response to deregulation, molding airline operations to the marketplace of today and tomorrow," said United's chairman, Richard Ferris.

What's really innovative about the arrangement is the selling of airline routes to a competitor. This will not only hasten the process whereby United gets bigger, but could set off a free-for-all among different airlines trying to outbid each other for foreign routes. Indeed, there has been talk about another airline stalking Pan Am's European routes from the American east coast. Although Pan Am Chairman C. Edward Acker claims that his firm's European routes are not for sale and never will be, Pan Am's competitor, TWA, is starting to worry about a possible takeover of its European routes. Its 1985 net market value was only $420 million, and analysts do not predict a healthy future for the airline because of its lack-luster management and high-priced structure. Indeed, domestic airlines such as American, Continental, and Northwest are eyeing TWA's potentially lucrative European routes.

Expansion into the Asian-Pacific market is a natural for United, which is very strong domestically in the western United States. In addition to the Asian-Pacific route deal, United is buying eighteen of Pan Am's airliners as well as all of its facilities in the Asian-Pacific region.

The demise of Pan Am's Asian-Pacific routes came about as the company began to focus its efforts on its North Atlantic–European routes. In fact, Pan Am executives admit that its whole future rests on flying passengers in and out of its New York and Miami hubs—doing what it can do the best. Pan Am simply does not have the $3 billion it needs to modernize its Asian-Pacific fleet and remodel its facilities. United, on the other hand, already flies to San Francisco from forty-two points in the United States, compared to Pan Am's six.

Bottom-line figures are another reason why Pan Am went for United's offer. In 1984, Pan Am lost a total of $107 million; however, it did make $110 million in its Atlantic division, while it made only $59 million in its Asian-Pacific division. Moreover, the company is $1 billion in debt, and the selling of its Asian-Pacific routes will allow it to pay $310 million of these obligations. The rest of the proceeds from the route sale might very well go to the parent holding company, Pan American Corporation, thus prompting rumors of diversification away from the airline business.

Labor-management conflict has been a proximate cause of Pan Am's recent misfortunes. During the spring of 1985, the

Sources: Colin Leinster, "Can Pan Am Survive?" *Fortune* (April 15, 1985), 49–50; "Pan Am Furls Its Flag Over the Pacific," *The Economist* (April 27, 1985), 77–78; Reggi Ann Dubin, "The Pan Am–United Deal: 'Truly a Win-Win' Situation," *Business Week* (May 6, 1985): 45–46.

airline was severely crippled when maintenance workers went on strike. The maintenance workers union, supported by the four other Pan Am unions, walked out in late February of that year. As a result, 70 percent of Pan Am's fleet lay idle for ten days. Even after workers returned to the job in early March, the airline could only operate half its scheduled flights until the end of the month. The company's misery and performance distress increased as travel agents and passengers switched to other airlines. This conflict situation made United's offer all the more attractive.

Selling off assets is nothing new to Pan Am, though. Even before Chairman Acker came on board in 1981, the airline was forced to sell its Intercontinental Hotel operations and the Pan Am building in New York in order to raise badly needed cash when the airline industry became chaotic right after deregulation.

As a final note, there are some potential "flies in the ointment" that could harm United. For one thing, it must somehow absorb 2,700 Pan Am employees into the United organization. Second, the transaction could confuse an already complex set of negotiations between the pilots and the airlines. And third, some business analysts believe that United's Asian-Pacific route takeover would consume most of United's management efforts and thus weaken its domestic operations.

QUESTIONS FOR DISCUSSION

1. How is the proposed sale related to the concept of enacted environment?
2. One condition that fosters interorganizational relationships is the cost/benefit concept. Do you think it was applied in this instance? Should more than economic cost/benefit analysis (e.g., psychological and sociological analyses) be performed?
3. Was Pan Am in a performance distress situation? How did this contribute to the route buyout?
4. As an alternative to the proposed route buyout, what other types of interorganizational relationships would be appropriate in this instance?

PART THREE

The Organization's Internal Environment

In this part of the book, we look inside organizations. Up to now we have been primarily concerned with the way the organization knows and deals with its environment. Now we ask, what are the processes that go on within the organization? How do organizations design themselves? What roles do strategy, delegation, and goals play in the life of the organization?

Chapter 7 is a transition piece that shows how coping mechanisms and strategies dealing with the external environment can also be used to keep the organization's internal components in proper adjustment. We then examine the goals and work systems of the organization.

What do organizations try to accomplish and how do they go about doing it? These questions and others are answered in Chapter 8. This chapter explains two important systems and how they must be intricately tied together if the organization is to succeed in the long run. The basis for organization activity (or work) is the pursuit of goals or purposes, and this chapter expands on that point and brings in various classifications and concepts in order to better understand it.

Chapter 9 is a general discussion of the entire field of organization design and how it relates to organization structure. The various organization design patterns are discussed, and the characteristics of effective structure are reviewed. This chapter logically follows the discussion of the goal and work systems because design is concerned with building the structure and processes that tie the various work patterns together into an effective whole aimed at achieving goals.

Chapter 10 explains in some detail the different kinds of structures—how they are put together and the various forms and configurations they can take. In essence, it fleshes out the general concepts described in Chapter 9.

Chapter 11 is geared toward examining two of the most important concepts of organization theory. To a large extent, the size and complexity of the differentiation and integration processes determine the effectiveness, or conversely, the cumbersomeness, of the organization as an entity. Determinants and measurements of both size and complexity are presented, as is their relationship to structure.

Chapter 12 exams the role of technology as it affects the organization, its growth, and even its maturation or deterioration. Technology is viewed not only as it relates to the core processes of the organization, but also as it affects the organization as an external force.

These six chapters look at the organization's micro or internal environment. These concepts are significant, not only for understanding the inner workings of the organization itself, but for better understanding the organization's relationship with its macro environment.

7

Organizational Strategy: Coping with the External Environment

No Christmas at Bethlehem

When the directors of Bethlehem Steel Corporation chose Donald Trautlein to be chairman of this decaying steel giant in 1980, they hoped that he, as an accountant and an "outsider," would find ways to turn around the organization's fortunes. By the spring of 1986, however, Trautlein had resigned and Bethlehem was in deeper trouble than ever. The company was so strapped for cash that it was forced to sell some of its few remaining viable assets, including part of its corporate jet fleet. Profits have steadily declined since 1981, with losses close to $2 billion. Debt as a percentage of total capital stood at 52 percent, and its remaining plants were running at 59 percent of capacity, the lowest in an already depressed industry. Indeed, some Bethlehem executives stated that "bankruptcy is not impossible."

Analysts claim that the cause of Bethlehem's demise was a series of strategic errors and paralyzing indecision. While other steel companies decided to adopt diversification strategies, Trautlein did exactly the opposite. He believed that steel's downturn in the early 1980s was a "cyclical phenomenon," and that the way to revitalize Bethlehem was to cut costs and modernize operations, thus staying primarily in the steel business. From 1980 through 1986, Trautlein pushed through the following changes: eliminated 38,000 jobs; shut down the eighty-year-old Lackawanna, New York plant (laying off 7,000 employees); purchased ultramodern casting equipment for still-operating plants; and decentralized Bethlehem's management structure into independent business units at each plant.

However, these and other measures failed to stop the slide. Critics argue that the strategy of focusing on steelmaking in the declining steel industry was suicidal. Trautlein did not attempt to identify a few promising niches in the market where Bethlehem might have been successful; rather, he chose the supermarket approach whereby Bethlehem continued to manufacture a wide variety of steel products that could not compete against foreign imports. The Bethlehem chairman also failed to liquidate certain unprofitable businesses that had little or no future—railroad car manufacturing and bar, rod, and wire manufacturing.

Trautlein failed to accurately read the external and internal environments in which his organization operated. He wrongly believed that the federal government would impose mandatory steel import quotas—it did not. And by the summer of 1985, foreign imports accounted for over 20 percent of the U.S. market. Trautlein also believed that the U.S. auto industry would revitalize to the point where Bethlehem products would be in heavy demand. Again, Trautlein was wrong, as evidenced by GM's successful wrenching of price cuts from Bethlehem in combination with declining steel orders. He thought the rank and file of the United Steel Workers would be receptive to wage and benefit cuts—they were, but only to a point. In the spring of 1986, union representatives walked out of contract talks after learning of Trautlein's and other senior Bethlehem executives' "golden parachutes," generous severance packages in the event of a takeover. And white-collar workers suffered serious morale problems because of massive layoffs. Finally, restructuring away from centralization only led to confusion and indecision as plant managers were faced with making decisions in areas in which they had

Sources: Gregory L. Miles and John P. Tarney, "Is Bethlehem Investing in a Future It Doesn't Have?" *Business Week* (July 8, 1985), 56–57; J. Ernest Beazley and Carol Hymowitz, "Steel Target: Critics Fault Trautlein for Failing to Revive an Ailing Bethlehem," *The Wall Street Journal* (May 27, 1986), 1; George McManus, "Will Trautlein Be Blamed for All of Steel's Woes?" *Iron Age Metals Producer* (July 4, 1986), 76.

no experience or expertise (e.g., labor relations, accounting, and even product advertising).

Reversing himself in 1985, Trautlein decided that diversification might be the proper strategy for Bethlehem. Bethlehem's single venture into this area was the purchase of J. M. Tull Industries, a small steel distributor, for $95 million (sixteen times its earnings). Within a year, however, Bethlehem had to sell this acquisition for much-needed cash. So much for diversification. And bankers became skittish when Trautlein announced future plans to spend $250 million for other acquisitions.

In fairness to Trautlein and Bethlehem, other steel corporations that did choose different strategies in the 1980s have often met with something less than complete success. Republic's merger with Jones and Laughlin has only doubled the amount of problems for the new entity, and Armco's diversification into the insurance business almost bankrupted the company. But the important difference is that other steel organizations did not put all their eggs in one basket; thus, they have not suffered as badly as Bethlehem. Moreover, if the steel industry continues to decline as predicted, other steel companies have choices besides steel manufacturing available to them. Bethlehem does not. It has to stick with steel and hope that both demand and price increase, because the company simply does not have the necessary money to expand into other areas.

Trautlein departed Bethlehem in 1986 and was replaced by Walter Williams, who believes that a diversification strategy would be in the best interest of the company. However, he stated, "Right now we don't have the resources to do a lot of the things we'd like to do—like growing in other businesses."

Bethlehem Steel is failing because it did not devise an effective strategy for dealing with its turbulent environment. By not properly analyzing his organization's internal and external environments and by failing to develop an appropriate strategy, Trautlein's actions precipitated the multiple crises at Bethlehem.

Today's organizations must understand and practice strategic management—the development and implementation of a long-range plan for the organization that is carefully thought out in terms of environmental opportunities and constraints. Failure to do so, as seen in the above example, can very well lead to the organization's instability and ultimate failure.

CHAPTER PLAN

This chapter examines the concept of strategic management and how organizations develop and implement long-term strategic plans in order to cope with the environment. First, the role of strategy and strategic management is discussed, with emphasis on the strategic typology developed by Miles and Snow. We next study the strategic management process, concentrating on the following areas: environmental analysis and forecasting, including scenario analysis; customer/market analysis; strategic planning premises, or assumptions the organization makes about the future; internal organization assessment; and, finally, definition of the organization's mission in view of the steps previously discussed.

We then focus on the variety of strategies available to the organization. These fall within two broad types. Generic corporate-level strategies are those adopted and followed by the organization as a whole; generic business-level strategies are those used by the organization to promote a particular product or service. The chapter closes with a summary of the strategic management process as it pertains to the study of organization theory.

In Chapter 4 we looked at the organization's external linkages, and we described some strategies an organization can use to cope with its environment. In Chapter 5 we saw how organizations process information and make choices based on this information. In Chapter 6 we examined how organizations form interorganizational relationships. Much of the material we presented gave a rather static, descriptive view of how an organization deals with its environment. In this chapter, we attempt to be more dynamic and analytical in our examination of organizational adaptation. Specifically, we address such issues as why organizations adopt particular strategies, the consequences of such strategies, and what types of deliberate managerial decisions need to be made to maximize organizational interface.

The purpose of this chapter is to provide an opportunity to integrate and apply the concepts we reviewed in Chapters 4–6. These are rather difficult concepts. Yet by applying them in a strategic framework, your knowledge of the concepts should be enhanced. In this chapter we present a broad overview of the essentials of strategic management. This is a rich and rapidly growing field in organizations; you may wish to consult the references at the end of the chapter for more information. Some of the questions we examine in this chapter include the following: Are organizations aware of the consequences of the reactive as well as the proactive strategy they employ? Do they conscientiously examine all choices and make a logical decision as to the most appropriate strategy? Do organizations seem willing to change strategy in the face of new environmental demands? Are organizations accurately assessing their task and potential task environments? What are the important decision-authority centers involved in organizations? Do organizations examine the degree of stability and heterogeneity in the environment and respond appropriately?

ROLE OF STRATEGY AND STRATEGIC MANAGEMENT

Boundary spanners play a critical role in the strategic planning function of the firm by establishing "formal linkages between external elements of the organization and internal decision-making or resource allocation functions."[1] Hence, the way an organization links with its environment is determined by and has a profound effect on the strategic decision making in the firm.

Strategic Management

Strategic management involves making basic and fundamental decisions in the following areas:

1. Assessing the external environment
2. Formulating organization purpose, philosophy, mission, and key goals
3. Making major choices of a particular set of long-term objectives and grand strategies needed to achieve them
4. Developing short-range objectives and allocating resources to achieve them
5. Designing organizational structures and systems to achieve the goals[2]

We define *strategic management* as the process of adapting the organization to its environment to better accomplish organizational purposes and to sustain the organization's long-term viability by enhancing the value of its products and services. *Strategic decisions* are those key decisions that tie the organization's mission and purpose to its environmental opportunities and constraints. They are long-term decisions that have a major impact on the organization. This relationship is shown in Figure 7.1. These decisions are usually made at the very top of the organization.

Strategic decisions and strategic management give rise to *organizational policy*. The terms *policy* and *strategic management* are virtually inseparable today.[3] At one time, organizational policy referred to the broad guidelines followed in reaching goals and objectives; when referring to policy at a lower (unit or department) level, it still has this meaning. However, organizational policy is used interchangeably with the concept of strategy when referring to organization-wide decisions.

Strategic Typology

In Chapter 4 we identified four basic environmental linkage strategies: imperviousness, selective imperviousness, adaptation, and action-adaptation. Each of these linkage strategies is associated with a different form of strategic management. For example, organizations that adopt an imperviousness strategy will make strategic decisions to isolate and protect their technical core from the influence of a threatening outside environment. An action-adaptation posture should reflect a strategic management decision to be heavily involved in attempting to influence the organization's outside environment while at the same time adjusting as deemed appropriate to parts of that environment.

The strategic decisions made at the organizational level will result in one of the linkage strategies we have discussed. Several researchers have developed a typology of basic strategic management decisions that can be used to classify strategic decisions much as the linkage strategies are used to classify boundary-spanning strategies. One of the more popular typologies was developed by Miles and Snow.[4]

Miles and Snow identify four basic organizational strategies for dealing with the environment, each with a particular mix of technology, structure, and process that is consistent with it. Each strategy is briefly defined below.

FIGURE 7.1

Strategic Management Is an Interactive Process

DEFENDERS. These are organizations with a relatively narrow line of products and market domains. Top managers in these organizations are experts in their organizations' limited domains but avoid seeking new market opportunities. Because of this relatively narrow focus, these organizations concentrate on improving the efficiency of their operations and are not concerned with major adjustments in technology, structure, or methods of operation. The Baskins-Robbins ice cream shop chain is an excellent example of this type of organization. It insulated itself from the market by maintaining its old store decor and repertoire of standard flavors while its competitors, such as Steve's Ice Cream and Häagen-Dazs, captured a significant market share through fancy store design and the introduction of more exotic flavors.

PROSPECTORS. These organizations are always looking for new market opportunities. They experiment with new products and services in response to new environmental trends. They tend to create uncertainty and change in the marketplace, to which their competitors must respond. However, these organizations are usually not efficient since they are continually experimenting with new services, products, and markets. Duquesne Systems of Pittsburgh exemplifies this type of organization. Duquesne is a new company that specializes in developing software to boost the efficiency of IBM and IBM-compatible computer mainframes. Although its software products are unique and well received by the market, the company does have its management problems as it attempts to design an organization structure to better boost efficiency and effectiveness.

ANALYZERS. These firms have one product in a stable market and one in a changing market. In the stable market they operate rather routinely and efficiently by using formalized structures and processes. In the rapidly changing markets, they closely watch their competitors and then adapt as best as they can. The Schering-Plough Corporation, a manufacturer of pharmaceuticals, can be typed an analyzer. Known for producing mostly "me too" drugs, the company has one stable product, the antibiotic Garamycin, that has been the mainstay of its prescription drug line. As Schering-Plough watched its competitors advance in the biotech field, it embarked on a crash program to develop the drug Interferon, once thought to be a miracle cure for cancer and viral infections. Analyzers seldom if ever start a new program or trend; instead they copy successful operations of others.

REACTORS. These organizations have top managers who frequently perceive changes and uncertainty in their outside environments but cannot marshal organizational resources to respond effectively to them. These organizations lack a consistent strategy-structure relationship and are unlikely to make major adjustments until environmental pressure becomes pronounced, and some fail to adjust altogether. Bethlehem Steel, discussed in the introductory case to this chapter, is a prime example of a reactor organization. Unable to adjust to the acute decline of steel manufacturing in the United States, this company now faces a life-or-death situation.

Each of these basic strategies sets the decision processes in motion for determining the organization's technology, structure, and process. Each strategy explicitly recognizes the organization's basic posture in relating to the environment in determining these internal factors. Consequently, the role of boundary linkage and boundary-spanning units is profoundly affected by the strategic posture taken. For example, organizations with a defender strategy are likely to use an imperviousness strategy in boundary linkage, while analyzers might follow an adaptation linkage strategy.

Even though Miles and Snow maintain that the strategies operate the same regardless of industry, recent evidence suggests that this is not so. Hambrick found that differences existed depending on the industry environment examined.[5] That is, the choice of strategy should be a function of an organization's particular environment and the type of performance that an organization seeks at the time.

THE STRATEGIC MANAGEMENT PROCESS

The basic posture of the organization toward its environment sets the framework or foundation for the development of specific strategies. This process is called *strategic analysis* and is considered an essential part of the overall strategic management and planning process.

While the specific steps in the strategic management and planning process vary from author to author, for our purposes we use the process depicted in Figure 7.2.[6] This process lays out the essential steps involved in strategic management and planning. The plan-operationalization phase deals with operational management and objectives and is discussed in Chapter 8, where we study goal setting and attainment.

Let's examine each step in the process depicted in Figure 7.2.

Environmental Analysis and Forecast

As we have pointed out numerous times elsewhere in this text, understanding the outside environment is critical for organizational functioning. The strategic management and planning process begins with this

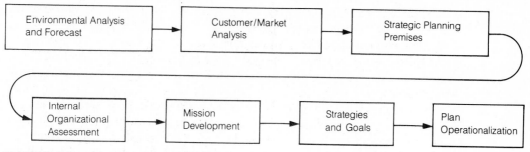

FIGURE 7.2

The Strategic Management and Planning Process

Source: William P. Anthony, "The Strategic Planning Process," in *Practical Strategic Planning: A Guide and Manual for Line Managers* (Quorum Books, a division of Greenwood Press, Inc., Westport, Conn., 1985), 5. Copyright © 1985 by William P. Anthony. Reprinted with permission.

understanding. Two steps must be accomplished here: (1) determine the present state of the environment, that is, the status quo, and (2) forecast what is likely to happen. Although determining the task environment and domain is emphasized, the organization should also scan the potential and non-task environments.

In general, the following aspects of the outside environment should be examined and forecasted:

Economy

Social and demographic trends

Political/legal factors

Technology

Industry

Competitors

These sectors will vary depending on the type of organization. For example, a large multinational organization, such as General Motors, will be more concerned with the global economy and worldwide political/legal trends than will a local or regional company, such as the Peter Pan Bus Company that operates primarily in western New England.

In all environmental areas being examined, an attempt is made to describe what exists now in each area, or sector, and what is likely to happen in the future. Depending on the organization's planning horizon—the period for which planning is being done—the organization's forecast may be from two to ten years, with a five-year limit being common.

One major objective of the environmental analysis and forecast is to assess the opportunities and constraints (or threats) in the environment. In designing its plans and strategies, the organization will want to take advantage of the opportunities while minimizing or deflecting threats or constraints. Again, we refer to the introductory case of this chapter where we mentioned how other steel companies, such as Republic, Jones and Laughlin, and Armco, attempted to deflect the environmental threat of declining steel prices and demand by adopting merger and diversification strategies.

Before we leave this step in strategic management, let's briefly examine the stakeholder concept. *Stakeholders* are groups of people who have a vested interest in the operation and outcomes of the organization. Although not all stakeholders exist in the outside environment (e.g., employees are stakeholders), many of them do (e.g., owners, government regulatory agencies, customers). These stakeholders should be examined at some point in the process. In our model, all stakeholders except customers and employees should be examined during this step. (Customers are examined in the next step and employees in the assessment phase.)

The primary difficulty here is reconciling the different expectations held among stakeholder groups (e.g., owners want a high return on investment while EPA regulators want a new pollution control system). One key element of strategic management is reconciling different stakeholder expectations.* This requires accurately reading their expectations and then using political and negotiating skills to fashion a compromise. No organization can be all things to all people—that is, no organization can completely satisfy every group making a demand on it. Rather, what the organization can do is to make important stakeholder groups at least reasonably well satisfied.

THE FORECAST. Strategic management deals with the future. Consequently, any strategic plan and set of strategic decisions are only as good as the forecast that predicts the future. To the extent that predictions are accurate, the building blocks for plans and decisions will be solidly constructed.

A complete discussion of forecasting is beyond the scope of this book**; however, we do briefly discuss a few key concepts. Most forecasts are based on a *trend analysis*. A historical trend is discerned from a set of data. Using a regression technique, a line is extended into the future. This trend may be straight line or curvilinear. The curvilinear trend may be cyclical, and thus relatively predictable, or it may be discontinuous, such as the oil price shocks of the early and late 1970s. Figure 7.3 shows these three types of trends.

---

*Readers desiring more information on this subject should read R. Edward Freeman, *Strategic Management: A Stakeholder Approach* (Boston: Pitman, 1984).

**Readers are referred to Jay Mendell, *Nonextrapolative Methods in Business Forecasting: Scenarios, Vision, and Issues Management* (Westport, Conn.: Quorum Books, 1985).

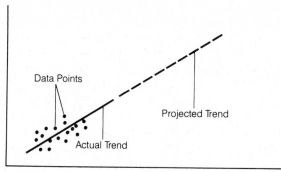

A. Straight Line

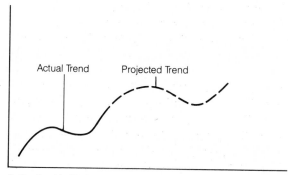

B. Predictable Cycle

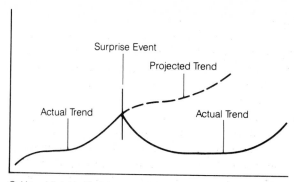

C. Unpredictable Cycle

FIGURE 7.3

Projection Techniques and Trend Analysis

Scenario analysis is also used in forecasting. Alternative future scenarios are constructed about future events; probabilities are assigned to the scenario; and contingency plans are developed for the most likely scenarios. Payoffs can be constructed for each alternative scenario and both pessimistic and optimistic scenarios projected. Planning for the most pessimistic scenario is called *worst-case planning* and is often done so the organization is prepared if everything goes wrong. In other words, the organization develops a method to cut its losses if its plan doesn't work. The key question in worst-case planning is, "If we've chosen the wrong plan, how easy is it for us to get out of the situation?" The military frequently uses this technique as a planning tool for engagements. A more traditional example would be the case of Boeing Company, the airplane manufacturer. Forecasting increased defense spending, the company has embarked on a strategy of producing more military aircraft (the company has previously concentrated its efforts on commercial aircraft). However, should defense spending be significantly curtailed, Boeing also has a simultaneous strategy of enhancing its commercial manufacturing operations through its development and acquisition of leading-edge technology. Moreover, should the demand for military aircraft not materialize as envisioned by Boeing, much of its effort can be transferred to the commercial side because the technologies and operations are somewhat similar.

Table 7.1 shows an example of scenario planning. Four possible scenarios (I–IV) are chosen, with the probability of each occurring ranging from 5 percent to 50 percent. The maximum benefit occurs in the second scenario, with a 30 percent chance of occurring. In this case, plan *RST* will yield a benefit of $75,000. The worst-case scenario only has a 5 percent chance of occurring, and will result in a $15,000 loss. Going back to the Boeing example, we could say that company forecasters foresee only a 5

TABLE 7.1

Scenario and Contingency Planning

Scenario	Probability of Occurrence	Plan	Financial Benefit
I. $A + B + C + D$	50%	XYZ	$50,000
II. $E + L + M$	30%	RST	$75,000 (maximum)
III. $H + P + Q$	15%	VWX	$10,000
IV. $C + D + G + N$	5%	UV	−$15,000 (minimum) Worst case

percent chance that defense spending will be cut in the future, and, if this were to happen with the company geared up for defense production, losses would be, say, $150 million. This would then be weighed against other scenarios, one of which could state that there is a 60 percent chance of defense spending increasing by 10 percent per year. Should the company effect a plan to manufacture military hardware to meet this forecasted opportunity, then Boeing would earn, say, $500 million.

Customer/Market Analysis

The next step in the strategic planning process focuses on an explicit analysis of both the customer and client groups served by the organization and the general nature of the market. Specifically, the organization tries to answer these questions:

1. How is our present customer/client group changing?
2. What new customer/clients should we be serving?
3. What forces are shaping the industries in which we operate?
4. What is the nature of our competitive advantage in our competitive environment?

Let's briefly examine each of these factors.

CHANGING CUSTOMERS/CLIENTS. Strategic planning and decision making focus on the future. Consequently, the focus here is on how the customer/client group is changing. The question is, "What will the customer be like in the future?" The answer to this question becomes the basis for preparing a strategic management program today.

The specific factors in customer analysis will vary depending on the specific organization. Certainly a multi-product/service company, such as Procter and Gamble, that uses a market segmentation strategy will want to describe several customer groupings. Regardless of the exact nature of the focal organization, however, some factors to analyze include such demographics as age, income, family size, geographic location, and education. Psychological factors include product meaning, symbolism, status, and prestige associated with product use.

Too often, organizations design strategic plans based on historical information about the customer or client. Instead, the emphasis should be on designing plans to serve the customer of tomorrow; hence, the analysis and forecasting of trends in customer characteristics become critical.

NEW CUSTOMERS/CLIENTS. As part of the analysis of future factors of the customer base, new customer groups should be examined. Can we appeal to a larger segment of our existing market (getting more babies to eat our baby food)? Can we appeal to new markets (enticing people with bad teeth to eat our baby food)? Can we develop new products for new markets (developing a frozen fruit dessert on a stick)? Can we acquire existing companies and increase customers (acquiring a children's clothing manufacturer)? All these questions deal with expanding the customer/client base and should be examined, at least in a preliminary fashion, at this stage of the analysis.

INDUSTRY FORCES. In most industries, there is a set of underlying forces that shapes industry characteristics such as growth, profitability, and competitiveness. For example, oil prices, safety and pollution laws, and foreign competition are the main factors that shape the domestic auto industry. Mortgage rates, new household formation, family size, and land costs are some of the factors that shape residential home construction. Every industry has underlying forces that must be understood if the organization is to remain viable in its industry. Failure to understand these keys to success required to compete effectively in an industry has doomed many once-successful organizations when they have moved into an unfamiliar industry.

The case of Baldwin-United Corporation provides an excellent example. Baldwin pianos were known the world over for their quality. As the company grew, it entered into the financial services market—annuities, insurance, mutual funds, and so on—an industry it knew little about. After a few short years the company filed for bankruptcy, not because it was unable to compete in the piano market, but because it failed to compete in the financial services market.

COMPETITIVE ENVIRONMENT. What is the nature of our competition? Why would someone buy our product or use our service rather than another company's? Who are our major competitors, and what is our differential advantage over them? In what areas are we weakest compared to our competition? Who is the industry leader and where do we rank? Are there any substitutes for our products or services provided by organizations outside our industry? These are some of the important questions that must be answered by the organization.

A renewed interest in being competitive, caused in part by increasing foreign competition, has spurred many organizations to rethink their competitive strategy.* Indeed, one of the reasons Boeing is concentrating more on military aircraft is because of the new foothold Europe's Airbus has gained in the world commercial aircraft market.

Even government organizations such as public schools and state uni-

---

*See Michael E. Porter, *Competitive Strategy* (New York: The Free Press, 1980) and Michael E. Porter, *Competitive Advantage* (New York: The Free Press, 1983) for excellent discussions on ways to become and remain competitive.

versities are trying to be more competitive because they realize that private schools can drain away both students and teachers. Many government units such as hospitals, mail services, prisons, vocational rehabilitation facilities, and so on now face competition from the private sector. This heightened awareness of the competitive environment is necessary if today's organizations are going to survive. The discount pricing actions of air carriers as well as the emergence of discount carriers are the result of this newly competitive environment in airlines. Much more attention and resources need to be devoted to meeting and beating competition in today's extremely competitive environment.

Strategic Planning Premises

Because any strategic action rests on certain assumptions about the future, the third major step in strategic management and planning involves developing a set of key premises or assumptions about the future. At this stage, the organization makes explicit the key factors developed in the first two steps of the process, environmental analysis and forecasting and customer/market analysis. The attempt here is to boil down the previous analyses to six or eight key assumptions. Table 7.2 shows the key planning premises of a bank. Notice their brevity as well as their significance to the bank in preparing its strategic plan.

Internal Organization Assessment

At this fourth stage, the organization attempts to examine its own internal operations in order to determine its strengths and weaknesses. The

TABLE 7.2

Key Planning Premises of a Bank

---

1. Deregulation of banking will level off; that is, most deregulation has already occurred.
2. The competitive environment will become more intense as banks continue to learn to live in a deregulated environment.
3. The economic outlook for the next three years is very favorable to growth at low rates of inflation.
4. Banks will continue to become more marketing-oriented, emphasizing retailing strategies even more.
5. Profit margins in banking will narrow.
6. The age of the megabank (large multistate operations) is just beginning.
7. Convenience will dominate customer preferences in banking.
8. Technology will revolutionize the delivery of banking services.

---

idea here is to build a set of strategic actions that capitalize on strengths while simultaneously overcoming weaknesses.

The strategic assessment of the organization usually examines at least the following organizational factors:

People

Financial resources

Facilities and equipment

Location

Management

General operations

Product/service offering

Image/reputation

Many methods are used at this stage. Some organizations survey managers and employees to glean opinions on the strengths and weaknesses in each of the above areas. These surveys may involve both paper-and-pencil questionnaires as well as face-to-face interviews. Consultants may be brought in to assist, and in other cases strategic planners might engage in group discussions to reach a consensus on the strengths and weaknesses of the organization. In still other instances, a market survey may be performed.

Sometimes this effort is called an *operations analysis, internal audit,* or *management audit*. Regardless of what the process is called, the objective is the same—to determine the internal state of affairs of the organization in order to generate a set of data and information on which plans for the future can be built.

BOSTON CONSULTING GROUP MATRIX. One technique that has been widely used in the assessment phase is the Boston Consulting Group Matrix (BCGM), which attempts to evaluate the product/service offerings of a multiproduct/multiservice organization. The purpose is to determine the organization's product/service offerings relative to competitors.[7] (Some of this analysis will occur in the previous step, market analysis.)

The basic matrix is shown in Figure 7.4. *Star* products are those with high growth rates and high market share. These products are likely to require capital investment over and above the cash flow they generate in order to maintain their market share. Eventually they become *cash cows* with high share and low growth as the market becomes saturated. Here capital investment can be reduced and net cash income greatly increased. In other words, cash cows can be milked. An example of a star product would be the Apple II computer. It later became a cash cow, and the Macintosh machines are replacing it as a star.

Relative Competitive Position (Market Share)

Business Growth Rate		HIGH	LOW
	High	Star Product Performers	Question Marks
	Low	Cash Cows	Dogs

FIGURE 7.4

The Boston Consulting Group Product Growth-Share Matrix

Products with low market share and high growth possibilities are *question marks* for the firm. Should capital expenditures be increased to try to increase market share? Should the products be allowed to decline and disappear instead? Should the products be sold? Many questions are presented to the company by products in this box. Many of Chrysler Corporation's larger automobiles were questionable products when Lee Iacocca took over as chairman of the board in the late 1970s. In fact, several models were allowed to die.

Dogs are products with low growth and low market share. If nothing is done with questionable products they often fall into this category. Conventional wisdom says these products should be abandoned. However, a firm may hold on to some of these products in order to offer a complete product line to customers or to add to a positive cash flow for the entire company. For example, a hardware store that prides itself on a complete line of products may continue to carry seldom-asked-for bolt and screw sizes.

The BCGM provides guidance for a multiproduct firm to analyze its products and determine where they fall in the matrix. Based on where they fall, strategic management decisions on growth, investment, and goals for the products can be formulated. While there are some problems with the matrix (e.g., products for many firms do not clearly fall into one of the four categories), it is a useful analytical tool for formulating strategy.* It specifically takes into account market share, an important part of the firm's task environment when making strategic decisions.

---

*The model has been refined and further developed by General Electric with the aid of the Boston Consulting Group and McKinsey and Company. See M. G. Allen, "Strategic Problems Facing Today's Corporate Planner," speech before the thirty-sixth annual meeting of the Academy of Management, Kansas City, Mo. (August 12, 1976). Also see D. D. Monieson, "An Overview of Marketing Planning," *Executive Bulletin*, The Conference Board in Canada, 1978.

Mission Development

The mission of the organization ties the organization specifically to its environment by serving as the underlying rationale for the organization's existence. It is the basic purpose of the organization and answers the question, "What business are we in?" Thus, it establishes the organization's identity.

When examining mission, organizations will frequently use models for comparison. For example, a computer company might ask, "Do we want to be like IBM or more like Apple?" A university might ask, "Do we want to be more teaching or research oriented? The idea is to establish or reinforce an identity.

Questions of mission probably will come up at an earlier stage of the analysis, especially in the customer/market analysis phase. This is normal, but the *formal* examination and establishment of the mission should occur after the environmental analysis, market analysis, strategic planning premises, and assessment phases are completed. The organization should fashion its identity and purpose based on its own strengths and weaknesses as well as the opportunities and constraints presented by the outside environment and market. Too often the reverse happens: An organization determines a mission and then attempts to find an environmental niche where it can fit. Instead, the organization should first look to the environment and then fashion a mission that allows it to specifically meet certain needs in the environment and market.

Three sample mission statements are presented in Table 7.3; note their brevity and clarity.

Strategies and Goals

We now come to the heart of the strategic management and planning process, the point at which the organization establishes its game plan. Specifically, it addresses the question of what it will do to meet or beat its competition.

There is a set of strategies that is *generic* in nature. These are distinctly identifiable, basic strategies that an organization may choose to follow. The appropriateness of each strategy for a particular organization depends on the environmental opportunities and constraints, market, internal strengths and weaknesses, and mission of the particular organization. The formation of the particular strategy evolves over time and will change as the situation changes.

Two primary levels of generic strategy will be discussed: corporate, or organization-wide, and business, or industry-level. In a single-product company operating in one line of business or industry, there is virtually no difference between corporate-wide and business-level strategies.

TABLE 7.3

Three Example Mission Statements

To provide adequate and dependable electric service to both present and future members of the Cooperative, within the twelve-county service area. This service must be provided in the most responsible, efficient, and cost-effective manner so as to promote the Cooperative philosophy to the membership as the most desirable method of receiving electric service.

Clay Electric Cooperative (Florida), 1986

To offer original equipment manufacturers a wide range of solutions based on industry standards, and to offer these solutions at the component, board, and system levels, based on three key strategies: to increase Intel's architectural and technological leadership; to be our customer's preferred supplier; and to be a world-class manufacturer.

Intel Corporation, 1986

The Ameritech Companies are the leading suppliers of advanced communications products and services in Illinois, Indiana, Michigan, Ohio, and Wisconsin. Five Bell operating companies serve more than 11.4 million business and residential customer accounts, most concentrated in the major metropolitan centers in these states. The unregulated subsidiaries are leaders in advanced cellular mobile telephone service, Yellow Pages, and other forms of directory advertising, state-of-the-art communications equipment, and systems software products. This market is worldwide.

Ameritech, 1986

Table 7.4 summarizes the types of strategies found at each level. Let's briefly examine each one.

GENERIC CORPORATE-LEVEL STRATEGIES. These are strategies adopted and followed by the organization as a whole. They fall into four main categories: growth, stability, defensive, and combination.

Growth Strategies. Most organizations wish to grow. As a matter of fact, a study by Glueck of 358 *Fortune* companies indicated that 54.2 percent pursue this strategy.[8] A *concentration* growth strategy means that the organization plans to focus its growth on a single product or a group of closely related products, as is the situation with Coors Breweries.

There are three ways to pursue a growth strategy. First, the existing market can be developed by expanding market share or moving into new geographic regions. Second, the product can be slightly changed or developed. Perhaps a new or closely aligned product can be added (e.g., Coors and Coors Light). Third, a concentration growth strategy can be achieved through horizontal integration. Here, another product in the same busi-

TABLE 7.4

Generic Corporate- and Business-Level Strategies

I. Generic Corporate-Level Strategies
  A. Growth strategies
    1. Concentration
      a. Market development
      b. Product development
      c. Horizontal integration
    2. Vertical integration
      a. Backward integration
      b. Forward integration
    3. Diversification
      a. Concentric
      b. Conglomerate
    4. Implementation of growth strategy
      a. Internal growth
      b. Acquisition
      c. Merger
      d. Joint venture
  B. Stability strategy
    1. Neutral
    2. Harvest (milk the investment)
  C. Defensive strategies
    1. Turnaround
    2. Divestiture
    3. Liquidation
    4. Bankruptcy
    5. Captive
  D. Combination strategies
II. Generic Business-Level Strategies
  A. Overall cost leadership
  B. Product/service differentiation
  C. Market segment focus
  D. Preemptive strategies

ness is added, usually through buying an organization, as when Dr. Pepper bought Canada Dry in 1982.

The James River Corporation, a Virginia paper goods manufacturer, is aggressively pursuing a growth strategy using the methods discussed above. First, the company is attempting to expand its market share by pushing its product in the northeastern states. Second, it is developing a host of new paper products, such as coated paper plates, that it hopes will win a large share of the $500 million-per-year paper plate market. Third, through the process of horizontal integration, it has purchased other paper goods companies, such as Connecticut's Dixie Northern.[9]

Vertical integration is another way to achieve growth. Here, the organization can either acquire its suppliers (backward integration) or acquire its distributors (forward integration); some organizations do both. Miller Brewing has purchased its own aluminum can manufacturing facilities in addition to acquiring some of its distribution channels.

The third way growth can occur is through *diversification*. Diversification occurs when an organization moves into products or services that are clearly different from its current businesses. There are two forms of diversification. Concentric diversification occurs when related but clearly differentiated products or services are developed or obtained. Coca-Cola's purchase of Minute Maid is an excellent example. Conglomerate diversification occurs when the firm diversifies into an area totally unrelated to the product or service. Bic's development of the disposable safety razor resulted in a product totally unrelated to its pen business.

The *implementation of growth strategies* can be accomplished through four basic methods: internal growth, acquisition, merger, and joint venture. Although these strategies were discussed in Chapter 6, they are briefly reviewed here. Internal growth occurs when current market share with current products is expanded (e.g., GM sells more Chevrolets relative to competitive brands). An acquisition occurs when one company buys another and absorbs it; a merger occurs when two companies join to form a new company. A joint venture occurs when two or more companies work together for a specific project such as oil exploration and drilling; they pool their resources and risk for a specific endeavor.

Stability Strategies. As opposed to growth strategies, stability strategies attempt to maintain the status quo. There are two basic stability strategies: neutral and harvest. *Neutral* strategies are do-nothing approaches. The organization just keeps doing what it always has done without a growth goal in mind. A *harvest* strategy, sometimes called a "milk-the-investment" strategy, represents an end-game strategy identified by Harrigan.[10] The idea here is to retrieve the value of earlier investments—the firm intends to sell its assets and get out of the business.

Defensive Strategies. A third set of corporate-level strategies involves actions taken to reverse a negative situation or overcome a crisis or problem. These are often called *retrenchment* strategies. There are five basic defensive strategies an organization can adopt. *Turnaround* strategies are designed to reverse a negative trend, such as falling profits or increasing costs. Layoffs, cutting wages, reducing expense accounts, and cutting advertising are all forms of turnaround strategies. LTV Steel, for example, postponed paying $180 million in pension fund contributions in order to cut costs.[11] Recently, the company declared bankruptcy and could not pay bonuses to employees who had taken early retirement.

A second type of defensive strategy is *divestiture*. This occurs when an organization sells or divests itself of a business or part of a business, as ITT did with many of its operations during the mid-1980s. In a *liquidation*, the organization is either sold or dissolved. DeLorean Motor Company, which was dissolved several years ago, and Walter E. Heller Corporation, a financial investment company, which was sold to Fuji Bank of Japan in 1984, are good examples of this strategy.

Since the Bankruptcy Reform Act of 1978, *bankruptcy* is now being used as a defensive strategy. Chapter 11 (in Title 11 of the United States Code), which involves a reorganization, is the device most used to rehabilitate corporate debtors having financial difficulties; it can be a way to escape a heavy debt load, contracted high wages, or even legal claims. Continental Airlines used Chapter 11 to negate its labor contracts with its unions, while Manville Corporation used this method to avoid high legal costs caused by asbestosis claims.

The final defensive strategy is to become a *captive* of another organization. This occurs when an organization allows another organization to manage it in return for promising to buy a certain amount of the captive's products or services. This often occurs between a small- to medium-sized supplier and a major manufacturer or retailer.

Combination Strategies. The last major set of corporate-level strategies occurs when an organization simultaneously uses different strategies for different units. Next to growth strategies, this strategy is the most common one. Large diversified corporations frequently use this; they acquire new companies while selling others. They carve out market segments and develop new products, and they acquire suppliers and distributors, and so on. General Motors's recent actions in dropping and adding models, while acquiring Hughes Aircraft and EDS, are a good example of using a combination strategy.

GENERIC BUSINESS-LEVEL STRATEGIES. Business-level strategies are strategies employed by an organization for one of its particular product or service lines. It answers the question, "What is the plan of each business to compete in the industry?" This type of plan tends to be less generic than corporate-level strategies because it must be tailored to fit the unique circumstances of each organization. However, four basic strategy types are often used to classify business-level strategies: (1) overall cost leadership, (2) product/service differentiation, (3) market segment focus, and (4) preemptive strategies.

Overall Cost Leadership. This involves producing the product or service cheaper than the competition and thus cutting prices. This can be done because of extensive experience, cheap labor, size (economies of scale), reduced overhead, or more efficient technology. By providing cheaper goods and services, an organization can either sell at a lower price than its competition, garner a larger share of the market, or maintain price and achieve a higher profit margin.

Product/Service Differentiation. This involves creating a perception in the market of the uniqueness of a product or service. A *brand image*, such as Bud Light beer or Polo sportswear, a *quality image*, such as Mercedes or Rolls Royce, or *customer service*, such as IBM offers, are but three ways to achieve this differentiation. Differentiation relies on convincing customers that the product or service is so unique that the customer should buy it.

Market Segment Focus. This strategy attempts to carve out a part of the market and focus organizational efforts on serving it. This may be done on the basis of a demographic factor such as age, income, family size, geographic region, and so on. The idea is to achieve a competitive advantage within a narrowly focused market segment rather than to appeal to a broad market. A high-fashion men's clothing store and Porsche automobiles are examples of a market segmentation strategy.

Preemptive Strategies. These are strategies undertaken to disrupt the normal state of affairs in an industry or product line.[12] This strategy essentially rewrites the rules of the game to compete in the industry. Such preemptive strategies may occur because of new product developments, such as happened with Xerox in the office copier market or as in the case of Edwin Land with the Polaroid camera. Or they may occur with market segmentation in an unsegmented market, as happened when Miller Brewing developed the first low-calorie beer (Miller Lite). This type of strategy could also be based on cost, as was the case when People Express Airlines was built around the concept of low price and discount air fares.

In each of these cases, the organization came up with an innovative product or tactic that caught the competition off guard. Hence, the competition had to scramble to remain viable.

The process of searching for generic corporate- and business-level strategies is not a smooth one; strategy usually evolves gradually. Some companies jump from one strategy to another, often reversing themselves at great peril. Bethlehem Steel initially sought to diversify, then decided to stick with steel, then reversed itself and decided to diversify after all. This had disastrous results, as we discussed in the introductory case to this chapter. Other companies stick to a strategy even though competitive trends indicate other courses of action should be pursued. Chrysler Corporation in the late 1970s, prior to Lee Iacocca's presidency, pursued a conservative strategy that almost resulted in the organization's bankruptcy.

Most large companies employ several strategies simultaneously, depending on market conditions and industry characteristics. For example, Ford began emphasizing quality, new styling, and high-state electronics in an attempt to beat Japanese competition in the mid-1980s. At the same time, they lobbied hard in Washington for increased voluntary and mandatory trade import protectionism for the entire industry.

The overall goals of the organization should be very clearly linked with its strategies. For example, if the organization wishes to differentiate its product to appeal to a larger share of the market, then a market share goal should be developed. If a market segmentation or focus strategy is used, then a goal of capturing a certain percentage of a geographic region or demographic grouping is appropriate.

Strategies should follow goals; organizations should decide what they wish to accomplish and then decide on the strategy to achieve it. However, in reality, strategies and goals are often formulated jointly. A goal may be established (e.g., to become the dominant manufacturer in an industry) and then a strategy formulated (e.g., cost leadership), which then causes a rethinking of the goal and perhaps a modification. This happens because, after further investigation, the organization may realize that its costs cannot be cut enough to allow it to become the dominant force in the industry. The organization decides, instead, to increase its presence in the industry as opposed to dominating the industry.

Plan Operationalization

The last step in the strategic planning and management process for the organization is to decide on the specific steps necessary to carry out the strategy in order to reach desired goals. This involves deciding on:

Who will do what?

When?

At what cost?

How will we know it gets done?

This step of the strategic management process deals with implementation issues such as setting operational objectives, action planning, assigning work to units, specifying individual accountability, developing schedules, allocating budgets, and setting up monitoring and tracking systems. These aspects are discussed in Chapter 8.

SUMMARY

Organizational strategy refers to the way in which the organization copes with the external environment in order to accomplish its purposes. The model of strategic choice we described in this chapter is basically a seven-step one:

1. Environmental analysis and forecast
2. Customer/market analysis
3. Strategic planning premises
4. Internal organization assessment
5. Mission development
6. Strategies and goals
7. Plan operationalization

In most organizations, strategy evolves. It is seldom "scientifically" established once and for all. There is usually much flexibility and change in this process. Although an organization may cover the seven basic steps above, it often does so by jumping from step to step rather than following them in precise order.

There are many generic corporate-level and business-level strategies. Generic organization-wide strategies generally fall into four categories: (1) growth, (2) stability, (3) defensive, and (4) combination. Four basic business-level or industry-specific strategies are (1) overall cost leadership, (2) product/service differentiation, (3) market segment focus, and (4) preemptive strategies.

In Chapter 8 we examine how organizations set and operationalize goals and deal with the question of effectiveness. These issues are central to the implementation and evaluation of strategy and ultimately can lead to adjustments, changes, or reaffirmations of the organization's decision posture with respect to its environmental interface.

QUESTIONS FOR REVIEW AND DISCUSSION

1. What is strategic management?
2. Explain the Miles and Snow four-category strategic typology for dealing with the environment (defenders, prospectors, analyzers, and reactors).
3. What is scenario planning? What are worst-case scenarios and what role do they play in strategic planning and management?
4. What role does customer/market analysis play in strategic management and planning?
5. Why is an internal assessment critical to the strategic management and planning process?

6. What is meant by the term *organizational mission* and what role does it play in strategic planning and management?
7. What is the difference between generic corporate-level strategies and generic business-level strategies?
8. List and explain four major growth strategies.
9. What is the difference between stability strategies and defensive strategies?
10. Why do you think so many organizations use combination strategies?
11. List and briefly define the four generic business-level strategies.
12. Why do you think strategy usually evolves, as opposed to being scientifically set, in an organization?

ENDNOTES

1. William R. Boulton, William M. Lindsay, Stephen G. Franklin, and Leslie W. Rue, "Strategic Planning: Determining the Impact of Environmental Characteristics and Uncertainty," *Academy of Management Journal* 25 (September 1982): 501.

2. John A. Pearce II and Richard B. Robinson, Jr., *Strategic Management* (Homewood, Ill.: Richard D. Irwin, 1982), 4–5; and Leslie W. Rue and Phyllis G. Holland, *Strategic Management* (New York: McGraw-Hill, 1986), 4–20.

3. C. Roland Christensen, Norman A. Berg, and Malcolm S. Salter, eds., *Policy Formulation and Administration* (Homewood, Ill.: Richard D. Irwin, 1980), 1–9.

4. Raymond E. Miles and Charles C. Snow, *Organizational Strategy, Structure and Process* (New York: McGraw-Hill, 1978), 29–30.

5. Donald C. Hambrick, "Some Tests of the Effectiveness and Functional Attributes of Miles' and Snow's Strategic Types," *Academy of Management Journal* 26 (March 1983): 5–26.

6. William P. Anthony, *Practical Strategic Planning* (Westport, Conn.: Quorum Books, 1985).

7. Seymour Tilles, "Strategies for Allocating Funds," *Harvard Business Review* (January–February 1966). Also see Betsey D. Gelb, "Strategic Planning for the Underdog," *Business Horizons* 25 (November–December 1982): 871; and Donald C. Hambrick, Ian C. MacMillan, and Diana L. Day, "Strategic Attributes and Performance in the BCG Matrix: A PIMS-Based Analysis of Industrial Product Businesses," *Academy of Management Journal* 25 (September 1982): 510–531.

8. William F. Glueck, *Business Policy and Strategic Management*, 3d ed. (New York: McGraw-Hill, 1980), 290.

9. Kimberly Carpenter and John P. Tarpey, "A Southern Papermaker's Yankee Campaign," *Business Week* (October 14, 1985), 77–82.

10. Kathryn R. Harrigan, *Strategies for Declining Businesses* (Lexington, Mass.: D. C. Heath, 1980).

11. William C. Symonds, "It's Every Man for Himself in the Steel Business," *Business Week* (June 3, 1985), 76.

12. Ian C. MacMillan, "Preemptive Strategies," in *Handbook of Business Strategy*, ed. W. G. Guth (Boston: Warren, Gorham, and Lamont, 1985).

ANNOTATED BIBLIOGRAPHY

Baird, Inga S., and Thomas, Howard. "Toward a Contingency Model of Strategic Risk Taking." *Academy of Management Review* 10, no. 2 (April 1985): 230–243.
A model of strategic risk taking incorporating environmental, industrial, organizational, decision-maker, and problem variables is presented. The model is intended to be both a preliminary conceptualization of strategic risk taking and a stimulant for future research on risk taking in strategic management decisions.

Bourgeois, L. J., III. "Strategic Management and Determinism." *Academy of Management Review* 9, no. 4 (October 1984): 586–596.
Contingency theories of management and economic theories of industrial organization both contribute to a mechanistic view of the strategic manager as analyst. In this view, the secret to managerial effectiveness is through the application of scientific laws or principles, be they "laws of organization" or "laws of the marketplace." This paper argues for a view of strategic management as a creative activity and suggests a dialectic between free will and determinism in conceptualizations of strategic behavior.

Camilus, John C. *Strategic Planning and Management Control*. Lexingon, Mass.: D. C. Heath, 1986.
This book is one of the first to integrate strategic planning and management control in organizations at both the strategic and operational levels. The author incorporates the latest developments in techniques and systems derived from both the literature and his own successful consulting practice to provide a deeper and more practical understanding of the design of planning systems.

Chaffee, Ellen E. "Three Models of Strategy." *Academy of Management Review* 10, no. 1 (January 1985): 89–98.
Three models of strategy that are implicit in the literature are described—linear, adaptive, and interpretive. Their similarity to Boulding's (1956) hierarchical levels of system complexity is noted. The strategy construct is multifaceted, and it has evolved to a level of complexity almost matching that of organizations themselves.

Chakravarthy, Balazi S. "Adaptation: A Promising Metaphor for Strategic Management." *Academy of Management Review* 7 (January 1982): 35–44.
Strategic management is the process through which a manager ensures the long-term survival of the firm. This paper provides a comprehensive framework for strategic management based on adaptation, a metaphor that succinctly captures the endeavors of an organization to be better fitted to its environment.

Ford, David, and Farmer, David. "Make or Buy—A Key Strategic Issue." *Long Range Planning* 19, no. 5 (October 1986): 54–62.

This paper is based on a research project that examined what are commonly known as industrial "make-or-buy" decisions. The project stemmed from the simple idea that decisions about which activities should be carried out within the company and those that should be contracted out can be crucial to business effectiveness. In making this choice, management faces complex issues as to which elements of manufacturing, marketing, and operations services should be provided in-house and which should be brought in.

Fredrickson, James W. "The Comprehensiveness of Strategic Decision Processes: Extension, Observations, Future Directions." *Academy of Management Journal* 27, no. 3 (September 1984): 445–466.

A recent study in an industry with an unstable environment reported a negative relationship between comprehensiveness (a measure of rationality) and organizational performance. An extension of that study establishes a positive relationship between comprehensiveness and performance in a stable environment.

Houlden, Brian T. "Developing a Company's Strategic Management Capability." *Long Range Planning* 19, no. 5 (October 1986): 89–93.

Organizations vary widely in their strategic management capabilities. Some still rely almost entirely on "fire-fighting," while others are slowly developing their capabilities. But there are only a few that give special attention to strategic issues and implement their decisions effectively. To be effective, a corporate planner must assist this process of development of strategic ability and must adapt his or her role as the company's capability changes. The author suggests that there is a largely untapped market for consultants to assist organizations in developing strategic capabilities.

Hrebiniak, Lawrence G., and Joyce, William F. *Implementing Strategy*. New York: Macmillan, 1984.

This text builds on a clear model of the iterative interaction between strategy and structure at several levels of the organization, beginning with corporate strategy and primary structure and moving through mid-level operating objectives and operating structure to incentives and controls at the most basic level. The book seeks to link the hierarchical levels of strategy with the corresponding levels of structure from macro to micro, from the organization as a whole to its impact on individuals.

Kanter, Rosabeth M., and Buck, John D. "Reorganizing Part of Honeywell: From Strategy to Structure." *Organizational Dynamics* 13, no. 3 (Winter 1985): 5–25.

The authors define tactical or response planning—a way to ensure that overall strategy and structure in an individual department are aligned with overall business strategy and structure. Five circumstances that can provide impetus for a departmental study and reorganization are identified in addition to selection criteria. The authors point out that it is important to collect data on business plans and priorities, the needs and interests of customers, current and potential department activities, and the views of department members.

Leemhuis, J. P. "Using Scenarios to Develop Strategies." *Long Range Planning* 18, no. 2 (April 1985): 30–37.

Structured approaches that fully use scenarios for strategy development have only emerged in the last few years. This paper describes such an approach as practiced by Shell Nederland and focuses on the business environment with reference to the norms and values of the organization.

Miesing, Paul, and Wolfe, Joseph. "The Art and Science of Planning at the Business Unit Level." *Management Science* 31, no. 6 (June 1985): 773–786.

This paper attempts to relate the conditions that require different planning approaches. A theoretical planning framework is presented that considers the confidence of causal linkages coupled with the extent of environmental change. Prior planning research is synthesized to speculate on the appropriate leadership and decision-making styles for single businesses, nondiversified firms, or divisions of diversified firms. Examples of computational, consensual, contingency, and conceptual planning systems are also provided.

Miles, Raymond E., and Snow, Charles C. "Designing Strategic Human Resources Systems." *Organizational Dynamics* 13, no. 1 (Summer 1984): 36–50.

The authors reach three major conclusions: (1) human resources management units and their selection, development, and reward practices must be tailored to organizational strategy; (2) organizations pursuing multiple strategies must also follow multiple human resource management approaches; and (3) human resources management units are generally not encouraged to participate in overall corporate planning.

Miles, Robert H., and Cameron, Kim S. *Coffin Nails and Corporate Strategies.* Englewood Cliffs, N.J.: Prentice-Hall, 1983.

This is the story of how complex organizations adapt under conditions of externally imposed stress and crisis. It focuses on the choices made by strategic managers of traditionally competitive corporations in the U.S. tobacco industry in coping with a fundamental threat of their right to do business by antismoking groups.

Schwenk, Charles R. "Management Illusions and Biases: Their Impact on Strategic Decisions." *Long Range Planning* 18, no. 5 (October 1985): 74–80.

Strategic decision making often involves a great deal of uncertainty and ambiguity. Because managers are subject to bounded rationality, their cognitive processes may result in systematic decision biases. This paper summarizes research in the areas of cognitive psychology and behavioral decision theory dealing with human cognitive biases that may influence strategic decision making.

Tozer, Edwin E. "Developing Strategies for Management Information Systems." *Long Range Planning* 19, no. 4 (August 1986): 31–40.

All businesses need to plan. Correspondingly, they all need to plan their information systems in one form or another. While the need for business planning is well recognized, the planning of information systems is all too often left to chance. Therefore, this article presents a formal and practical approach for developing an information systems strategy.

Wheelan, Thomas C., and Hunger, David. *Strategic Management and Business Policy.* Reading, Mass.: Addison-Wesley, 1983.

This text discusses all the key concepts in business policy and strategic management, and is written to provide the reader with a more thorough understanding of the business corporation. A strategic model integrates the text by providing a map throughout, while a strategic audit provides a structured approach to complex case analysis.

ADDITIONAL REFERENCES

Beard, Donald W., and Dess, Gregory G. "Corporate-Level Strategy, Business-Level Strategy, and Firm Performance." *Academy of Management Journal* 24 (December 1981): 663–688.

Bracker, Jeffrey. "The Historical Development of the Strategic Management Concept." *Academy of Management Review* 5 (April 1980): 219–224.

Chandler, A. D., Jr. *Strategy and Structure.* Cambridge, Mass.: MIT Press, 1962.

Dymsza, W. A. *Multinational Business Strategy.* New York: McGraw-Hill, 1972.

Fredrickson, James W. "The Strategic Decision Process and Organizational Structure." *Academy of Management Review* 11, no. 2 (April 1986): 280–297.

Fry, Fred L., and Stoner, Charles R. *Strategic Planning for Small Businesses.* Cincinnati: Southwestern, 1987.

Gupta, Anil K., and Govindarajan, Vijay. "Resource Sharing Among SBUs: Strategic Antecedents and Administrative Implications." *Academy of Management Journal* 29, no. 4 (December 1986): 695–714.

Harrigan, Kathryn R. "Formulating Vertical Integration Strategies." *Academy of Management Review* 9, no. 4 (October 1984): 638–652.

Harrison, E. Frank. *Policy, Strategy, and Managerial Action.* Boston: Houghton Mifflin, 1986.

Hayden, Catherine. *The Handbook of Strategic Expertise.* New York: The Free Press, 1986.

Herbert, Theodore T. "Strategy and Multinational Organization Structure: An Interorganizational Relationships Perspective." *Academy of Management Review* 9, no. 2 (April 1984): 259–271.

Hartley, R. F. *Marketing Mistakes.* Columbus, Ohio: Grid Press, 1976.

Lamb, Robert, ed. *Advances in Strategic Management.* Vol. I. Greenwich, Conn.: JAI Press, 1983.

Lubatkin, Michael, and Shrieves, Ronald E. "Towards Reconciliation of Market Performance Measures to Strategic Management Research." *Academy of Management Review* 11, no. 3 (July 1986): 497–512.

Melin, Leif. "Strategies in Managing Turnaround." *Long Range Planning* 18, no. 1 (February 1985): 80–86.

Odiorne, George S. *Strategic Management of Human Resources: A Portfolio Approach.* San Francisco: Jossey-Bass, 1984.

Pennings, Johannes M., and Associates. *Organizational Strategy and Change: New Views on Formulating and Implementing Strategic Decisions.* San Francisco: Jossey-Bass, 1985.

Porter, Michael E. *Competitive Strategy.* New York: The Free Press, 1980.

Richards, Max D. *Setting Strategic Goals and Objectives.* 2d ed. St. Paul, Minn.: West, 1986.

Romanelli, Elaine, and Tushman, Michael D. "Inertia, Environments, and Strategic Choice: A Quasi-Experimental Design for Comparative-Longitudinal Research." *Management Science* 32, no. 5 (May 1986): 608–617.

Rumelt, R. *Strategy, Structure, and Economic Performance.* Cambridge, Mass.: Harvard University Press, 1974.

Salancik, Gerald R., and Meindl, James R. "Corporate Attributions as Strategic Illusions of Management Control." *Administrative Science Quarterly* 29, no. 2 (June 1984): 238–254.

Szilagyi, Andrew D., Jr., and Schweiger, David M. "Matching Managers to Strategies: A Review and Suggested Framework." *Academy of Management Review* 9, no. 4 (August 1986): 626–637.

TenDam, Hans. "Strategic Management in a Government Agency." *Long Range Planning* 19, no. 4 (August 1986): 78–86.

van der Merwe, Andre, and van der Merwe, Sylvia. "Strategic Leadership and the Chief Executive." *Long Range Planning* 18, no. 1 (February 1985): 100–111.

Venkatraman, N. and Grant, John H. "Construct Measurement in Organizational Strategy Research: A Critique and Proposal." *Academy of Management Review* 11, no. 1 (January 1986): 71–87.

```
C    A    S    E
```

A Growing Giant

Giant Supermarkets are the darlings of supermarkets in the Washington, D.C.–Baltimore corridor. Giants are trendy, offer lots of service, have gourmet items galore, and can (and have) won out over national competitors such as Grand Union and Pantry Pride in price wars.

Giant dominates because it knows what it is doing with its three-pronged strategy: (1) stylish retailing, (2) exceptional service, and (3) unparalleled vertical integration. Stylish retailing is well evidenced by the ambience one finds along its sparkling clean, well-lighted aisles, where specialty merchandise such as flowers, baked goods, designer chocolates, exotic cheeses, prime meats, and seafood are mingled in with the more mundane supermarket/pharmacy items. All this takes place in a 55,000-square-foot building (the average of competitors is 27,000 square feet).

Contrary to the self-service concept found within competitors' supermarkets, Giant CEO Izzy Cohen stresses personal service to the shopper. Rather than having ready-made bakery products shipped in, the company installed ovens in its supermarket bakeries that are tended by bakers in white uniforms and hats who also double as customer service representatives. Indeed, the bakeries look more like French patisseries than supermarket

Source: Joshua Mendes, "The Giant of the Regional Food Chains," *Fortune* (November 25, 1985), 27–36.

baked goods departments. Seafood buyers can purchase live trout, lobster, and clams from seafood service experts. The delicatessen sections are staffed by on-site cooks who offer such specialties as six kinds of smoked salmon and Italian buffalo milk mozzarella. These gourmet items are not only found in special sections—$4.39 a can soup shares space with Campbell soups, and Lipton has 267 other teas to keep it company.

If a customer has a complaint or suggestion, he or she might meet personally with Izzy or with Alvin Dobbler, Senior Vice President for Operations. Other consumer complaints and suggestions are handled by Esther Peterson, the head of Giant's consumer affairs department. She was the former federal Director of Consumer Affairs during the presidency of Lyndon Johnson.

Although Giant takes pride in its high-priced gourmet items, it still has low-priced basics as well. Believing in the premise that high-volume sales determine long-term success, Giant will sacrifice short-term profitability to ensure long-term high sales volume. Cohen maintains and wins price wars because of the third prong of his strategy, vertical integration. The company produces many items with its own private label, an indispensable weapon that allows for both distributor and retailer markup. For example, Giant runs its own warehouses and produces its own baked goods, milk, and ice cream. In 1985, it opened its own soft-drink bottling plant and an ice cube plant. That's why Giant appeals to blue-collar Baltimore customers in addition to the multitude of Washington-area "yuppies." And that's not all. It recently opened its own flower (the colorful, blooming type) warehouse and had its own in-house construction unit design and manufacture equipment for flower arranging. Speaking of this in-house construction unit, it occupies a two-acre building where carpenters, millwrights, and electricians put together much of a new store's interior while the shell is being constructed at the site. Indeed, Giant's construction operations are so renowned that the company is diversifying into the construction business. It has subcontracted work for the CIA and is the prime contractor for six new shopping centers where Giant supermarkets will be located.

Giant does not even contract out its information-processing needs. The company developed its own computer hookup called the Uniform Communication Standard, which analyzes and reports such things as current stock and sales, warehouse space, promotion schedules, purchasing and receiving, invoicing, and transportation by its own fleet of ve-

hicles. This computer capability is now putting Giant into the banking business. In 1985, Giant formed a joint venture with a Maryland bank to install automatic teller machines in its stores; however, unlike other such joint ventures, Giant operates the machines, earning money on each transaction.

Giant is so successfully reaping the benefits of its overall strategy that it is now able to develop diversification strategies that will enable the company to operate in areas heretofore untouched by supermarkets (e.g., in-house photo processing, computer maintenance, and so on) in addition to the banking, construction, and florist aspects previously discussed. Izzy Cohen and his associates not only know their business and present opportunities, they also know how to make their own future opportunities, thereby helping to ensure Giant's long-term health and growth.

QUESTIONS FOR DISCUSSION

1. How would you label Giant's overall strategy?
2. What are the advantages and disadvantages of Giant's overall strategy?
3. What advice would you give Izzy Cohen if he consulted you in your role as a management expert?
4. How would you determine if Izzy's approach to planning and operations fits the discussion in this chapter?
5. What major factors in the macro environment must Izzy watch out for? How should he go about this?

8

Organizational Effectiveness and Goals

Steeltown Blues

When LTV Corporation acquired Republic Steel in the summer of 1984, the hope was to salvage the best of these two struggling steel companies and turn them into a single, more efficient, and profitable operation. For example, combined LTV/Republic operations permitted raw materials inventories to be reduced by hundreds of thousands of tons. In terms of capital investments, LTV was able to build one electrogalvanizing line instead of the two that would have been needed had the merger not occurred. But foreign imports have caused the economic recovery of the 1980s to bypass the steel industry, and LTV has shifted its major goal of making a profit from steel to just being able to weather the crisis.

With this new goal in mind, LTV President David W. Hoag was forced to set new objectives, one of which was to cut LTV's white-collar work force of 12,000 employees by 25 percent. The implementation of this new objective has had a negative impact on LTV. When the merger was first being planned, executives at both LTV and Republic thought that such a move would benefit both companies because they believed a productive, cooperative spirit would develop between the two heretofore different white-collar groups. However, this spirit never developed; rather, sagging morale now characterizes the white-collar work force at LTV. Although this objective was achieved by April 1985, Hoag must still maximize blast furnace efficiency, improve raw materials and finishing operations, and complete the combination of two different sales forces and computer systems.

LTV Executive Vice President James J. Poulos is presently faced with another major objective that he must accomplish if LTV is to prosper—to keep the company above water financially. This is an almost impossible feat because, in 1984, there was only a disappointing 8 percent increase in domestic steel shipments, while foreign steel imports jumped to over 30 percent of the U.S. market. Thus, Poulos finds that he must somehow wring cash from the sale of surplus assets and keep the firm's lenders and shareholders "in the fold."

When LTV decided to acquire Republic, most analysts believed that the demand for domestic steel would rebound, particularly in view of voluntary import quotas negotiated by the Reagan administration that were supposed to cut imports' share of the market to 20.5 percent. Because this national goal was not met, LTV's overall market share dropped from 15.5 percent to 13.8 percent. Expected profits of $200 million for 1985 were, in reality, transformed into a $175 million loss.

Although the phasing out of many white-collar employees has saved the company millions of dollars, LTV must still take other measures to keep itself financially afloat. For example, the old J & L facilities in Aliquippa, Pennsylvania, are prime candidates for closing. In 1986, the company hopes it can pare an additional $220 million by closing plants and reorganizing activities. Moreover, unless the demand for domestic steel grows, LTV will further sink as it fails to meet its planned technological efficiencies.

Should the current cash flow crisis continue at LTV, the organization might be faced with having to sell assets from its defense and energy subsidiaries. This was *not* its purpose in acquiring Republic. LTV might drop out of the steel business rather than weaken the rest of the company.

Sources: George McManus, "David Hoag Tells About LTV's Merger," *Iron Age Metals Producer* (February 1, 1985), 42–43; Todd Mason, Zachary Schiller, and Gregory L. Miles, "Why LTV Is Stymied in Steel," *Business Week* (April 1, 1985), 65–66; D. B. Thompson, "LTV Steel: Casting a New Company," *Industry Week* (April 29, 1985), 46–48.

Win or *You* Lose

Eastern Michigan University (EMU) has developed a new policy to enhance its athletic program. From now on, coaches' salary increases will be tied to win-loss records, attendance, and student athletes' grades. The EMU policy sets a formula whereby coaches will receive annual merit raises. Factors to be considered include winning percentage, conference standings compared to the previous year, athletes' academic performance, an athletic program's adherence to budgets and conference rules, and fan attendance. According to EMU's Director of Information Services, Kathleen Tinney, the new policy's goal is to consistently achieve championships and motivate others.

Tinney also states that the formula would be based on objectives set for each coach before the season. In short, the formula will help ensure that coaches improve their programs to the level of those who consistently win.

Some of the coaches at EMU aren't too happy with the new policy. To quote one, "If you're going to judge a coach on his win-loss record, you better make sure he has an equal amount of money for recruiting, an equal number of scholarships, facilities that compare with his opponents, and a comparable travel and equipment budget. At Eastern, in many sports, that just isn't the case."

Source: Glen Macnow, "Eastern Michigan's Plan to Tie Coaches' Pay to Performance Derided on Other Campuses," *Chronicle of Higher Education* (July 17, 1985): 27–28.

Switch On; Switch Off

ITT Corporation, the communications giant, is faced with a crucial test—launching "System 12," its most expensive project ever in the United States. System 12 is a new telephone switch that routes calls and provides other services to telephone companies. ITT's success in this venture is of paramount importance to the company's future, particularly in view of its hopes to become a contender in the global, and especially American, telecommunications market.

To recover its huge investment in System 12, the firm must sell at least $12 billion worth of switches and related products, and the breakup of the Bell System in the United States is giving ITT a chance to put a foot in the door before its competitors.

However, if past performance is any indicator of success, ITT might face serious problems in meeting its $12 billion goal. The company has been as much as two years late in handing over workable switches in some of its foreign markets because of computer software problems. In fact, ITT has shipped only about 10 percent of switches ordered by foreign countries. Moreover, to attain its objective of becoming preeminent in the U.S. switch market, ITT must face the fact that U.S. standards and feature requirements are different and more demanding than those of foreign countries. The firm must spend heavily to adapt System 12 switches to the U.S. market. In 1985, ITT spent over $105 million meeting U.S. requirements.

As the company overcomes technological problems with the new system, it expects to ship switches for 2 million phone lines by the end of 1986. This optimism is based on the fact that ITT recently managed to meet its delivery schedules in two of its foreign markets and, even better, is three months ahead of scheduled deliveries to its potentially largest foreign customer, the People's Republic of China.

Because digital switching systems are expected to become the backbone of a worldwide communications network, ITT must go forward with System 12. As one Wall

Street analyst reported about the potential effect of the system on the telecommunications business, "It's the difference between showing 10 percent growth and no growth." Regarding the United States, ITT must succeed with System 12 because the United States currently accounts for one-third of the world market. To quote M. Peter Thomas, former System 12 division head, "If it wants to hold its position worldwide, ITT has to prove itself in the United States."

Source: Peter W. Barnes, "ITT Faces a Big Test: Selling Its New Switch to Phone Firms in the U.S.," *The Wall Street Journal* (December 19, 1985), 1.

As these short excerpts illustrate, organizations are goal-seeking entities. As you read the material in the chapter, you will realize that goals, often in and of themselves, are what give the organization its purpose and identity. For any organization to succeed, it must set various goals for itself and, in turn, design its work system and operations to achieve these goals. As we saw in the excerpts above, the success, even the survival of the organization, depends to a large degree on how well it has achieved the goals that it or others have established.

The organization's goal and work systems are an integ[r]
ternal environment. This chapter explains what goals [
attainment means to the organization, and how work re[
tainment of goals. We describe classes of objectives, or g[
at why an organization establishes a particular goal or o[
further look at some techniques that organizations can use[
setting process.

Because not all goals can be attained in the short run, th[e
tion must establish a type of hierarchy, or priority list, as we
sures or standards, to determine whether objectives have bee[
plished. The last part of this chapter explains the various c[
work necessary to attain these objectives.

In short, this chapter is a brief explanation of the establishn[

goals and a description of the work necessary to attain them.

Because most people are social, they spend a considerable amount of time in organizations. They hope to accomplish personal goals or purposes through their association with these organizations. Their lives in organizations are governed to a great extent by the pursuit of these goals and purposes.* This is a key concept in understanding how organizations function. Organizations are the means for not only personal but also group accomplishment.

GOALS AND THEIR ATTAINMENT

At the same time that every member seeks a personal need satisfaction (or goal accomplishment) from an association with the organization, that organization itself has a group or system of goals to accomplish. These goals or purposes are defined and sought quite separately from the members' personal goals. In other words, the organization takes on an identity of its own with its own goals.

The objectives of an organization serve three main purposes: (1) They

*In this book, goals, purposes, and objectives are considered to have the same meaning.

blish a future state that the organization is trying to realize, and thus they set down guidelines for the organization to follow; (2) they legitimate the existence of the organization; and (3) they provide a standard for assessing the efficiency and effectiveness of the organization.[1] In conjunction with these functions, clearly formulated objectives make it easier for organization subunits to work toward some common purpose and so lend consistency and intent to the style of management throughout the organization.

Members join and remain in organizations to attain personal goals, and they are willing to contribute to organization goals in return for the realization of their personal goals. The individual joins the organization with a sense of expectations and a value set. That individual must be willing to modify his or her behavior in order to gain full membership in both the formal and informal organizations. At the same time, however, the individual is capable of modifying the group's expectations and objectives. The result of this interaction is what Bakke[2] terms "the fusion process," a situation in which the individual and group change to reconcile their respective values into one integrated pattern of expectations and objectives.

This fusion process has a synergistic effect on the organization's performance. Individuals are better motivated and committed to an organization whose goals closely fit their own.

When personal goals and organization goals conflict, job dissatisfaction and low productivity are common. Disenchantment and preoccupation with this conflict take away from member satisfaction and organization productivity. Given this tendency, it is important for management to bring about a reconciliation, or fusion, of the goals of the formal and informal organization with those of the individual so that job satisfaction and organization productivity are at least possible. Although the attainment of organization goals is influenced greatly by the attainment of the personal goals of its members, these alone do not determine the organization's goals, as we see below.

WHO BENEFITS FROM THE ORGANIZATION?

Organizations must satisfy a number of client groups that can be divided into two basic categories: *primary beneficiaries* and *secondary beneficiaries*.

The primary beneficiary group is comprised of the people that the organization is established to serve. The customer is the primary beneficiary of a retail food store; students are the primary beneficiaries of a university; and patients are the primary beneficiaries of a hospital. The needs and desires of these groups set the foundation for defining the organization's basic purpose or objective. In our ITT excerpt at the beginning of this chapter, the primary beneficiaries of ITT's System 12 telephone switching system are the multitude of telephone companies that will purchase and use such switches and relays.

In addition to the primary beneficiary group, all organizations have secondary beneficiary groups that they try to serve or satisfy. Examples include employees, owners, and the general public. These groups want satisfaction from their association with the organization. Employees want good pay and working conditions as well as job assignments that are interesting and meaningful. Owners want a reasonable return on their investment and a reasonable assurance that it is safe. The general public wants a pollution-free environment, good and safe products and services, and evidence of social concern from organizations. Although the primary beneficiary of Eastern Michigan University's new athletic policy should be the entire university, think of all the secondary beneficiaries who must be satisfied—fans, alumni, athletes, students, faculty, and so on.

It is no simple task to satisfy all these objectives; indeed, if you were to examine a given organization at any particular time, you would find some priority or hierarchy of objectives. This indicates that management realizes the possibility of not achieving all its goals in the short run and so has placed some order of importance on their attainment. In the long run, of course, all the organization's goals must be attained or it will cease to exist. The following section deals with classes of objectives that organizations establish for both their primary and secondary beneficiaries.

CLASSES OF OBJECTIVES

For our purposes the following scheme is convenient and simple for classifying goals. Any classification is a way of arranging information about a given subject area, so a goal classification scheme can be helpful in cataloging what we know about goals and the role they play in organization life.

The scheme that we use relies heavily on the one proposed by R. C. Davis in his classic work *The Fundamentals of Top Management*.[3] A summary of it is presented in Table 8.1.

Primary Objectives

Those objectives that are tied directly to satisfying the needs and desires of the organization's primary client group (primary beneficiaries) are called *primary objectives*. Whatever type of organization is considered, it is basically established to provide goods and services to some special group that may be called the *primary client group*. For example, ITT's primary objective with its new System 12 is to develop those telephone

TABLE 8.1

Classification of Objectives

Type of Objective	Focus	Serves	Examples
Primary	Production and distribution of goods and services	Primary beneficiary groups	To increase sales of widgets by 10% by end of the fiscal year 1990
Secondary	Support functions to achieve production and distribution of goods and services	Secondary beneficiary groups	To meet all major occupational safety and health standards (OSHA) by 1990
Short-term	One year or less or accounting cycle	Primary and secondary groups	To reduce the number of quality control rejects by 20% within the next 12 months
Long-term	Two to twenty years or more	Primary and secondary groups	To increase market share to 31% by January 1, 1995
Equilibrium	Maintain status quo with environment	Resource preservation	To maintain market share at 10% through 1995
Improvement	Increase operating efficiency and effectiveness	Primary and secondary beneficiaries	To reduce electrical consumption (kwh) by 15% by January 1
Explicit (formal, official)	Publicly stated	External groups and top management	To increase the hiring of minorities by 10% by January 1, 1990
Implicit (operational, unofficial)	What people actually work toward	Operational managers	To fill 6 positions as soon as possible

switches and relays that individual telephone companies, the primary clients, will purchase.

This primary objective is of paramount importance to the organization because it establishes the base for defining other supporting objectives by setting the basic purpose of the organization. Also, it can be a determining influence on the structure and process used in the organization. It sets the stage for an organization's operations because the process, technology, and even personnel are selected on the basis of what is required to produce and distribute products and services that will satisfy primary client needs and desires.

The value contained in products and services, then, becomes the foundation of primary consumer support. Without this support (in the form of purchases), the means of satisfying other client groups would be severely restricted because the income flow would be considerably reduced if the organization lost the support of its primary client group.

Although the specific statement of this primary objective will vary among organizations (perhaps even among those in a single industry), the definition is basically the same for all. That is, the primary objective of an organization is to produce and distribute those goods and services that have the ability to satisfy its primary client group. Thus, it is critical for an organization to define accurately its primary client group so that it may cast its primary objectives accordingly.

Secondary Objectives

All organizations must satisfy the needs and desires of a variety of *secondary client groups*, and these needs and desires become the basis for defining the organization's *secondary objectives*.[4] For example, the organization's employees expect certain utility from the organization in return for their contributions to it. This utility can take many forms. Wages and salaries, pleasant working conditions, and a host of fringe benefits are but a few examples. Whatever form they take, however, secondary goals are the personal goals of secondary client groups that can be satisfied only if the organization concentrates on providing the utility that the group desires. Here again we see the importance of achieving the fusion process.

Let's consider some examples. Government frequently demands certain utility from organizations. This can be seen in the form of taxes that organizations pay, regulations governing the environment and enforcing safe working conditions, and laws concerning the hiring of minorities. These conditions may not be in keeping with the basic purpose of the organization, as the organization was probably not established primarily to pay taxes, to provide clean environments and safe working conditions, or to hire minorities. Nevertheless, it must satisfy the desires and demands of government if it is to stay in existence. In other words, in this case the organization must satisfy the secondary client group as a means to an end, that of satisfying the primary client group. This is not to say that one group is more important than the other; rather, it indicates that the organization must concern itself with satisfying groups other than the primary client group if it is to succeed over the long run. Consequently, it must establish goals or objectives that are aimed at this satisfaction.

In addition to outside groups, such as government, that must be satisfied, the organization must establish secondary objectives for internal groups that are also secondary beneficiaries of the organization. For example, the quality control department has certain expectations of the manufacturing department; the manufacturing department expects certain goods and services from the purchasing department; the marketing department has expectations of the personnel department; and so on. In other words, within the organization, subunits have expectations of each other; they expect utility to satisfy these expectations, and so the organization as a whole must set objectives to provide the necessary utility required of all its parts. Otherwise, the whole organization suffers from internal disruption that will affect its ability to attend to secondary groups outside the organization as well as the primary client group.

Both primary and secondary objectives should be viewed from an integrated time perspective that provides both a short- and a long-term view of objectives and the time period required for their attainment.

Short- and Long-Term Objectives

Organizational objectives can be classified as short- and long-term. This classification is not a new category per se but a different way of looking at primary and secondary objectives from the viewpoint of establishing some sort of time boundary for them.

Short-term goals[5] are those that the organization hopes to accomplish within a year, for instance. Accounting cycles are often used as the time frames for these short-term goals. The organization then strives to attain this type of goal within the bounds of its accounting cycle.

Short-term goals serve to point the organization's resources to accomplishing those projects that are the daily, weekly, and monthly assignments of its members. An example of a short-term objective might be "to increase sales by 10 percent over last year's amount within the current accounting cycle." Accepting this objective then sets the stage for assigning resources to projects concerned with its attainment. As we read in the LTV excerpt in the introductory cases to this chapter, that company set the short-term goal of earning $200 million in profits for 1985. As you know, this short-term goal was not met.

It is important that management keep long-term objectives in mind when setting short-term goals. This is necessary to avoid inadvertently deflecting the organization from its long-term purpose by pursuing short-term goals.

Long-term goals[6] are those that cannot be accomplished within the time frame of a year or so. Former definitions of the long term ranged from five to ten years; now that period has been prolonged to range up to twenty years. The reason for this is that technology (such as simulation) has greatly increased management's ability to forecast. Organizations concerned with population growth and resource supply, for example, would certainly have to define a long-term goal to be at least twenty years. A long-term objective for an electrical utility might be to completely convert to nuclear power by January 1, 2000. Government programs in the areas of energy and social security are based on twenty-five- to fifty-year projections. On the other hand, rapid change is making it difficult for some organizations to forecast beyond about five years. They believe that rapidly changing conditions make planning beyond five to seven years impractical.

Whatever its definition, the long-term objective of an organization will provide the overall direction for it for a considerable number of years. LTV chose to acquire Republic Steel in 1984 because it believed this was an appropriate means of achieving its long-range goal of becoming an efficient and profitable steelmaking operation. Likewise, the various provisions of Eastern Michigan University's new athletic policy all strive to help attain the long-range primary goal of winning athletic championships. ITT's long-term goal is to become a contender, if not the leader, in the world telecommunications market.

It is important to keep the long-term objective in mind when setting short-term objectives so that their accomplishment can directly contribute to the attainment of long-term goals. At the same time, it is important for management to review the long-term goals each year in order to reaffirm or alter them as the base for the future direction of the organization, whether the organization desires to be in a state of equilibrium or improvement.

Equilibrium Objectives

Those organizations that wish to remain in or achieve a steady state will develop what might be termed *equilibrium objectives*. These objectives are such that their attainment would allow the organization to preserve its relative share of the market and its relative share of resources over time.

Basically, an organization that adopts equilibrium objectives makes a conscious decision also to adopt the adaptation strategy for staying in tune with its macro environment. This means that it will monitor this environment with a view to making internal changes that will allow it to remain in consonance with outside pressures. This also means that the organization is in a reactionary mode in that it is reluctant to adopt objectives that would require shaping or molding the macro environment. An equilibrium objective might be considered a kind of gyroscope that ties the organization to its outside environment.

In February 1986, Ford Motor Company's chairman, David Peterson, announced 1987 equilibrium goals for his company—maintaining an approximately 20 percent share of the car market and an approximately 30 percent share of the truck market. Peterson decided on these equilibrium objectives because the U.S. auto industry was operating within an environment characterized by heavy competition and uncertainty; by establishing such objectives, Ford would be able to minimize its risks. Peterson stated, "When you consider all that's happening and all that is going to happen and the extraordinary explosion of competition, I think it's valid for us to aspire to be a 20 percent company in the car business and a 30 percent ± company in trucks. I think anything beyond that on a just-in-case basis, with all the uncertainties, would be unsound."[7]

Improvement Objectives

The desire to improve operations and to accomplish projects more efficiently is one of the universal goals of most organizations in the United States. Improvement has been a keynote of the U.S. economy. As part of our culture, we are taught from an early age the virtue of doing things in a better way; thus, it is natural for our organizations to have an improvement objective.

In contrast to Ford's Peterson, Chrysler's Lee Iacocca announced a variety of improvement objectives for his organization in 1987. His objectives, unlike Peterson's, are not stated in terms of percentages; rather, they are stated in terms of new product development, such as the introduction of a convertible in the upper-middle price range, a more expensive mini-van with a bigger engine, and a bigger luxury car to compete with Cadillac.[8]

So, for reasons of efficiency, conservation, and tradition, today's organization counts the improvement objective among its goals. Together with the other classes of goals discussed above, the improvement objective completes the classification of organization goals. This classification scheme for examining objectives can help an organization focus attention on individual and organization goals and how they are related to each other. This sharper focus can enable the organization to set more realistic goals than might otherwise be the case. Setting all these goals is an important and sometimes complicated process that is examined later in the chapter.

Explicit Objectives

Organizations frequently set formal, official objectives that are printed and circulated primarily to those outside the organization (e.g., owners, government, or the media). These might appear in the annual report, in press releases, or in other organization pronouncements. These objectives may not even be the actual objectives of the organization; they may be formally stated only for public-relations purposes.

As we saw in our introductory case examples, organizations publicize a variety of explicit objectives. LTV wants to be efficient and profitable in the steel industry; Eastern Michigan University wishes to win athletic championships; and ITT's explicit goal is to become number one (or close to it) in the manufacture and sale of telephone switches and relays.

Implicit Objectives

The actual or unofficial objectives that the organization works toward in reality might be different from the formally stated (official) objectives. This might occur for several reasons. Lower-level managers may not be aware of explicit objectives and may, therefore, formulate their own objectives. Explicit objectives may be deemed unrealistic or unattainable, and less ambitious ones may be implicitly set. Finally, personal objectives of managers may cloud or even negate formal objectives. For whatever reason, it is important to note that formally stated objectives (explicit objectives) may not be the actual objectives that guide behavior in organizations. For example, LTV's explicit objective of becoming a profitable steelmaker has been replaced, by necessity, with the implicit objective of "just being able to weather the crisis" facing the U.S. steel industry in the 1980s.

Responsibility for Goal Setting

One of the most important tasks facing managers is setting goals for their organizations. This is a particularly challenging assignment because most of us have a difficult time setting definite courses of action. This requires us to think about our values and how they can best be protected while setting both personal and organizational objectives.

The process of setting organization goals should ideally begin at the top levels of the organization in order to set the basic direction for the entire organization. As we saw above, Ford's Peterson and Chrysler's Iacocca are responsible for setting their organizations' respective goals. Even though the ultimate responsibility for goal setting rests with the top management group, it is important that they gather sufficient input from within and without the organization to make intelligent decisions about the goals that the organization will seek.

First-line managers and production workers can add valuable input to production-oriented goals, and the same can be said for sales managers and the sales force about establishing sales goals. These members are most familiar with the conditions surrounding the process of goal achievement. At the Japanese-owned Honda plant in Marysville, Ohio, for example, workers believe in and are involved with the automated factory in which they work. Indeed, Honda workers see automation in assembly operations as an investment in job security. The result is that many ideas contributing to and enhancing production goals come directly from the factory floor.

The management group at every level should set goals for their respective departments and divisions. Goal-setting responsibility should be shared, involving all members of management and often nonmanagers as well, depending on management philosophy, technology, and so on. At the Marysville Honda plant, responsibility for goal setting is shared. All Honda employees, from top to bottom, are referred to as "associates." The plant is run "democratically," with the result that Honda's primary goal of increased profitability is being achieved. Some important determinants of who is to be involved in the goal-setting process are discussed below.

Often objectives are set by a *dominant coalition* of managers, experts, or those with special interests and influence in the organization. These individuals might not, in fact, be charged with the formal responsibility for goal setting. Nevertheless, they can be very influential when it comes to establishing those goals toward which the organization works, both formally and informally.

As a matter of fact, such coalitions can subvert the organization's formal goal hierarchy. (See page 292 for a more complete discussion of goal hierarchy.) A classic example of such a situation can be seen in cases of organization sabotage or spying, or in situations in which sales agents strive to increase their personal incomes through the bonus plan. Production objectives can be jeopardized due to an imbalance of emphasis placed on the sales objective. If the members of the credit department cooperate with this tactic, the sales agent can further cause an imbalance in the goal hierarchy.

Because of the impact, actual as well as potential, that it can have on goal setting, the dominant coalition must be considered when goals are set.

Determinants of Organization Goals

An organization's management group must consider a variety of factors and forces when setting goals. The following are some of the major ones; they are common to all organizations and are summarized in Figure 8.1.

CONSUMER NEEDS. All organizations exist to serve some consumer group(s) (primary beneficiaries), so they must carefully identify those people they will attempt to serve. A clear understanding of these consumer needs is necessary for a management group to establish primary organizational goals. For example, in recent years Americans of all creeds have "fallen in love" with the bagel. To capitalize on this consumer affectation, an Israeli company, Betavon, was formed in 1986 with the goal of

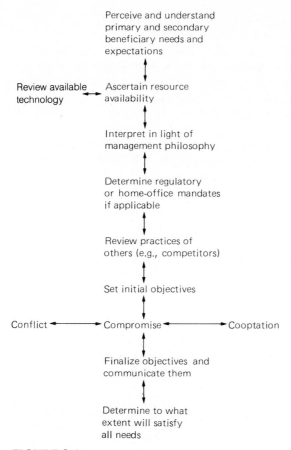

FIGURE 8.1

Determination of Objectives

whetting America's appetite for a variety of Jewish foods (in addition to bagels).

In addition, at this point the organization should examine needs of secondary beneficiary groups. As Betavon gears up for exporting Jewish foods to the United States, it must seriously think of ways to satisfy two extremely important secondary beneficiaries: the Israeli government (that might lend money to the company) and American supermarkets (that will retail the products).

In this way there can be an integrated set of goals aimed at satisfying primary consumer groups that also takes into account the needs of the secondary groups such as government, distributors, and so forth.

TECHNOLOGY. Organizations tend to change their goals to accommodate technological advances. The classic example of this is the computer. Once it became generally available, organizations began to change goals in accordance with the computer. Production and sales quotas were revised upward as technology made more rapid and efficient production and distribution possible. Such actions were tied to goals affected by the availability of the computer and its capability of increasing organizational efficiency.

The improvement of a given state of technology can itself become an organization goal. Such was the case with the space program in the United States during the 1960s. The U.S. government established a national goal of developing the technology required to put a person on the moon within the decade. This goal became a guiding influence for many organizations embracing a wide variety of types and sizes of industries. From this national goal came many individual organization goals that were directly related to the proposed moon landing. Goals to establish new products and processes were the bases for new activities in established organizations, as well as the impetus for beginning new organizations.

RESOURCES. Among the most critical aspects of goal setting is recognizing the role of resources. It is not practical, for instance, to set objectives that require more resources than the organization can reasonably expect to acquire. It would be a mistake to establish an organization with the hope of capturing 50 percent of the steel market in the United States if the firm could only command a capital structure of $1 million. The steel industry simply requires far more than $1 million of capital if competition in it is to be successful. Can Eastern Michigan University achieve its goal of winning athletic championships without recruiting the best athletes, having adequate money for scholarships, and building the finest sports facilities?

MANAGEMENT PHILOSOPHY. Because top management is ultimately responsible for establishing the organization's goals, the values that this group holds will exert a major influence on the statement of goals. This set of values guides all of management's decision making, and it is recognized here that goal setting is a major choice area. The goals of the organization can even be taken as a reflection of the values that the management group seeks for the organization since goals represent a desired end-state for the organization. Note how Ford's and Chrysler's goals reflect the philosophies of their chairmen, Peterson and Iacocca, respectively. The point to be made here is that the formal recognition of the management philosophy of the firm should be made at the time goals are set and again whenever progress is evaluated.

PRACTICES OF OTHERS. Often an organization sets its goals in response to what others in its industry are doing. For example, when a competitor brings out a new product, others in the industry must take this into account when setting sales and production goals for the coming period. Lee Iacocca wants Chrysler to build and market a larger luxury car in order to compete successfully with GM's Cadillac. This is not to say that a goal to bring out a competitive product must be set, but an attempt must be made to gauge the potential effect of such a competitive move.

In order to attract students as well as faculty, universities try to bring out new courses and majors in response to the practices of other colleges and universities. Consider the area of computer science recently. Presently, there appears to be a general move to emphasize the liberal arts more.

Competition can exert a force on an organization. The goals of others can actually determine the goals of an organization. The simplest case of this happening can be seen in a conglomerate where the parent company allocates a "a 10 percent contribution to the profit objective" to one of its members.

Whether the practices of competitors are adopted, it is sound to take them into account when setting goals. Consequently, this factor must be given considerable weight by a management group when it is establishing goals for its organization.

MANDATES. Occasionally, organizations are mandated, in effect, to set a particular goal. This can be demonstrated in the case of actions of the Environmental Protection Agency (EPA) of the U.S. government. When setting goals that can affect the environment, organizations must abide by the rules and regulations of the EPA. Environmental impact studies must be conducted to measure the projected effect of certain construction projects, for example. In cases such as housing developments, the developer must establish a goal to protect the surrounding environment. Manufacturers are required to observe certain pollution standards. Again, the automotive industry can be cited as an example of a case in which mandates (both environmental and safety) affect goal setting. Mandates, then, can have a significant impact on the entire process of goal setting and measurement.

Figure 8.2 summarizes, in a kind of flow process, these various determinants and how they fit together in the function of determining objectives. In addition to the basic determinants, the figure also shows the steps beyond setting objectives that close the cycle of goal setting. The first six parts of the figure summarize the determinants; part 7 contains three examples of how decisions on the goals themselves can be reached;

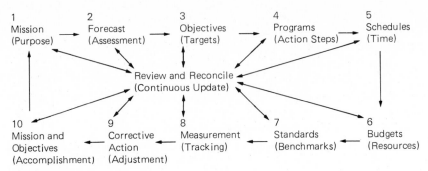

FIGURE 8.2

The Management by Objectives Process

Source: Adapted from George Morrisey, *Management by Objectives and Results* (Reading, Mass.: Addison-Wesley, 1970): 17.

parts 8 and 9 complete the decision process and provide for the elements of evaluation and control.

The goal-setting process must be carried out with due consideration of these and other factors. Although the particular techniques used by a given management group will vary to some degree with the situation, the following discussion describes some popular techniques used to set goals in the modern organization.

SOME GOAL-SETTING TECHNIQUES

Officially, organizations often have a formal and explicit means for establishing goals, whether by a vote of the stockholders or the board of directors or by some other means. In actuality, the setting of goals or objectives is often quite different from the formal means that the organization espouses. In reality, there are many factors that come into play in establishing goals, some of which were mentioned above. Internal politics frequently exert a great influence on the process. A strong group or an individual in a key place can exert an inordinate amount of influence on setting goals and also on determining their priority once they have been selected. A prominent faculty member can, for example, decide how many merit scholars to recruit for a college or a department.

The following sections briefly discuss four popular techniques that can be used to establish organization goals and the priority placed on them.

Conflict

Setting goals by conflict can create the type of discussions that result in the development of an effective base for conflict resolution.* This means that conflict can provide the impetus for the type of interaction that brings out the factors affecting the goals of all parties. Without the conflict, one of the parties might set a goal that would require the other(s) to set either suboptimal or unreachable goals.

Conflict, because it does focus attention on its own resolution, points the way to effective goal setting. Unchecked conflict can be potentially disastrous to an organization, and yet a healthy level of conflict can bring pressure to bear on the setting of realistic goals. A management group can use it as a process to bring about the establishment of a sound goal program for the organization.

Compromise

It is not unusual for managers to set goals that are quite ambitious in their initial form in order to establish a base for compromise as well as for an increased share of resources. Every organization has its own set of rules for such practices, and these rules of the game play an important role in setting courses of action for the organization.

Managers who expect to use compromise set a given level of goal in the hope of bargaining away some of the advantages that might be associated with this level for other benefits. For example, a college administrator might set the goal for his or her unit's share of capital funds at an optimistic level in the hope of bargaining with superiors for a larger share of current expense money. In other words, there is a deliberate attempt to establish a base from which to "retreat" in an effort to gain an overall advantage through compromise.

Cooptation

When one organization or a group of people absorbs another, the act is termed *cooptation*. As mentioned earlier, this can be seen when a company becomes a member of a larger organization. It is customary for its goals to be set in accordance with guidelines furnished by the parent organization. This means that the goals of the parent will determine to a large extent which goals of the members will fit into the overall goal structure of the conglomerate.

Let's take the case of Buckingham Corporation, the distilled spirits distributor, to prove this point. In 1980, after being purchased by North-

*Rensis Likert and Jane Gibson Likert, *New Ways of Managing Conflict* (New York: McGraw-Hill, 1976), 141–145, contains a good section on integrative goals and conflict.

west Industries, Buckingham was ordered to increase its business. Thus, Buckingham's CEO, Richard Newman, created a new marketing department and cleared out bloated inventories of Cutty Sark. These actions, along with other measures, increased Buckingham's profits on three different occasions from 1980 to 1984. However, back in 1983, Northwest sold Buckingham to Beatrice. A year after the sale, Beatrice decided to get out of the liquor business; therefore, it sold Buckingham to Julius Wile and Sons. The Wile organization was more interested in enhancing its two star products, Mouton Cadet Bordeaux and Finlandia Vodka. Therefore, Wile eliminated many of Buckingham's operations and slashed the latter's staff by three-fourths. In short, as Buckingham changed from owner to owner, its goals were changed.[9]

The goals of the conglomerate itself can be affected by the practices of its members. The management of the conglomerate must take the conditions and objectives of all its members into account when setting the goals of the entire organization. Therefore, cooptation can be viewed as a two-edged effect, with influence flowing from both the top and the bottom of the organization.

Organizations must use some system that will produce a meaningful purpose for them and the groups they serve. In other words, they must seek a balance among competing objectives. As yet, there is no fail-safe means for doing this, although there are several static models for approximating balance. Essentially, they all involve the assignment of some degree of utility (or desirability) to each goal, and so they enable management to at least subjectively rank goals in their order of importance. Once this can be done, management can focus attention on the most important goals and can assign resources to them with some degree of deliberateness. Such a process can help ensure that all goals are assigned their relative importance to the organization and so help contribute to better management practice.

One such system of goal setting is management by objectives. It is being adopted for its systematic approach to the goal-setting process as well as for its structured measurement of goal accomplishment. It is discussed briefly below in order to demonstrate how it can be used to establish the organization's objectives.

Management by Objectives[*]

Although it has been in existence as a process for quite a long time, management by objectives (MBO) is a relatively new concept as far as its use as

---

[*]The system of management by objectives explained here is based on the approach designed by George Morrisey that is described in more detail in *Management by Objectives and Results* (Reading, Mass.: Addison-Wesley, 1970).

a formal system is concerned. First put forth formally by Peter Drucker in 1954, MBO has enjoyed considerable success as a management tool in the intervening years.

Management by objectives is founded on a philosophy of participation and on a leadership style that encourages considerable involvement of organization members in the operation of the system. Thus, MBO requires a high degree of understanding and communication between superiors and subordinates.

The following is a concise description of the various phases of a typical MBO system of management. There can be variations of this scheme, but all versions of MBO will contain basically the same components. The process is summarized in Figure 8.2.

MISSION. The MBO system provides for the involvement of every manager in the process of establishing the organization's basic purpose or mission. After an initial draft of basic purpose (mission) is provided by the superior, the subordinate establishes a basic purpose for his or her unit that is in keeping with that of the superior. This "linking pin" approach is carried out in order to provide maximum vertical integration of purpose for the entire organization. This is an important step in the whole MBO process because unless this sense of overall purpose can be translated into subunit purposes, there can be little hope for coordinated effort within the organization. Morale and efficiency both suffer when members have no overall purpose in mind; they fail to see how their actions relate to the accomplishment of their personal objectives, let alone those of the organization as a whole. A sense of directionlessness that can cause innumerable difficulties results.

FORECASTS. Once the mission of every manager has been set, the conditions that are likely to affect it must be forecast. The means for conducting forecasts vary according to philosophy, economics, and technology, among other things. Whatever means are used, however, it is important to project the conditions (e.g., economic, political, and cultural) that are likely to bear on the mission.

It is also important at this stage to assess the internal operations of the organization by asking the questions "What are we doing well?" and "What are we doing poorly?" This internal assessment will aid the organization in identifying strengths and weaknesses that can serve as the basis for building objectives. Objectives that capitalize on strengths and that correct weaknesses can then be developed.

OBJECTIVES. When forecasts have been completed, the long-term mission can be used to set short-term (one year, say) objectives that provide the base for daily activities. These short-term goals, set through a process similar to that used to establish mission, provide the foundation for the measurement of accomplishment and progress of the organization.

PROGRAMS. After objectives are established, major activities required to accomplish them can be determined and made part of operational procedure. It is important to spell out all these major activities—the program—that will be required to accomplish each objective so that those who are responsible can know exactly what will be necessary for proper attainment. This is also known as *action planning*. The program, or action plan, then not only guides activities, it also helps deploy resources effectively, serves as the basis for training members of the organization, and helps in the measurement of accomplishment.

SCHEDULES. When all objectives are programmed, it is necessary to determine an appropriate schedule for their attainment. It is suggested that, where practical, each step in a program have its own schedule in order to facilitate the tracking of progress. In those instances where it is not feasible to attach a schedule to every step in the program, it is important to fix a schedule for the entire program; again, this is done to facilitate the tracking process.

BUDGETS. Budgeting for each objective involves the commitment of all resources needed to accomplish that objective. Not only dollars, but also space, materials, personnel, and all other relevant resources should be assigned or budgeted to each objective. By doing this, management is in a better position to control the objectives.

Establishing the organization mission, forecasts, objectives, programs, schedules, and budgets is collectively the concern of management *planning* efforts. The remaining aspects of MBO are the setting of standards, the measuring of performance, and the taking of appropriate corrective action—all parts of the management function of *control*.

STANDARDS. Once the planning phase of an MBO program is completed, it is necessary to begin work on the control aspects. The first step in the MBO program of control is setting standards that can be used to determine the degree of success of goal accomplishment. For every organization there will be a variety of standards ranging from quality control to sales quotas. Because of their critical role, it is imperative to set standards that are realistic and attuned to the particular situation.

MEASUREMENT. Once standards are established, they must be applied to determine whether goals are being attained; this process is measurement. Again, a number of techniques can be used, but it is important to note several considerations with any measurement program.

One key to an effective measurement system is the development of a management information system (MIS). An MIS is a system of information that provides accurate and relevant data to managers at the time, place, and in the format they desire for effective decision making. Such a system is critical for making MBO work. Because an MIS is usually computer-based, a good MIS for use in tracking and measuring MBO will help managers avoid drowning in a sea of paperwork.

Aside from the obvious effect on production, there are also psychological and sociological dimensions to a measurement program. Often a degree of anxiety is experienced when a formal measurement program is installed. Members, not unlike students facing an examination, feel this sense of anxiety and perhaps frustration when they are evaluated. This means that care should be taken to explain the standard and how it will be applied to measure performance.

Competition among various groups can be successfully employed to raise production levels if, among other things, measurement is properly handled. This sense of competition has positive psychological and sociological effects that can benefit both the organization and its members.

CORRECTIVE ACTION. The measurement program can reveal situations in which goals are not being attained. When such situations are found, it is important to take immediate and positive corrective action to remove the cause(s) of deviation. Corrective action should always be taken by the responsible manager. For instance, it would be proper for the supervisor of a work group to be responsible for correcting difficulties on a work project. To allow an inspector to make needed adjustments would create a condition in which the workers might feel a sense of loyalty or obligation to the higher officer, thus undermining the authority and position of the lower one. This is not to suggest that workers themselves should never correct their own mistakes, but merely to note where the *managerial* responsibility for corrective action lies.

When corrective action is required, it should be taken with a preventive approach. In other words, management should take the long-term outlook when making corrections with a view to preventing a recurrence. At the same time, corrective action should be taken with a positive, learning-oriented approach rather than with a punitive one. Learning from mistakes can be a positive influence on future behavior; undue punishment can dampen one's morale and creativity.

A management system of MBO, then, can bring a systematic approach to setting objectives and to their attainment. It can be adapted to fit any size or type of organization; therefore, any management group can benefit from its use. Patience is the watchword for the installation of the program, however, because it does require a three- to five-year period for maximum benefits to be realized. It appears to be worth the effort, because it has been demonstrated time and again by a variety of organizations to be a significant management aid.

Whether an organization uses MBO or some other system for formulating and tracking its objectives, it is important that some priority or hierarchy of importance be established. This goal hierarchy can serve to focus attention and resources on those areas of most significance to the organization rather than emphasizing objectives randomly. Setting such a hierarchy plays a vital role in the goal-setting process.

THE GOAL HIERARCHY

At the head of the list of organization objectives must be placed providing the goods and services to the primary beneficiaries the organization attempts to satisfy. As noted earlier, the organization must also establish a group of secondary objectives that serves to satisfy the needs of secondary clients such as government, suppliers, employees, owners, and so on.

The organization must also operate economically and effectively to conserve its limited supply of resources. But management should not allow economy and effectiveness to become so important that the organization begins to exist solely to achieve these goals. Satisfying the basic client groups should never be ignored. An ideal hierarchy would place the primary objective of serving the basic client group at the top and follow it with the secondary objectives of serving secondary client groups and achieving the goals of economy and effectiveness. Occasionally, however, an organization experiences a displacement of goals in its desired hierarchy.

Goal Displacement

Goal displacement is a situation in which an original goal is given a different place in the hierarchy or is substituted by some other goal for which the organization was not created.[10] Consequently, these other goals have not had resources allocated to them nor have they been recognized externally or internally as properly placed goals.

Goal displacement can originate from the top of the organization when the executive group alters the amount of attention and resources given a particular goal after having approved the original hierarchy. For example, the goal of economy might be shifted to a high priority relative to production if the organization finds itself in financial difficulty caused by an unusual amount of doubtful accounts receivable. Economic recession can surely be the cause of such a situation, and so management makes a deliberate decision to move the objective of economy to a higher position in the hierarchy. Again, we refer to LTV. Recession in the steel industry forced this industrial giant to modify its lofty goal of becoming a profitable steelmaker. Survival is now the primary goal of this organization.

Undue attention to rules and procedures can also divert the organization from its original plan. Government regulations, for example, affect organizations of all types and can subtly shift the priority of goal attainment. Organization members can find themselves so occupied with complying with regulations that there is scarcely time left to attend to original goals. This can be a major cause of goal displacement over a period of time, yet on a daily basis the shift might go unnoticed.

Union rules and regulations, particularly within large manufacturing organizations, can displace the organization's original goals. For example, at AMC's Jeep plant in Ohio, the company has consistently failed to achieve its primary goal of manufacturing high-quality jeeps for a number of reasons, among them being the plethora of union rules that it must follow. How can AMC realize manufacturing efficiency when the United Auto Workers union demands that three different individuals move parts from inventory to the assembly line when only one individual is really needed to do this job?

The settlement of a labor dispute can be seen as another example of how goals can get displaced. The secondary objective of providing for the conditions sought by the labor force can occupy the full attention of management in the short run. When the dispute is settled, the original hierarchy can be reestablished. Even during the dispute, however, management still retains an underlying concern for continuity of operations and optimum productivity.

There are also occasions when the production goal, for example, can be disproportionately emphasized to the detriment of sales and finance goals. This often causes the organization to operate in an unbalanced condition that can have serious long-term effects. In a university, the research goal can be given undue emphasis relative to the teaching goal, with the result being dissatisfaction on the part of the student body.

Attribution of goals can also cause the displacement of goals in a given hierarchy. In goal attribution, an observer imputes or attributes a goal to a particular undertaking so as to make the undertaking rational or congruent with the observed behavior. A lack of information about the formal goal hierarchy coupled with the attribution of goals to given acts can cause confusion. For example, assume that a supervisor is unaware of the formal mission of the inspection department, which is to optimize the efficiency of resource use. The supervisor could easily attribute an objective of effectiveness to the inspection department and thus be confused by the inspector's decision to reduce the amount of a scarce resource in a given product batch. This confusion can lead not only to interpersonal friction but also to lower organizational productivity.

The message is simple: All members of the organization should be conscious of goal attribution in order to be able to compare attributed goals with formal goals and thus to avoid confusion and misunderstanding.

These are but a few examples of how goals are displaced or relegated to subordinate positions in the original hierarchy. When management deliberately alters a goal hierarchy, the condition is termed *suboptimization.* As noted, there are times and situations when such a choice is best for the organization in the short run. Care must be taken, however, to ensure that the alteration is only temporary. Otherwise, the organization's original purpose can be permanently changed. Without an original hierarchy, management would have no frame of reference for knowing or correcting conditions of goal displacement.

Goal displacement is an ever-present possibility as far as the goal hierarchy is concerned. Whether done consciously or unconsciously, displacement of goals can have far-reaching effects on the organization's performance as well as on individual member job satisfaction.

MEASURES OF ACCOMPLISHMENT

Whatever its type or particular mission, an organization needs some benchmarks or standards by which to measure its success. As we pointed out in our discussion of MBO, management is responsible for establishing the means of determining if objectives are attained. The following are some suggested measures that can be used to determine the degree of success of goal attainment.

In business organizations, there has traditionally been a single measure that has taken the prime position among standards—profit. Certainly, this is an important goal for business organizations to strive for, although its precise measurement has been and continues to be difficult. In spite of the difficulty of measurement, however, profit must continue to occupy an important place among business organizations' measures of success.

Even though we traditionally think of profit maximization as the key measure of accomplishment, Simon argues strongly that because of bounded rationality (discussed in Chapter 2), organizations actually try to "satisfice" rather than maximize.[*] Because it is difficult to achieve per-

---

[*]Herbert A. Simon, *Models of Man: Social and Rational* (New York: John Wiley & Sons, 1957). Simon argues that once people find a workable solution to a problem, the search for alternatives ends. This solution works although it might not be the very best. Simon uses the term "satisficing" to describe the search for the workable solution, based on the concept of bounded rationality. Objective decisions are based on a kind of triangle of rationality limited by one's skills, values, and knowledge of the decision subject, and decisions made within these limits are called "satisficing" decisions.

fect rationality, decision making can best be characterized as "satisficing" rather than maximizing. The maximum efficiency-effectiveness criterion may be replaced by a "satisficing" one for those organizations operating under bounded rationality. Therefore, in viewing measures of accomplishment for an organization, particularly one in a changing, unpredictable environment, we may wish to use the criterion of "satisficing" rather than maximizing.

In addition to business organizations, there are many other types of organizations in our society that must somehow attempt to measure their success. The measures discussed here are by no means exhaustive; they are merely representative. These standards are also stated in rather general terms—it is necessary to apply more specific definitions to each of them when they are used to evaluate an actual organization.

Effectiveness

All organizations must at some point determine how effectively they have used their resources to accomplish their goals or objectives. In other words, they must know whether they accomplished what they undertook to accomplish. This is easier said than done, for a number of reasons. The thorny issue rests on the definition of the term *effectiveness*.

When we speak of effectiveness, just what is it that is being discussed? Is it the number of units of product produced? Is it the amount of specific profit earned? Is it the number of lunches served or the patients successfully treated? There is even the question of the source of the definition. Should it come from society or from the organization? In other words, do the citizens of a community or nation have anything to say about the matter, or should the organization be left to define its own terms?

Customers might say that a mythical organization is effective if, over the long haul, they have been served a quality product at a reasonable price. A citizens group might condemn the organization for polluting what was once a pristine lake. At the same time, the local chamber of commerce might extol the virtues of the organization as the town's largest employer and taxpayer, while both employees and stockholders might be less than enthusiastic because they received low wages and profits. All constituencies affected by the organization have their own definition of organization effectiveness. As you see, a conclusive definition of organization effectiveness is elusive.

Even respected organization theorists disagree on the proper definition of effectiveness. If we take a historical perspective, we see that each different school of thought had its own particular standards for defining effectiveness. Frederick W. Taylor, the founder of scientific management, thought that effectiveness was determined by such factors as production maximization, cost minimization, technical excellence, optimal utilization of resources, and task specialization. Henri Fayol, who was the principal thinker of the Principles of Management school of thought, believed that effectiveness was a function of clear authority and discipline within an organization, unity of command and direction, order, equity, stability, initiative and *esprit de corps*. Elton W. Mayo and adherents of the Human Relations school attributed effectiveness to productivity resulting from employee satisfaction, and satisfaction through attention to workers' physical and emotional needs. Other historical thinkers in the management discipline, such as Herbert Simon, Rensis Likert, Douglas McGregor, and so on, all had their own views concerning effectiveness in organizations. The point here is that throughout the history of management and organization theory, there has never been consensus about what organization effectiveness is.

Kim S. Cameron, writing in *Organizational Dynamics*, provides an incisive summary of modern divergent views on the subject by examining four major models of effectiveness.[11]

The *goal model* defines effectiveness in terms of how well an organization accomplishes its goals: The closer the organization comes to meeting its goals, the more effective it is. However, if an organization's goals are ill-defined or complex, this model is inadequate. Moreover, as Cameron points out, if the organization's goals are too low, misplaced, or harmful, then this model cannot be used. For example, in the 1960s Boise Cascade Company set a 20 percent growth in earnings per share per year as its major goal. The firm reached and even surpassed this goal for a number of years; however, in order to reach this goal, the organization took on risky projects and ignored certain important environmental groups. The result was that Boise Cascade declared bankruptcy and had to reorganize under court order in 1972. Thus, even though Boise Cascade reached its goal, it was not an effective organization, the goal model notwithstanding.

The *systems resource model* claims that effectiveness is attained to the extent that the organization acquires needed resources from the environment. The reasoning behind this model is based on the proposition that there is a clear connection between system inputs from the macro environment and organization performance. Cameron clearly points out the shortcomings of this model with his discussion of the Seattle Supersonics basketball team. This team managed to win the NBA championship in 1979 despite the fact that it did not succeed in acquiring superstars for the roster and even had a rookie coach. Thus, organizational output per se is not necessarily a function of obtaining the "best" resources from the environment.

The third major approach for determining effectiveness is what Cameron calls the *internal processes model*. This model defines effective organizations as those having an absence of undue internal strain. In other words, an effective organization is a "healthy" organization. Information flows smoothly, both vertically and horizontally; there is little conflict; and relations in the organization are characterized by trust and benevolence. Again, using a sports example, Cameron shows the inapplicability of this approach in all circumstances. The New York Yankees won the World Series in 1978 and 1979 despite the fact that the team was plagued by fights between coaches and players, threatened firings, and turnover in key personnel.

The *strategic constituencies model* is the fourth major approach discussed by Cameron and rests on the assertion that effective organizations are those whose strategic constituencies, groups of individuals who have a stake in the organization, are at least minimally satisfied. Although this model can apply to those organizations whose constituencies have major influence on the organization, and the organization reacts to constituencies' demands, it, too, has its defects. Note in our example above how the customers, citizens group, local chamber of commerce, employees, and stockholders all had differing views concerning the mythical organization's effectiveness.

Recognizing these and other issues, we propose the following definition: Organization effectiveness is a condition in which a focal organization, using a finite amount of resources, is able to achieve a stated objective(s), as measured by a given set of criteria. Further, and as an integral part of the concept, this definition must be viewed from the perspective of the affected constituency. This point is illustrated by the issues raised in the preceding paragraph.

The values, perspectives, and so on of the evaluator can also affect the definition of the term. Referring again to the mythical organization at the beginning of this section, the citizens group was not particularly interested in defining a "polluter" as being effective, while the customers did not have environmental protection high on their agenda. And there is subjectivity even in objectivity. Who is to say, for example that "X" units of production per day is "good" output? Even though there may be some snags in the process, there is no alternative to establishing and using some type of criteria for measuring effectiveness.

John Campbell and his colleagues prepared a comprehensive list of standards for establishing organizational effectiveness. They range all the way from the state of morale to absenteeism, and constitute a rather exhaustive compendium of generally accepted standards, both subjective and objective.[12] Because Campbell's list is recognized by most management scholars as being the most universally representative, we present it in Table 8.2.

TABLE 8.2

Campbell's List of Effectiveness Criteria

Overall effectiveness	Productivity
Efficiency	Profit
Quality	Accidents
Growth	Absenteeism
Turnover	Job satisfaction
Motivation	Morale
Control	Conflict/cohesion
Flexibility/adaptation	Planning and goal setting
Goal consensus	Internalization of organizational goals
Role and norm congruence	
Managerial task skills	Managerial interpersonal skills
Information management and communication	Readiness
	Utilization of environment
Evaluations by external entities	Stability
	Value of human resources
Participation and shared influence	Training and development emphasis
Achievement emphasis	

Source: Adapted from J. P. Campbell, "On the Nature of Organizational Effectiveness," in *New Perspectives on Organizational Effectiveness*, eds. P. S. Goodman and J. M. Pennings (San Francisco: Jossey-Bass, 1977), 36–39.

Depending on who is doing the measuring, an organization can be effective or ineffective. It would be a rare case in which everyone involved with an organization would use the same measures and reach the same conclusions. The student of organization theory must be aware of this situation when evaluating the organization's effectiveness.*

For example, using an open-systems perspective, we can define an effective organization to be one that remains in harmony with its environment, regardless of other outcomes. On the other hand, we can take a more closed-systems view and say an organization is effective if it makes a profit.

It is not productive to attempt to measure all organizations against a single measure nor is it fruitful to apply any one measure to all organizations. Connolly, Conlon, and Deutsch put this issue into clear focus: "We see no particular merit in an obsessional search for the single measure of

---

*Karl Weick's article, "Re-Punctuating the Problem," in *New Perspectives on Organizational Effectiveness*, eds. Paul S. Goodman, Johannes M. Pennings, and associates (San Francisco: Jossey-Bass, 1977), 193–225, is an interesting, though offbeat, enunciation of some fascinating criteria. Weick maintains that organizations are garrulous, clumsy, superstitious, hypocritical, monstrous, octopoid, wandering, and grouchy.

merit on which organizations can be compared."[13] In spite of the power of this statement, Gerald Salancik proposes a unique means of measuring a single value that he maintains reveals organization effectiveness, regardless of circumstance.[14] Salancik argues that it is theoretically possible to measure organization effectiveness by assessing the extent to which an organization promotes valued outcomes, regardless of who prefers those outcomes. The key to this solution lies in determining the value of outcomes on the basis of relationships among outcomes as opposed to individual orientations toward them. For our purposes, however, we will adopt the former perspective.

So, the elusive term *effectiveness*, though quite difficult to define and measure, is nevertheless a critical construct in organization theory. It is fitting to close this section by citing six questions developed by Cameron. He suggests organizations should ask them in order to choose the best criteria for measuring effectiveness.[15]

1. What domain of activity is being focused on (e.g., internal or external activities)?
2. Whose perspective, or which constituency's point of view, is being considered?
3. What level of analysis is being used (e.g., individual effectiveness, subunit effectiveness, or overall organizational effectiveness)?
4. What time frame is being employed? (short-term or long-term)?
5. What type of data is to be used (subjective or objective)?
6. What referent is being employed (comparative, normative, or goal-centered)?

Efficiency

A companion standard for effectiveness is efficiency, the relationship between expenditure of resources and results. To be efficient means to get the most of whatever goal an organization wishes to pursue—the most growth, the happiest employees, the highest quality products, and so on. Efficiency means the greatest benefit for the costs.[16] Each expenditure of resources should bring an accompanying positive result. An organization can be effective but not efficient: For example, an organization might accomplish its objectives, but at a net loss of revenue. Such an organization could not be considered efficient because it did not realize a net return from its resource use. Yet, it could be considered effective in that it did accomplish what it set out to accomplish.

Effectiveness might be considered a long-term measurement, and efficiency could be classified a short-term measurement. This is the case because the organization cannot exist over time if it operates at a net loss

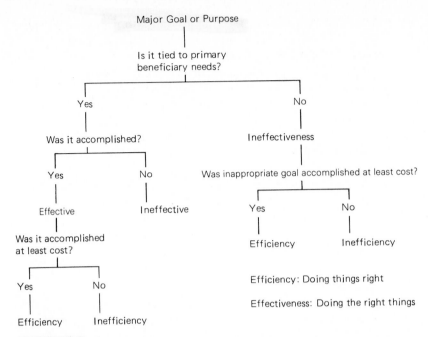

FIGURE 8.3

Efficiency and Effectiveness

of income in the long run, even though it might be successful in its overall purpose.

The definition of efficiency must be carefully established or the organization can be misled into concentrating on effectiveness at the expense of efficiency. Both effectiveness and efficiency must be counted among the measures of success for any organization. Their relationship is depicted in Figure 8.3. Note that an organization can be effective without being efficient and can be efficient without being effective.

Humanism

In today's organizations attention is increasingly focusing on concern for the human element (humanism). Along with effectiveness and efficiency, people in the organization are now being taken into account when evaluating its success. There are many reasons for including the humanism standard in the set of benchmarks of success. Chief among them are the cultural and legal forces that have placed pressure on managers to treat members as individuals and to recognize their special needs and desires.

To observe this standard of humanism, the organization must modify (where necessary) its definition of effectiveness and efficiency. For example, an organization that is considered by its members to place undue emphasis on production standards to the exclusion of concern for member needs and desires is likely to be faced with high turnover and other personnel problems. This condition can hamper, in the long run at least, the organization's ability to attain all its goals.

There are those organization theorists today who would define the basic role of the manager as one concerned with developing a climate that fosters the personal and professional growth of organization members. These theorists argue that an organization that can create and maintain such an internal environment will succeed, according to traditional measures of success in the long run, as a direct result of efforts to develop members to their fullest. However strongly a management group feels about this responsibility for development, it must be aware of the human element to some extent if it is to retain member support and loyalty necessary for success.

Of course, all of the above measures must be defined within the particular environment of the organization. Although the concern here has been on a general treatment of the measures, in practice, management must set specific definitions for the measures so that all concerned will know on which standards their performance is to be judged. Time and effort spent in defining measures of success can bring more-than-proportional results to management and to the organization as a whole.

CLASSES OF WORK

An organization accomplishes its goals through the performance of various types of work. The Classical School of management thought was founded, to a large extent, on division of labor, a term used to refer to the work arrangements that would allow the desired degree of specialization required to attain organization goals. So, goals exert a determining influence on work definitions and arrangements.

From this basic tenet of thought has come today's approach to work division, although it is more oriented toward concern for the human element than was the original "one-best-man" concept that characterized the early emphasis on work division. According to the "one-best-man" approach, work was to be defined and grouped into jobs or positions that could serve as the basis for selecting and training the individual most capable of performing them.

Following this approach, management would define the type of work necessary to accomplish objectives and then select that person who possessed the qualities to perform it most successfully. To this basic talent, management would add proper training and tools to improve the person's ability. The reasoning was that the organization was bound to prosper from an arrangement where the job to be performed was determined by the objectives and, in turn, was the basis for selecting, deploying, and developing organization members. Everything revolved around the work to be performed.

As indicated earlier, this trend in job design has been modified to account for the human element—the interests of the members themselves. Of course, such a practice must be evaluated in the final analysis by its effect on the attainment of overall organization objectives. Its adherents believe that the practice of designing jobs around incumbents is not contrary to the best interests of the organization in the long run.

Whatever its philosophy of work design, any management group must build both management and operative work units into an effective whole if objectives are to be attained. The following parts of the chapter discuss these classes of work with a view to showing not only their basic composition but also their relationships with each other. A summary of these classes of work, with examples, is shown in Table 8.3.

TABLE 8.3

Classes of Work

Class	Focus	Examples
Managerial work	Decision making and influence	Planning, organizing, controlling, leading, coordinating, obtaining resources
Operative work	Production and distribution of utility	Fabricating a part, making a sale
Line operative work	Production and distribution of primary utility (manufacturing and distributing products and services for primary consumers/clients)	Assembling a product, counseling a client
Staff operative work	Production and distribution of secondary utility (support activities for line operative work)	Determining wage rates, keeping sales records

Managerial Work[17]

In any organization there are basic tasks that should be assigned to the management group, and the decision about what these tasks should be is critical. Basically, management is assigned the twin tasks of decision making and influence, as discussed in Chapter 1. There are many versions of what the basic tasks of the manager are or should be; they range from planning, organizing, and controlling to marshaling resources, leading, and coordinating. The present treatment was chosen because it includes the essential features of many of, if not all, the various versions, and yet it has the advantage of simplicity. Therefore, for our purposes, *management work* consists of decision making and influence.

An organization employs a manager to make the type and quality of decisions that are required to guide it toward its objectives. These decisions involve every facet of operation and organization, from defining goals, to selecting resources, to evaluating performance. Decisions are made to set the policy and process network that ties activity into an effective whole of organization and operation.

If these decisions are to bring results, however, management must implement them. This process requires that management influence people to carry out decisions effectively and efficiently, drawing on both its power and its authority. In other words, management must draw on positional and personal influence sources in order to implement its decisions.

In addition to the management functions of decision making and influence, the organization must ensure the proper execution of operative work.

Operative Work

To accomplish objectives, an organization must produce and distribute utility in the form of products and services desired by its clients. This utility is produced and distributed through the execution of *operative work*. Operative work is the basic activity that directly enables the organization to realize its objectives.

Everyone, including managers, engages in operative work of one form or another. It is the form of work that pervades every unit of responsibility in the organization: A production worker assembling the parts of the product, a salesperson taking a customer's order, an engineer designing the product or the production process, a personnel clerk processing an employment application, and a manager scheduling a work day are all doing operative work. Activities that do not involve the supervision of subordinates and that result in the production and distribution of utility are classified as operative work.[18]

Management work of decision making and influence is carried out to ensure the proper performance of operative work, the basic building block of the organization. Therefore, operative work can be classified as a key ingredient in the building of structure and process. This is true since both structure and process are built around production and distribution of utility, the concern of operative work. Operative work can be further classified as line or staff work.

LINE OPERATIVE WORK. *Line* (or primary) *operative work* is that which is concerned with the production and distribution of primary utility. It takes the form of those activities that result in the manufacture and distribution of products and services for the primary consumer. For example, all activities carried out in the assembly of a product are line activities. Likewise, the activities carried out by sales and delivery personnel are line activities because they result in getting the product to the customer.

Both production and distribution are classified as line operative activities because they are directly associated with the organization's attempt to attain its primary objective. The statement of this objective is the basis for defining the exact nature of line operative work. Consequently, it is through proper performance of line operative work that the primary objective is attained.

STAFF OPERATIVE WORK. In addition to the execution of primary work, the organization must perform a host of activities concerned with secondary objectives. This type of activity is termed *staff* (or secondary) *operative work* and is aimed at producing and distributing the utility that is desired by secondary client groups.[19]

An example of staff operative work is that of a personnel department whose major responsibility is the administration of policy governing wages, working conditions, and fringe benefits that go toward satisfying the desires of employees. The accounting department also performs staff operative work when it keeps accurate records and advises on the proper use of the organization's resources. The payment of accounts and dividends is also an example of staff operative work performance. Quality control, the legal function, and the research function in a manufacturing plant are also classified as staff operative functions. They produce and distribute utility that is consumed in the organization's attempt to operate as economically and effectively as is practicable.

Staff operative work is concerned with the attainment of secondary objectives. When management defines the exact nature of these goals, it determines the basis for the composition of staff operative work units. In turn, these units form the basis for the building of staff or secondary elements in the structure.

FIGURE 8.4

The Relationship Between Work, Objectives, and Beneficiaries

Both line and staff operative work must be properly defined and grouped into effective units of responsibility for the organization to have a sound structural and procedural network. The differentiation of these work units must be tied together through a process termed *integration* that is discussed in Chapter 9.

Managers have an important task in defining and grouping managerial and operative work units into an effective pattern in order to realize the organization's goals. These two components, goals and work, must be included in a general theory of organizations. Figure 8.4 shows the relationship between the various kinds of work and their respective ties to objectives and beneficiaries. Goals and work must be tied together into an overall system that is concerned with the satisfaction of all client groups with which the organization is concerned. In brief, the goal system should determine the work relationships concerned with producing and distributing the utility needed to satisfy the goal system.

SUMMARY

Today's organization manager faces an important assignment—setting goals or objectives that are aimed at satisfying the needs and desires of primary and secondary client groups. Every organization must serve both groups, so it is necessary to formulate objectives for them.

Primary objectives are concerned with the primary consumer group and are satisfied when the organization produces and distributes primary utility in the form of goods and services to its primary client group. Secondary consumers are satisfied by the organization's production and distribution of secondary utility, again, in the form of goods and services. Effective wage and salary programs, reasonable dividend programs, and quality-control programs are examples of attempts to satisfy secondary client groups, both within and without the organization.

Whatever its goal structure, the organization must recognize some type of short-run hierarchy that places primary objectives at the head of the list. Otherwise, the organization can find itself drifting about aimlessly, devoting its resources to unsuccessful projects that satisfy no one.

There must be long-term goals if the organization is to have a grand sense of purpose and to have a frame of reference to guide it over time. At the same time, there are equilibrium goals that keep the organization in tune with its environment, and there are improvement objectives that are concerned with enhancing ability to accomplish all goals effectively and economically.

Management is ultimately responsible for setting the goals of the organization. Among the factors that affect decisions about goals and how they should be set are consumer needs, technology, resources, management's philosophy, the practices of others, and mandates from government agencies and home offices.

The goal-setting process can be carried out using conflict as the means for reaching decisions. Such conflict often stems from competition and can result in hammering out a goal structure that is superior to one that might be set unilaterally by management. Compromise is often used to reach agreement on goals as is cooptation, the absorbing of one organization or unit by another, thus impacting the goal setting of the absorbed unit. However it is set, the goal hierarchy is an important organization theory construct.

A popular system of management today is management of objectives (MBO). This system is aimed at improving managerial planning and control by providing for (1) a systematic involvement of organization members in the goal-setting process, and (2) insurance that proper action is taken to monitor progress and to take corrective action when necessary. The system is composed of (1) planning activities such as missions, forecasts, objectives, programs, schedules, and budgets, and (2) controlling activities such as standards, measurement, and corrective action. If properly installed in an organization, it can bring rich rewards to everyone concerned.

Often objectives get displaced from their original position in the hierarchy. This can be illustrated by the case of a labor strike, when management turns its attention to settling the dispute at the expense (momentarily, at least) of the primary objective. Displacement can also occur without the knowledge or deliberate effort of management.

Conflict between personal and organization goals and the attribution of goals to observed behavior can also cause goal displacement. When there is perceived conflict between these two types of goals, the individual is likely to pursue personal goals at the expense of organization goals. This tendency can also cause the individual to pursue secondary objectives, such as better wages and working conditions, to the detriment of the primary objective. This conflict can elevate a secondary objective over the primary objective in the mind of the individual.

When an individual attributes goals to performance, this also causes a form of goal displacement. The confusion that goal attribution causes can divert attention from formal goals and their placement in the hierarchy to attributed goals, which might be higher or lower than the formal goal or even be outside the hierarchy. Therefore, management must establish some means for determining when goal displacement occurs if the entire formal goal hierarchy is to be achieved.

Effectiveness, efficiency, and humanism can be used to measure organization success. Management must, of course, provide more specific definitions of these guides to ensure that all who use them fully understand them and how they will be used.

Objectives are accomplished through the execution of work. This work can be classified as managerial (decision making and influence) and operative (the actual production and distribution of utility). Line operative work is concerned with producing and distributing primary utility to the primary client group, and staff operative work is devoted to producing and distributing secondary utility to secondary groups within and without the organization.

These work units of line and staff operative types must be held together in a well-integrated fashion if the organization is to survive and be effective in the long run.

This chapter has analyzed the organization's goal and work systems, two of the most important systems in any organization. Chapter 9 continues this discussion by applying it to the design of the organization.

QUESTIONS FOR REVIEW AND DISCUSSION

1. What is the real significance of formally stated goals for an organization?
2. Why is it important for an organization to identify and classify the beneficiaries of its goods and services?
3. How is a formally stated goal hierarchy of importance to an organization?
4. Under what conditions would an organization deliberately establish a goal of equilibrium?
5. How can an organization go about the task of goal formulation?
6. What are some of the major determinants of the exact nature of an organization's goal structure?
7. Why is it important to distinguish between personal and organization goals?
8. What is the fusion process? Why is it important to organization theory?

9. What is an attributed goal? Why is this an important concept in organization theory?
10. What are the essential ingredients of a system of management by objectives? Will this system work in all types of organizations?
11. How can an organization determine if it is achieving its objectives?
12. Discuss the various classes of organization work and relate them to the organization's goal hierarchy.

ENDNOTES

1. Amitai Etzioni, *Modern Organizations* (Englewood Cliffs, N.J.: Prentice-Hall, 1964).

2. E. Wight Bakke, "Concept of the Social Organization," in *Modern Organization Theory*, ed. Mason Haire (New York: John Wiley & Sons, 1959), 60–61.

3. R. C. Davis, *The Fundamentals of Top Management* (New York: Harper & Row, 1951), 95–109.

4. Ibid.

5. Leslie W. LaRue and Lloyd D. Byars, *Management: Theory and Application*, 4th ed. (Homewood, Ill.: Richard D. Irwin, 1986), 432–433.

6. Ibid.

7. Jerry Flint, "Ford's Defensive Posture," *Forbes* (December 5, 1986), 49.

8. Ibid.

9. Jeremy Main, "Companies that Float from Owner to Owner," *Fortune* (April 28, 1986), 39–40.

10. George S. Odiorne, "Management by Objectives and the Phenomenon of Goal Displacement," *Human Resources Management* 13 (Spring 1974): 2–7.

11. Kim S. Cameron, "Critical Questions in Assessing Organizational Effectiveness," *Organizational Dynamics* 9, no. 2 (Autumn 1980): 66–80.

12. J. P. Campbell, "On the Nature of Organizational Effectiveness," in *New Perspectives on Organizational Effectiveness*, ed. P. S. Goodman and J. M. Pennings (San Francisco: Jossey-Bass, 1977).

13. Terry Connolly, Edward J. Conlon, and Stuart Jay Deutsch, "Organizational Effectiveness: A Multi-Constituency Approach," *Academy of Management Review* 5, no. 2 (April 1980): 211–217.

14. Gerald R. Salancik, "A Single Value Function for Evaluating Organizations with Multiple Constituencies," *Academy of Management Review* 9, no. 4 (October 1984): 617–625.

15. Cameron, "Critical Questions," 75.

16. Henry Mintzberg, "A Note on the Dirty Word 'Efficiency,'" *Interfaces* 12 (October 5, 1982): 101–102.

17. R. C. Davis, *The Fundamentals of Top Management* (New York: Harper & Row, 1951).

18. Ibid.

19. Ibid.

ANNOTATED BIBLIOGRAPHY

Cameron, Kim. "Critical Questions in Assessing Organizational Effectiveness." *Organizational Dynamics* 9, no. 2 (Autumn 1980): 66–80.

To gain meaningful results from any organizational evaluation, the concept of organizational effectiveness must be clearly defined and limited. Managers must ask questions focusing on: (1) What domain of activity is being focused on? (2) Whose perspective is being considered? (3) What level of analysis is being used? (4) What time frame is being employed? (5) What type of data is to be used? and (6) What referent is being employed?

Chacko, Thomas I.; Stone, Thomas H.; and Brief, Arthur P. "Participation in Goal-Setting Programs: An Attributional Analysis." *Academy of Management Review* 4 (July 1979): 433–438.

This is an examination of the goal-setting process in the light of attribution theory to explain why increased participation in goal-setting programs has not shown positive results in general. Attribution theory suggests that more research should be directed at individuals' perceptions of the causes of success or failure of goal-setting programs.

Davis, Ralph C. *The Fundamentals of Top Management*. New York: Harper & Row, 1951.

This is a discussion of the functional aspects of organizations and the ways in which top management approaches each functional area. The style of managerial philosophy that top management holds will directly influence the manner in which these functions are exercised.

Dollinger, Marc J. "Environmental Boundary Spanning and Information Processing Effects on Organizational Performance." *Academy of Management Journal* 27, no. 2 (June 1984): 351–368.

The boundary-spanning activity of the entrepreneur is used to examine the strategic management process in small business. In a sample of eighty-two owner/operators, intensive boundary-spanning activity was strongly related to organizational performance, and information-processing capability significantly affected the performance–boundary-spanning relationship.

Erez, Mirian; Earley, P. Christopher; and Hulin, Charles L. "The Impact of Participation on Goal Acceptance and Performance: A Two-Step Model." *Academy of Management Journal* 28, no. 1 (March 1985): 50–66.

Past research has tested goal-setting strategies and found high and invariant levels of goal acceptance. The present research consisted of two studies—one laboratory and one field experiment—hypothesizing a two-step model (participation $\xrightarrow{1}$ acceptance $\xrightarrow{2}$ performance) with which participation could be tested more effectively. Hierarchical regression analyses demonstrated that the participative and representative groups outperformed the assigned groups under conditions in which individual goal acceptance varied. The findings support the two-step model and offer an explanation as to why previous research has failed to differentiate empirically between participative and assigned goal setting.

Granger, Charles H. "The Hierarchy of Objectives." *Harvard Business Review* 42 (May–June 1964): 63–74.

Granger discusses the conceptual framework of objectives, the characteristics of the criteria for selecting objectives, and the most effective results achieved from well-developed and implemented objectives.

Hughes, Charles, L. *Goal Setting: Key to Individual and Organizational Effectiveness*. New York: American Management Association, 1965.

This is an in-depth coverage of goal formation, goal-achievement orientation, goal processes, and goal-setting systems. It provides adequate coverage of the integration of individual and organizational goals.

Mahoney, T. A., and Frost, P. "Goal Setting and the Individual: An Interactive Influence on Individual Performance." *Organizational Behavior and Human Performance* 17 (December 1976): 328–350.

An experiment was conducted to determine the effects of goal characteristics on individual performance. Specifically, goal characteristics such as acceptance and difficulty were studied to determine if these goal characteristics, coupled with other variables such as wages, would be strong motivators to the employee.

Umstot, Denis. "MBO and Job Enrichment: How to Have Your Cake and Eat it Too." *Management Review* 66 (February 1977): 21–26.

Goal setting for productivity, goal setting as part of job design, how goals affect jobs, and integrating goal setting with job enrichment are all discussed. Umstot believes job design, incorporated with goal setting and enrichment characteristics, may concurrently lead to greater employee motivation, job satisfaction, and productivity.

Zammuto, Raymond F. "A Comparison of Multiple Constituency Models of Organizational Effectiveness." *Academy of Management Review* 9, no. 4 (October 1984): 606–616.

Four sets of multiple constituency models of organizational effectiveness that employ relativistic, power, social justice, and evolutionary perspectives are reviewed. Comparison of these perspectives shows that the construct of organizational effectiveness is both value-based and time-specific. The implications of these findings are examined in the form of potential directions for research on organizational effectiveness.

ADDITIONAL REFERENCES

Aiken, M., and Hage, J. "Organizational Interdependence and Intra-Organizational Structure." *American Sociological Review* (1968): 912–930.

Bourgeois, J. J., III. "Strategic Goals, Perceived Uncertainty, and Economic Performance in Volatile Environments." *Academy of Management Journal* 28, no. 3 (September 1985): 548–573.

Burch, John G., Jr.; Strater, Felix R.; and Grudnitski, Gary. *Information Systems: Theory and Practice.* 2d ed. New York: John Wiley & Sons, 1979.

Cameron, Kim S. "Domains of Organizational Effectiveness in Colleges and Universities." *Academy of Management Journal* 24, no. 1 (March 1981): 25–47.

Campion, M. A., and Lord, R. G. "A Control System Conceptualization of the Goal-Setting and Changing Process." *Organizational Behavior and Human Performance* 30 (1982): 265–287.

Chacko, George K. *Management Information Systems*. Princeton, N.J.: Petrocelli Books, 1979.

Connally, Terry; Conlon, Edward J.; and Deutsch, Stuart J. "Organizational Effectiveness: A Multiple-Constituency Approach." *Academy of Management Review* 5, no. 1 (January 1980): 211–217.

Mintzberg, Henry. *The Nature of Managerial Work*. New York: Harper & Row, 1973.

Odiorne, George S. "Management by Objectives and the Phenomenon of Goal Displacement." *Human Resources Management* 13 (Spring 1974): 2–3.

Price, J. L. "The Study of Organizational Effectiveness." *The Sociological Quarterly* (1972): 3–15.

Rappaport, A. "Corporate Performance Standards and Shareholder Value." *Journal of Business Strategy* 3, no. 4 (1983): 28–38.

Reid, D. M. "Human Resource Planning: A Tool for People Development." *Personnel* 54 (March 1977): 15–25.

Urwick, L. F. "V. A. Graicunas and the Span of Control." *Academy of Management Journal* (June 1974): 349–354.

Weick, Karl E., and Daft, Richard L. "The Effectiveness of Interpretation Systems." In *Organizational Effectiveness: A Comparison of Multiple Models*, edited by Kim S. Cameron and David A. Whetten. New York: Academic Press, 1982.

Weiner, J. L. *Conflict and Control in Health Care Administration*. Beverly Hills, Calif.: Sage, 1975.

```
C        A        S        E
```

Trouble on the Mountain

The Mountaineers of West Virginia University (WVU) have a dream "of a vibrant land grant university—a richly financed 'flagship' institution—leading the state into a new era of prosperity. Both teaching and research at the university are first-rate. Its salaries are competitive, its facilities are outstanding, and its programs of public service and extension are among the best." In short, the goal is preeminence.

How to achieve this goal in West Virginia, a state suffering through a virtual depression, is an unanswerable question that WVU is struggling to answer. Unemployment is at 16 percent; the coal industry is in deep trouble, and so are the steel and glass industries. In spite of this bleak economic prospect, WVU leaders have found a sense of purpose with their dream. President E. Gordon Gee has taken a number of steps to enhance his institution: He has restructured administrative procedures, reassessed academic programs, expanded the university's involvement in statewide economic development, cultivated political ties, and pushed for a broad public awareness of the school's actual and potential value to the people of West Virginia.

A recent report, the Berendum Study, was a comprehensive review and evalua-

Source: Robert L. Jacobson, "The Dream Versus the Reality at West Virginia University," *Chronicle of Higher Education* (February 27, 1985), 12–15.

tion of WVU's present condition. It raises some interesting points about the practicality of the university's achieving its goal of preeminence. Some of the study's conclusions are: (1) The university is "grossly underfunded" with no rational formula for annual allocations by the state board of regents; there is no appreciation of the necessary costs related to WVU's role as a land-grant, doctoral-degree-granting university in the state; (2) the academic program should be overhauled; and (3) the university needs greater freedom to manage its own affairs. On a positive note, the study did conclude that the university has made the most effective use possible of its available resources.

In order to persuade the state to provide it with the resources and freedom it needs to attain its potential, the university has adopted two strategies, inside and outside. The former includes program reviews with broad faculty participation. For example, the doctoral internal review committee has targeted thirty-one doctoral programs for elimination that had averaged fewer than three graduates per year. Standards for eliminating these programs focus on the number of degrees awarded over a period of time and the quality of the faculty and its research. Similar reviews are underway for masters and undergraduate programs. The inside strategy also includes an orderly reallocation of university-controlled funds and priorities based on a focal program's merit.

From the outside viewpoint, the university gained the approval from its board of regents to receive $28 million in bonding authority for a new engineering and science complex as well as $87 million in bonding authority to replace its teaching hospital.

Complementing the university's efforts is its athletic program. Indeed, one WVU administrator stated that the challenge is to translate popular enthusiasm for the university's athletic program into fervor on behalf of its academic program. Recently, WVU announced plans for a $6 million expansion of its four-year-old stadium. As more citizens become involved with athletics, President Gee believes this will give him the opportunity to talk to them "about the good things we are doing" and raise the level of public awareness about what it is a state university can contribute.

Even with these signs of progress, the university faces such serious financial shortcomings that the Berendum Study concluded that "continuing failure to budget *according to mission* [emphasis added] will propel WVU toward mediocrity." The problem, however, is not just one emanating from the state's depressed economic condition. The university competes with fifteen other state colleges and universities for funds. The state allocates monies to its colleges and universities on an "incremental funding of the past" formula. WVU has asked that this procedure be changed so that the total state higher education formula "differentiates the funding needs of a comprehensive, research-oriented, land-grant institution from those of two- to four-year teaching colleges." Indeed, there is a certain element of friction and even conflict between WVU and the other state institutions of higher education.

The university's goal of preeminence has resulted in the formation of secondary objectives that must be attained for total success. As WVU attains these secondary objectives, it pushes itself toward its ultimate goal; however, success depends on economic and political factors beyond its control.

QUESTIONS FOR DISCUSSION

1. Is the goal of preeminence a reasonable one for a major state university such as WVU? Why? Why not? How can the material in this chapter help you answer these questions?
2. How would you suggest the effectiveness of WVU's efforts be measured? By what criteria? By whom?
3. Explain what you would consider the proper role for the faculty, the students, the administrators, the governing body, the legislature, and the governor to play in goal setting at WVU.
4. What should WVU use as its referent(s) when setting goals (other state universities in West Virginia, in the East, and so on)?
5. What would you look for to determine if primary goals have been displaced by secondary goals? Is this important to know? Why? Why not?

9

Organization Design: An Overview

Listening to TV/Watching the Radio?

"There has been a lot of discussion over the years about the National Association of Broadcasters' (NAB) structure. Should it be a single, closely integrated organization for all phases of broadcasting? Or a federation, with separate operating divisions? Or should it be split completely to represent the separate forms of broadcasting?

During these years I have been one of the industry's strongest supporters of a single, integrated-system organization. But developments in the real world in recent years have created a gnawing doubt in my own mind about the soundness of my long-held judgment on this subject. And in mulling over the pros and cons of this issue in the light of experience, I have come to the conviction that NAB's effectiveness is hampered—both for radio and television—by an outdated organization structure. I now believe that, like most modern enterprises—GE and General Motors are examples—NAB must have separate operating divisions, each responsible for doing a full-service job for its members and its branch of the industry.

Basic changes in our industry itself demand this. Television grew out of radio, and for a while common management of the two media was typical. Industry interests and concerns were common to radio and television, and NAB Board members shared these common interests. Today, the radio and TV boards are completely different in makeup, interests, and outlook.

New media for program distribution and information processing affect radio and television quite differently. The television world has its own complexities, and many of its problems are far outside the interests and concerns of radio broadcasters. And the reverse is equally true.

There are some common elements—sales and audience goals are essentially the same, and all broadcasters are concerned about undue government interference—even though that area is beginning to affect radio differently from television. Yet the means of developing these two media and of dealing with these issues are sharply different and, in some ways, conflicting.

Certainly a strong umbrella organization is appropriate, but radio and television should have their own operating divisions to tailor make positions and services to the needs of each. There should always be an NAB parent. The conventions should be joint efforts. The board meetings should continue together. But radio and television can deal with their respective government problems more effectively as separate divisions with separate and distinct lobbying efforts.

The idea that the two groups should be combined to deal with Congress is not true—in fact, I can point to cases where the reverse is true. Radio should not have been delayed in obtaining deregulation legislation because of television; and television should not be subjected to restrictions resulting from an imbalance on a forty-six-member joint Board.

Other separations may follow, but in many instances, staff services could be pooled. For example, the law department could serve both divisions, providing service to two clients, as is done in many industry organizations, including those in the broadcast and publications fields. In time, other NAB units might be added to the two basic ones I've just mentioned.

I don't expect any immediate bandwagon result from these comments. Change is always difficult. It requires a breakaway

Source: Farewell paper delivered to the NAB Joint Board by Peter B. Kenney, Vice President, Washington, D.C., National Broadcasting Company, "Viewpoint," *Television/Radio Age* 31, no. 3 (August 15, 1983): 55.

from safe harbors and long-established habits. It is even more difficult when the decision has to be made by a constantly changing board where it is easier to send things to committee and 'let the next board do it.' However, a task force created now could bring a reorganization plan to the January board, and the change could be in place no later than 1986.

I urge you to face the upcoming years by asking yourselves whether the NAB, in its present form, is best organized and equipped to deal with futures. If you have any doubts, I hope you will analyze this question impersonally and thoughtfully, and take action. And do it yourselves, through *this* board. Don't leave it for someone else to handle. If you do that, you would have lost

your opportunity to make an important contribution."

Mr. Kenney's farewell paper emphasizes the necessity for an organization to design itself to meet contingencies in the environment as well to accommodate work and goals. Indeed, as you read the material in this chapter, you will realize how modern organizations must pay strict attention to the basic tenets and philosophies of organization design in order to successfully accomplish their missions.

As indicated by the title, this chapter is an overview of the basic considerations and forces involved in designing an organization structure-process network. We examine the nature of organization design and relate design to the two basic concepts of differentiation and integration, which, when considered independently and together, constitute the two fundamental considerations to take into account when building or designing an organization.

Organizations should be designed in order to carry out the work necessary to achieve the organization's goals and objectives. In other words, the goals of the organization should dictate how organizations organize themselves. In the previous chapter, we examined the organization's goal and work system. In this chapter and the next, we discuss how organizations design themselves to carry out their work.

THE NATURE OF ORGANIZATION DESIGN

The design of an organization can have two meanings because the word "design" can be used as a verb or a noun. When used as a verb, organization design refers to the process of setting up an organization. Just as an architect designs a building, so is an organization designed. As a noun, organization design refers to the results of the designing process. It deals with the question, what does the organization look like?

In this chapter, our primary emphasis is on the use of design as a noun, although occasionally we do discuss design as a process. We are interested in the results of the design process: what organizations look like.

Design versus Structure

The two concepts of design and structure are closely related. There is some confusion in the literature on the meanings of the two terms. We will use Mintzberg's definition of organization *structure*: "the sum total of the ways in which [the organization] divides its labor into distinct tasks and then achieves coordination among them."[1] This definition recognizes the two essential aspects of structure: *differentiation* and *integration*. Differentiation involves breaking up the work to be done into tasks, and integration refers to coordinating these tasks. The structure of an organization is usually depicted through a formal *organization chart*. This chart shows authority relationships (who reports to whom or the chain of command), formal channels of communication, formal work groups, and formal lines of accountability—all issues discussed later in the chapter.

Organization design, on the other hand, is viewed as a broader concept than structure. It includes structure but it also includes more. For example, Mintzberg identifies design parameters that use such aspects as unit size, unit grouping, planning and control systems, behavior formalization (policies and rules), and decision-making decentralization.[2] Thus, there are process issues design is concerned with as well as structural issues. As shown in Figure 9.1, design is an umbrella concept. Think of structure as the human skeleton. It is the framework on which muscles, nerves, blood vessels, and other aspects of the organization are attached. These items make the skeleton (structure) come alive, and all items, including the skeleton, make up the design of the whole body.

Formal versus Informal Organization

In examining organization design and structure, we see that organizations create an officially sanctioned structure known as the *formal organization* or *de jure* organization. This structure is often depicted by a formal organization chart such as that seen in Figure 9.2. Notice that this chart shows various authority and reporting relationships depicted by the lines that connect each point on the chart. Each point represents a position in the organization occupied by one person. Each horizontal level of points represents a level of authority in the organization. (Not all subordinate positions in the organization are shown. The department heads would have subordinate supervisors reporting to them, and these subordinate supervisors would have operatives reporting to them.)

ORGANIZATION DESIGN

Structure	Process
Differentiation	Planning and Control Systems
Integration	Behaviorial Formalization
	(policies, procedures, rules)
	Decision-making

FIGURE 9.1

Organization Design and Structure

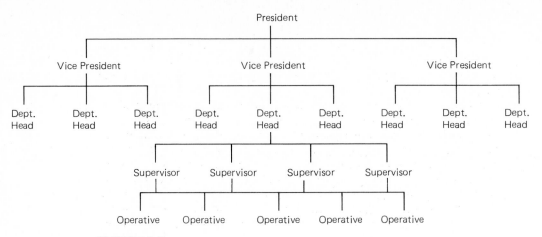

FIGURE 9.2
A Formal Organization Chart

A formal or "objective" organization chart presents the official structure explicitly sanctioned by the organization. But this is only half the story, for superimposed on these relationships are *informal* or *de facto* relationships that are not necessarily sanctioned by the organization, although they might be perceived to actually exist and are thus considered by some to be the real structure. These include informal work groupings of employees, informal leaders, informal channels of communication, and informal power and status differentials. Some of these are depicted in Figure 9.3.

Our focus in this chapter is primarily on the formal organization structure, although we will examine the impact of the informal structure on the formal structure when it can be significant.

Differentiation and Integration: Key Elements of Structure

All organizations must split up their work into units called *tasks*. As we saw earlier in this chapter, this is called *differentiation*. In the vast majority of organizations today, it is physically impossible for one individual to do all the tasks. As soon as a secretary is added to do typing or a part-time bookkeeper is hired to keep the books, the organization has begun differentiating the tasks to be done. A large business corporation such as General Motors typifies the very complex and extended process of specialization often found in today's organization.

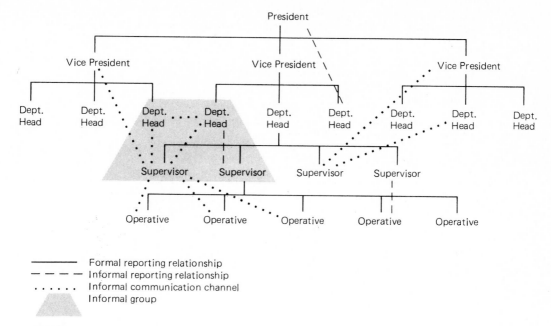

- ———— Formal reporting relationship
- — — — Informal reporting relationship
- · · · · · · Informal communication channel
- Informal group

FIGURE 9.3

Some Aspects of the Informal Organization

Just as organizations split up the work to do, they must also coordinate this work. As we discussed earlier, this is called *integration*. Basically, this includes the means that organizations use to pull together the highly differentiated tasks that have been established.

This need for differentiation and integration and some of the methods that can be used to achieve them are of critical concern to the organization structure question. We will examine these methods in more depth later in the chapter.

Organization Design and the Environment

As we pointed out earlier, the environment has a great impact on how organizations design themselves. We indicated in Figure 4.8 (see page 150) that two key variables in the environment—stability and homogeneity—have a major impact on organization decisions. In general, the more stable and homogeneous is the environment, the less complex and more centralized is the organization design. The more unstable and heterogeneous the environment, the more complex and decentralized is the design.

Note in NBC retiring Vice President Kenney's remarks, which serve

FIGURE 9.4

The Relationship of the Organization's Environment, Objectives, Work, Design, and Policy

as our introductory case, how he wished to split the NAB structure into two divisions, one for television and one for radio. Kenney believed this to be the proper course of action for his organization because the old NAB structure was no longer responsive to demands placed on it by the volatile macro environment, particularly the political component. When the NAB was formed, the old, centralized structure was able to serve both television and radio interests; however, this is no longer the case.

Thus, because design determines complexity and facilitates or hinders the decentralization process, we examine the influence of the environment on various aspects of the organization design process later in this chapter.

Organization Design, Objectives, Work, and Policy

As we indicated previously, organizations should be designed to facilitate the accomplishment of objectives. The structure of the organization should organize work flows so that objectives are easier to accomplish.[3] By the same token, organization policy should be developed so that work flows are enhanced.* Figure 9.4 shows the relationship between design, objectives, work, and policy from a normative or ideal perspective. Notice that the organization's goals and objectives provide the framework for organizing the work flows. This, then, provides the basis for design. The role of policy is to provide guidelines of action that should be followed by all the working members of the organization so that objectives can be achieved, part of the behavioral formalization issue as identified by Mintzberg. It ties the environment to the functional operation of the organization.

Policy decisions tend to be decisions of "strategic choice." They are important decisions that refer to the way organizations formulate objec-

*Jay R. Galbraith, *Organization Design* (Reading, Mass.: Addison-Wesley, 1977). He uses the notion of *strategic choice* to refer to the way the organization makes design decisions to integrate the organization domain, goals, and individual goals.

tives to take advantage of environmental opportunities. They also refer to the way the organization establishes a design to carry out work. Thus, we can think of broad overall policy making in the organization as the making of strategic-choice decisions to tie an organization to its environment through goals, work, and design.

We can see real-life applications of the concepts described above with the Celanese Corporation, the textile manufacturer. In 1982, this organization, after being trounced by textile imports, embarked on a strategy of retrenchment (we discussed this type of strategy in Chapter 7) to cut costs. In order to better meet its goals vis-à-vis this retrenchment strategy, Celanese conducted an "activity-value analysis" that required employees to keep excruciatingly detailed time logs of what they were doing over several months. Managers and employees then got together to determine which tasks could be cut back, performed at other organizational levels, or even eliminated.[4]

Often, design results from the personalities of managers or from tradition. Work flows may change without commensurate change in design. Old policies may continue in force even though organization objectives, work, and structure have changed. Organization theory regarding design is normative or prescriptive but, in reality, real-world experiences are often different from what theory prescribes.

However, probably of greatest concern is the lack of change in design as organization objectives change. Many organizations change objectives annually, particularly if they are under a system of management by objectives (MBO), discussed in Chapter 8. Are we saying that structure must change annually? Not necessarily. The key to this is the kind of change that occurs in the organization's objectives. If organization objectives change significantly in terms of products and services produced and markets or clients served, then design should change, especially if this change in objectives requires a change in work flows. On the other hand, if changes in objectives are minor and can be substantially accommodated by present work flows, then little or no design change needs to be made.

Of course, the degree to which organization objectives change from year to year is substantially influenced by the environment the organization faces. A changing, heterogeneous environment will likely cause a greater change in objectives as the organization attempts to cope with this environment (as explained in Chapter 4), than a stable, homogeneous environment. Thus, environmental changes can cause objectives to change, which will ultimately result in structural change. Conversely, an organization facing a stable, homogeneous environment will likely experience little change in objectives and design over time. It need not be as flexible or adaptive as an organization facing a dynamic environment.

But this still does not give us the whole story, for even with an organization facing a dynamic environment, one does not often see dramatic design changes on a year-to-year basis. This is because organizations often respond to changes in the environment and in their objectives by instituting changes in work flows rather than structure. Work flows are modified within the existing structure or hierarchy. This occurs for many reasons, most of which lie in the operations of the informal organization. Changes in structure, a *reorganization*, cause changes in authority and reporting relationships, which often cause changes in individual power, status, and prestige in the organization. New work groups are constituted that may be substantially different from old ones and that often require individuals to break old friendships and establish new ones. People often feel comfortable with the present structure, and management is often unsure about making wholesale changes in structure without knowing in advance whether these changes will necessarily enhance objective achievement. In addition, some structural changes would require an innovative response on the part of managers, many of whom are unable or unwilling to make such a response. Managers often feel comfortable with the traditional pyramidal structure and may be unable to conceptualize or cope with something substantially different. Indeed, DuPont, the nation's giant chemical concern, was reluctant to redesign its organization structure in the past because "DuPont managers had a sense of complacency stemming from a half-century of preeminent success until the energy debacle."[5] Environmental changes demanded an organization restructuring, which DuPont eventually accomplished in 1985.

On the other hand, work flows often can be modified within the existing structure. Duties and tasks can be added to or subtracted from organization positions and jobs. New positions can be added within a job category to handle the new work flow without substantially changing structure.

In our Celanese example above, the result of the activity-value analysis was not a change in structure; rather, the organization changed the volume and direction of its work flows. Some organizations restructure in response to a changing environment. For example, Mercury Marine cut out an entire management layer just below the divisional layer within its old organization structure. This layer was comprised of approximately 200 individuals who provided sales and marketing expertise to each division. After performing an analysis of Mercury's objectives and work flows, top management decided that these 200 positions should be consolidated at the corporate level. Unlike Celanese, Mercury felt obliged to radically alter its structure in response to environmental conditions that were similar to those facing Celanese.[6] Mercury officials dealt with these conditions by repositioning a layer of management personnel; at Celanese, unnecessary work was eliminated. From these situations, we can conclude that changing organization design is a consequence of the interaction of the constructs discussed above.

Personnel with different types of expertise or with ability to handle new work tasks can be substituted for existing personnel in certain positions without changing the structure. Temporary task forces or committees can be established to handle a work project without changing the organization's permanent structure. Informal work groups can develop to expedite the new work flow. All of these are alternatives to new structure and are commonly used by organizations to meet changing objectives.

Organization Design and Organization Development

Organization analysis involves a critical examination of the elements that make up an organization's structure and processes. Problems are identified, usually as a first step to designing a better organization. The process of analyzing the organization and developing ways of implementing elements of a new organization design—in structure or process—is called *organization development*.

The concepts of organization design and organization development are often confused. Organization development refers to the changes an organization makes so that it can better state and achieve its goals. It is a way to achieve organizational effectiveness and efficiency. It may involve a change in structure, but it also usually involves training and development programs for managers and other personnel. It can also include a comprehensive review of organization policy and work flows. So, as a part of an organization development program, an organization can, and often does, undertake a comprehensive study of its design to determine if the organization can be designed in a more effective and efficient manner.

Another relationship between organization design and organization development exists. Organizations should be designed so that the organization development process is facilitated and enhanced. This can come about in several ways. Periodically, the organization can create organization development task forces to assess organization effectiveness. Or, a permanent committee on organization development can be established with rotating members who represent various sections of the organization. The structure should facilitate feedback, particularly from clients or customers and operative employees. Such feedback should be provided to decision centers (as explained in Chapter 4) so appropriate evaluations of organization effectiveness and resultant adjustments of organization activity can be made. These methods are helpful in assuring continuing, periodic organization development activities.

Finally, we should point out that some organizations view *every* organization development problem as a structural problem. Those organizations facing problems believe that they can be resolved by internal restructuring, by moving the boxes around on the organization chart.

Thus, organizations following this philosophy ignore other aspects of the development process, for example, training and development, policy reviews, or stipulation of more appropriate objectives, and probably have contributed to the confusion over the meanings of organization design and organization development. We will return to the topic of organization development in Chapter 16.

Results of Effective Design

Why are we interested in the concept of organization design? Is it not less important than the competency and motivation of personnel, the financial and physical resources of the organization, and the market opportunities an organization faces? In other words, do these factors not outweigh the design issue in determining the effectiveness of organizations? Those that believe this believe that competent people will perform well regardless of the structure in which they work. While this may be so, we do not believe that they will perform as well as they could if the structure facilitated their effective performance. Effective organization structure should enhance the performance of any and all levels of resources. Although a ship with a square bow will eventually cross an ocean if enough horsepower is applied, that same level of horsepower will move the ship faster and more efficiently if the bow is V-shaped.

Thus, effective organization structure should enhance organization performance. What do we see in an organization that has effective structure? First, lines of authority and accountability can be clearly identified. Individuals know to whom and for what they are accountable, and they know clearly who is accountable to them and for what. Second, the organization differentiates its activities in such a way so that the activities are performed efficiently and effectively. Third, the organization is able to effectively and efficiently coordinate or integrate the various types of differentiated activity so that organizational objectives are achieved. Fourth, the communication process in the organization is efficiently constructed in that information needed by decision makers is provided accurately, efficiently, and rapidly. Fifth, the formal structure allows for deviations in behavior and, indeed, recognizes the necessity of informal or de facto structure. In fact, informal structure is viewed as a way to complement and enhance the operation of formal structure. Sixth, the structure allows for an appropriate amount of decentralization and complexity so that the organization can respond to the contingencies of the environment.

There are two other results of an effective organization design. Effective structures will help reduce or eliminate organization gaps and organization overlaps. An *organization gap* exists when an important task or function of the organization that is necessary for goal achievement goes undone. For example, if the goal of a construction organization is to construct a building, a gap would occur if no one put on a roof because no one was assigned to do it. An *organization overlap* exists when an important task or function is performed by two or more organizational units at the detriment of task accomplishment. In the building case, an overlap would occur if two units were assigned the same job of building the roof. An effective organization structure will help reduce the instances of gaps and overlaps by clearly specifying responsibility, accountability, and authority for various organizational tasks and functions.

THE ROLE OF DIFFERENTIATION

The very reason for the existence of organizations is that they can perform tasks more effectively and efficiently than individuals working alone. Through the process of differentiation organizations divide the overall task to be accomplished into subtasks and assign them to various units within the organization and to individuals within each unit. This process of differentiation enables the organization to divide a total complex task into more specialized tasks that can be performed more efficiently. Units and people can concentrate on a particular subset of the overall task and become proficient at it.

Nature and Process of Differentiation

Two basic types of differentiation occur in organizations.* *Horizontal differentiation* refers to the division of work to be done into tasks and subtasks. As we saw in our introductory case, Kenney recommended that the NAB be horizontally differentiated into two divisions, one for television and one for radio. This division is represented by the vertical lines in Figure 9.5. Each line represents a segmentation of one task or set of tasks from another. Some refer to this as *functionalization*.[7] However, since the differentiation may be done on some other basis than function (which is explained later in this chapter), we will call this horizontal differentiation.

Vertical differentiation refers to the division of work by level of authority. This is often referred to as the *scalar process*.[8] Here work is di-

---

*It should be noted that differentiation also occurs on the basis of status and power. Differentiation in status is best discussed in an organization behavior text. That based on power is discussed in Chapter 14.

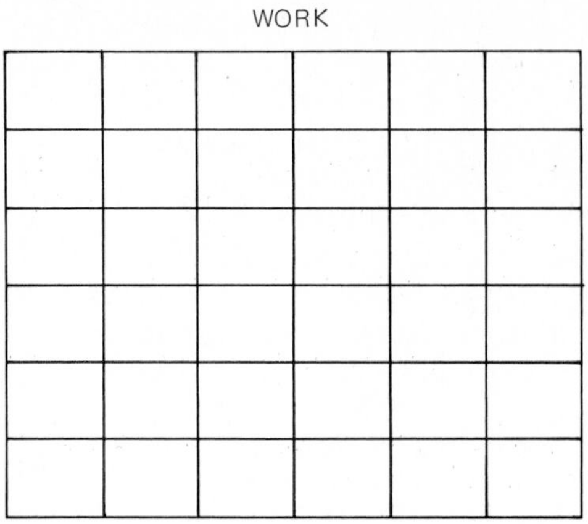

WORK

Vertical lines represent horizontal differentiation
breaking the work up into tasks.

Horizontal lines represent vertical differentiation
breaking the work up by level of authority.

FIGURE 9.5

Horizontal and Vertical Differentiation

vided on the basis of the authority each unit or person has over each other
unit or person in the organization. This is represented by the horizontal
lines in Figure 9.5

You will observe the vertical differentiation process in the end case to
this chapter where we discuss Standard Oil's (Indiana) Real Estate Department. You will see, for example, that under the position of "Manager, Real
Estate Development," there are two vertical layers of authority designed
to manage Standard's vast real estate projects. One might expect only one
layer would be necessary, but Standard officials believed that, in their situation, two vertical layers would be more effective.

The *level of complexity* of an organization is largely determined by
the degree of horizontal and vertical differentiation that exists.[9] Complexity is often related to organization size, but it need not be. Large organizations are often more differentiated than smaller ones, but a small
organization, such as a medical clinic, can have a high degree of vertical
and horizontal differentiation and be quite complex. From this, one
might conclude that size per se does not necessarily determine complexity. Of course, the typical large organization is generally more complex
than the typical small organization. But differentiation is not always a
function of size.

There are two basic ways in which the differentiation process can

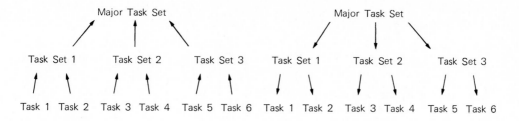

A. Bottom-Up Approach (Synthesis)   B. Top-Down Approach (Analysis)

FIGURE 9.6

Bottom-Up and Top-Down Approaches to Building Structure

occur in organizations. Building organizations from the bottom up focuses on combining specialized tasks into larger and larger sets of tasks. This "bottom-up" approach is called *synthesis* and is shown in Figure 9.6A. The "top-down" approach looks at the overall work of the organization at the top and splits this into increasingly more specialized tasks as one moves from the top to the bottom of the organization, as shown in Figure 9.6B. This type of approach is called *analysis*.

Both approaches are used in an organization. When organizations are growing, top-down analysis is often used because it is easy to visualize the sets of tasks to be done and then to break these sets down into specific tasks and subtasks. The bottom-up (synthesis) approach is often used during periods of retrenchment when organization growth has stabilized or even declined, because combining tasks often eliminates positions, jobs, or even whole units.

Differentiation and Decentralization

Decentralization is the passing down of authority to levels of the organization closer to where the task is performed. It is the sharing of authority with horizontal levels in the organization. Vertical differentiation splits up authority into horizontal levels in the organization so that each given level has more authority than the level below it. Therefore, the differentiation process is a way to achieve decentralization if, at the time of vertical differentiation, authority to direct organizational tasks is left with the level responsible for task completion.

Equating authority with task completion is similar to the concept that authority equals responsibility. This concept holds that the level of the organization responsible for completion of a set of tasks should have enough authority to make decisions to ensure task completion. At

DuPont, for example, the company redesigned its structure because managers did not have appropriate authority to make important decisions. At the corporate headquarters, several management layers were eliminated entirely; departments that had two vice presidents now have one; and plants with seven or eight levels of supervision now have only four. Individual DuPont plant managers now have the authority to make research and marketing decisions that, before 1985, would have required approval from a plethora of corporate management layers. For example, in 1984, John McAndrews, the vice president for the finishes and fabricated products group, needed *three* months and *thirty* signatures in order to get a report authorizing facilities for a new polymerization process.[10] One would have expected a corporate vice president to have fewer restrictions placed on him for making such a decision.

THE ROLE OF INTEGRATION

At the same time an organization differentiates itself, it must also integrate the activities, tasks, and sets of tasks performed into a coordinated whole. This is a prime responsibility of a person in a managerial position. The very functions of management—decision making and influence—imply coordinating and integrating a set of activities.

However, even though a manager must integrate the differentiated tasks of the organization, the organization structure itself can facilitate or hinder this integrating process. Lawrence and Lorsch studied the degree of differentiation and integration in three industries: plastics, foods, and containers.[11] They found that dynamic and complex environments require a good deal of differentiation on the organization's part, as we discussed previously. But they also found that, regardless of the stability of the environment, the requirement for integration is present.

Spans of Control

One way to approach the issue of integration is by examining the concept of span of control. The *span of control* refers to the number of immediate subordinate positions that a superior position controls or coordinates. In other words, a manager with seven immediate subordinates has a span of control of seven. The job of the manager in the superior position is to integrate the activities and tasks of those in immediate subordinate positions.

The old rule of thumb that used to be suggested for the best number of immediate subordinates was five to seven. It was thought that if a manager tried to integrate the activities of fewer than five people, he or she was being used inefficiently because there was enough time to handle more people. On the other hand, if a manager tried to coordinate more than seven people, it would be difficult to achieve integration of tasks with the larger number.

This thinking, however, has been replaced by a different approach to determining spans of control and the degree of integration that can be achieved. No rule-of-thumb number is specified as appropriate for all managers and positions. Rather, the approach taken now holds that the appropriate span depends on a number of factors. These factors include the following:

1. The ability and expertise of the manager in the integrating or controlling position
2. The ability and expertise of those in subordinate positions
3. The degree of interrelatedness of the tasks performed in the subordinate positions
4. The degree of geographic dispersion of those in the subordinate positions
5. The stability of the tasks performed by subordinates
6. The amount and type of interaction required by the superior position with higher-level positions.

In general, the more competent the manager and subordinates, and the less interrelated and more stable the tasks of the subordinates, the wider the span of control can be.* Also, the less the degree of geographic dispersion, all other things equal, the greater the span can be. Finally, the less often the manager in the superior position has to interact with superiors and others in the organization, especially on routine matters, the greater the span can be.

Closely related to the issues of span of control and degree of integration is the concept of delegation. *Delegation* is the way in which decentralization occurs in the organization. It is the process of passing authority and responsibility down through the organization. A high level of delegation results in a decentralized organization.

Flat versus Tall Organizations

Organizations with wide spans of control have been characterized as *flat organizations*. That is, there are few horizontal layers of management in

---

*However, there is some research to show that with highly professional subordinates, for example, engineers, accountants, and so on, superiors tend to have narrow spans of control because of the professional needs for frequent interaction with their subordinates and for quick decisions on recommendations and requests for materials. This, of course, assumes little delegation has occurred. Actually, more can occur in these cases. See Marshall Meyer, "Expertness and the Span of Control," *American Sociological Review* 33, no. 6 (December 1968): 944–951.

the organization, but each layer is composed of a relatively large number of managers reporting to each superior manager. As previously discussed, DuPont's organization structure has been significantly "flattened" due to the elimination of several management layers within its structure.

A *tall organization* has opposite characteristics: There are many horizontal layers of management relative to the number of people in each horizontal level, and each horizontal level has few managers reporting to each superior manager. Military units are excellent examples of tall structures, with many subunits designed for the effective control that is so essential in these types of organizations.

Figure 9.7 depicts these organizations. Thus, the span of control determines the degree of flatness or tallness of an organization.

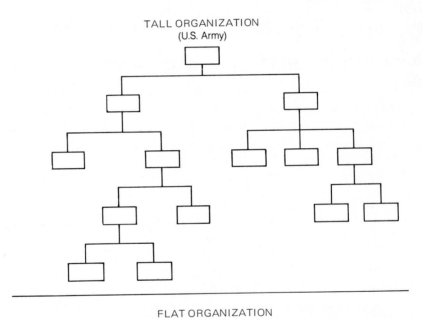

TALL ORGANIZATION
(U.S. Army)

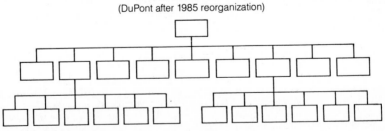

FLAT ORGANIZATION
(DuPont after 1985 reorganization)

FIGURE 9.7

Tall versus Flat Organization Structures

SUMMARY

All organizations need structure, both horizontal and vertical, in order to differentiate and integrate the work to be done. Structure provides reporting relationships, formal channels of communication, determination of task responsibility, and delegation of decision-making authority. The environment of the organization has a major influence on structure: In general, the more differentiated and dynamic the environment, the more differentiation and decentralization are required in the organization's structure.

We are concerned with the whole issue of structure because effective structure is required for effective organizational operations. Structure should facilitate effective performance. Characteristics of effective structure include clear lines of authority and accountability, effective differentiation and integration, and well-developed and clear communication and information-processing systems.

This chapter has reviewed the more important concepts involved with structure without actually indicating how these concepts are applied. In the next chapter, we review the application of these concepts as they result in various types of patterns of organization design.

QUESTIONS FOR REVIEW AND DISCUSSION

1. What is meant by the term *organization structure?* Do all organizations need structure? Explain.
2. What does an organization chart depict?
3. What bearing does the environment have on the issue of organization structure?
4. What is the relationship among organizational objectives, policy, work flows, and structure? Should structure be changed every time an organization changes its objectives or work flows? Why or why not?
5. What is meant by the term *reorganization?*
6. What is the relationship between organization design and organization development?
7. How do we know when an organization has been designed effectively?
8. Explain the concepts of differentiation and integration. How do these concepts relate to a manager's job?
9. Explain the "bottom-up" and "top-down" approaches to design.
10. What factors determine how wide a manager's span of control should be?
11. What is the difference between flat and tall organizations?

ENDNOTES

1. Henry Mintzberg, *The Structuring of Organizations* (Englewood Cliffs, N.J.: Prentice-Hall, 1979), 2.

2. Ibid., 66–67.

3. Michael McCloskey, "An Introduction to Organization Design," *California Management Review* 17 (Winter 1974): 13–20.

4. Maggie McComas, "Cutting Costs Without Killing the Business," *Fortune* (October 13, 1986), 70.

5. Alix M. Freedman, "DuPont Trims Costs, Bureaucracy to Bolster Competitive Position," *The Wall Street Journal* (September 25, 1985), 1.

6. McComas, "Cutting Costs Without Killing the Business," 76.

7. Keith Davis and John W. Newstrom, *Human Behavior at Work*, 7th ed. (New York: McGraw-Hill, 1985), 283.

8. Ibid.

9. Richard Hall, *Organizations: Structure and Process* (Englewood Cliffs, N.J.: Prentice-Hall, 1972), 143.

10. Freedman, "DuPont Trims Costs," 19.

11. P. R. Lawrence and J. W. Lorsch, *Organization and Environment* (Boston: Harvard Business School, Division of Research, 1967).

ANNOTATED BIBLIOGRAPHY

Blau, Peter M. "A Formal Theory of Differentiation in Organizations." *American Sociological Review* 35 (April 1970): 201–218.

Blau builds a theory of organizational differentiation on these basic empirical generalizations: (1) Increasing organization size generates differentiation at a decelerating rate, and (2) differentiation enlarges the administrative component of organizations required for coordination.

Blau, Peter M. "The Hierarchy of Authority in Organizations." *American Journal of Sociology* 73, no. 4 (January 1968): 453–467.

The study confirms previous implications that organizations requiring higher personnel qualifications are more decentralized. Also, it lends credence to the belief that such organizations have more superiors and narrower spans of control.

Child, John. "Predicting and Understanding Organization Structure." *Administrative Science Quarterly* 18 (June 1973): 168–185.

This work finds that organization size is the single most influencing factor in determining organization structure. Complexity is also an important factor, with differentiation the major component of complexity.

Davis, Stanley M. "Two Models of Organization: Unity of Command versus Balance of Power." *Sloan Management Review* (Fall 1974): 29–40.

The author describes how and why business management adheres to the pyramid model in principle while, in reality, it behaves according to a balance-of-power model. He discusses how a better correlation between administrative theory and practice would reduce the gap between management's preference for the unity of command and a business environment that requires interdependence and shared power.

Donaldson, L. "Organization Design and the Life Cycle of Products." *Journal of Management Studies* 22 (January 1985): 25–37.

This paper presents a model that elaborates the relationship between organization design and the product life cycle (PLC). Consideration is given to the structural implications of corporations that have multiple products at different phases in their life cycles. This involves a theoretical synthesis of work on PLC with that on degree of product diversification.

Drucker, Peter F. "New Templates for Today's Organizations." *Harvard Business Review* 52 (January–February 1974): 45–53.

New organization designs are appropriate for modern organizations. Traditional designs have difficulty handling the complexity of today's organizations. Specifically, modern organizations must act to develop a strategy for determining appropriate design.

Evers, Frederick T.; Bohlen, Joe M.; and Warren, Richard D. "The Relationships of Selected Size and Structure Indicators in Economic Organizations." *Administrative Science Quarterly* 21, no. 2 (June 1976): 326–342.

This study explores the feasibility of extending formal organization theory and structure to organizations of less than fifty people. It suggests that formal structures can be effective for groups over ten people, but in smaller groups the informal structure will dominate.

Freeland, James R., and Moore, Jeffrey H. "Implications of Resource Directive Allocation Models for Organizational Design." *Management Science* 23, no. 10 (June 1977): 1050–1059.

This article uses a linear programming model to develop mechanisms for resource allocation in decentralized organizations. It discusses the problem of degeneracy and arrives at a solution. The article is very specific and may be of use if this type of problem arises.

Greenwood, Royston, and Hinnings, C. R. "Centralization Revisited." *Administrative Science Quarterly* 21, no. 1 (March 1976): 151–155.

This is a research-based article prepared as an extension to the organizational structure studies made by Pugh. It addresses the idea that a correlation exists between delegation of decision making and more rule making.

Lorsch, Jay W. "Organization Design: A Situational Perspective." *Organizational Dynamics* 6, no. 2 (Autumn 1977): 2–14.

This is a very complete article on appropriate organization designs. It discusses in detail the problems of integration and differentiation. Lorsch stresses the necessity of having an organization design that is consistent with management's preferred method of leadership.

McCaskey, Michael B. "An Introduction to Organizational Design." *California Management Review* (Winter 1974): 13–20.

The author presents a synthesis of key concepts and findings from research on the design of organizations, the complex tradeoffs involved in designing the structures and processes of an organization examined from the contingency approach viewpoint. Empirical research provides guidelines for fitting together organization form, the people in the organization, and the task environment, and some important areas for further research are identified.

Montanari, John R., and Freedman, Sara M. "Organization Structure and Administrative Control: A Question of Dimensionality." *Journal of Management* 7, no. 1 (Spring 1981): 17–31.

A large, diverse sample of national firms was used to investigate the relationship between specialization, formalization, and centralization in the functional work unit. A finding was that the three variables compose a single dimension of organization structure. Another finding was that, within this dimension, specialization, formalization, and centralization were negatively related, thus indicating that these are alternative mechanisms for achieving administrative control.

Pitts, Robert A. "Toward a Contingency Theory of Multibusiness Organization Design." *Academy of Management Review* 5, no. 2 (April 1980): 203–210.

The author develops a contingency model of organization design for multibusiness enterprises—those competing simultaneously in several different business areas—and compares this model to the one underlying most single-business contingency research. Three important differences emerge: (1) the degree to which management influences contextual variables; (2) the nature of the causal relationship between contextual and organizational variables; and (3) the way in which these two kinds of variables are distributed.

Rice, George H., Jr., and Bishopricke, Dean W. *Conceptual Models of Organization.* New York: Appleton-Century-Crofts, 1971.

This excellent book develops the conceptual foundations of many models of the organization. Comparative advantages and disadvantages are readily apparent.

Tolbert, Pamela S. "Institutional Environments and Resource Dependence: Sources of Administrative Structure in Institutions of Higher Education." *Administrative Science Quarterly* 30, no. 1 (March 1985): 1–13.

Two theoretical perspectives are combined to explain the pattern of administrative offices in institutions of higher education. The first perspective, resource dependence, is used to show that the need to ensure a stable flow of resources from external sources partially determines administrative differentiation. The second perspective, institutionalization, emphasizes the common understandings of organization behavior and structure considered appropriate and nonproblematic, and suggests conditions under which dependency will and will not predict the number of administrative offices that manage funding relationships. The results of the analyses indicate that dependence on nontraditional sources of support is a strong predictor of administrative differentiation.

Urwick, Lyndall F. "V. A. Graicunas and the Span of Control." *Academy of Management Journal* (June 1974): 349–354.

In a personal recollection of the thoughts of Graicunas, Urwick clarifies the concept and application of the span of control. Additionally, he reaffirms the continuing importance of applying the principle properly.

Walton, Eric J. "The Comparison of Measures of Organization Structure." *Academy of Management Review* 6, no. 1 (January 1981): 155–160.

The author reports that the low convergence between survey and institutional measures of organization structure reported in three recent studies challenges assumptions about the interchangeability of these two approaches. In addition, the author suggests that current formulations of convergence appear to be too broad, and this inadequacy has contributed to the low convergence observed in the studies.

ADDITIONAL REFERENCES

Bacharach, Samuel B., and Aieken, Michael. "Structural and Process Constraints on Influence in Organizations: A Level-Specific Analysis." *Administrative Science Quarterly* 21, no. 4 (December 1976): 623–642.

Blau, Peter M. et al. *The Structure of Organizations.* New York: Basic Books, 1971.

Cummings, L. L., and Berger, Chris J. "Organizational Structure: How Does It Influence Attitudes and Performance?" *Organizational Dynamics* 5, no. 2 (Autumn 1976): 34–49.

Ford, Jeffrey D. "Departmental Context and Formal Structure as Constraints on Leader Behavior." *Academy of Management Journal* 24, no. 2 (June 1981): 274–288.

Ford, J. D., and Hegarty, W. Harvey. "Decision-Makers' Beliefs About the Causes and Effects of Structure: An Exploratory Study." *Academy of Management Journal* 27 (June 1984): 271–291.

Galbraith, Jay. "Organization Design: An Information Processing View." *Interface* 4 (May 1974): 28–36.

Galbraith, Jay, *Organization Design.* Reading, Mass.: Addison-Wesley, 1973.

Gresov, C. "Designing Organizations to Innovate and Implement: Using Two Dilemmas to Make a Solution." *Columbia Journal of World Business* 19 (Winter 1984): 63–67.

Grinyer, Peter H., and Yasai-Ardekani, Massoud. "Strategy, Structure, Size, and Bureaucracy." *Academy of Management Journal* 24, no. 3 (September 1981): 471–486.

Khandwalla, Philip. "Visible and Effective Organizational Designs of Firms." *Academy of Management Journal* 16 (September 1973): 481–495.

Kimberly, John R. "Organizational Size and the Structuralist Perspective: A Review, Critique, and Proposal." *Administrative Science Quarterly* 21, no. 4 (December 1976): 571–597.

Kover, Arthur J. "Reorganization in an Advertising Agency: A Case Study of a Decrease in Integration." *Human Organization* 22, no. 4 (Winter 1962–1963): 252–259.

Magusen, Karl O., ed. *Organizational Design, Development and Behavior: A Situational View.* Glenview, Ill.: Scott, Foresman, 1977.

Mahler, Walter R. *Structure, Power, and Results: How to Organize Your Company for Optimum Performance.* Homewood, Ill.: Dow Jones-Irwin, 1975.

Melcher, Arlyn J. *Structure and Process of Organizations: A Systems Approach.* Englewood Cliffs, N.J.: Prentice-Hall, 1976.

Pearce, John A., II, and David, Fred R. "A Social Network Approach to Organizational Design-Performance." *Academy of Management Review* 8, no. 3 (July 1983): 436–444.

Pugh, D. S.; Hickson, J. D.; and Hinings, C. R. "An Empirical Taxonomy of Structures of Work Organizations." *Administrative Science Quarterly* 14, no. 1 (March 1969): 115–125.

Pugh, D. S.; Hickson, J. D.; Hinings, C. R.; and Turner, C. "Dimensions of Organization Structure." *Administrative Science Quarterly* 13, no. 1 (June 1968): 65–105.

Telem, M. "The Process of Organizational Structure." *Journal of Management Studies* 22 (January 1985): 38–52.

```
┌─────────────────────────────────────┐
│                                       │
│   C      A      S      E              │
│                                       │
└─────────────────────────────────────┘
```

Oil and Land

Standard Oil Company (Indiana) is one of the nation's largest corporations, and among its myriad functions are the acquisition and management of significant real estate holdings. In 1982, the corporation designed a specific real estate organization structure to manage all the real estate matters in which Standard was involved.

Before discussing Standard's real estate structure and organization chart, it is first necessary to discuss the history of this function within the Standard Oil organization. Twenty years ago, real estate matters were handled by a subsidiary, Amoco, whose real estate department was responsible primarily for the acquisition of service station sites. Other Standard subsidiaries, in turn, handled their own real estate matters through their district managers, plant managers, or administrative supervisors.

However, as Standard grew in size and sophistication, the company adapted to its new environment. Amoco's real estate department was transferred to the parent company, Standard. Additional staff were hired and the department's responsibilities were significantly increased. Shortly thereafter, Standard realized that real estate development per se could become a profitable venture. To this end, Standard then formed a separate corporation called Amoco Realty Company. From 1972 through 1982, Amoco Realty was involved in the acquisition and development of numerous large projects such as condominium developments and office parks.

In 1982, a Standard post-audit indicated that external real estate development would not remain a significant profit center according to the company's long-range investment strategy. Therefore, corporate decision makers decided that Amoco Realty should cease its efforts in looking for new projects unrelated to Standard's main business—energy acquisition, manufacturing, and distribution. Amoco Realty was absorbed into the parent corporation as a separate department, with the primary objective of developing real estate for use in the corporation's main business activities. New projects illustrating the real estate department's function include the Amoco Building in Houston and the Amoco Minerals Headquarters in Denver.

The current structure of the Standard real estate structure is depicted in Figure 9.8. Highlighting the real estate department's "closer-to-home" mission is the fact that the head of the department is the corporate secretary, who reports directly to the chairman of the board of Standard Oil Company (Indiana). Moving from left to right under the corporate secretary is the manager for real estate development. Reporting to this person are various project managers from throughout the country who are directly responsible for on-site projects. In turn, each project manager has a project coordinator under him or her.

Moving across the chart, Standard has several managers for real estate services, each with certain subsidiary companies assigned to his or her responsibility. Duties of these managers involve the selection and acquisition of sites for offices, manufacturing, and warehousing facilities (excluding gas, oil, and minerals).

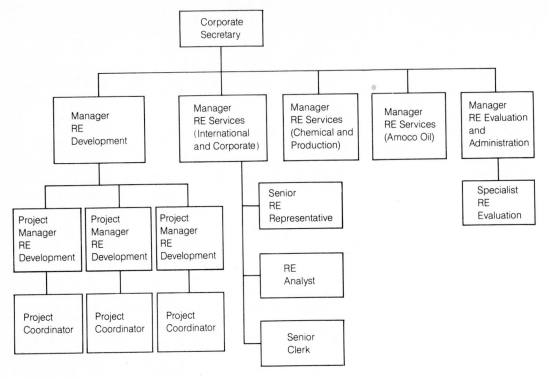

FIGURE 9.8

Standard Oil Company (Indiana) Real Estate Department Organization Structure

Source: James E. Healey, "The Structure of Standard's Real Estate Department," *Industrial Development* 153, no. 6 (November/December 1984): 35–37.

Note that the manager for international and corporate real estate services is reported to directly by a senior real estate representative, a real estate analyst, and a senior clerk. Amoco Oil has a separate manager of real estate services because this subsidiary is, in itself, a mature organization with tens of thousands of parcels of land that need to be separately managed. The last position to the right of the line is the manager of real estate evaluation and administration, who acts as the department's chief economist. This manager and the real estate evaluation specialist under him or her are responsible for completing all of the economic evaluations involved with Standard's real estate projects. This individual is also responsible for ensuring that all Standard real estate projects are in tune with current corporate financial standards against which all investments are measured.

In conclusion, as Standard Oil's mission has changed throughout the years, so has its structure for the management of real estate operations. Organization design and subsequent organization struc- tures mirror the corporation's evolution over time.

QUESTIONS FOR DISCUSSION

1. When designing a formal organization, such as at Standard Oil, how much emphasis should be placed on the informal structure? Why?
2. How would you characterize the design of Standard's real estate department? Evaluate its strengths and weaknesses.
3. Do you think Standard Oil's macro environment affected the design of the reorganization? If so, how? If not, why not?
4. Present what you would consider a rational, objective justification for the new design.
5. What part did differentiation play in the reorganized structure?

10

Patterns of Organization Design

KEY CONCEPTS

Functional design
Product design
Geographic design
Market-based design
Process design
Equipment-based design
Mechanistic or bureaucratic structure
Organic or adaptive structure
Line structure
Line-and-staff structure
Functionalized structure
Project matrix structure
Product matrix structure
Brand manager
Program matrix structure
Linking-pin structure
Liaison position
Strategic business unit (SBU)
Ad-hocracy
Joint venture arrangement
Laissez-faire structure
Industrial democracy

The Perfect Ten

In September 1984, Merrill Lynch CEO Bill Schreyer announced his plans for a complete reorganization of this huge investment firm. The basic purpose of this reorganization, as explained by Schreyer, was to make Merrill Lynch closer to its customers by deemphasizing its sales orientation and concentrating on the marketing function. "The emphasis on the future must be on what the customer needs and demands, not on what a financial services company wishes to offer," said the Merrill Lynch boss. He further added, "We want to become investment-services driven. Right now I'd rank us a five in marketing. We want to be ten. We have a long way to go."

To refocus his organization's efforts on the marketing function, Schreyer plans to reorganize Merrill Lynch into three main sectors: consumer markets, capital markets, and real estate and insurance. (Previously, these three areas were called individual services, capital markets, and real estate and insurance.) These three sectors will be subdivided into fifteen subgroups, each aimed at a specific customer group. Each of these fifteen subgroups will have individual profit-and-loss responsibility. Merrill Lynch also plans to reorganize its brokers-salespeople around customer types, the rationale being that individual salespeople won't have to know all Merrill Lynch products and services nor will they need a huge support staff for their operations.

At the time of the reorganization, Merrill Lynch also attempted to better control internal operating costs. This included employee layoffs, raising commission fees, and consolidating locations, particularly within

Source: Beth McGoldrich, "Bill Schreyer: No More Mr. Nice Guy," *Institutional Investor* (September 1984), 144–149.

New York City. Some analysts predicted that Merrill Lynch would have to reduce the number of "products" it manufactures—there were 200 of them in 1984—in order to avoid exorbitant overhead costs associated with new consumer-oriented product development and support.

Merrill Lynch's reorganization and cost-cutting efforts were criticized by some. Some analysts believed that the idea of pushing profit responsibility down to operating levels would be divisive. "Each subdivision," said analyst Perrin Long, "will be concerned about its own profitability. Two subgroups might not be inclined to work together on a project because they would have to charge each other for their help." As a result, the notion of teamwork would suffer within the entire organization. Concomitant with this criticism was the fact that the Merrill Lynch organization had always been prone to empire building. By setting up fifteen new "empires," management encouraged more of it, along with possible duplications in staff.

CEO Schreyer, however, planned to make the Merrill Lynch reorganization work and have subordinates accept it. Throughout the summer of 1984, he held a series of weekly breakfast meetings with key managers, and during the fall he toured Merrill Lynch offices in key cities, selling his gospel of reorganization.

Because Schreyer was attempting to redesign the Merrill Lynch organizational structure so that the organization would better fit the consumer/client component of the macro environment, he focused his efforts on redesigning the organization on the basis of the type of customer served. However, Schreyer also faced the dilemma of instituting overall integration within the organization while simultaneously differentiating his subunits in order to increase their proficiency. These concepts, along with others, form the basis for the current chapter, in which we explore the different devices available to organizations as they design themselves to achieve their mission.

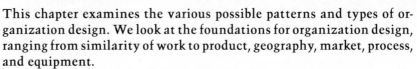

CHAPTER PLAN

This chapter examines the various possible patterns and types of organization design. We look at the foundations for organization design, ranging from similarity of work to product, geography, market, process, and equipment.

All designs can be classified into one of two basic contexts: bureaucratic or organic-adaptive. We explain each context and its respective types of design. By examining the types and characteristics of effective design, a more rational choice can be made when decisions about a particular design pattern become necessary.

In Chapter 9 we described the role of differentiation and integration in organization design. Special emphasis was placed on structure as a key element in the design process. In this chapter, we examine specific forms of organizations. The more common forms are emphasized primarily, but we also briefly discuss some of the newer forms that have been adopted.

In our systems approach to organizations, organization design is part of the transformation process in the input-output analysis. Design facilitates the use of inputs to produce outputs. In other words, effective design facilitates the efficient use of resources to achieve output goals.

An organization faces a basic dilemma with regard to design. The very reason an organization exists is because people working together can accomplish more than people working individually. This synergistic effect is achieved by providing for specialization (differentiation) so that people become proficient in a particular area. But the more differentiated the organization, the more difficult it becomes to integrate the various activities. Thus the dilemma: how to achieve differentiation in order to increase proficiency while at the same time providing means to coordinate (integrate) these differentiated activities.

In this chapter, we begin by examining two primary aspects of organization design. First are the bases that are often used for designing organizations. These are the foundations on which organizations differentiate and classify organization tasks. Second are the types of designs that organizations take. The types refer to the ways in which the differentiation is integrated in the organization.

BASES FOR ORGANIZATION DESIGN

Organizations can be differentiated on at least the following six foundations or bases: similarity of work or function, product, geography, market, process or interface, or equipment. In the first part of this section, we simply describe each type. In the second part, we provide some guidelines for managers to follow in selecting an appropriate type(s).

SIMILARITY OF WORK OR FUNCTION. This very common form of differentiation results in the classification of work done by the organization into the primary functional components that need to be carried out for the organization to operate. Such functions as production, marketing, finance, accounting, and personnel often serve as broad categories, as shown in Figure 10.1. Each function is differentiated into subfunctions or tasks that need to be carried out in order for the total function to be achieved, as indicated for the production function in this figure. For example, before its reorganization to a strategic business unit base in 1985, Eastman Kodak Company's photographic division, which accounts for 80 percent of that organization's $10.6 billion in annual sales, was differentiated according to its major functions such as marketing, production, research and development, and so on.[1]

PRODUCT. Differentiation based on product classifies tasks and positions on the basis of the product that is produced. An example of this basis for differentiation is shown in Figure 10.2. General Motors has long been differentiated on the basis of its products: Chevrolet, Pontiac, Oldsmobile,

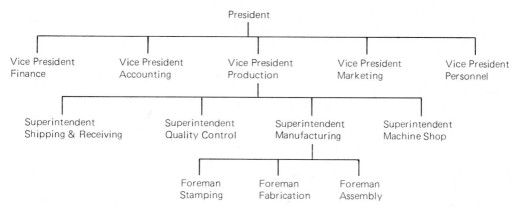

FIGURE 10.1

Differentiation on the Basis of Similarity of Work or Function

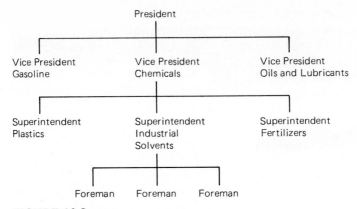

FIGURE 10.2

Differentiation on the Basis of Product

Buick, Cadillac, and GMC. Even its reorganization in 1984 was based on product—big cars and small cars. Likewise, DuPont Company, one of the world's largest chemical manufacturers, is also differentiated according to the types of products it makes—plastics, fibers, agricultural chemicals, and so on.

GEOGRAPHY. The basis of this differentiation is the actual physical location of the work that is done. This type of differentiation is most often found within the sales and marketing function of the organization, as indicated in Figure 10.3. Large real estate development organizations, such

FIGURE 10.3

Differentiation on the Basis of Geography

as Lincoln Property Company (discussed in Chapter 6), are differentiated on the basis of geographic region. Lincoln's organization structure is based on a system of regional partnerships, with each partner being responsible for projects in a specific geographic region of the United States.

MARKET. The fourth basis for differentiation is the customer served or the market for the product or service produced. This differentiation, like geography, is often used by the marketing or sales operation of an organization, as depicted in Figure 10.4. Hewlett-Packard reorganized in 1984 from a product-based organization structure to a market-based one. Its computer and instruments division has been subdivided into two groups; one concentrates on business customers and the other focuses on serving scientific and manufacturing customers. Likewise, as you read in our introductory case, Merrill Lynch reorganized to a market-based structure and is focusing its efforts on serving three large market segments: consumer markets, capital markets, and the real estate and insurance market.

PROCESS OR INTERFACE. A fifth type of differentiation can be done on the basis of the process that is performed and the interface of this process with other processes. This is a commonly used basis in the manufacturing or production area of a company, as shown in Figure 10.5. For example, at AMC's Jeep plant in Toledo, a variety of Jeep products, such as sports vehicles, pickup trucks, and wagons are rolled out on different assembly lines. This basis for organization design is reflected in the physical layout of the AMC plant, which is a maze of sixty-four interconnected buildings.

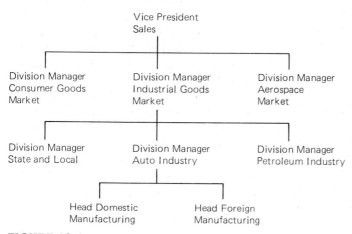

FIGURE 10.4
Differentiation by Market

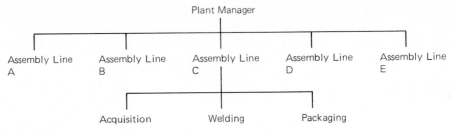

FIGURE 10.5

Differentiation on the Basis of Process or Interface

EQUIPMENT. The final type of differentiation we will discuss here is that based on the equipment used or worked on in a given process. This method of differentiation is often tied to a particular job skill or craft, as shown in Figure 10.6. We see this basis for organization design with the introduction of the computer that has caused the establishment of MIS departments in most large organizations. Also, hospitals have radiology departments that exist because of the X-ray machines they use. Even professional sports teams, particularly those within the National Football League, have equipment managers.

Most of these various bases for differentiation are often found in a single organization, especially if it is a large organization with a multiproduct line. Each level of the organization can be differentiated on the basis of a different foundation. One vertical slice of the organization might be organized on the basis of geography while another vertical slice, such as production, might be differentiated on the basis of function and process. Figure 10.7 shows how some of these bases could be used by a large corporation.

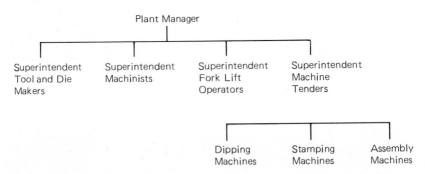

FIGURE 10.6

Differentiation by Equipment

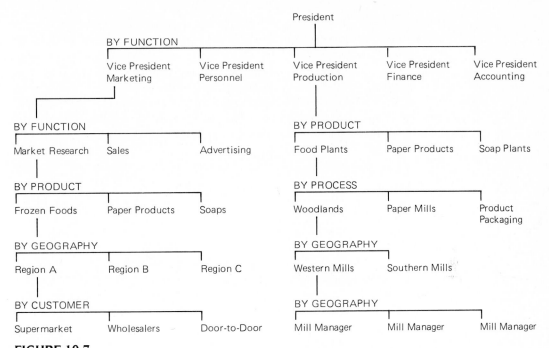

FIGURE 10.7

Differentiation on the Bases of Function, Product, Process, Geography, and Customer

Guidelines for Determining Bases

Because so many bases are used by organizations, guidelines for choosing which one is most appropriate for an organization at a particular time need to be followed. Koontz and O'Donnell provide some guidelines for determining an appropriate basis for differentiating functions.[2]

FUNCTION. Specializing on the basis of function reflects and provides visibility, power, and prestige of the major functions an organization must carry out. It also follows the principle of occupational specialization and simplifies training. Its disadvantages are that it tends to place responsibility for profit and economic efficiency at the top, it can cause overspecialization and a narrow viewpoint of key personnel, which can reduce coordination among functions and cause a lack of a systems view of the organization, and it limits the development of general managers.

In spite of these objections, functionalization has been used for many years by organizations and is still used frequently today, although it is often combined with other bases. It is best suited for use by a small- to medium-sized company where primary responsibility for task integration and profitability rests at the top with the general manager or president of the organization.

Differentiation on the basis of function is still widely used within small departments of large organizations. For example, the employee relations department within Honeywell Corporation's defense systems division is differentiated according to the various subfunctions within the purview of employee relations. These subfunctions include human resources development, safety and workers' compensation, compensation systems, community relations, and so on.

PRODUCT. In large, multiproduct organizations, differentiation by product has become increasingly more common. Its advantages are that it places attention and effort on product lines, which can improve coordination of functional activities needed for each product. It also is a way of placing responsibility for profit and economic efficiency at the divisional level, and it furnishes many training opportunities for general managers.

However, differentiation by product has its disadvantages. First, it requires more persons with general-manager abilities within the organization so that the functions for each product area can be coordinated effectively. It also makes it difficult to achieve functional coordination of the total organizational effort at the top since functional operations are usually decentralized within each product line. This can present top management with various control and interface problems.

We can see how problems associated with product differentiation can become dysfunctional for the organization by examining General Motors's operations in the early and mid-1980s. Because of a lack of coordination among the different product divisions, in addition to loose controls at the top-management level in the corporate headquarters, GM suffered greatly in the marketplace as customers became disenchanted and confused by the various GM products. Buicks looked like Cadillacs, which looked like Oldsmobiles; Chevrolets and Pontiacs became indistinguishable. Chrysler took advantage of this situation with its television advertisements pointing out the uniqueness of Chrysler products in comparison to GM's.

However, in a large, multiproduct company, differentiation on the basis of product at some level in the organization is almost a necessity. In the absence of product differentiation for such a company, the manager's job can become extremely complex in coordinating functions for a wide variety of organizational products. Product organization allows decentralization of functions based on product. It is almost as if the organization sets up mini-companies on the basis of each product so that organizational functions can be coordinated by product rather than across all products.

GEOGRAPHY. In organizations that are physically dispersed in their operations, specialization by location has become a popular form of differentiation. As we indicated earlier, this is often used for sales operations since the sale of an organization's products and services usually tends to be more widely dispersed geographically than the manufacture of its products. The idea behind this type of differentiation is that all activities in a given area or territory should be grouped and assigned to a manager.

Geographic differentiation has many of the same advantages and disadvantages as differentiation on the basis of product. It is a way to decentralize and place responsibility for economic efficiency at lower levels, and it is a good way to provide training for general managers. It also improves coordination of organization activities in a region. Finally, it is a way to emphasize local markets and problems and to improve communication with local interest groups and customers. However, it also requires more persons with general-manager abilities, and it can increase the problem of top-management coordination and control of organization functions across all organization regions.

The Trammell Crow Company, a Texas-based real estate giant, was forced to modify its geography-based structure in 1986 because of the reasons cited above. This far-flung real estate empire experienced phenomenal growth in the 1970s and 1980s, with the result that widely separated regional partners and managers, heretofore granted autonomy in their operations, began to compete with each other. In 1984, *three* Trammell Crow companies were involved in the construction of an Atlanta hotel. In other instances, different Trammell Crow units competed with each other for top graduates from schools such as Harvard and Stanford. Therefore, corporate executives decided to consolidate many commercial and residential developments under the authority of the corporate headquarters, establish a college recruiting department at the corporate level, and otherwise pull in the reins of its regional partners and managers.[3]

For widely dispersed organizations that need to be tuned to the needs of a particular locality, differentiation on the basis of geography is appropriate. It provides a way to decentralize operations and yet to achieve a degree of coordination at the local levels. It can be an effective means by which an organization can create boundary-spanning unit operations that key in on the differences in local markets.

MARKET. Differentiation by market also allows an organization to key in on the needs of a particular set of customers or clients.[4] It differs from simple product or geographic differentiation because the market for a product may be in several different regions and may include more than just one product. By keying in on this market, the organization creates products or services needed by the market and organizes itself to see that the market receives the product or service. This is another effective means of building boundary-spanning units that keep the organization in tune with a significant aspect of the task environment.

Hewlett-Packard reorganized on the basis of market precisely to keep in tune with its environment. Computers and related instruments were previously separate operations at H-P; however, H-P management discovered that industrial customers were increasingly buying computers linked with instruments for testing and control purposes. By reorganizing on the basis of market, computer and instrument operations were merged, thus allowing the organization to better serve and react to conditions in the industrial market.

Some disadvantages of specializing by market include the fragmentation that could result if the organization faces a very heterogeneous, changing market for its product. New structure might have to be created every time the market changes. (A heterogeneous, relatively stable customer group, however, is conducive to specialization by market because it allows the organization to effectively segment the market for its products.) Another problem might be the inability of the organization to provide products or services for all potential client groups. Specializing by market or potential market might cause an organization to try to serve all markets when that may not be the organization's mission or when the organization may not have the resources to do so effectively.

Although it may be used in other areas, organization by market is most often done in the sales and marketing function of the organization. In general, if an organizational unit's function is to provide a full range of services to a client, it may find it beneficial to organize by market segment. Office business-machine service representatives are often assigned to accounts where their job is to provide full servicing (sales, repair, and maintenance) to these accounts. AT&T experimented with assigning to phone installer-repairers a set of customers for service on the basis of customer product or service need rather than on the basis of geography or function. Other organizations, such as state welfare agencies, are experimenting with this approach by assigning a welfare case to a case manager whose job it is to ensure that the case receives the right types of services from the state's welfare service offerings.

PROCESS OR INTERFACE. The advantage of organizing by process or interface is that it allows for better coordination in bringing together a set of related tasks that need to be completed simultaneously or sequentially. An automobile assembly line is an example of process differentiation since the various tasks involved in scheduling, fabrication, logistics, assembly, and packaging are integrated and managed so as to achieve a smooth and efficient flow of materials through the line. People and materials are brought together in appropriate amounts at the appropriate times so that the process components interface properly in order to assemble the automobiles efficiently. A disadvantage of this type of differentiation arises when the process is extremely complex, with so many varied functions that it is difficult for one manager to coordinate all the tasks involved.

Technology plays a role here. At AMC's Toledo Jeep plant, operations are very complex, perhaps needlessly so. This is because AMC lacks automated equipment (among other reasons); and thus, in the opinion of many analysts, operations in Toledo are very inefficient. On the other hand, the automated Honda assembly plant in nearby Marysville, Ohio, although also differentiated on the basis of process, is a much more efficient and better-integrated operation because it uses high technology to facilitate its assembly-line production.

EQUIPMENT. Differentiation by equipment grew out of the process basis of differentiation and is similar to it. However, instead of differentiating on the basis of the process, the differentiation occurs on the basis of the machines that are used in the process. This allows some decentralization of the process based on the machines that are used. It also allows units and positions in the organization to be specialized by machine, which encourages those units to become extremely proficient in running that machine.

We see this most often in the electronic-data-processing (EDP) department in organizations. Here, because of the complexity of the machines used and the necessity to interface machine use with other organizational functions (e.g., billing, accounting, sales, personnel records, production records, research), people are often assigned to the data-processing machines. The disadvantage here (as anyone knows who does not have computer expertise and who has conversed with a computer specialist) is that those units specialized by machine may have trouble communicating with individuals in the organization who do not have expertise with the machine or process involved. Specialists tend to develop their own jargon that has meaning to other individuals in their specialty but may not to those outside the specialty. This can be a real problem for people in EDP because they are a service unit within the organization, processing information for other units. This interface role requires that they be able to serve as a communication link between EDP and the other units.

This is why many organizations, such as Rayovac Corporation in Wisconsin, have an oversight board comprised of representatives from all horizontal layers in the organization. The function of such oversight boards is to assure that the EDP (MIS) department's operations are synchronized with the total organization's work and objectives.

CONCLUSION. These guidelines developed by Koontz and O'Donnell do not provide us with enough information to specify the most appropriate bases for structure in each and every case. But, they do give us an appreciation for some of the advantages and disadvantages in using each basis.

Bases for differentiation are only part of the story. We also need to examine the way in which organizations integrate these differentiations. We label these as types of designs.

TYPES OF ORGANIZATION DESIGN

How does an organization integrate or coordinate the diverse specialties within it? What types of integrative structure are used to pull differentiated tasks together? We will look at five basic types of structure: line, line-and-staff, functionalized, matrix, and linking-pin. Each of these structures can be practiced in either one or two organization design contexts: mechanistic or bureaucratic, or organic/adaptive. It is possible (likely in large organizations) to find one department or subunit established in the mechanistic mode (the physical plant) and another in the organic/adaptive mode (research). Therefore, it is important to keep the unit of analysis in mind when discussing these concepts. We will discuss these contexts prior to examining each of the five integrative structures.

Mechanistic or Bureaucratic Context

As we saw in Chapter 1, Max Weber is perhaps the best-known writer on bureaucratic organizations, and his book *The Theory of Social and Economic Organization* is the classic text on bureaucracies.[5] Basically, Weber developed the concept of a bureaucracy as a way to improve the operation of organizations. Today we often use the term *bureaucracy* in a disparaging way; but in actuality it is a system of organization based on rational organizational principles. At the time Weber wrote his book, organizations were often structured and managed on the basis of haphazard hunches or hip-pocket reactions of managers. Favoritism and managerial biases characterized the way in which organizations were structured and operated. Weber believed this system should be replaced by a rational one based on logical analysis and economic efficiency. He saw bureaucracy as an important improvement in structuring organizations.

Weber's ideal type of bureaucracy holds the following:

1. Clear and explicit statement of organizational purpose and goals
2. Clearly specified organizational rules, procedures, and regulations derived from the goals based on the most rational procedure for attaining goals

3. Division of tasks among members of the organization so that each member has a limited sphere of activity that is matched to his or her own competency
4. A pyramid structure with each level of management having more authority than the level below it—thus, authority tends to be centralized at the top
5. Decision making based on officially established rules and criteria that are attached to a position
6. Detailed rules and procedures attached to each position so that, regardless of the person in the position, the same tasks and activities will be performed by the incumbent
7. Selection for organizational membership based on the person's technical competence[6]

In stable, relatively homogeneous environments these characteristics are probably appropriate for an organization, as we discussed in Chapter 4. In fact, in the Burns and Stalker study that examined twenty manufacturing firms in England and Scotland, it was found that a number of organizations facing a stable environment used this structure.[7] They labeled this a *mechanistic* structure in that the organizations had defined the decision-authority relationships and rules to the point of almost mechanizing them.

Are these concepts of bureaucracy or mechanistic organizations actually being practiced in real organizations? A number of studies by Pugh and his colleagues investigated this question in a series of studies at the University of Aston in England.[8] (These have come to be known as the "Aston" studies.) Forty-six organizations in a variety of industries, including government and education, were studied. Three bureaucratic or mechanistic characteristics were studied: specialization, standardization, and formalization. (Chapter 11 contains material that clarifies and further explains these concepts.) The researchers found these three characteristics to be highly correlated. They concluded that organizations do tend to structure or formalize activities.

Later replications tended to confirm these earlier findings. However, one study found that decision-making authority was not always centralized in these organizations.[9] Pugh and his co-workers concluded that there may, in fact, exist different bureaucratic structures, one where decision power is centralized and one where it is not.

Bureaucracy can be criticized on several grounds. Certainly it is not appropriate for organizations facing dynamic, heterogeneous environments (as we have discussed) since it tends to reflect a closed-system approach. It also largely ignores the operation of the informal or de facto organization by assuming that interpersonal relationships can be maintained on a formalized, impersonal basis and that socioemotional elements do not intrude into organization operations.[10] It also holds that there is one best way to achieve a goal, thus largely ignoring the concept of equifinality discussed in Chapter 2. Finally, it tends to be slow to change and tends to encourage rigid adherence to policy and rules in the face of new environmental requirements. These are the limitations that subject bureaucracy to so much criticism.[11]

Organic/Adaptive Context

The organic or adaptive context tends to have characteristics that are the opposite of the mechanistic or bureaucratic context. In overcoming the shortcomings of bureaucracy, it is a more appropriate means for integrating organizational tasks for those organizations facing a dynamic environment. Burns and Stalker found, for example, that:

> organic systems are adapted to unstable conditions, when problems and requirements for action arise which cannot be broken down and distributed among specialist roles within a clearly defined hierarchy. Individuals have to perform their special tasks in the light of their knowledge of the tasks of the firm as a whole.[12]

Even though the organic/adaptive structure overcomes many of the limitations of the mechanistic structure, it is not necessarily true that the organic/adaptive is the better structure. As Burns and Stalker point out, and as we pointed out in Chapter 4, it depends on the environment. Organizations facing a shifting, heterogeneous environment will find the organic/adaptive structure more effective, but organizations facing a stable, homogeneous environment will find the mechanistic structure suitable.

We stress throughout this text that, for the most part, today's organizations face a shifting, heterogeneous environment. Therefore, as was evident in our introductory case, organizations, such as Merrill Lynch, *must* develop organic/adaptive structures in order to successfully interact with the environment.

It is possible that various units and subunits within an organization can operate on either an organic/adaptive or a mechanistic basis. All units within an organization need not be either entirely mechanistic or organic/adaptive. A mix within an organization is possible, depending on the environment faced. If a particular subunit (e.g., the recruitment division of a personnel department) faces a dynamic environment, it should be structured as an organic/adaptive unit even though the total organization is not so structured.

Organizational Forms

Whether an organization creates a mechanistic or an organic context, there are five basic forms the organization can take to integrate differentiated activities. Each of these forms can be practiced in either the mechanistic or organic context. However, there is a tendency for the first three forms—line, line-staff, and functionalized—to be more mechanistic than the latter two of matrix and linking-pin.

LINE STRUCTURE. There are units in any organization that perform tasks that are directly involved in the production or distribution of primary utility. This primary operative work consists of the tasks, sets of tasks, and activities that are "directly concerned with the production or distribution of the utility required to satisfy the basic consumer/client groups of the organization."[13] Manufacturing, selling, and distributing are all examples of tasks directly concerned with the production or distribution of primary utility.

An organization can structure itself around the tasks involved in producing or distributing the primary utility it creates. This is called *line structure*. It is a relatively simple type of structure and tends to emphasize two basic functions of the organization, manufacturing and marketing, as seen in Figure 10.8. It has a serious disadvantage, though, in that many of the functions involved in the production of secondary utility have to be done by line managers. This requires that line managers be generalists capable of handling such traditional supportive functions as personnel, accounting, billing, and quality control—all supportive or staff functions.

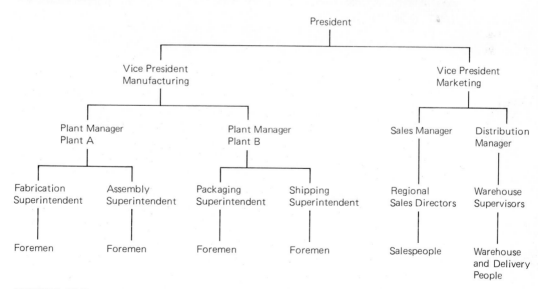

FIGURE 10.8

Line Organization Structure

Line structure serves as an integrating structure by allowing organization work to be grouped and coordinated around the two basic forms of primary operating work, manufacture and distribution of primary utility. Those activities that are involved in either of these two basic functions are grouped around each function. In this manner, line structure is integrative.

Line organization structure is often found in smaller organizations where a manager does not need to spend as much time on each of these staff activities and where there would be difficulty financially supporting a full-time organization unit to perform each staff activity. Managers who can efficiently handle primary and secondary operative work in a large organization are probably in short supply, and the complexity of the coordination required of both primary and secondary work would make it extremely difficult to accomplish, even by a highly skilled manager.

LINE-AND-STAFF STRUCTURE. As organizations grow, they usually add supportive staff to handle the secondary operative work involved in the production of secondary utility. This usually results in a structure known as *line-and-staff structure.* It is commonly found in larger organizations (see Figure 10.9). Here, because of the complexity of coordinating primary and secondary work and because the organization can achieve economies of scale in the production of primary utility, separate staff units are created. These staff units handle personnel, accounting, finance, billing, research, quality control, and other functions previously performed by line managers. The organization can afford to create separate units for these functions because of its size and the resultant economies of scale achieved; the actual cost of overhead per unit of products produced is relatively low.

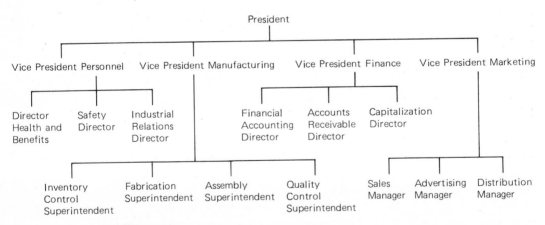

FIGURE 10.9

Line-and-Staff Structure

The staff components exist to facilitate the operations of line managers. They are properly viewed as service units in the organization that exist to serve the line managers engaged in the production or distribution of primary utility. For example, Honeywell Corporation's employee relations department within the defense systems division is designed to handle personnel work associated with that division's line operations. In short, it is a service unit. Therefore, the staff serves in a support role in that they advise the line management on activities, but they do not usually have command authority over primary operative work. This distinction between line and staff authority has blurred in recent years because staff operations of large organizations have grown to be very large and have acquired high levels of technical or specialized expertise. Thus, staff members often feel they can influence primary operative work. While the potential for this line-versus-staff conflict exists, it does not occur in all cases. Much depends on the formal authority and accountability assigned to line and staff managers by the organization and on the personalities of those involved.[14]

Line-and-staff structure achieves integration by grouping differentiated activities on the basis of whether primary or secondary work is being performed. Primary work is separated from secondary work and those activities that are required in each are grouped respectively. Explicit recognition is given to staff work, and an integrative structure is provided to coordinate it to ensure that it supports line work.

The big advantage of adding staff positions to the organization is that it frees line managers to concentrate on managing primary operative work. It also allows people to specialize in order to develop an expertise in various complex fields such as legal affairs, market research, and personnel. This enables the organization to work more efficiently and effectively to perform the secondary operative work. For example, in today's legal environment, it is difficult to imagine a production manager with the legal and personnel knowledge needed to hire, train, and place personnel in safe and healthful work environments without violating equal employment opportunity (EEO) guidelines or safety and health regulations. A competent personnel staff is a necessity.

In addition to the potential conflicts between line and staff personnel, there is another, more dangerous, problem that can arise. Line management may totally abdicate responsibility for performing any secondary operative work when staff positions are created. It is true that staff positions are created to assist line managers, but this does not mean that line managers give up *all* aspects of secondary operative work. For example, line managers should help personnel specify job criteria and qualifications for positions to be followed during the hiring process. If a staff planning department exists, this does not mean line managers should do no planning. By the same token, equal employment opportunity is not just the personnel department's job; rather, all line managers should share in the responsibility for following EEO guidelines.

FUNCTIONALIZED STRUCTURE. This third type of structure builds on the line-and-staff structure for the functional basis of differentiation discussed previously. It was originally developed by Taylor and called "functional foremanship." The functionalized structure ". . . is a line-and-staff structure that has been modified by the delegation of managerial authority to personnel outside their normal spans of control."[15] Thus, people in staff positions are given line authority over some aspect of the production or distribution of primary utility, as shown in Figure 10.10. For example, the personnel manager can actually decide who the foreman must hire. The quality-control manager can halt the production line if rejects exceed a certain level. Indeed, this is quite common in manufacturing organizations. At Davidson Rubber Company, before it significantly changed in manufacturing operations through automation, twelve quality-control inspectors had the authority to halt the work of 150 employees who manufactured flexible car bumpers.[16]

Functionalized structure integrates work by using the concept of line authority to bring together both staff and line work. The staff authority of various staff positions is made direct over operating managers. In this way, staff and line activities are brought together or integrated at various points in the organization.

The chief advantage of this structure is that it allows for maximum specialization, and it forces line management to follow the advice (decisions, in this case) made by staff experts. The major disadvantage, however, is that it violates the single accountability principle (or unity-of-command principle), which states that each subordinate should have only one immediate superior. In the functionalized structure, a subordi-

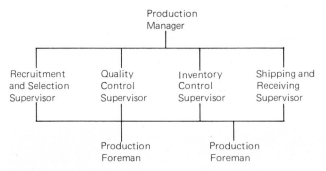

FIGURE 10.10
Functionalized Structure

nate may have two, three, or more immediate superiors who may give conflicting directions or orders. It is left up to the subordinate to decide which ones to follow and which ones to violate. This can be overcome, however, if each subordinate knows to whom he or she is accountable for which tasks. Such delineation of accountability is often difficult to achieve, and because of the confusion that results, comprehensive functionalized structures are seldom found in organizations.

PROJECT MATRIX STRUCTURE. An increasingly common type of structure, first used in aerospace and military-weapons-production industries, is called *matrix* management.[17] Matrix structure is also called *project* structure, *product* structure, and *program* structure. The terms are often used interchangeably, but there are differences among them. However, the essence of all three matrix forms is the same: Resources from vertical units are assigned to horizontal units based on the need in each unit. For example, a person who is administratively housed in the production department can be temporarily assigned to a project for a specific period of time to perform a specific set of functions. Once the role on the project is completed, the individual returns to the production home base to await reassignment to a new project.

Figure 10.11 shows an example of project matrix structure. People

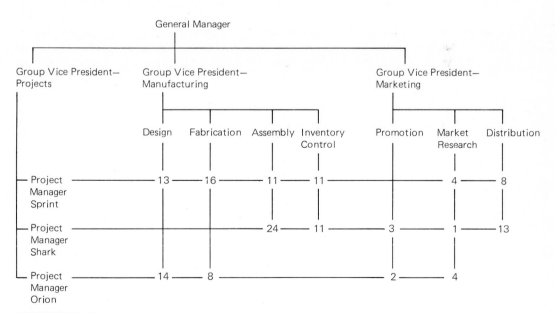

FIGURE 10.11

Project Matrix Structure

are assigned to various projects based on the stage of project development and the project director's need for personnel and other resources. The numbers in each of the cells in Figure 10.11 represent personnel assigned to each project director from their home base, which is indicated at the top of the cells. Not all people are assigned to a specific project at any given time. Individuals not assigned to a project can be performing staff work, such as conducting various studies or performing research and development, while they await assignment to a project.

Project managers are given complete authority for the project. Projects usually have a definite beginning and end, and it is the project manager's responsibility to manage the project throughout to ensure that the project is completed on time and within budget. When people are assigned to project managers, the project manager should have complete authority over them. That is, the home-base functional manager temporarily relinquishes authority over people assigned to a project to the project manager. This is to ensure that the project manager has the necessary authority to see the project through to completion. Project matrix structures have been successfully used in such organizations as TRW (for the development of space vehicles for NASA) and at Thermodyne Corporation (for the development of U.S. Army weapons systems).

Product matrix structure is similar to project structure and is shown in Figure 10.12. It differs from project structure in that there is not necessarily a beginning and end for each product. (Although products do go through a life cycle, this period is typically much longer than that for a project.) It is used in multiproduct organizations and is frequently used in new product introduction and in special promotional efforts for existing products. The product manager has complete authority to schedule and manage a major promotional effort for a product. In multiproduct, multibrand consumer organizations, the product manager is sometimes called a *brand manager*. When a major promotional effort is scheduled for a product or brand, the product manager is given the authority to ensure that sufficient quantities of product will be available for sale, necessary distribution will occur, and that dealers will promote the product. The product or brand manager may also be given the authority to coordinate advertisements for the product or brand, consumer mailings, distribution and redemption of coupons, establishment of point-of-purchase displays, and the provisions for dealer discounts.

For example, suppose a product or brand manager at Procter and Gamble for Bounty paper towels schedules a major promotional campaign for Bounty. The Bounty brand manager would work with the production unit to ensure sufficient product availability. A pricing strategy would be determined. Distribution to dealers would be arranged. Television and newspaper advertisements for the promotion would be written and scheduled; coupons would be printed and distributed; and

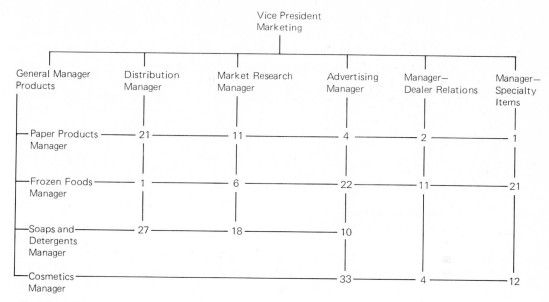

FIGURE 10.12

Product Matrix Structure

point-of-purchase displays would be constructed in each store. Once the promotional campaign was completed, normal sales activities for Bounty would resume.

The use of product or brand management is popular for special promotions and for introducing new products. Vesting one manager with the authority to coordinate all activities associated with the new product introduction or promotion helps to ensure that essential functions are coordinated across functional lines. In other words, matrix management is a good way to integrate differentiated activities.

The final type of matrix structure discussed here is *program* matrix structure. This is used when an organization wishes to coordinate a number of programs across a number of functional areas. A program is defined as a major work thrust that involves the coordination of a number of specialized activities from diverse areas in order to achieve a specific end. For example, market testing at a consumer products firm could be considered a program. It also differs from the project structure in that the life cycle of the program is typically longer than that for a project. In fact, an end for a program is typically not specified. If such an end is specified, then the program matrix takes on the characteristics of project structure.

Because program matrix usually involves continuing programs, it is becoming a more popular form of organization in service-oriented industries such as government and education. For example, Figure 10.13 shows how program matrix structure can work in a college of business. The individual program managers would acquire faculty from various functional areas to staff particular courses in each program. These faculty would not necessarily be assigned full time to each program manager, but may also teach a course or two in their functional area. As with all matrix structure variations, the program manager would evaluate the faculty member's performance in the program and report to the department chair as part of the evaluation process.

A variation of the project, product, or program matrix structure is the *multidimensional matrix* structure developed by Dow Corning.[18] This occurred when Dow Corning Corporation, a joint venture of Dow Chemical Company and Corning Glass Works, reorganized from a conventional divisional type of organization into a matrix form of organization. Although matrix organization had been successfully used for aerospace projects, Dow Corning was the first large corporation to adopt a matrix

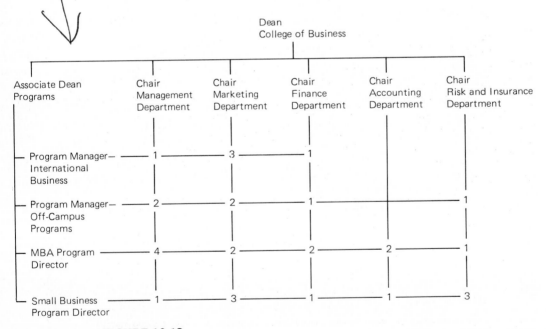

FIGURE 10.13

Program Matrix Structure

structure on a permanent basis. Dow views the matrix organization as a four-dimensional system composed of:

1. *Profit centers*—the different businesses of the company defined along product lines; for instance, rubber, encapsulants and sealants, resins and chemicals, and fluids, emulsions, and compounds.
2. *Cost centers*—the functional entities such as marketing, manufacturing, and research, as well as a number of supportive activities such as corporate communications, legal and administrative services, and industrial relations.
3. *Geographical areas*—for example, the United States, Europe, and Asia, which are considered both profit and cost centers.
4. *Space and time*—denotes fluidity and movement through time as the multidimensional organization is constantly changing. Decision making tends to be spread across the organization, with most of the decisions made at the middle management level based on group consensus.

Dow's experience shows that the matrix form can be modified or varied to meet the needs of a particular organization. The multidimensional matrix, as used by Dow, has elements of all three forms of matrix structure—project, program, and product.

The chief advantage of all forms of matrix organization is that they allow the proper technical advice, expertise, and other resources to be present at the proper location and time desired. The matrix organization is flexible. It allows for changes in shifting emphasis on projects, products, and programs. For this reason, matrix structures tend to be more organic/adaptive in nature than line, line-and-staff, or functionalized structures. But this is not necessarily always so; some organizations have adopted a matrix structure and still remain rigid bureaucracies in terms of policies, procedures, and rules. The structural aspect of design has been made more flexible, but in these organizations the other aspects of design have not been changed to be consistent with it. They have a flexible structure, but they attempt to make it work under rigid policies, procedures, and rules.

There are disadvantages to the matrix structure. First, it requires that the project, product, or program managers work cooperatively with the functional heads to handle conflict. It also requires the general manager of all these people to be able to mediate conflict between program, project, or product managers and functional heads when they cannot work out problems among themselves. The appropriate delegation needed under the matrix may not be forthcoming in some organizations. (Delegation and conflict management are discussed in Chapters 11 and 15.) Second, matrix structure, especially project matrix structure, may require a lot of relocation of personnel, which can cause behavioral traumas (e.g., breaking and forming new work and friendship groups, frequently moving one's family, and forming new superior-subordinate relationships based on mutual trust). Some individuals may have difficulty coping with these activities. Finally, if explicit authority is not assigned to project, program, or product managers vis-à-vis functional heads, the unity-of-command principle can be violated. Explicit authority differentiation between the matrix managers and functional heads needs to occur so people under the matrix know to whom they are accountable for what and for what time period.

These disadvantages can be overcome. Matrix structure gives the organization flexibility in assigning resources as priorities and projects change in response to changing environmental demands. Therefore, in those organizations facing shifting, heterogeneous environments, there is likely to be greater use of matrix structure as a means to integrate various differentiated organizational tasks.

LINKING-PIN STRUCTURE. This structure views certain key subordinates as occupying "linking-pin" positions. Developed by Likert, and refined by others, the linking-pin concept holds that subordinate managers do not just link a superior with a subordinate's subordinates, they link a team of managers with a team of subordinates.* It emphasizes the vertical and horizontal linkage role a manager plays in integrating the tasks of an organization, as shown in Figure 10.14.

There are two essential features of the linking-pin structure; the first is *conceptual*. It involves a different way of thinking about the organization. As seen in Figure 10.14, the traditional hierarchy essentially defines one-on-one relationships between superiors and subordinates. The linking-pin hierarchy, on the other hand, shows that *team* relationships exist. A subordinate of one team is a superior of another team and thus is a team link. In Figure 10.14, A links one team with B's and D's teams; B links with C's team, and D with E. Notice that there are no lines connecting the blocks. This is to connote interactive communication among all team members among themselves and with the team leader, not one-on-one communication as with the traditional hierarchy.

This conceptual view is essentially Likert's contribution, but others have added a second aspect to the linking-pin concept. That aspect is *structural* in nature and is represented in Figure 10.14 by position F. Here a *liaison position* or *horizontal* linking position has been created to link two units down in the hierarchy. This can be done if coordination and communication between these two units are needed. A person is given

---

*See Rensis Likert, *The Human Organization* (New York: McGraw-Hill, 1967); and for additional development, see Raymond E. Miles, *Theories of Management: Implications for Organizational Behavior and Development* (New York: McGraw-Hill, 1975), 85–88.

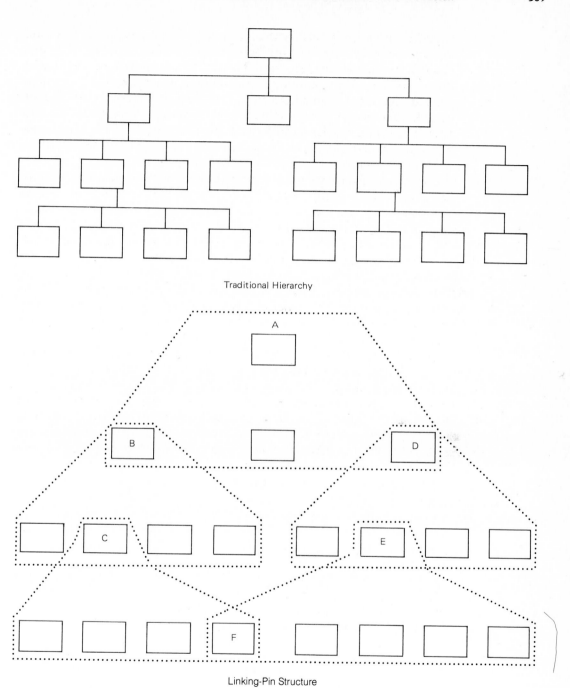

Traditional Hierarchy

Linking-Pin Structure

FIGURE 10.14

Traditional versus Linking-Pin Structure

the authority to work with both units. Such an arrangement is sometimes used in the telephone industry between outside plant construction and engineering. In a typical phone company, these two functions do not formally come together under one position except at the very top of the organization under the general manager. Yet, engineering and outside plant construction must work closely together on various projects. Without a liaison position, it is difficult to ensure that engineering designs can actually be constructed by the outside plant as they were designed. The liaison position can mediate conflict between these two groups.

The major potential problem with the liaison position is that it can violate the unity-of-command principle. This potential problem can be reduced or alleviated, however, if the authority differentiation is clearly spelled out for the people involved. For example, in Figure 10.14, clearly spelled-out authority for position F vis-à-vis C and E would help F understand to whom he or she is accountable and for what.

For the linking-pin system to work properly, it requires a participative management style. The linking-pin-manager and liaison positions play key roles in sharing information and in coordinating tasks. Thus, the actual structure is only half of the linking-pin approach; the other half is the managerial process that has to be used. If the philosophy of management that dominates the organization does not encourage joint goal setting and open information sharing, then the linking-pin structure will not work adequately.

The linking-pin structure can be an effective way to achieve the same results of the matrix structure without the complexity often found in a matrix structure. By using a participative approach and by using committees and task forces to implement linking-pin structure, the organization can achieve a degree of integration that may otherwise be difficult to attain. For this reason, we are likely to see the linking-pin structure used more in the future.

STRATEGIC BUSINESS UNITS. Organizational units established primarily for strategic planning and decision-making purposes are termed *strategic business units* (SBUs). Comprised of a group of related products or services directed to a distinct group of customers or clients, they are used mainly in diversified multiproduct/multiservice organizations.[19] SBUs are often structured differently for strategic planning purposes than for operations.

For example, suppose a diversified container manufacturer produced the following types of containers: glassware, bottles, plastic cups, tubs (e.g., toothpaste containers), and corrugated boxes. The formal organization chart for the manufacture (operations) of these might be as shown in Figure 10.15A. But because these products serve different customers, for strategic planning and decision purposes, the organization can be viewed

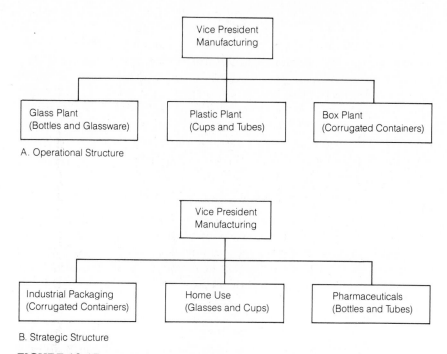

A. Operational Structure

B. Strategic Structure

FIGURE 10.15

Operational and Strategic Structures

as shown in Figure 10.15B. In other words, for planning and decision purposes, the products and decisions affecting them are grouped differently than they are for operations. This is done because in planning and decision making, *explicit*, narrowly focused recognition of the environment, customers, and competition requires that products facing common markets be grouped together in order to assure that decisions regarding them take special note of any unusual variables. Not to establish an SBU could jeopardize the quality of management practices.

The idea of SBUs was pioneered by General Electric (GE) as a way to streamline its strategic planning process. Imagine trying to develop a corporate-wide strategic plan for such a diversified company as GE, which has product lines ranging from toaster ovens to nuclear reactors, and from jet engines to construction equipment in addition to products in chemicals, light bulbs, electric motors, transformers, turbines, and so on.

Widely divergent products such as these face different environments. So, even though the production of glassware and bottles might be grouped in the same plant, they actually face as many as three distinct environments (homes, industry, and pharmaceuticals). Each environment presents different customers and competitive forces, so grouping products for planning purposes around common environments and markets helps lend both economy and efficiency to decision making.

Although the SBU framework might not be depicted as such on formal organization charts, it is a method of design that can help capture product similarities for purposes of centering attention in a coordinated way and helping hold organizational units together in a sensible fashion. Like the linking-pin structure, SBUs are another way of achieving integration within a diversified organization.

Miscellaneous Structures

There are a number of miscellaneous structures used by organizations today, which are briefly summarized here. Although these structures are used by few organizations now, they may be adopted more frequently in the future. We will simply introduce and define each structure here and will discuss it more fully when we speak of the future of organizations. The structures are ad-hocracy, joint venture, free-flowing or laissez-faire, and industrial democracy.

Ad-hocracy refers to a nonpermanent organization. It derives its name from the concept of ad hoc committees, which are set up to examine a particular issue and which disband once their report is made, much as a task force operates.* The concept is different, however, in that the whole structure—indeed, the organization—disappears once the issue or task is completed. It is a temporary organization structured to solve a particular issue. We often see this type of organization in the nonbusiness sector. For example, suppose an organization is put together to establish a civic center in a community. The organization would draw from various interest sectors in the community, such as labor, government, business, and universities, and would operate until the civic center became a reality, at which point it would disband.

Joint venture arrangements are similar to ad-hocracy, but they also contain elements of matrix structures. The difference is that two or more separate organizations pool resources to accomplish a particular project. Once the project is completed, the venture arrangement ceases, but the original organizations that furnished resources to the arrangement continue to exist. Such arrangements are often used by petroleum companies in locating and drilling for new oil reserves.

Free-flowing or *laissez-faire* arrangements are loose collections of people who are brought together for a period of time under a relatively loose style of management and control. They usually exist solely to sat-

---

*See Alvin Toffler, *Future Shock* (New York: Random House, 1970). The chapter "Organizations: The Coming of Ad-hocracy," explains this concept in greater detail.

isfy the desires of the members of the organization rather than the needs of some constituent or client group. A bridge club is an example of this. Someone must coordinate the scheduling of games, hosting, refreshments, tournaments, and so on, but it is usually done very informally. The leader may never be officially appointed but may just emerge from the group. On some occasions the leader may be elected by the group. He or she "governs" or coordinates with the consent of those "governed" and can be ignored or replaced if the group's wishes are not carried out. Other examples exist in the way some communes are organized.

Industrial democracy is somewhat like the laissez-faire structure except that it is more formal. In Europe this model is also known as *codetermination* because of the joint role that labor has in running the organization. Often the leaders are elected and serve a period of time in office. All membership groups and, in some cases, the organization's clients exercise voting rights in selecting leaders. Organizations of this type are usually flat with wide spans of management since there is considerable delegation of authority and individual autonomy. In fact, delegation has been said by some to flow *upward* in the organization as each group elects leaders who are to carry out its wishes.[*]

CHARACTERISTICS OF EFFECTIVE STRUCTURES

Up to now in this chapter, we have described the various ways organizations differentiate and integrate their tasks. We have discussed several bases for differentiation and several types of structure that are used to integrate activities. What we have not really addressed, however, are the characteristics of an effective organization structure. That is the purpose of this last section of the chapter.

Let us point out at the outset that *there is no one right structure* that is appropriate for all organizations.[20] There are structures that are more appropriate for a particular organization, given the circumstances in which that organization finds itself. Of course, as we have indicated several times in this book, a major determinant of an appropriate structure for an organization is the environment within which the organization operates. Other determinants are the competence of the personnel who make up the organization, the diversity of market segments, the diversity of product or service offerings, the geographic dispersion of operations, the type of technology employed in producing and distributing the prod-

---

[*]See Paul Blumberg, *Industrial Democracy* (New York: Schocken Books, 1969).

uct or service, the size of the organization, and the information-processing tasks of the organization.

Regardless of these circumstances, all organization structures should have certain characteristics if they are to be effective. These characteristics are goal accomplishment at least cost, encouragement of innovation, flexibility and adaptiveness, facilitation of human resource performance and development, facilitation of coordination, and facilitation of strategy.

Goal Accomplishment at Least Cost

Organization structure should encourage goal accomplishment with a minimum of resource expenditure. These criteria of effectiveness (goal accomplishment) and efficiency (at least cost) are prime criteria to evaluate the appropriateness of an organization's structure. As we indicated in Chapter 9, structure should facilitate goal accomplishment by being a skeleton or network of task differentiation and integration for the allocation and utilization of an organization's resources.

Innovation

Even organizations in static, homogeneous environments need innovation—the ability to generate more effective and efficient ways of operating. Structure should encourage innovation by providing the pooling of organizational resources and an appropriate communication and information system so that innovation can take place. This important concept is explained further in Chapter 16.

Eastman Kodak was forced to reorganize in the mid-1980s because its old functional structure stifled innovation. Long, rigid communication channels and cumbersome authority relationships were such that deliberation and procrastination were raised to a high art within this organization. At the "old" Kodak, a suggestion from a marketing manager for altering a manufacturing process would have to filter all the way up the management ladder and back down the managerial ranks. By the time the decision got back down, it was often distorted and no longer applicable. Kodak's new structure, based on seventeen entrepreneurial profit centers, now provides managers with authority over everything from design to production within their respective units.

Organizations in dynamic, heterogeneous environments require even more innovation if the organization is to stay in tune with and respond to its environment. Structure should thus facilitate effective operation of organizational sensors and boundary-spanning units. In particular, the structural linkage between sensors and decision-authority centers needs to be such that important information reaches the decision centers so that innovative responses occur.

Flexibility and Adaptiveness

Closely related to the characteristic of innovation are the characteristics of flexibility and adaptiveness. No organization exists in a truly static, homogeneous environment, even though some environments approach this in the short term. Therefore, all organizations need to be flexible and adaptive. The need to be flexible and adaptive to changes in the macro environment was the reason for Merrill Lynch's reorganization that we discussed in the introductory case to this chapter.

Structure facilitates flexibility and adaptiveness in a number of ways. Once again through boundary-spanning units, environmental information is passed from sensors to decision-authority centers allowing the organization to design and implement appropriate responses. Structure can provide for decentralization, which allows for the placement of decision centers closest to where the work or boundary interface occurs. Structure can encourage changes in organizational processes as required. Finally, structure itself should change in response to the environment and the needs of the organization.

Facilitation of Human Resource Performance and Development

Probably the most common complaint about organization structure made by organization members is that, instead of facilitating performance, structure often hinders or blocks effective performance. Usually, this complaint reflects a concern over a rigid, bureaucratic structure with detailed and often outmoded policy, procedures, reporting relationships, and rules. Superimposed on this is a centralized decision policy that requires top-level clearance for even the most routine decisions. Of course, because of the element of certainty inherent in bureaucracies, human performance can be facilitated. Routinization permits individual employees to know exactly what their tasks are while well-established career ladders provide employees with a clear direction and goals to be attained within their careers.

Structure—even bureaucratic structure—need not be inhibiting and rigid. Weber, when writing about bureaucracies, probably never envisioned "buck-passing" and red tape, yet people in bureaucratic structures adopt these defensive mechanisms. Structure should encourage high-level performance by providing a framework, be it rigid or flexible, whereby organization members can work at their highest level of ability in areas of their interests and competencies. It should encourage employees to grow on the job by learning new job skills and accepting increasing responsibilities as they become more experienced. It should provide a clearly defined career path or ladder of organization jobs or positions, and a system whereby employees can get the necessary training that will qualify them for higher level jobs. Highly differentiated dead-end jobs (such as those on an auto assembly line) do not do this. Organizations need to be more sensitive to human resource performance and development when designing jobs.*

Facilitation of Coordination

Another characteristic of an effective structure that we will discuss here is the degree to which structure contributes to an overall coordinated effort on the part of the units in the organization and the organization itself. Organizations usually do a pretty good job of differentiating their activities on the basis of function, geography, process, machine, and so on, but often they have a difficult time integrating these activities. In fact, as we indicated before, much of what is taught as management is really an emphasis on the necessity of integration and coordination. After all, planning, organizing, controlling, communicating, and leading—popular topics covered in management—are skills that need to be employed by a manager if integration and coordination of tasks are to be achieved.

However, as we pointed out, structure should facilitate, indeed achieve, integration. The manager who is highly skilled in the typical managerial skills still will have a difficult time achieving integration and coordination without the assistance of a structure. By the same token, a structure that integrates tasks well will not guarantee overall coordination unless the manager also has planning, organizing, leadership, and other important skills.

Facilitation of Strategy

In Chapter 7 we presented a broad overview of the essentials of the strategic management process. Within that chapter, we specifically discussed how organizations perform an internal operations analysis and subsequent strategy operationalization plan as part of this process. These two

---

*There is some evidence that organizations are becoming more sensitive to the effect of structure and job design on human resource performance and development. The whole concept of "job enrichment" is an attempt to add more responsibility and freedom of discretion to highly differentiated routine jobs. Several companies are experimenting with this approach. For example, see Robert N. Ford, "Job Enrichment Lessons from AT&T," *Harvard Business Review* (January–February 1973): 96–106.

aspects of strategy point out how important it is for the organization to understand its own internal operations and procedures in order to formulate and implement strategy.*

In the present chapter, we focus on how organizations design various structures so that tasks can be carried out and goals accomplished in the most efficient and effective manner(s). We now ask, "What, if any, relationships exist between an organization's structure and strategy? Are there elements of various structures that facilitate, or alternatively, hamper strategy development and implementation?"

J. W. Fredrickson, of Columbia University, has made a significant contribution to this aspect of organization theory by providing a synthesis of the research pertaining to the relationship between structure and strategy.[21] Fredrickson has shown that there is a growing body of literature suggesting that there is a major effect from structure to strategy, "i.e., once a structure is in place, it will influence a firm's strategic decision process, and eventually, its strategy."[22] This relationship exists because structure delimits responsibilities and communication channels. Moreover, structure enables management to control the decision-making environment and facilitate the processing of information. Indeed, when management designs a particular structure for the organization, it not only provides a framework for current operations, but also the communication channels through which environmental and strategic information will flow.

Fredrickson looked at three distinct dimensions of structure—centralization, formalization, and complexity—and studied the various effects they have on the strategic decision process. Table 10.1 summarizes Fredrickson's findings.

By examining Table 10.1, we see how structural dimensions affect strategy formulation and implementation. For example, with a large, laissez-faire structure, it appears that it would be difficult for management to effect meaningful strategic decisions because of organization members' parochial perceptions. Within a highly complex and mechanistic structure, strategic action would be hampered by the fact that its rigid system(s) permits only certain environmental variables to be monitored. A highly centralized structure would have problems formulating strategy because of the cognitive limitations on the part of top management, although strategic decision implementation would be greatly facilitated.

Fredrickson's work provides an excellent introductory framework for analyzing strategic effectiveness vis-à-vis the structural dimensions of centralization, formalization, and complexity. In addition, this work should enable researchers to devise more sophisticated methodologies

---

*We will discuss these three dimensions of structure in detail in Chapter 11.

TABLE 10.1

The Relationship Between Structural Dimensions and Strategy

Increased Centralization	Increased Formalization	Increased Complexity
Strategic decision process initiated by top management.	Strategic decision process initiated in response to problems that occur in variables that are frequently monitored.	Organization members will not recognize strategic issues, or they will ignore them.
Strategic decision process will be aimed at achieving proactive, "opportunistic" goals in spite of changes in the means to their end.	Strategic decision process will be aimed at achieving precise, remedial goals.	Strategic decisions will be made to satisfy a group of organization members, not to achieve organization goals.
Strategic actions are the result of intensely rational choices. Moves will be major departures.	Strategic actions are the result of standardized organizational processes. Moves are incremental.	Strategic actions are the result of internal processes of political bargaining. Moves are incremental.
Top management's cognitive limitations are the primary constraint on comprehensiveness; high integration of decisions.	Level of detail achieved by standardized organizational processes will inhibit comprehensiveness; intermediate integration of decisions.	Biases of organization members' parochial perceptions will constrain comprehensiveness; low integration of decisions.

Source: Adapted from James W. Fredrickson, "The Strategic Decision Process and Organizational Structure," *Academy of Management Review* 11, no. 2 (April 1986): 284.

for studying the structure-strategy relationship in terms of specific organization structures such as those discussed in this chapter.

SUMMARY

The basis for structure is the environment in which the organization finds itself and the goals it hopes to accomplish. Organizations attempt to differentiate and integrate a set of tasks that need to be carried out in order to accomplish goals. The resultant pattern of differentiation and integration and the associated authority levels and reporting responsibilities are what we call organization structure.

Organizations can be differentiated on at least six foundations: similarity of work or function, product, geography, market, process/

interface, or equipment. Each of these bases has its advantages and disadvantages, and there is no best one for all organizations. In most large organizations, a combination of bases is used. Organizations attempt to integrate their activities by creating a design that coordinates the various differentiated tasks. These integrative structures include line structure, line-and-staff structure, functionalized structure, matrix structures, and linking-pin structure. Each of these has its advantages and disadvantages, and no one structure is best for all organizations.

Effective structure should maximize efficient goal accomplishment. It should also encourage innovation, flexibility, and adaptiveness. It should bring out the best in its members so that human resources are developed and performance is maximized. Finally, it should facilitate coordination of overall organization activity in addition to strategy formulation and implementation.

This chapter has focused on various types of organization structure. In the next chapter, we will more closely examine the evolution of these types of structure, from the simple and informal to the complex and formal. As you will read, this evolution occurs as organizations change themselves in response to growth.

QUESTIONS FOR REVIEW AND DISCUSSION

1. What are the bases for differentiating organizations? When should each be used? Why do organizations often use a combination of bases for different functions and at different levels in the organization?

2. What is a line structure? How does it differ from a line-and-staff structure? Why does line-staff conflict exist in so many organizations? How can it be reduced?

3. What is a functionalized structure? When should it be used?

4. Contrast the mechanistic or bureaucratic model with the organic or adaptive model. Why did Weber develop the bureaucratic model?

5. What is matrix structure? What are its advantages and limitations?

6. What is linking-pin structure? Does it violate the unity-of-command principle? Explain.

7. Pick an organization with which you are familiar. Examine its organization chart. How might this chart be recast into either a matrix or linking-pin structure?

8. Do you see much future for ad-hocracy and venture arrangements? Why or why not?

9. Are laissez-faire structural arrangements appropriate only for

mutual benefit type organizations such as bridge clubs? Could a business be organized this way? How?

10. What should an effective organization structure accomplish?

11. Why does it seem that managers are often unwilling or unable to experiment with new forms of structure?

ENDNOTES

1. Barbara Buell and Rebecca Aikman, "Kodak Is Trying to Break Out of Its Shell," *Business Week* (June 10, 1985), 92.

2. Harold Koontz and Cyril O'Donnell, *Principles of Management: An Analysis of Managerial Functions*, 5th ed. (New York: McGraw-Hill, 1972), 266–281.

3. William Cellis, III, "Trammell Crow's Realignment Moves Stir Fears of Change in the Partner Ranks," *The Wall Street Journal* (February 2, 1986), 5.

4. Mark Hanon, "Reorganize Your Company Around Its Markets," *Harvard Business Review* 52, no. 6 (November–December 1974): 63–74.

5. As translated by A. M. Henderson and Talcott Parsons (New York: The Free Press, 1947).

6. As summarized by Richard H. Hall, *Organizations: Structure and Process* (Englewood Cliffs, N.J.: Prentice-Hall, 1972), 15–16.

7. T. Burns and G. M. Stalker, *The Management of Innovation* (London: Tavistock Institute, 1961).

8. Derek S. Pugh, D. J. Hickson, C. R. Hinings, K. M. MacDonald, C. Turner, and T. Lupton, "A Conceptual Scheme for Organizational Analysis," *Administrative Science Quarterly* (1963–1964): 289–315; and Derek S. Pugh, D. J. Hickson, C. R. Hinings, and C. Turner, "Dimensions of Organizational Structure," *Administrative Science Quarterly* (1968): 65–105.

9. Derek S. Pugh, D. J. Hickson and C. R. Hinings, "An Empirical Taxonomy of Structures of Work Organizations," *Administrative Science Quarterly* (1969): 115–126.

10. Hall, *Organizations*, 16.

11. Bernard Reimann, "On The Dimensions of Bureaucratic Structure: An Empirical Reappraisal," *Administrative Science Quarterly* 18 (December 1973): 462–471.

12. Burns and Stalker, *Innovation*, 5–6.

13. B. J. Hodge and Herbert J. Johnson, *Management and Organizational Behavior* (New York: John Wiley & Sons, 1970), 122.

14. Philip Browne and Robert T. Golembiewski, "The Line-Staff Concepts Revisited: An Empirical Study of Organizational Images," *Academy of Management Journal* 17 (September 1974): 406–416.

15. Hodge and Johnson, *Management and Organizational Behavior*, 163.

16. Maggie McComas, "Cutting Costs Without Killing the Business," *Fortune* (October 13, 1986), 72–73.

17. Jay Galbraith, "Designing Matrix Organizations," *Business Horizons* (February 1971): 29–40.

18. William C. Goggin, "How the Multidimensional Structure Works at

Dow Corning," *Harvard Business Review* 52, no. 1 (January–February 1974): 54–65.

19. Lester A. Digman, *Strategic Management* (Plano, Tex.: Business Publications, 1986), 154–160.

20. Y. K. Shetty and Howard M. Carlisle, "A Contingency Model of Organization Design," *California Management Review* 15 (Fall 1972): 38–45.

21. James W. Fredrickson, "The Strategic Decision Process and Organizational Structure," *Academy of Management Review* 11, no. 2 (April 1986): 280–297.

22. Ibid., 281.

ANNOTATED BIBLIOGRAPHY

Ackoff, R. J. "Toward Flexible Organizations: A Multidimensional Design." *OMEGA, The International Journal of Management Science* (May 1977): 649–662.

The author considers how to increase organizational flexibility and responsiveness by dividing the organization into units whose survival depends on their ability to produce at a competitive price, which creates a "marketplace" within an organization. Multidimensional organizational design is not restricted to the traditional structure that deals only with two dimensions—responsibility and authority. Units of a multidimensional design (which has much in common with "matrix organizations") are relatively independent of each other and can be manipulated more easily than in conventional organizations.

Allen, Stephen A. "Organizational Choices and General Management Influence Networks in Divisionalized Companies." *Academy of Management Journal* (September 1978): 341–363.

Using an empirical taxonomy for identifying key choices faced by managers in organizing and reorganizing divisionalized companies, the author traces patterns of reorganization in a sample of companies studied in 1970 and again in 1974. The impact of organizational choice on the influence that various levels of general management exert over divisional policy decisions is also explored. The results indicate that divisionalized organizations represent a diverse family of institutional arrangements differing from one another in terms of divisional self-containment, extent of divisionalization, and complexity of coordinative devices. Further, general management influences are affected but not fully determined by different combinations of these organizational choices.

Bennis, Warren. *American Bureaucracy.* New Brunswick, N.J.: Aldine, 1970.

This is a collection of essays by distinguished writers in the field. The bureaucracy and its relation to democracy, motivation, conflict, and change are topics of discussion. Also included is a good symposium on the innovating organization. Bennis contributes two articles on the future of bureaucracy and its leadership.

Bourgeois, L. J.; McAllister, Daniel W.; and Mitchell, Terence, R. "The Effects of Different Organizational Environments Upon Decisions About Organizational Structure." *Academy of Management Journal* 21, no. 3 (September 1978): 508–514.

This paper reviews three studies designed to test the following hypotheses: (1) Managers who encounter turbulent environments will react by "pulling in the reins"; (2) a more stable environment will result in a manager's "loosening up" into a more organic style; and (3) given a stable environment that subsequently becomes turbulent, decision makers will tend to shift from an organic to a mechanistic structure and vice versa. The studies supported the first two hypotheses, but not the third. Although a shift to a more mechanistic mode was noted when turbulence followed stability, there was no shift to a more organic mode when the environment became more stable. The support for the first two hypotheses raises the issue of directionality of causation between environmental uncertainty and organization structure.

Dewar, Robert, and Hage, Jerald. "Size, Technology, Complexity, and Structural Differentiation: Toward a Theoretical Synthesis." *Administrative Science Quarterly* (March 1978): 111–136.

This paper suggests and finds that the most important determinant of differentiation is the scope of an organization's task (a technological dimension) and not organization size. The authors believe neither horizontal nor vertical differentiation is determined by size, while the scope of the task is a determinant of horizontal differentiation. Using data collected on each of sixteen social service organizations in 1964, 1967, and 1970, the findings, however, support only a moderate causal connection between either size or task scope and differentiation. These findings suggest that the relationships among size, complexity, technology, and structural differentiation are more complex than the authors previously thought.

Filley, Alan C., and Aldag, Ramon J. "Characteristics and Measurement of an Organization Typology." *Academy of Management Journal* (December 1978): 578–584.

This paper describes an organizational typology based on adaptive strategies. Their findings from over 400 retail and manufacturing firms suggest that there are three different patterns of organization: (1) craft firms that are stable and nonadaptive, (2) promotion firms organized to exploit some type of unique competitive advantage, and (3) administrative firms that are formalized and professional, utilizing differentiated personnel. The authors conclude that organizations may be classified by types or profiles of characteristics as well as by single traits such as size, technology, or industry type.

Galbraith, Jay. *Matrix Organization: Design for High Technology.* Cambridge, Mass.: MIT Press, 1971.

The author makes a strong case for using the matrix organization concept. Specifically, he argues that the matrix design is most appropriate for complex or advanced technologies. Considerable effort is devoted to management strategies involved with the matrix approach.

Greiner, Larry E., and Schein, Virginia E. "The Paradox of Managing a Project-Oriented Matrix: Establishing Coherence Within Chaos." *Sloan Management Review* 23, no. 2 (Winter 1981): 17–22.

Projects that require the flexible coordination of multidisciplinary teams have tended to adopt a matrix structure to accomplish complex tasks. Yet these project-oriented matrix structures themselves require careful coordination if they are to realize the objectives set for them. The authors identify the basic organizational questions that project-oriented matrix organizations must face. They examine the relationship between responsibility and authority, the tradeoffs between economic efficiency and the technical quality of the work produced, and the sensitive issues of managing individualistic, highly trained professionals while also maintaining group cohesiveness.

Hoskisson, Robert E. "A Time Series Test of the Structure/Performance Relationships Given General Environmental Influences." In *Academy of Management Proceedings 84*, edited by John A. Pearce, II and Richard B. Robinson, Jr., 178–181. Boston, Mass.: Academy of Management, 1984.

This research examines the impact of structural change on financial performance in six organizations. Historical case analysis is used to specify the year of structural change and the time series methodology is used to test the impact of the new structural form. Results indicate that reorganization to the multidivisional form has a positive impact on financial performance, even given general environmental fluctuations.

Litterer, Joseph A. *The Analysis of Organizations.* 2d ed. New York: John Wiley & Sons, 1973.

This is Litterer's update of his excellent first-edition work. He spends worthwhile effort on analyzing individual and group behavior in organizations, as well as the process and consequences of organizational differentiation. The importance of adaptation to the changing environment is also handled in depth.

Lorsch, Jay W. "Organization Design: A Situational Perspective." *Organizational Dynamics* (Autumn 1977): 2–14.

An approach to organization design based on a situational theory, not a theory that explains cause-and-effect relationships, is presented. The author maintains that the organization design must fit both the environment and the individual member's needs. The organization designer must, therefore, create a structure, rewards and measurements, and other elements compatible with the external environment, strategy, tasks, organization members, top management style, and existing culture. Problems in applying such an approach to organization design are also addressed.

Mansfield, R.; Todd, D.; and Wheeler, J. "Company Structure and Market Strategy." *OMEGA, The International Journal of Management Science* (April 1978): 133–138.

The article reports a preliminary study of twenty-four companies. It investigated the relationships between strategies (diversification and geographic dispersion) and structural variables (the number of structural differentiations in the company, the decentralization of decision making, and functional specialization). The two strategic variables have different structural implications: geographic dispersion is particularly associated with structural differentiation and diversification is associated with decentralization.

Middleton, C. J. "How to Set Up a Project Organization." *Harvard Business Review* (March–April 1967): 73–82.

The author treats the basics of installing a project-type organization. Included are appropriate cautions and advice on managing the finished product.

Newman, Derek. *Organization Design*. London: Edward Arnold, 1973.

This is a pragmatic, analytical approach to the design of organizations. A short review of organization theory is presented, followed by an elaboration of available design options within various types of organizations.

Perrow, Charles. "A Framework for the Comparative Analysis of Organizations." *American Sociological Review* (April 1967): 194–208.

Perrow classifies organizations according to their technologies. The major subcategories deal with the number of exceptions handled by the technology and the type of search procedure used, that is, routine or nonroutine. Task structure varies with technology, while social structure varies with both technology and task structure.

Pfeffer, Jeffrey, and Salancik, Gerald R. "Organization Design: The Case for a Coalitional Model of Organizations." *Organizational Dynamics* (Autumn 1977): 15–29.

The authors believe that organizations need to strike a balance between the need for adaptation, which requires less institutionalization, and the need for action, which requires substantial institutionalization. The authors develop an alternative perspective to the rational model of organization design called a "coalitional model," a loosely coupled model of organizations having subunits, each of which deals with specific environmental interests and each of which is only minimally interdependent with the rest of the organization.

Routamaa, Vesa. "Organizational Structuring: An Empirical Analysis of the Relationships and Dimensions of Structures in Certain Finnish Companies." *Journal of Management Studies* 22, no. 5 (September 1985): 489–522.

The relationships of structure and structural factors at a general level are examined on the basis of data from a Finnish sample of mostly small- and medium-sized industrial organizations. The sample, which consists of shoe and clothing firms, is homogeneous in terms of basic technology and industrial environment. The structural relationships are examined from the point of view of size so that the interaction or concurrence of size and specialization is seen as a primary determinant of the systems of structural relationships.

Stuckenbruck, L. C. *The Implementation of Project Management: The Professional's Handbook*. Reading, Mass.: Addison-Wesley, 1981.

This handbook provides a step-by-step approach for developing the right type of project management by covering all the important aspects of a project—laying the groundwork, defining the duties of the manager, integrating the system, and delegating authority.

Thompson, James D., and Bates, Frederick L. "Technology, Organization and Administration." *Administrative Science Quarterly* 2 (December 1957): 325–342.

This early perceptive work found that the elaboration of technology leads to increasing organizational complexity, and that, to some extent, technology governs structure. A comparative analysis also found relationships between technology and administrative processes.

Tushman, Michael L., and Nadler, David A. "Information Processing as an Integrating Concept in Organizational Design." *Academy of Management Review* (July 1978): 613–624.

The authors suggest an approach to design that builds on the view of organizations as information-processing systems facing uncertainty. Organizations will be more effective, they say, when there is a match between information-processing requirements facing the organization and information-processing capacity of the organization's structure. This implies that design should first consider the composition and structure of organizational subunits and then consider mechanisms for linking them together. As information-processing requirements change, so, too, must the organization's structure.

Yasai-Ardekani, Masoud. "Structural Adaptations to Environments." *Academy of Management Review* 11, no. 1 (January 1986): 9–21.

According to the model presented in this paper, objective industry environments influence managers' perceptions of their environments, and managers' perceptions influence structural adaptations. Individuals' characteristics and organizational structures also influence managers' perceptions. Finally, managerial choice and organizational slack also influence structural adaptions to environments.

Weick, Karl E. "Organization Design: Organizations as Self-Designing Systems." *Organizational Dynamics* (Autumn 1977): 31–46.

The author is concerned with design as a process and with putting that process into the hands of "insiders." The article states that the concept of self-design, which requires individuals to integrate themselves into the design, is so new that concrete illustrations of it are rare. Furthermore, since self-design is as much a strategy as it is an object, it is not obvious what it would look like or where it would be visible. The author examines six general characteristics of self-design, concluding that self-design involves a different way of thinking about what is valuable and what is worthless in organizations and generating alternative designs based on one's findings.

Zey-Ferrell, Mary, and Aiken, Michael. *Complex Organizations: Critical Perspectives.* Glenview, Ill.: Scott, Foresman, 1981.

This anthology takes a sociological approach to the study of organizations. Structure, power, goals, politics, and management strategy are all examined from critical nontraditional viewpoints. The articles on structure are particularly noteworthy.

ADDITIONAL REFERENCES

Bennis, Warren. "Beyond Bureaucracy." *Transactions* (July–August 1965).

Blackburn, R. S. "Dimensions of Structure: A Review and Reappraisal." *Academy of Management Review* 7, no. 1 (January 1982): 59–66.

Blau, Peter. "The Hierarchy of Authority in Organizations." *American Journal of Sociology* (January 1968): 453–467.

Cleland, David I. "Understanding Project Authority Requires Study of Its Environment." *Aerospace Management* 2, no. 1 (Spring/Summer 1967): 5–14.

Cleland, David I. "Why Project Management." *Business Horizons* 7, no. 4 (Winter 1964): 81–88.

French, Wendell. "Processes Vis-à-Vis Systems: Toward a Model of the Enterprise and Administration." *Academy of Management Journal* 6, no. 1 (March 1963): 46–57.

Fry, Louis W., and Slocum, John W., Jr. "Technology, Structure, and Work-group Effectiveness." *Academy of Management Journal* 27, no. 2 (June 1984): 221–246.

Galbraith, Jay R. "Designing the Innovating Organization." *Organizational Dynamics* 10 (Winter 1982): 5–25.

Halvacek, James D., and Thompson, Victor A. "Bureaucracy and Venture Failures." *Academy of Management Journal* 3, no. 2 (April 1978): 242–248.

Hedburg, Bo L. T.; Nystrom, Paul C.; and Starbuck, William H. "Camping on Seesaws: Prescriptions for a Self-Designing Organization." *Administrative Science Quarterly* 21 (March 1976): 41–65.

Hill, Richard M., and Halvacek, James D. "Venture Team: A New Concept in Marketing Organization." *Journal of Marketing* 36 (July 1972): 1–7.

Huber, George P.; Ullman, Joseph; and Leifer, Richard. "Optimum Organization Design: An Analytic-Adoptive Approach." *Academy of Management Review* 22, no. 4 (October 1979): 567–578.

Kingdom, Donald R. *Matrix Organizations: Managing Information Technologies.* New York: Harper & Row, 1973.

Litwak, Eugene. "Models of Bureaucracy Which Permit Conflict." *American Journal of Sociology* (September 1961): 177–184.

McKelvey, Bill, and Kilmann, Ralph H. "Organization Design: A Participative Multivariate Approach." *Administrative Science Quarterly* 20 (March 1975): 24–36.

Mee, John F. "Ideational Items: Matrix Organizations." *Business Horizons* (Summer 1964): 70–72.

Nystrom, Paul C., and Starbuck, William H., eds. *Handbook of Organizational Design.* Vol. 1, *Adapting Organizations to Their Environment.* New York: Oxford University Press, 1981.

Nystrom, Paul C., and Starbuck, William H., eds. *Handbook of Organizational Design.* Vol. II, *Remodeling Organizations and Their Environment.* New York: Oxford University Press, 1981.

Osborn, Richard N.; Hunt, James G.; and Jauch, Lawrence R. *Organization Theory: An Integrated Approach.* New York: John Wiley & Sons, 1980.

Parsons, Talcott. *Structure and Process in Modern Society.* New York: The Free Press, 1960.

Rowen, Thomas D.; Howell, C. Douglas; and Gugliotti, Jean A. "The Pros and Cons of Matrix Management." *Administrative Management* 41, no. 12 (December 1980): 22–59.

Shull, Fremont. "Dimensions of Matrix Organization Structure: Humanism, Temporariness and Variability." In *Management Research and Practice,* edited by William Frey. Amherst, Mass.: Eastern Academy of Management, 1970.

Stinchcombe, Arthur. "Bureaucratic and Craft Administration of Production: A

Comparative Study." *Administrative Science Quarterly* 4 (September 1959): 168–187.

Tung, R. L. "Dimensions of Organizational Environments: An Exploratory Study of Their Impact on Organization Structure." *Academy of Management Journal* 22, no. 4 (October 1979): 672–693.

```
C    A    S    E
```

Fuel Efficient

As oil prices dropped dramatically in the mid-1980s, the world's largest energy producer, Exxon, began a major restructuring effort aimed at eliminating layers of management, shrinking the work force, and altering the lines of command in order to quicken the pace of decision making.

Before restructuring began, Exxon had fourteen regional and operating organizations. Now they have nine—Exxon Chemical Company, Exxon Coal and Minerals Company, Exxon Company International, Exxon Company U.S.A., Exxon Enterprises, Exxon Research and Engineering Company, Imperial Oil Ltd. of Canada, Reliance Electric Company, and Exxon Production Research.

Oil and gas operations, the heart of Exxon's business, are the main focus of the redesign. These operations, which will absorb 90 percent of Exxon's $8 billion in 1986 capital expenditures, will be handled by three of the Exxon entities—Exxon U.S.A., Exxon International, and Imperial Oil of Canada.

Of special interest is the revamping of Exxon U.S.A., which represents about one-fourth of the total Exxon work force of over 160,000 people. Formally comprised of sixteen departments, Exxon U.S.A. will be divided into three separate divisions, two of which will be fully inte-

Source: Allanna Sullivan, "Exxon's Sleeker Look Starting to Emerge," *The Wall Street Journal* (June 2, 1986), 6.

grated operating businesses. One will handle exploration, production, and natural gas, while the second will handle refining and marketing. The third division will center its activities around corporate and financial affairs.

According to Exxon U.S.A. President Randall Meyer, "Our objective is to combine under one management those activities which are similar in nature and closely related." The company's new organization chart calls the three major divisions "upstream," "downstream," and "financial." Each will decide its own strategic and business plans, handle its own management recruitment and development, and be independently able to call on support services from the corporate headquarters (e.g., public affairs, law, medical, employee affairs).

By establishing clear-cut profit centers, Exxon U.S.A. has made it easier to determine where it is making money and where it isn't.

Exxon U.S.A. isn't the only Exxon entity to undergo a radical restructuring. At corporate headquarters, four departments are being eliminated, and the functions of several others have been combined (e.g., the public affairs and secretaries departments have been combined to form a new corporate affairs group).

Exxon International will undergo the most sweeping reorganization. While other Exxon entities restructured existing operations, International is creating a whole new entity. Regional management of all international operations will be eliminated and foreign affiliates will now report to the U.S. headquarters rather than to regional offices.

Although the official organization chart for Exxon International had not been released to the public at the time of this writing, its myriad functions have been remolded into four divisions—exploration/production, gas, petroleum products, and financial/corporate affairs. In short, operations previously divided by geography will now be aligned according to business line. As a result, the following Exxon companies have ceased to exist—Exxon International, Esso Exploration, Esso Europe, and Esso Inter-America.

As the Exxon behemoth's domain has shrunk as a result of declining oil prices, it has, in turn, instituted a parallel shrinking of its organization structure to accommodate for this changed environment.

QUESTIONS FOR DISCUSSION

1. Besides profit, what other indicators of good design are there?
2. Why could Exxon management have thought a business base was better than a geographic base?
3. How would you suggest the company now hold the various organizational units together in a coordinated way?
4. Will the new organization require different management skills? If so, why, and what would they be?
5. If it is true that an organization chart cannot show how a company really works and how it makes decisions, why would you think a company would bother to have one?

11

Organization Size and Complexity

Tea Time

In 1984, Kraft, the giant U.S. food processor and distributor, bought Celestial Seasonings for $50 million. Celestial, the marketer of "soothing teas for a nervous world," was and still is famous for its herbal brews with names like Red Zinger, Grandma's Tummy Mint, and Sleepy Time. Why Kraft paid $50 million for a company that was founded in 1971 with only $10,000 in capital is an interesting story that illustrates how small companies, if and when they become successful, have a tendency to become large and complex organizations.

The legend of Celestial Seasonings' founding began in 1971 in Boulder, Colorado. Two young hippie dropouts, Mo Siegel and John Hay, spent the summer picking various mountain herbs, such as mountain spearmint, in the Rocky Mountains. Siegel and Hay dragged 125-pound bags of herbs back to Siegel's home where their wives sewed bulk tea bags from muslin cloth. Mo and John screened the herbs they collected and mixed them in batches that were then crammed into the bags sewn by the wives. Next, the full herb tea bags were taken by pickup truck to natural food stores in the Boulder area where the herbal tea mixtures were sold to health food devotees.

The two "entrepreneurs" decided to make their herbal tea endeavors official by forming a company. Hay's mother guaranteed a $5,000 bank loan and Siegel borrowed $5,000 from a friend. They named the company after Hay's brother's girlfriend, a flower child with the moniker "Celestial Seasonings." Thus, the company was born.

Sources: Sandra D. Atchison, "Kraft Is Celestial Seasonings' Cup of Tea," *Business Week* (July 28, 1986), 73; Nora Gallagher, "We're More Aggressive Than Our Tea," *Across the Board* 20, no. 7 (July–August 1983): 46–50; and Eric Morgenthaler, "Herb Tea's Pioneer: From Hippie Origins to $16 Million a Year," *The Wall Street Journal* (May 6, 1981), 1, 22.

Within five years, something happened that neither Siegel nor Hay expected—the general public fell in love with their herbal teas. By 1976, the company was making and marketing thirty-two different types of herbal teas that were no longer found just on the shelves of obscure health food stores—supermarket chains such as Safeway were now carrying Celestial products. Herbs were no longer collected from the nearby Rockies; Celestial purchased various herbs from throughout the United States and from foreign countries as well. And finally, operations had moved from Siegel's house to a facility within a Boulder industrial park. Celestial was no longer a two-men-and-their-wives cottage industry—it was becoming a big business.

Despite the company's growth and rapidly expanding wealth, Siegel and Hay were still able to maintain a laid-back atmosphere in Boulder. Even though there were almost 100 employees by 1976, there were still volleyball games every lunch hour; toddlers wandered throughout the buildings; a silent grace preceded each lunch in the company-owned cafeteria; and *all* employees participated in day-long company meetings to thrash out company philosophy and policies.

Five years later in 1981, Celestial Seasonings was earning $16 million per year, making forty different teas, and was the leader in the herbal tea industry, which grossed over $70 million in 1980. Celestial Seasonings had managed to grow at an annual rate of 39 percent since 1976. These impressive figures caused a number of large companies to avariciously eye the then still-small Boulder organization. General Mills was particularly interested. Its takeover attempt of Celestial was thwarted two years prior, in 1979, when Siegel bought the $1 million worth of stock from a shareholder-friend who had been tempted by General Mills to sell his stock.

Other changes were noticeable at Celestial Seasonings during its tenth anniversary year. Siegel had signed up for seminars conducted by the American Management Association, and his favorite reading materials, formerly comprised of superuniverse, ascetic writings such as *The Urantia Book* had been replaced by the works of Peter Drucker, the famous management scholar and writer. Celestial products were advertised in magazines such as *Redbook* and *McCall's*, the direct result of the efforts of marketing professionals who had been brought in from such companies as Pepsi Cola, Procter and Gamble, Quaker Oats, and Lipton. Celestial was fast becoming mainstream, big-time American business.

This growth and its accompanying changes did not set well with some of the company's original free spirits, such as John Hay's younger brother Wyck, who left the company that year. Said Wyck, "When the whole onslaught of former Pepsi and former General Foods and former Quaker Oats people starting drifting in, I definitely opted to drift out."

Mo, despite his original intentions of running a very small, laid-back company, had decided that his company had to be run like a real American business; hence, significant changes were made in 1981. The year 1981 was noted as being the year of expansion within Celestial. The company developed vitamins, body care products, and snack foods. These new product ideas were developed under the leadership of Kenneth E. Bren, formerly of Pepsi, and, in 1981, the executive vice president for marketing at Celestial. Bren, who also headed Celestial's new research and testing department, set a goal of having Celestial products sold in 75 percent of all supermarket chain stores by 1983.

When 1983 arrived, sales were $27 million a year. John Hay left the company, although he was still Siegel's good friend and a major stockholder. There were almost 200 employees working within a five-building complex. Visitors to Celestial had to first pass through a public relations department and were never left alone—they were escorted from one building to another by management guides. The volleyball games and company-wide meetings had become memories. Managers and workers were formally differentiated; the former wore suits and the latter wore jeans. Although some of the workers wanted to form a union in 1980, management was able to convince employees not to unionize. Said Siegel, "I'm not anti-union. It's just not the way we work here." Workers were kept happy with traditional benefits such as group life and health insurance and profit sharing. Job rotation had been introduced to eliminate some of the boredom associated with the assembly-line type work that had slowly but surely been introduced as the company expanded its operations.

The whole system for acquiring, processing, and packaging the herbs had become elaborate and complex. Celestial buyers traveled to such countries as Egypt, Chile, and Spain to purchase herbs. There were even formal contracts between Celestial and some growers. From the fields, the herbs were shipped to a warehouse in the Boulder complex where they were inspected. If nothing was wrong, they were then shipped to a second warehouse to be cleaned, milled, and blended. An elaborate, high-tech vacuum system removed most of the dust from the sifting process in order to protect workers from "green lung."

Once blended, the various herbal teas were then sealed in two giant freezers to prevent the different aromas from mingling. The following stage of the process was packaging, which took place in a separate building. Huge, Italian-made machines made boxes that were glued and sealed by two other machines. Most of the work in the packaging department had become automated. Workers were even paid a cash bonus if they could figure out a way to eliminate their own jobs! They were then put on a first-hire-back list.

Even before a new tea or other product was introduced, it had to go through arduous processes, beginning with the marketing concept, where ideas were hashed out and tested in the research and testing department's laboratories. From the labs, new products were consumer tested. For example, the Boulder swim team tested a shampoo conditioner, and women's clubs through the western United States tested Country Apple tea. Each new product came under the control of a product manager.

Certainly, this was a far more complex and larger operation than that which existed twelve years before when Celestial Seasonings was a simple four-person business.

In 1986, after Celestial had been part of the Kraft empire for two years, Siegel left the company. Barnet Feinblum, the former treasurer for Celestial and an expert in finance, became the new president. Because the trendy herbal tea market had been discovered by competitors such as Lipton it became essential for Celestial to be owned by a company such as Kraft that had the clout to deal with rivals the size of Lipton. Kraft pro-vided Celestial with $1.5 million per year for advertising; Celestial ads have now been on national television. Most important, through Kraft's distribution system, Celestial can now be found on the shelves of every major supermarket in both the United States and Canada.

Celestial Seasonings was originally intended to be a small, friendly company. Success, however, forced changes on it that its founders did not envision in 1971. Because Celestial is now part of Kraft, most analysts believe that whatever vestiges remain of the old Celestial culture and way of doing things will soon be nothing but memories.

The Celestial Seasonings saga is an excellent illustration of how organizations can grow and become complex entities. As you read the material contained in this chapter, you will begin to understand the transformation process that occurs within organizations as they increase in size and complexity. You will also see how management attitudes and organization structures must adapt to these dimensional changes.

CHAPTER PLAN

In this chapter we examine the variables of organization size and complexity, particularly their effect on organization structure and processes. First, we define organization size and show its consequences on the organization as a whole. We then discuss the stages of an organization's growth patterns and explain what happens to an organization internally when it increases in size.

We next treat the relationship between size and structure, particularly vis-à-vis the concepts of delegation and integration. In this treatment, we show that complexity is a function of these two concepts. The chapter ends with a discussion of the interrelationships between complexity, centralization, and formalization within organizations.

In this chapter we examine two of the most important dimensions of organizations: size and complexity. These aspects are important both in building and understanding organizations. Consequently, the following discussion is aimed at exploring these concepts and how they affect the organization and its interaction with its environment.

We tend to associate an organization's ability to grow with its success in attracting resources and consumers. When an organization is started, its owners (at least implicitly) expect it to prosper and to attract an increasing share of the market. Today, for example, virtually every university in this country has a program for attracting more and better students and faculty. Almost all types of business engage in one form or another of advertising that is aimed at attracting more customers. Advertising itself is a major business.

With increasing size comes complexity. As an organization grows, its operations and structure invariably become more difficult to manage. A manager's challenge thus becomes to balance the advantages of size with the limitations of complexity.

WHAT IS ORGANIZATION SIZE?

There are many ways to measure the size of an organization. Share of the market is one indicator. Those organizations that dominate the marketplace are considered large by some standards. Giant corporations, as well as "megaversities," provide ready prototypes of how market share can indicate large organizations. Conversely, organizations with only a fraction of the marketplace are considered small.[1] For example, we all know that GM is a large organization for many reasons, not the least of which is its perennially significant share (43 percent in 1986) of the U.S. auto market.[2] Likewise, we can consider Celestial Seasonings to be a large organization because of its significant share of the herbal tea market.

When firms open branches in other cities, we tend to think of them as being large. Universities that have branch campuses or overseas programs are considered larger than those with a single campus. In the same vein, the renowned law firm of Finley, Kumble, et al., with its home office in Miami, is considered to be one of the largest in the nation because of its many branches in major U.S. cities and foreign countries.

Manufacturing plants with multiple product lines may also be considered big. Many national firms have acquired diversified companies that make a variety of products. These firms are not only large but complex as well. Thus, asset size and number of facilities are indicators of size. Maytag Company, whose repairmen are the "loneliest guys in town," is now a much larger organization through its acquisition of Magic Chef, another home appliance manufacturer. Maytag now produces six different brands of refrigerators.[3]

Although all the indicators just mentioned can measure size, we have chosen the number of full-time employees in an organization as the measure of size. The number of employees provides a simple measure of the size of an organization, and is the measure mostly commonly used in the literature.[4]

Because all organizations have employees or members, this number is a convenient common denominator. Whether its share of the market is large or small, whether it has branch operations, or whether it has multiple product lines, the organization can be compared to others on the basis of the number of employees or members it has. It is also a less subjective measure than market share, product lines, or other methods of measuring size (though it might be somewhat misleading in terms of power, influence, or ability to survive).[5] Despite GM's market share, which we mentioned above, we can also consider this organization to be gigantic because it has 800,000 employees. Indeed, it currently has over 130,000 white-collar employees just for its North American automobile operations.[6]

WHERE ORGANIZATIONS TEND TO GROW FIRST

In order to place the beginning of growth in perspective, let us follow the case of someone who starts an automobile repair shop. The person who begins such a business will usually possess the skills required to correct problems related to the operation of automobiles. Although this might include a wide range of skills, it is not enough to manage the entire operation.

When repairs are done, they must be properly recorded; invoices must be prepared; taxes must be computed and paid; and inventories must be maintained. These are but a few of the support activities needed, each requiring a different kind of skill than that required to repair automobiles.

In the beginning, these activities might be quite simple and undemanding on the owner/mechanic. They probably will require little time and perhaps no special talent. As the garage experiences success and begins to grow, however, they will doubtless take more time and expertise.

As the number of customers increases, the owner usually finds that he or she is unable to perform all the support work as well as the repair work itself. There is probably not enough time to do bookkeeping. The business needs an employee to carry out this support (or staff) function.

Success can also bring the need for other talents. In addition to bookkeepers, someone might be needed who has knowledge of selling and advertising. People with supervisory skills in managing other mechanics might be needed as the business grows. Finally, mechanics might begin to specialize in a single type of repair: Some may work only on transmissions, others might do body repair work, and still others might only do simple tune-ups. As you saw in our introductory case, as Celestial Seasonings grew and became more successful, it needed to hire individuals with marketing and advertising expertise.

In short, as the business grows, it finds itself faced with the need for specialized knowledge required to support the main operations. All this means is that the effects of success and growth are seen within differentiation of the primary duty (repairs) and in those areas that are not directly related to the basic function of repair.[7]

STAGES OF AN ORGANIZATION'S GROWTH

Henry Mintzberg has developed a convenient and effective means of tracing an organization's growth through its several stages, which we will use here.[8] It follows growth from the beginning of the informal group to the final stage of the matrix structure. The scheme appears to fit all forms of organizations, from commercial to government to unions.

An organization can follow each of these stages or it can begin in the second or subsequent stages. It might not complete the entire cycle, especially if it ceases to exist. The movement might be smooth or jerky. Parts of an organization can even remain in one stage while others move on to subsequent ones.

The First Stage (A): Craft Structure

This type of organization is exemplified by an informal group (perhaps friends) that start a business, as Mo Siegel and John Hay did with Celestial Seasonings. In this stage, informality dominates all aspects of the organization. There will generally be no rules, no formal procedures, and management is frequently shared by all. Even if there is a recognized leader, he or she generally works along with everyone else. The structure is simple because there is no need for it to be formally established.

The First Stage (B): Entrepreneurial Structure

Growth brings about the need for some form of management of the group's members and their activities. Without coordination and guidance the group can become misdirected and its efforts can become ineffective. As Mintzberg puts it, "new levels of management must develop and direct supervision must be more relied upon for coordination. This signals the arrival of the entrepreneurial stage."[9]

So movement into the entrepreneurial stage brings about at least the beginnings of a separation of duties in the organization. A cast of managers is needed to steer the organization on its course; here labor specialization is seen in its basic form. The organization probably will remain basically informal; there still might be instances of crossover between management and operational duties, with managers perhaps still performing nonmanagerial work. The separation of duties has, nevertheless, begun.

This type of structure existed at Celestial Seasonings in 1976. Although still a basically informal organization, Celestial had almost 100 employees at this time; some type of bureaucratic structure had to evolve as the work involved with herb acquisition, blending, packaging, and marketing became more complex and specialized.

The Second Stage: The Bureaucratic Structure

From the time of Max Weber, attention has been directed to this stage of growth. Weber saw the need to "de-personalize" the organization to the extent feasible by imposing job specifications, rules, regulations, and the like on it. This, he believed, was imperative if the organization were to continue over the long term when individuals left it for whatever reason. Otherwise, there would be no possible continuity.

Growth, at some point, demands the elaboration of an administrative structure based on formal differentiation of duties. As work units increase in number and size, they require some form of supervision, and as the number of supervisors increases, another level of supervision for their management. The management structure thus emerges.[10]

By 1981 the bureaucratic structure was firmly established at Celestial Seasonings. Formal departments and functional units, such as research and testing, marketing, packaging, and so on, in addition to an executive hierarchy, were well in place at this time.

Along with this development comes the formality of virtually all operations that Weber described. Paper begins to substitute for personal contacts, and rigidity and formality replace flexibility and informality. The organization begins a movement toward bureaucracy.

The Third Stage: Divisional Structure

This stage of growth sees the organization expand into other markets or begin operations at different sites. In order to coordinate and control activities on such diversified fronts, it becomes necessary to establish another variation of structure. The organization must develop what amounts to a form of bureaucracy for each site or product line. In order to hold the entire organization together, then, it is imperative to create divisions of the organization.[11]

General Motors is an excellent example of such an arrangement. It has created several divisions to deal with its various products. There is a Chevrolet division, a Pontiac division, an Oldsmobile division, and so forth. Each separate division of the corporation is operated to maximize its success. Yet the corporation itself must be able to tie these various units together in such a way that the entire corporation is not endangered by the uncoordinated efforts of its members. This task becomes the job of the headquarters group.

Growth of an organization, therefore, can cause it to create a number of divisions to cope with special problems and interests associated with a particular site or product. Not all organizations reach this stage, but many do as we see in all types of concerns, whether they be business, government, or universities with their several companies or branches.[12]

The Fourth Stage: Matrix Structure

This form of structure is almost a return to the kind of organization structure seen in the early stages of growth. It is an attempt to use more than one base on which to build the organization. This combination of bases will enable management to place talent at the point where it is needed most, often only temporarily.

Although the matrix structure is thoroughly explained in Chapter 10, let us look at an example. The committee form of governance in universities is well established and can be seen as an example of a matrix structure. Universities are generally organized along functional or disciplinary lines. There can be several colleges (or discipline groups) within a university. These colleges, in turn, are subdivided into departments, as can be seen in the case of a college of arts and sciences with its many departments, ranging from, say, chemistry, physics, and English to a college of business with finance, accounting, management, and other departments.

Faculty from these and other departments within the university are members of various committees that attend to university-wide matters. The undergraduate planning committee, for instance, might be composed of faculty from the departments of chemistry, English, and management among others. They leave their respective disciplines and assume a broader, more universal perspective that is basically discipline-free in order to attend to the entire undergraduate curriculum. They elect a colleague to head the group and voluntarily agree to follow the head's general lead, reserving the right, of course, to disagree and to change leaders if need be. This specialized group cuts across traditional department lines to bring together a diversity of talents to solve problems and issues that run through the entire university. This adaptation combines both disciplines and types of issue in its organization base.

Although this stage of growth is not inevitable, it is possible to find many examples (such as NASA) of organizations that have moved into it. It is an attempt to combine the advantages of nearly all stages of growth, but primarily to retain the flexibility and innovation associated with the craft and entrepreneurial stages.

In order to develop a solid base in high technology, Daimler-Benz, the West German manufacturer of Mercedes, recently acquired three West German firms known for their expertise in this area. Daimler formed a matrix structure it called "Prometheus" that combined engineers from the parent company and two of the new acquisitions to design a traffic control system in which sensors and computers in cars and trucks will help drivers avoid hazards and traffic jams. This is an example of the project matrix structure, discussed in Chapter 10.

An organization can remain in any one stage, or it can move through all the stages. Although the movement can be smooth and orderly or discontinuous, today's turbulent environment augurs for the latter, especially for a rapidly growing concern. When we think of growth, Mintzberg's model can aid in appreciating how an organization increases in size and what conditions explain its movement through the various stages.

WHAT HAPPENS WHEN ORGANIZATION SIZE INCREASES?

Just as people change as they grow and mature, organizations experience different "passages" as they move through the stages of their growth cycle. Generally speaking, organizations become more formal and more differentiated as their size increases. These effects are a direct result of the necessity to divide the increased work in the organization. There comes a point when one person (or even a few) can no longer do all that must be done to make the organization work effectively and efficiently.[13] The addition of people to the organization requires that it be more formal and precise. In the following sections we examine some of the major consequences of organization growth.

Formalization

In the small, beginning organization there are a few members who come into close contact with each other daily. Because they know each other personally, there appears to be little need for written rules and the like. When communication is necessary, the members simply talk face-to-face; there is little place for records and procedures. Note that Celestial Seasonings, when it had less than 100 employees, had company-wide meetings where everybody had a say in determining company philosophy and policies. Now that the company has grown, however, formality and structure have replaced these meetings.

The situation begins to change rapidly, however, once the organization starts to grow. New personnel are added to the group, and they perhaps do not know the other members on a personal basis. Continued employment growth eventually brings about a condition in which it becomes impossible for every member to know the rest of the group. Members may be geographically separated and may not see each other regularly. Yet, the need to communicate with other members and to coordinate their work still remains. The logical means to do this appears to be to use rules, memos, and policy to substitute for the personal contacts that are no longer possible.

This formalization enables managers to delegate the more routine decisions to lower ranks in the organization. At the same time, this process facilitates decentralization of major decision making as well because it adds at least an element of certainty to the decision environment. Rules and procedures enable several decision makers to observe the same decision values and so preserve some consistency and control in the decisions they make. The formalization process, consisting as it does of basically stringent means to control organization behavior, is a seeming unavoidable consequence of growth. This formalization is what many of us think of when we hear the term "bureaucracy."[14]

Apple Computers was founded by two friends, Steve Jobs and Steve Wozniak, much like Celestial Seasonings was founded. Until 1985, when the two founders left Apple, this organization was still managed informally, even though its success and subsequent growth would appear to have demanded a more formalized structure. When the present CEO, John Sculley, reorganized Apple in 1985, he took long-overdue action to formalize this company. Now there are rules, strict financial controls, formal reporting relationships, and tough product development deadlines.

Sculley had to formalize Apple because it had become a $2 billion company with 5,000 employees. Its laid-back culture, patterned after the co-founders' beliefs and management styles, was simply not congruous with its environment. Thus, conflict, confusion, and financial losses were endangering the company before Sculley took over in 1985. (For a further examination of Apple's woes before its 1985 reorganization, read the introductory case to Chapter 15.)

Differentiation

As was identified in Chapters 1 and 9, differentiation is merely the process of dividing the work of the organization into manageable units, and it involves both managerial and operative tasks. In the initial stage of growth, members might adapt to growth simply by working longer hours; eventually, however, continued growth will render this technique ineffective.

When the work load reaches the point where it causes undue fatigue and frustration or begins to interfere with the members' personal lives, the decision to add additional people will have to be made. This will generally involve adding operative personnel. As more and more operatives are added, the need for additional supervisors (and even middle and top managers) becomes apparent.

To make a logical division of work, then, requires vertical differentiation (the distinction between managerial and operative work) as well as horizontal differentiation (the distinction between what operatives do). A kind of labor specialization thus begins, and the specific assignments of both managers and operatives become more detailed and formal.[15]

Once the organization has decided on the pattern of its differentiation, it must turn its attention to integrating the various functional groupings: Some device must be established to hold the pattern together and to keep it working smoothly. Integration can thus be seen largely as a means of achieving coordination among the various units so they work in harmony.

Specialization

Growth brings about the necessity for organization members to concentrate their time and talents. A set of job skills that is required by increased and perhaps more diversified work loads needs to be developed. The Mom-and-Pop grocery store has little need for sophisticated skills and technology. A nationwide supermarket operation, however, demands highly skilled personnel as well as technology if it is to maintain control of its operations. It needs produce buyers, accountants, computer specialists, and the like. Mom and Pop, on the other hand, are required to be jacks of all trades in order to manage their neighborhood grocery. They have to do everything without the benefit of special skills and equipment, even if they could afford them.

When Mo Siegel and John Hay formed Celestial Seasonings in 1971, little did they know that their organization would eventually hire MBA graduates to handle the company's marketing and financial affairs and a Ph.D. in fruit technology to develop new herb products.

Routinization

Another result of growth is the tendency to develop set routines for the performance of work. This is especially true of operative work where machines often are able to perform tasks previously done by people. This substitution of machines for people is only possible because of the ability to develop routines for the performance of the organization's work.

As you read in the Celestial Seasonings case, the work at that organization became very routine as the company grew in size and complexity. In fact, the work became so routine that management instituted job rotation so that employees would not become too bored. Also, note how the work at Celestial eventually became automated.

Routinization also allows for delegation of authority and responsibility to lower ranks because it minimizes the need for judgment. This condition thus reinforces both vertical and horizontal differentiation.

Desktop procedures can be developed to explain the proper routine for task accomplishment, and this minimizes the dependence of the organization on particular personnel who might carry the organization's know-how with them when they leave. Such procedures also facilitate the training of replacements.

A More Impersonal Work Environment

In an organization that is undergoing the conditions we describe, a more impersonal atmosphere in the workplace is bound to develop. At some point it becomes impossible for all the members of a large organization to know each other personally. Friendship groups tend to be limited to a few co-workers, and knowledge of the overall work of the organization is known to but a few, if any.

Paperwork begins to take the place of daily personal contacts, and many begin to feel like they are "just another number." This condition easily breeds alienation and other measures of job dissatisfaction. Therefore, one price that a growing organization might have to pay is alienation of its members, caused by a more impersonal workplace, and characterized by paperwork.[16] This is certainly the case now at Apple Computers, at least according to one former employee. Peter Quinn, who was a design engineer for Apple, stated, "You're a cog in a wheel. It's just another big, boring company."[17]

However, as noted in the previous chapter, not all subsystems must experience this condition. It is quite possible in large organizations to find small personable work groups. So, again, it is necessary to keep the unit of analysis in mind.

Less Direct Involvement by the Chief Executive Officer

Often the founder of an organization takes a direct part in its operations. He or she might even be involved in operative work. As the concern grows, however, this is no longer feasible or even possible. Delegation becomes absolutely necessary.

Even if the chief executive officer of one of our giant corporations had the time (or talent) to be involved with daily matters, he or she might be legitimately faulted for improperly using valuable time. It becomes necessary to involve others and to delegate the responsibility for daily operations to them. This means the CEO must rely on subordinates to make the necessary decisions on a daily basis, and this eventually means using formal guidelines such as policy and procedure.[18]

Let us return to the law firm of Finley, Kumble, et al., that we mentioned at the beginning of the chapter because of its many branch offices. Steven J. Kumble, one of the firm's founders and senior partners, stated that he would rather practice real estate law in his firm. However, because his firm is so large, he must spend his time managing the enterprise at the top level. The actual legal work is handled by the firm's 200 partners and 300 associate attorneys.[19] Meanwhile, the support work is headed by William Long, a CPA, who directs the firm's administrative, financial, personnel, and data-processing functions.

The Total Effect of Individual Factors

These effects of growth, though they can exercise individual forces on the organization, tend to reinforce each other as the organization grows. It is important for the management group to be aware of what happens as their organization moves through its various stages of growth and to control the effects of growth so that these do not destroy the organization.

There are other effects of growth on the organization. The ones that we have discussed have been singled out as examples only. When a conscious decision to promote growth is made, then it should be against this background of effects.

ORGANIZATION SIZE AND STRUCTURE: A RELATIONSHIP?

Much has been said and written about the relationship, if any, between size and structure. Needless to say, there has been no unanimous agreement, and the debate continues. The positions range from causal (with size determining structure) to a random connection. This section will examine the basic aspects of this discussion and cite relevant support for them.

A large organization frequently "looks different" from a small organization, and even from itself when it was smaller. The speed of growth and whether it was smooth and orderly has relevance for structure and its design: Not only the size variable but how fast growth occurred must be considered. Ordinarily, slow growth can be controlled more easily than stop-and-start advancement.

Some organizations find the need to adjust rapidly to growth, as has been the case of university colleges of business recently. The adjustment to increased student demand has consequences for staff and faculty. Departments and programs might need to be added and expanded. But before this is done, management must judge whether this demand will cause permanent or temporary growth. If the judgment is that it will be relatively permanent, and it is to be accommodated by adding faculty and staff on a permanent basis, a mistake can be costly. If enrollment declines later, it would be difficult to reduce the number of faculty with tenure or clerical staff who are covered by government civil service programs. In this instance, rapid growth adjusted for by adding permanent faculty and staff results in a structure that is more difficult to dismantle or otherwise alter than if adjunct, part-time faculty, and temporary personnel had been added.[20]

The more predictable the environment, the more it is possible to make considered adjustments to growth. There can at least be an attempt to provide an adaptable structure. When decisions have to be made "under fire," managers generally do not have this luxury. In fact, as the organization grows rapidly in an uncertain environment, there is a tendency for the organization to grow willy-nilly by tacking on a function or department here and there based on a whim or a wish. In other words, when organizations increase in size rapidly and make structural decisions under fire, systematic and rational structures usually do not develop. There is little time to thoroughly consider planning and rational structure.

The story of the Baldwin-United Company provides an excellent example to prove this point. This company, which originally made pianos, rapidly expanded in the late 1970s and early 1980s into a variety of other endeavors, particularly financial services. When one of your authors wrote to the company to obtain a copy of its organization chart, he received a chart that looked like a Christmas tree because of the number of pen and pencil additions and deletions. This company grew so fast that it didn't even have time to print an up-to-date organization chart! Consequently, two structures of the same size in the same industry might be different simply on the basis of how rapidly they grew and the uncertainty of the environment.

Recent research has elaborated on the size-formality-structure relationship. For example, Marsh and Mannari studied fifty Japanese factories and found that structural differentiation and formalization were more a function of size than technology.[21] Gringer and Yasai-Ardekani found that "the strategy, structure, bureaucracy nexus is clearly size-dependent."[22] Their study of forty manufacturing companies in electrical engineering in the United Kingdom showed that more complex, bureaucratic organizational structures may be a response to difficulties in coordination and control caused by size.

Although earlier studies on size and the proportion of administrative personnel showed that as size increases, the proportion of administrative personnel decreases, a recent study by Ford of twenty-four school districts showed this not to be the case.[23] Moreover, the relationship between strategy and structure has been shown to exist apart from an organization's size.[24] Finally, size has been found not to be a primary determinant of the span of control.[25] Rather, the amount of position specialization appears to be the primary factor affecting the size of the span.

The debate on size-structure relationships continues. Resolving it calls for continued research studies, both cross-sectional and longitudinal. Although impossible to generalize given our current understanding, it is obvious that size and structure are tied together in various ways that bear recognition (and possible action) by management.

SIZE AND DELEGATION

In the typical condition of growth (a situation that is probably normal for a successful organization), there will be an increase in overall work load. To cope with this increase initially, managers might hire more personnel or assign additional duties to present subordinates. Thus, a manager can deal with growth by adding personnel to the group of subordinates or by giving the subordinates some of the duties that other personnel previously performed. Along with this assignment of duties (the basis of responsibility) must go a concomitant amount of authority (the right to perform these duties). This act of passing duties and rights to subordinates is termed *delegation* and is the means of accommodating for organization growth or for implementing a decision to rearrange a prevailing pattern of job assignments.

We should add here that as modern organizations become increasingly large and complex, there may come a point at which an organization can no longer effectively delegate authority and responsibility within its own ranks, particularly in the face of an uncertain environment. Therefore, some organizations have deliberately decided to shrink themselves, and, rather than delegate authority and responsibility for different functions that would normally be within the purview of the organization, they contract these out. For example, Mega Corporation is now just one-third of the size it was in the late 1970s. This is because (among other reasons) top management at Mega has contracted out a great deal of its engineering, data collection and analysis, and advertising work to satellite concerns nearby. Previously, these functions were conducted at various levels within the Mega organization.[26] Whether this phenomenon will continue and become a well-established organization structure of the future is unknown at this time.

DELEGATION AND INTEGRATION

The concept of delegation is closely related to the concept of integration. Essentially, delegation is the means for assigning the tasks that must be accomplished in order to attain goals. Once this assignment of tasks is made, management must be concerned with integration, the state of coordination and control in which the various task assignments are tied together into an effective whole.[27]

Integration is necessary in all types of large organizations, regardless of structure. Even organizations that are designed on a profit-center basis need to have their activities well integrated in order to avoid organizational dysfunction. For example, GM's five car divisions had historically been run as individual profit centers, and this design worked quite well when the world was "simpler," and competition, particularly from Japan, was not so fierce. However, by the mid-1980s a lack of integration between the five divisions resulted in styling overlaps, duplication of effort, a bloated bureaucracy, and general inefficiency. Thus, in 1984, GM was reorganized from five profit centers to two: one for small cars—

Chevrolet, Pontiac, Canada (CPC); and one for large cars—Buick, Oldsmobile, Cadillac (BOC). Of course, integration will still be required to ensure that the activities of these two groups are efficiently and effectively coordinated.

The Effect of Delegation on Integration

The extent of delegation in an organization has a direct and immediate effect on integration. Without some mechanism to achieve a coordinated effort among its various members, the organization would suffer from a multitude of inefficiencies. In other words, management must ensure that task differentiation and delegation are controlled if efficiency and effectiveness are to be preserved.

The necessity for effective integration is a direct function of the degree of delegation that is practiced. The more delegation there is, the more there is the necessity for integration, a type of organization glue that holds the entire set of differentiated tasks together in a coherent pattern of coordination and control.

The role of integration can be best appreciated, perhaps, by an example of its absence. Consider the case of a manufacturing company with an aggressive sales force that is committed to an increase in sales volume. Assume that management has delegated responsibility and authority to the sales division to accomplish this goal. This sales force is likely to increase its promotion efforts in an attempt to reach its goal. If management also grants to the sales force the authority to extend credit to customers, it is likely to provide them with a potent opportunity to overextend production capacity. In other words, the sales personnel, in their enthusiasm to increase sales, might well pursue this goal with tunnel vision. They could secure more orders than the production department could reasonably be expected to provide. When this condition occurs, the company is faced not only with the inability to produce sufficient goods but with angry customers. The result could be the loss of goodwill and orders in the future.

On the other hand, we can see integration perfected with Toyota's "kanban," just-in-time inventory system, where assembly and logistics functions are so tightly integrated (partially as a result of technology, partially as a result of good management) that one Toyota assembly line can produce *six* different Toyota models without any slowdown or stoppage of the assembly line.[28]

ORGANIZATION COMPLEXITY

Today's organizations range from the simple Mom-and-Pop type grocery store to the highly sophisticated organizational giants found in industry and government. The question of organization complexity is one that requires consideration when a manager decides how much authority and responsibility to delegate to subordinates. This is true because these decisions are affected in large measure by the type of task differentiations involved in organization complexity.

The Nature of Complexity

Although there are several aspects of complexity, Hall[29] identifies three basic components of complexity, and they should be considered collectively in order to obtain a true picture of the exact nature of complexity (see Figure 11.1). In the first place, Hall sees complexity as involving horizontal differentiation. This is the way that work is divided into jobs among the members of the organization, as we saw in Chapter 9. Jobs can be quite large and require a wide range of talent and ability, such as professionals' assignments, or they can be quite minute and require no special talent or ability, such as unskilled tasks.

The process of dividing the work of the organization is carried out by delegation. Therefore, delegation of work assignments among members of the organization creates a degree of complexity, the amount depending on the extent of the delegation.

Vertical differentiation is also an element of complexity, according to Hall. This condition refers to the number of levels in the organization structures. It can be determined by simply counting the number of levels from the top to the bottom of the structure. The more levels there are, the more complexity there is and the more potential there is for coordination and integration problems. Certainly by this standard, GM is an extremely complex organization with its mammoth bureaucracy, comprised of vertical layer after vertical layer of managers, departments, and committees.

Finally, Hall considers spatial dispersion, the geographic distribution of activities, as a component of complexity. When an organization oper-

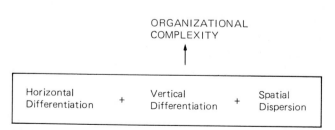

FIGURE 11.1

Hall's Factors Affecting Organizational Complexity

ates on more than one site, for example, coordination can be a problem. Lack of physical contact can take away one of the contributing factors for integration—daily contact and communication. This surely accentuates the effect of organization complexity and makes integration much harder to attain.

Perhaps you will remember our short discussion of the Trammell Crow organization in Chapter 10, where we pointed out how this very large real estate development company, differentiated on the basis of geography, was experiencing integration difficulties as some of its various geographic units competed with each other in the areas of project bidding and college recruiting.

The Relationship of Size and Complexity

Although one might intuitively predict that size and complexity are quite closely related, Hall and Child found little evidence of this condition. Hall found that other factors such as the type of work being performed and the separateness of the work (geographic dispersion) were more important factors. Child found that the degree of formalization had a more direct relationship with complexity than did size. He did find, however, that size was the major predictor of decentralization.[30]

From the findings of Hall and others, it appears there is little evidence for making any hard-and-fast conclusions about the relationship between size and complexity. What the findings do suggest, however, is that management would be well advised to take note of possible reinforcing effects between the two. This suggestion is based on the contention adopted by Hall that indicators of complexity as related to size are classifiable into three categories: hierarchical differentiation, intradepartmental specialization, and spatial dispersion. Delegation, of course, affects all three.

So, based on the work cited, size and complexity are difficult to tie together in any cause-and-effect relationship, but they are major factors in delegation.

The Relationship Between Complexity, Centralization, and Formalization

Fredrickson provides us with a summary model of the relationship between complexity, centralization, and formalization. This model is shown in Figure 11.2.[31] The model summarizes a number of relationships discussed in this chapter.

Fredrickson draws on Mintzberg's work to show how Mintzberg's purest structure forms tie together the three concepts of complexity, centralization, and formalization. A *simple structure* is informal and highly centralized. It has little or no support staff, little differentiation, a loose

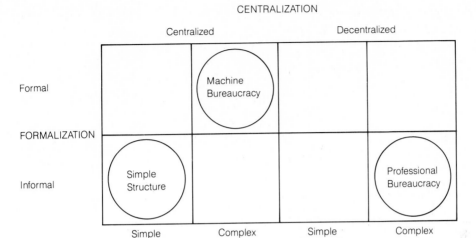

FIGURE 11.2

The Relationship Between Complexity, Centralization, and Formalization

Source: James W. Fredrickson, "The Strategic Decision Process and Organizational Structure," *Academy of Management Review* 11, no. 2 (April 1986): 291.

division of labor, and a very small managerial hierarchy. The chief executive makes all the decisions and there is minimal planning, training, or liaison work. A small restaurant with an owner-manager, cooks, waitresses, and waiters exemplifies this type of structure. This structure is similar to the implicitly structured organizations defined by Pugh, Hickson, and Hinings.[32] The simple structure works best in a simple environment (relatively homogeneous) that is changing. In such an environment, the CEO can keep up with the few key variables and can make quick decisions about them. Certainly, this was the situation at Celestial Seasonings in the early 1970s when Siegel and Hay, along with their friends and wives, ran the company as a small, democratic "family."

The *machine bureaucracy* is also centralized, but it is much more formal and complex than the simple structure. It relies on standardized, very formalized procedures, proliferation of rules and regulations, and formalized communications. It has large, functionally grouped units at lower levels and an elaborate administrative staff at the top. This structure works best in a simple and stable environment. It can monitor the few key critical variables and apply established standards in performing its work and responding to these variables. However, this structure does not respond well to a changing environment where new, critical variables may go untracked or rapid changes in monitored, critical variables may be met by the established, standardized response.

General Motors is an excellent example of a machine bureaucracy that no longer works within the context of the volatile, heterogeneous environment of the 1980s. A machine bureaucracy can be hard to change, particularly when it is so well-entrenched and gigantic as GM. A person or a group long accustomed to being told what to do cannot easily make independent decisions when the need arises. Even though GM is making a conscientious effort to dismantle part of its bureaucracy and push authority down the ranks, "learned helplessness" still abounds. A GM stamping plant in Pittsburgh became so reliant on orders from Detroit that plant managers were at a loss when told to set their own goals and solve their own problems.

The third organization structure is a *professional bureaucracy*. This is the structure most frequently used in hospitals, universities, school systems, and social service agencies. It is complex, informal, and decentralized. Highly trained individuals are expected to meet professional standards in their respective disciplines and thus control their own work. This leads to decentralization. The law firm of Finley, Kumble, et al., is a professional bureaucracy. Each of its branch offices is an autonomous law firm that is comprised of specialists dealing with individual legal areas such as litigation, banking, real estate, administrative law, and so on.

In a professional bureaucracy, detailed knowledge of specialized skill areas results in specialization and horizontal differentiation. Vertical differentiation is limited. This structure works best when it faces a complex, yet stable, environment. The specialized skills of its members allow the organization to deal with complexity. The professional standards allow an appropriate response. But if the environment changes rapidly, the professional bureaucracy has a difficult time adapting. It also has a difficult time forming a consensus and unity of action among the wide variety of highly specialized skill groups represented.

Fredrickson uses Mintzberg's three basic models—simple structure, machine bureaucracy, and professional bureaucracy—to provide a template for showing how centralization, formalization, and complexity are related. None of the models adapt well to a rapidly changing environment. Some of the structures examined in Chapter 10, such as the matrix, linking-pin, and SBU framework appear to do a better job.

SUMMARY

Organizations, if they are successful, can generally expect to increase (at least somewhat) in size as a result. This growth can be measured with a number of indicators such as market share, the presence of branch operations or products, or by the number of full-time employees or members.

We selected this last measure because we believe it to be a convenient, simple, common denominator for all organizations, and because it is more objective.

Although growth can be experienced at virtually any point in the structure, because of environmental pressures that require technical expertise, growth will be seen first (or certainly very early) in the support or staff elements. Labor specialization in the form of technical personnel begins to show in the form of record keeping, personnel activities, and such.

Mintzberg developed the model used in this chapter to depict the stages of an organization's growth. His growth stages begin with the craft organization, made up of an informal group in which the leader (if one is even recognized) works alongside the other members of the group. Organizations in this stage are generally quite small.

The entrepreneurial stage sees the emergence of vertical differentiation and the presence of more managers. Informality continues to characterize the organization, however.

The bureaucratic structure arises in the next stage. Formality (rules and procedures) starts, as does the elaboration of an administrative structure. The structure tends to become more rigid and even less innovative.

When the organization moves into other markets or locations, we find the divisional structure. Here each product or site develops its own bureaucracy, and a headquarters group is needed to hold the divisions together.

Finally, some organizations reach what Mintzberg termed the matrix structure. Here more than one base is used to support the structure, such as is the case with committee governance in universities.

When organizations begin to move through these various stages, several things tend to happen. The organization becomes more formal, differentiation increases, specialization begins, and there is more routinization. A more impersonal work environment that can breed alienation is observed. Finally, the chief executive officer devotes less and less time to daily operations.

Although much has been written about the relationship between size and structure, there is still some disagreement about what that relationship is. About the only conclusion that can be drawn with certainty is that more research is needed.

Delegation is the primary means of increasing the organization's size, but when it is practiced, management must use a variety of integration devices to hold the structure in a unified pattern.

Large organizations are often thought of as being complex. Organization complexity, according to Hall, contains three elements: horizontal differentiation, vertical differentiation, and spatial dispersion.

Finally, by examining Fredrickson's theoretical work, we saw that a series of relationships exists between the three dimensions of structure (centralization, formalization, and complexity) and Mintzberg's three structural types (simple structure, machine bureaucracy, and professional bureaucracy).

QUESTIONS FOR REVIEW AND DISCUSSION

1. What is organization size, and how can it be measured?
2. Where do organizations tend to grow first? Why?
3. How, specifically, can you use Mintzberg's model to understand organization growth?
4. Under what conditions would you use a matrix structure in a business organization? Why would you consciously decide not to use one?
5. How can you relate formality, differentiation, and size?
6. Is routinization always associated with large organizations? Explain.
7. Is there a causal relation between size and structure? Present a thorough analysis of this issue.
8. Relate delegation, integration, and organization size.
9. Does a large organization have to be complex? Explain.
10. What is machine bureaucracy? How does it differ from the simple structure and professional bureaucracy?

ENDNOTES

1. Dennis S. Mileti, David F. Gillespie, and J. Eugene Haas, "Size and Structure in Complex Organizations," *Social Forces* 56, no. 1 (September 1977): 208–217.

2. Anne B. Fisher, "GM Is Tougher Than You Think," *Fortune* (November 10, 1986), 56.

3. Kathleen Deveny, "Maytag's New Girth Will Test Its Marketing Muscle," *Business Week* (February 16, 1987), 68.

4. J. D. Ford and J. W. Slocum, Jr., "Size, Technology, Environment, and Structure of Organizations," *Academy of Management Review* 2, no. 4 (October 1977): 561–575.

5. John R. Kimberly, "Organizational Size and the Structuralist Perspective: A Review, Critique and Proposal," *Administrative Science Quarterly* 21, no. 4 (December 1976): 557–597.

6. Fisher, "GM Is Tougher Than You Think," 60.

7. John Child and Roger Mansfield, "Technology, Size, and Organization Structure," *Sociology* 6, no. 3 (September 1972): 369–393.

8. Henry Mintzberg, *The Structuring of Organizations* (Englewood Cliffs, N.J.: Prentice-Hall, 1979), 242–248.

9. Ibid., 242.

10. Mileti, Gillespie, and Haas, "Size and Structure in Complex Organizations," 208–217.

11. Paul R. Lawrence and Jay W. Lorsch, *Organization and Environment* (Cambridge, Mass.: Harvard University Press, 1967).

12. Stewart Ranson, Bob Hinings, and Royster Greenwood, "The Structuring of Organizational Structures," *Administrative Science Quarterly* 25, no. 1 (March 1980): 1–17.

13. Thomas A. Mahoney, Peter Frost, Norman F. Crandall, and William Weitzel, "The Conditioning Influence of Organizational Size on Managerial Practice," *Organizational Behavior and Human Performance* 8, no. 2 (October 1972): 230–241.

14. Richard H. Hall and Charles R. Tittle, "Bureaucracy and Its Correlates," *American Journal of Sociology* 72, no. 3 (November 1966): 267–272.

15. Richard L. Daft and Patricia J. Bradshaw, "The Process of Horizontal Differentiation: Two Models," *Administrative Science Quarterly* 25, no. 3 (September 1980): 441–456; also see Jonn W. Meyer and Brian Rowan, "Institutionalized Organizations: Formal Structure as Rite and Ceremony," *American Journal of Sociology* 83, no. 2 (September 1977): 340–363.

16. Paul M. Nemiroff and David L. Ford, Jr., "Task Effectiveness and Human Fulfillment in Organizations: A Review and Development of a Conceptual Contingency Model," *Academy of Management Review* 1, no. 4 (October 1976): 69–82.

17. Katherine M. Hafner, "Apple Is Getting a Few Gray Hairs," *Business Week* (January 19, 1987), 88.

18. Stanley Lieberson and James F. O'Connor, "Leadership and Organizational Performance: A Study of Large Corporations," *American Sociological Review* 37, no. 4 (August 1972): 119.

19. John Nielson, "An Upstart Law Firm Comes of Age," *Fortune* (September 29, 1986), 36–38.

20. David A. Whetten, "Sources, Responses, and Effects of Organizational Decline," in *The Organizational Life Cycle*, ed. John R. Kimberly and Robert H. Miles (San Francisco: Jossey-Bass, 1980), 342–374.

21. Robert M. Marsh and Hiroshi Mannari, "Technology and Size as Determinants of the Organizational Structure of Japanese Factories," *Administrative Science Quarterly* 26, no. 1 (March 1981): 33–57.

22. Peter H. Gringer and Masoud Yasai-Ardekani, "Strategy, Structure, Size, and Bureaucracy," *Academy of Management Journal* 24, no. 3 (September 1981): 484.

23. Jeffrey D. Ford, "The Administrative Component in Growing and Declining Organizations: A Longitudinal Analysis," *Academy of Management Journal* 23, no. 4 (December 1980): 615–630. For a rationale for the negative relationship between size and administrative personnel, see Peter M. Blau, "A Formal Theory of Differentiation in Organizations," *American Sociological Review* 35, no. 2 (April 1970): 201–218.

24. Peter H. Gringer, Masoud Yasai-Ardekani, and Shawi Al-Bazzaz, "Strategy, Structure, the Environment and Financial Performance in 48 United King-

dom Companies," *Academy of Management Journal* 23, no. 2 (June 1980): 193–220.

25. Robert D. Dewar and Donald P. Simet, "A Level Specific Prediction of Spans of Control Examining the Effects of Size, Technology, and Specialization," *Academy of Management Journal* 24, no. 1 (March 1981): 5–24.

26. Amanda Bennett, "Growing Small: Big Firms Continue to Trim Their Staffs, 2-Tier Setup Emerges," *The Wall Street Journal* (May 4, 1987), 1, 12.

27. Don Hellriegel and John Slocum, "Organizational Design: A Contingency Approach," *Business Horizons* 16 (April 1973): 59–68.

28. Joel Dreyfuss, "Toyota Takes Off the Gloves," *Fortune* (December 22, 1986), 78.

29. Richard H. Hall, *Organizations: Structure and Process* (Englewood Cliffs, N.J.: Prentice-Hall, 1972), 143–147.

30. Ibid., 114; and John Child, "Predicting and Understanding Organization Structure," *Administrative Science Quarterly* 18, no. 2 (June 1973): 168–185.

31. James W. Fredrickson, "The Strategic Decision Process and Organizational Structure," *Academy of Management Review* 11, no. 2 (April 1986): 290–297.

32. D. S. Pugh, D. J. Hickson, and C. R. Hinings, "An Empirical Taxonomy of Structures of Work Organizations," *Administrative Science Quarterly* 14, no. 1 (March 1969): 115–126.

ANNOTATED BIBLIOGRAPHY

Atherton, Roger M. "Centralization Works Best When Managers' Jobs are Improved." *Human Resources Management* 16 (Summer 1977): 17–20.
    Centralization often adversely affects the company's work climate and the confidence of its subordinates. Decentralization of individual responsibility may correct these adverse effects of centralization and also may be instrumental in improving the morale of individual managers.

Brown, David S. *Managing the Large Organization: Issues, Ideas, Precepts, Innovations.* Mt. Airy, Md.: Lomond Publications, 1986.
    This book emphasizes the unique management needs of the large organization, which are quite different from those of the small organization. Few writers on management have yet dealt directly with large organizations, or even acknowledged that size makes a difference. One compelling chapter deals with the significance of the culturally derived characteristics within the individual that the large organization is likely to overlook.

Cullen, John B., and Baker, Douglas D. "Administrative Size and Organization Size: An Examination of the Lag Structure." *Academy of Management Journal* 27, no. 3 (September 1984): 644–653.
    In order to understand the relationship between administrative size and organization size, two basic questions were addressed in this paper: (1) Does the explanatory power of within-organization models of the administrative/ organization size relationship vary by time lag of organization size? and (2) Given the discovery of differences among the time-lag models in terms of ex-

planatory power, can the differences be attributed to other organizational factors?

Cummings, Thomas G., and Srivostria, Surech. *Management of Work: A Socio-Technical Systems Approach*. Kent, Ohio: Kent State University Press, 1977.

This book is a systems approach to delegation within the organization. Delegation as it relates to power and responsibility, the allocation of equity within the company, the structuring of managerial roles, and the decision-making process are all covered.

Dewar, Robert D., and Simet, Donald P. "A Level Specific Prediction of Span of Control Examining the Effects of Size, Technology, and Specification." *Academy of Management Journal* 24, no. 1 (March 1981): 5–24.

This paper develops and tests a model that states in level specific terms the effects that size, routineness, and the number of different specialties have on the span of control. The number of specialties supervised was found to decrease spans at lower and middle levels, and increase them at upper levels. Routineness had little effect at any level. Size had little effect at lower levels, but a positive effect at middle ones.

Fisch, Gerald G. "Do You Really Know How to Delegate?" *The Business Quarterly* 54 (Autumn 1973): 17–20.

Addressed are the problems a manager must confront before delegating. Five suggestions that may be instrumental in determining who should receive the delegation are listed.

Ginzberg, Eli, and Vojta, George. *Beyond Human Scale: The Large Corporation at Risk*. New York: Basic Books, 1985.

The authors quickly and clearly introduce their thesis in Part I: The increasing scale and complexity of the large corporation results in the underutilization of its management personnel. This relationship is traced to the contention that the corporation is increasingly mismatched with its volatile market environment and values of its managers.

Haynes, Marion E. "Delegation: Key to Involvement." *Personnel Journal* 53 (June 1974): 454–456.

The author believes productivity and job satisfaction may be improved by involving personnel more in the organizational decision-making process. This involvement may be achieved through delegation.

Miller, Danny, and Friesen, Peter H. *Organizations: A Quantum View*. Englewood Cliffs, N.J.: Prentice-Hall, 1984.

The theoretical contribution of this book consists of the quantum perspective of organization structure, process, and change. This perspective embodies two propositions: (1) There exists clustering among organizational variables that is statistically significant and predictively useful and that reduces the variety of organizations to a small number of rich configurations and types, and (2) major organizational change takes place on a quantum basis, that is, because of the pressures for internal consistency among the variables of a configuration, organizations maintain their configurations for a long period of time and resist piecemeal or incremental change.

Perrow, Charles. "The Bureaucratic Paradox: The Efficient Organization Centralizes—Decentralizes." *Organizational Dynamics* 5, no. 4 (Spring 1977): 3–14.

This article assesses the question of how an organization can increase delegation while, at the same time, having an increase in bureaucratization. Bureaucracy is assumed to involve the centralization of authority. Therefore,
how can rules, standardization, specialization, and hierarchy produce more
decentralized decision making? This can be accomplished by minimizing
some first-order controls, thus decentralizing, and imposing second-order
controls, thus centralizing.

Weisse, Peter D. "What a Chief or Group Executive Cannot Delegate." *Management Review* 64 (May 1975): 4–8.
Weisse feels that certain degrees of responsibility cannot be delegated.

ADDITIONAL REFERENCES

Allen, Louis A. "How to Stop Upward Delegation." *Nation's Business* (July
1973): 16–22.

Alutto, Joseph, and Belasco, James A. "A Typology for Participation in Organizational Decision-Making." *Administrative Science Quarterly* 17, no. 1 (March
1972): 117–125.

Azumi, Koya, and McMillan, Charles J. *Subjective and Objective Measures of Organizational Structure.* New York: American Sociological Association, 1974.

Baron, James N., and Bielby, William T. "Bringing the Firms Back In: Stratifica-
tion, Segmentation, and the Organization of Work." *American Sociological
Review* 45, no. 5 (October 1980): 737–765.

Benson, Kenneth J.; Kunce, Joseph T.; Thompson, Charles A.; and Allen, David L.
Coordinating Human Services. Columbia, Mo.: University of Missouri Regional Rehabilitation Center, 1973.

Biggart, Nicole W. "The Creative-Destructive Process of Organizational Change:
The Case of the Post Office." *Administrative Science Quarterly* 22, no. 3
(September 1977): 410–426.

Bolman, Lee G., and Deal, Terrence E. *Modern Approaches to Understanding and
Managing Organizations.* San Francisco: Jossey-Bass, 1984.

Brewer, John. "Flow of Communication, Expert Qualifications, and Organizational Authority Structure." *American Sociological Review* 36, no. 3 (June
1971): 475–484.

Cullen, John B.; Anderson, Kenneth S.; and Baker, Douglas D. "Blau's Theory of
Structural Differentiation Revisited: A Theory of Structural Change or
Scale?" *Academy of Management Journal* 29, no. 2 (June 1986): 203–229.

Daft, Richard L., and Becker, Selwyn W. "Managerial, Institutional, and Technical
Influences on Administration: A Longitudinal Analysis." *Social Forces* 59
(1980): 392–413.

Daft, Richard L., and Bradshaw, Patricia J. "The Process of Horizontal Differentiation: Two Models." *Administrative Science Quarterly* 25, no. 3 (September
1980): 441–456.

Davis, R. C. *The Fundamentals of Top Management.* New York: Harper & Brothers, 1951.

Drucker, Peter. *The Practice of Management.* New York: Harper & Row, 1973.

Etzioni, Amitai. *A Comparative Analysis of Complex Organizations*. New York: The Free Press, 1975.

Fisch, Gerald G. "Toward Effective Delegation." *CPA Journal* 46 (July 1976): 66–67.

Freeman, John H., and Hannan, Michael T. "Growth and Decline Processes in Organizations." *American Sociological Review* 40, no. 2 (April 1975): 219–228.

Greiner, Larry E. "Evolution and Revolution as Organizations Grow." *Harvard Business Review* (July–August 1972): 37–46.

Hart, Stuart; Boroush, Mark; Enk, Gordon; and Hornick, William. "Managing Complexity Through Consensus Mapping: Technology for the Structuring of Group Decisions." *Academy of Management Review* 10, no. 3 (July 1985): 587–600.

Hostiuck, K. Tim. *Contemporary Organizations: An Introductory Approach*. Morristown, N.J.: General Learning Press, 1974.

Ivanavich, John M., and Donnelly, James H., Jr. "Relation of Organizational Structure to Job Satisfaction, Anxiety, Stress, and Performance." *Administrative Science Quarterly* 20, no. 2 (June 1975): 272–280.

Kaufman, Herbert. *The Limits of Organizational Change*. University, Ala.: University of Alabama Press, 1971.

Lehman, Edward W. *Coordinating Health Care: Explorations in Interorganizational Relations*. Beverly Hills: Sage, 1975.

Lorsch, Jay, and Morse, John. *Organizations and Their Members*. New York: Harper & Row, 1974.

Melcher, Arlyn L. *Structure and Process of Organizations: A Systems Approach*. Englewood Cliffs, N.J.: Prentice-Hall, 1975.

Miller, George, and Conraty, Joseph. "Differentiation in Organizations: Reconciliation and Cumulation." *Social Forces* 59 (1980): 265–274.

Moch, Michael K. "Structure and Organizational Resource Allocation." *Administrative Science Quarterly* 21, no. 4 (December 1976): 661–674.

Ouchi, William G. "The Relationship Between Organizational Structure and Organizational Control." *Administrative Science Quarterly* 22, no. 1 (March 1977): 95–113.

Roberts, Karlene H.; Hulin, Charles L.; and Rousseau, Denise M. *Developing an Interdisciplinary Science of Organizations*. San Francisco: Jossey-Bass, 1978.

Sisk, Henry L. *Management and Organizations*. 3d ed. Cincinnati: South-Western, 1977.

Stunn, D. "Control: Key to Successful Delegation." *Supervisory Management* 17 (July 1972): 2–8.

Taylor, James C. "Some Effects of Technology in Organizational Change." *Human Relations* 24, no. 2 (April 1971): 105–123.

Van de Ven, Andrew H., and Delbecq, André. "A Task Contingent Model of Work Unit Structure." *Administrative Science Quarterly* 19, no. 2 (June 1974): 183–197.

Yarmolinsky, Adam. "Institutional Paralysis." *Daedalus* 104, no. 1 (Winter 1975): 61–67.

```
C     A     S     E
```

People Problems

In 1981, People Express was the marvel of the airline world. As a small, just-starting company, it instituted a novel management philosophy and style—minimal bureaucracy, group organization of workers, rotation of staff through a variety of jobs, salaries tied to profits, and "manager" titles for everyone.

By the summer of 1986, the airline was in deep trouble, facing huge financial losses and even bankruptcy. To many business analysts, the organization's experiment in "popular" management, which was so successful when People was just starting out, became inappropriate as the company grew and its operations and operating environment became more complex.

Many companies throughout the 1970s and 1980s have experimented with participatory management styles (e.g., layers of authority have been replaced with peer or self management, decisions have been pushed to the lowest possible level). However, such styles, particularly within the long-term successful organization, should be sharply circumscribed. Dana Corporation, an auto parts manufacturer, gives its divisions broad latitude in such matters as hiring and firing, though *within limits* [emphasis added] specified by the corporate headquarters. At GM's Saginaw plant, workers and

Source: Amanda Bennett, "Airline's Ills Point Out Weakness of Unorthodox Management Style," *The Wall Street Journal* (August 11, 1986), 17.

managers consult one another on production problems, but only within their own areas of expertise.

At People, however, the participatory practices went much further. Each operating group of 250 people decided how it would carry out its assigned tasks. Employees moved from job to job, sometimes daily, and *everyone* had to deal with customers. Even the company's chief financial officer flew once a week as a flight attendant.

As the People organization grew rapidly, the jack-of-all-trades philosophy backfired. Complexity demanded stability among People employees, both in terms of their duties and the depth of their knowledge. For the rapidly growing organization, the lack of a tight organizational structure had detrimental effects. "Their unwillingness to put in a formal management structure was a key element to the current difficulties," noted an aviation analyst who has followed the company quite closely during the past two years.

By reducing commitment to specific tasks and encouraging job hopping, People lost a sense of stability and structure that is necessary to effectively manage large organizations. If management is left unstructured, then it is absolutely necessary to structure operations. "If you let your people roam free, then your machine part had better be pretty damn good," said Nicholas Radell, the president of a New York management consulting firm. By "machine part," Radell was referring to People's lack of a sophisticated computer, telephone reservation system, and baggage-handling system.

By shunning formal lines of authority and standard reporting procedures, the People "system" became unwieldy as the airline grew. As employees became more numerous, it became increasingly difficult to depend on phone calls and face-to-face meetings to make decisions, keep information flowing, and goals aligned.

People should've taken a lesson from other companies in similar predicaments. As Jim Manzi, chairman of Lotus Manufacturing Company in Boston, notes, "Managing a company with 1,200 employees isn't twice as difficult as one with 600. There's a multiplier effect." Lotus went from eight to 1,300 employees within four years, and just finished organizing itself into divisions that will allow it to retain the freedom of a small company in a more organized way. "It's not uncontrolled," said Manzi, "it's decentralized."

Finally, as People grew, it failed to set standards. Without standards, employees could not measure performance nor maintain a certain level of service. Indeed, if People Express Airline wished to remain a small, counter-culture airline, it could have maintained its viability for a much-longer period of time. However, as the company grew, it failed to realize that any given management style and structure are not appropriate throughout the organization's lifetime. Therefore, at the end of 1986, People Express Airline became a very easy takeover victim for Frank Lorenzo and his Texas Air conglomerate.

QUESTIONS FOR DISCUSSION

1. Evaluate the effect of size as a factor in the decline of People.
2. How could People's organization problems have been minimized, if not eliminated?
3. What action(s) would you suggest to fix whatever organization problems might exist? Justify your proposed action.
4. Give a complete examination of why a complex organization is more difficult to manage than a simple one.

12

The Role of Technology

Assembly-Line Work—No People Need Apply

The Allen-Bradley Company is a Milwaukee manufacturer of industrial controls and electronic components. As the 7:30 A.M. workday begins, the world's most advanced assembly line comes to life. Without any human intervention, small plastic casings begin rolling through the twenty-six automated assembly stations. Bar code labels, somewhat similar to the ones found on supermarket products, tell each assembly station what tiny different parts to install and in what combination. Mechanical arms, automatic screwdrivers, and laser printers now do the complex work that once required highly skilled human dexterity. When the casings are completed, they are packaged, sorted into customer orders, and directed to various chutes for shipment—all automatically. There are only four human technicians involved with this assembly process, and they are on standby just in case something goes wrong. The total time for the assembly run is forty-five minutes.

This automated assembly process, begun in April 1985, has put Allen-Bradley in the vanguard of the development and utilization of computer-integrated manufacturing (CIM), the ability to make different versions of a product at mass production speeds in lots as small as a single unit. Allen-Bradley can and does sometimes make a single unit out of an assembly run, without slowing down or stopping the line.

Because of its automated assembly system, Allen-Bradley has established itself as a leader in the highly competitive world of industrial controls/electronic components manufacturing. In the very recent past, the Europeans and the Japanese were the prime sources for these products. The industrial control devices manufactured by foreign firms (called IEC because they meet the standards of the International Electrotechnical Commission) were one-third the size and one-third the price of similar American products. As U.S. firms imported more foreign machinery, they also imported the foreign IEC parts. Prior to 1985, Allen-Bradley only manufactured American-type devices; thus, the firm was quickly losing out to foreign competition.

Deciding against using cheap foreign labor to build IEC devices, Allen-Bradley executives decided to invest $15 million in new technology that would be able to manufacture IEC devices in an effective and cost-efficient manner. Even though Allen-Bradley management realized that the ROI (return on investment) for such technology would be long-term, it tackled the "factory of the future" challenge in order to ensure concomitant long-term success.

The main technological problem facing the host of engineers and technicians on this project was finding the key to identifying the various products and their assembly components so that the assembly line would not have to be stopped for different versions. The key turned out to be the use of bar codes. The bar codes stand for the catalogue number of the product being manufactured, tell the machinery exactly what operations have to be performed and what parts are needed, and are printed on the spot at each assembly station by a laser printer. Indeed, these bar codes work so well that Allen-Bradley now uses the just-in-time inventory system (i.e., practically no inventory other than those materials needed for a day's assembly runs). Different components are manufactured in house the day before a run, or are shipped to the plant by outside suppliers the night before they are needed.

Sometimes a bar code can't be read because of a printing defect or a loose label; however, when this happens, an alarm

Source: Gene Bylinsky, "A Breakthrough in Automating the Assembly Line," *Fortune* (May 26, 1986), 64–66.

sounds and one of the four standby technicians fixes the problem in a matter of seconds, or at worst, minutes. Quality control for the entire operation is ensured by scores of computer-controlled sensors that can detect deviations as small as one-sixth the diameter of a human hair.

Tracy O'Rourke, Allen-Bradley's president, now claims that no competition anywhere can beat his company on the price and quality of IEC components. For U.S. companies, the Allen-Bradley experience shows that CIM is a viable technological process that can help U.S. industry regain its competitive edge within the world market.

High technology has come to Allen-Bradley and myriad other organizations throughout the world. Technology can be both a means and an end as high-tech processes manufacture high-tech products. As you study the present chapter, you will realize that technology is more than just computers and new ways of doing things. It is a major force, in and of itself, that affects all aspects of organization life.

CHAPTER PLAN

In this chapter we examine a very important component of organization theory, technology. We present our working definition of the term and show how it contains elements of both art and science. The Aston Group studies, with their well-known classification scheme based on the way technology is used in organizations, are discussed as is the relationship of technology to that most significant function in today's organizations, information processing.

Next, we present the macro aspects of technology by looking at technology and the environment. Here, we argue for an open-systems perspective in order to understand the interface of technology and the macro environment.

Following this discussion, we turn to various ways organizations behave in order to protect their core technology, that technology the organization utilizes to convert its resources into outputs. We then show how technology is diffused throughout society by examining five basic categories of adopters.

Woodward, Thompson, and Perrow give various schemes for classifying the types of technology, and we briefly describe each.

The relationship of technology and organization design is the next section of the chapter, and the final section presents sociotechnical systems and how they relate to technology.

This chapter is an overview of the concept of technology and how it affects organizational life on a daily basis. The real-life examples show that technology, though an abstract concept, is used in common business situations.

Technology has a profound impact on organizations. Manufacturing firms, retail establishments, hospitals, universities, and other organizations are each uniquely affected by the technologies they adopt. Although the search for technology began with the use of fire and primitive tools, it was not until the Industrial Revolution of the late eighteenth century that organizations began to develop and exploit the technology of machine manufacture. Adam Smith, in *Wealth of Nations* (1776), showed how the production of pins could be increased many fold through specialization and the use of better tools. The writings of Taylor, Gilbreth, and others advocating scientific management (reviewed in Chapter 1) focused on the better use of technology in manufacturing.

We briefly explained technology as an important part of the macro environment in Chapter 3. In this chapter, we focus on technology as a major aspect of the macro environment that is internalized by the organization. We explore some of the effects that technology has on organization operations. All organizations must employ a technology—a way of doing things—in order to exist. In designing and using a technology, organizations take from the outside environment. Perhaps no other aspect of the macro environment affects an organization as much as the technologies in that environment.

The discussion in this chapter is somewhat more technical than in other chapters. This is so because of the nature of technology; it is difficult to discuss technology without being technical. Consequently, in various parts of this chapter we highlight some of the important research studies that have been conducted on the effects of technology in organizations. This research is relatively new and there are many unanswered questions. We are likely to see more research on the issue as organizations strive to develop and use new technologies in order to survive and compete in our increasingly complex world.

WHAT IS TECHNOLOGY?

Definitions of technology vary from writer to writer. Some focus on machinery used in manufacturing. Others focus on the knowledge used. Still others examine human-machine interaction. The use of materials as part of technology is explored by still others. For the purpose of our treatment of organizations we take a rather broad view of technology and define it as the *art and science employed in the production and distribution of goods and services.*

This definition implies that technology incorporates the idea of the *way* an organization uses resources to produce products and services. In other words, technology deals with the *throughputs* in our systems model. It deals with the question, how are resources used in producing goods and services?

For example, we can envision the technology used in an automobile assembly line. Certain machinery is used in the process, and the machinery is placed in an appropriate configuration. Certain products are needed at the right time and place in the right quantity and quality. People with appropriate skills are needed to operate the line. All these factors make up the technology of producing an automobile using the principles of mass production.

Let us explore some other implications of our definition of technology.

Technology as Art and Science

Technology is very much affected by the level of scientific advancement in a society. Even primitive societies employ technology as goods are made and crops are grown. However, in advanced industrialized countries we view their technology as quite primitive, and we view ours as quite sophisticated.

Technology depends on science, but it also depends on the *use* of science. The use of scientific principles is often an art; that is, some discretion and judgment are inherent in the use of technology. For example, the manufacture of automobiles relies on a rather sophisticated technology based on many scientific principles. But the design of automobiles and the methods used to employ a given technology to produce the desired automobile is also an art requiring sophisticated skills as well as knowledge of scientific principles.

In Chapter 5, we discussed information processing and the important role played by MIS managers within modern organizations. We also discussed how important it was for these individuals to have managerial knowledge in addition to the technical knowledge required for computer-based information processing.

We return to this subject in the present chapter to further show how technology is both an art and a science. That is, technology is a "science" because it is founded on scientific research, processes, and principles. Technology is an "art" because human judgment and values are used in order to ensure that technology best serves the organization and society in general.

As an illustration of this dual nature of technology, note that many large organizations, such as American Airlines, Exxon, and Pillsbury, among others, have created a senior executive position called Chief Information Officer (CIO). Individuals holding CIO positions are not just technocrats; they are executives who have the ability, both technical and managerial, to straddle the historic gulf between the nontechnical people in the boardroom and the MIS managers from the data-processing department. CIOs look for ways to better harness the power of new information technology in order to slash costs, boost productivity, improve sales and marketing, and even help design the organization's overall grand strategy. For example, at Pillsbury, John M. Hammett, vice president for information management, is responsible for developing a company-wide strategy for new technology adoption. In order to carry out this responsibility, Mr. Hammett must be well versed in the art of management in addition to the science of technology.[1]

Production and Distribution

Although many writers in technology look strictly at production technology, we are also interested in distribution technology. Using our input-output model, we are concerned not only with how an organization produces goods and services but also with how it distributes them. We are also concerned with the process that a firm uses to acquire raw materials and other input resources.

In our introductory case, we read not only how the Allen-Bradley Company uses high technology to manufacture electrical components (throughputs), but also how it uses high technology in order to obtain the various parts for its components (inputs) in addition to sorting the completed components for distribution (outputs).

Goods and Services

Many writers focus only on product technology, but we are also concerned with the technology involved in the production and distribution of *services*. Services are intangible offerings of value that do not have physical form provided to a customer or client. For example, in the automobile industry, repairs, warranties, and financing are all services provided by auto manufacturers. Another excellent example demonstrating service technology is American Airline's SABRE reservation system, whereby computers allow American customers to make reservations for any flight on any airline at any time at any airport.

Some organizations provide only a service and no tangible product beyond, say, a document. For example, universities provide educational services to students; banks provide financial services; lawyers, doctors and other professionals provide services for individuals. In providing these services a certain technology is employed. Consider the university setting, for example: Educational services are provided through a technology that uses students, faculty, classrooms, books, and support materials in a certain configuration. Students meet in a class under the guidance of an instructor and discuss topics. Assignments from books and articles are read by the students and instructor. Students may do a paper or project thereby using writing instruments, paper, and typewriters. In some courses, movies, overhead transparencies, and slides may be used. Duplicated material may be distributed by the instructor or by individual students to the class. Almost always a chalkboard is used.

In some universities, the computer is used to provide individually tailored learning experiences and testing. For example, Florida State University has the PLATO learning system that allows a student to interact on an individual basis with the computer to progress through a set of learning experiences or problems. The advantage of this system is that it allows students to progress at their own pace and to go to the learning situation at their convenience instead of meeting in a scheduled class. One disadvantage of this system is that its initial adoption is costly, although over time it may be cheaper on a per-student basis than employing a large number of professors. Another disadvantage is that exclusive reliance on this method deprives the student of the opportunity to discuss ideas with other students and an instructor. Finally, the process requires a major change in professor and student behavior and course structure.

The technology of the delivery of most educational services has changed little from the time of Socrates, although books and other reading materials are certainly more readily available today. Still, the predominant technology employed is one of student-instructor interaction in a classroom setting. The use of more sophisticated technologies, not only in education but also in other service areas, is likely to be a continuing challenge.

Some organizations are neither clearly oriented toward manufacturing nor clearly service oriented. There are, for example, organizations that prepare food (manufacturing in a sense) as well as serve it (service). Today, many organizations, even though they offer a product, contain large and vital service elements (e.g., the U.S. Postal Service delivers mail, banks provide money, and stockbrokers trade stocks). From these few examples, you can see that simple, straightforward classification is difficult in today's environment. Figure 12.1 summarizes the manufacturing-service continuum in an effort to help place the classification system into perspective.

ASTON GROUP. In order to further clarify the classification issue, a group of researchers from the University of Aston in Birmingham, Great Britain, developed a scale classifying both service and manufacturing technologies.[2] They used the following classification factors:

1. *Automation of equipment.* This criterion can be utilized to distin-

MANUFACTURING	SERVICE AND PRODUCT	SERVICE
Steel	Restaurants	Hospitals
Automobiles	U.S. Postal Service	Law Firms
Mining	Stockbrokers	Universities
Rubber		

FIGURE 12.1

Examples of Service and Manufacturing Technologies

Source: Adapted by permission from Richard L. Daft, *Organization Theory and Design,* 2d ed. (St. Paul, Minn.: West, 1986), 143. Copyright © 1986 by West Publishing Company. All rights reserved.

guish between organizations whose machinery or technology can be placed on a continuum, with one terminus being "self-operated" and the other terminus being conditions in which work must either be performed or directed by people. Of course, the operations at the Allen-Bradley Company are highly automated, while some assembly line operations, such as those performed at AMC's Jeep plant in Toledo, involve a higher degree of interaction between people and machinery.

2. *Work flow rigidity.* This classification scheme is concerned with the degree of flexibility in both human skills and machinery capabilities. For example, a recent development occurring within engineering organizations is the introduction of computer-aided engineering (CAE) workstations. These workstations, according to Richard Nedbal, the president of Personal CAD Systems, are capable of handling about 80 percent of the work usually done by engineers.[3] Certainly, this is a very flexible technology considering the complexity of engineering work. On the other hand, an organization whose machinery is basically single-purpose (e.g., a stamping machine) would be considered rigid.

3. *Specificity of evaluation.* This factor refers to the degree to which work flow can be measured quantitatively as opposed to subjective evaluations made by managers. For example, high technology is now hitting the farming industry with the introduction of indefatigable and versatile robots that can do everything from picking oranges to milking cows. By measuring the number of oranges picked or gallons of milk collected, one can be quite specific in measuring the quantity of work performed by using this type technology. On the other hand, the trend in today's economy is to find organizations that must be evaluated and classified subjectively. An example of this type of organization might be service organizations such as universities, chambers of commerce, and so on. Even though these types of organizations might very well use a wide range of technologies in their operations, we cannot always measure their work flow using quantitative methods.

Combining these factors into a measure called *workflow integration*, the Aston researchers used a twenty-one point scale to study fifty-two organizations. They found that manufacturing firms had higher scores than service firms, which meant that manufacturing firms had higher degrees of automation of equipment, greater rigidity of work, and more precise measurement of operations than service firms. Firms that were rated high in workflow integration included a vehicle manufacturer, a food processor, and a metal goods manufacturer. Service-oriented units, including a savings bank and department stores, received a considerably lower score, indicating virtually the opposite characteristics from manufacturing firms.

It should be noted that the Aston studies were conducted in the mid-

1960s in Great Britain before the automation wave hit the retail trade in the late 1970s. The heavier use of automated equipment in retailing and banking might result in different scores if the study were conducted today, especially in the United States. However, many manufacturing firms have also become more automated, as exemplified by the Allen-Bradley case that introduced this chapter. Therefore, although the total scores might go up for both types of organizations, the relative scores might well stay the same.

As you can see, these studies provided fundamental bases for classifying organizations that can still be useful today, more than twenty-five years later.

Information Processing/Knowledge Technology

Our detailed discussion of the subject in Chapter 5 leads us to consider technology in another way: Technology is also used as a means to gather, process, store, and transmit information and knowledge. This occurs between the organization and its outside environment as well as within the organization. In a sense, this facet of technology is related to the service-producing aspect discussed previously. Technology is being used to produce information—a service activity essential to the functioning of an organization.

A person writing with pen and paper is using a particular technology to store and communicate information. But what really gave impetus to this view of technology was the development of computers, which focused attention on how sophisticated technology can be used to handle information. The invention of the microchip is continuing the electronic computer revolution, and the use of personal computers in home and office is proliferating. Technology and knowledge are likely to be two very closely related concepts in the future.*

TECHNOLOGY AND THE ENVIRONMENT

In this section we discuss the role of technology in a society and focus on how the organization ties in to the technological framework found in the society. Organizations deal with the technology available to them in dif-

---

*Galbraith relates information processing and knowledge issues to organization technology and design by pointing out that "... the greater the uncertainty of the task, the greater the amount of information that has to be processed between decision makers during the execution of the task." See Jay R. Galbraith, *Organization Design* (Reading, Mass.: Addison-Wesley, 1977), 36. Perrow also addresses this issue, but from a different perspective. He argues that the knowledge industry has been stimulated by the development of technology. See Charles Perrow, "Is Business Really Changing?" *Organizational Dynamics* (Summer 1974): 31–34.

ferent ways. Some are innovators and actually create new technology. Others are late followers and only adopt technology after it has been used by competitors for some time.

Macro Aspects

A certain state of technology exists within every society, whether it be primitive or advanced. The technology that exists is not always developed in a particular society but may instead be borrowed from other societies. The Arab countries, for example, are adopting much technology from the Western world in their industrialization effort.[4]

Sometimes the adoption of this new technology conflicts with existing social and cultural values and mores. We see this also in the Arab countries, but especially in Iran. The Iranian Islamic Revolution was an attempt by certain sectors in Iranian society to maintain and preserve aspects of the Iranian culture in the face of a massive infusion of Western technology under the Shah.

Sometimes technology is misapplied or misunderstood in a society. For example, the people in parts of Melanesia were completely unable to cope with the technological shock brought on by World War II. These islands were used as supply and staging areas; B-17s and B-29s would land on runways cut out of the jungle and deposit large amounts of cargo for use in the war. Once the war ended, the natives constructed crude small-scale models of airplanes and runways. Using incantation and ceremony, they hoped to attract planes that would leave more cargo for them.

Cargo cults such as those in Melanesia have arisen in other primitive societies that have experienced a sudden impact of sophisticated technology from an outside country. The people are so shocked by this technology and are so unable to understand it that their adjustment to it is irrational. It is dealt with from a magic or religious perspective, not from a scientific one.

Even when a technology develops primarily from within a society, there is often resistance to it. For example, during the Industrial Revolution in England in the early nineteenth century, people known as Luddites rioted and smashed the new looms and machinery in textile mills, claiming that the new technology would soon put them out of jobs. Such radical reactions to technology have occurred in other societies. The Mennonites and Amish religious groups in parts of Pennsylvania, Ohio, and Indiana even today shun automobiles, electricity, modern machinery, and modern clothes in favor of a lifestyle typical of the 1880s. Most of them are farmers and still use horse-drawn plows, horse-drawn buggies, and kerosene lamps. In the late 1960s and early 1970s there was an anti-technology movement in the United States precipitated by the sophisticated use of technology, including napalm bombing, by the

United States in Vietnam. Groups demonstrated not only against the war in Vietnam but also against the pervasive use of and dependency on technology. The counterculture prevalent at that time argued for a return to a less hectic, back-to-the-land existence. Partly as a result of this anti-technology movement, farm communes were formed, natural foods were advocated, the supersonic transport (SST) was killed, and environmental protection legislation was passed.

On the other hand, there can be an insatiable demand for high technology and its products by segments of society. An excellent example of this has been the introduction of the compact disk and compact disk player in the music industry. Indeed, so high is the demand for these products by the music-loving segment of society that companies such as CBS Records and Polygram Records are running out of capacity to produce them. For the music lover, compact disks bring the concert hall into the home. Certainly, there is no anti-technology movement among the millions of compact disk devotees.

Thus, we see that the rise of technology in a society has many effects on that society. One major result is the effect on values. A certain technology embodies a set of values. For example, new technology embodies the values of efficiency and innovation. These values might conflict with existing values of tradition and stability, which in some societies are more important than change and innovation.

Technology might also give a different meaning to existing values in society. For example, in New Guinea during World War II, the natives were given metal axes by the Allied military to replace the stone axes they were using. The metal axes were extremely more efficient and allowed the native to more easily cut trees and clear land, but the social effect of this new technology was disastrous. Stone axes were the primary means of expressing status: They were passed down from generation to generation and represented far more than a device to cut wood. The elaborateness of the ax, who had used it, and how long it had existed all had symbolic meaning. Replacing these tools with identical metal axes completely eliminated the important social function they had played. The metal axes cut better, but they had no social meaning. Devising other means to express social status and meaning took time, and in the interim the society was in turmoil.

Another example comes from American society. Prior to Henry Ford's introduction of the Model T, automobiles were the playthings of the rich. People who had cars had high status and prestige. The cheap Model T enabled everyone to own a car, and car ownership no longer carried its previous status. (Of course, luxury cars still carried status, but car ownership in and of itself did not.)

Automobiles are not the only products that technology has made available to the masses. When compact disks and compact disk players were first introduced, they cost an average of $22 and $1,000, respectively. However, as the technology associated with their production advanced, the prices dropped to an average of $12 and $250, respectively. Thus, in 1984, 5.8 million compact disks were sold, while one year later, this figure rose to almost 15 million.[5]

Interface

Rousseau strongly argues that the technological component of the macro environment must be viewed from an open-systems perspective today especially because it interfaces with organizations so intricately.[6] No longer is it appropriate to view technology from a simplistic, closed-systems point of view. Rousseau states quite effectively that one of the shortcomings of the study of organizational technology has been its narrow, closed-systems view. The application of the newer, open-systems perspective can help organizations understand the truly turbulent technological developments that occur daily. We do know that organizations interact with their environments and adopt existing technology that is viewed as consistent with their particular operations. Some organizations even create technology, through a research and development effort, which they may adopt and may sell to other organizations. Basic research in universities and research companies such as Battelle Memorial Institute and the RAND Corporation results in technology that is used by others. Research performed under the guidance of the National Aeronautics and Space Administration (NASA) has resulted in the creation of much technology by a variety of firms.

How an organization links up with the macro environment for technological adoption can be expressed in Figure 12.2. Here, the *core* represents the technology used by the organization in its internal processes. The *infrastructure* technology is composed of various organization buffers that organizations use to incorporate and mediate the influence of technology in the outside environment.[7] For example, the infrastructure might consist of purchasing, shipping, and personnel departments. Each of these departments employs a technology in obtaining resources for the organization and in distributing goods and services produced. The infrastructure might also consist of engineering departments and research and development (R & D) departments whose job it is to find and locate technologies in the outside environment that can be used by the organization. Engineering and R & D might also create a new technology for use by the organization by modifying existing outside technology.

The technology employed in the core is most certain in that it is well known since it is in use; the organization has had experience with it. Technology in the macro environment is more uncertain in that the organization has had little, if any, experience with it. This is why an organi-

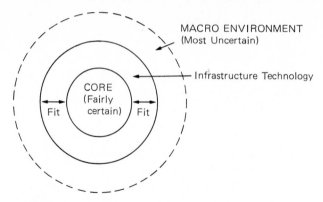

FIGURE 12.2

Macro-Micro Interface and Technology

Source: Adapted from Mariann Jelinek, "Technology, Organizations and Contingency," *The Academy of Management Review* 2, no. 1 (January 1977): 22.

zation may be reluctant to adopt a new technology even if it has proved successful in other firms. There is always the nagging question, "Will it work here?"

Core Technology

Thompson identifies the actual technology employed by the organization as the *core technology*.[8] This is the technology the organization uses to convert its resources into output. It occurs in the transformation box in our input-output systems model of the organization. For example, in 1985, IBM's core technology was primarily directed at the manufacture of its best-selling mainframe, the 3080. In addition, core technology is also employed in the development of new products, as we can see in the case of IBM. While it was producing the best-selling 3080, it was at the same time developing the next generation of mainframes, the 3090.

Thompson argues that, under norms of rationality, organizations seek to "seal off" and protect their technical cores from the disturbing influences of environmental uncertainty. (*Norms of rationality* refers to an organization's operating in a planned, rational way as opposed to one acting in a helter-skelter manner.) He states that organizations seek to protect their technical core by using the following methods: *buffering, smoothing, anticipating,* and *rationing*. The four methods are actually used by the organization, according to Thompson, to protect the technical core from *any* changes in the outside environment, not just technological ones. However, since we are concerned with changing technology as it affects the technical core, we discuss them here. Where applicable, we will show how IBM used these methods to protect both its 3080 mainframe production and 3090 mainframe development.

BUFFERING. This refers to methods used to protect the technical core from fluctuating levels of inputs and fluctuating market demand. For example, stockpiling raw material such as coal in an inventory is a way of buffering varying delivery schedules. Thus, if there is a delay in coal delivery, the organization need not close down but can tap its inventory. By the same token, storing finished goods in a warehouse buffers the organization from changing market demand or difficulties experienced by shippers.

SMOOTHING. This method refers to leveling or smoothing out incoming raw materials or departing products produced. Whereas buffering absorbs environmental fluctuations, smoothing or leveling involves attempts to reduce fluctuations in the environment. Retail organizations may offer special sales during off or slow periods such as in late January or February. Airlines might provide a reduced fare at night or during traditionally slow days.

Let's examine IBM operations to better illustrate this point. When IBM customers held off on their purchases of the 3080 mainframe in anticipation of the introduction of the newer 3090, IBM simply cut the price of its 3080 models in order to move them faster.

ANTICIPATING. Organizations can also forecast resource availability on the input side and demand on the output side. Their forecasts are then incorporated into plans for operations. If a slack period is forecast the company may schedule layoffs or may close for retooling. If a tight market for a key resource, such as oil, is forecast, alternative energy supplies might be located. At IBM, executives anticipated increased demand for its 3090 mainframe. Therefore, the company moved up its production and delivery schedules for this new product.

RATIONING. When all else fails, organizations may ration resources on the input side or sales on the demand side. Because IBM could not deliver its 3090 mainframe to all the customers who had ordered it, the company promised its biggest and best customers that they would receive first priority. In other words, IBM rationed (for a short while) the 3090.

Rationing occurs on the input side when a multiplant operation allocates limited resources to each plant operation in the face of a serious shortage. All plants are kept in operation, but each plant is on a reduced work week because of the unavailability of a key raw material or semifinished product. Plants may even be closed down on a rotating basis.

Diffusion

The last topic we address in this section is the question of the diffusion of technology. How rapidly is technology adopted by the organization? Although not addressed by Thompson, the question of technological diffusion is a major one for the organization. The technical core must be protected from massive, dysfunctional influences of new technology but cannot be so protected that new technology is never adopted. The question becomes, how can new technology be incorporated into the technological core yet minimize dislocations and other dysfunctional effects?

This question is a key one in many industries in the United States today as firms attempt to revitalize and adopt new technology. Because of the concern with sagging productivity and foreign competition, many organizations are faced with finding ways to adopt new technology in a rapid yet orderly manner while reducing the adverse consequences. For example, in the automobile industry the need to automate much of the production process by using robots is a key technological question that must be answered if the U.S. auto industry is to remain cost-competitive with foreign imports. The use of sophisticated technology in steel, railroads, and other basic industries in order to increase productivity to remain competitive is also required.

Organizations need to develop and use methods to incorporate the new technology with available financial resources and in a way that minimizes the impact on human resources. Questions that need to be addressed include the following:

1. Shall we provide protection from layoff and termination for our employees as we adopt new technology?
2. Can our employees be retrained and replaced in light of the new technology?
3. Will we be able to hire the right kind of employees with skills appropriate for the new technology?
4. What effects will the new technology have on employee morale and wage rates?
5. How can we work with the union in adopting the new technology?
6. If the work force is to be cut, can we do it through normal attrition?

RCA provides a good example of where new technology was introduced in the production of color television sets in such a way that productivity was enhanced and employee security was protected. RCA is now competitive with Japanese manufacturers of color television sets because it was able to borrow and adopt a sophisticated technology from the Japanese and introduce it with minimal adverse effects.[9] In fact, an employee is quoted as saying:

Machines are more accurate. Transistors and integrated circuit boards have wiped out many of my old jobs, but now we make a much better TV set—and faster, too.

This attitude is representative of RCA employees. They view advancing technology as a necessity in order to remain competitive. The fact that RCA was able to introduce the technology while guaranteeing present employees job security by providing other training and jobs in the company no doubt contributed to this positive view by employees.

Studies on the diffusion of technology evolved from studies on new product adoption found in studies of adoption in agriculture. A taxonomy developed by rural sociologists explains how new products and techniques are adopted.[10] There are five basic categories of adopters, which are briefly discussed below. These categories help us to understand how organizations adopt new technology in that they help us to classify the behavior of organizations. They also show us that technology is adopted in phases; that is, certain organizations adopt technology prior to other organizations. Technological improvements do not appear at once throughout an industry.

INNOVATORS: VENTURESOME. These are the adventurous risk takers, similar to the prospectors in the Miles and Snow typology that we discussed in Chapter 7, who are eager to try something new. They are the first to adopt a new technology. Innovators travel in a friendship clique and share information among themselves even if they are separated by great geographic differences. Innovators must control substantial financial resources to absorb the loss of an unprofitable innovation and must have the ability to understand and apply complex technical knowledge. Rogers places only 2.5 percent of adopters of technology in this category.[11]

In the 1980s, demands from the competitive and consumer/client components of the macro environment are requiring organizations to become much more technologically innovative than they have been. Companies such as 3M, Paragon Optical, and Polymer Technology can be considered innovators in the development of new polymer chemicals used in extended-wear contact lenses. Older style extended-wear contacts, because of their chemical composition, had been linked to an alarming rise in eye infections. Therefore, these companies are on the cutting edge to develop and adopt these new polymers.

EARLY ADOPTERS: RESPECTFUL. This is the second group to adopt innovations. Early adopters have a local orientation as opposed to the more cosmopolitan orientation of innovators. Early adopters are leaders viewed with respect in their community and are considered as the people to consult by others who later make an adoption. Rogers places 13.5 percent of adopters as early adopters.[12] A respectful early adopter would be a company such as Superior Market Research, a Utah-based organization that recently acquired the rights for a new technology that will allow for the self-refrigeration of beverage cans.

EARLY MAJORITY: DELIBERATE. The third group of adopters adopts new ideas just before the average members of a social system. Their link between the early adopters and late-to-adopt groups makes them important in the process of legitimizing innovations. This group deliberates for some time before adopting a new idea, and follows a longer adoption period than either of the first two groups. Rogers puts about 34 percent of adopters in this category.[13]

A company such as CBS Records can be considered a deliberate early adopter of compact-disk technology. It accepted this new way of recording music after the idea was first adopted and put into mass production by Sony, an early respectful adopter.

LATE MAJORITY: SKEPTICAL. This is the group that adopts new ideas just after the average person in a social system. This group is much like Miles and Snow's reactors. The weight of public opinion must be in favor of the innovation before the late majority is convinced. This group responds to social pressure in adoption and does not adopt until a clear majority of others have adopted the idea. Rogers states that 34 percent make up this group.[14]

Certainly, GM falls into this category. It was very late in adopting and implementing the robotics technology utilized for automobile assembly operations.

LAGGARDS: TRADITIONAL. This group is the last to adopt an innovation, and they correspond to Miles and Snow's defenders. They are the most local oriented of all adopter categories and many are near-isolates. Their focus is on the past and tradition. Change, change agents, and new ideas are generally resisted. This group primarily reacts with others who greatly value tradition. The adoption process of this group is slowed to a crawl. In fact, by the time they adopt the innovation, the innovators may have already replaced the innovation with a new technology. Of course, some in this category never adopt the new ideas or innovation. Rogers places 16 percent of the relevant social population under study in this group.[15]

Even though an organization can be termed a laggard according to our definition above, this does not necessarily mean that a given organization is unsuccessful. Nabisco, the maker of Shredded Wheat, has been making the *same* biscuit with the *same* technology for 100 years! At the company's Niagara Falls, New York plant, over 38 million pounds of shredded wheat were produced in 1986, with machinery that was patented in 1886 and installed in that plant in 1901.[16]

We are now ready to explore the types of technology employed in organizations.

TYPES OF TECHNOLOGY

There have been several ways to type or classify existing technologies. In this section, we review each of the major classification schemes that has been developed.

Woodward

One of the first studies of the effect of technology and organizations was completed by Joan Woodward, whom we briefly discussed in Chapter 1. For her study she classified technology into one of three classifications:

1. *Unit*—where production runs consist of only a few units at a time, such as that found in a specialty job shop.
2. *Mass*—where many units are produced at one time, such as that found on an automobile assembly line.
3. *Continuous*—where the production runs continuously with no start-ups and down times on a daily or weekly basis, such as in refining gasoline or producing fertilizers and chemicals.[17]

Woodward's classification scheme is helpful but it has some disadvantages. First, it focuses solely on manufacturing and ignores technology employed in nonmanufacturing sectors such as education and other service sectors. Second, it examines the core technology employed and does not deal with the technology used in the infrastructure. In other words, it does not examine distribution technology. Third, it is not useful in all cases as a method of classification. For example, in a steel mill or glass plant there is continuous operation because it is very expensive to have the furnace and machinery sitting idle, and it is very expensive to turn the furnace off and on. Yet glass and steel plants are also engaged in mass production. Hence, where should they be classified, as mass production technology or continuous process technology?

Thompson

Thompson's scheme partially overcomes the limitations of Woodward's. He develops three types of technology: long-linked, mediating, and intensive, which we also briefly reviewed in Chapter 1.

LONG-LINKED TECHNOLOGY. This is the technology used when one step must be completed after another step. In other words, the steps must be done in a specified order:

A ⟶ B ⟶ C ⟶ D ⟶ E

Long-linked Technology

The automobile assembly line is a classic example of long-linked technology, since various parts must be manufactured and then assembled in a specific order. Building a home is another example of long-linked technology. One would not try to install plumbing and electrical work after the drywall has gone up. A channel of distribution in retailing is also an example of long-linked technology since the product is shipped from company warehouse to wholesaler to a regional distribution center to a local retail store in a specified sequence. As you read in our introductory case, the Allen-Bradley Company uses a very automated form of long-linked technology.

MEDIATING TECHNOLOGY. Here the technology brings together organizations with complementary needs. For example, banks bring together borrowers and depositors. Real-estate agencies bring together home buyers and home sellers. Employment agencies bring together employers with open jobs and employees seeking work. Wholesalers bring together manufacturers with products and retailers with a need for product to sell. The Social Security Administration brings together those seeking benefits and government providing the benefits. In fact, many government agencies are examples of mediating technology. American Airline's SABRE reservation system is also an excellent example of this type of technology in that it brings together reservations agents and airline customers.
     The mediating technology can be depicted as follows:

Facilitating

Organization with Need ⟶ ◯ ⟵ Organization with Resource

Organization

Mediating Technology

INTENSIVE TECHNOLOGY. The last technology type discussed by Thompson involves the technology used to assemble a variety of techniques and methods in order to accomplish a specific goal. Here, a variety of different techniques, methods, and skills is brought together for a specific time period in order to accomplish a specific purpose, as depicted below:

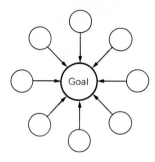

Intensive Technology

The intensive-care ward of a hospital is one example of this technology, as is NASA in developing rockets and the space shuttle. A multidisciplinary consulting firm that can solve organization problems such as reducing job turnover is also an example of intensive technology. A large counseling center designed to provide a range of counseling skills to patients or clients with emotional problems is another. One might also argue that a university with a variety of schools, colleges, and course offerings for students is also an example of intensive technology.

Certainly, an organization such as Polymer Technology, which is devoted to the development of safe extended-wear contact lenses, is involved with intensive technology. Chemists, engineers, and optometric experts must all work together to ensure that this new technology and its resultant products are successfully developed.

Thompson's framework certainly improved on Woodward's in that it is more generalizable to both the service sector and the infrastructure. But it, too, has limitations. For example, what classification would one use for General Motors, which uses an intensive technology in its R & D department, a long-linked one in its assembly line and distribution operations, and mediating technology in its financing through GMAC? Also, how would the services of a specialist such as a brain surgeon or heart specialist be classified? Finally, Thompson does not deal explicitly with the issues of complexity or variability of technology in a given case. For example, some long-linked technologies are quite complex and allow variability and exceptions (e.g., assembling different automobile models with color and option combinations), while others are fairly simple and allow for few variations (e.g., the assembly of bicycles).

Perrow

The final typology we examine was developed by Charles Perrow.[18] His typology is a bit more complex than either Woodward's or Thompson's. Essentially, he defines technology along two dimensions: *exceptions* and *analyzability of problems*. With regard to exceptions he classifies technology by the number of exceptions the technology allows. Those technologies with high routine have few exceptions; those with a varied routine have many exceptions:

The degree of flexibility allowed in organization operations, then, depends to some extent on the number of exceptions allowed by the technology. If the technology is highly routinized with few allowable exceptions, such as in the continuous operations of a refinery, organization operations are likely to be less flexible. If the technology is varied and allows many exceptions, organization operations can vary more easily.

The Allen-Bradley Company, whose automated assembly operations serve as the focal point of our introductory case, is an organization whose technology allows many exceptions. Remember how bar codes are printed at each assembly point in order to produce different electrical components, thereby maximizing flexibility.

Perrow's second dimension for classifying technology is the analyzability of problems. Problems can vary between easily analyzable and unanalyzable:

Easily analyzable problems can be solved fairly easily by organization decision makers. There is a routine for solving them and the organization has had experience with them. Updating job descriptions would be an example of this type of problem. Problems that are unanalyzable are so complex and foreign to the organization that the organization's decision makers have a very difficult time solving them. Designing a service delivery system tied to a management information system in social welfare services exemplifies an unanalyzable problem for many county and state social welfare service agencies. When you read the end case to this chapter, you will see how American automobile manufacturers have encountered many unanalyzable problems as they attempt to master the high technology they rapidly introduced to their operations in the mid-1980s.

Using the two dimensions of exceptions and the ease of solving problems, Perrow develops a four-category taxonomy of technology as shown in Figure 12.3. The four categories are *craft, nonroutine, routine,* and *engineering.* Craft technologies deal with relatively few exceptions and unanalyzable problems, such as those of specialty glass manufacturing. Nonroutine technologies deal with many exceptions and unanalyzable problems, such as those of aerospace firms. Routine technologies deal with few exceptions and analyzable problems, such as those of tonnage steel mills and screw and bolt manufacturers. Finally, engineering technology, such as that used in heavy machinery manufacturers, deals with many exceptions but easily analyzable problems.

Perrow's scheme is more comprehensive than either Woodward's or Thompson's, yet using the two criteria of the analyzability of problems and the amount of exceptions allowed can create some problems. What might be an unsolvable problem for one organization using one technology may be solvable for another organization in the same industry using a different technology. By the same token, one organization may be able to build in flexibility with a particular technology while another in the same industry may not because of the way the particular technology has been employed in that organization. Nevertheless, Perrow's scheme helps to hypothesize the effect technology has on other organization variables such as goal setting, structure, job design, and control.

Table 12.1 presents a summary of the three technology types discussed here.

FIGURE 12.3

Perrow's Technology Model

Source: Charles Perrow, "A Framework for the Comparative Analysis of Organizations," *American Sociological Review* (April 1967): 194–208.

TABLE 12.1

Summary of Technology Types

Name	Types	Examples
Woodward	Unit	Machine shop, shipbuilding, construction
	Mass	Auto assembly line, electronics assembly
	Continuous	Refineries, chemicals, fertilizers
Thompson	Long-linked	Auto assembly line, channel of distribution
	Mediating	Banks, real-estate agents, employment agencies
	Intensive	Intensive-care ward, NASA, university
Perrow	Craft	Specialty glass, handicraft shop
	Nonroutine	Aerospace, weapons systems
	Routine	Tonnage steel mills, screw and bolt manufacturing
	Engineering	Heavy machinery, construction

TECHNOLOGY AND ORGANIZATION RELATIONSHIPS

Researchers have tried to determine the relationship between technology and certain organization variables. In these studies technology is usually treated as an independent variable, and its effect on certain dependent variables is analyzed. In this section we do not propose to cover all research in this area; rather, we highlight only a few of the more important relationships.

Before beginning this discussion we should mention some of the limitations of the previous research on technology. First, the research on technology and organizations is relatively recent and somewhat spotty. The sample organizations studied have been few and the number of variables examined and their relationships are rather limited. Second, most researchers look at technology only as it exists in core technology and ignore it in the infrastructure for the most part. Third, the research treats technology as an independent (causing) variable; it may be a dependent (caused) variable or an interactive variable (dependent in some situations, independent in others). Fourth, the research generally ignores interactive effects of dependent variables and technology. Finally, much of the research either ignores or holds constant the role technology plays in the macro environment in which the organization finds itself. Bearing these limitations in mind, let us examine some of the relationships.

Technology and Organization Design

No doubt the technology employed by an organization has a substantial effect on the way the organization designs itself. Design refers to two major components: organization structure and the organization policies, procedures, and operations that make the structure work.

Most of the early work in technology focused on the effect technology had on human behavior at work, as shown in Figure 12.4. Issues such as worker alienation, job enrichment, and job design were addressed. Currently, much of the research examines the technology-structure relationship. What many researchers define as organization structure we label organization design. Design includes structural plus other elements, as we pointed out earlier.

Woodward studied six aspects of design and related them to her three taxonomies of technology. She found the following:

1. The number of management levels was greatest under continuous technology and smallest under unit technology.
2. The ratio of direct to indirect labor was highest under unit technology and lowest under continuous.
3. The ratio of line to staff positions was highest under unit technology and lowest under continuous technology.
4. The span of supervision was greatest in mass and smallest in continuous production.

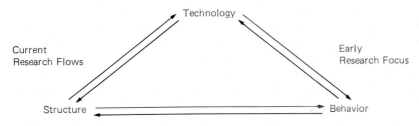

FIGURE 12.4

Research in Technology, Structure, and Behavior in Organization Theory

Source: David F. Gillespie and Dennis S. Mileti, "Technology and the Study of Organizations: An Overview and Appraisal," *The Academy of Management Review* 2, no. 1 (January 1977): 13.

TABLE 12.2

Woodward's (1965) Technology and Design Dimensions

Structural Dimension	Technology		
	Unit	Mass	Continuous
Median scalar levels[a]	4	5	7
Median span of supervision	23	48	15
Median direct to indirect labor	9:1	4:1	1:1
Median line to staff labor	8:1	5½:1	2:1
Formalization	Low	High	Low
Centralization (decision making)	Low	High	Low

[a]Includes supervisory management levels plus one level of nonsupervising employees.

Source: Joan Woodward, *Industrial Organization: Theory and Practice* (London: Oxford University Press, 1965).

5. Formalization, as evidenced by rules, policies, and procedures, was highest in mass production and low in both unit and continuous production.
6. Decision making was most centralized under mass technology and least centralized under both unit and continuous technology.

Table 12.2 summarizes the relationships she found.

Woodward's research tells us that certain characteristics are associated with each type of technology:

Unit Technology
   Few levels of management
   Medium span of supervision
   High ratio of direct to indirect labor
   High ratio of line to staff positions
   Low formalization
   Low centralization of decision making

Mass Technology
   Medium levels of management
   Wide span of management
   Medium ratio of direct to indirect labor
   Medium ratio of line to staff positions
   High formalization
   High centralization of decision making

Continuous Technology
   Many levels of management
   Narrow span of management
   Low ratio of direct to indirect labor
   Low ratio of line to staff positions

Low formalization
Low centralization of decision making

Even though Woodward's study involved a relatively small number of companies in England, her work is of major importance because, for the first time, it produced research evidence that shows how technology affects some of the major concepts in organization theory.

Since Woodward's study, additional studies have been done. Ford and Slocum provide us with a summary of the research on the relationship of technology to certain organization design issues, as listed in Table 12.3. What this research summary shows us is that as technology allows for more routine, repetitive tasks, the following variables increase:

1. Administrative intensity (a ratio of managerial and administrative positions to nonadministrative positions)
2. Horizontal differentiation (the degree of specialization by task or function)
3. Vertical differentiation (the number of administrative or management levels of authority)
4. Formalization (the degree to which policies, procedures, and rules are formally stated in written form)
5. Centralization (the degree to which decision-making authority is located toward the top of the administrative hierarchy)

A negative relationship exists between routine tasks and personnel differentiation, the degree of differences in personal expertise. No relationship is demonstrated by the research reviewed between the degree of task routine and spatial differentiation, that is, the degree of geographic dispersion.

This summary tells us that as organizations adopt more routine technologies that allow few variations, we are likely to see more complex organizations that have high formalization, centralization, and a large number of administrative positions. Some might say that task-routine technologies lead to centralized bureaucracies. In other words, as technology that leads to very standardized ways of producing a product is adopted, the organization tends to become more like a traditional bureaucracy. However, if technology that allows flexible task routines is adopted, the organization tends to be the opposite of bureaucracy. We have seen in previous chapters that decentralized, flexible organizations are often what are needed.

More recent evidence suggests that vertical differentiation is actually *decreasing* as more technology is introduced to organizational operations. John Naisbitt, author of the best-selling *Megatrends*, and famous futurist, wrote in 1985 that "There will be a tremendous whittling away of middle management." Naisbitt bases his statement on the premise that

TABLE 12.3
Technology and Organization Design

| | Administrative Intensity | Complexity | | | | Formalization | Centralization |
		Horizontal Differentiation	Vertical Differentiation	Spatial Differentiation	Personnel Differentiation		
Technology							
Routine	Increases	Increases	Increases	No Relationship		Increases	Increases
Nonroutine					Decreases		

Source: Adapted from Jeffrey D. Ford and John W. Slocum, Jr., "Size, Technology, Environment and the Structure of Organizations," *The Academy of Management Review 2* (October 1977): 571.

450

middle managers serve largely as passers and processors of information, and the computer now appears to be spelling the end of the hierarchical structure in organizations. Therefore, as a direct result of the introduction of computer technology within organizations, Naisbitt believes that organizations will develop along horizontal, not vertical lines.[19] Indeed, many companies, such as DuPont, Kodak, and Texas Instruments, among others, have abolished entire middle management layers during recent restructurings. As many organizations introduce automation in the workplace, large assembly and production departments have correspondingly shrunk, further lessening the need for supervisory and middle management layers. Note the title to our introductory case, "Assembly Line Work—No People Need Apply."

Finally, recent evidence indicates that technology is causing some companies to get bigger while simultaneously causing others to fail. This is because technology is very expensive. Let's take the example of the $145 billion U.S. telecommunications industry. With the breakup of the Bell System in 1984, analysts now believe that only those telecommunications companies with the resources to offer competitive pricing, the most advanced technology, and the best customer service will survive.[20] Smaller companies, without the necessary resources, must either drop out of the business or consolidate with other organizations, the latter course of action being necessary to consolidate research and development costs. Thus, we see organizations such as Communication Satellites and Centel merging in order to compete with such giants as AT&T and MCI. This phenomenon also applies to organizations outside the telecommunications industry. Intel and IBM have entered into a five-year technology exchange agreement; Motorola and Toshiba of Japan recently agreed to exchange technology; and DuPont has been buying promising smaller high-tech companies in order to increase its efficiency and balance sheet.

Before we leave the topic of technology, we shall explore briefly the relationship of technology and the design of tasks and jobs in organizations.

TASK DESIGN AND TECHNOLOGY: SOCIOTECHNICAL SYSTEMS

The use of a particular technology in an organization results in a particular set of tasks. These tasks are then grouped into a particular set of *jobs*. A job is a grouping of tasks within a prescribed unit or units of work. A job encompasses a set of duties, functions, and responsibilities. Secretary, supervisor, engineer, electrician, clerk, vice president are all examples of job units.

In this section we do not provide a complete overview of task and job design; that is better left to a book on personnel management or organizational behavior. Our objective is to briefly examine how technology affects the way tasks and jobs are designed.

There are two basic approaches to job design. The first and more traditional approach to job design is to *fit people to jobs*, the second is to *fit jobs to people*. Each of these approaches differs in philosophy and technique, as we see below.

Fitting People to Jobs: The Traditional Industrial Ethic

Using this approach, a technology that is best from the standpoint of productivity and economic efficiency is employed. This results in a set of jobs to be filled. People are then selected and trained so that they can perform the jobs. The industrial engineer is the kingpin in this approach. People are viewed almost as an extension of the machine. They are engineered to fit the jobs that the technology (machines) dictates. The job is considered almost as an inflexible socket determined by the technology, and the person is pliable rubber that can be made to fit the socket. This relationship is shown as follows:

This is the traditional manner in which jobs are designed as a country industrializes. It is conducive to job specialization and assembly-line operations.

Fitting Jobs to People: The Task of a Post-Industrial Society

Under this approach, the capabilities of an available labor force take precedence over the technology to be employed. The skills, abilities, and aspirations of the available labor force are first analyzed, and a technology is adopted that results in jobs consistent with the available skills and abilities. The industrial psychologist is the kingpin in this approach. The job is viewed as moldable rubber and the person is viewed as rather rigid and unbending as he or she presents available skills, abilities, and aspirations to the organization. We can depict this as follows:

Those who agree that jobs should be designed with people in mind advocate this approach. Much of the job-redesign and job-enrichment literature that argues for more challenging and inherently motivating jobs rests ultimately on the idea that jobs should be redesigned to better fit people who occupy them.

We normally think of this latter approach as the mode of the future, but Davis argues that this was the approach used by early industrialists in the United States to take advantage of the hordes of unskilled immigrants that came to this country around the turn of the century.[21] He argues that very specialized jobs were created through mass production and assembly-line techniques that were easily learned by uneducated and unskilled immigrants. That is, the technology of the period was well suited to the labor force.

Whether this situation was caused consciously by managers at the time or was a happy coincidence is undetermined, although there is some evidence it may have been a conscious effort. As long ago as 1835, Babbage argued strongly for the use of division of labor and for highly specialized jobs that could be easily learned by the unskilled.[22] Whether these industrialists knew of and used Babbage's ideas in designing jobs for immigrants is unknown.

Today, the argument is made that jobs of the future should be designed to tap the higher skills, abilities, and aspirations of a developed work force. Unchallenging jobs should be done by machines, specifically robots. People should be left to do the challenging jobs associated with the service aspect of the economy. Hence the argument that designing jobs to fit people is the challenge of a post-industrial society.

On the other hand, there is some evidence that people with lower IQs and those who have difficulty in handling complex relationships prefer highly structured jobs—what many of us would consider routine unchallenging jobs. Thus, there will likely be a place for highly structured jobs that do fit the needs of a particular segment of the labor market.

Sociotechnical Systems: A Middle Ground?

Perhaps neither of the above approaches is appropriate. Perhaps jobs should be designed while considering the people and the technology simultaneously. The industrial engineer and the industrial psychologist should work together; neither should rule the roost.

FIGURE 12.5

The Sociotechnical Systems Approach to Job Design

Sociotechnical systems is the field that explicitly recognizes both the human factor (socio) and the technical factor (technology) in designing jobs. This explicit recognition of each factor considers each as equally occurring within a holistic systems framework. The whole person is considered, and the range of factors that impinge on the human-machine interface is explicitly considered in a systems framework, as shown in Figure 12.5.

The use of the sociotechnical approach has its roots in both group dynamics and *ergonomics*, the science of studying how tools and equipment can be adapted to human use. For example, the design of a doorknob would take into consideration how the human hand works and average strength of the hand. The design of chairs would consider average weight and height of people plus the structure of the human body. The design of tools and equipment in construction and plant manufacturing would consider various aspects of the human body as well as strength, fatigue, and movement. Ergonomics, coupled with how people act in work groups, helps us to better understand the human-machine interface.

Applying the sociotechnical systems concept in individual cases requires consideration of the individuals in the particular organization. Brousseau presents a model that shows the factors that need to be considered in assessing the job-person fit (Figure 12.6).[23] This is a dynamic process and gives explicit consideration to the specific factors associated with the individual (career stage, current needs and abilities, previous job experience, and developmental sequence) and the organization (organizational context of the job). The organizational context of the job is where the technology used by the organization would be manifested.

The sociotechnical approach extends ergonomics considerably and

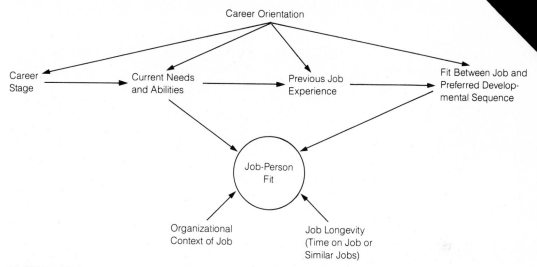

FIGURE 12.6

A General Model of Job-Person Dynamics

Source: Kenneth R. Brousseau, "Toward a Dynamic Model of Job-Person Relationships: Findings, Research Questions, and Implications for Work System Design," *Academy of Management Review* 8, no. 1 (January 1983): 38.

uses group dynamics principles to take a much broader approach. Because it gives explicit consideration to both the human factor and the machine, it serves as a good base for understanding job design issues in organizations. Technology cannot be fully understood in the organization apart from its relationship to people; however, since this text focuses on macro organization issues, further discussion of the people-technology interface is best left to a text in personnel management or organizational behavior.

The sociotechnical approach, in and of itself, however, is not a panacea for increased productivity. Within the past decade, a multitude of organizations have introduced computer workstations, particularly within offices. These workstations, designed for the efficient and effective interaction between people and machines, can be indispensable tools for the secretary and white-collar manager. However, as reported in *Fortune*, the payoff from many of these computer workstations has been "puny."[24] This is because of inadequate supervision, machine underuse, and improper work-flow design. In many cases, managers do not scrutinize their

ıtions before they automate with these new workstations. When
do automate, they then often go through a painful learning process.
y Bancroft, a manager in Digital Equipment Corporation, stated, "If
le are doing the wrong things when you automate, you get them to do
ırong things faster."[25] Therefore, it is imperative, when considering
ociotechnical approach for job design, that the organizational con-
ιεχι of the job, in addition to other factors, be considered from an interactive systems viewpoint.

SUMMARY

Technology has a major effect on organizations. Our broad view of technology defines it as the art and science involved in the production and distribution of goods and services. We are concerned not only with the core
technology of an organization but also with its infrastructure technology—the technology used to link the organization with its environment—and the technology of the macro environment. Our open-systems
model makes it plain that the macro environment provides a technological state that affects not only the organization's structure and design but
also the design of its jobs. Further, technology has an interactive effect
with cultural values of the society.

Rogers has given us a taxonomy that illustrates how new technology
is diffused through a society. His five classes of technology adoption are
innovators, early adopters, early majority, late majority, and laggards.

Various writers have developed typologies of technology. Woodward
examined unit, mass, and continuous technologies. Thompson looked at
long-linked, mediating, and intensive technologies. Perrow developed a
comprehensive classification system of craft, nonroutine, routine, and
engineering technologies based on the number of exceptions allowed and
the analyzability of problems addressed by the technology.

Much of the research in the area of the organization technology linkage suffers from several faults. Technology is almost always treated as an
independent variable rather than as a dependent or interactive one. The
macro environment for technology is frequently excluded from analysis;
core technology is usually the focus of the research; and little has been
done to study the infrastructure technology.

Finally, the issue of job design brings to focus the relationship of technology to the design of jobs and the people who fill them. Even though a
detailed discussion of job design is beyond the scope of this book, we are
interested in sociotechnical systems as a way of understanding the marriage of social and technical factors in organizations.

QUESTIONS FOR REVIEW AND DISCUSSION

1. What is technology?
2. What role does technology play in the macro environment?
3. Distinguish between core technology and infrastructure technology.
4. How is technology diffused throughout the organizations in a given society? (Consider Rogers's five categories of adopters.)
5. Explain the three typologies of technology described in the chapter (Woodward's, Thompson's, and Perrow's). In your opinion, which is the best typology and why?
6. What are the basic findings of research in the area of relationships between technology and organization design and structure? What are the limitations to this research?
7. What are task and job design? What are the two basic approaches to job design?
8. What is meant by sociotechnical systems? How are they related to ergonomics and group dynamics? How does this approach reconcile the two basic approaches to job design?
9. Pick a job you have held in which technology had an immediate and direct impact on how the job was designed. Why did it have such an impact and how did it affect what you did?
10. Think of a job you have held in which technology had little impact. Why was there little impact? How did the role of technology in that job affect what you did?
11. In what ways did the job of question 9 differ from that described in question 10, from a technological perspective?
12. What is the technology employed in the learning situation in the class for which you are using this text? Is it appropriate? How could this technology be improved?

ENDNOTES

1. Gordon Bock, Kimberly Carpenter, and Jo Ellen Davis, "Management's Newest Star: Meet the CIO," *Business Week* (October 13, 1986), 160–172.
2. D. J. Hickson, D. S. Pugh, and D. C. Pheysey, "Operations Technology and Organizational Structure: An Empirical Reappraisal," *Administrative Science Quarterly* 14, no. 1 (March 1969): 91–114.
3. John P. Newport, Jr., "How PCs Shook an Industry," *Fortune* (September 16, 1985), 105–106.
4. Karen Elliot Huene, "As Saudi Wealth Rises, Traditional Values Fall and Anxieties Spread," *The Wall Street Journal* (June 2, 1981), 1.
5. Brian Dumaine, "The Compact Disk's Drive to Become the King of Audio," *Fortune* (June 8, 1985), 104.

6. Denise Rousseau, "Assessing the Technology in Organizations: Closed Versus Open Systems Approaches," *Academy of Management Review* 4, no. 4 (October 1979): 531–542.

7. Mariann Jelinek, "Technology, Organizations, and Contingency," *Academy of Management Review* (January 1977): 21.

8. James D. Thompson, *Organizations in Action* (New York: McGraw-Hill, 1967), 14–24.

9. Raymond A. Joseph, "Automation Helps RCA and Zenith Keep Color-TV Leadership in Face of Imports," *The Wall Street Journal* (May 5, 1981), 56.

10. Everett M. Rogers, *Diffusion of Innovations* (New York: Macmillan, 1962), 168–171.

11. Ibid.

12. Ibid.

13. Ibid.

14. Ibid.

15. Ibid.

16. "Shredded Wheat Biscuits Reap More in Sales than Niagara Company Sows," *The Tallahassee Democrat* (April 15, 1987), 16D.

17. Joan Woodward, *Industrial Organization: Theory and Practice* (London: Oxford University Press, 1965).

18. Charles A. Perrow, "A Framework for the Comparative Analysis of Organizations," *American Sociological Review* (April 1967): 194–208.

19. John Naisbitt, "Re-inventing the Corporation," *FE* (March 1985), 40.

20. John J. Keller, "As the Big Get Bigger, the Small May Disappear," *Business Week* (January 12, 1987), 90.

21. Louis Davis, "The Design of Jobs," *Industrial Relations* (October 1966): 21–45.

22. Charles Babbage, *On the Economy of Machinery and Manufacturers,* 4th ed. (New York: Charles Knight, 1835), 119–122, 172–190.

23. Kenneth R. Brousseau, "Toward a Dynamic Model of Job-Person Relationships: Findings, Research Questions, and Implications for Work System Design," *Academy of Management Review* 8, no. 1 (January 1983): 33–45.

24. William Bowen, "The Puny Payoff from Office Computers," *Fortune* (May 26, 1986), 20–24.

25. Ibid., 22.

ANNOTATED BIBLIOGRAPHY

Aldag, Ramon J., and Brief, Arthur P. *Task Design and Employee Motivation.* Glenview, Ill.: Scott, Foresman, 1979.
This is an excellent summary of research on job design and enrichment. It incorporates some aspects of sociotechnical systems.

Alexander, Judith W., and W. Alan Randolph. "The Fit Between Technology and Structure as a Predictor of Performance in Nursing Subunits." *Academy of Management Journal* 28, no. 4 (December 1985): 844–859.
Regression analyses of a field study of twenty-seven nursing subunits sup-

ported the hypothesis that a simple measure of fit between technology and structure is a better predictor of quality of care than either technology or structure alone, or the two together.

Betz, Frederick. *Managing Technology: Competing Through New Ventures, Innovation, and Corporate Research.* Englewood Cliffs, N.J.: Prentice-Hall, 1987.

This book focuses on bridging the cultures within an organization—between technical and other functional personnel (e.g., marketing and finance). The author begins by covering the overall process of introducing new technology, from the invention of technical knowledge to its commercialization. He next discusses entrepreneurship that is required to manage technological innovation into successful new business ventures. After stressing the need for organizations to manage research so that they can maintain technical competitiveness, Betz closes the text with a summary of the R & D infrastructure of the nation.

Bigoness, William J., and Perreault, William D., Jr. "A Conceptual Paradigm and Approach for the Study of Innovators." *Academy of Management Journal* 24, no. 1 (March 1981): 68–82.

An operational approach for measuring an organization's innovativeness is proposed. This procedure draws on measurement theory to overcome problems often associated with single product and composite measures of innovativeness. A criterion variable is used to test the relationship between selected organization characteristics and firm innovativeness. Firms possessing internal technical expertise were found to be more innovative than firms without such expertise.

Blauner, R. *Alienation and Freedom.* Chicago: University of Chicago Press, 1964.
This is a review of the concept of alienation and its relationship to individual freedom. It points out the role of technology, among other factors, that affects alienation, and discusses the relationship between technology and cultural values.

Ford, J. D., and Slocum, J. W. "Size, Technology, Environment, and the Structure of Organizations." *Academy of Management Review* 2 (April 1977): 561–575.
This article is an excellent review of the research on organization design as it relates to size, technology, and the environment. Summary matrix tables relate technology to various organization design issues such as complexity, formalization, and centralization.

Gerwin, D. "The Comparative Analysis of Structure and Technology: A Critical Appraisal." *Academy of Management Review* 4 (October 1979): 41–51.
This article is a good review of the pitfalls of current research in organization structure and technology. It points out the major problems with current research and suggests future directions for research.

Hackman, J. Richard. "The Design of Work in the 1980s." *Organizational Dynamics* (Summer 1978): 3–17.
This article is an excellent look at the two routes to job design and their consequences. Route One is described as fitting jobs to people and Route Two is described as fitting people to jobs. The author speculates that a Route Two approach will prevail in the 1980s even though he favors a Route One approach.

Marcus, A. A. "Policy Uncertainty and Technological Innovation." *Academy of Management Review* 6, no. 3 (September 1981): 443–448.

This article considers the key impact of government policies on organizations and innovations. Some key factors affected by public policy are economic stability, research and development, improvement in communication channels, and the overall cultural and social environment.

Noble, David F. *A Review of Forces of Production: A Social History of Industrial Automation.* New York: Alfred A. Knopf, 1984.

Noble develops a plausible case that the development of numerical control systems in organizations followed a path leading to high levels of sophistication due to social and political rather than technological forces. Moreover, an intriguing account of the quest for a factory without workers and the role of military priorities in shaping the development of technology are presented.

Perrow, C. "A Framework for the Comparative Analysis of Organizations." *American Sociological Review* 32 (1967): 194–208.

Perrow's typology of technology and how it was derived are presented. Examples of each type are shown.

Rogers, Everett M. *Diffusion of Innovations.* New York: Macmillan, 1962.

This is the classic work on the adoption of new ideas, products, and technologies. It contains original work done with the adoption behavior of farmers. It also develops the five categories of adoption.

Rousseau, Denise M., and Cooke, Robert A. "Technology and Structure: The Concrete, Abstract, and Activity Systems of Organizations." *Journal of Management* 10, no. 3 (Fall 1984): 345–361.

The authors develop a framework that specifies the qualitatively different components that constitute technology in organizations, the hierarchical arrangement of these components, and the nature of organizational structuring. The components considered are those associated with the concrete, the abstract, and the activity systems that characterize organizations. These system components are then integrated into a model of technology and structure.

Sahal, Devendra. *Patterns of Technological Innovation.* Reading, Mass.: Addison-Wesley, 1981.

The major contribution of this book lies in formulating an evolutionary theory of technological capabilities. This theory has led to the development of a unified, general conceptual framework for analysis and management of technological change. In addition, a number of patterns of industrial innovation processes are identified and explained, and their policy implications are defined.

Thompson, James D. *Organizations in Action.* New York: McGraw-Hill, 1967.

This book presents Thompson's typology of technology and develops propositions on how national organizations protect their technical core from environmental influences.

Tushman, Michael L., and Moore, William L. *Readings in the Management of Innovation.* Marshfield, Mass.: Pitman, 1982.

This book presents a variety of readings covering a broad range of topics such as industrial and consumer products and services, high and low technology, short and long product life cycles, major corporations and small firms attempting to grow, setting strategy and direction for innovation, and the anatomy of successful innovations.

Woodward, J. *Management and Technology*. London: Her Majesty's Office, 1958. This is the first and classic study of the effects of technology on structure. It develops typology of mass, unit, and continuous technologies.

ADDITIONAL REFERENCES

Adler, P. A. "New Technologies, New Skills." Harvard Business School Working Paper 9-784-086, 1984.

Billings, R. S.; Klimoski, R. J.; and Breaugh, J. A. "The Impact of a Change in Technology on Job Characteristics: A Quasi-experiment." *Administrative Science Quarterly* 22 (1977): 318–339.

Cherns, A. "The Principles of Sociotechnical Design." *Human Relations* 29 (1976): 783–792.

Child, J., and Mansfield, R. "Technology, Size and Organization Structure." *Sociology* 6 (1972): 369–393.

Cooper, R., and Foster, M. "Sociotechnical Systems." *American Psychologist* 26 (1971): 467–474.

Dewar, R., and Hage, J. "Size, Technology, Complexity, and Structural Differentiation." *Administrative Science Quarterly* 23 (1978): 111–136.

Edwards, Frank L., and Larwood, Laurie. "Strategic Competitive Factors in the Acquisition of Technology: The Case of Major Weapon Systems." In *Academy of Management Proceedings 86*, edited by John A. Pearce, II and Richard B. Robinson, Jr., 289–298. Chicago: Academy of Management, 1986.

Glisson, C. A. "Dependence of Technological Routinization on Structural Variables in Human Service Organizations." *Administrative Science Quarterly* 23 (1978): 383–395.

Greene, K. B. *Sociotechnical Systems: Factors in Analysis, Design and Management*. Englewood Cliffs, N.J.: Prentice-Hall, 1973.

Hackman, J. R. "Work Design." In *Improving Life at Work*, edited by J. R. Hackman and J. L. Suttle, 96–162. Santa Monica, Calif.: Goodyear, 1977.

Herbst, P. G. *Socio-technical Design*. London: Tavistock, 1974.

Hickson, D. J.; Pugh, D. S.; and Pheysey, D. C. "Operations Technology and Organization Structure: An Empirical Reappraisal." *Administrative Science Quarterly* 14 (1969): 378–397.

Hirschhorn, Larry. *Beyond Mechanization*. Cambridge, Mass.: MIT Press, 1984.

Martin, Michael J. *Managing Technological Innovation and Entrepreneurship*. Reston, Va.: Reston Publishing, 1983.

Trist, E. L., and Bamforth, K. W. "Social and Psychological Consequences of the Long Wall Method of Coal-Getting." *Human Relations* 4 (1951): 6–38.

Van de Ven, A., and Delbecq, A. "A Task Contingent Model of Work-Unit Structure." *Administrative Science Quarterly* 19 (1974): 152–163.

```
C    A    S    E
```

Glitches

By the late 1970s, Detroit finally realized that Japan's automakers had become a significant competitor in the U.S. auto market. Not only were Japanese cars averaging $1,500 cheaper than comparable U.S. models, they were also better. This new fact of life set in motion a massive attempt by U.S. automakers to improve the productivity of their plants and the quality of their products. By June 1986, the "Big Three" had spent over $40 billion to build highly automated, state-of-the-art plants that were intended to put the United States back in the forefront of world automobile manufacturing.

Plans have gone awry. In 1983, Japanese cars averaged $2,500 cheaper than comparable models and were still better quality. On the surface, Detroit's new high-tech plants are as sophisticated as anything in Japan; however, productivity and quality are mediocre at best.

The reason for this debacle is the multitude of "glitches" Detroit has encountered with new production processes and equipment. For those unfamiliar with high-tech jargon, a glitch is "an unexpected technical mishap." Ford's ultra-

Source: John McElroy, "Project Saturn: GM's Great Leap Forward," *Automotive Industries* (January 1984), 27–29; John McElroy, "T-Wagon Plant: Chrysler's Productivity Show Place," *Automotive Industries* (February 1984), 57–58; Arthur Flax, "Assembling Big Trucks Defies Mass Production Methods," *Automotive News* (December 30, 1985), 12–13.; Russell Mitchell, "Detroit Stumbles on its Way to the Future," *Business Week* (June 16, 1986), 103–104.

modern assembly line had so many glitches that the company had to postpone by four months the introduction of its Sable and Taurus cars. At GM's Hamtramck plant, continuing glitches have resulted in a 30 percent shortfall in new car production quotas. Similar problems are facing GM at its Buick City complex, which, on the surface, is a copycat of Japanese high-tech auto plants.

Why are American auto manufacturers having such problems with the high technology that was supposed to revitalize the industry? The answer, says David Cole of the University of Michigan, is that "They're now discovering that if you don't have good management, you'll end up with a rotten automated plant." In other words, Detroit assumed that technology, in and of itself, would be the panacea to all its production and quality problems.

General Motors's Hamtramck plant best exemplifies the problem. Designed to produce luxury cars with state-of-the-art technology, this plant's multitude of computer-controlled robots sat idle for months while GM employees tried to figure out the software needed to make them run. In the Hamtramck paint shop, software problems forced GM to ship unpainted autos to a nearby conventional plant for painting. In addition, a highly complex inspection station was placed at the wrong spot on the assembly line; therefore, many defects were not caught.

On the other hand, older technology is working just fine for GM at its NUMMI joint-venture-with-Toyota plant in California. The key to NUMMI's success, say analysts, is Toyota's management style, which focuses on thorough training of employees, participative management, lean layers of middle management, and decision making pushed as close to the assembly line as possible.

GM hopes to take its NUMMI success one step further with its Saturn project. Saturn's goal is to build small cars in the United States that can match or even surpass the Japanese in terms of cost, quality, safety, and handling. In order to attain this goal, GM will implement the most advanced manufacturing and assembly technologies. But even as GM builds Saturn in Tennessee, problems develop with new technologies that must be debugged before successful operations can begin. For example, Saturn will utilize a robotic loading dock, whereby a robot will "see" various cartons of parts from the back of delivery trucks. However, in order for the robot to unload the right carton, the carton must be in the exact place in the unloading sequence. Should the carton be out of sequence or move along the rollers a fraction of a second out of time, then the whole system will shut down.

At present, Chrysler has best adapted to the new technology among the U.S. "Big Three." That's because Chrysler took the time to develop thorough training programs to prepare workers to handle the new technology. For example, Chrysler's Windsor, Ontario, plant is the company's most modern and sophisticated assembly operation. At Windsor, Chrysler employs a factory information system (FIS) that monitors most of the automated and semiautomated assembly equipment. The FIS scrutinizes production and maintenance operations and can even locate machine failure or provide an early warning for potential breakdowns. What keeps the FIS and other high-tech equipment working properly are Chrys-

ler's highly trained and motivated employees. When the Windsor plant was being converted in 1983 from manual to automated production methods, employees at all levels underwent extensive training in the new high-tech equipment. Indeed, the operations at Windsor were running so smoothly that in 1984 the vans produced there had the lowest number of defects of any Chrysler product manufactured anywhere.

Ford is now facing up to its past mistakes. "We didn't do an adequate job of planning the whole process," admits John A. Betti, Ford executive vice president. With Ford's old system, it took forty-two days to get a new assembly line into "production-run" order—now it takes twice as long. At Ford's Kentucky truck plant in Louisville, a sign reads, "Warning: This machine subject to break down at times of critical need." Moreover, because many large trucks are special ordered, standardized automated assembly methods are not always the best way to build them. However, in fairness to Ford, we must note that many high-tech operations at the Kentucky plant run at maximum efficiency because of Ford's Employee Involvement Program, which seeks inputs from employees concerning the best ways that humans and machine can work together.

Although neither Ford nor GM is retreating from new technology, both organizations are now taking a long, hard second look at the different ways they can effectively manage high technology within their plants. GM's subsidiary, Electronic Data Systems, is currently looking at already existing GM technology and systems that work well with a view toward improving them. At the GM Saturn plant, which is expected to open in

1989, planners have been delegated more authority for designing operations with the help of computer simulation.

Detroit is finding out the hard way that technology is not an independent miracle system. Rather, it is a two-edged sword that must be managed and integrated with other organizational systems.

QUESTIONS FOR DISCUSSION

1. Using the classification system in this chapter, describe in detail the type of technology contained in this excerpt.
2. Is it significant that the technology in question is the auto industry's core technology? Explain your answer in terms of its consequences to the organization's structure and interface systems.
3. What are the consequences of this high technology for job design?
4. Does the traditional "fit people to jobs" approach still apply in high-tech companies? If not, what alternative approach would you suggest and why?
5. Speculate on the configuration of the design of an organization engaged in high-tech production. In your answer, be careful to include a rationale for it.

PART FOUR

Organizational Dynamics

T he four chapters in this last section of the text concern those parts of organization theory that are a bit more "energetic" than those discussed up to this point. They bring the balance of the text to life.

Chapter 13 defines culture and shows how it forms within an organization. We briefly define culture as that mix of values, beliefs, assumptions, meanings, and expectations that members of a group hold in common and that guide their behavior and decision making. An organization's culture can be seen and felt by observing the ceremonies and rituals of the organization, its symbols, slogans, language, myths, and stories, and even its physical environment. Where culture is adopted by a large portion of the organization and is seldom questioned, it is said to be *thick*; if it is not widely adopted, it is said to be *thin*. We also discuss some means for maintaining cultural flexibility and show how culture is related to commitment. Because it is important to manage culture, it is necessary to audit it, and so we treat this function in the chapter. The final section deals with the ties between an organization's strategy and culture, and we talk about ways of dealing with these ties. Culture is an integral part of organization theory, and Chapter 13 will help you appreciate its important role.

Power, authority, and politics are the subjects of Chapter 14. Here, we discuss the nature of power and authority and relate both concepts to organization behavior. We also examine the foundations of power and authority. We then show how responsibility and accountability are tied together. The last sections of the chapter deal with power, authority, and politics. We discuss the dynamics and sources of power and how to assess their role in organization theory. Commitment and external dependency are examined and, finally, how power is used in organizations is covered.

Chapter 15 contains material that is needed to understand some of the potential consequences of using power and authority within an organization. This chapter explains how organizational conflicts come to be and the various coping strategies that can be used for dealing with situations full of conflict.

In Chapter 16 we look at how change affects the organization and how the organization adapts. Sources of change and how to plan for them are included as is a particular examination of macro environmental change and its effects. The management of organizational change is also covered in this last chapter, with special attention given to organizational development. We close with an appraisal of the bureaucratic structure and speculate briefly on what tomorrow's organization is likely to be like. This last section of the text places the other parts of organization theory into a dynamic evaluation of organizations and how they work.

13

Organizational Culture

Steppin' Up

The best-selling book *In Search of Excellence* notes that "excellent" companies are those with a strong, or thick, culture—"a set of shared values, norms, and beliefs that gets everybody heading in the same direction."

Successful companies and thick cultures do not just happen. Just as a successful company makes deliberate plans to produce a product or service that will sell, it must also develop a "socialization" plan for new employees, a plan whose goal is to attain social conformity, or thick culture, throughout the entire organization. This is done because a high degree of social conformity enables organizations to work better.

The great U.S. companies (e.g., IBM, Procter and Gamble, and Morgan Guaranty Trust) have perfected their socialization processes to acculturate new employees. As a result, these organizations have a great deal of internal consistency concerning operations and role relationships. Internal consistency is based on shared attitudes, habits, and values that, in turn, foster cooperation, integrity, and communication.

For example, at IBM there is conformity among employees regarding dress, behavior, and lifestyle. These are the superficial aspects of thick culture that make it easier for people to be comfortable with each other and work together. More important, employees are dedicated to the three cornerstones of IBM's philosophy—respect for the dignity of the individual, customer service, and excellence.

Organizations that do not promote the development of a thick culture through socialization invite conflict and capriciousness into their organizational lives. For example, at Atari, the electronic games manufacturer,

Source: Richard Pascale, "Fitting New Employees into the Company Culture," *Fortune* (May 28, 1984), 28–40.

there were no clear values and rules of behavior. Managers and routines were constantly changing, with the result that employees became burned out as the company lost both direction and profits in the mid-1980s. At Atari, individuals' social roles were unclear; no one spoke the same "language"; and trust and communications had broken down. Some organizations rely totally on formal rules and regulations to guide behavior without any reference to informal culture and values; thus these organizations are often associated with rigidity, bureaucracy, and "oversteering."

By synthesizing information from IBM, Procter and Gamble, and Morgan Guaranty Trust, we can observe a seven-step process that successful companies use to socialize individuals into the mainstream organizational culture.

Step 1 involves a rigorous selection process, whereby thick-culture companies tell the applicant the bad side of their organization as well as the good. Indeed, corporate recruiters prod applicants to take themselves out of contention if they believe the organization will not fit their own values and beliefs. At Procter and Gamble, the person conducting the first interview is a member of the elite cadre of line managers who have been specially trained to identify those applicants who best fit the Procter and Gamble culture, which is based on such values as "the ability to turn out high volumes of excellent work, to identify and understand problems, and to reach thoroughly substantiated and well-reasoned conclusions that lead to action."

In *Step 2*, the organization subjects newly hired employees to experiences designed to induce humility and make them question prior beliefs, behavior, and values. At Morgan Guaranty Trust, new employees often work until the wee hours of the morning and have to travel extensively. At Procter and Gamble, the newcomer may be required to color in a map of sales territories. The message is, "While you may be accomplished in many respects, you are in kindergarten as far as what you know about this organization."

Step 3 puts the new employee in the "trenches," where he or she masters one of the disciplines at the core of the organization's business. The employee is put in the field to gain hands-on experience, and, moreover, to learn to work up through the ranks. At this stage the employee gets a feel for the business as well as a feel for people and skills.

Step 4 involves evaluation and rewards. The company measures the operating results achieved by the new employee, and rewards him or her accordingly. At Procter and Gamble, for example, a new manager is measured against three factors deemed crucial for a product's success: building volume, building profit, and conducting planned change. At IBM, however, if the new manager does not measure up to standards, he or she is placed in the "penalty box," a meaningless job where one contemplates the errors of one's ways.

With *Step 5*, the individual is inculcated with the more intangible and transcendental values of the organization. Here, the new employee learns the values that connect the organization to human values of a higher order than those of the marketplace, such as serving humankind, providing a first-class product for society, or helping others to learn and grow. At Delta Airlines, the dominant transcendental value is "family feeling," which means that sacrifices may sometimes be required in terms of pay cuts and fewer working hours. In other words, the individual will make a sacrifice for "the good of the (Delta) family."

The history and folklore of the company are the essential ingredients of *Step 6*. The organization constantly harps on watershed events in its history to the new employee that reaffirm the importance of the former's values and beliefs. For example, at the old Bell System, story after story extolled the virtues of employees who kept the phones working despite disasters. By learning the myths, sagas, and legends of the organization, the employee's mind set is further molded into those channels of thought that exemplify the organization's culture.

The final step, *Step 7*, occurs when the employee is provided with a mentor, or role model. Nothing communicates more powerfully to younger employees than the example of superiors who are recognized by the organization as winners. The younger employee watches his or her mentor make presentations, handle conflict, perform routine administrative tasks, and so on. By closely watching his or her mentor, the new employee will try to duplicate the traits that work most effectively. At Procter and Gamble, the mentor is usually one of the brand managers who exhibits extraordinary abilities in the areas of analytical thought, energy, and motivation.

Once the new employee has accomplished these seven steps, he or she is acculturated, or socialized, into the organization, and thus becomes a valued member of the team. From the company's point of view, the individual is now part of a strongly cohesive culture that will endure and provide the direction for success. A strong, consistent set of implicit understandings provides a body of "common law" for both individual and organizational action. An IBM manager, knowledgeable of his firm's socialization process, puts it this way: "Socialization acts as a fine-tuning device. It helps us make sense out of procedures and quantitative methods. . . . Formal controls, without coherent values and culture, are too crude a compass to steer by."

The above case illustrates the importance that successful organizations place on culture. Until quite recently, organization theory was more concerned with studying the formal and static ways in which organizations conducted their business. However, a comprehensive study of today's organizations requires us to analyze those dynamic aspects that make an organization unique—the shared values, beliefs, and norms that comprise culture. As you read the chapter material, you will become aware of the critical role that culture and its manifestations exert on all facets of organization life.

Values, beliefs, and attitudes govern our behavior and decision-making activity. Together, we think of these concepts as culture. Because culture plays such a central role in organization life, this chapter is devoted to examining it.

We first define culture and show how it develops. Next, we look at cultural manifestations: ceremonies and rituals, symbols and slogans, language, and myths and stories. Because the physical environment both affects and reflects an organization's culture, it is examined briefly.

Culture can either be widely adopted throughout the organization, and so termed *thick*, or narrowly adopted and thus termed *thin*. This thickness factor relates directly to how flexible, or changeable, culture is, which in turn relates to organizational commitment.

Because culture affects management's effectiveness, it must be monitored or audited, and so a portion of the chapter discusses culture audits. Finally, the relationship between culture and strategy is examined.

This chapter shows the part that culture plays in modern organization theory.

The concept of culture is a relatively new entry into the terminology of organization theory, although the idea of culture is as old as society itself. Because it deals with such a central issue, culture is not likely to become just another buzzword or fad. We believe it will take its place along with the other components we discuss to form the core of organization theory itself. Culture appears to be an idea whose time has come.[1]

Because of its pervasiveness, culture affects the totality of organizational composition and behavior, and has an especially significant effect on managerial thought and action. Therefore, this chapter is devoted to examining this central construct.

CULTURE DEFINED

A review of the literature and common experience shows that there is little agreement on a precise definition of culture. It is necessary to glean some common ideas from several sources in order to get an understanding of the term.

Consider the following definitions as examples of efforts to provide meaning to the term *organizational culture*:

> Culture is the set of important understandings (often unstated) that members of a community share in common.[2]

> ... Culture is most usefully thought of as the taken-for-granted and shared meanings that people assign to their social surroundings.[3]

> ... the amalgam of beliefs, ideology, language, ritual, and myth we collapse into the label of organizational culture.[4]

> Most authors argue that "corporate culture" refers to a set of values, beliefs, and behavior patterns that form the core identity of an organization.[5]

> ... a pattern of basic assumptions—invented, discovered, or developed by a given group as it learns to cope with the problems of external adaptation and internal integration—that has worked well enough to be considered valid, and, therefore, to be taught to new members as the correct way to perceive, think and feel in relation to these problems.[6]

These definitions have a general theme in common. The members of the group, organization, or society have a common conception of their basic values, beliefs, behaviors, understandings, and meanings that guide their behavior and their efforts to solve problems. From this general theme, we propose the following definition of organizational culture for the purpose of this text:

> Organizational culture is the mix of values, beliefs, assumptions, meanings, and expectations that members of a particular organization, group, or subgroup hold in common and that they use as behavior and problem-solving guides.

For example, because the basic values and beliefs that underlie our form of government are contained in our Constitution, it can be thought of as a reflection or product of our national culture. Many companies have credos or codes of beliefs that similarly reflect their culture. We can see at least one indication of culture in such documents.

THE FORMATION OF CULTURE

Because culture is a group phenomenon, it is necessary to examine briefly how groups form and produce culture. The key concept in culture is sharing, for without shared values, goals, norms, and so on, there would be no group culture. Commonality is vital to culture formation.

People form groups seeking need satisfaction. They bring goals, values, and even hopes to the group process and endeavor to find a situation in which, for the most part, they can achieve what they want. Schein has an excellent treatment of the stages of group formation and growth, and it is used as the basis for this discussion.[7] Throughout the following discussion, remember that group formation and maintenance depend on shared norms, values, and so on as the glue that holds members together, so they constantly seek to find and preserve commonality.

Stage one is what Schein terms the "confrontation of dependency/ authority" issue. Here, the matter of who will lead the group is the focal point, and culture is easily seen as a force in it. The group looks for someone to give it direction. What individual members think and value is evident when one suggests that a person be selected because of age, experience, or sex. None of these characteristics alone is reason enough for selecting (or accepting) one person or another, even though some may think so. Images of authority and dependency come to the fore: "She's too young to be president"; "Experience is the key to leadership"; "It takes a real man to lead a bunch of outlaws." All these statements point out issues that surface in this first step of group development.

Historically, these initial leaders and founders have had a great impact on the future culture of their organizations. The J.C. Penney Company still reflects its founder's beliefs about customer satisfaction, and the company gives its best to achieve it. Henry Ford's ideas about the color of Ford's early cars were carried forward by the Ford organization for a long time. He supposedly told one of his engineers to paint the car any color he wanted, as long as it was black.

Founder beliefs about how to treat employees also affect future culture. Frederick Taylor's "one-best-man" approach showed employees to be extensions of their machines, to be treated as such. This is in contrast to Chester Barnard's New Jersey Bell culture, based on participation, involvement, and an appreciation for the worth of the employees, individually and collectively.

The second stage of group formation is what Schein terms "confrontation of intimacy, role differentiation, (and) peer relationship issues." Successful first efforts to deal with the authority issue (stage one) are likely to produce a feeling of success and good feelings about membership that are likely to occupy the group's attention for the rest of its existence.

Imagine the good feeling that prevailed among the team members in NASA who carried out the mission that put Neil Armstrong on the moon, or among the members of the Green Bay Packers when they beat Kansas City 35-10 in the first Super Bowl in 1967.

Confronting the creativity/stability issue is the third stage. Here the group begins to cope with the innovative approaches that brought its initial success as they come in conflict with the need for order and a stable, predictable way of behaving. The creativity that formed the initial impetus to formation can now threaten to disrupt its order.

This clash can be seen in a company such as Apple Computers, founded by the energetic Steve Jobs. The creativity and energy that founded the company have come face to face with the values necessary to keep the company stable and ongoing.

Finally, the group matures only to encounter a confrontation of survival/growth issues. Here the group learns whether its values, norms, and so on are capable of keeping it in consonance with its environment, or whether it should disband and abandon its mission in favor of perhaps a newer group.

The airline industry has been the scene of several failures, takeovers, and reorganizations in recent years. Eastern was taken over by Texas Air, and Braniff went bankrupt, only to later reorganize. These airlines experienced the survival/growth issue and made various adjustments in their cultures. Lee Iacocca, on the other hand, almost single-handedly saved Chrysler by being the driving force behind a major change in its cultural values. The "old" Chrysler culture was characterized by aversion to risk, pessimism, one-way communications (top-down from management), and insularity of the different Chrysler subunits. Under Iacocca's leadership, Chrysler's culture has been positively transformed. The company is now very aggressive in pursuing new markets, products, and technology; optimism pervades, two-way communication channels have opened between management and employees, and the various subunits now work together toward attaining a common goal.

Throughout these stages, the group tries to solve problems of leadership, role, and other issues that affect its style and survival. The underlying question throughout all these stages is whether the group can forge the type of culture needed to survive. This is true, even though members are not necessarily aware of their attempts to form a viable culture; it can be an almost unconscious event. Table 13.1 summarizes these four stages of culture formation in groups.

Group experience, both emotional and cognitive, becomes the foundation of the group's culture, which provides a sense of order and emotional comfort for members. Critical events, especially those that require critical choices, have major influence in the early establishment of culture. As we saw earlier, these choices are frequently made by group founders, so the personalities of these leaders make an indelible stamp on the organization's culture. So, an understanding of the formation of a group should be based, at least in part, on a study of its founders who can convert, through critical choice and role modeling, personal values, norms, and so on into the organization's culture.

TABLE 13.1

Culture Formation in Groups

Stage	Dominant Assumption	Group Focus
1. Dependency/ authority confrontation	A leader will guide the group to its maximum benefit.	Leadership selection
2. Confrontation of intimacy, role differentiation, peer relationship issues	The group is successful and the members like each other.	Normative consensus; harmony
3. Creativity/stability issue	The group can be innovative and stable at once.	Team continuity and accomplishment
4. Survival/growth issues	The group has endured and so must be "right."	Group's attention on status quo/resistance to change

Source: Adapted from Edgar A. Schein, *Organizational Culture and Leadership* (San Francisco: Jossey-Bass, 1985), 191.

Thick and Thin Cultures

From our brief account above, we see how groups come to be and attempt to form a "good" culture based on members' shared experiences and expectations. If they are successful, they build a culture that holds its members together as they pursue both personal and organizational endeavors. Organizational culture is said to be *thick* if it is widespread and accepted throughout a given population, that is, if the overwhelming majority of the group adopt and internalize it. For example, take the case of company creeds that contain the basic values for which the organization stands. At Ford Motor Company, the organizational creed is carried on a three-inch by five-inch plastic card by all employees. The message is simple: At Ford, the quality of the product, as well as the service, is an extension of the employee.[8] These cards constantly remind employees of the company's corporate culture. Now Ford is attempting to transplant the importance of quality and customer satisfaction into its dealers with a President's Award based on service rather than sales. Both the cards and awards help make Ford's culture thicker by exposing employees and dealers to a core value, customer satisfaction.

If successful, Ford has a better chance of keeping a uniform sense of value throughout the organization and its dealerships. Thick culture is a strong tie that can hold the total organizational system together. Another method to inculcate thick culture in an organization is through employee orientation programs. Referring to our introductory case, we saw how successful companies maintain a thick culture throughout their organizations by establishing a series of indoctrination stages through which new employees must pass.

Thin cultures, on the other hand, are not as central to the group. The contents of these cultures are peripheral in a sense. An example of a component of a thin culture might be seen in the case where dress codes (considered as a manifestation of value) vary among units of the same organization. Compare this to the dark suit, white shirt, and muted tie one finds among male IBM employees. The IBM code represents part of a thick cultural component because of its general adoption. The varying dress code, on the other hand, is considered part of a thin culture because no single dress code has been adopted and internalized by the organization as a whole.

Thick cultures help organizations channel energy into productive behavior because they fend off politics and ambiguity. When you read the case at the end of this chapter, you will see how the thick culture at Goldman, Sachs and Company precludes politics and conflict in that particular organization. This, of course, is not the case with a thin culture like the one that existed at Atari, which we mentioned in the introductory case. One former Atari executive summed up the situation well by asserting that employees were never taught the Atari way because there *wasn't* an Atari way. Contrast this to Ford's thick culture and you can see the effect of culture on stability and focus for organizational behavior.

CULTURAL MANIFESTATIONS

Culture is often difficult to pin down because it is structureless in a sense. Yet we know it exists and affects the organization. One way to further appreciate culture is to look at some of its manifestations, or things that result from it. The following sections discuss some of the typical manifestations of a group's, or organization's, culture.

Ceremonies and Rituals

Every group develops certain habits or ways of life that we can call *ceremonies* and *rituals*. Simple, everyday group life is filled with them, from retirement dinners replete with speeches, plaques, and the proverbial gold watch to the morning coffee break. Other rituals, such as our description in the introductory case of how new Procter and Gamble managers are required to color in sales-territory maps, are specifically designed to inculcate new employees with organizational culture.

Some ceremonies and rituals are formal, even to the point of being described in a program or company history, while others are quite informal and private, and might only be known to members, as is the case with fraternal-order initiation rites. Members know the routine and their place in it. They can even stake out certain seats they occupy when the group meets.

Ceremonies and rituals hold the group together. Indeed, the group often comes together simply to carry out a ceremony or ritual. This can be seen in religious gatherings, or homecomings held at universities. The present and former students of a university generally look forward to homecomings as a way to tie the various classes together and to the university over a long period of time. These ceremonies and rituals thus manifest the beliefs and values of the various members of a university community. They give it a sense of continuity and stability and bind the group members together.

Symbols and Slogans

Firms spend considerable effort developing means of ready recognition of their organizations and products. Much effort goes into the selection of just the right logo or slogan. "We try harder" is the Avis Company's way of saying the company is working to please its customers. Eastern Airlines, before it became a subsidiary of Texas Air, had a similar slogan, "We earn our wings every day," while Delta uses the slogan "Delta gets you there" to convey the same customer-oriented values.

Logos and trademarks also indicate cultural values and beliefs. The Coca-Cola Company's "wave," Nike Shoe Company's "swoosh," and Mercedes-Benz's "triangle" are statements of identification with these organizations and their cultures. Remember how AT&T changed its corporate logo from the bell to the striped globe after the organization was forced to break up by the federal government. As AT&T changed its emphasis from service to marketing, it came up with a new logo to signify its new direction and culture.

Language

One of the marks of any group is its tendency to develop a language or jargon. Members develop a kind of organizational vocabulary, and members are expected to use it in their daily contacts with each other. In the Goldman, Sachs case at the end of this chapter, you will see how members of the firm use laudatory language with each other to instill a sense of teamwork. In the nonorganizational world, CB radio owners quickly learn the language of "10s," as in "10-4," meaning that a message is understood or agreed with, or "10-36," which is a request for the correct time of day. Professional groups develop a sophisticated jargon, as can be seen with doctors, lawyers, and computer specialists. Language, then, can be seen as a result of the common culture of a group.

Myths and Stories

Groups develop a history of operations and events over time, and this history is handed down from one generation to another in the form of myths and stories, or tales about organizational life. In the introductory case to this chapter we saw how successful organizations relate the history and folklore of their organizations to new employees in order to re-affirm the importance of the organization's values and beliefs. Hard times or heroic deeds that "saved the company from certain ruin" cement members together. School spirit is often built on stories of how the team "won one for the Gipper." Indeed, President Reagan relied on the spirit, commitment, and determination contained in that simple statement from his role in the *Knute Rockne Story* to demonstrate his optimism and commitment to victory.

Even though these stories probably get exaggerated (certainly altered) over time, they still serve to initiate new members and reassure old ones that their culture is worth observing and preserving.

The Physical Environment

People in organizations work in physical environments. As simple and straightforward as that sounds, this aspect of culture has generally been lightly treated in the literature. But as you will soon learn, physical structure, symbols, artifacts, and stimuli are an integral part of any organization's culture and organizational life.

One need only consider a few basic issues to appreciate this part of culture. Office size and location, for instance, can tell a lot about culture. A large office, well appointed, says that its owner is a valued member of the organization who can exert influence on it. Just who has an office on the second floor, a reserved parking space, or a reserved table in the executive dining room reveals much about who and what is important. These physical symbols tell us much about the degree of formality, warmth, and support that underlies the status, power, and cultural values in an organization.

Tim Davis summarizes the importance of the physical environment vis-à-vis culture.[9] He contends that this environment is composed of three basic elements: physical structure, physical stimuli, and symbolic artifacts. Together, these components exert considerable influence on organizational culture.

PHYSICAL STRUCTURE. Davis sees the physical structure to be made up of three areas. First, the actual design of the building and one's location in it are important. It has been stated that, at first, people design buildings to serve a need and then the building determines, because of its shape and design, what can be done successfully in it. Consider, for example, how limiting and difficult it would be to convert a hospital into a basketball gym.

The case of Levi Strauss is pertinent at this point in our discussion. Levi Strauss's corporate culture is one characterized by openness, friendliness, flexibility, and innovation. In the late 1970s, because of increased business, the company decided that it had to move its headquarters into a more spacious building. Levi Strauss moved into a high-rise glass tower in San Francisco that was not amenable to its culture. The corporate headquarters were scattered throughout various floors; offices were closed in; and there were few common areas in which organization members could meet. Such a physical structure might very well have served a bureaucratized, more rigid company; however, for the Levi Strauss organization this new headquarters was inhibiting. Therefore, in 1982, Levi Strauss built its own new corporate headquarters, consisting of a set of four-story buildings around a central, open courtyard. Offices were open, faced the courtyard, and were interconnected. In short, Levi Strauss realized that its culture demanded a corresponding physical structure, and thus acted accordingly, despite the fact that the company had to pay considerably for breaking its lease in the glass tower.

The Levi Strauss example shows that we tend to associate with those near us and so share a kind of culture based on proximity. Friendships are made or broken on such a simple matter as a change in office location. We look approachable or aloof based on the size of the office and its furnishings—they can appear to be bright and friendly or cold and forbidding. Whether a subordinate is assigned to the main administration building could tell the organization how much the business thinks of him or her. Friendships can develop quickly when people are in a small building or office complex designed to facilitate contact and communication.

Furniture type and location can affect, and at the same time reflect, culture. In recent years, doctors' offices have surely come to exemplify attempts to make both doctors and their offices more "patient-friendly." What were once bland environments are being made homey and appealing. They can even help to reduce anxiety!

The furniture size and shape can tell much about an organization's culture. Round tables, for example, connote more equality than do long, highly polished ones. The width of a table can determine who talks with whom. Because we tend to talk to those near us, wide tables invite conversations between those seated next to each other as opposed to those seated across from one another. So, a kind of "table culture" can form among members of a group simply by the size and shape of the table they share.

The issue of open versus closed offices is still another indicator of culture. A closed office indicates more status consciousness and formality than an open one, which invites frequent contact among all ranks, even though Sundstrom, Burt, and Kemp found that all members of their study indicated a preference for privacy and visual inaccessibility.[10]

PHYSICAL STIMULI. Davis terms the second major aspect of the physical environment *physical stimuli*. These are parts of the physical environment that gradually come into members' awareness. Such things as mail delivery, time clocks, and telephone calls are examples of physical stimuli. These are often in the form of distractions—the delivery of mail to a manager's desk can even become a ritual, with a certain time of day and a particular placement of envelopes on the desk as key aspects. These physical stimuli have a great deal of influence on what people do and how they behave.

SYMBOLIC ARTIFACTS. Finally, we must consider symbolic artifacts— ". . . aspects of the physical setting that individually and collectively guide the interpretation of the social setting."[11] These things send cues about culture. Spartan surroundings convey one image; the staid oppulence of old, established firms conveys another. Public relations firms do much to build the "right" image for corporate officers and managers. Whether managers have access to the corporate jet, or whether they "brown bag" lunch with the staff is a cue or commentary on the nature of culture and its role.

Jimmy Carter, when he assumed office, was frequently seen carrying his own luggage. This was a cue to how "down home" he was trying to appear to the public. It was supposed to indicate his rural culture and his closeness to "ordinary" people.

From this brief treatment of cultural manifestations, we see that they are both a result and reflection of an organization's culture. They are an integral part of organizational culture and must be considered along with the other, more abstract components of an organization's cultural mix. Table 13.2 presents a convenient picture and discussion of various cultural manifestations.*

HOW CULTURE AFFECTS THE ORGANIZATION

Our previous discussion of thick and thin cultures mentioned how these two cultural characteristics can affect the organization. We now expand on this theme by examining the work of Kilmann, Saxton, and Serpa, who suggest that there are three aspects of culture's effect on organizations: direction, pervasiveness, and strength.[12] *Direction* refers to the way cul-

---

*Our discussion of cultural manifestations is a representational sampling rather than an exhaustive narrative of the Trice and Beyer list.

TABLE 13.2

Cultural Manifestations

Manifestation	Description
Rite	Relatively elaborate, dramatic, planned sets of activities that consolidate various forms of cultural expressions into one event, which is carried out through social interactions, usually for the benefit of an audience.
Ceremonial	A system of several rites connected with a single occasion or event.
Ritual	A standardized, detailed set of techniques and behaviors that manage anxieties, but seldom produce intended, technical consequences of practical importance.
Myth	A dramatic narrative of imagined events, usually used to explain origins or transformations. Also, an unquestioned belief about the practical benefits of certain techniques and behaviors that is not supported by demonstrated fact.
Saga	An historical narrative describing the unique accomplishments of a group and its leaders.
Legend	A handed-down narrative of some wonderful event that is based in history but has been embellished with fictional details.
Story	A narrative based on true events—often a combination of truth and fiction.
Folktale	A completely fictional narrative.
Symbol	Any object, act, event, quality, or relation that serves as a vehicle for conveying meaning.
Language	A particular form or manner in which members of a group use vocal sounds and written signs to convey meanings to each other.
Gesture	Movements of parts of the body used to express meanings.
Physical setting	Those things that surround people physically and provide them with immediate sensory stimuli as they carry out culturally expressive activities.
Artifact	Material objects manufactured by people to facilitate culturally expressive activities.

Source: Harrison M. Trice and Janice M. Beyer, "Studying Organizational Culture Through Rites and Ceremonials," *Academy of Management Review* 9, no. 4 (October 1984): 655.

ture affects goal attainment; it can push the organization toward its goals or away from them. It can be either a positive or negative influence on behavior and accomplishment. For example, if a firm's culture fosters a "market-leader" approach to sales, any effort to gain experience from observing others enter the market first will be thwarted. This attitude of the "be-first" part of culture pushes the organization toward its basic mission of market leadership and helps it resist contrary efforts.

The degree to which members share a culture is an indication of its *pervasiveness*. As we mentioned above, widespread adoption is characterized as thick, while thin culture is not pervasive. We saw pervasive, or thick culture at Ford and a nonpervasive, or thin culture at Atari.

Strength of culture refers to its impact on members. Some religious sects have what amounts to a compelling force over their members. Take the case of Jim Jones, who commanded 700 of his followers to commit mass suicide in Guyana. Compare this with the strength of a culture of a political party (medium effect) or the very temporary culture of a collection of people on an airplane flight.

Observing the effects of culture on organizational behavior and decision making can show how culture affects goal attainment (direction), how thick it is (pervasiveness), and how it impacts organization members (strength). These three facets of culture show how it affects the organization, its behavior, and course of action. Although authors point out that more research needs to be done on this subject, there is little doubt that culture can have either a positive or negative impact on organizational behavior and performance.

Concomitant with the concepts of direction, pervasiveness, and strength are two other cultural concepts that affect organizational behavior and decision making—flexibility and commitment. *Flexibility* refers to a culture's ability to be accommodating to different demands placed on the organization. *Commitment* is the catalytic effect that culture has on organization members' actions and work efforts.

Cultural Flexibility

It is essential for the management group to work diligently to ensure that their organization's culture remains flexible and accommodating to both the internal and external environments. The case of Johnson and Johnson illustrates why this is so.

Known for manufacturing and distributing consumer health and beauty aids, Johnson and Johnson's culture was characterized by decentralization and autonomy among its 170 units. However, perceiving the tremendous impact that high technology will have on the health care industry, Johnson and Johnson chairman, James E. Burke, embarked on a program of high-tech acquisition and manufacturing in the early 1980s.

The problem with the implementation of this new strategy has been the old culture at Johnson and Johnson. Coordination among units is vital for the company's push into high technology, but the old culture is not used to working that way. For example, two Johnson and Johnson executives quit the company rather than participate in a centralized ordering-and-distributing effort deemed critical to maintaining the organization's position in the hospital supply business. Chairman Burke acknowledges that persuading his company's units to work together will require a tremendous change in attitude among managers so used to independence. Johnson and Johnson is now faced with the task of making its corporate culture more flexible.

Jay Lorsch suggests several means that can be used to keep an organization's culture flexible.[13] One technique involves establishing a senior management position(s) whose incumbent is basically a questioner of proposed actions and the status quo in general. These managers should have considerable experience with the organization so they can see the situation from a total organizational perspective. They can serve this role well because they do not owe allegiance to any particular department or cause. These managers can play devil's advocate by dissenting simply to stimulate a reevaluation of existing elements in the culture.

Rotating "outsiders" onto governing boards is another way to prevent a "frozen" culture. By remaining at least somewhat aloof from daily operations, they can offer a more objective perspective. Some organizations rotate these members frequently in an effort to prevent their being coopted by the group itself. Not to do so would negate any advantage their presence can bring to the decision-strategy process. These members also can serve as boundary spanners, keeping the organization in touch with its environments.

Lorsch also suggests bringing in an outside senior manager to provide a fresh spark. This can have some undesirable side effects, such as lowered morale of those insiders who were passed over. To be effective, this tactic must balance the concern for objectivity with the actual and potential costs of attaining and maintaining it.

Finally, flexibility can be encouraged throughout the organization. Cross training (where managers learn the jobs of other managers, perhaps even by assuming them) can go a long way toward this end. Frequent reassignments can keep allegiances from becoming too strong. The organization should think "cultural flexibility." Indeed, this is the tactic being used by Johnson and Johnson's Burke. He has increased the movement of managers between Johnson and Johnson companies in addition to placing more importance on corporate-level committees whose function is to facilitate the exchange of information between companies.

Lorsch pinpoints and analyzes a variety of means that organizations can utilize to keep culture/strategy decisions tightly integrated, yet flexible and in tune with their total environmental network.

Culture and Commitment

The strength of a culture, which we discussed previously, is reflected by the degree of commitment shown by organization members. Commitment is a condition in which members of a group give their abilities and loyalties to the organization and the pursuit of its goals in return for satisfaction. In other words, member and organizational interests are clearly identified, there is little membership resistance, and there is anticipated mutual benefit for the group and its members.

Culture aids the attainment of member commitment by laying out the mission and the values to be observed in its pursuit. Commitment means choosing one set of options in preference to another.[14] It is a type of emotional (and perhaps financial) investment in the group.

Reinforcers of commitment take the form of varying rewards, ranging from salary to the physical environment. Indeed, as we saw in our introductory case, negative reinforcement can be used to obtain commitment. Remember how IBM put new managers in the "penalty box" when they did not demonstrate the proper amount of commitment to the organization's mission and culture.

Culture, by its nature, contains many elements of reinforcement to help attain organizational commitment. Being accepted as a member of a desirable group gives an individual a strong incentive to adopt its culture as a way of life and to work for its preservation. Think for a moment about someone who wants to join a social fraternity or sorority. Willingness to adopt the group's rituals, handshakes, and way of life is essential to acculturation. Over time, after initiation rites are over, the individual feels a sense of identity with the group and is even willing to make sacrifices for it. The feeling of sharedness and acceptance leads one to be committed to the group's continuation.

Thus, one of the prime requirements for, or conditions of, commitment is the sense of oneness that culture provides. All of its rites and symbols, so evident in fraternal groups, are excellent examples of the critical role that culture plays in attaining organizational commitment, the necessary condition for long-term group survival.

THE CULTURE AUDIT

Just as they conduct financial and management audits, organizations today are beginning to put their cultures under the microscope. The basic purpose of such investigations is to ensure that the organization's culture fits and has a net positive effect on the organization and its mission.

Alan Wilkins cites what appear to be two key reasons for the recent interest in organizational culture.[15] The tremendous upheaval in the world economic structure (triggered by the roller coaster ride of the oil industry) sent many executives scurrying to find ways to prop up their organizations and to gird against the waves of shock felt. Concomitant with this came a flood of writing, speaking, and research on the Japanese way of doing things.* As a result, there is a new awareness of culture's role in organizational life. At the same time, managers began studying other countries' cultures and how they affect organizations. For example, the Japanese spend considerable effort inculcating philosophy and culture into their employees, who expect to remain with their organization for a lifetime. There appears to be more of a feeling of family in Japanese firms, and it can be a strong motivator. By serving as a basis for organizational normative consensus, culture can exert strong pressure.

Wilkins talks about how culture seems to "creep" into assumptions that members make every day, from simple to complex tasks. Over time, it becomes almost second nature, a type of normative consensus, to wear a tie or get to work on time or answer your own phone. Only when some change occurs do members become conscious of values, assumptions, and their role structure in general.

The Informal Culture Audit

As noted earlier in this chapter, culture tends to be a constant, and, over time, we don't think of it much in our daily lives. Wilkins notes this general condition but states that there are occasions when culture does become apparent.[16]

Role changes are prime causes for attention to culture. When we enter a new situation (think of your first days in college), we meet it immediately by attempting to see if our old culture fits. We try to learn about the accepted ways of doing things in our new environment; we examine dress codes and word usage, for example. We try hard to learn the "pecking order" and jargon so that we are not so awkward as to stand out in the crowd.

The acculturation process involves both the newcomer's attempt to learn and adopt the prevailing culture and the "old-timer's" attempt to mold the newcomer to the culture. We saw this process at work in the introductory case to this chapter. This type of adjustment is frequently addressed formally by orientation programs aimed at teaching new members the official culture. The informal culture, however, must also be learned. How things are *really* done is probably different from what is

---

*See especially William G. Ouchi's seminal contribution, *Theory Z: How American Business Can Meet the Japanese Challenge* (Reading, Mass.: Addison-Wesley, 1982).

written in the procedures manual. How one *really* behaves is probably not in the code of conduct.

Subculture conflicts also call attention to what members come to believe and take for granted about the organization. Think about the results of a job reassignment in which an engineer joins workers on the line only to find that the intellectual bent of the former clashes with the practical, let's-get-it-done orientation of the latter. The engineer will feel a certain amount of culture shock, no doubt, even if he or she has been a member of the company for a long time. The line group will also be affected. Here values, beliefs, orientations, and even dress will be examined and tested with a view toward achieving cultural fit. These encounters cause us to examine facets of both group and organizational culture that otherwise might not have been looked at.

How top managers behave also causes members to monitor culture. What these executives say and do goes far to show an organization's culture. Remember in our introductory case how top firms provide new employees with a mentor, or role model, from the senior managerial ranks. Whether top managers stress detail over concept, outside or inside matters, and how they control the reward system reveal their ideas about organizational culture. Officials at the top, of course, have more power to alter or mold their organization's culture, so it is not surprising that they have an important impact.

A cultural audit, then, is basically a look at values, beliefs, and so on and consists of monitoring, evaluating, and perhaps changing various components of culture. Audits show much about both the formal and informal rules by which members of an organization operate, and today's managers must think seriously about them and their uses.

Culture audits can be conducted by asking questions aimed at finding out how members feel and think about the organization and their places in it. You can do the same kind of audit of your school or social organization—all you do is ask questions such as, "What do we believe about student participation?" "What do we believe about academic freedom?" "How are our faculty members rewarded?" These and other questions can be quite revealing in showing the underlying culture of your college or university.

The Formal Culture Audit

Our previous discussion focused on ways that individuals can informally audit the culture of their organizations. However, simply being observant and asking questions will not always get the right answers. Therefore, we will now turn our attention to a formal, ten-step, culture audit methodology developed by Schein, based on his consulting experiences.[17]

1. *Entry and focus on surprises.* In this step, an organizational "outsider" actually enters the group and begins to observe and "feel" its culture and watch for surprises, that is, things that are not expected.
2. *Systematic observation and checking.* Here, the observer attempts to ensure that the "surprises" really are surprises.
3. *Locating a motivated insider.* Outsiders would probably have a difficult time analyzing a group's culture, so it is quite helpful to talk to a member who knows and can evaluate the culture. This contact can reduce the time necessary to audit culture as well as ensure a more accurate assessment.
4. *Revealing the surprises, puzzlements, and hunches.* In this step, the outsider reveals his or her assessments to the insider in order to get reactions about their appropriateness and accuracy. Candor is essential here.
5. *Joint exploration to find explanations.* The outsider is told by the insider whether observations are accurate and of what significance they are. Together, the outsider and insider attempt to fit observations with guiding assumptions to explain behavior.
6. *Formalizing hypotheses.* At this point, the outsider and insider collaborate to form statements about the culture based on observations and data gathered about it. These hypotheses become a kind of model of the culture.
7. *Systematic checking and consolidation.* The outsider now has enough information to know what to ask about. Additional information is needed, and questionnaires, interviews, and stories can be used to gather it.
8. *Pushing to the level of assumptions.* Once the hypotheses are validated, the evaluator is ready to derive cultural assumptions and see how they affect what members do and what they believe. In other words, at this stage, efforts are made to build a kind of program that drives member behavior.
9. *Perpetual recalibration.* Here the model of culture is fine-tuned. It is tested on other insiders to see if it actually reveals the underlying assumptions that are manifest in culture. Schein argues for caution here less embarrassment or defensiveness skew the results, for there are those who might not even be aware of their assumptions or are reluctant to admit them.
10. *Formal written description.* In this final step, the outsider reduces the model to writing to see if a true description has been found. If the data are accurate, this is possible; otherwise, something is amiss. Of course, once written, the cultural description document must be kept current because, as we will see, culture can change over time.

Schein's process can be a useful tool of cultural analysis because it is succinct yet explanatory. It also provides order and direction to the audit and helps prevent misreadings of the group's culture. Management can thus use this methodology to understand and manage their organization's culture.

CHANGING CULTURE

The proper management of an organization requires that managers not only understand culture and its role, but stand ready to alter its composition and direction of force.

These are two basic approaches to this task: top-down and bottom-up. In the *top-down* approach, the Theory X assumptions of Douglas McGregor are used. Top management generally "decrees" the different norms of behavior to be observed. If the way things are done is to be changed, this approach can be implemented rather quickly. The effects might not be long lasting, however, because organization members might feel the "order" to change was given without consulting them. In the case at the end of the chapter, you will see how Goldman Sachs has quite successfully used this approach to manage its corporate culture.

The *bottom-up*, or participative approach, involves group members in the process of change. This is a slower but perhaps more long-lasting approach because it involves ego-involvement, identification, and commitment of members. People will give stronger and more long-lasting support to projects with which they are deeply involved. This approach concentrates on changing the assumptions governing behavior, as opposed to the norms of behavior associated with the top-down approach. Both the top-down and bottom-up approach can be employed singularly or in combination.

The recent breakup of AT&T is a classic example of perhaps the most massive change in organization culture in corporate history.[18] Here is the case of a company with a deeply imbedded culture based on thoroughly ingrained values and beliefs about service and their relationship to success.

To alter the organization's culture, the managers of AT&T devised a three-step process to fit the new business environment that revolved around marketing, as opposed to the old service orientation that guided AT&T for so many years. First, it was necessary for management to perform a culture audit to learn the elements of the current culture and their impact on operations and employees. Then the elements to be retained had to be separated from those to be discarded. Finally, action to carry out the desired changes had to be taken.

Management conducted a thorough study by surveying 6,000 employees, getting recommendations from twenty key managers, and employing management consultants. This study was aimed at getting a fix on the nature and extent of culture's effect on the company.

Chairman Charles L. Brown took personal charge of the transition in the new culture. He submitted copies of the study report to his "cabinet," comprised of fifteen top officials, and a special meeting was called to discuss the report. This effort centered on an informational front, with broad dissemination of findings and recommendations through seminars, video tapes, and so on.

The AT&T case is an excellent example of managing cultural change. In it, both top-down and bottom-up approaches were used to change norms and assumptions that had to be altered to move AT&T from a service to a marketing orientation. New ads, new images, as well as a new logo, helped to signify to employees, customers, and the general public that, indeed, a new company was beginning. Because it takes as much as a decade to completely effect such a drastic change as cultural change, especially in an organization so vast and complex as AT&T, this change is still evolving.

Stages of Change

Cultural change basically involves four stages.[19] At the outset, managers should be aware that the tendency of any culture is to resist change, because past observance of it has brought reasonable levels of satisfaction. Managers need to be aware of this tendency if changes are to succeed.

Lorsch and his colleagues conducted investigations in several companies and found that the first condition required for change was for top managers to be aware of the need for change. At first, the managers studied denied the necessity of altering culture in response to external events that were applying pressure on their organizations.

Once an awareness did occur, it was followed by a period of what Lorsch calls "confusion." Faced with changing conditions that did not fit familiar culture constructs, managers had no clear sense of direction. These firms responded by bringing in new leadership for top positions. Most of these leaders came from within the organization; they brought in a new perspective but still appreciated the past. This allowed the companies to build new approaches while keeping old, operable parts of the culture alive.

Upon taking office, these new managers began to develop a strategic vision. This vision was based on the definition of their companies' future capabilities. As much as possible, these capabilities were built on parts of the old culture in order to minimize the natural resistance to change.

It was then appropriate for the firms to begin experimenting with various means of determining new directions. Among these were the acquisition of other firms and internal development as part of an overall thrust to open new markets. Through trial and error, these companies settled on new members and products that would set their future course of action.

Cultural change can take years to carry out because it requires fundamentally new values and ideas that can go against existing culture. Through this type of evolution, though, companies can eventually alter their basic cultural fabric.

CULTURE AND STRATEGY

Because of their crucial roles in organization performance, it is necessary to look at the relationship between culture and strategy. Strategic choices are made to pledge the organization's resources to the pursuit of its long-term purpose(s). These forces set the fundamental agenda of organization action, and culture, as we have seen, is the values, norms, and assumptions that members observe when striving to implement strategic choices. Managing strategy and culture is at the root of managing organizational behavior and performance. These relationships are shown in Figure 13.1. As can be seen in the figure, culture and strategy interact with other organizational components to produce performance.

In Figure 13.1, we see how culture is comprised of two types of be-

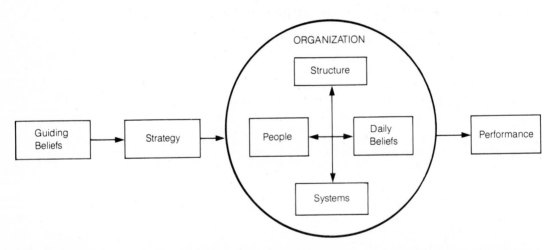

FIGURE 13.1

The Relationship of Culture to Strategy

Source: From Stanley M. Davis, *Managing Corporate Culture* (Cambridge, Mass.: Ballinger, 1984), 6. Copyright 1984 by The Human Resource Planning Society. Reprinted with permission from Ballinger Publishing Company.

liefs. *Guiding beliefs* are the philosophical roots and principles upon which the organization is built. At IBM, as we have already seen, these are respect for the individual, customer service, and excellence. Guiding beliefs provide the overall direction and strength of the strategy. *Daily beliefs* are the rules and feelings about everyday behavior (e.g., the dress code at IBM). Daily beliefs are one of the four mutually reinforcing components of the organization, the other three being structure, systems, and people. Taking our systems view of organizations, culture is the input that guides strategy, which is developed by the throughput process (the interaction of the four components). The system output, of course, is organizational performance.

There is no management of culture without the element of risk, and Schwartz and Davis provide some guidelines for choice in this area.[20] They suggest four possible positions: (1) Ignore the culture; (2) manage around the culture by changing the strategic implementation plan; (3) try to change the culture to fit the strategy; and (4) change the strategy to fit the culture, perhaps by reducing performance expectations.

Ignoring Culture

Based on our discussion so far, it would appear impossible to ignore any cultural dimensions of strategy. If for no other reason, organizational inertia would tend to preserve the status quo and so inhibit any but the most rare strategic choice making. Indeed, even if it were possible to do so, no responsible manager would attempt to ignore culture. It is simply not a viable option. Think how imprudent it would be for a firm doing business in the Middle East to ignore its very different and very thick culture.

Managing Around Culture

Another implementation approach is to recognize culture but attempt to minimize its influence as much as possible. Using this approach, the organization tries to neutralize culture's influence. An example of this would be a company trying to enter a foreign market characterized by strong ideas about sex roles, particularly those of women. The company might consider sending only those employees who share the local views. In these situations, the company recognizes local culture but tries to keep it from affecting strategic decisions.

Another example can be seen when a strategy conflicts with the organization's internal culture. For example, a company (such as Johnson and Johnson) that wishes to enter the high-tech field might want to form a matrix-type structure to enhance innovation and creativity. However, the autonomous culture of various organizational subunits would inhibit this strategic approach. Therefore, the company would manage around the culture through job reassignments and the formation of committees, program coordinators, and so on (as Johnson and Johnson actually did).

Changing Culture

As we saw in our previous discussion, cultural change in an organization can be a complex and time-consuming process. Indeed, there are situations in which it is not unreasonable to imagine a situation in which change would be "too late." For example, if a strategic decision to enter a foreign market would take five years to implement, and it would take eight years for managers to become fluent in the requisite language, it would be impossible to change culture in time. In other situations, however, it might be wise to make the effort. To do so, management must project (guess?) what a nurturing culture would be like; analyze and evaluate current culture; decide what parts should be changed; decide how to go about a proposed change; and, finally, be prepared to reinforce the new culture with a reward/penalty system. This option would be extremely expensive in every sense of the word.

Changing Strategy

Situations can arise in which the preferred strategy is incompatible with the organization's or community's culture. Because the values, beliefs, and norms simply won't accommodate the proposed course of action, the strategy must be changed. For example, there are communities whose school boards have seen their proposed curricula in sex education thwarted because of local cultural beliefs that the subject matter would be better taught at home. Television and radio commercials about alcohol have likewise been affected (or in some cases cancelled) for the same reasons.

When mergers occur, there is invariably a clash between the respective cultures of the firms, with strategy (or the reason for the merger in the first place) being affected as a result. When American firms combine with foreign producers to capitalize on a particular market condition, they are frequently faced with this situation. Consider the case of an American firm merging with a South American firm to introduce a new birth control product in a country where religious beliefs are strongly opposed to birth control. It is not unlikely that the strategy will bring resistance and low productivity from workers in the new company operating in South America. If the resistance and lack of acceptance of the product are intense enough, both market and product strategy will have to be changed.

USX (formerly U.S. Steel), under the leadership of CEO David Roderick, has embarked on a strategy of diversification, foreign purchases, mergers, and cost cutting in an attempt to get away from the declining U.S. steel market. However, its corporate culture has always emphasized steel, job security, and a belief that anything not made in the United States was not worth having. Roderick and his colleagues are having trouble successfully implementing this strategy because it goes against the company's long-term culture. "The whole company is beset with uncertainty—and the changes it has been through inevitably have triggered depression and a feeling of disbelief among staff."[21] Although we do not suggest USX's strategy is wrong in view of the environmental threats facing the organization and the steel industry in general, we do assert that more planning for culture's role could have been done.

From our discussion, we can see the intimate relationship between strategy and culture. Today's manager must consider and account for this relationship any time strategic choices are made. A conscious choice must be made from the above approaches about how to match culture and strategy if organizations are to be successful over time.

Schwartz and Davis suggest a construct for appreciating the effects of culture on strategy. They identify a four-step process for doing this:

1. Define the relevant culture and subcultures in the organization (i.e., perform a culture audit). Management must know its culture(s) before it can deal with it and so must develop statements about it.

2. Organize statements about the firm's culture in terms of manager's tasks and their key relationships. For example, the task of managerial communications might support statements such as "Avoid confrontations" or "Withhold information from adversaries." Likewise, a manager's peer relationships could be characterized by "Guard information."

3. Assess the risk the company's culture presents to the realization of the planned strategic effort. In this step, management attempts to evaluate the potential impact that culture can have on a proposed strategy. For example, interdepartment cooperation and coordination might be variables affecting the strategic plan; however, these variables might not be strong characteristics of the organization's culture. Therefore, what risk does this present to the proposed strategy (e.g., unacceptable, manageable, or negligible)?

4. Identify and focus on those specific aspects of the company's culture that are both highly important to strategic success and incompatible with organizational approaches that are planned. For example, if interdepartmental cooperation and coordination are absolutely essential for strategic success, and have been identified in Step 3 as constituting an unacceptable risk to the strategy, then

management must take action to enhance cooperation and coordination, or, alternatively, minimize their negative effects.[22]

When formulating and implementing strategy, it is necessary to consider culture's thickness. It is a difficult task for management to achieve just the right thickness to promote both innovation and implementation. For example, a thin culture can foster innovation, while a thick culture can promote implementation. An organizational culture with little variation can stifle innovation while promoting implementation. Heterogeneous, or thin, cultures have the opposite effect. Thus, the analysis of culture we discussed in the culture audit section can be useful in appreciating the culture/strategy fit.

Although it is clear from our discussion that culture and strategy are closely tied together, too many organizations simply do not pay attention to this relationship. Strategy simply cannot be formulated and implemented without considering culture. The modern organization executive cannot afford to overlook this relationship if success is a long-term objective.

SUMMARY

This chapter has explored the role of culture in the overall scheme of organization theory and demonstrated how organizations must know and manage their cultures for long-term survival. Culture is a complex concept that has a major influence on organizational life. It is defined as those values, beliefs, assumptions, meanings, and expectations that members of a group hold in common and that guide their behavior and problem-solving efforts.

Culture forms as groups come together and strive for goal attainment. Groups deal early on with a dependency/authority issue in the selection of leaders. The group must next find solutions to intimacy, role differentiation, and peer relationships issues, during the stage in which members learn to cope with success. Then, it is necessary to balance creativity (needed for innovation) with stability (needed for continuity). Finally, members encounter a confrontation of survival and growth whose resolution determines whether the group survives or is replaced by a new one.

When cultural forces are spread widely through the organization's membership, culture is said to be *thick*. These forces will doubtless be at the core of organizational life. Peripheral culture is termed *thin* because it is not central to everyday activity.

One can study culture by looking at organizational ceremonies, rituals, symbols, slogans, and language, as well as myths and stories that tell of organizational life and history. The physical environments of organizations, including structures, stimuli, and symbolic artifacts, are intertwined with organizational life and must be accounted for when examining culture.

Culture affects the organization in a variety of ways. The Kilmann, Saxton, and Serpa study showed this effect to be three-pronged: direction, pervasiveness, and strength. Culture can push the organization in the direction of goal attainment or away from it. Pervasiveness refers to the degree to which organization members share the culture, and strength refers to just how forceful culture is on member behavior.

Managers should work hard to make their organization's culture capable of adaptation and change. In a word, they must make it flexible. This can be done by establishing a senior management position whose incumbent plays devil's advocate. Outside members on governing boards can also help, as can bringing in outside, unbiased, senior managers. Cross-training can also be effective in achieving cultural flexibility.

Culture can foster commitment of members to organization goals by fusing their beliefs and values together for the benefit of all. It is a type of bonding or emotional investment process.

Many large organizations now perform culture audits, the basic purpose of which is to ensure that the organization's culture fits and has a net positive effect on the organization and its mission. Cultural audits can be done informally by organization members, or management can bring in a specialized consulting team to formally ascertain and analyze the nature of the firm's culture.

Culture can be changed from a bottom-up or top-down approach, with the former being more democratic than the latter, which tends to rely on management "decrees." Regardless of approach, there are four basic stages involved: awareness, confusion, strategic vision, and experimentation.

Culture and strategic decision making are closely tied together, and so adjustments must be made for each. Rarely can culture be ignored; sometimes it is necessary to change it; and, at other times, it is necessary to change the proposed strategy because culture is too strong and hard to change. A prescriptive analysis is necessary to determine the right course of action.

Culture has taken its rightful place in organizational literature as an integral part of organization theory.

QUESTIONS FOR REVIEW AND DISCUSSION

1. Speculate on why culture has only recently become such a popular part of organization theory.
2. Under what conditions would a thick culture be desirable? Undesirable?

3. Under what conditions would a thin culture be desirable? Undesirable?
4. How would you describe the culture of your college or university?
5. Describe the importance of culture in achieving and maintaining commitment in a group. Can commitment ever be undesirable? Under what circumstances?
6. Of the manifestations of culture, which one(s) is easiest to establish? To destroy?
7. Show by real-life examples instances of the uses of various techniques for maintaining cultural flexibility.
8. Using Schein's model, conduct a culture audit of both a formal and informal group of which you are a member and describe the results. Note especially the primary differences in the two audits.
9. Show in detail and by example the relationship of culture and strategy.
10. What factors would affect your personal approach to changing a group's culture?

ENDNOTES

1. Ralph H. Kilmann, Mary J. Saxton, and Roy Serpa, "Issues in Understanding and Changing Culture," *California Management Review* 27, no. 2 (Winter 1987): 92–93.

2. Vijay Sathe, "Implications of Corporate Culture: A Manager's Guide to Action," *Organizational Dynamics* 12, no. 2 (Autumn 1983): 6.

3. Alan L. Wilkins, "The Culture Audit: A Tool for Understanding Organizations," *Organizational Dynamics* 12, no. 2 (Autumn 1983): 25.

4. Andrew M. Pettigrew, "On Studying Organizational Cultures," *Administrative Science Quarterly* 24, no. 4 (December 1979): 572.

5. David R. Denison, "Bringing Corporate Culture to the Bottom Line," *Organizational Dynamics* 13, no. 2 (Autumn 1984): 5.

6. Edgar H. Schein, *Organizational Culture and Leadership* (San Francisco: Jossey-Bass, 1985), 9.

7. Ibid., 163–165.

8. Arthur Flax, "Ford Brings its Culture to its Dealers," *Automotive News* (March 12, 1986), 1.

9. Tim R. V. Davis, "The Influence of the Physical Environment in Offices," *Academy of Management Review* 9, no. 2 (April 1984): 271–283.

10. E. Sundstrom, R. E. Burt, and D. Kemp, "Privacy at Work: Architectural Correlates of Job Satisfaction and Job Performance," *Academy of Management Journal* 23, no. 1 (March 1980): 101–117.

11. Davis, "Influence of the Physical Environment," 276.

12. Kilmann, Saxton, and Serpa, "Understanding and Changing Culture," 88–89.

13. Jay W. Lorsch, "Managing Culture: The Invisible Barrier to Strategic Change," *California Management Review* 26, no. 2 (Winter 1986): 105–109.

14. Pettigrew, "Studying Organizational Cultures," 578.

15. Wilkins, "The Culture Audit," 24.

16. Ibid., 34–36.

17. Schein, *Organizational Culture and Leadership*, 114–119.

18. W. Brooke Tunstall, "The Breaking Up of the Bell System: A Case Study in Cultural Transformation," *California Management Review* 26, no. 2 (Winter 1986): 110–124.

19. Lorsch, "Managing Culture," 101–104.

20. Howard Schwartz and Stanley M. Davis, "Matching Corporate Culture and Business Strategy," *Organizational Dynamics* 9, no. 1 (Summer 1981): 42–48.

21. J. Ernest Beazley and Carol Hymowitz, "Strike at USX Shows How Far Steelmaker Has Fallen from Glory," *The Wall Street Journal* (August 7, 1986), 1.

22. Schwartz and Davis, "Matching Corporate Culture and Business Strategy," 47.

ANNOTATED BIBLIOGRAPHY

Adler, Nancy J. "A Typology of Management Studies Involving Culture." *Journal of International Business Studies* 14, no. 2 (Fall 1983): 29–41.

As a methodological review, this paper delineates six approaches to researching cross-cultural management issues: parochial, ethnocentric, polycentric, comparative, geocentric, and synergistic. For each approach, assumptions are discussed concerning the similarity and difference across cultures and the extent to which management phenomena are or are not universal.

Cummings, Larry L. "Compensation, Culture, and Motivation: A Systems Perspective." *Organizational Dynamics* 12, no. 3 (Winter 1984): 33–44.

The author develops a system for describing and diagnosing the components of an executive influence system. The key to intervening on the basis of the diagnosis lies in assessing the congruence among five key causes of executive behavior (compensation, promotion, competence development, control, and decision making). To yield maximum effect, compensation systems must be designed and implemented to send signals to executives that are consistent with the other four elements. As guidelines for action, he provides three examples of diagnosis and intervention in three different organizational cultures.

Ebers, Mark. "Understanding Organizations: The Poetic Mode." *Journal of Management* 11, no. 2 (Summer 1985): 51–60.

As a system of understanding reality, the organizational culture and symbolism perspective is similar to Romanticism. Both movements arose out of the recognition of the inadequacies of rationalism, and both attempt to chart areas of the human experience through the imagination in terms of metaphors, symbols, and myths. A comparison of the two, therefore, serves to explain the rise of the cultural and symbolic perspective in organizational studies and its theoretical basis.

Gardner, Meryl P. "Creating a Corporate Culture for the Eighties." *Business Horizons* 28, no. 1 (January–February 1985): 66–72.

Corporate cultures developed in the 1960s don't work as well in the 1980s because the heterogeneity of the work force has increased and lifestyles and values have changed. Corporate cultures are as important as ever, though, and can be adapted to meet the needs of this decade of workers.

Harris, Stanley G., and Sutton, Robert I. "Functions of Parting Ceremonies in Dying Organizations." *Academy of Management Journal* 29, no. 1 (March 1986): 5–30.

This paper advances a theory about the functions that parting ceremonies serve for members displaced by organizational deaths. The theory is grounded in data from eleven parties, picnics, and dinners that occurred in six dying organizations. The authors propose that parting ceremonies create settings in which people can exchange emotional support and can edit self, social system, and even schemata. The authors also assert that such gatherings provide opportunities for managers to influence the course of organizational demise.

Heller, Trudy. "Changing Authority Patterns: A Cultural Perspective." *Academy of Management Review* 10, no. 3 (July 1985): 488–495.

This paper focuses on the theme of loss of authority as it appears in the management literature. Drawing on longitudinal and descriptive studies, the paper discusses the loss to both organizations and the leaders who represent them. The treatment of this theme is contrasted with the perspective provided by a model of cultural change as a process of loss and substitution.

Jaeger, Alfred M. "The Transfer of Organizational Culture Overseas: An Approach to Control in the Multinational Corporation." *Journal of International Business Studies* 14, no. 2 (Fall 1983): 91–101.

Organizational control has traditionally been described within the framework of the ideal type of Weberian bureaucracy, in which rules and regulations specify desired behavior, and rewards are based on explicit performance measures. This paper describes an alternative organizational ideal type that relies on an organizational culture for control. In this type of system, behavior is specified by an organizational culture, and performance is maintained via mechanisms of social pressure.

Morey, Nancy C., and Luthans, Fred. "Refining the Displacement of Culture and the Use of Scenes and Themes in Organizational Studies." *Academy of Management Review* 10, no. 2 (April 1985): 219–229.

The move to displace the concept of culture traditionally used in anthropology and organizational research is discussed. Issues surrounding the culture concept and the juxtaposition of culture and organization are given special attention. Current thinking about the nature of the process of displacement is refined. Examples of an ongoing study of a city transit organization are used to demonstrate the use of cultural scenes in organizational research.

Moscowitz, Milton. "Lessons from the Best Companies to Work For." *California Management Review* 27, no. 2 (Winter 1985): 42–47.

What do the 100 best companies to work for in America have in common?

The answer goes beyond just good pay and strong benefits, and beyond just being a successful company. The author explains how and why he made his selection of the 100 best companies to work for in America and offers a number of illustrations of successful corporate personnel policies.

Sathe, Vijay. "Some Action Implications of Corporate Culture: A Manager's Guide to Action." *Organizational Dynamics* 12, no. 2 (Autumn 1983): 4–23.

This parag—Sathe shows that by distinguishing between culture and behavior and examining both simultaneously, it is possible to see more clearly why culture can be both an asset and a liability, and why it has such a subtle, but powerful, influence on organizational life. Not all cultures are equally powerful, however. Sathe presents some approaches for diagnosing a culture and understanding its strengths along with some implications for managerial action.

Schall, Maryan S. "A Communication-Rules Approach to Organizational Culture." *Administrative Science Quarterly* 28, no. 4 (December 1983): 557–581.

This paper suggests that organizations, cultures, and cultural "rules" can be synthesized as communication phenomena, using a communication-rules perspective. The synthesis is operationalized by an inductive, multifaceted method designed to test the effectiveness of describing an organizational culture through a composite of its communication rules.

Schein, Edgar H. "Coming to a New Awareness of Organizational Culture." *Sloan Management Review* 25, no. 2 (Winter 1984): 3–18.

If one really wants to decipher an organization's culture, Schein claims that one must dig below the organization's surface—beyond the "visible artifacts"—and uncover the basic underlying assumptions, which are the core of an organization's culture. To do this, he provides a tool—a formal definition of organizational culture that emphasizes how culture works. With this definition in hand, Schein feels that one cannot only come to understand the dynamic evolutionary forces that govern a culture, but also can explain how the culture is learned, passed on, and changed.

Smircich, Linda. "Concepts of Culture and Organizational Analysis." *Administrative Science Quarterly* 28, no. 3 (September 1983): 339–358.

This article examines the significance of the concept of culture for organizational analysis. The intersection of culture theory and organization theory is evident in five current research themes: comparative management, corporate culture, organizational cognition, organizational symbolism, and unconscious processes and organization. Researchers pursue these themes for different purposes and their work is based on different assumptions about the nature of culture and organization.

White, Jerry. "Corporate Culture and Corporate Success." *Management Decision* 22, no. 4 (1984): 14–19.

Some organizational cultures encourage productivity; many do not. This article considers some of the factors at work in the relationship between productivity, management, and culture.

Wilkins, Alan L., and Ouchi, William G. "Efficient Cultures: Exploring the Relationship Between Culture and Organizational Performance." *Administrative Science Quarterly* 28, no. 3 (September 1983): 468–481.

Contrary to popular notions of organizational culture, the authors claim that the existence of local organizational cultures that are distinct from more generally shared background cultures occurs relatively infrequently at the level of the whole organization. Wilkins and Ouchi also argue that, with respect to organizational performance, particular properties of local organizational culture are more important than others and that local organizational culture will be more critical to performance in one range of organizations than others.

ADDITIONAL REFERENCES

Barley, Stephen R. "Semiotics and the Study of Occupational and Organizational Cultures." *Administrative Science Quarterly* 28, no. 3 (July 1983): 393–413.

Barney, Jay B. "Organizational Culture: Can It Be a Source of Sustained Competitive Advantage?" *Academy of Management Review* 11, no. 3 (July 1983): 656–665.

Beadle, Carson E. "Firms Revising Remuneration Policies to Support Corporate Culture and Values." *Management Review* 72, no. 12 (December 1983): 30.

Deal, Terrence E., and Kennedy, Allan A. *Corporate Cultures: The Rites and Rituals of Corporate Life.* Reading, Mass.: Addison-Wesley, 1982.

Denison, Daniel R. "Bringing Corporate Culture to the Bottom Line." *Organizational Dynamics* 13, no. 2 (Autumn 1984): 5–22.

Gregory, Kathleen L. "Native-View Paradigms: Multiple Cultures and Culture Conflicts in Organizations." *Administrative Science Quarterly* 28, no. 3 (July 1983): 359–376.

Hofstede, Geert. "The Usefulness of the Organizational Culture Concept." *Journal of Management Studies* 23, no. 3 (May 1986): 253–257.

Katz, D., and Kahn, R. L. *The Social Psychology of Organizations.* 2d ed. New York: John Wiley & Sons, 1978.

Kelly, Charles M. "Effective Communications—Beyond the Glitter and Flash." *Sloan Management Review* 26, no. 3 (Spring 1985): 69–77.

Martin, J. "Stories and Scripts in Organizational Settings." In *Cognitive Social Psychology,* edited by A. Hastorf and A. Issen, 255–305. New York: Elsevier-Holland, 1982.

Morgan, G.; Frost, P. J.; and Pondy, Louis R. "Organizational Symbolism." In *Organizational Symbolism,* edited by Louis R. Pondy, P. J. Frost, G. Morgan, and T. C. Dandridge, 3–38. Greenwich, Conn.: JAI Press, 1983.

Peters, Thomas J., and Waterman, Robert H., Jr. *In Search of Excellence: Lessons from America's Best Run Companies.* New York: Harper & Row, 1982.

Riley, Patricia. "A Structuralist Account of Political Culture." *Administrative Science Quarterly* 28, no. 3 (July 1983): 414–437.

Shivastava, Paul. "Integrating Strategy Formulation with Organizational Culture." *The Journal of Business Strategy* 5, no. 3 (Winter 1985): 103–110.

Smith, Kenwyn K., and Simmons, Valerie M. "A Rumpelstiltskin Organization: Metaphors on Metaphors in Field Research." *Administrative Science Quarterly* 28, no. 3 (July 1983): 377–392.

Thompson, Michael, and Wildavsky, Aaron. "A Cultural Theory of Information Bias in Organizations." *Journal of Management Studies* 23, no. 3 (May 1986): 273–286.

Tunstall, W. Brooke. "Cultural Transition at AT&T." *Sloan Management Review* 25, no. 1 (Fall 1983): 15–24.

Turner, V. S. *The Ritual Process.* Chicago: Aldine, 1969.

Whorton, J. W., and Worthley, J. A. "A Perspective on the Challenge of Public Management: Environmental Paradox and Organizational Culture." *Academy of Management Review* 6, no. 2 (April 1981): 357–361.

```
C     A     S     E
```

Knowing Who We Are

Goldman Sachs and Company, a New York investment banking firm, is so successful that each of its seventy-five partners earn $5 million per year. Their earnings cannot be casually explained in terms of sales and commissions—it's something else; that is, a unity of beliefs, values, and ethics throughout the entire organization. In the words of co-chairman John Whitehead:

> There are some things about Goldman as an institution that make it unique: its team spirit, the pride in what we do, the high standard of professionalism, the service orientation . . . That's the essence of Goldman Sachs' culture, the things that have made us what we are, and I would say that culture has been the key to our success.

Culture not only binds the Goldman Sachs organization together, it *feeds* it. Throughout all layers, there is a well-forged emphasis on entrepreneurial aggressiveness, self-effacing teamwork, a shared knowledge of what the business will and will not do, homegrown talent, and, moreover, a commitment to serving the customer above all other interests. The *esprit de corps* is so strong that one partner noted, "If you polled people here and asked them why they work so hard, they would probably say that there's

Source: Beth McGoldrich, "Inside the Goldman Sachs Culture," *Institutional Investor* (January 1984): 53–67.

nothing else in their lives that gives them nearly the charge their work does."

Let's examine this "super" culture and see how it operates within the Goldman Sachs firm.

First, Goldman Sachs is in business to make money, and at this particular investment banking firm, this means, as the members of the firm term it, *greed*. Greed is at the hub of the wheel of cultural energy that drives the organization. However, unlike its competitors, Goldman Sachs channels greed in such a way that it works for and benefits the entire firm. There is no backstabbing or selfishness. There is no "star system" at Goldman Sachs; rather, it's "all for one and one for all."

There is an indomitable team spirit at Goldman Sachs. Partners and staff "gang tackle" problems with a near mania for interdepartmental and interpersonal communication and coordination. For example, if a corporate client is interested in a merger, then analysts from Goldman's merger and acquisition department explain what effect a merger will have on the client's stock. The arbitrage, syndicate, and trading departments advise on structuring and pricing offers. Then the new business department and corporate finance department give their views. There is even ritual involved with this: "An astute young person quickly learns that the way to win around here is to send around long memos that give credit loud and clear to everyone who worked on a given task."

To ensure the acculturation of the teamwork and other values at Goldman Sachs, the organization "grows" its own talent. Recruiters go after the cream of the crop at leading business schools to find the right person whose character is still pliable enough to be molded. The thirty individuals per year who get jobs at Goldman Sachs (over 1,500 apply) are the ones with brains, humor, motivation, confidence, maturity, and needless to say, an inclination to play on the team. Once a young person is hired, he or she usually spends a career with the same department. Therefore, all departments within Goldman Sachs have a deep bench of expertise with viewpoints that are quite similar.

Of course, inbreeding can and does cause insularity—a pariah in other organizations, but not in Goldman Sachs. This firm takes pride in its aloofness, and, moreover, is not even interested in how its competition does things. Outsiders are rarely brought into the organization, and the great majority of the firm's seventy-five partners have been with the company from ten to twenty years. In combination with employee inbreeding and longevity, insularity has become a corporate asset, not a liability.

Concomitant with this "isolation" is a calculated choosiness about clients. Goldman Sachs strictly adheres to certain standards about who it will do business with. Clients must have sound management of their operations, produce only high-quality goods and services, show profit for all their businesses, and also benefit the public in some way. Other such standards include Goldman Sachs's refusal to underwrite any deal involving nonvoting stock (a violation of the belief that shareholders should have voting rights) and its refusal to participate in unfriendly tender offers.

Service to the customer is paramount at Goldman Sachs. While the competition shuns seats on the boards of the corporations they serve, the two senior partners at Goldman Sachs, John Weinberg and John Whitehead, sit on a total of thirteen boards of directors. Indeed, Goldman Sachs would rather "hurt the (Wall) street" than not serve the needs of its customers. For example, Goldman Sachs' management of Ford Motor Company's debt deals drew criticism from other Wall Street bankers because the latter considered Ford's debentures unprofitable. Although this attitude works well for Goldman Sachs in the United States, it has caused problems for the company in Europe, where there is a tendency for bondhouses to consider the overall effects of their decisions on their industry as a whole.

Likewise, the firm is very cautious about expanding into new areas. Opportunities are studied, studied, and studied some more. This results in very few mistakes being made, although the inordinate amount of time spent in the decision-making process can and does cause some opportunities to be lost.

Finally, the culture at Goldman Sachs emphasizes a unique "loose-tight" management style. The organization is rigidly controlled at the top concerning operational procedures and overhead; however, each department is allowed autonomy concerning entrepreneurship and innovation. The status quo in structure and operations is maintained by the firm's inbreeding of long-term employees, who know their place within their respective departments and the overall organization. In addition, the firm is very hesitant to increase its staff. Compensation is used more as a control than as a motivational device. Most partners' wealth is on paper; salaries are modest; the percentage one earns on investments is fixed; and ostentatiousness is frowned on. Doing a job well and working on the team are the lubricants for smooth in-house operations. Professional employees who do not make partner are kept happy with perquisites and symbolic offerings such as the vice presidents' dining room, which has the same food and decor as the partners' dining room.

The culture at Goldman Sachs did not just happen. It's the long-term result of the joint leadership of the two co-chairs, Weinberg and Whitehead. Having been with the firm since the late 1940s, the two planned how they would run the company if given the chance. They were given the chance in 1976 when former chairman and CEO Gus Levy died. Since that time, Weinberg and Whitehead have subordinated their individual egos through power sharing and teamwork for the good of the firm. Hence, the values and beliefs of the organization are now theirs.

The culture works—for this organization. Its profit margins are the widest in the investment banking industry; it's the biggest dealer in commercial paper in the United States; and its market share of mergers and acquisitions is envied by competitors. But there is a human price to pay—working until 2:00 A.M., marital breakups, and the psychological problems inherent with the total subordination of ego and personal life to business. Thus, the challenge facing Goldman Sachs is to maintain its culture by finding individuals suited for it, while simultaneously reinforcing the culture for those already within the organization.

QUESTIONS FOR DISCUSSION

1. How do you think Goldman Sachs has been successful in maintaining such a thick culture?
2. What, if any, risk does Goldman Sachs run in maintaining the present state of its culture and insularity?
3. Goldman Sachs seems to be successful in obtaining an inordinate amount of commitment from its executives. Based on chapter material and this case, analyze this condition from the perspective of culture's role.
4. How can Goldman Sachs make its symbols and rituals believable to newcomers?
5. Explain the advantages and disadvantages of Goldman Sachs' promotion-from-within policy in light of organizational culture.

14

Power, Authority, and Politics in Organizations

Do It My Way!

Successful corporations are invariably led by very powerful individuals who do not hesitate to use their considerable power and authority to do whatever they deem necessary to make their organizations profitable and efficient. Some of these individuals are so powerful that they are able to rule by decree, while others need to form political alliances, both within and without their organizations, in order to get their way.

Perhaps one of the most ruthless leaders of modern industry is Hisao Tsubouchi, one of Japan's leading industrialists. He personally owns a group of almost 200 companies, ranging from movie theaters and hotels to taxi services and a sake brewery. His main industrial strength, however, rests with his shipbuilding empire, where he's made a reputation as a ruthless and all-powerful boss.

The stereotype of the successful Japanese manager presents an image of a company man who rules by consensus. Tsubouchi, however, became a leading Japanese industrialist by managing his own way. He is a tough, autocratic boss who earned his reputation by breaking unions, firing large numbers of employees, and instilling fear in his subordinates.

Tsubouchi likes power. One way he obtains power is by identifying and acquiring previously unprofitable companies. In 1984, he took control of Hokodate Dock Company, his fifteenth shipbuilding concern, thus making him the second largest shipbuilder in Japan. His first shipbuilding takeover occurred in 1953 when he took over Kuroshima Dockyard Company, which had just gone bankrupt. Tsubouchi's style quickly became apparent. He fired workers, bargained hard

Sources: "A Japanese Boss Whose Consensus Is the Iron Fist," *Business Week* (November 19, 1984), 176–177; Phyllis Berman, "A Quixotic Father's Acquisitive Son," *Forbes* (October 20, 1986), 105–108; Colin Leinster, "The Would-Be Queen of Revlon's Beauty Business," *Fortune* (January 6, 1986), 76–80.

for cheaper steel and parts, and made a reputation for building the least expensive ships in Japan.

He first caused people, especially those in the Japanese government, to notice him when, in 1978, he bought Sasebo Heavy Industries, Japan's eighth largest shipbuilder. He immediately fired half of Sasebo's 6,000 workers, pared the management staff from over 400 to less than 40, sharply reduced wages, cut employees' lunch hours in half, pressured his workers to work overtime without extra pay, and forced his suppliers to accept significant price cuts or lose Sasebo's business.

Tsubouchi's character was molded by his World War II experiences in a Soviet labor camp. There he learned that, for him personally, "joy doesn't come from luxury." On the contrary, it comes from "thriftiness and hard work." After the war, he took over a string of ailing movie theaters from his father. His unorthodox management methods, such as putting film on larger reels, enabled him to reduce the number of projectionists per theater from four to one. After his success in this business, Tsubouchi went on to other ventures where he's made his mark on the Japanese economy.

Tsubouchi begins his average work day before dawn and tries to visit at least three of his companies each day. He has even been known to call management meetings on weekends. Justifying his management style, Tsubouchi polled his companies' employees to find out what they liked in a boss and found that they admired someone who lives frugally, is serious, treats employees well, and has no mistresses. States Tsubouchi, "I have done my best to become the model boss."

Unlike most Japanese businesses, which try to foster a sense of loyalty to the company by employees, Tsubouchi has created a personality cult. Employees call him "Owner Tsubouchi," and workers are told that bo-

506

nuses come directly from his pocket. When workers at one shipyard doubled productivity, Tsubouchi sent $200 to each employee and a similar amount to their wives so the latter would encourage their husbands to work even harder.

Tsubouchi uses special training sessions that involve grueling self-criticism to teach employees the "joy of working." And they work. "His people work like field mice," says Hajimi Murakami, head of educational affairs for one of Tsubouchi's companies. "He can brainwash people into wanting to work hard."

This giant of Japanese industry is not without detractors. When he announced that 800 employees had to go at one of his shipyards, almost 500 voluntarily quit because Tsubouchi had the reputation of being such a tough boss. Periodicals that once honored him with laudatory praise as the savior of Japanese shipbuilding now refer to him as the "Stalin of Japanese business."

Though not as extreme as Mr. Tsubouchi, Ralph Ingersoll, II, the chief executive officer and chairman of the Ingersoll Group, the fifteenth largest newspaper chain in the United States, also has a reputation for being a very tough boss. He is a tight-fisted and cost-conscious manager who will not hesitate to lay off or fire workers if such moves will improve his newspapers' profitability. For example, in 1973 he fired 600 printers when he converted his newspapers from hot metal to cold type. Mr. Ingersoll also believes in keeping tight control over work operations. For example, all 115 Ingersoll newspapers must follow a specific manual that spells out in minute detail how the newspaper will be run. This manual includes directions for advertising space, time to compose a page, cost of solicitation of advertising, and so on. Thus, Ingersoll newspaper editors do not possess any significant power or authority to run newspapers as they see fit. Ingersoll also maintains control

of his newspapers through special deals with investment firms such as Drexel Burnham and E. M. Warburg, Pincus, and Company. Although these investment firms have considerable stock ownership in the Ingersoll Group, Ingersoll himself owns the majority of the voting stock.

Power and authority in successful business firms are not necessarily vested only in males or owners. Linda Wachner, the former president and chief operating officer of Max Factor's U.S. operations, is well-known throughout the cosmetics and women's apparel industry as a "fiery, single-minded, and imperious" ruler.

Throughout her twenty-year career in the industry, Wachner has made her mark as a no-nonsense boss. While running Max Factor's U.S. operations, her fondness for spiral notebooks earned for her the fear and loathing of both colleagues and subordinates. Wachner used these spiral notebooks to take detailed notes of every meeting, then used quotes from her notes during following days to see how her instructions were followed. During follow-up meetings, she would publicly unleash her fury on any culprit who failed to do as he or she was told.

Wachner gained her power in the cosmetics and women's apparel industries through her superior knowledge of and insight into customer needs and wants. She has a tremendous capacity for long and hard work, and has made a reputation for herself by darting into stores selling Max Factor products to grill both sales people and customers about what was moving and what was wanted.

When Wachner was first hired by Max Factor in 1978 to run its U.S. operations, the company was losing approximately $16 million per year. Within two years, she stopped the flow of "red ink" and produced a $5 million profit for the company. By 1982, she was promoted to president and chief operating officer—over the heads of many males who thought they had the inside track. Her success with Max Factor can be traced to her business relationship with David Mahoney, the chief of Norton Simon (the then-parent company of Max Factor). She impressed Mahoney with her outstanding performance at Max Factor, which not only consisted of raising revenues, but cutting waste and extravagance at all levels, even if this required mass firings. These firings also increased Wachner's power base as she filled vacant positions with her own loyalists.

Wachner left Max Factor in 1984 after the company was taken over by Beatrice. Wachner engineered a power play to make Max Factor private, a move that would ostensibly give her the opportunity to become the company's chairperson and chief executive officer. According to some associates, that move failed because her power play backfired due to the long-term resentment and jealousy felt by many Max Factor executives. She is now with the New York investment firm of Adler and Shaykin, where plans are in the works to take over Revlon from Pantry Pride. Should these plans succeed, Wachner will assume the dual roles of chairperson and CEO of this very successful cosmetics firm.

As the preceding excerpts illustrate, powerful business owners and executives will not hesitate to use their considerable power and authority to get the job done "their way." With the exception of Wachner (who did not own Max Factor), Tsubouchi's and Ingersoll's management styles perfectly exemplify the formal theory of authority that will be discussed later in this chapter. As you read further and study the information contained in this chapter, you will realize that power and authority are integral parts of organization theory. These two concepts, as well as the by-product of their interaction, politics, are the core around which the chapter material revolves.

CHAPTER PLAN

No discussion of organizations would be complete without a study of power, authority, and politics. We first examine the nature of formal authority in organizations and how it differs from power. Although these two concepts are intrinsically related, they are different and interact to form the basis for organizational behavior.

We next examine the foundations of power: rational/legal, reward, coercive, referent, charismatic, and expert. Following this discussion, we review the foundations of authority: managerial, staff, situational, and operative.

We then turn to the nature of responsibility, which is the obligation to perform a task, and the nature of accountability, which is the obligation to report on one's or another's performance of a task.

The use of power and authority often leads to organizational politics, that is, activities undertaken to acquire power and/or resources for the attainment of preferred outcomes. We further discern that politics involves a relationship between power and decision making, and, moreover, that a political model of organizations is a useful tool in helping to explain the dynamics of organization activities.

It is necessary to assess power in organizations; therefore, we study some of the methods used for this purpose. We also expand on our earlier discussion of the foundations of power in order to further clarify the relationship between power and politics.

Many lower order participants in organizations wield tremendous power even though they occupy relatively low positions within the hierarchy. Therefore, we analyze the attainment and uses of lower-order-participant power.

We next examine the relationship between power and commitment and power and external dependency. We end the chapter with a broad discussion of the everyday use and applicability of power within today's organizations.

All organizations depend on power and authority. Every day in every kind of situation, managers and operatives alike use their power and authority to get their jobs done: a manager hires a secretary; a staff specialist prepares a report; an inspector rejects a batch of product. All of these are instances of the use of power and authority.

Managers are hired to ensure that organizational goals are accomplished, and they do this by making choices among alternatives. This decision-making process would be only an exercise if the manager could not put these decisions into effect. Power and authority are the means for accomplishing this purpose. Moreover, as managers within organizations use their power and authority to make decisions, politics is often the result. That is, managers will undertake activities and form into groups or alliances to ensure a particular outcome.

THE NATURE OF POWER AND AUTHORITY

This section of the chapter examines the component parts of power and authority and how they fit together to provide the influence a decision maker needs to make choices and to get them accepted and implemented.

Authority

The word *authority* probably brings to mind a picture of a parent scolding a child or of a sergeant giving a command to the troops. In other words, we probably think of a superior guiding or altering the behavior of subordinates. One person gives a command or issues an order in an attempt to elicit some form of desired behavior from another.[*]

What happens when a superior issues an order or a command? First, the superior makes the decision or choice; this requires the right to do this. In other words, the superior must be given approval or sanction to make decisions in the name of the organization, and this requires some form of recognition by the organization itself. In the case of a formal organization, such as a factory or a retail store, this approval ultimately comes from the owners, who have the right to direct the use of their property. Owners, in turn, get their right to own property (the factory or the store) from the fact that our government recognizes the right of its citizens to own and use private property as long as this ownership and use do not unduly interfere with the rights of others. This explanation of authority, which traces its source to societal approval, is called the *formal theory of authority*.[1]

---

[*]The following discussion deals with managerial authority. This is only one form of authority; others will be discussed later. But this treatment helps explain the entire concept of authority.

In essence, the formal theory of authority says that the right of a manager to make decisions and to issue orders, instructions, and so on comes from the ownership and control of property. The passing along of this right from the owners to a management group and then, in turn, from one manager to the next is termed *delegation* and was discussed in detail in Chapter 11.

We can see a real-life application of the formal theory of authority by looking at the top management within CBS. CBS is owned by its thousands of stockholders, who elect a fourteen-member board of directors and its chairman. The chairman happens to be William S. Paley, the CBS founder who also owns 8 percent of CBS stock. The board and its chairman, as representatives of all the CBS owners, are responsible for selecting a president and chief executive officer to run the company's operations and make major decisions. In the case of CBS, the president and chief executive officer are vested in one person, Lawrence A. Tisch, who also happens to own 25 percent of CBS stock. Of course, Tisch cannot possibly make all the decisions necessary to run a large organization such as CBS; therefore, he has to delegate authority to subordinate managers, such as Howard Stringer, who is in charge of CBS news operations. Under Stringer is a multitude of subordinate managers who are responsible for such functional areas as producing, directing, reporting, writing, editing, and so on. As we can see from this example, all authority legally stems from the stockholders, the owners of the CBS organization.[2]

Directing the behavior of others is based on two "subrights": (1) the right to decide and (2) the right to issue appropriate implementing instructions or directions. Without the right to decide, no manager could be a successful planner, and without the right to issue orders and instructions, the manager's plans would be worthless because there could be no assurance of the implementation of the plans. Thus, authority is fundamental to every organization because the nature of managerial responsibility involves decision making and influence.

The essence of authority is rights. These rights are determined (ideally, at least) by obligations. The obligation (responsibility) should determine the nature of the right (authority), and so they should be "equal" or in balance. A manager accepts the obligation or responsibility to use organization resources effectively and efficiently and to guide others in the accomplishment of organizational objectives. So, it is this obligation of a manager that should determine how much and what type of authority he or she must have if he or she is to be adequately equipped to discharge this responsibility. Therefore, it is quite important for the organization to strive to ensure a proper balance between authority and responsibility in the organization.

Two points emerge from the above discussion. First, authority is a right determined* by an obligation, and, second, authority is solely associated with the formal organization that has formal sanction or approval from society.

Thus, we can define authority as the formal right to make decisions and to influence behavior to implement those decisions based on formal organizational relationships. The organization must, therefore, officially recognize the organizational relationship between manager and subordinates if the superior is to be granted authority. Otherwise, the influence of the superior must be considered informal, that is, outside the sanction of the formal organization. This informal influence is defined as power.

Power

Power is the ability (potential or actual) to impose one's will on others;[3] it is the ability of one person to affect the behavior of someone else. This ability can be based on a number of factors, such as knowledge, personality, and even on authority. Authority is simply power that the organization formally sanctions. In other words, power is a larger concept than authority and, indeed, subsumes it as a formal power relationship.

Power, unlike authority, is influence that is not based on organizational position; consequently, power applies to any interpersonal influence that exists either within or outside the bounds of formal organizational relationships.**

An example will clarify the difference between power and authority. Consider the situation in which a supervisor issues directions to subordinates that require them to carry out a normal work routine. These directions are considered by both the supervisor and the subordinates to be legitimate or official. The supervisor, in this instance, can be said to be using power in the form of position authority, which attaches to his or her role as a manager and which has been delegated to him or her by superiors in order to get certain organization goals accomplished.

Now assume that the supervisor directs a subordinate to do a personal errand for him or her. This errand is clearly outside the official relationship between superior and subordinate; therefore, the instructions cannot be founded on authority. This instruction, then, is an attempt to use power as the basis of influence. In other words, if the subordinate does the errand, the supervisor has exercised power over him or her. In the

*This statement applies to all forms of authority, even though the discussion here centers on managerial authority.

**Although power can be considered both a macro and a micro concept, the present discussion deals with power from the micro perspective only. Chapter 6 deals with power from a macro point of view and treats an organization's power relative to other organizations in the environment.

event that the subordinate elects not to do the errand, the power attempt will have been unsuccessful.

In this example, there is a dependency relationship between the superior and the subordinate. Even though this relationship is not based on formal job relationships, the subordinate depends on the superior for various rewards so is likely to submit to the power influence of the superior. Formal relationships often have a kind of carry-over effect into informal relationships.

The extent to which an individual can exercise power can be viewed as a function of the dependency relationship that exists between the parties. If B depends on A (for knowledge, income, and so forth), then A is in a position to exercise influence or power over B to that extent. The more dependent that B is on A, other things being equal, the more power A can exercise over B.

POWER, AUTHORITY, AND ORGANIZATIONAL BEHAVIOR

Because authority is a formal organization concept, its use is limited to those organizations that are formally recognized by society. As a part of this recognition and sanction, these organizations are given the right, or authority, to use their resources in whatever manner is appropriate for accomplishing their objectives. This authority can be subdivided among organization members to whatever extent is appropriate.

As they perform their tasks, all members of a formal organization exercise some form of authority. Because organizational behavior is channeled by the use of authority, it must be considered one of the most effective means of shaping and controlling behavior in the formal organization. All relationships that are officially recognized by the formal organization are held together and made effective by the use of authority. Power, on the other hand, is one of the important adhesives for holding unofficial relationships together and for making them effective. Power and authority are both necessary in order to control and guide total organizational behavior.

There are many informal relationships in any organization that are cemented by power. For example, every organization has social groups that are not necessarily related to formal positions. The group that takes its coffee break together, the group that plays on the company basketball team, and the group that plays poker on Friday evenings all are based on informal or social ties. The members might not even belong to the same department or have any official contact on their jobs. Nevertheless, in these groups leadership roles can be recognized based on influence not necessarily tied to the formal organization. The social leader's ability to shape the behavior of the group is founded on power rather than on authority.

It is important to point out here the necessity of examining power within the organization units themselves. The following brief discussion will center around the influence that accrues to various departments and other organizational units as a result of the organization's dependency on them. Members of these departments generally enjoy prestige as well as power.

The organization's interaction with its environment also affects the power of an individual department or unit. Environmental forces frequently are felt first by the organization in its staff or secondary units. For example, many organizations set up particular departments to deal with OSHA requirements. Safety departments, because of their knowledge of the rules and regulations, have knowledge that the organization needs to avoid government action were it not in compliance.

The budget office in many organizations likewise enjoys a power position because of the role it plays in organization life. All managers in an organization depend to some extent on information and perhaps even on a favorable decision from budget personnel if they are to be effective managers. This power frequently transcends the normal budgeting function. For example, many personnel matters are affected by their budgetary considerations as defined by the budget department. Consequently, this office occupies a critical position with respect to the determination of personnel matters that might permeate the entire organization.

Hickson and his colleagues[4] discuss a model that could be used to predict departmental power within organizations. The ability of a subunit to deal successfully with organizational uncertainties and contingencies is the first element of the model. Uncertainty or lack of knowledge creates a power dependency relationship.

The second part of the Hickson model deals with a concept called *substitutability*. If an individual department's power is shared by other departments, its relative power is diminished to that extent. The ability to control a scarce resource is an important source of power for any department, but that power diminishes to the extent that other units in the organization gain control over or make determining decisions about the use of that resource.

The final predictor of departmental power in the model is the pervasiveness of the uncertainty to the organization. To the extent that an environmental pressure is felt by the entire organization, and to the extent that one department can deal with that uncertainty, that organizational unit has power. If, on the other hand, the environmental turbulence affects only one department, then the ability to deal with that uncertainty does not produce power to the extent that it might were the uncertainty felt throughout the organization. For example, a faculty group with the ability to change the basic curriculum of the university would have more power than would a faculty group in an individual department able to change only the requirements for graduation with a degree in that discipline.

We can see the concept of departmental power in organizations at work within the American Express (AmEx) organization. As part of his strategy to increase cooperation and coordination among the various AmEx enterprises, a plan called "One enterprise," CEO James Robinson granted the manager of the corporate strategy department, Ursula Burke, the authority to make monthly reports citing the progress various AmEx managers and their divisions have made toward collaborating with each other. Should these managers and their divisions make "bad grades" (a "No Progress" citation), then these individuals soon hear from top-level management. In other words, the corporate strategy department at AmEx, although a separate unit within the corporate headquarters, has tremendous influence over that organization's multitude of various business units and divisions.

The Hickson model helps us understand that power is not only an individual concept, but also a departmental concept. The Hickson model helps us understand that such departmental power can be a function of the ability of a department to deal with organization uncertainty, the substitutability of departmental capabilities, and the pervasiveness of the uncertainty in the organization.

Power and authority are two of the most important aspects of organizations, and no theory of organization would be complete without treating them in some depth. The following section examines the foundations of power, and later sections deal with authority and politics.

THE FOUNDATIONS OF POWER

Influence based on power is rooted in several possible bases. The following sections briefly review each of them.[5] This review describes these bases in order to help you understand how power, coming from one or more of them, gains its support and potency. A summary of the bases is presented in Table 14.1.

Rational/Legal Power

Similar to what Max Weber termed rational/legal authority, rational/legal power stems from one person's acceptance that its exercise by another person agrees with some set of rules or protocol considered legitimate by both parties. In other words, there is little or no question about whether its use is considered proper. Certainly, Tisch's power at

TABLE 14.1

Foundations of Power

Type	Meaning	Example
Rational/legal	Accepted as legitimate by those involved	Obeying commands of police officer
Reward	Granting of benefits to others	Working hard for a promotion or recommendation
Coercive	Punishing others	Disciplinary action of a three-day suspension
Referent	Identification with person in a power position	Hero worship
Charismatic	Dynamic personality	Religious leaders
Expert	Extensive knowledge or high-level skill	Computer programmer

French & Rovem - In the eyes of the beholder - perceived

CBS stems primarily from the legal authority vested in him by that company's board of directors, and there is little doubt in the organization about its validity.

This condition of legitimacy is a function of culture that is instrumental in helping define societal norms. For instance, in countries of the Far East, it is considered legitimate for the older members of a group to be shown more deference (and thus be given more power) than younger members. In other cultures, such as ours, this might not be the case. Other factors might account for power, as can be seen when power is traceable to knowledge, ability, or some other factor. Whatever its particular source, if members of a society consider it legitimate to accept this type of influence, power is properly classified as rational/legal power.

Reward Power

Power that comes from one's ability to control and dispense benefits to another is termed *reward power.*[6] The controller of the benefits has the ability to shape the behavior of others by the simple act of dispensing or withholding these benefits.

The strength of this type of power is primarily determined by two major forces: the size of the reward and the belief that it will, in fact, be dispensed. In other words, A's reward power over B increases as the size of the benefit increases. The proposition is that, other things being equal, a large reward gives A greater power over B than would a small reward.

If A can pay B twenty dollars to mow a lawn, B is more likely to perform the task than if A can pay only five dollars. At the same time, if B perceives the probability that A will dispense the benefit is low, this fact will lessen the potency of A's reward power over B, regardless of the size of the reward. In this case, B considers the reward large and desirable but does not consider it likely that A will give the reward.

In the above example, B might not be willing to mow the lawn for an offer of twenty dollars if B does not assign a high probability to receiving the reward upon completion of the task. B might even be more willing to perform the task for a five-dollar payment if the probability of receiving it seemed higher than that of receiving the twenty-dollar fee.

In the use of reward power, it is also important that A have some means of determining whether B performs the desired task. In the case of mowing a lawn, it is relatively easy to measure task accomplishment. But there are other cases (for example, if A instructed B to teach a group of students how to write a publishable poem) when such is not the case. Task measurement, then, is a key dimension of the use of reward power.

This means that if reward power is to have its maximum impact, the user must be able to demonstrate the desirability of a benefit as well as a high probability that the reward will be dispensed upon determination that the assignment is complete. To the extent that one of these conditions is absent, reward power is less potent. On the other hand, successful use of reward power increases its potency for future use. It appears that the use of reward power strengthens its use in the future, much like a case of operant conditioning.

Hisao Tsubouchi, the Japanese industrialist who is one of the focal points of our introductory case, is a believer in the use of reward power. Note how he gave bonuses of $200 to shipyard workers after they had doubled productivity. Certainly, this "reward" will prime his workers to increase their efforts at his shipyards.

Coercive Power

The ability to coerce or punish another is a strong foundation of power or influence.[7] This ability is often strong motivation and can, in many ways, be viewed as the obverse of reward power. Where reward power relies on the dispensing of rewards for its strength, coercive power depends on the meting out of punishment for its effectiveness.

At IBM, new managers who do not measure up to standards are placed in the "penalty box," a meaningless and sometimes degrading job in which the young managers have the opportunity to consider the errors of their ways. And we have already seen in our introductory case how Hisao Tsubouchi will not hesitate to fire workers if he believes they are not working productively.

During childhood we all witnessed the use of coercive power. We saw an angry parent punish a child for misbehaving, or watched a leader of a street gang punish a member for "improper" behavior or attitude. What happens when coercive power is used successfully in instances like these? First, there is a compliant level of behavior demonstrated. This means that A will be able to obtain a minimum level of desired behavior from B because B wants to avoid further punishment. Additionally, it is likely that B will feel more estranged from A after the use of coercive power. This estrangement is likely to take the form of resentment and possibly even a deep-seated desire to retaliate. This sense of resentment and latent frustration can have serious dysfunctional consequences in a relationship, especially over time.

A situation in which there is merely compliant behavior will require close observation in the future to ensure that at least that level of behavior is demonstrated. The proposition is that, in the absence of close observation, it might not be exhibited. For example, it is not unreasonable to imagine a change of objectives and behavior on the part of those being punished—a change from normal performance to doing as little as possible to avoid punishment.

Again, the effectiveness of coercive power depends on the definition of punishment, its perceived impact, the probability that it will be used, and the measurement of desired behavior. For example, if the possible punishment is not defined as such by the "offender," if it is seen to be relatively mild, or if the chance of its being used is slight, coercive power is made less potent. Likewise, coercive power cannot be used unless "undesirable" behavior can be observed.

Referent Power

Referent power can be defined as the influence A has over B because of B's identifying with A.[8] This sense of identification makes A capable of influencing B's behavior even though neither A nor B may be aware of the identification or the sense of identification.

This type of power can be illustrated in the case of hero worship. Star athletes are worshipped by aspiring youngsters who see that their own abilities can be enhanced by emulating the star's behavior. Because everyone at one time or another has known this feeling of identification with success, this is a common foundation of influence or power.

Kirk Cottrell, the founder and owner of Island Water Sports, a Florida surf shop chain, has this type of power with young people. "I watch this guy with young people, and believe me, it's uncanny," stated Nancy Lyman, a friend and former classmate of this young entrepreneur, who succinctly stated the case of hero worship of Cottrell by young surfers and employees.[9]

People with whom others identify might not be aware of their own referent power. This fact makes it difficult to completely trace power relationships. Secret admiration of a successful person is a case in point. Such relationships would be difficult to identify and analyze, even though such relationships are undoubtedly common and have a tremendous impact on interpersonal relationships. Thus, referent power is significant to the understanding of organization behavior.

Charismatic Power

Influence based on personality can be defined as charismatic power. There are those who have an almost undefinable magnetic quality about their personalities that attracts others to follow them.[10] Hitler exercised this type of influence in Germany before and during World War II. The same has been said of John F. Kennedy and many religious leaders.

Those who possess charisma find it relatively easy to influence their followers. One of the dimensions of charismatic power that helps explain its potency is that charismatic leaders also help their followers attain personal goals. By following such a leader, the followers can realize their own objectives even though they might primarily be serving the leader's purposes.

Allen H. Michels, the entrepreneur who built Convergent Technologies into a $400 million-a-year computer business in only five years, is renowned in management circles because of his enormous energy and charisma.[11] Likewise, Lee Iacocca's power within Chrysler Corporation can be partially attributed to his charisma and ebullient personality.

No special effort is required to exercise charismatic power. The base itself remains stable and changes very little. Charles Manson, the leader of a group convicted of the bizarre murders of Hollywood personalities, is still said to have some magical hold over his followers even years later. Such influence is potent, indeed. Charismatic power is a formidable type of influence for managers and organization theorists to appreciate.

Expert Power

There are those who wield influence because of their knowledge or special skills. They are respected for this knowledge or skill that gives them expert power. Nobel scientists, professional artists, and consultants are examples of those with expert power. P. Roy Vagelos, the CEO of Merck and Company, the New Jersey pharmaceuticals concern, wields tremendous power in his organization because, among other reasons, he is a medical doctor. Thus, he understands medical research methodology and pharmacology.

Those who admire this expertise or who need it to solve problems are willing to subordinate themselves in return for the expert's assistance. A student who needs a teacher's help in solving a problem is an example. The student attributes the power of knowledge to the teacher and behaves in a manner that will enable him or her to have the advantage of the teacher's knowledge in solving problems.

Successful use of expert power within its sphere of influence tends to increase or at least maintain its potency, while its use outside its prescribed area of appropriateness tends to weaken its strength.[12] For example, an expert auto mechanic might enhance his influence if he restricts his influence to automotive repair, but he might lose it if he attempts to apply it to areas where it does not fit, for example, the repair of television sets. The latter application can cause suspicions about whether the knowledge is, in fact, "expert" since its user is unaware of the limits of its application. So it is wise to appreciate the sphere of expert power and to restrict its use to these bounds.

The foundations of power discussed above help clarify the sources of power and thus help explain the potencies of power. Power, the ability to influence without the sole sanction of the formal organization, is a dependency-causing force with which all people concerned with the workings of organizations must deal. This discussion should improve your ability to deal with it successfully. The other influence source in the organization is authority.

THE FOUNDATIONS OF AUTHORITY

Authority is the mainspring of influence in the formal organization. It has its roots in the official recognition of the organization by society. It is a prime mover for guiding the organization and its various membership groups toward their objectives. Several forms of authority are discussed below and are summarized in Table 14.2. Additionally, the discussion will treat the components and uses of authority in order to demonstrate how this force affects organizational behavior.

Managerial Authority

Managers of formal organizations are responsible for acquiring, deploying, and controlling resources needed to accomplish objectives. To do this, managers must have the right to make and enforce necessary decisions. This right is termed *authority* and is possessed by all who hold managerial positions. Managerial authority is composed of the right to choose among alternatives and the right to enforce those choices based on official position. Without both these components, no manager can

TABLE 14.2

Foundations of Authority

Type	Meaning	Example
Managerial	Right to make and enforce decisions	Decision to order a new glass-making machine
Staff	Right to make suggestions and recommendations	Study recommending a change in job descriptions
Situational	Right to make binding decisions within a very restricted area or scope	Accountant deciding proper accounting methods
Operative	Right to work without undue supervision	Tool and die maker rejecting poor raw material

successfully carry out responsibilities. This is true because all managers, regardless of their positions in the organization structure, are charged with the responsibility of making decisions and ensuring that they are carried out. Thus, managerial authority is the key means for executing managerial responsibility.

The exact nature and amount of managerial authority required at any given location in the organization structure should be a function of the responsibility located there. Consequently, the manager's responsibility should be a determining factor in deciding the amount of authority that the manager is granted. This balance between responsibility and authority is in keeping with the *principle of parity of authority and responsibility*, a long-recognized guide to building and maintaining a sound organization structure. The principle simply states that a balance between authority and responsibility is desirable because this balance prevents the dysfunctional consequences of managers' (as well as other members') being responsible for a project and not having the authority to carry it out effectively. Also, it prevents a condition in which a manager's authority exceeds his or her responsibility.* All managers, then, possess managerial authority and use it to enforce the decisions needed to carry out their responsibility for the accomplishment of organization objectives.

Let's take the example of Howard Stringer's role within CBS News. Stringer is responsible for managing all CBS operations relating to news

---

*Even though this principle is discussed here in connection with managerial authority, it is also appropriate to consider it in connection with the other types of authority.

reporting and coverage. His mandate from CEO Tisch also requires him to determine if the news division is overstaffed and too bureaucratic. Therefore, in order to make CBS news operations more efficient, Stringer has the concomitant authority to eliminate positions and lay off employees.

Staff Authority

Every day, members of an organization make suggestions and recommendations about the solutions to problems, procedural changes, or how their jobs could be made easier or more attractive. Each time this happens, staff authority is being exercised. Even though we normally associate this type of authority with expert or professional personnel, it is actually possessed by every member of the organization. In other words, everyone in an organization has the right to recommend, to suggest, to advise, and to attempt to exert influence to gain acceptance for ideas.[13] This means that every subordinate has the right to make recommendations and suggestions or to give advice.

Even though we might best understand the use of staff authority when we see a subordinate attempt to gain the superior's acceptance of an idea or suggestion, it should be noted that there are many other paths over which staff authority can flow. For instance, suggestion systems that are commonly used today are prime examples of the use of staff authority, because the organizations in which such systems are used have given official recognition to them.

One possibly confusing aspect of the use of staff authority is the fact that subordinates often do not elect to use their staff authority for one reason or another. In addition, some superiors discourage their subordinates from using it. This situation can be compared to the right to vote. There are those who voluntarily choose not to exercise their voting rights, and there might be occasions where they are virtually prohibited from doing so by others. Whether they are used, however, voting rights are possessed by all qualified citizens. So it is with staff authority; it is possessed by all organization members even though its actual use might be limited for any of several reasons.

In the case where a decision is made by the organization to employ a consultant, a slightly different use of staff authority might be made. For example, it is a common practice to hire accountants to aid in the proper management of organization resources. These experts are often given specific grants of staff authority by the organization to make suggestions or to advise management on organizational or procedural aspects of financial management. This authority affects many, if not all, phases of the organization and its operations. Basically, an expert is hired to extend the abilities of management into an area where special skill and knowledge are required. One might say that staff authority in these instances becomes a type of technological necessity due to the complexity of work involved.

The type of staff authority associated with a consultant was used by Michael Blumenthal, CEO of Burroughs Corporation, when his organization purchased Sperry Corporation. Blumenthal hired a team of psychologists to treat "merger syndrome," the demoralization that often cripples a newly acquired company. These psychologists have the responsibility and concomitant authority to form and direct teams of managers from the two companies, the objective being to create teamwork and organizational bonds.

Whether it is used by a subordinate to advise or to make suggestions to a superior on general issues, or whether it is used by an expert to advise on special issues, staff authority must be capably used if the organization is to function properly. Sometimes, staff authority evolves into situational authority.

Situational Authority

Situational authority is a type of hybrid authority in that it contains elements of both managerial and staff authority. Generally, it is delegated to a staff expert who is restricted rather severely in the areas of organization structure and function in which it can be exercised. This expert is given the right to make *binding* decisions (an element of managerial authority) about a given function in the organization structure.* Because of the potentially wide area of application in the structure, it is important to restrict the use of situational authority to a very limited functional scope.

This type of authority relationship often begins as a staff authority relationship. An accountant, say, is given the right to make recommendations, give advice, or make suggestions on the matter of proper accounting methods. As time passes and the expert's superior gains confidence in the quality of the advice, the expert might be given a grant of situational authority that is approved by the manager who supervises the chief accountant.

This type of authority enables the accountant to interact directly with other members of the organization to implement decisions about accounting procedures without having to confer with her superior. This means that the accountant issues decisions that have the prior approval of the superior through the grant of situational authority. Therefore, it is

---

*The word *binding* is emphasized here since it is important to understand that situational authority is something more than merely emergency decision making.

not necessary to involve the superior in every decision. This frees the superior to attend to other matters and gives more effect to the decisions of the accountant, who, in this case, is acting as the superior's agent on matters falling within the accountant's area of expertise.

Situational authority is less cumbersome and more efficient than staff authority. If the accountant in this instance had only been given staff authority, she would have had to confer with the superior and obtain approval for the decision. The superior, in turn, would have been required to convince the appropriate manager of the part of the organization where the decision was to be implemented of the validity of the idea. Upon acceptance of the idea, this manager would have used managerial authority to achieve its implementation. Situational authority, because it enables its holder to interact directly at the point of implementation through the use of binding decisions, avoids considerable communication contact. Thus, if properly used, situational authority can be an effective managerial aid.

Because of the increasing importance of the information-processing function within organizations, information managers have become vested with ever-increasing situational authority. For example, at Air Products and Chemicals, line workers in natural gas production operations were responsible for reading meters, writing reports on the condition of equipment, keeping inventory, and so forth, and then mailing everything to corporate headquarters in Allentown, Pennsylvania. However, Peter Mather, the vice president for management information services at Air Products and Chemicals, saw a way to save time in the performance of these line tasks by having computers do the work. Mather, through situational authority, spearheaded the creation of a $30 million system that now ties computers from the natural gas plants to a central computer at headquarters. The result of this use of situational authority has been a 14 percent savings, or $25 million a year, in the organization's costs for natural gas production.[14]

Situational authority can be quite disruptive to the organization if it is misused. For instance, the accountant could issue decisions that bind members to follow what might be a poor direction for the organization or to install an ineffective accounting procedure. Such could be the case if the accountant has inadequate or erroneous information, or if the accountant is attempting to gain undue influence. With the force of situational authority behind them, the accountant's decisions could bring undesirable effects without the safeguard of staff authority. This safeguard would require the accountant to advise rather than to issue binding decisions.

Situational authority is a potent right. It should only be delegated after careful consideration and it should have some safeguards about over what activities it can be exercised.

Operative Authority

All members of an organization have the right to make certain decisions about how, in what order, and with which tools they will carry out their assignments. The right to work without undue supervision is also commonly considered to apply to all members. These rights, taken collectively, are operative authority.[15]

Providing for operative authority among low-level assembly workers at the joint GM-Toyota NUMMI plant in California has enhanced productivity there. Workers are organized in teams of ten to twelve people for a given assembly operation, and the team members themselves can make their own decisions about how to divide the work within the group.

Even though it is not frequently mentioned as an authority type, operative authority is included here because it is necessary to completely explain all the rights of organization members. For example, we have all experienced job assignments in which certain decisions were necessary that did not involve others in any way, as do decisions involved with managerial, staff, and situational authority. We have had to decide about priorities, schedules, and tools and materials to be used. These decisions required that we be given some form of authority to make them. Since in these cases no other individuals were directly involved with the decision process, the decisions were made using operative authority.

Operative authority is made up of two basic rights: the right to carry out responsibility and the right to determine, within reason, how and when it will be done. Whether one is a manager, a technician, or an unskilled laborer, one has these minimum rights. Without them, it would not be possible to plan and carry out one's personal responsibility.

All the authority types described above have two components, one of them being common to all types. All types of authority contain the right of decision. Without it, no one could plan; no subordinate or expert could advise; no expert could make binding decisions; and no member could carry out personal responsibility. In addition to the right of decision, managerial authority has the right of official enforcement; staff authority has the right of recommendation, suggestion, and advice to accompany the decision; situational authority has the right to issue binding decisions at appropriate points in the structure; and operative authority has the right to work without undue supervision in order to carry out personal responsibility.

Along with the concepts of power and authority, an organization must consider responsibility and accountability as important organization variables. The next sections discuss these concepts and show how they are related to the organization's power and authority network.

THE NATURE OF RESPONSIBILITY AND ACCOUNTABILITY

Responsibility is among the most important parts of organization theory. It is the obligation that members assume to carry out their duties to the best of their ability in accordance with directions, procedures, and policies. Thus, responsibility has its roots in work differentiations that are needed to attain organization goals.

Because people accept a general obligation to perform their duties when they join an organization, they expect to be held liable for their actions. In other words, there is a general expectation that one will give up a certain amount of freedom in return for a position and rewards for proper behavior. We have seen that employees expect to get certain rewards from their association with an organization. For example, in the case of a part-time student/worker, it might be money for school expenses or even the gaining of work experience that might help secure a better job in the future. In order to acquire funds or experience, the student/worker expects to do some task at an acceptable level of performance—expects, in other words, to fulfill some obligation to carry out his or her responsibility.

The basis of this responsibility is the performance of a task or group of tasks that have been grouped together to form a position. This positional responsibility becomes the foundation for the delegation of authority, the right to carry out such responsibility. Responsibility, as noted earlier, is a prime determinant of the amount and type of authority required for proper performance of the task obligation.

Authority and responsibility should be kept in a reasonable balance so that minimum opportunity for poor performance and frustration exists. The balance is brought about by defining and delegating authority to fit the demands of responsibility, not vice versa. Whether an individual is given a grant of managerial, staff, situational, or operative authority should be determined by whether the person has the obligation to carry out managerial, staff, expert, or operative responsibility, respectively. Of course, a given individual can have a combination of these responsibilities and, thus, can have a corresponding grant of authority types to accompany it.

Once authority has been delegated to an individual to complement his or her responsibility, that person should be held accountable for its proper use in carrying out the obligation. *Accountability* is the obligation to submit a report (in whatever form) to one's superior about how well responsibility has been discharged. The superior, in turn, can use this report not only to judge the quality of performance but also to determine the worth of the individual to the organization.

At American Express, the responsibility for the development and implementation of the "One Enterprise" strategy has been delegated by

FIGURE 14.1

Authority and Responsibility Serve as the Basis for Accountability

the CEO to the manager for corporate strategy. She, in turn, requires reports from AmEx managers on their progress in carrying out the plan. Through these reports, AmEx division managers are accountable to the manager for corporate strategy, who, in turn, submits a consolidated report to the CEO.

Accountability is the obverse phase of responsibility since responsibility determines authority, and together responsibility and authority form the basis for accountability, as we see in Figure 14.1. Control of the organization obviously depends heavily on how well responsibility and authority are balanced so that meaningful and legitimate accountability reports can be expected. Therefore, management must be given the right to require these accountability reports and to use them to carry out responsibility for goal attainment.

The Determinants of Responsibility

Responsibility is a product of matching people and jobs or tasks. When people are assigned jobs in an organization, they assume the obligation to perform those jobs to the best of their abilities and in accordance with directions, procedures, and policies. This, in essence, is the nature of responsibility.

Responsibility is, then, made up of two essential ingredients—a task and a person; and the organization hopes there is a match or balance between the two. Decisions about work differentiations and their grouping into positions have a significant influence on the hiring, utilization, appraisal, and rewarding of the person assigned to carry out the positional responsibility.

So, in the final analysis, responsibility is determined by its work component and how well it is used to match people and their talents to it.

When there is a proper match, responsibility and authority can be balanced to form the proper base for accountability.

Determinants of Accountability

When people are provided with the proper authority, resources, and sense of direction for carrying out their responsibilities, a proper base for accountability exists. This means simply that a vital part of managerial responsibility must be to provide these essential prerequisites if a meaningful accountability base is to exist. Management must be alert to changes in any or all of these conditions if accountability is to be properly required.

Because organizational success depends to a large extent on how sound the accountability base is, it is an important variable to be included in a theory of organizations.

POWER AND AUTHORITY RELATIONSHIPS

Earlier in the chapter, we examined power and authority relationships in organizations. Here we examine the relationship that power has to political forces within the organization. Our focus is on how the political processes at work in the organization affect the power and authority relationships.

Most of us spend much of our lives in one form of organization or another. We start at a very early age in an educational institution and work our way through secondary school, and then some of us find our way into college or become prepared for a career. But how many of us have stopped to think who governs these institutions? In other words, who *really* has the power and authority to make the kinds of decisions that determine the course and governance, not only of schools and universities but also of giant corporations, churches, and social institutions in our country?

Think of a particular organization of which you are a member. Can you name those people or that person who governs the organization? Take your own college or university, for example. Is it the alumni? the governing board? Is it the president? a vice president? a dean? your instructor? To pose such questions is to indicate the difficulty in finding an answer to them. For at the same time we could say that no one group or person mentioned above governs your college or university, we could also say that, in a sense, each one does.

The alumni exert influence on the course and direction of your college or university. The governing board issues rules and regulations. The president, vice president, and other administrators make decisions and issue directives that are a kind of governance system. Yet, to consider only these formal organizational influence wielders is not to get the full picture.

We have all seen individuals exercise far more influence in their organizations than their formal authority would indicate that they should. For example, a dean's secretary, because of the position, can serve as a kind of gatekeeper to let individuals into, or to deny them access to, the dean's office. Some faculty members, because of their distinguished academic backgrounds, may almost be granted immunity from the formal structure.

Both faculty and students often form coalitions in order to get their way in the organization. For example, on many campuses it is traditional to have students run for office, such as that of student body president. These contests can become quite heated, and it is not unusual for a "greek" versus "nongreek" polarization to develop in the student body where many of the members of fraternities and sororities support one candidate while the independents might support another. The coalitions are not formally recognized by the university, but they are nonetheless influence centers in changing the way the university might operate.

POLITICS DEFINED

These examples indicate the necessity for a clear definition of politics in organizations. Jeffrey Pfeffer has suggested a concise and useful definition:

> Organizational politics involves those activities taken within organizations to acquire, develop, and use power and other resources to obtain one's preferred outcomes in a situation in which there is uncertainty or dissensus [sic] about choices.[16]

This definition of politics is not restricted to the formal organization; it can apply to any exercise of influence in order to secure a particular outcome. From this short description, we can see that issues are resolved both through the formal and informal use of power. Formal power is used in the case when the president or governing board makes a decision or issues a directive, and in the case of faculty and student coalitions that form in order to prevail in a particular situation, much of the power involved is informal.[17]

Power and Decision Making

Among the primary activities that are performed in any organization is decision making. Daily operations require a multitude of decisions covering every aspect of the organization. Choices must be made about markets, products, prices, inventories, and whether to hire employees.

Decisions are made by all members of the organization and are made for a variety of purposes; however, they all affect the organization in some manner, either directly or indirectly. For this reason, it is important to understand why these choices impact organization life and to understand the bases on which they are made.

Decisions are choices that are intended to affect behavior in some manner. Some decisions are limited in their consequences to an individual, as when one elects to perform one task instead of another or whether to attend class. Other decisions are aimed at affecting the actions of others, as when a manager gives an order or an instructor gives a class assignment.

In any organization there are decision makers who are formally recognized as such and, thus, who are expected to make choices on behalf of the organization. These managers are selected to guide the organization toward its objectives, and members expect them to make choices and to follow their lead. In sororities and fraternities, for example, members elect officers each year. These officers occupy official positions and are vested with the authority to make necessary decisions within the purview of their respective offices. In other words, these officers are given the requisite authority to carry out their duties.

The basis for decision making in these instances is formal, organizational authority. Members recognize the necessity for choices and for some official recognition of the rights of officers to make those choices. This is true whether the organization is voluntary (as is the case with sororities and fraternities), a government agency, or a private business. This means, then, that formally recognized organizations have a group of people who are expected to make required decisions. These decisions are classified as managerial (when they directly affect the work and behavior of formal subordinates). An example is a supervisor issuing a work order to a technician. Nonmanagerial decisions, on the other hand, take a "noncommand" form, as when a worker determines a priority for work or selects a particular tool or material with which to work. Even though they are different in their scope and impact on the organization, both managerial and nonmanagerial decisions are founded on authority that has been defined and delegated.[18]

There are many other decisions, however, that are made daily on the basis of power or informal influence. A good example can be found in the informal group activity that goes on within the formal organization. Think of a friendship group you belong to. Each group has a generally recognized (at least by the members) leadership structure. People who occupy those positions make choices that affect the group. Examples could include when to meet and what to do. Other informal organizations include juvenile gangs, crime syndicates, and drug rings, among others.

At the Honda assembly plant in Marysville, Ohio, informal groups of assembly workers are well established and even encouraged by management. All Honda employees, from top to bottom, refer to each other as "associates"; all wear white coveralls with their first names stitched above the pocket; there are no enclosed offices; no reserved parking spaces; and no executive dining room or lounges. In short, Honda is running this plant as one big informal group.

There is a norm of behaviors in each of these groups, and certain members expect to be given "orders" by others. Decisions and orders in these groups are based on power rather than on authority simply because the groups are not officially recognized by our society.

Therefore, we can see that decisions can be based on either authority, power, or a combination of both. The discussion here assumes that decisions are based on power; that is, we will concentrate on informal rather than formal decisions, because there are many more of them made in organizations. Also, it is important to portray the "power" or "political" side of organizations as well as the "authority" side, which has generally been given the major emphasis in the literature.

These informal decision makers make their choices in order to "get their way." They try to control their environment so they can optimize their benefits, especially vis-à-vis their disadvantages. Some have more influence than others, of course, and so a kind of power structure can be drawn from this informal hierarchy. Membership in this hierarchy can be fluid, with different actors taking the lead as the situation or issue changes. Pfeffer sums this up as follows:

> It is generally agreed that power characterizes relationships among social actors. A given social actor, by which we mean an individual, subunit, or organization, has more power with respect to some actors and less with respect to others. Thus, power is context or relationship specific.[19]

So, it is important to note that power is relative and situation-specific. Change any part of the decision context, or change actors or issues, and the power structure will likely take on a new configuration occupied by different choice makers. Keep this in mind as we proceed with our examination of power and politics—that process we use to acquire power for ourselves or to minimize that of others.

A Political Model of Organizations

Although several models attempt to explain organization structure and behavior, we have selected a political perspective simply because we believe it best fits with a discussion of power. As power is used to make choices in an informal setting, a political view sees the organization from the basis of decisions that stem from power rather than those based on authority that aim to attain the formal organization's overall goal network.

Power decisions can be examined to learn more about organization activity.[20] Much of the activity and energy of an informal group is spent vying for power that can be used to alter favorable events on one's behalf. One type of decision that must be made in the informal setting arises because of the presence of conflict. Disputes are bound to arise simply because the informal organization is really a mosaic of several organizations, each trying to protect its turf. These groups frequently have interlocking memberships, so the power structure encompasses several groups. Bargaining is commonplace within this structure; of course, one's ability to bargain successfully is a function of power to a great extent.

We can see the political model of organizations at work in the case of GAF when that organization went through a period of political turmoil in 1983. One informal group, headed by Samuel J. Heyman, a major stockholder, was comprised of those stockholders who wanted to sell GAF's chemical businesses in order to pay long-term debts and obtain the necessary capital for future acquisitions. Another group, headed by then-CEO Jesse Werner, and consisting of his loyal coterie of stockholders, wanted to sell GAF's building materials operations. Neither of these two groups was an official organizational subunit; however, they vied with each other, through conflict and bargaining, for control of the organization, with the result that Heyman became CEO in 1983. Certainly, this major change in direction for GAF did not come about entirely through the organization's official structure and operating mechanisms; rather, the changes at GAF were also brought about by the political clash between the two stockholder groups.

An analysis of decision types and their makers in order to understand organizations, then, is a simple explanation of the political model of organizations. It is a view maintaining that conflict, bargaining, and other maneuverings are the essence of organization life. The study of the use of power is a very effective way to study this activity.

HOW TO ASSESS POWER

Because power permeates the organization, and all its members are, in some way, affected by it, it is important to find some means to measure or assess it. Only if they are able to assess power can the members find their places in the power structure. There are, according to Pfeffer,[21] several means of assessing or measuring power, which the following sections describe.

Power Determinants as a Measure of Power

To measure power by its determinants requires a judgment about how much of a particular type of power a given actor possesses. We saw earlier in the chapter the six types or sources of power. Determinants (or origins) of power are *indirect* measures of the particular type of power that a given actor has at a particular time.

An example of the determinants of power as a measure of power might be useful here. When people have expert power, it means that they have special expertise or knowledge about a given field; their power originates from this expertise. If they appear to have considerable in-depth knowledge, we may tend to assign disproportionate power to them. The more fields in which they effectively demonstrate expert power, the more powerful they can be as employees.

Employees, of course, can behave in a way that creates the impression that they have more power than they actually do by using "double talk" and by appearing quite sure of their positions. Only experience with a given employee can reveal whether that power is based on legitimate expert (or some other type) power.[22]

Power Consequences

Another means of assessing power is to determine the effects or consequences of the decisions made by various actors. A look at who makes the significant organizational decisions gives a good indication of who has the most power in the organization. It is important, however, to distinguish between who *makes* the decisions and who *announces* them. For example, the president of a corporation might announce a merger plan that was actually the work of a close advisor. A dean might announce a plan to allocate the school's budget that could really be the work of a staff assistant.

An excellent example of this point can be seen in the case of Liz Claiborne, the apparel company. Although Liz Claiborne, herself, is the president of the organization, her husband and co-chairman of the board, Arthur Ortenberg, makes all the pronouncements. Ken Wise, the company's former marketing director, stated, "He's the man behind the door—intellectual and godlike, Socratic, and dogmatic."[23]

Those actors called on to make the decisions that cause the most severe consequences or alter the behavior of the most important actors are those whose power can be measured by the consequences of its use. Consider, for example, the various magnitudes of impact of the following decisions:

Mergers

Building new plants

Introducing new products

Budget allocations to departments

Hiring new employees

Although there are countless other types of decisions, there exists a hierarchy of power consequences. Each organization has its own power hierarchy, and it is generally fluid, meaning that consequences vary in importance to the organization, depending on the total decision environment.[24]

Power Symbols

Those who have power generally like to display the trappings of their office. Large offices, carpets, reserved parking spaces, and styles of dress can all indicate the presence of power. In one university, the floor on which the faculty have their offices indicates the value of the faculty (and hence their power). Offices on the same floor as that of the dean of the college hold the most powerful faculty, while the third floor is reserved for those with little power. The first floor is occupied by those with medium influence. Lieutenant Colonel Oliver North of the 1987 "Irangate" scandal certainly exemplifies this point. How many Marine lieutenant colonels have their own offices in the White House?

Even though symbols signify power, it is impossible to generalize their applicability. It might well be the case, for instance, that spartan conditions have a kind of reverse symbolism. Those managers in the original office wing near the plant might be viewed as having more power than the new employees located in the new wing somewhat removed from the plant.

Reputation of Actors

Still another means to measure power is the reputation employees have for possessing and using influence. Following this means, one would simply ask members of an organization who possesses power and over what issues it can be employed. Of course, this assumes that the respondent (1) will tell the truth and (2) knows about power distribution.

We have all known individuals who are naive about how their organizations work and about who makes the critical decisions. Answers from these people would obviously create a false power structure. There are also those who do not care to know, preferring to "just do their jobs." So, there can be cases in which the actor has more power than the actor's reputation justifies. There can also be actors who have a greater reputation for having power than they actually possess. Therefore, one must be careful to gather and evaluate information about reputation.

An excellent example demonstrating the reputation of an actor to show his or her power can be found in Richard N. Perle, former assistant secretary of defense for international security policy in the Reagan administration. While in this position, he had a reputation in government circles for exercising an inordinate amount of power in the area of United States–Soviet relations, even though his official position was well below that of Caspar Weinberger, then secretary of defense. Perle had considerable power and influence over other executive departments, most notably the Department of State and the Department of Commerce. For example, he managed to single-handedly forestall United States–Soviet trade agreements that he believed would be detrimental to the United States because of technology transfer to the Soviets. Perle was well known and even feared in Washington because of his influence with President Reagan and Secretary Weinberger. He was a powerful person for a number of reasons, not the least of which is his *reputation* for being powerful.[25]

Representational Indicators

These measures, according to Pfeffer, ". . . assess the position of social actors in critical organization roles such as membership on influential boards and committees or occupancy of key administrative posts."[26] If a mid-level manager is the head of a special company task force as well as chairperson of several organization-wide committees (such as the budget committee, for example), this indicates considerable influence in the entire organization. It might also indicate the person's popularity with senior management who appointed him or her to the posts.[27]

In every organization there are key jobs or offices that represent power, some by their title (executive vice president) or by their function (budget officer). The control of resources is important in any kind of organization, so the making of key budget decisions represents power. In other areas of control the key offices can vary, thus title might not be sufficient to measure the power of a chancellor or a president because these terms are used differently in different systems. For instance, the chief executive officer is called president on some campuses and chancellor on others.

We can see the relative power reflected in position titles by examining the hierarchy of titles within the Hewlett-Packard organization. Under the board of directors and its chairman, the person responsible for running the organization is called the chief executive officer (CEO). Second in command is the chief operating officer (COO), while third is the executive vice president. Therefore, we can assess who has power within Hewlett-Packard by observing who has what position title within top management. It is important, then, to learn about specific situations when one looks for things, events, and conditions that represent power.

There appears to be no overall best way to assess power. One measure is best in one circumstance while another would measure power better in another. We simply describe these indicators and suggest that a prescriptive use of them be made.

Whatever measure is used, it is imperative to be able to assess power if one is to be an effective member of any organization. This is doubly true of managers. These measures can aid in this effort.

THE SOURCES OF POWER

Influence can come from a number of sources, but the sources all revolve around the dependency of one actor on another. The ability to create dependency is among the most important determinants of the amount of power any actor can wield. The most simple case of dependency can be seen in the parent-child relationship. Here, the child (at least in early life) is almost totally dependent on its parents to provide all the necessities of life. There is no participation in decision making, and so the child is, for all practical purposes, powerless except for its ability to attract attention by crying. As the child matures, dependency is lessened, and he or she can make more and more decisions on his or her own. This process generally continues until the child eventually severs the dependency on the parents.

The achievement of independence from parents, however, is replaced by dependence on others—on teachers for information; on friends for support; on employers for jobs. The point is simple: All of us depend to some extent on others and therefore are subject to their influence. At the same time, we have influence of some strength over others. So, the dependency factor that is so vital to the exercise of control is really a network of relative forces.

Power Through the Control of Resources

Every organization must have resources to convert into product or service. Without a sufficient amount and proper distribution of such resources, the organization will soon cease to exist. Thus, members who can control resources exercise a tremendous influence on the organization.[28]

The more widely used the resource in the organization, the more its control produces power. For example, money affects almost all aspects of organization life, so those who make decisions about who gets how much money are especially powerful actors. The same could be said about decisions to hire personnel. Thus, the more pervasive the use of the resource, the more powerful is its controller.

Position Power

A certain amount of power attaches to the various offices in the organization. The chief executive officer assumes the power of office upon being hired or elected. The power of the office of the president of the United States is awesome. The incumbent has the influence to significantly alter the course of world events. Choices made by the president can help or hinder underdeveloped nations, can begin and end wars or help preserve peace, and can affect our natural environment.

The organization charts of most organizations generally depict the hierarchy of formal power because position power is basically authority. Note, however, that because of the formal position, the chief executive officer is often quite influential in informal relations. For example, a secretary in the shipping department would hardly refuse a request from the CEO even though he or she is not the immediate supervisor!

Personal Qualities

Knowledge, charisma, and skill possessed make some actors more important to the organization than others. They can consequently exert influence on the organization, and the more prized these qualities, the wider the range of influence. There can exist what amounts to a multiple set of rules, for example. If a university had a Nobel Laureate on its faculty, that person could get by with more rule violations (parking and traffic regulations, for instance) than a beginning assistant professor probably could.

Some individuals attempt to hoard information so that the organization cannot do without them. These people obviously are reluctant to share with others, lest their power be reduced. Organizations can minimize this dependency by having written rules and the like. This allows others to know how to perform and thus to reduce the power of some actors.[29]

Persons who can deal with uncertainty successfully are usually more powerful than those who can handle only stable, structured situations. Because organizations today exist in a turbulent, unstable environment, an organizational requirement is that at least some actors have the ability to quickly grasp situations and to gather information about them from a macro perspective. Many, not few, decisions require this ability today, so the possession of this trait allows an individual to exert considerable power in most present organization forms, regardless of position or title held.

We can observe the acquisition of power by individual entrepreneurs who have the foresight and ability to venture into previously uncharted frontiers created by the deregulation of the telecommunications, transportation, and health maintenance industries. For example, representatives of the new power elite emerging within American industry are such individuals as William McGowan of MCI Communications, Frederick Smith of Federal Express, and David Jones of Humana Hospitals. These individuals and others like them have accumulated power because they have successfully dealt with uncertainty.

Control of the Agenda

The people who have the right to decide the agenda for action are in powerful positions. In legislatures, for example, the chairperson can frequently decide the fate of a bill simply by not allowing it to come before a committee or the entire body.

Pehr Gyllenhammar, the chairman of Sweden's Volvo, is a very powerful man, and not just because of his chairmanship of the Volvo board of directors. In addition to his rational/legal power, Gyllenhammar is even more powerful because he controls the Volvo board's agenda. He accomplished this by forcing the resignation of board members opposing him and handpicking new appointees from among his friends and supporters.

Professionalism

Once someone acquires professional recognition, that person's stock of power is generally increased. A bookkeeper who earns a certified public accountant certificate suddenly becomes more influential in the organization. What were once mere suggestions now become directives, and the CPA finds his or her sphere of influence spreading. Certainly, CEO Vagelos' power within Merck Pharmaceuticals is enhanced by the fact that he is a medical doctor.

The more central the special knowledge is to the organization, the more potent and widespread can be its use. For example, a CPA probably will have more influence in a manufacturing concern than would a certified association executive. Professional certification, nonetheless, is a source of power in most organizations.[30]

Substitutability

In our discussion of the Hickson model at the beginning of this chapter, we discussed the concept of substitutability and its relationship to power. We now expand on this concept by referring to an article written by Dr. Rosabeth Kanter.[31] Kanter pointed out that power in organizations is often based on substitutability, that is, the extent to which an individual's or department's function can be performed by another. As we discussed in Chapter 11, some organizations are deliberately decreasing their size and complexity by contracting out certain functions that were previously performed by their own in-house functional units. Specifically, we described in that chapter how Mega Corporation had contracted out to outside firms many of its advertising, engineering, and data collection and analysis functions. Therefore, we can say that individuals and departments within Mega that used to perform these functions now have significantly less power because others are readily available to do their work.

LOWER-ORDER-PARTICIPANT POWER

As we have mentioned, every member of an organization has some amount of power for at least some situation. Having noted how leaders gain their power, let us now examine briefly the power that lower order participants (LPs) have. (When you read the end case in this chapter, you will see many real-life examples of the tremendous power that LPs can exert within their organizations.)

Because of its significance to the understanding of power, David Mechanic's work will provide the primary scheme for the discussion of this important topic.[32] The term *LP* refers to those people who occupy positions on lower levels of the organization structure, but it also refers to any subordinate, be it an accountant, a department manager, or a vice president. The comments made here apply equally to any superior-subordinate relationship.

LPs come to the organization expecting to take orders from higher-order participants (HPs). Any subordinate can acquire power, according to Mechanic, by having control over these elements: information, persons, and instrumentalities.

Mechanic defined information as follows:

> *Information* includes knowledge of the organization, knowledge about persons, knowledge of the norms, procedures, techniques, and so forth.[33]

This definition is quite inclusive and not limited to expert knowledge of a subject discipline such as law or accounting.

His definition of persons is:

> *Persons* include anyone within the organization or anyone outside the organization upon whom the organization is in some way dependent.

Again, this is quite a broad definition.

He defines instrumentalities as follows:

> *Instrumentalities* include any aspect of the physical plant of the organization or its resources (equipment, machines, money, and so on).

This definition appears to cover the physical aspects of the sources of power and control.

People who have access to information, persons, and instrumentalities have more power and influence than those who do not. The higher in the organization the person to whom a member has access, the more power the member has. For example, an accountant who is a friend of the president of the company can probably talk with the president often to learn more about developments and perhaps can influence proposed actions. At the same time, colleagues, perhaps fearing retaliation from the president, might allow the accountant extra privileges.

Another subtle form of power can be seen in the way an organization is structured. The vice president whose division includes personnel, controller, and budget offices can be more influential than another vice president simply because these functions affect the whole organization.[34]

In the case of LPs' power vis-à-vis that of HPs, we see a kind of inverted dependency in which the LPs have considerable control. Every HP depends to a certain extent on LPs who furnish information and advice, and who help implement decisions made by HPs. LPs can misinterpret directions, misunderstand orders, and forget to pass on information to HPs. No HP can prevent these possibilities, and the consequences can be especially negative in organizations whose employees are protected by civil service requirements and union contracts. These make the subordinates particularly difficult to terminate, and so they add to the power base of LPs.

When LPs are indispensable, the force of dependency inversion is even more acute. As Mechanic points out, the longer an LP is in the organization, the more likely he or she is to have access to the sources of power (information, persons, and instrumentalities).[35] The long-term LP who makes the effort to acquire access to these sources can become very powerful. This is true for all kinds of organizations, but it can be easily seen in the case where a newly elected public official inherits a staff of seasoned bureaucrats. The official is almost completely dependent on the staff, especially in the first days of office. The staff knows the routine, knows what needs to be done, and serves as a form of organization memory. This places them in a position to almost tell the official what to do. So, in the short run at least, the power of the LP in this situation is considerable.

Another point should be kept in mind when examining conditions that foster LP power. As organizations grow and become more complex, the LP becomes ever more important to the organization.[36] Even a newly elected or appointed HP can learn how the organization works and what its technical core is if it is small and employs a relatively simple technology and employs a few people. This becomes impossible in a large corporation, the federal government, or a nationwide charity, for example. There must be dependency on LPs in these organizations because of the quantity of tasks to be done and the amount of specialized knowledge required for proper execution.

For these and doubtless other reasons, many HPs insist on the right to bring their personally selected staffs with them to the new job. Although that does not prevent a power inversion, it can help minimize its effects. LPs who have long tenure still can exert a great deal of influence, even to the point of sabotage.

LPs can also exert power by combining into groups on the premise that no organization can afford a wholesale housecleaning. This condition can also be seen in the case where entire departments combine their power in an effort to promote their views or positions on issues. If, for instance, the production and sales departments combine into a coalition, they could exercise a great amount of influence on top management.

Finally, Mechanic suggests that organization rules can be used by LPs as power sources.[37] No organization can successfully survive an exact enforcement of its rules. By simply following the rules, LPs can be quite powerful, and the more important their tasks are to the organization the more powerful they can be.

COMMITMENT AND POWER

Another important aspect of power is its relationship to the commitment of organization members. Any type of organization, to be successful, must have its members' commitment in order to retain their services.

Commitment is composed of three elements: satisfaction, identification, and involvement.[38] These elements, when present in the membership, make the exercise of power more effective. When members derive personal satisfaction from their tasks, they will tolerate more direction and control than if they are dissatisfied. In other words, they will follow orders more willingly lest they lose their membership.

When members perceive that their personal goals are congruent with those of the organization, they identify with it and believe that their association with it benefits them. This condition, therefore, promotes the use of power over them. Members who can actively participate in organization affairs (especially decision making) also feel a sense of commitment and are more willing to subordinate their interests to those of the organization.

Barnard summed up the effects of commitment with his "zone of indifference," described in Chapter 15. The more narrow this zone, the more difficult it is to control subordinates. The higher the level of commitment, the wider the zone, and so if a superior wishes to exercise maximum control over subordinates, he or she should strive for their commitment.

Managers, therefore, can expand their spheres of influence by providing, in so far as practicable, those conditions that promote member commitment. Members who are satisfied with their assignments and work environments, who identify with the organization, and who are involved with its activities in a meaningful way seem to be more committed to, and so more subject to, control.

Unfortunately, this degree of commitment is not present in many organizations, and its absence is one of the main causes of declining productivity in the United States. Throughout several chapters of this text, we have referred to the shoddy operations at AMC's Jeep plant in Toledo. At Jeep, the workers are more committed to their union and themselves than they are to the company and its mission. Thus, management does not have the control over employees that is absolutely necessary for successful operations.

For example, during one balmy Friday in May 1986, the beckoning weekend proved so alluring at Jeep that *15 percent* of its work force did not show up for work, forcing management to close down the plant and send the other 85 percent of employees home without pay. The very same day at the Honda plant in Marysville, Ohio, however, where workers are committed, absenteeism was only 2 percent.[39]

We are not suggesting that managers manipulate members to create the illusion of the presence of these conditions; rather, they should work to create genuine conditions for member commitment based on mutual trust and confidence. The entire organization can benefit as a result, because the internal political structure of organizations (especially voluntary organizations) affects the level of support of organization activities that members show.[40] Commitment is, indeed, an important facet of power and politics in any organization.

EXTERNAL DEPENDENCY AND POWER

All organizations, regardless of their nature or purpose, must interact with their environment; they depend on it for both resources and clients or customers. What happens in the environment affects organizational activity and the balance of power within it. As a matter of fact, as Pfeffer and Salancik point out with their resource dependence model, the endurance of the organization itself is interconnected with its environment, for without a reliable group of suppliers and customers no organization can survive.[41]

A recent phenomenon occurring within U.S. industry has been the rising power and influence of investment banks. Investment banking firms, because of their ability to harness huge amounts of capital, the *basic* resource of the U.S. economy, are now critically important power centers in and of themselves. Thus, for many organizations, particularly those undergoing a merger or acquisition or restructuring requiring huge infusions of capital, the control of a most critical resource is directed from an extraorganizational entity. Thus, we see how an investment banking firm such as Drexel, Burnham, and Lambert has the power to push a giant industrial organization such as USX "to the wall" because the former provides the conduit of capital that is absolutely necessary to save the ailing steel giant.[42]

Organizations must exert their power to keep in tune with environmental forces. They must attempt to counteract those external forces that threaten them and to control the environment to the extent necessary to ensure the continued flow of inputs and outputs.

Perhaps there was a time when an organization (for example, a monastery) could isolate itself from its surroundings. It could provide its own food, clothing, and shelter without depending on the outside world. Even in the case of monasteries, however, there was eventually the need for some interaction with the environment. If nothing else, there was the need to recruit new members.

To the extent that an organization cannot control its environment, it is dependent on it. This is to say that outside agencies can dictate actions of an organization. An important customer, for example, the government in the case of defense contractors, can dictate organization behavior. The government can, through contract specifications, determine what products and departments, what hiring practices, and what working conditions will have the most importance in the contracting organization. The company that depends on these contracts must adjust its behavior and products because it obviously has little power.[43]

We discussed the open-systems concept in Chapter 2. There we made the point that organizations constantly interact with environmental forces; they adjust to demands while at the same time attempting to control them. We saw how turbulence in this environment made it difficult to stay in balance with it. Interaction allows external forces to alter the power structure of the organization dramatically, so the organization must continuously monitor these outside forces if it is to succeed.

When there is considerable dependency on factors in the environment, an organization can be controlled by outside sources. The dependency of our economy on foreign sources of oil is a classic example. During the oil crises in the 1970s, Middle Eastern governments almost dictated how our economy behaved. As a result there have been moves to lessen this dependency. Conservation and more emphasis on domestic production are two obvious examples of how our economy reacted. Likewise, as we previously pointed out, investment banking firms, with their ability to muster huge amounts of capital, have become a dominating external power force on today's organizations.

Organizations' attempts to lessen dependency on their environment are typical, but they can never be totally successful. They *can*, however, succeed in recognizing and mitigating the effects of these forces. In sum, dependence on external forces is a crucial element of any power relationship, whether it be within or between organizations.

THE USE OF POWER IN ORGANIZATIONS

We have discussed a number of concepts relating to organizational power as well as the power of individuals within the organization. We have seen that power is a complex, ever-changing force in any group: It can arise from a number of sources and be possessed to some extent by all members. Basically, though, power is used to alter events and circumstances to fit the holder's preferences. This is true whether we are concerned with organizational or individual power. For the sake of simplicity, we will concentrate the following discussion on the use of individual power, recognizing its general applicability, even to the organization level.

We said earlier that one requirement for the effective use of power was effort: A person must exert some amount of energy, and perhaps ingenuity, to have influence. Power vacuums exist in all groups; it remains for someone to spend the energy to fill them.

At Bendix Corporation, there was a power vacuum that existed between Chairman William Agee and his top managers, whom he did not trust. This vacuum was soon filled by Mary Cunningham, who acted as the chairman's alter ego and guarded him constantly. Cunningham was soon appointed by Agee as executive vice president of Bendix, and wielded her newly acquired power by taking Agee's calls, screening his mail and visitors, writing his speeches, and making his appointments. Eventually they married. The Agee-Cunningham relationship, as you might already know, received wide press and media coverage. All this came to pass at Bendix because a power vacuum existed, and an ambitious woman saw a golden opportunity.

Some functional areas make the effort to fill a power vacuum quite worthwhile. Organizations rely on information about their financial health, and so an enterprising member of the budget department has a golden opportunity to store up this valuable resource. The budget officer can, for instance, devise an allocation system known only to himself or herself so that no one else can gain access to needed information without permission. This, of course, is dangerous for the organization, but it nonetheless makes the budget officer powerful. This condition can easily permit the budget officer to make "unauthorized" budget allocations that contradict the organization's intent. Suppose a top management official in the marketing department has just refused a request from a district sales manager to purchase a word processor. The reason behind this refusal was that the vice president of marketing knew of a proposal being considered that the company buy an integrated information-processing system that would fit the entire organization. To approve the request for the word processor would have been contrary to this major direction planned by the company. Suppose further that the district sales manager and the budget officer were close friends and that the budget officer did not know of the company's plans. The district sales manager could have asked for funds for the word processor directly from the budget officer, and the request could have been honored, thus subverting both the directive of a top management official and the overall intention of the company.

This condition can lead to further subversion of the organization by people who control important information and hoard it for themselves. Such people can quickly develop a multitude of "friends" seeking favors. The position of the budget officer is even stronger to the extent that he or she can prevent others from controlling such information. This is a case where a single individual can divert resource allocations from the official intent of the organization.[44]

A similar situation can occur even in the formal decision process. Consider a member of the company's long-range planning committee who enjoys considerable social status in the organization, especially among the committee's membership. This person can line up the necessary votes to impose his or her preferences on the organization's future. Thus the values of this person can be formally transformed into those of the organization itself.[45]

Coalitions of members are potent forces in an organization. Because we are all part of many different organizations, we have had experience in observing and probably participating in these various groups. Every organization seems to have an "in group" and an "out group." Regardless of the type of organization, there always appears to be a relatively small "in group" that determines what happens. Consider your home town: It has a formal structure composed of both elected and appointed officials who are charged with directing its affairs. Yet we all know that certain influential citizens also form a kind of power structure that may override the formal government structure. If the city commission, say, wants to get its program of objectives approved, it must have the blessing of this group. So, even though they are not in formal decision-making roles, this power group can actually determine the course of the city—from annexation, to road projects, to the levying of additional taxes. It can even be that the formal program must be sanctioned by this group before it comes before the commission for approval.

Although we used an example of city government, the same conditions can apply to all organizations, from corporations to universities and even churches. This social network can have a powerful effect on the organization. It remains management's role to understand and to coopt it into the formal structure (if possible) if there is to be some form of central thrust for the organization.

Power is a dynamic force used by many organization members for many purposes. A snapshot of the power structure is not adequate today—we need a high-speed, full-length motion picture of it in order to appreciate it as a part of organization life, composed as it is of all those activities that characterize the members' efforts to use power for their benefit.

SUMMARY

Because they are the prime means of influence in both formal and informal organizations, power and authority are among the most important aspects of organization life. Power is the ability to exert influence over others without the sole backing or official sanction of the formal organization. This means that power is not dependent on society's recognizing its existence.

Power is both a personal and departmental force in the organization. One proposed model for explaining departmental power is based on three factors: ability of a department to deal successfully with environmental forces and uncertainties; substitutability, or the possession of power by more than one department; and the pervasiveness of the uncertainty in the organization.

Rational/legal power is that which is generally recognized as proper, such as in the case of a parent disciplining a child. Reward power is based on A's ability to dispense rewards to B. A can have coercive power over B if A has the ability and willingness to dispense punishment to B. Referent power can be traced to B's identifying in some way with A. Influence that is traceable to the power of personality is charismatic power. If some influence can be exercised because A has some special knowledge or skill needed by B, the type of power is expert power.

Authority is a form of influence that is associated solely with the formal organization. It is the right to take action required to carry out one's responsibility. It is a form of legitimate power that all employees can possess in one form or another. Managers exercise managerial authority, the right to make decisions and to enforce their implementation. All personnel can be given the right to make recommendations, suggestions, and so on about the implementation of their decisions. This type of authority, staff authority, is also commonly delegated to expert personnel. These experts are sometimes given situational authority, the right to issue binding decisions about their area of expertise throughout portions of the organization. A final type of authority is operative authority, the right to work without undue interference and to determine work priorities affecting only oneself. Authority in its many forms is a complement to power as a form of organizational influence.

No discussion of power and authority would be complete without a treatment of responsibility and accountability. The obligation to carry out an assignment to the best of one's ability and in accordance with directions, procedures, and policies is responsibility. It is a major determinant of authority delegations. Once the base of responsibility and authority has been determined, accountability can be properly required. This obligation to report on how well responsibility has been discharged is accountability. People, resources, and tasks are thus the essence of responsibility, the base for authority, and the foundation of accountability. Management must make careful choices in the area of power and authority relationships because of their impact on organization performance and because they are possible causes of conflict.

Power and authority are related to conflict, responsibility, and accountability. These elements are involved in every organizational decision.

The politics of power involve those activities members perform to acquire the power and other resources needed to gain their preferences. Much of everyday life in organizations is devoted to this end. The power structure in the organization is made up of the hierarchy of relative power held by members. Although it can be analyzed at a point in time, it is quite fluid. New actors joining the group or new issues to be decided can easily cause ripples in the power structure. In our examination we use a political model of the organization. Within this model it is necessary to assess the power bases or strengths of the organization's members. There are several ways to do this, including the use of determinants or sources of power. The effects of a power choice also indicate strength, as some members can affect large numbers of others while others can make only inconsequential choices. Symbols such as titles and office furnishings also measure the amount of influence of the member. Some members are believed by others to hold power, so reputation can indicate a member's strength in the organization. Finally, representational factors such as membership on important committees are a measure of power.

Whatever its specific source, power is a function of dependency, and the more dependency a member can create, the more powerful he or she can be. When one can control resources, has an important office and attractive personal qualities, can control the decision agenda, and has professional status, one can derive and utilize power from a variety of sources.

The power of any lower order participant can be traced to his or her control of information, persons, and instrumentalities. Access to these forces supports decisions of lower order participants and, to the extent that access is great, there can be a power inversion in which control can actually shift to lower order participants, especially if they are indispensable to the organization.

When members are satisfied in the group, identify with it, and are involved with its activities, they can be said to be committed to it. This condition makes them more susceptible to power decisions; thus we must be cognizant of the role of commitment when we discuss power.

Dependency of any organization on outside forces brings an added dimension to the analysis of power within it. In today's organizations this factor is significant because the macro environment is highly turbulent and diversified and, as such, causes more interorganizational linkages than ever before. This, in turn, makes it possible for more outside influence to be brought upon the organization to shape its behavior to a large extent.

Power is a fascinating topic for both organizational behavior and organization theory, and although the treatment here has been brief, it is intended to present a political view of organization life. This is an accurate way to view organizations, we believe, and we suggest that everyone should be familiar with how their organizations work from a power-and-politics perspective.

QUESTIONS FOR REVIEW AND DISCUSSION

1. Define authority and tell how it is related to formal and informal organizations.
2. How does power differ from authority?
3. Why is a knowledge of both power and authority important to an understanding of organization theory?
4. Select one of the types of power discussed in the chapter and describe a situation in which you have observed its use.
5. How are the types of authority discussed in the chapter related to total organizational performance?
6. Briefly explain how responsibility, authority, and accountability should be related to each other in the ideal organization.
7. What is organization politics and why is it important to management? Does the type of organization in which it is practiced matter? If so, how?
8. Why is it important for members of the organization to be able to assess the power of other members?
9. How can management prevent the existence of an informal power structure within the organization? Can this effort ever be completely successful? Explain.
10. We suggested in this chapter that power is context- or situation-

specific. Can you think of a situation or condition in which this is not true?

11. Select an organization in which you are an active member and enumerate those decisions that are truly crucial to its overall direction. Determine who makes those decisions and how they are able to make them.

12. Is there a single most effective way to acquire power? Does the type of organization under consideration make any difference?

13. How, specifically, would you, as a recent graduate with a major in engineering, go about acquiring power in a high-tech company?

14. Why should top management be concerned with the power of lower order participants?

15. Can management provide the necessary commitment to be able to completely control the organization? Explain.

16. Can any organization today reduce its dependency on its environment to the point that it can put little emphasis on it when making decisions? Explain.

ENDNOTES

1. B. J. Hodge and H. J. Johnson, *Management and Organizational Behavior* (New York: John Wiley & Sons, 1970), 38–40.

2. Peter B. Barnes, "CBS' Tisch Seeks Review of News Unit, Reportedly Wants to Cut Up to $50 Million," *The Wall Street Journal* (February 9, 1987), 4.

3. H. Joseph Reitz, *Behavior in Organizations* (Homewood, Ill.: Richard D. Irwin, 1977), 463–464.

4. D. J. Hickson, C. R. Hinings, C. A. Lee, R. E. Schneck, and J. M. Pennings, "A Strategic Contingencies Theory of Intraorganizational Power," *Administrative Science Quarterly* 16 (1971): 216–229.

5. J. R. P. French and B. Raven, "The Bases of Social Power," in *Studies in Social Power*, ed. D. Cartwright (Ann Arbor: Institute for Social Research, 1959), 150–167. Also see J. S. Adams and A. K. Romney, "The Determinants of Authority Interactions," *Decisions, Values and Groups*, Vol. 2, ed. N. F. Washburne (New York: Pergamon Press, 1962), 227–256.

6. B. H. Raven, "Social Influence and Power," in *Current Studies in Social Psychology*, ed. I. D. Steiner and M. Fishbein (New York: Holt, Rinehart and Winston, 1965), 374.

7. B. H. Raven, "Legitimate Power, Coercive Power, and Observability in Social Influence," *Sociometry* 21 (1958): 83–97.

8. French and Raven, "Social Power," 162. See also Walter R. Nord, "Development in the Study of Power," in *Concepts and Controversy in Organizational Behavior*, 2d ed. (Pacific Palisades, Calif.: Goodyear, 1976), 437–438.

9. David Bailey, "Kirk Cottrell: Riding the Crest of a Retailing Wave," *Florida Trend* (May 1987), 38.

10. W. Jack Duncan, *Organizational Behavior* (Boston: Houghton-Mifflin, 1978), 313.

11. John W. Wilson, "Can Ely's Magic Turn Convergent Around?" *Business Week* (January 21, 1985), 33.

12. A. S. Tannebaum, "Control in Organizations," *Administrative Science Quarterly* 7, no. 2 (1962): 236–237.

13. Hodge and Johnson, *Management*, 143–144.

14. Gordon Bock, Kimberley Carpenter, and Jo Ellen Davis, "Management's Newest Star: Meet the CIO," *Business Week* (October 13, 1986), 162.

15. Hodge and Johnson, *Management*, 145–147.

16. Jeffrey Pfeffer, *Power in Organizations* (Marshfield, Mass.: Pitman, 1981), 7.

17. Henry Mintzberg, *Power In and Around Organizations* (Englewood Cliffs, N.J.: Prentice-Hall, 1983), 26–30.

18. Ibid., 4–6.

19. Pfeffer, *Power in Organizations*, 3.

20. Ibid., 27–29.

21. Ibid., 43–61.

22. V. L. Huber, "The Sources, Uses, and Conservation of Managerial Power," *Personnel* 58, no. 4 (1981): 62.

23. Patricia Selle, "The Rag Trade's Reluctant Revolutionary," *Fortune* (January 5, 1987), 38.

24. M. Jelenik, J. Litterer, and R. Miles, eds., *Organization by Design: Theory and Practice* (Plano, Tex.: Business Publications, 1981).

25. "Richard Perle: The Pentagon's Powerful Headliner on Soviet Policy," *Business Week* (May 21, 1984), 130.

26. Pfeffer, *Power in Organizations*, 57.

27. Mintzberg, *Power*, 68.

28. Jeffrey Pfeffer and G. R. Salancik, "Organizational Decision-Making as a Political Process: The Case of a University Budget," *Administrative Science Quarterly* 19, no. 4 (June 1974): 135–151.

29. R. W. Allen, D. L. Madison, L. W. Porter, P. A. Renwick, and B. Y. Moyes, "Organizational Politics: Tactics and Characteristics of Actors," *California Management Review* 22, no. 1 (1979): 78.

30. A. M. Pettigrew, "Information Control as a Power Resource," *Sociology* (1977): 187–204.

31. Rosabeth M. Kanter, "Power Failure in Management Circuits," *Harvard Business Review* (July–August 1979): 65–75.

32. David Mechanic, "Sources of Power of Lower Participants in Complex Organizations," *Administrative Science Quarterly* 7, no. 3 (December 1962): 349–364.

33. Ibid., 352.

34. A. B. Wildavsky, "Budgeting as a Political Process," in *International Encyclopedia of the Social Sciences* 2, ed. D. C. Sills (New York: Cromwell, Collier, MacMillan, 1968), 191–193.

35. Mechanic, "Sources of Power," 353.

36. Ibid., 357.

37. Ibid., 362–364.

38. James G. Houghland and James R. Wood, "Control in Organizations and the Commitment of Members," *Social Forces* 59, no. 1 (September 1980): 92.

39. John Merwin, "A Tale of Two Worlds," *Forbes* (June 16, 1986), 105.

40. David Knoke, "Commitment and Detachment in Voluntary Organizations," *American Sociological Review* 46 (April 1981): 154.

41. Jeffrey Pfeffer and Gerald R. Salancik, *The External Control of Organizations* (New York: Harper & Row, 1978), 2.

42. Anthony Bianco, "American Business Has a New King Pin," *Business Week* (November 24, 1986), 77–83.

43. M. D. Richards, *Organizational Goal Structures* (St. Paul, Minn.: West, 1978), 78–82.

44. Wildavsky, "Budgeting as a Political Process," 192.

45. Mintzberg, *Power*, 23.

ANNOTATED BIBLIOGRAPHY

Aram, John D., and Salipante, Paul F., Jr. "An Evaluation of Organizational Due Process in the Resolution of Employer/Employee Conflict." *Academy of Management Review* 6, no. 2 (April 1982): 197–204.
A need for organizational procedures to resolve employer-employee conflict has been stimulated by expanding definitions of employee rights, greater statutory protection of employees, and the opportunity for corporate adaptation in the area of employee dissatisfaction. The utility of internal systems of conflict resolution rests on the formulation of specific objectives and values, a high degree of decision-maker independence, balanced formality of procedures, and matching types of conflict with means of resolution.

Bacharach, Samuel B., and Lawler, Edward J. *Power and Politics in Organizations.* San Francisco: Jossey-Bass, 1980.
This new approach to intraorganizational relations focuses on the group as the primary unit of analysis. The authors examine the processes occurring within and between coalitions in discussing conflicting interests.

Bell, Peter. *Organizations as Bargaining and Influence Systems.* New York: Halsted Press, 1975.
Technology, power, and influence are intraorganizational dimensions. The need to integrate these dimensions within the organizational framework is the focal point of this work.

Biggart, Nicole W., and Hamilton, Gary G. "The Power of Obedience." *Administrative Science Quarterly* 29 (Spring 1984): 540–549.
Organizational roles provide actors with moral constructs for the enactment of power. Indeed, actors evaluate each other's acts of power on the willingness to obey role prescriptions. For a person to sustain power in an organizational setting, he or she must self-consciously exercise power so as to signify the awareness of role obligations. Organizational power, paradoxically, stems from obedience to roles. The authors illustrate these points with interview data from the California gubernatorial administrations of Ronald Reagan and Jerry Brown.

Brass, Daniel J. "Being in the Right Place: A Structural Analysis of Individual Influence in an Organization." *Administrative Science Quarterly* 29 (Spring 1984): 518–539.

This research examined the relationships between structural positions and influence at the individual level of analysis. The structure of the organization was conceptualized from a social network perspective. Measures of the relative positions of employees within work flow, communication, and friendship networks were strongly related to perceptions of influence by both supervisors and nonsupervisors and to promotions to the supervisory level. A comparison of boundary-spanning and technical-core personnel indicated that contacts beyond the normal work requirements are particularly important for technical-core personnel to acquire influence. Overall, the results of this study support a structural perspective on intraorganizational influence.

Cavanaugh, Dennis J.; Moberg, Dennis J.; and Velasquez, Manual. "The Ethics of Organizational Politics." *Academy of Management Review* 6, no. 3 (July 1981): 363–374.

Political uses of power demand explicit consideration of ethical restraints, in part because current management theory focuses on the value of outcomes rather than the means chosen. The authors have developed a normative model of ethics that can be helpful in determining what these restraints are. The model integrates three kinds of ethical theories: utilitarianism, theories of moral rights, and theories of justice.

Cotton, C. C. "Measurement of Power-Balancing Styles and Some of Their Correlates." *Administrative Science Quarterly* (May 1976): 307–319.

This article lists three hypotheses: (1) Organizational members who hold lower levels of power use one of four methods of balancing power as a preferred power-balancing style; (2) biographical correlates are associated with these styles; and (3) the preferred style will be overrepresented in the organization. These hypotheses are supported by a study of 214 faculty members.

Fox, William S.; Payne, David E.; Priest, Thomas B.; and Philliber, William W. "Legitimacy of Authority Structure and Acquiescence to Authority." *Social Forces* 55 (1977): 966–973.

Results are given from an interview of 549 average workers in an Ohio town who were interviewed on the subject of influence within their organization. These workers were asked to describe their feelings about the authority structure at their workplace, their perceptions of the legitimacy of this authority structure, and, in general, their attitude about authority.

Franklin, Jerome L. "Down the Organization: Influence Processes Across Levels of Hierarchy." *Administrative Science Quarterly* 20, no. 2 (June 1975): 153–164.

Empirical studies were conducted on the direction and form of influence processes across levels of hierarchy. Also, linkages between social and psychological factors across levels of hierarchy were covered.

Gandz, J., and Murray, V. V. "The Experience of Workplace Politics." *Academy of Management Journal* 23, no. 2 (June 1980): 237–251.

Recent graduates of a business school report on the impact politics has in their organization. The article investigates the perceived politicization of organizational processes by recent graduates as well as their beliefs about workplace politics.

MacMillan, Ian C., and Jones, Patricia E. *Strategy Formulation: Power and Politics.* 2d ed. St. Paul, Minn.: West, 1986.

This textbook is for both practicing managers and management students. It provides a framework for thinking about strategy with a political perspective. The thrust of the argument is that managers, as strategists, must take into account the behavioral and political components of internal and external stakeholders when they formulate strategies in order to ensure the success of the organization they manage.

Margulies, Newton, and Raia, Anthony P. "The Politics of Organization Development." *Training and Development Journal* (August 1984): 20–23.

OD professionals have remained consistently aloof from claiming a political perspective. But political savvy needn't conflict with the OD process or its underlying values. In fact, the ability to perform effectively in the political arena is essential to successful organizational change.

Mintzberg, Henry. *Power In and Around Organizations.* Englewood Cliffs, N.J.: Prentice-Hall, 1983.

This text synthesizes the current research and writings on power from the perspective of organizations. The book draws on a wide range of academic disciplines, including management, political science, sociology, economics, and anthropology.

Pfeffer, Jeffrey. *Power in Organizations.* Marshfield, Mass.: Pitman, 1981.

Power is examined from a political perspective. Power and decision making, ways to assess power, conditions for its use, sources of power, political strategies, and ways to perpetuate power are examined from an organizational standpoint.

Salancik, Gerald R., and Pfeffer, Jeffrey. "The Bases and Uses of Power in Organizational Decision Making: The Case of a University." *Administrative Science Quarterly* 19, no. 4 (December 1974): 453–473.

Organizational decision making is affected by subunit power. The effects on the organization of subunit power and the losses of subunit power are considered.

ADDITIONAL REFERENCES

Astley, W. G.; Axelson, R.; Butler, R. J.; Hickson, D. J.; and Wilson, D. C. "Decision-Making: Theory III." Working paper, University of Bradford Management Center, 1980.

Blau, P. M. *The Dynamics of Bureaucracy.* Chicago: University of Chicago Press, 1963.

Brodford, B. Boyd, and Jensen, J. Michael. "Perceptions of the First-Line Supervisor's Authority: A Study of Superior-Subordinate Communications." *Academy of Management Journal* 15, no. 1 (September 1972): 331–342.

Farrell, Dan, and Petersen, James C. "Patterns of Political Behavior in Organizations." *Academy of Management Review* 7, no. 3 (July 1982): 403–412.

Galbraith, J. R. *Designing Complex Organizations*. Reading, Mass.: Addison-Wesley, 1973.

Kemelgor, B. H. "Power and the Power Process: Linkage Concepts." *Academy of Management Review* 1 (October 1976): 143–149.

Kipnis, D. "The Powerholder." In *Perspectives in Social Power*, edited by J. T. Tedeschi, 82–122. Chicago: Aldine, 1974.

Lerner, Allan W. *The Politics of Decision Making: Strategy, Cooperation and Conflict*. Beverly Hills, Calif.: Sage, 1976.

Levitt, L. "Public Relations as a Source of Power." *Public Relations Review* 11 (Fall 1985): 309.

McDaniel, S. W. "Social Power Bases of Marketing Executives: The Relationship with Organizational Climate." *Journal of Business Research* 13 (February 1985): 77–85.

Nord, Walter, R. "Development in the Study of Power." In *Concepts and Controversy in Organizational Behavior*. 2d ed., 437–438. Pacific Palisades, Calif.: Goodyear, 1976.

Pfeffer, J., and Salancik, G. *The External Control of Organizations: A Resource Dependence Perspective*. New York: Harper & Row, 1978.

Riker, W. H. *The Theory of Political Coalitions*. New Haven: Yale University Press, 1962.

Ross, I. "How Lawless Are the Big Companies?" *Fortune* (December 1, 1980), 56–64.

Salancik, G. R., and Pfeffer, J. "Who Gets Power and How They Hold On to It: A Strategic Contingency Model of Power." *Organizational Dynamics* 5 (Winter 1977): 3–21.

Saunders, Carol S., and Scawell, Richard. "Intraorganizational Distributions of Power: Replication Research." *Academy of Management Journal* 25, no. 1 (March 1982): 192–200.

Schein, Edgar H. *Organizational Psychology*. 3d ed. Englewood Cliffs, N.J.: Prentice-Hall, 1980.

Scovilla, Norma. "The Persistence of Charisma: A Re-interpretation of Routinization." *Review of Social Theory* 2 (May 1974): 91–108.

Thibodeaux, Mary S., and Powell, James D. "Exploitation: Ethics Problems of Organizational Power." *Advertising Management Journal* 50 (Spring 1985): 42–44.

Wiley, Mary Glen, and Eskilson, Arlene. "The Interaction of Sex and Power Base on Perceptions of Managerial Effectiveness." *Academy of Management Journal* 25, no. 3 (September 1982): 465–499.

<table>
<tr><td>C</td><td>A</td><td>S</td><td>E</td></tr>
</table>

Rising Through the Ranks

Women today are gaining ever-increasing power and authority in the organizations in which they work. In some instances, women occupy very high positions within an organization's hierarchy, and, thus, their rise in the corporate world is quite evident. In other cases, examining a corporation's organization chart will not depict all the power and/or authority relationships that exist in a given company. Indeed, close scrutiny of life in the executive suites throughout the nation might very well reveal a significant power center that isn't on the chart—the executive secretary to the firm's CEO.

There are two reasons for the developing power of executive secretaries in today's organizations. First, technological advances, such as the word processor, have eliminated the need for executive secretaries' constant attention to simple tasks such as typing and filing. These women are now free to handle more challenging administrative tasks. Second, the women's movement has done much to raise the general consciousness of women's roles in organizational life in addition to reducing the amount of time they spend on "wifely" chores, such as getting

Sources: Pat Allen, "Secretaries' Role Develops, Expands," *Savings Institutions* (July 1984), 138–139; Mark Hanauer, "A Friendly Frontier for Female Pioneers," *Fortune* (June 25, 1984), 81; R. Rowan, "America's Most Wanted Managers," *Fortune* (February 3, 1986), 23; Laurie Baum and John A. Byrne, "Executive Secretary: A New Rung on the Corporate Ladder," *Business Week* (April 21, 1986), 74–75.

the boss's coffee or running his personal errands.

Take Nanette Buckhout, for example, the assistant to President John Sculley of Apple Computers. She is encouraged by her boss to submit her own proposals to improve the company's internal operations. And there's Jean C. Jones, executive secretary to Intel's chairman, Gordon E. Moore. Most of Jones's influence and power derives from her control of information and access to her boss. She is the one who decides how much of the thirty-inch stack of mail her boss will see and how many of the 125 phone calls per day will gain his ear. Charlotte Bimonte, the secretary to the chairman and president of the First Federal Bank of Connecticut, states that she learns from her boss' reactions which people he wants to see and which ones he doesn't. She often will probe a caller and redirect him or her to another executive or department within the bank.

Knowledge is power. Kathy Habiby is the executive secretary to Nelson Doubleday, the CEO of Doubleday and Company, one of the nation's leading publishing houses. Her physical location at the right hand of the head of Doubleday enables her to witness most, if not all, of his private conversations. "I have a lot of power," she stated. "I can act in Mr. Doubleday's absence. I know everything he is doing. He wants people to be able to rely on me as much as they rely on him." Nancy Sutton, the executive secretary to a senior vice president at the Georgia Federal Bank, FSB, in Atlanta reports that she conducts a lot of research and project-oriented studies that enable her boss to make major decisions. Thus, she has accumulated tremendous power by being able to determine which research will get her boss's attention and which will not.

Many of today's executive secretaries are armed with higher academic degrees, computer skills, and even their own staff, and thus they are able to carve out their own decision-making niche within the executive suite. Indeed, some make over $50,000 per year, and for others, the executive secretary position is a springboard to higher managerial jobs, both within and without the organization. Hilda Gerstein started out fifty-nine years ago as the sixteen-year-old secretary to Milton J. Petrie, chairman of Petrie Stores Corporation. In 1986, at seventy-five, she was the vice chairman of the corporation and was earning $350,000 per year. Kathleen Kallman, executive secretary to Beatrice's former chairman, James Dutt, parlayed her job into an assistant vice presidency of Beatrice within four years. On the other hand, because the role of the executive secretary has expanded so much in recent years, some incumbents feel that the position is a career in itself. Joan Sutcliffe, an executive secretary at the Coral Gables (Florida) Federal Savings Institution, stated, "There are no limits in this job. . . .I can set my own limits and the sky is it."

In order to perform their jobs well and gain power, most executive secretaries become their bosses' alter egos. At Apple, CEO Sculley ". . . listens to me and treats me as his confidante," said Buckhout. "He views me as an equal." Many executive secretaries sublimate their own personalities and adopt the persona of their bosses. Former Secretary of State Cyrus Vance's secretary, Elva Murphy, would prefer to speak her mind to some of the people who waste her boss's time; however, she adopts a "diplomatic" manner when dealing with the many petitioners at Vance's office. As their bosses' alter egos, executive secretaries are a "jewel of rare price" and "indispensable."

So entwined are these executive secretaries with their bosses' careers that their rise to and fall from power parallel those of the CEOs they serve. When Beatrice's CEO Dutt was ousted in 1985, Kallman walked out the same day. She said of leaving, "They attacked the chairman and anyone nearby is expendable in a power play." Even when they stay in their jobs, many executive secretaries are resented by the organization's managers because of their power. Even before she left Beatrice, Kallman noted that many people felt threatened by her. Beatrice executives still viewed her as a secretary and treated her that way, despite the fact that she was the "right hand" of the most powerful man in the company.

Of course, the executive secretary route is not the only method that women are using to gain power within modern business organizations. As many young women graduate with valuable degrees from colleges and universities, they find that many business firms are anxious to hire them and move them up the corporate ladder on the "fast track." For example, there is Sandra Kurtzig, who at thirty-seven is the chairperson of ASK Computer Services. With degrees in chemistry, mathematics, and aeronautical engineering, Kurtzig first worked for General Electric, where she developed computer software and rose rapidly through the managerial ranks. Leaving General Electric in 1980 to start her own business (ASK), Kurtzig now rules a company with a net worth of $150 million. In other business endeavors, such as retailing, there is

Jane Evans, who at forty-one is the president and CEO of Monet Crystal Brands. Fluent in French, German, Spanish, and Italian, Evans started out as an assistant buyer for Genesco. Promoted rapidly by that organization, she was elevated to the presidency of Genesco's I. Miller subsidiary by the age of twenty-five. By 1979, Evans had left Genesco to become the executive vice president for Crystal Brands' fashion group. When Monet was spun off from Crystal Brands, Evans was the natural choice to become the new subsidiary's president and CEO, thus running the world's largest costume jewelry company.

Whether they be executive secretaries, top-level managers, or independent entrepreneurs, women in organizations have obtained power and/or been delegated authority to an unprecedented degree.

QUESTIONS FOR DISCUSSION

1. Explain how power can get converted into authority when a person is promoted.
2. Once a person acquires power, how can the organization be sure it is used properly?
3. Executive secretaries are sometimes promoted to even more responsible positions, as the case noted. When this happens, what are the consequences for maintaining an integrated structure?
4. Does the authority vested in a subordinate position somehow reflect the power of the superior position? Explain your answer.

15

Conflict in Organizations

One Bad Apple

Morale at Apple Computers fell to a new low during the early spring of 1985. Within the Apple II division, the developer and manufacturer of Apple's mainstay and workhorse, the Apple II personal computer (PC), there were rumors of general dissatisfaction and even defections of the division's key managers. The cause for this drop in morale at Apple II was the "lavish" attention and resources being spent on Apple's new computer product, the Macintosh, or "Mac," which Apple executives hoped would be able to strongly compete with IBM, the leader in the manufacture and sale of business PCs. Indeed, at the corporation's annual meeting in January 1985, Steve Jobs, Apple cofounder and chairman of the board, devoted most of the program to the new Mac. While Mac division employees watched Jobs's presentation from front-row seats in the auditorium, Apple II personnel watched the proceedings from closed-circuit television in a separate room.

Throughout the January annual meeting, little was said of the Apple II or the people who have kept it a top-selling product since its introduction to the marketplace in 1978. After the meeting, harsh words were exchanged between Jobs and Steve Wozniak, the other Apple cofounder, and between Wozniak and John Sculley, the Apple CEO. Wozniak warned his two colleagues to give credit where credit was due. It was natural for Wozniak to be incensed over the attention and resources being directed at the Mac group because he was the developer of the Apple II. Within a week of this heated exchange, Wozniak left Apple, taking with him six key managers from the Apple II division.

CEO Sculley acknowledged the conflict between the Apple II and Mac divisions to the press, but insisted that Apple II was not being ignored or being denied adequate resources to do its job. Sculley ordered the Apple II head, D. W. Yocam, who also doubled as Apple executive vice president, to gain more public recognition for the division as well as to move the Apple II division to the corporate headquarters. The reason for this physical move was necessary, according to Sculley, ". . . because the II group was physically remote, and that only contributed to its being a second-class citizen."

This was the conflictful situation that Apple found itself in during early 1985. By late spring, matters had worsened, and the conflict between the two product divisions had become even more acute. Most notably, a "fatal" conflict developed between Jobs and Sculley and between Jobs and the Apple board of directors. The causes for this increasing turmoil were both business and personal. As worsening conditions came to a head during the end of May 1985, Apple reorganized in a rush, fired 20 percent of its work force, announced its first-ever quarterly financial loss, and, most important, stripped Jobs of *all* operating authority within the organization.

Following is the series of events from the January annual meeting to the May "calamity."

Apple's board of directors, comprised of no-nonsense managerial types, periodically ordered Sculley during the spring of 1985 to assert his authority over the entire organization and Jobs in particular, despite the fact that the latter was a cofounder of Apple and chairman of the board. Although Jobs and Sculley were once close friends and appeared amicable toward one another in public, the crisis between the two came to a head

Sources: Deborah C. Wise and Geoffrey C. Lewis, "A Split That's Sapping Morale at Apple," *Business Week* (March 11, 1985), 106–107; Edward Nee, "Sculley Confirms Rift with Jobs," *Electronic News* (July 29, 1985), 22; Bro Uttal, "Behind the Fall of Steve Jobs," *Fortune* (August 5, 1985), 20–24; and Deborah C. Wise, "Steve Jobs vs. Apple: What Caused the Final Split," *Business Week* (September 30, 1985), 48.

when Sculley learned in late May that Jobs was plotting to oust him as CEO.

Jobs's dissatisfaction with Sculley arose out of the latter's plans to improve Apple's retailing and marketing operations. In effect, this meant reducing the company's nine decentralized divisions, based on product, into functional areas such as engineering, manufacturing, and marketing. Previously, in 1984, Sculley had managed to reduce Apple from nine to three divisions—a sales division for all products, Apple II, and Mac; however, this was not the complete reorganization based on function that Sculley wanted. This, of course, sharply conflicted with Jobs's near mania for focusing Apple's efforts on product development, particularly the new Mac. Moreover, as Mac sales failed to reach expectations by the end of 1984 (150,000 units were expected to be sold; only 50,000 actually were), Jobs and Sculley began to bicker. Sculley accused Jobs of failing to deliver the new Macs on time, while Jobs retorted that Sculley didn't understand how high-tech products were developed.

At its April 11, 1985, meeting, the Apple board of directors discussed a sweeping reorganization plan for the company, part of which called for bringing in a more competent manager for the Mac division. The board members continued to urge Sculley to more fully assert his authority over Jobs. Finally, at this meeting, the board voted to eventually remove Jobs from his Mac position and replace him with Jean-Louis Gassee, the head of the highly successful Apple France operation.

Jobs, of course, was infuriated by this move and began suggesting to his Apple cohorts that "Apple was too small" for both him and Sculley. On May 23, 1985, Jobs told his aides that he wanted Sculley ousted. Getting wind of Jobs's plan, Sculley called a meeting with the Apple executive board and Jobs.

During this three-hour meeting, the executive board stuck to the earlier decision made by the whole board of directors to strip Jobs of all operating authority within Mac and, moreover, stated that it could find no operating role at all for Jobs within the Apple organization. Jobs walked out of this meeting and volunteered to take a "long-needed" vacation.

With Jobs gone, Sculley and his staff completely reorganized Apple from May 29 to May 31, 1985. Engineering, manufacturing, and distribution were herded into one functional area; product development went into another; and marketing and sales made up the third. In terms of product development, all Apple PCs would now be designed to be "friendly" to (i.e., compatible with) other systems' software, a move heretofore vigorously opposed by Jobs.

On September 17, 1985, Jobs officially resigned from Apple. But the conflict between Jobs and Apple was not over. Jobs announced that he would start a new computer company and take key Mac personnel with him. Apple's board considered this as "treachery" because board members believed that Jobs planned this move and recruited while he was still officially with the Apple organization. Moreover, Jobs "assured" Apple that he would not develop computers that would compete directly with Apple products; however, analysts believe that Jobs's proposed new computer company would develop products that will directly compete with the Mac.

Although by the end of 1985 the Mac people were the ones disillusioned and suffering from low morale, with even insiders stating that many Mac employees wished that Jobs had taken them with him when he left the company, their fortunes may be looking up because of the current "hot" state of the Apple Macintosh.

As the above case illustrates, conflict was rife at Apple Computers, existing at both the interpersonal and intraorganizational level. Although the conflict situation at Apple might seem extreme (partially because it was so well publicized by the press), conflict is a reality that pervades *all* organizations, and it can take a multitude of forms at any level within an organization. As you read the material in this chapter, you will learn why conflict, with all its various forms and levels, is such an important ancillary of organization theory.

CHAPTER PLAN

In this chapter we examine the phenomenon of organizational conflict. To better understand this phenomenon, we present a historical perspective of thought on the subject. We briefly examine the anticonflict attitude that exists within organizations and U.S. society.

We then analyze each of the various levels of conflict: intrapersonal, interpersonal, intragroup, and intergroup. We next describe some of the causes of conflict within each of these levels.

The next section of the chapter presents some representative models of the dynamics of the conflict episode. We discuss Pondy's stages of conflict, Rahim's stages of conflict, and Deutsch's six factors.

In order to understand the "why" of conflict in terms of its various levels and causes, we examine Pondy's three models of conflict. This is followed by a discussion of Wheeler's model of industrial conflict.

We close the chapter with a discussion of the various means available to the organization to manage and control conflict so that it benefits, rather than hinders, the organization's operations.

No organization can escape conflict. At some point, people will experience it in some form, be it frustration over not getting a promotion or disagreement over the quality of a production run. Because of its centrality to organization life, we need to examine conflict in some detail. This chapter will provide you with a concise, yet comprehensive look at this facet of organization theory.

Conflict occurs when two or more individuals or groups that have opposing goals, ideas, philosophies, or orientations confront each other in some way. They might oppose each other by vying for resources, support, and so on to ensure that their position prevails. Conflict leads to some form of frustration or confrontation within the organization; often this is on an interpersonal level. It may also be a conflict brought on by an organizational system that does not allow enough freedom or by a clash of values caused by job requirements.

There are many forms of conflict between organizations; however, here we will focus on conflict within the organization. The rationale for this view is that the majority of the concepts in this book are also discussed at the micro level.

ORGANIZATIONAL CONFLICT: A HISTORICAL OVERVIEW

As we mentioned above, conflict is today a given in organization theory. Its management is one of the most difficult, yet important, jobs for any manager. Regardless of organization type, conflict is recognized as a fact of life, and so the issue is not whether to have it, but how to manage it.

No theory of organizations is complete without a treatment of conflict. Indeed, a content analysis conducted by M. A. Rahim in 1981 found that the subject was fifth on a list of sixty-five most frequently mentioned topics for M.B.A. students in organizational behavior courses.[1] The topic of conflict finds a proper place in both organization theory and organizational behavior curricula.

This acceptance of conflict has not always been the prevailing view, however. Conflict was once thought to be highly undesirable— something to be stifled at almost any cost. Such was certainly the view of the Classical School of organizational thought.

Such classical writers as Henri Fayol and Frederick W. Taylor assumed that conflict was a negative force in the workings of the organization and so was to be avoided in favor of harmony. This approach is most evident in the rules and types of organization structures they suggested as models. They spelled out conditions specifically and in detail to try to prevent conflicts. At least that was their aim.

Fayol put forth what he termed "universal principles" for the management of any type of organization, maintaining that their application would provide a basis for governing. Additionally, he explained the job of managing in terms of functions (such as planning, organizing, and so on) that he argued could be taught to prospective managers who would then apply the knowledge and principles to achieve organizational effectiveness in the absence of conflict.

Taylor was more "shop-oriented," preferring to center his analysis on workers at the bottom of the organization structure. His view was that management should find the one best worker; divide work into small units; teach the worker how to do the task; provide the best tools; and finally, pay "high" wages. This was to be done in a structure Taylor called "functional foremanship." Basically, it rested on using several supervisors, each specializing in one phase of management responsibility instead of aggregating these functions into a single job. For example, one supervisor was responsible for scheduling, another for expediting, another for maintenance, and so on. Again, Taylor assumed harmony was the backdrop for his scientific management approach. He simply did not provide for conflict.

Max Weber's seminal work on bureaucracy also treated conflict as undesirable. The rules, job specifications, and so forth that characterized his structure were aimed at providing the type of order where there would be little or no conflict.

The Classicists, thus, assumed a closed system of organizations, one characterized by rules, procedures, and structures that were oriented toward order and harmony as the means to organizational effectiveness.

Neoclassicists, on the other hand, founded what has been termed the "Human Relations School" of organizational thought. Centered on job context, this school regarded conflict as undesirable, as did the Classicists. The means for achieving desired harmony, however, were a bit different.

Whereas Classicists sought harmony through rules, procedures, structures, and such, the Neoclassicists believed that the social system was the key. By having a nurturing, accommodating social network, organization members would tend to be happy, and happy workers were productive workers, so went the argument. Happiness and harmony were seen as the best ways to obtain the desired level of organizational effectiveness.

The Value of Conflict

Today's view of the role of conflict is quite different from either of these schools of thought. Conflict is sometimes seen not only as unavoidable, but even desirable. It can stir emotions and creativity alike because, by definition, conflict creates tension and frustration that augur for action of a different type than the "usual peaceful" approaches to organizational problem solving.

We've all been involved, for example, with devil's advocate roles that are acted out precisely to cause conflict with its attending diverse and opposing views. We also know how inventive solutions can come from situations in which our position is opposed. This tension can stimulate invention.

Paul Lawrence and Jay Lorsch, two respected organization theorists, argue that some level of conflict between departments in an organization can have a very beneficial effect.[2] That is, as different departments, or groups, within an organization vie with each other over such matters as goals, scheduling, and so on, members within each department or group will often forget their individual differences and work together more cohesively toward completing their task.

Conflict, if not carried to an extreme, can have other beneficial effects to the organization. As we pointed out in Chapter 8, conflict can serve as a mechanism for fine-tuning the organization's goal hierarchy. In other situations, a conflict episode in an organization, after its resolution, can help clarify the proper power and authority relationships between different organizational members or subunits.

The modern view is not to oppose conflict, but to provide for it. The aim is not to eliminate fire, or have a wildfire, but to have a "controlled burn." Managers, like foresters, must know when conditions are right for "burning" and when there has been enough. Seen from this perspective, conflict can be considered healthy, not inhibiting, in the organization's striving for effectiveness.

A Philosophy of Avoiding Conflict

If conflict is unavoidable, and it certainly appears to be, why does the Classical view still dominate organizations? One plausible view has been suggested by Stephen P. Robbins.[3] According to Robbins, the anticonflict attitude begins virtually at birth. As children, we are taught that the role of the child is to be seen and not heard. In other words, the child is to accept the parents' role as decision makers and quietly obey what they say.

These roles are reinforced in school, where the teacher "is always right." Punishment generally follows confrontation; confrontation is viewed as disruptive and counterproductive. A quiet class is sometimes rewarded for its behavior. If quiet and calm prevail, perhaps homework will not be excessive.

Robbins goes on to point out that anticonflict sentiment is the keystone of religious beliefs, as epitomized in the teachings of the Roman Catholic church, where peace and the infallibility of the pope are core values to the institution.

So, it is small wonder that many believe in the traditional view of conflict—that it should be suppressed. We are exposed to its suppression at an early, impressionable age and see this suppression reinforced daily in virtually every group setting. Even the U.S. armed forces are seen as *defensive* units.

As we can see, conflict carries with it a distinctly negative connotation. As a matter of fact, "getting along with people" is one of the most sought-after qualities in a manager. There doesn't currently appear to be any movement away from the traditional view of conflict as something to be avoided. Even if this traditional view persists, modern scholars recognize conflict's inevitability and the necessity to manage it productively.

LEVELS OF CONFLICT

As a means of further understanding conflict, we will briefly examine its various levels and their importance. Basically, there are four levels of conflict: intrapersonal, interpersonal, intragroup, and intergroup. All four are treated here, even though, for our purposes, interpersonal and intergroup are most significant because they involve two or more component parts of an organization. Intrapersonal and intragroup conflict are more closely allied with organizational behavior. The following is a concise look at each level.

Intrapersonal Conflict

This type of conflict is that which is felt within a person and is caused by being pushed in two or more directions at once. For example, we have all been subject to conflicting directions from our parents or bouts of conscience over a social situation. We have probably experienced what can be termed *intrarole conflict* in these situations.

In our introductory case, we noted the conflict between Apple CEO John Sculley and the Apple chairman and cofounder, Steve Jobs. Because these two individuals had previously been close friends, think of the intrapersonal conflict experienced by Sculley as he was forced by the Apple board of directors and general business conditions to strip Jobs of all operating authority within the Apple organization.

When managers delegate responsibility to their subordinates, they often create intrapersonal conflict within the latter group. Managers can create role overload for subordinates even when they assign compatible tasks, simply by expecting too much from subordinates. In order to cope, subordinates must set priorities for themselves that can differ from those of fellow workers and managers. This constant strain is seen as intrapersonal conflict for a given individual.

Interpersonal Conflict

This type of conflict involves strain (or *interrole conflict*) between two or more people and, if not managed properly, can impede any organization's attempt at effective goal accomplishment. Take the case of Ross Perot's recent role at General Motors, for example. As head of the dynamic Electronic Data Systems Corporation that he founded in 1962 with $1,000, Perot was the "point guard" of a highly dynamic organization accustomed to getting things done quickly and efficiently. In 1984, Perot sold EDS to GM for $2.5 billion and assumed a seat on the GM board of directors. Then the clash began, particularly between Perot and GM Chairman Roger B. Smith. Perot ran headlong into the "blundering" bureaucracy that is GM and concluded, "GM is moving neither fast nor effectively enough to reduce its slide."[4] Basically, Perot and Smith disagreed as to whether GM's reorganization into a large-car and small-car company was working. Perot's prodding and "poking," as he put it, made other GM board members uncomfortable. Even though some individual board members applauded Perot, and Smith himself publicly stated that he had "no complaints" with Perot, it was clear that interpersonal conflict was widespread where Perot was concerned. Eventually, in early 1987, Perot resigned his position on GM's board, thus ending the interpersonal conflict between himself, Smith, and other members of the board.

Pfeffer and Salancik provide some valuable insight into the phenomenon of interpersonal or interrole conflict.[5] These two authors state that an individual's partial inclusion in many groups within an organization, or even within many different organizations, places demands on the individual that require different behaviors for different situations or structures. Thus, two or more individuals who experience no conflict in one organizational setting might experience conflict in another. For example, the CEO of a corporation might get along very well with the corporation's president concerning a variety of day-to-day business matters. However, conflict between the CEO and president might erupt before the board of directors on a matter involving strategy. Indeed, such a situation actually did occur in 1984 when Dr. Armand Hammer, CEO and chairman of Occidental Petroleum, fired his president and chief operating officer, A. Robert Abboud, when the latter sided with a dissident board member over matters relating to Occidental's long-term strategic direction. Before this conflict erupted between Hammer and Abboud, the two had gotten along magnificently. Indeed, Abboud had previously been chosen by Hammer to be his successor to the Occidental chairmanship!

Intragroup Conflict

People form into groups for many reasons, not the least of which is to accomplish more than they can as individuals. However, members quite often fail to work together harmoniously. Intragroup conflict to some degree of intensity is the result.

According to Hamner and Organ, there are three basic types of intragroup conflict: role conflict, issue conflict, and interaction conflict.[6] We briefly describe each of these below.

ROLE CONFLICT. Role conflict occurs in the course of carrying out one's assigned activity in the group or organization. In carrying out these assignments, members frequently experience some degree of conflict that occurs when members experience various expectations from other members. For example, there are times when a member is given orders or directions from two different superiors. Consider the case of a department secretary who receives work assignments from all faculty in a given department. Each faculty member wants his or her work done first, and some can even be impatient! Confusion and conflict often result.

Hamner and Organ cite research that shows ". . .that high levels of role conflict are related to low levels of job satisfaction, low confidence in the organization, a high degree of job-related tension, and a high propensity to leave the organization."[7] Pressure to perform according to different standards and/or expectations, thus, has many undesirable consequences for the organization and its members, who, at some point, will act to reduce it by some means.

ISSUE CONFLICT. When members of a group come together to make a decision or solve a problem, their individual values and orientations can conflict. We can see this happen when a member has a different goal or "answer" that is not generally agreed on by the group. Conflict can become intense if this member possesses a strong personality or has power. This type of confrontation produces conflict that can be helpful or detrimental to group activity, depending on the way it is managed.

Issue conflict within a group frequently occurs in the boardrooms of major corporations. For example, in the early 1980s, the board of directors of Salomon Brothers, a New York investment banking firm, became embroiled in a controversy about whether the company should focus its efforts on securities or commodities trading. The issue was resolved in September 1983, when John Gutfreund, a firm believer in securities trading, became chairman and CEO.

INTERACTION CONFLICT. Simply being a member of a group requires some cooperative behavior. When working together, members enjoy success or failure. If projects succeed, individual members can take credit. If projects fail, individual members tend to blame others, thus creating a conflictful outcome. Resentment can easily carry over to subsequent interactions, causing a lasting effect not necessarily traceable to the original conflict.

These types of intragroup conflict occur every day in any group, and it behooves the student of organization theory to appreciate them and their consequences.

Intergroup Conflict

Various departments in an organization can come into conflict over the *type of work* they perform. Take, for example, the conflict that can easily result between researchers and purchasing agents. Researchers are basically concerned with experimentation and publications; they generally care little about the rules and regulations purchasing agents are required to enforce. The researcher comes to a point in an experiment where a special instrument is needed and sees the bidding process as an unnecessary impediment. The purchasing agent, on the other hand, is specifically assigned the responsibility of obeying the rules and regulations of proper purchasing. A conflict between these two groups is virtually inevitable.

Different opinions over the "proper" *assignment of responsibility* also cause intergroup conflict. This can be seen, for example, in the fund-raising efforts of today's colleges and universities, where it is not uncommon to find more than one group seeking public support dollars. Foundations seek to raise funds for the university as a whole, and individual departments try to raise money for their particular needs. These groups frequently call on the same donors, thus causing conflict not only between the departments and the foundation, but also between donors and the college or university. So, conflict results over the question of who is responsible for fund raising. The reverse situation can also occur when foundations expect help from departments that do not see fund raising as part of their assignment.

Groups are often brought into conflict over *limited resources*, particularly at universities. Maintenance departments vie for funds to repair their physical plants, while academic units argue for increased numbers of faculty, scientific equipment, and library materials. The student division wants more money for student services and activities, while the public affairs group wants increased spending for publications and image building. Likewise, as we read in the introductory case to this chapter, conflict between the Mac and Apple II groups within Apple Computers was partially based on the latter group's perception that it was being denied an adequate share of the Apple organization's resources. It is not surprising to see conflict exist between groups in such situations.

Robbins points out that such conflict is more likely to occur when there is *low formalization* in the organization.[8] In these situations, there are few rules and little order to help prevent conflict by regulating the conditions that breed it.

Intergroup conflict can result from perceived *status incongruities*, as can be seen in the case where a financial crisis can cause the budget officer and the controller in an organization to be awarded undue status because of their knowledge and roles in resolving this type of situation. Production takes a back seat, and resentment, jealousy, and conflict can easily occur. Remember how members of the Apple II division in Apple Computers felt that they were being treated like second-class citizens compared to the Mac division.

Finally, conflict between groups in an organization can result from what is termed *ethnocentrism*, the application of one group's values and attitudes to those of another group. Judgments of inferiority are causes for conflict between groups when they are made. Many groups succeed, indeed, to the extent that they are able to attribute subordinate qualities to other groups. If you have fraternities or sororities on your campus, you may have noticed how one Greek organization will put down another. As we saw in our introductory case, the Mac group, as the "darlings" of the Apple organization, felt superior to the older, established Apple II group.

Intergroup conflict can be generalized to the level of interorganizational conflicts (e.g., Coke versus Pepsi) and national conflicts (e.g., United States versus U.S.S.R.). We have centered our attention here primarily on the micro or internal organizational aspects of intergroup conflict. Because intergroup conflict in organizations is of such paramount importance to the general study of conflict within organizations, we will treat this subject further in subsequent sections of this chapter.

As we see, conflict can occur at four different levels within an organization. These four levels of conflict are summarized in Table 15.1. Today, we must understand and be aware of the types of conflict that can occur at each of these levels if we are to appreciate how organizations form and operate.

BASES OF CONFLICT

Conflict, as we have previously discussed, can take many different forms and can exist at different levels within the organization. Although we have already mentioned some of the bases, or causes, of conflict, the fol-

TABLE 15.1

Levels of Conflict in an Organization

Level	Definition	Examples
Intrapersonal	Conflict that occurs within an individual as a result of intrarole pressures	An individual is required to perform a task that is incompatible with his or her goals or values.
Interpersonal	Conflict that occurs between two or more organization members at the same or different levels	Two or more individuals argue over different goals, values, or task assignment.
Intragroup	Conflict that occurs among members of a group or between two or more subgroups within a group	Individuals within a group argue over different role expectations or issues facing the group.
Intergroup	Conflict that occurs between two or more units or groups within an organization	Different organizational units initiate conflict over such issues as task interdependence, assignments of responsibility, competition for resources, and status incongruity. Low formalization within the organization and ethnocentrism within a group can enhance conflict at this level.

lowing section presents an expanded view of these bases, which are summarized in Table 15.2.

Role Conflict

People are often thrown into a conflict situation when their roles are changed or when different expectations are applied to established roles. New behavior patterns can cause conflict when they require significant change on the part of the individual. At the same time that intrapersonal conflict occurs in these cases, it is probable that interpersonal conflict occurs between an individual and another imposing the change.

TABLE 15.2

Bases for Conflict

Base	Meaning	Example
Role conflict	Change in role expectation and/or standards of performance and behavior	Changing the method for evaluating sales performance
Change in delegation	Reducing or increasing a person's authority	Reducing the scope of a manager's authority to make budget decisions without obtaining prior approval from $5,000 per purchase to $1,000
Change in status	Increasing or reducing a person's status	Change in job title from general manager to office manager
Change in goals	Goals redefined or given a different priority	Movement from a research to a teaching emphasis in a university
Organization overlap	Two or more people assigned to carry out the same task	Bussers and waiters assigned task of keeping tables clean
Resource competition	Two or more people or groups in an organization competing for scarce resources	Different academic departments in a university competing for faculty salary dollars
Culture conflict	Individuals or groups within an organization clashing because of different values, norms, and behavior patterns	American workers clashing with Japanese managers in a Japanese-owned American plant

Change in Delegation

Changes in delegation can cause conflict. For example, when the authority of a manager is reduced, there can be intrapersonal conflict. The manager can perceive himself or herself to be less important to the organization, and this perception can cause severe emotional disturbance. He or she can view this reduction of authority as an undermining of the ability to act independently. When a new delegation requires a new contact point for execution, the manager might experience or cause conflict in this different situation with different subordinates who are not accustomed to his or her style or expectations.

Change in Status

Changes in status, especially when they disturb a given accepted hierarchy, can bring conflict in virtually every form possible. For example, such simple things as changes in title can be a significant cause of conflict. If an individual perceives that the change in title from general manager to office manager means a reduction in status, he or she is bound to feel disappointment and perhaps even resentment. Another example along this line can be seen when the titles of two seemingly equal jobs in an organization are not perceived to convey equality. The chief fiscal officer might be given the title of vice president while the chief budget officer is given the title of director of budgets. The incumbents in these positions might infer some difference from their titles and feel conflict toward each other (or toward whoever decided which titles to confer).

Change in Goals

A change of goals can also bring conflict to an organization's members. For instance, conflict would probably occur between members of a university faculty if the primary goal of the university were changed from a research to a teaching orientation. Research-oriented faculty would be in conflict with those who place teaching as their top priority. The research faculty would be frustrated and would doubtless attempt to reverse the emphasis, thus causing conflict with the teaching faculty.

Indeed, major changes in an organization's mission or goals are common causes for conflict, particularly within large organizations facing a volatile environment. For example, McGraw-Hill, the publishing giant, recently changed its primary mission, thus precipitating conflict throughout and between all organizational layers. McGraw-Hill's historical mission has been to publish advertising-based magazines and education textbooks. However, under the leadership of CEO Joseph Dionne,

McGraw-Hill is redirecting its efforts to selling statistics and editorial services electronically to just about any individual or organization having a computer. In order to accomplish this change in mission, Dionne has reorganized the company, formerly structured around six major divisions, into nineteen focus groups concentrating on market segments. This sudden "dismemberment" has caused conflict, turmoil, and confusion throughout the organization. Executives in the magazine publishing area see the restructuring and change of emphasis as nothing short of neglect and mismanagement, and 10 percent of the employees in McGraw-Hill's econometric forecasting company, Data Resources, resigned after the company was scattered throughout six focus groups. States Dionne, "We had people who grew up with one medium, who loved it, revered it, and tended to expand upon that medium. But we believed the market for information was going to change, and if we were going to participate, we would have to master the new technologies."[9]

Organization Overlap

When two or more people are assigned to carry out the same task, organization overlap occurs.* Overlap causes interpersonal strain or conflict almost by definition. If bussers and waiters were both assigned the task of keeping the tables in a restaurant clean, there would undoubtedly be situations in which conflict could occur. It might also cause conflict with their superior if neither group did the work while assuming the other was responsible. Overlap must be avoided because it has tremendous potential for undesirable organizational conflict.

Resource Competition

Two or more people or groups who are competing for the same resources or rewards are thrown into conflict as a result. Their energy and attention are diverted from pursuing their basic purpose to gaining a larger share of resources or rewards. If you closely examined the inner workings of your college or university, you would probably notice conflict occurring between the different academic departments as they vie with each other for faculty salary dollars. For example, English Literature faculty might think the Engineering faculty obtain a disproportionate share of allocated salaries.

---

*Organization overlap should not be confused with group membership overlap in organizations, even though similar behavioral consequences may result. See Allen Cohen, Stephen Fink, Herman Gadon, and Robin Willits, *Effective Behavior in Organizations* (Homewood, Ill.: Richard D. Irwin, 1976), 137–138.

Culture Conflict

In Chapter 13, we defined culture as ". . .the mix of values, beliefs, assumptions, meanings, and expectations that members of a particular organization, group, or subgroup hold in common and that they use as behavior and problem-solving guides." Close examination of this definition shows that culture can easily be the spur to a conflictful situation. Heterogeneous cultures bring values and attitudes into conflict quite easily. We saw this briefly when we discussed ethnocentricity and how a clash of values can cause intergroup conflict.

We see this basis of conflict daily. There are those who feel strong moral obligations to withhold their employment from companies that make munitions or that make or distribute alcohol. Some hospitals today are experiencing low occupancy rates and so have begun advertising campaigns to make their organizations more "patient friendly." These are moves that have agitated some members who hold more traditional views.

Cultural conflict can be seen in the case of Sanyo Manufacturing Company, the huge Japanese television and microwave company, after it opened a factory in Forrest City, Arkansas. The Japanese style of management, which stresses quality, harmony, and sacrifice, was alien to American workers, who, through their union, desired traditional American benefits such as seniority, union-negotiated wages and benefits, and so on. This culture clash erupted in a violent twenty-one day strike in 1985.

Subordinate cultures develop within any group of size. Martin and Siehl describe three types of subcultures, one of which is likely to produce conflict.[10] The authors describe two of these subcultures as follows:

> An enhancing subculture would exist in an organizational enclave in which adherence to the core values of the dominant culture would be more fervent than in the rest of the organization. In an orthogonal subculture, the members would simultaneously accept the core values of the dominant culture and a separate, unconflicting set of values to themselves.[11]

The third type of subculture is termed "counterculture" according to Martin and Siehl, and it presents values that ". . .should present a direct *challenge* to the core values of the dominant culture."[12] Such a challenge was evident in this country during the "Hippie Revolution" of the late 1960s and early 1970s, in which predominantly young people dropped out of the mainstream of the dominant culture and espoused views that shocked it. Subculture dress, speech, behavior, and lifestyle came into what was sometimes physical conflict with the dominant culture.

Counterculture groups, by definition, conflict with the dominant culture. The level of such conflict seems to be a function of the relative strengths of the two cultures, coupled with their respective inclination to engage in conflict behavior.

STRATEGY-CULTURE CONFLICT. As we discussed in Chapter 13, the cultural orientation of a group can conflict with an organization's proposed strategy or main direction. Let us revisit McGraw-Hill to prove this point. Before CEO Dionne embarked on his strategy of making the company electronically market-oriented, its corporate culture was characterized by entrepreneurial decentralization; that is, each of the former six operating divisions was basically an autonomous profit center. Managers infrequently interrelated with their counterparts in other divisions, and in some instances, they even competed with each other. McGraw-Hill's data resources group and publications group offered similar reports to the same customers. Now, with the company reorganized into market focus groups, intergroup coordination and cooperation are essential. The resulting conflict and turmoil within the McGraw-Hill organization can partially be explained because of this strategy-culture conflict. Indeed, Dionne readily admitted that he knew beforehand that this cultural change would cause such problems.

Thus, cultural conflict can be viewed as a restriction on the adoption of strategy, a condition to be resolved if an effective, acceptable course of action is to be put in place. Resolution can be difficult, however, because as Schwartz and Davis point out, ". . .managers have had no method for thinking through the relationship between culture and the critical success factors on which strategy is contingent."[13]

Management must perhaps intuitively assess how culture relates to strategy and whether a conflict is likely. As we explained in Chapter 13, managers then have the following options: manage around culture; attempt to change the culture; or change the strategy. Whatever action management undertakes, cognizance of culture-strategy conflict is imperative.

PHYSICAL SETTINGS AND CONFLICT. High on the agenda of any individual or group is adequate space, be it an office or parking. Physical proximity, or its absence, has a definite effect on communications and coordination. Competition for preferred space occurs within and between organizations.

Power is manifest in physical settings. Aspiring executives long to abandon offices in the field for those in the headquarters building. A simple move can change the balance of power in favor of either more or less conflict. Consider the stress that can develop between two associates, one who is located near the boss and one who is housed in a remote location. Access to the seat of power is seen as power, so the absence of that access can cause conflict. Note in our introductory case how Apple CEO Sculley decided to move the Apple II group from its remote location to the corporate headquarters in order to ease the intergroup conflict that was tearing apart the Apple organization.

Seating arrangements can also invite conflict. A circular arrangement of chairs with no table invites more cooperation than a rectangular one with one "side" facing an "opposing" group at the onset of a meeting. Who sits next to the president, who sits opposite, and who is unable to gain a seat at the main table are all related to power, status, and conflict potential.

From this short treatment, we can see that the physical setting and trappings affect the level of conflict in organizations. This physical setting dimension of conflict must not be overlooked when studying organization theory.

These bases of conflict point out the sources or causes of conflict so that they can be better understood and controlled. Although we have not discussed all possible types of conflict, the ones we have mentioned show that there are many different sources or origins of organizational conflict, a most important variable in modern organizations.

THE CONFLICT EPISODE

Because of the frequency of its occurrence, it is important to examine the conflict episode in some detail. By examining the theoretical works of Pondy and Rahim, we will see how a conflict episode can be viewed as a series of events, or stages. Although Pondy and Rahim describe different stages in their explanations of the conflict episode, both scholars view conflict as a *sequential* process. Deutsch, on the other hand, views the conflict episode from a *holistic* point of view, arguing that the simultaneous interplay of a variety of factors determines the course of a conflict and its resolution by third-party intervention.

Pondy's Stages of Conflict

The work of Louis R. Pondy is widely cited when conflict is discussed.[14] Pondy's stages of conflict help place the issue into the type of perspective that generally prevails today. His model of conflict episode, shown in Figure 15.1, is comprised of five stages: latent conflict, perceived conflict, felt conflict, manifest conflict, and conflict aftermath.

The *latent stage* of conflict consists of those conditions that can breed conflict. Included here are such conditions as competition for scarce resources, drives for autonomy, and divergence of subunit goals. Each of

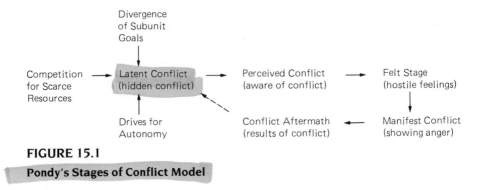

FIGURE 15.1

Pondy's Stages of Conflict Model

these situations is fertile ground for the growth and development of a condition full of conflict.

If one is vying for a portion of resources, one will doubtless find oneself opposed by others attempting to gain their share. Individuals who desire the right to act without interference from others are quite likely to experience opposition. The statement of organizational goals that requires concerted effort from two or more divisions in the organization is likely to cause a conflict situation. Because all these conditions are frequently found in organizations, latent conflict is a common occurrence.

The second stage of a conflict episode is the *perceived conflict*, a condition in which one or more parties becomes aware of the potential for conflict. This has been labeled the cognitive aspect of the episode because some significance is attached to stimuli that bring about an awareness of conflict. Almost any type of information about opposing forces can bring an individual or group into this phase of a conflict episode.

The third stage of conflict is termed *felt stage*, and it is reached when emotions are excited and feelings become hostile. We have all experienced this sense of anger toward another and realized that it could be a prelude to adversary behavior in some form.

When adversary behavior is exhibited, it represents the fourth stage of the episode, *manifest conflict*. There are several types of manifest conflict that range from aggression to apathy to strict adherence to rules (a kind of subtle rebellion). In order to determine if there is, in fact, manifest conflict, one must understand the situation in which the episode occurs. For example, a pat on the back can be considered a show of positive affection or a show of aggression, depending on the context and intentions of the parties involved.

Conflict aftermath is the condition that results after manifest conflict has occurred. The situation can result in resolution of the conflict or it can be the basis of a recycling of the episode to a further stage of latent conflict. For instance, open aggression can produce a condition of understanding (as in the case of a heated debate), or it can produce a desire to continue the conflict (as in the case of physical encounters). Thus, the conflict episode should be viewed as a continuous cycle.

Rahim's Stages of Conflict

M. A. Rahim developed a five-stage model of the conflict episode by synthesizing the works of various scholars in the field.[15] The model, which is shown in Figure 15.2, can be used to describe interpersonal, intragroup, and intergroup conflict episodes. The solid lines show how the stages are sequentially related (from top to bottom in the figure), while the dashed lines show how the stages are connected to explain future conflict episodes.

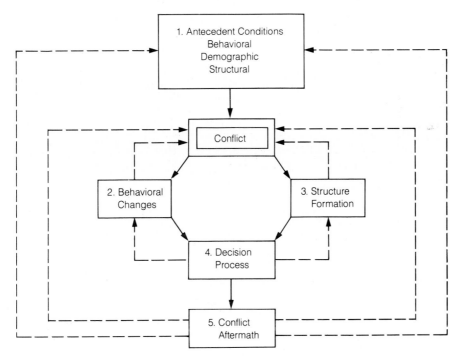

FIGURE 15.2

Rahim's Stages of Conflict

   Source: M. Afzalur Rahim, *Managing Conflict in Organizations* (Praeger Publishers, Division of Greenwood Press, Inc., 1986), 60, copyright © 1986 by Praeger Publishers. Reprinted with permission.

Antecedent conditions, the first stage, are those conditions within the individual(s) or group(s) that exist just prior to conflict occurring. These conditions are behavioral, structural, and demographic in nature.

Behavioral conditions refer to the personalities, philosophies, and orientations of the conflicting parties. *Structure* refers to both organizational structure and task structure. Loose structures (e.g., low formalization), where authority relationships are unclear, can foster conflict, while more rigid, bureaucratized structures have a tendency to preclude certain types of conflict. Likewise, the task structure indicates the extent to which a task is simple or complex. Simple tasks, where goals and procedures are clearly defined, tend to produce less conflict than do complex tasks. *Demographic conditions* refer to such variables as the conflicting parties' age, sex, education, tenure in the organization, and so on.

Behavioral changes, the second stage, occur after the conflict is initiated, and they refer to aggressive behavior accompanied by a reinforcing attitude. Attention of the group is diverted from goal accomplishment to "winning." Relative strength is tested and attributions and perceptions are altered, thus making future cooperative behavior more difficult. At this stage, the conflicting parties begin to think of each other as enemies, and it is not uncommon for the parties to describe each other in terms of negative stereotypes. In our introductory case, we could say this stage occurred after the April 11, 1985, meeting of the Apple board of directors when Steve Jobs considered "Apple too small" for both him and his former friend, John Sculley.

As the parties to the conflict become more rigid in their interaction, *structure formation*, the third stage, occurs; that is, the parties rely on rules and written communications for their interactions. Parties are often addressed by title instead of familiar, informal names. In other words, the conflict is institutionalized and as formal as possible.

The fourth stage is *decision process*, in which the parties devise a substitute process or structure of decision making to take the place of the usual methods. For instance, labor-management conflict is often resolved by negotiation or even arbitration instead of friendly discussion and consensus. In other instances, a superior issues a directive to resolve a conflict with a subordinate, or a common superior is called on for a decision when peer groups are in conflict.

Conflict aftermath, the fifth and final stage, occurs after the conflict is resolved. There can be bitterness and resentfulness if one party perceives that it is a loser. These feelings can easily carry over into future interactions and cause latent conflict to be a factor of some significance. On the other hand, where a conflict is resolved from a general consensus point of view, both parties can approach future encounters on a more positive and cooperative note, committed to the agreed-on resolution.

Rahim's stages of conflict are a dynamic and useful description of just what leads to and happens in a conflict episode.

Deutsch's Six Factors

Morton Deutsch argued in 1969 that there are six factors that determine the actual course of a conflict episode.[16] The first of these is *process*, which means the kind of tactic used in the conflict. For example, coercion, threat, mutual problem solving, and persuasion often lead to different outcomes, with the latter two generally being associated with some form of cooperation and the first two being concerned with some form of competition.

The second factor that Deutsch suggested is the *prior relationship between the parties*. The experiences that we have had in competition and cooperation are likely to significantly influence what happens in the course of a particular conflict. If a bond of friendship exists between the parties, destructive outcomes are less likely.

The *nature of the conflict* is the third major factor in determining the course of a conflict episode. Deutsch argued that small conflicts are easier to deal with than large ones. For example, conflict that involves two individuals would be easier to contain and manage than a conflict that involves two nations. Deutsch used the term "issue rigidity" to describe the lack of satisfactory alternatives to conflict. The idea here is that individuals who are mentally and emotionally rigid are much more difficult to manage in a conflict episode than those individuals who are more flexible. This rigidity sets the parties on a collision course with conflict.

The *characteristics of the parties* to the conflict are also important in determining conflict courses. There are those who seem to have a penchant for controversy and conflict while others seem to want to find a peaceful solution, sometimes at almost any cost. Personality and the belief patterns of the parties affect outcomes.

The tendency of the parties to continue to pursue conflict is affected by their respective *estimates of outcomes*. Not many thinking people, for example, would continue in a physical contest against an individual who obviously had more strength and agility. Such conflicts are quickly resolved in favor of the individual with superior ability.

The final factor affecting conflict is what Deutsch termed the *third party*. Involvement of an outsider who has resources and who is skillful can often encourage the parties to reach some kind of resolution in order to make the conflict short-lived. Figure 15.3 shows how Deutsch's six factors work together to determine the course of a conflict episode.

When one analyzes a given conflict episode, it is important to keep these factors in mind not only to understand conflict but also to help predict the outcome of the conflict episode.

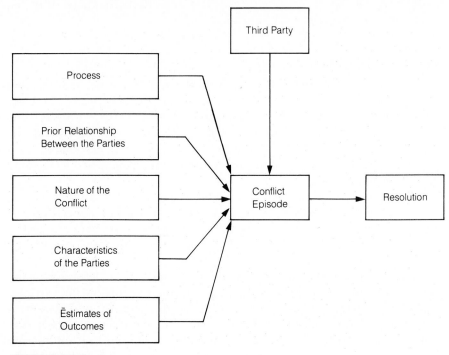

FIGURE 15.3
Deutsch's Six Factors

MODELS OF CONFLICT

As we saw in the preceding section, organization theorists devise models of the conflict phenomenon in order to better understand the dynamics of the conflict episode. In this section, we look at four different conflict models. The first three were developed by Louis Pondy and attempt to describe the "why" of conflict by synthesizing material concerning the levels and bases of conflict. The fourth model, developed by Wheeler, is a specialized depiction of an extremely important and particular type of organizational turmoil, industrial conflict.

The Pondy Models

Drawing on Pondy's work, we describe three models of conflict that occur in organizations. Pondy's models, as summarized in Table 15.3, use many of the concepts we have discussed in previous sections of this chapter.

TABLE 15.3

Pondy's Models of Conflict

Model	Meaning	Example
Bargaining	Competition for scarce resources	Collective bargaining (union-management negotiations)
Bureaucratic	Superior exercising authority over a subordinate (vertical conflict)	Asking secretary to make coffee for the office
Systems	Obtaining coordination and cooperation among units (lateral conflict)	Sales making commitment for product delivery that cannot be met by transportation department

A common form of organizational conflict occurs when members of an organization compete for scarce resources, with each striving for a "just" share. The type of model that explains this conflict is termed the *bargaining model* by Pondy.[17] The essence of the bargaining model is that each party to the conflict attempts to find what, hopefully, will become a common solution to the problem. This model represents a collaborative process that allows for give and take between conflicting parties.

Even a bargained solution to conflict, however, can leave the seeds for future conflict if one of the parties perceives that a loss has occurred. But even if only one conflict episode can be resolved in this manner, at least the parties know where they stand. As Veiga and Yanouzas put it:

> Bargaining might also be viewed as an intervention bridge to either elevate a stalemated power-play situation from a covert "loss of face" condition to a situation in which both parties have at least made an explicit—albeit "hard" or power-based agreement in their mutual interest.[18]

Bargaining, thus, can be a means of equating power (or resources) among the parties so that more harmonious, collaborative relations are at least possible in the future.[19] Management can simultaneously attempt to increase the organization's resource base as a further attempt to control conflict for future interactions between the parties. Labor-management relations have a high potential for conflict because of competition for scarce resources. Indeed, labor-management negotiations are an excellent example of the bargaining model.

What Pondy terms the *bureaucratic model*[20] explains those conflicts that occur when a superior attempts to control the behavior of subordinates. This conflict takes a vertical form. We can better comprehend this form of conflict if we imagine that there is a series of zones of indifference around a subordinate, much like a target. At the center of the target is a relatively small zone in which the subordinate will have little reason to experience conflict. For example, when a superior issues orders and instructions that are clearly job-related, the subordinate is not very likely to find conflict.

The next ring of indifference contains some potential for conflict. For example, if the superior asks the subordinate to serve coffee to some guests, it is possible that the subordinate might see this request as being outside the subordinate's area of responsibility, so the request could result in some form of manifest conflict (perhaps resentment).

The outer ring of indifference has the most potential for manifest conflict. It can be demonstrated in the case where a superior asks a subordinate to do a personal errand, such as to take the superior's laundry to a local cleaner. Such a request is clearly outside the scope of formal organizational responsibility for the subordinate, so the potential for conflict is high.

As we see, the subordinate has several zones of indifference (areas where the subordinate has varying degrees of sentiment about following orders) that affect how he or she will respond to orders and instructions from a superior. The nearer to the center zone such orders and instructions fall, the less chance there is for manifest conflict; the farther from the center they fall, the greater are the chances for manifest conflict.

Thus, the bureaucratic model helps explain vertical forms of conflict, a rather common occurrence in organizations. Remember that the perceived balance of power and authority between superior and subordinate will be important in determining if manifest conflict actually occurs.

Finally, Pondy proposes the *systems model*[21] to explain lateral conflict in the organization. Lateral conflict often stems from situations that require a high degree of cooperation and coordination. This can be seen in the case where the sales and advertising divisions make a concerted effort to inform the public about the introduction of a new product and, in their desire to compete successfully in the market, make commitments for delivery that are beyond the capacity of the transportation division to meet. Failure to deliver the product as promised can be a sure cause of conflict among the sales and transportation divisions.

Research conducted by Blake and Mouton helps explain the subject of lateral, or systems, conflict.[22] Managers from a large company were placed into competing groups of nine to twelve members each and given overnight to solve a problem. They were told that there would be "winning" and "losing" groups. Blake and Mouton observed the following outputs from the exercise:

1. *Increased group cohesiveness.* Members worked closely together, forgetting their individual differences.

2. *Distorted perceptions.* All groups saw themselves as superior.
3. *Distorted judgment.* Each group thought its decisions were best and downgraded the other groups' decisions.
4. *Unequal knowledge.* Each group had a better understanding of its solution in spite of efforts to explain all solutions to all groups.
5. *Group loyalty.* After the exercise, each group elected a member to negotiate with a member of each of the other groups to decide which one had the better solution. In only two of thirty-three sessions did a member "admit" the superiority of the other group's solutions.

This experiment clearly points out how loyalty to one's group impaired an attempt to reach a best solution to a problem. We should keep these results in mind when trying to control lateral conflict, especially if there is a real or perceived power differential between the parties.

Daft's work presents a concise explanation of why lateral conflict occurs in organizations by looking at those factors that seem to determine the frequency, extent, and intensity of this type of conflict.[23] He maintains that *environmental factors* are one explanation. This can be seen when departments are created to deal with the external environment and so are differentiated accordingly, thus distancing them from other departments. Conflict now occurring between the market focus groups at McGraw-Hill is partially due to the fact that each group is differentiated to deal with a different subgroup within the customer/client component of the macro environment. Likewise, at Apple Computers, the Mac group developed its product for business applications, while the Apple II group sought to develop a product for individual and family use.

As organizations increase in *size*, there are more departments, wider power gaps, and more potential for conflict among the departments.

Technology frequently requires interaction between task-interdependent departments, such as those using assembly lines, and conflict potential thus increases. You will remember in Chapter 12 how we discussed the various types of technology developed by Thompson—long-linked, mediating, and intensive. Each of these technologies requires different organizational subunits and members to come together to complete a task. The last type of technology that Thompson mentions, intensive technology, is the most complex. Moreover, the more complex the technology and interactions, the greater the possibility that uncertainty will enter the processes for completing a specific task. Of course, it thus follows that uncertainty can often cause disagreement and conflict. This is particularly true with Perrow's technology types, also discussed in Chapter 12. As you remember, Perrow placed technology types along a continuum ranging from analyzable to unanalyzable. The more unanalyzable (uncertain) the technology, the greater the possibility of conflict occurring between organizational members and departments involved with technology. As you read in our introductory case, one of the reasons for the conflict at Apple Computers was Jobs's disagreement with Sculley concerning the intricacies involved with developing high-tech products.

As we have already discussed, departments tend to pursue *operative goals* that are frequently at cross-purposes with those of other departments. We see this situation occur in the case where the sales department has made promises of delivery that the transportation department cannot honor.

As we saw previously when we discussed Rahim's five stages of conflict, the type of *structure* an organization utilizes causes groups to form and come into contact with other groups. Depending on the type of organization structure, then, a given group shares resources with another group that might not be compatible.

Finally, the *reward system* for the organization can affect lateral conflict. When incentives for cooperation and coordination are ineffective, there is a propensity for interdepartmental conflict.

We thus see how Pondy's work, as augmented by work from other scholars, helps explain the various conditions that can promote conflict within the organization. Every manager must come to grips with each of these conditions in the course of business, and Pondy's three models can be a valuable managerial aid in dealing with the pervasive condition of conflict.

Wheeler's Integrative Theory of Industrial Conflict

Because industrial conflict is the most commonly observed and publicized form of organizational conflict, we devote special attention to a model developed by Hoyt Wheeler to explain this phenomenon.[24] One of the most publicized news events of 1986–1987 was the strike and ensuing violence that took place at the Hormel plant in Austin, Minnesota; and we have previously discussed the strike conducted by Sanyo workers at the company's Arkansas plant. Because this type of organizational conflict can have such a tremendous impact not only on the organization, but on the entire nation as well, Wheeler's incisive work merits special attention.

As shown in Figure 15.4, Wheeler suggests that there are five "pillars" that support and maintain industrial conflict: innate human predispositions, material and social dominance roots of industrial conflict, employee expectations and achievements, three paths to readiness for aggressive action, and collective aggressive action. Following is a capsule of each pillar.

FIGURE 15.4

Wheeler's Five Pillars of Industrial Conflict

INNATE HUMAN PREDISPOSITIONS. Basically, this pillar rests on the proposition that humans are biological in nature, meaning that we all have certain predispositions to behave based on human nature. We listen to the "whisperings within," as Wheeler puts it. These predispositions influence how we behave and what we want in life.

MATERIAL AND SOCIAL DOMINANCE ROOTS OF INDUSTRIAL CONFLICT. This pillar revolves around the assumption that we all have a propensity to pursue material return in response to our efforts in the organization. In effect, it assumes an "economic man" theory of behavior. We want maximum return for minimum effort or pain. Thus, the main reason for the Hormel strike (according to the strikers) was the fact that Hormel management demanded ever-increasing wage and benefit concessions from hourly workers. Workers perceived this as unfair in light of previous wage and benefit concessions, thus leading to an inequitable condition under which employees felt they were not being paid fair wages and benefits for the work they performed.

In addition, we create hierarchies of dominance in the form of social systems and organization structures. When groups form, a hierarchy of authority and power results, a hierarchy that can conflict with or reinforce one's preference for freedom or subordination. Whatever preference, we see power and authority as legitimate possessions of the dominant members.

EMPLOYEE EXPECTATIONS AND ACHIEVEMENTS. Members of a group inevitably bring a set of expectations to the group and compare their achievements against it. The size of the gap (perceived or real) between expectations and achievements is a necessary condition for conflict. The dominant members generally control the conditions that affect the ability of the subordinates to close the gap, thus creating the conditions surrounding the propensity for conflict.

When Sanyo took over the manufacturing plant in Forrest City, Arkansas, in the late 1970s, workers expected full employment, high wages, and a variety of benefits, and, according to union officials, they worked hard to achieve these benefits. Japanese managers, on the other hand, demanded sacrifice, loyalty, and ever-increasing productivity. Thus, Sanyo workers' expectations were not met, although they believed they had done the work expected of them.

THREE PATHS TO READINESS FOR AGGRESSIVE ACTION. Wheeler suggests three paths to a readiness for aggressive action. In the first, *frustration-aggression*, he explains that when individuals seek some objective and their attempts are blocked, they develop a readiness for aggression. Such aggression might not occur if fear dominates the group members, or if they merely resign themselves to that frustration.

The *threat* path is an avenue to aggression that is observed when an individual is threatened or attacked. When this occurs, conflict is virtually inevitable. Consider the case of your home being threatened by a burglar. Sanyo workers felt threatened when half the factory labor force was laid off, when management removed such amenities as chairs and benches from the employee restrooms, and, in particular, when the president of the union local was fired.

Finally, there is the *rational calculation* path to aggression. If we assume that individuals attempt to maximize pleasure (as they define it) and to minimize pain (again, as they define it), it is not unreasonable to project courses of action deliberately aimed at such end states. Obstacles create conflict.

COLLECTIVE AGGRESSIVE ACTION. In this, the fifth pillar of Wheeler's model, regardless of the path members have taken to it, open and often violent conflict occurs. Conditions have become intolerable; and members perceive that aggressive action is justified. They exhibit the type of behavior that they believe will reduce their anxiety and frustration, and so conflict begins. At Sanyo, aggressive action took the form of strikers holding placards that read "Japs Go Home" and "Remember Pearl Harbor." In addition, rocks were thrown, windows broken, shots fired, and, at one point, workers charged the plant and would have overtaken it had they not been stopped by police.

Wheeler's model of industrial conflict and the conditions that lead to it will help you identify and understand this pervasive kind of conflict.

CONFLICT MANAGEMENT

Conflict is often considered to be neither good nor bad, but rather a natural condition in the organization. Managers today are well advised to

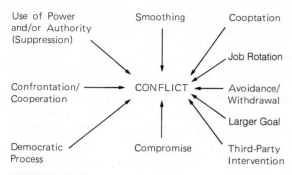

FIGURE 15.5

Conflict Resolution Methods

accept this situation and to devise some strategy, such as those shown in Figure 15.5, for coping with conflict.

One position that can be adopted is to use power and/or authority to put down conflict (*suppression*). Management simply orders the parties to cease their conflict, or one party can order the other party to cease the conflict. When you read the end case to this chapter, you will note how General Electric's chairman suppresses conflict in his organization by wielding his tremendous power over subordinates. Obviously, this technique has questionable effectiveness in organizations that do not have chairmen or managers with the power that GE has. Management might not have enough power and authority to suppress the conflict, in which case conflict not only continues, but management loses relative power and status to the conflicting parties.

Another technique for dealing with conflict is *smoothing*.* Managers who use this technique attempt to defuse the conflict by consoling the conflicting parties. They use supportive, affective language in restoring peaceful relations among the parties. We can see parents use this approach with children. Basically, the technique is an attempt to restore normal or peaceful relations through the use of consolation.

Avoidance is another means of dealing with conflict. Here, one or more parties attempts to divert attention from the conflict or simply ignores it. In a heated debate, for example, the chairperson can change the subject to a less controversial one. In a situation in which conflict seems inevitable, one party can physically leave (as in the case of an impending fight) by walking away. Another example might be seen when a subordinate observes a superior taking money from the company's petty cash

---

*The following techniques for dealing with conflict were adopted from Robert F. Blake and Jane S. Mouton, *The Managerial Grid* (Houston: Gulf, 1964), 162–166.

fund without official authorization. In order to avoid conflict with the superior, the subordinate may simply "look the other way." This technique is an attempt to deal with conflict by skirting or ignoring the issue.

As noted earlier, managers should develop skills for *compromise* because it can be an effective means for dealing with conflict. The manger (or anyone else for that matter) seeks to establish a middle ground, yielding somewhat from an original position that is part of the conflict. If both parties can move to a middle position, conflict can be controlled. Labor-management relations are frequently based on this approach, in which both parties establish original positions and then move to a position toward the middle, each party yielding some of the original demands. The compromise approach to conflict management is basically one of bargaining.

Fred Jandt and Paul Gillette have put forth an intriguing scheme for bargaining that they term the *mini-max strategy*.[25] The basic purpose of this bargaining strategy is to reach a solution to conflict that is acceptable to both parties, based on the proposition that people are willing to give up something in order to get and keep something they prefer. According to Jandt and Gillette, negotiators must ask themselves four questions before beginning negotiations:

1. What is the minimum I can accept?
2. What is the maximum I can ask for without getting laughed out of the room?
3. What is the maximum I can give away?
4. What is the least I can offer without getting laughed out of the room?[26]

The answers to these questions provide a framework for resolving conflict. They establish values to be given and accepted by both parties. Thus, the approach has promise for effective conflict resolution.

Third-party intervention is also an effective means for dealing with conflict. Here, one or more people who are not a party to the conflict are brought in to find a means to resolve the conflict issue. Labor arbitrators are often effective in resolving labor-management disputes. Since third parties frequently bring about a compromise in the situation, their involvement is one means of negotiating a compromise solution.

Lawrence and Lorsch, whom we cited earlier in this chapter, suggest that an effective use of third parties to manage conflict can be found in the person of an "integrator."[27] Lawrence and Lorsch define an integrator as an individual assigned the task of achieving coordination and cooperation between different departments or subunits in an organization. Indeed, this integrator position is similar to the linking-pin position we discussed in Chapter 10. Certainly, in addition to helping to achieve coordination and cooperation between different departments, an integrator can be very influential in helping to resolve interdepartmental conflicts if and when they develop.

When one group takes over or subsumes another group, the condition is termed *cooptation*, and it can be useful in resolving conflict that might have existed among the groups. Corporate mergers provide an excellent example of this technique. Often these mergers are brought about only after bitter and sometimes drawn-out proxy fights among the stockholders of the organizations involved. Once the merger has taken place, the means for peaceful resolution can exist.

The *democratic process* can be used to resolve conflict. Faculty and student governing body meetings can be forums for airing debate and opposing views. After the views have been discussed, the group frequently will vote on the issues, with the majority vote prevailing; thus conflict can be dealt with simply by voting. In the GE case at the end of the chapter, workers at one of the company's participative management plants decided *by themselves* to cut back production and eventually lay themselves off when economic conditions adversely affected plant operations. Had the workers not reacted to the problem in this manner, labor-management conflict might have resulted.

Through each of the means of conflict resolution runs the persuasive abilities of the parties. By whatever means, one party attempts to persuade the other of the correctness of its views. Skillful persuaders hold the upper hand when attempting to resolve conflict, regardless of the means they use.

Conflict can sometimes be managed by the simple method of *job rotation*. When members work together with other groups, they can come to appreciate others' tasks, attitudes, and orientations, possibly removing some conditions that cause unhealthy conflict.

When competing groups can see a *larger goal* than their individual group's objective, they can begin to cooperate rather than compete. Organizations faced with a matter of survival can be seen as examples where this can occur.

Finally, conflict can be dealt with by *confrontation*—the objective recognition that conflict does in fact exist and that an attempt to deal with it should be based on facts rather than on emotions. This is a mature approach to conflict because it is founded on realism. Its use requires that the parties face the fact that conflict exists and that a straightforward approach to its management should be taken. Confrontation does not suggest that emotions should be ignored; it suggests that objectivity and facts should be emphasized rather than emotions. Because conflict, by its very nature, involves feelings and emotions, the approach cannot be entirely emotion-free. Confrontation simply attempts to minimize the role of emotions and stress the importance of facts and objectivity.

Because conflict is central to organizational life, managers must devise some means of monitoring and controlling it. Some companies have gone so far as to differentiate separate organizational units for this purpose. This third-party intervention is an attempt to monitor and control conflict. Other organizations have designed "cooling-off" periods and procedures of decision review to ensure that objectivity and power distribution are as optimal as is practicable. Whatever technique used, conflict, because of its inevitability and potential harm, must be managed properly.

Throughout our discussion of conflict management we must keep in mind the concept of personal commitment. When parties feel strongly about an issue, they are committed to a successful resolution that will preserve their feelings about or positions on the issue. Once a public commitment is made, individuals become more ego-involved with the outcome of a conflict and so make its resolution more difficult. The message is clear: One must be careful when forcing others to make a public commitment on an issue, because this makes it more difficult to resolve conflict.

From these brief descriptions, we see that parties can use one or a combination of means for dealing with conflict. These techniques provide a variety of approaches and, taken together, can be effective methods for conflict management.

SUMMARY

This chapter has examined the organizational phenomenon known as conflict. Today, some level of conflict is inevitable in organizations, regardless of their size. So a theory of how organizations form and operate must include a treatment of this important variable. Simply put, we can say that when individuals or groups have opposing goals, ideas, philosophies, orientations, and so on, conflict results. We discussed this outcome from a micro perspective, based on the overall treatment of organization theory that we have adopted for the text.

Even though conflict today is an organizational given, such has not always been the case. The Classical School thought conflict was undesirable and should be stifled at almost any cost. Such Classical scholars as Henri Fayol, Frederick W. Taylor, and Max Weber firmly argued this view. These writers were followed by Neoclassical contributors who adopted the Classical School's basic premise, but argued that, rather than center on the job, rules, regulations, and so on as a means of eliminating conflict, management should concentrate on making workers happy, believing that happy workers would work effectively together in cooperation and harmony.

Today, we view conflict as a part of everyday life, and so must concentrate on understanding and managing it. A line of anticonflict thought, however, still pervades society at large. The reason for this is that from birth we belong to institutions (the family, school, and church) that propose peaceful interaction among groups.

The various levels of conflict are classified intrapersonal, interpersonal, intragroup (including role conflict, issue conflict, and interactive conflict), and intergroup. The causes of intergroup conflict range from type of work, proper assignments of responsibility, limited resources, low formalization, and perceived status incongruities, to ethnocentrism.

Bases of conflict include role conflict, changes in delegation, changes in status, changes in goals, organization overlap, resource competition, and culture conflict. Culture conflict can be studied by focusing on how subgroup cultures frequently conflict with the dominant culture's values. Two subcultures, enhancing and orthogonal, do not cause conflict, though a third, counterculture, almost by definition, does. Cultural values can conflict with the development and implementation of an organization's strategy. The physical setting in organizations, as a reflection of culture, can either inhibit or advance conflict situations.

The dynamics of the conflict episode can be examined using three models. Pondy's model describes the conflict episode as a sequential event, consisting of the latent stage, perceived conflict, the felt stage, manifest conflict, and conflict aftermath. Rahim also sees the conflict episode as sequential and consisting of five stages: antecedent conditions (behavioral, demographics, and structural); behavioral changes among the parties; structure formation where the conflict becomes formalized; the decision process, where the parties devise a structure for dealing with the conflict; and conflict aftermath. Deutsch sees the conflict episode as a holistic interaction of six factors: process, the prior relationship between the parties, the nature of the conflict, the characteristics of the parties, the estimate of outcomes, and the intervention by a third party.

Pondy's three models can be used to better understand the conflict phenomenon in general terms. His first model, bargaining, sees conflict occurring when organization members strive for a "just" sharing of resources or power. The second model, bureaucratic, represents conflict as vertical (that which exists between superiors and subordinates). The third model, systems, examines lateral, or intergroup, conflict. This third model can be expanded by citing the works of Blake and Mouton, who see such conflict as a function of group loyalty. Daft's research, in turn, helps to explain the frequency, extent, and intensity of systems conflict in organizations.

Because industrial conflict is of such paramount importance to both organizations and the economic health of the nation, Wheeler's integrative theory of industrial conflict is significant. Wheeler suggests that such conflict rests on five pillars: innate human predispositions, material and social dominance roots, employee expectations and achievements, the three paths to readiness for aggressive action, and collective aggressive action.

Finally, we dealt with the issue of conflict management. We discussed a variety of methods that organizations can utilize to better control conflict situations that exist within their organizations. These include suppression, confrontation/cooperation, the democratic process, smoothing, compromise (including the mini-max strategy), cooptation, avoidance/withdrawal, job rotation, the establishment of a larger goal to bring the conflicting parties together, and third-party intervention.

QUESTIONS FOR REVIEW AND DISCUSSION

1. This chapter states that conflict is virtually inevitable. Do you agree or disagree? Present examples to support your answer.
2. Several causes of intragroup conflict are discussed in the chapter. Describe several situations that you have personally been involved with that can be explained by these causes.
3. Take a situation in which you were a party to interpersonal conflict and describe it in terms of Pondy's stages-of-conflict model.
4. Describe a situation in which the physical setting itself was a cause of conflict. Do you think that conflicting parties are always aware of the role the physical setting plays when conflict occurs? What is the significance of your answer?
5. Cite examples of intergroup conflict based on Pondy's three models.
6. Which of the various means of dealing with conflict do you personally use, in general? Which of them would you not (except in dire circumstances) use?
7. Write a short paper in which you describe a real-life situation in which you could use the mini-max strategy for negotiation.
8. Cite examples of situations in which conflict was inevitable because of antecedent conditions described by Rahim.

ENDNOTES

1. M. A. Rahim, *Managing Conflict in Organizations* (New York: Praeger, 1986), 4.

2. Paul R. Lawrence and Jay W. Lorsch, *Organization and Environment* (Homewood, Ill.: Richard D. Irwin, 1969).

3. Stephen P. Robbins, *Organization Theory*, 2d ed. (Englewood Cliffs, N.J.: Prentice-Hall, 1987), 336–338.

4. Todd Mason, Russell Mitchell, and William J. Hampton, "Ross Perot's Crusade," *Business Week* (October 6, 1986), 60.

5. Jeffrey Pfeffer and Gerald R. Salancik, *The External Control of Organizations* (New York: Harper & Row, 1978), 31.

6. W. Clay Hamner and Dennis W. Organ, *Organizational Behavior: An Applied Psychological Approach* (Dallas: Business Publications, 1978), 342.

7. Ibid., 343.

8. Robbins, *Organization Theory*, 341.

9. Stuart Gannes, "Marketing Is the Message at McGraw-Hill," *Fortune* (February 17, 1986), 35.

10. Joanne Martin and Coren Siehl, "Organizational Culture and Counterculture: An Uneasy Symbiosis," *Organizational Dynamics* 12, no. 2 (Autumn 1983): 53–55.

11. Ibid., 54–55.

12. Ibid., 54.

13. Howard Schwartz and Stanley M. Davis, "Matching Corporate Culture and Business Strategy," *Organizational Dynamics* 9, no. 1 (Summer 1981): 36.

14. Louis R. Pondy, "Organizational Conflict: Concepts and Models," *Administrative Science Quarterly* 12, no. 2 (September 1967): 296–320.

15. Rahim, *Managing Conflict in Organizations*, 59–63.

16. Morton Deutsch, "Conflicts: Productive and Destructive," *Journal of Social Issues* 25, no. 1 (1969): 27–29.

17. Pondy, "Organizational Conflict," 312–314.

18. John F. Veiga and John N. Yanouzas, *The Dynamics of Organization Theory*, 2d ed. (St. Paul, Minn.: West, 1984), 299.

19. Ibid.

20. Pondy, "Organizational Conflict," 314–316.

21. Ibid., 316–319.

22. Robert R. Blake and Jane S. Mouton, "Reactions to Intergroup Competition Under Win-Lose Conditions," *Management Science* 7 (1961): 420–435.

23. Richard L. Daft, *Organization Theory and Design*, 2d ed. (St. Paul, Minn.: West, 1986), 451–452.

24. Hoyt N. Wheeler, *Industrial Conflict* (Columbia, S.C.: University of South Carolina Press, 1985), 7–29.

25. Fred E. Jandt and Paul Gillette, *Win-Win Negotiating* (New York: John Wiley & Sons, 1985), 199–228.

26. Ibid., 201.

27. Paul R. Lawrence and Jay W. Lorsch, "New Management Job: The Integrator," *Harvard Business Review* 45 (November–December 1967): 142–151.

ANNOTATED BIBLIOGRAPHY

Aram, John D., and Salipante, Paul F., Jr. "An Evaluation of Organizational Due Process in the Resolution of Employer/Employee Conflict." *Academy of Management Review* 6, no. 2 (April 1982): 197–204.

A need for organizational procedures to resolve employer-employee conflict has been stimulated by expanding definitions of employee rights, greater statutory protection of employees, and the opportunity for corporate adaptation in the area of employee dissatisfaction. The utility of internal systems of conflict resolution rests on the formulation of specific objectives and values, a high degree of decision-maker independence, balanced formality of procedures, and matching types of conflict with means of resolution.

Barton, Robert A. "Reducing Organizational Conflict: An Incompatible Response Approach." *Journal of Applied Psychology* 69, no. 2 (May 1984): 272–279. Anger and aggression can both be reduced by exposure to events that generate positive states incompatible with these reactions. To determine if this principle could be applied to the reduction of organizational conflict, subjects played the role of executives and discussed important organizational issues with another person. This individual was actually an accomplice, who disagreed strongly with other views. Such disagreement was expressed either in a calm and reasonable manner or in an arrogant and condescending fashion. Subjects were then exposed to one of three treatment conditions designed to induce states incompatible with anger (sympathy, gratitude, and amusement) or to a no-treatment control. Finally, the subjects rated their current mood, indicated their impressions of the accomplice, and reported on their likelihood of handling future conflicts through collaboration, avoidance, competition, compromise, or accommodation. Results of the study indicated that the three incompatible-response-generating treatments improved subjects' moods, enhanced their impressions of the accomplice, and increased their preference for constructive as opposed to destructive modes of dealing with conflict.

Bazerman, Max H., and Neale, Margaret A. "Improving Negotiation Effectiveness Under Final Offer Arbitration: The Role of Selection and Training." *Journal of Applied Psychology* 67, no. 5 (October 1982): 543–548. Recent research has shown that final-offer arbitration increases resolution behaviors of labor-management negotiators. Under final-offer arbitration, if negotiators do not reach an agreement, each must submit a "final offer" to the arbitrator. Rather than compromising, the arbitrator must choose a final offer from one of the parties. Empirical evidence confirms that resolutions occur more frequently under final-offer arbitration than under more traditional resolution mechanisms. This article presents theoretical and empirical work suggesting that selection and training mechanisms improve resolution frequency under final-offer arbitration.

Bedeian, Arthur G., and Armenakis, Achilles A. "A Path-Analytic Study of the Consequences of Role Conflict and Ambiguity." *Academy of Management Journal* 24, no. 2 (June 1981): 417–424. This study achieves its primary purpose of evaluating the consequences of role conflict and ambiguity within a multivariate causal context. In addition, it also serves the secondary purpose of underscoring the need for future investigations into the impact of additional factors (e.g., individual characteristics, differences in contexts, tasks, work settings, and personal controls) on role perceptions. The increased knowledge resulting from the incorporation of such variables in future research will greatly enhance the understanding of role theory and, hence, knowledge of human behavior in organizations.

Blake, Robert R., and Mouton, Jane S. "Overcoming Group Warfare." *Harvard Business Review* 62, no. 6 (November–December 1984): 98–111.

The authors of this article present two very different approaches to resolving conflicts between embattled groups. In one method, a neutral facilitator tries to mediate between the two groups by offering compromises and trying to get each group to see the other's point of view. In the other method, the groups form their own views of what their ideal relationship should be and a neutral administrator helps them go through steps to achieve it.

Cochran, Daniel S.; Schnake, Mel; and Earl, Ron. "Effect of Organizational Size on Conflict Frequency and Location in Hospitals." *Journal of Management Studies* 20, no. 4 (October 1983): 442–456.

The purpose of this paper is to report significant findings concerning the effect of organizational size on the frequency and location of intraorganizational conflict within the hospital purchasing decision-making process. The independent variable tested, hospital size, was measured by beds ranging from under 99 beds (small hospitals), 100–199 beds (medium-sized hospitals), and over 200 beds (large hospitals). Conflict was defined as "difference of opinion" between individuals involved in the purchasing decision-making process: administrator and board, administrator and medical staff, board and medical staff, purchasing manager and administrator, and the purchasing manager and medical staff.

Cochran, Daniel S., and White, Donald D. "Intraorganizational Conflict in Hospital Purchasing Decision-Making Process." *Academy of Management Journal* 24, no. 2 (June 1982): 324–332.

Empirical data collected from administrators and purchasing managers in fifty-six general short-term hospital facilities, together with in-depth interviews conducted in nine hospitals, provided insights as to the frequency, location, and nature of purchasing-related conflict.

Dowling, John B., and Schaeffer, Norbert V. "Institutional and Anti-Institutional Conflict Among Business, Government, and the Public." *Academy of Management Journal* 25, no. 3 (September 1982): 683–689.

If conflict management within a society is to be a social objective, a systematic study of the forms of conflict is an important diagnostic procedure. In this article, two forms of conflict are developed—institutional and anti-institutional. These two forms of conflict are then applied to an examination of changes in the relationships among business, government, and the public.

Greenhalgh, Leonard. "SMR Forum: Managing Conflict." *Sloan Management Review* 27, no. 4 (Summer 1986): 45–57.

While conflict is not necessarily bad, or something that should be squelched (it is inherent in organizational life), it can impair relationships among people who need to interact effectively. Therefore, conflict needs to be managed. The author synthesizes much of the diverse writing on conflict management and presents a useful model that can help people diagnose a conflict situation and thus plan tactics for managing it.

Holzworth, James. "Intervention in a Cognitive Conflict." *Organizational Behavior and Human Performance* 32, no. 2 (October 1983): 216–220.

The cognitive conflict paradigm, developed within the framework of social judgment theory, was used to determine effects of intervention in interpersonal conflict. Task predictability and the third party's knowledge of task characteristics were manipulated as independent variables. After being trained to have different policies, judges were brought together to work on a common set of judgment problems. During the conflict session, a third party intervened to assist judges in making joint predictive judgments. Task predictability was found to have more effect on conflict reduction than did intervention. Overall, intervention did not appear to effect conflict reduction; however, mediator characteristics were significantly correlated with an objective measure of a mediator's relative usefulness.

Kabanoff, Boris. "Potential Influence Structures as Sources of Interpersonal Conflict in Groups and Organizations." *Organizational Behavior and Human Decision Processes* 36, no. 1 (August 1985): 113–127.

It is argued that conflict in organizations can be interpreted, in many cases, as conflict over who is to exert influence, and that this conflict, in turn, is caused by structural incongruities in the distribution of potential influence in groups and organizations. Potential influence is described in terms of the structural relations defined by structural role theory. At the psychological level, conflict is explained as a result of incompatible expectations among people about their relative influence, their desire to protect valued roles, and to maintain a sense of freedom.

Raelin, Joseph A. "An Examination of Deviant/Adaptive Behaviors in the Organizational Careers of Professionals." *Academy of Management Review* 9, no. 3 (July 1984): 413–427.

A model of professional deviant/adaptive career behaviors is presented to clarify the negative behavioral effects experienced by some salaried professionals and proposed as being caused by conflicting expectations with their management. The nature of and precursors to these conflicting expectations are delineated. The cognitive state, attitudes, and specific behaviors, which are the results of the expectations, are discussed. Behavioral outcomes are presented in terms of four career elements: management, job, self, and career.

Schwenk, Charles R. "Devil's Advocacy in Managerial Decision-Making." *Journal of Management Studies* 21, no. 2 (April 1984): 325–337.

There is some debate about the potential value of using devil's advocates in top-level organizational decision making. In this paper, the contrasting views on this question are summarized briefly and the field and laboratory research on the devil's advocate and related techniques is discussed. This research is then used as the basis for detailed suggestions on the effective use of devil's advocates in improving managerial decisions.

Schwenk, Charles R. , and Thomas, Howard. "Effects of Conflicting Analyses on Managerial Decision-Making: A Laboratory Experiment." *Decision Sciences* 14, no. 4 (Fall 1983): 467–482.

Researchers in a variety of disciplines have recommended using multiple conflicting data analyses to improve managerial decision making through the challenging of assumptions. This study deals with the effects of single data analyses and conflicting analyses on managers' solutions to a case analysis task. Results showed that managers who received conflicting analyses produced solutions with higher expected profits than those who received single analyses.

ADDITIONAL REFERENCES

Abell, P. *Organizations as Bargaining and Influence Systems.* New York: Halsted, 1975.

Bernardin, J. H., and Alvares, K. M. "The Managerial Grid as a Predictor of Conflict Resolution Method and Managerial Effectiveness." *Administrative Science Quarterly* 21, no. 1 (March 1976): 84–92.

Bomers, G. B. J., and Peterson, R. B., eds. *Conflict Management and Industrial Relations.* Boston: Kluwer-Nijhoff, 1982.

Brown, L. David. "Managing Conflict Among Groups." In *Organizational Psychology: A Book of Readings,* edited by David A. Kob, Irwin M. Rubin, and James M. McIntyre, 377–389. Englewood Cliffs, N.J.: Prentice-Hall, 1979.

Byrnes, J. D. *Conflict Resolution.* New York: AMACOM, 1987.

Cole, D. W., ed. *Conflict Resolution Technology.* Cleveland: Organization Development Institute, 1983.

Cosier, R. A. "Methods for Improving the Strategic Decision: Dialectic Versus the Devil's Advocate." *Strategic Management Journal* 3, no. 4 (October–December 1982): 373–374.

Cosier, R. A., and Ruble, T. L. "Research on Conflict-Handling Behavior: An Experimental Approach." *Academy of Management Journal* 24, no. 4 (December 1981): 816–831.

Deutsch, Morton. "Fifty Years of Conflict." In *Retrospections on Social Psychology,* edited by L. Festinger, 46–47, 259–265. New York: Oxford University Press.

Filley, A. C. "Some Normative Issues in Conflict Management." *California Management Review* 21 (1978): 61–66.

Hacon, R. J. *Conflict and Human Relations Training.* New York: Pergamon Press, 1964.

Harnett, D. L., and Cummings, Larry L. *Bargaining Behavior: An International Study.* Houston: Dame, 1980.

Himes, J. S. *Conflict and Conflict Management.* Athens, Ga.: University of Georgia, 1980.

Janis, Irving L., and Mann, Leon. *Decision Making: A Psychological Analysis of Conflict, Choice, and Commitment.* New York: Free Press, 1977.

Kilmann, R. H., and Thomas, K. W. "Four Perspectives on Conflict Management: An Attributional Framework for Organizing Descriptive and Normative Theory." *Academy of Management Review* 3, no. 1 (January 1978): 59–68.

Kochan, T. A. "Collective Bargaining and Organizational Behavior Research." In *Research in Organizational Behavior,* Vol. 2, edited by B. Staw and L. Cummings. Greenwich, Conn.: JAI Press, 1980.

McNeil, E. G., ed. *The Nature of Human Conflict.* Englewood Cliffs, N.J.: Prentice-Hall, 1965.

Pruitt, D. G. "Achieving Integrative Agreements." In *Negotiations in Organizations,* edited by M. H. Bazerman and R. J. Lewicki, 35–50. Beverly Hills: Sage, 1983.

Robert, M. *Managing Conflict: From the Inside Out.* Austin, Tex.: Learning Concepts, 1982.

Smith, K. K. *Groups in Conflict: Prisons in Disguise.* Dubuque, Iowa: Kendall/ Hunt, 1982.

Sullivan, Jeremiah; Peterson, Richard B.; Kameda, Naoki; and Shimada, Justin. "The Relationship Between Conflict Resolution Approaches and Trust—A Cross Cultural Study." *Academy of Management Journal* 24, no. 4 (December 1981): 803–815.

Thomas, K. W., and Pondy, Louis R. "Toward an Intent Model of Conflict Management Among Principal Parties." *Human Relations* 30 (December 1977): 1089–1102.

Wall, J. A., Jr. *Negotiation: Theory and Practice.* Glenview, Ill.: Scott, Foresman, 1985.

C	A	S	E

Progress at General Electric

John F. (Jack) Welch, Jr., the chairman of General Electric, has transformed this industrial giant into one of America's economic bright spots during a period in which other old-line American corporations, such as GM and U.S. Steel (now USX), have sunk into a morass of decay and mediocrity. Since becoming chairman in 1981, Welch has utterly transformed GE by stripping away entire echelons of its management, selling off over $6.5 billion worth of "dog" businesses such as Utah Mining, and shifting resources from sterile manufacturing units to fast-growing services and high technology. Welch has told his business managers that their operations would be sold or shuttered if they did not become number one or number two in their markets. He further stepped on managers' toes when he grouped the fifteen GE businesses (excluding RCA) into three "circles": services (such as GE Credit Corporation and nuclear plants); high-tech products in high-growth areas (such as jet aircraft engines and plastics); and the old GE core businesses (such as light bulbs and electric motors).

This turnaround has not occurred without conflict. When waste is rooted out and unneeded managers and workers are fired, there is often resistance, from

Sources: Peter Petre, "What Welch Has Wrought at GE," Fortune (July 16, 1986), 43–47; Bill Saporito, "The Revolt Against Working Smarter," Fortune (July 21, 1986), 59–60.

both organizational subunits and individuals alike. But Jack Welch was not in a compromising mood with those who challenged his goals and methods. He made it plain to his subordinate managers that they had to achieve unsurpassed quality at "Scrooge-like" cost in addition to capturing market share. If they failed, they went. And many managers at GE have gone. One executive working at one of GE's old core businesses stated, "Morale stinks. People are looking for jobs or waiting for a nice severance package. They talk openly about it."

By eliminating managers, Welch has also eliminated management layers. Businesses within the three circles have been further broken down into twenty operating divisions. Managers in these operating divisions, trained to act like conservative bureaucrats by the old GE, have been instructed to act as if they were entrepreneurs. Welch also promotes open communications between the operating division managers and the corporate headquarters. This is an alien concept to the old-line GE manager who previously "got ahead by knowing a little bit more than the employee who works for him." Welch's view of open communications breaks the hierarchical bonds of authority that formerly characterized communications at GE. Welch seeks information from any source in the organization, be it high or low. Thomas Thorsen, GE's chief financial officer until 1984, noted, "If you're a manager who gets upset if the boss goes around you, you'll spend a lot of time being upset."

It is interesting to note here that GE was one of the first experimenters with participative management or quality circles in the United States. General Electric began this experiment over twenty years ago in twelve of its plants. The experiment only lasted at two, however, due to layoffs, management rotation, union reaction, and the benign neglect of GE's old management. Now, under Welch's leadership, there is increased interest in this management style. For example, the Newark, Ohio, plant was specifically built for participative management in 1973 and is now being studied by other GE operations because of its success. When this plant, which makes quartz tubes used in producing semiconductors, was racked by the slowdown of the computer industry in the mid-1980s, the workers *themselves* decided to slow down production and eventually lay themselves off. At GE's Ravenna, Ohio, plant, where participative management/quality circles were introduced in 1982, productivity has increased by 25 percent. Welch does hold the line, however, when it comes to grievances based on incidents on the shop floor, such as reprimands or suspensions. He does not consider them matters for discussion for the quality circle groups. Thus, in 1985, workers at the Lynn, Massachusetts, plant went on strike for a month over this issue.

Welch thrives on debate. In January, 1986, he hosted a workshop for seventeen of GE's corporate officers at the organization's lavish training center in upstate New York. The seventeen executives barraged Welch with questions about growth and complained that GE was not growing fast enough internally, and, moreover, they wanted to have a greater voice in selecting future acquisitions and deciding how GE should allocate its capital. The participative management concept stopped here as Welch told his managers that he was not willing to share power with them. Rather, he would be willing to

debate budgeting policies and acquisition priorities.

One of Welch's most notable achievements was the acquisition of RCA by GE in 1985. After dumping so many unprofitable businesses in the early 1980s, GE's board of directors became anxious to acquire anything that would add profit potential to the organization. Welch argued at that time that it would be best to wait until the *right* acquisition opportunity presented itself. Board member Lewis Preston noted that ". . .Jack had the right sense to wait until the right one came along." With the RCA acquisition, GE's annual revenues leaped from $28 billion to $40 billion in a single year.

One problem with this acquisition was the divergent views of GE and RCA concerning television manufacturing. GE, which also manufactured televisions, wanted to get out of the business, while RCA had ambitions about expanding television production. Welch alleviated this conflict by hiring three consulting firms to study television technology, marketing, and manufacturing. Being a good listener, Welch wanted to lay out the facts before deciding whether to quash RCA's television manufacturing plans.

One final accomplishment by Welch and GE was the turnaround in the major appliance section. In the late 1970s, GE's major appliance division was stumbling, disorganized, and laying off thousands of workers. Welch chose senior vice president Roger Schipke to turn the division around in 1982, with instructions to "clean house" and automate. Managers who disagreed with Schipke were summarily fired or offered early retirement. Schipke and Welch, over the objections of the so-called "experts," introduced the manufacture of rotary compressors in its new Tennessee plant for installation in GE's major appliances, such as refrigerators. The "experts" thought rotary compressors were impractical for this purpose because they must be made to tolerances unheard of in mass manufacturing. Welch and Schipke managed to quash this controversy by pulling aircraft-engine and automation experts from elsewhere in the company to help design the new plant and assembly processes. The plant is a huge success, and, moreover, is probably the most automated in the world. Welch's penchant for automation is being pushed organization-wide, and he has union backing by agreeing to retrain displaced workers.

Jack Welch has managed to make GE a success despite objections from many individuals and subunits within the organization. He has succeeded because he believes in his own vision for the company, listens to people, and, most important, will not hesitate to use his enormous power to stop those conflicts that could interfere with his long-range strategic vision for GE.

QUESTIONS FOR DISCUSSION

1. How would a knowledge of theories of (or attitudes about) conflict help you understand the GE situation better?
2. Do you see any element of an anti-conflict attitude in this case? Cite the situation in which it occurs and evaluate its influence.
3. Determine if you can find an example of each level of conflict in this case.
4. There are several bases of conflict described in the chapter material. Apply as many as you can to this case.
5. Show how each technique of conflict management can be used in the case.

16

Organizational Renaissance

Keep on Truckin'

"We had a strong motivation to embrace change.

Change is frightening. It can paralyze powerful executives. It can cause entire organizations to drag their corporate feet. It's the stuff sleepless nights are made of.

Not long ago, International Harvester was in the shadow of an even more frightening prospect.

The reaper was already at our doorstep. We had to change. Or else.

We had to streamline operations. Greatly improve productivity. And find new ways to compete.

The fact that you're reading this today is testimony to how well our people rally to change.

We consolidated facilities. Eliminated five levels of bureaucracy. Doubled manufacturing productivity. Cut inventory by two-thirds. And orchestrated the largest private debt restructuring in history.

An old company, set in its ways, changed. And was reborn as Navistar International Corporation.

In doing so, we learned a lesson.

Change is not a nemesis. It's vital to our organization. To any organization.

Properly managed, change is progress. It's the road to improved quality, and to new products that will help our customers meet their changing needs.

It's a competitive edge. Change helps us further strengthen our number one position.

Yet we know we must never change merely for the sake of change. Change is not a goal. It's the means to a goal. Today, we're still changing.

We're growing. Improving. And finding better ways to serve our customers.

Change, however, still keeps us awake at night.

But these days it's because we're dreaming of new ways to accomplish it."

NAVISTAR
The Rebirth of International Harvester

Source: "We Had a Strong Motivation to Embrace Change," [advertisement], *The Wall Street Journal* (July 2, 1986), 9.

International Harvester (IH) is no more. On January 7, 1986, Chairman Donald D. Lennox presented a new name to the organization's remaining 15,000 members—Navistar International Corporation.

As IH, the company suffered more than $3 billion in losses since 1980, and in 1984 was on the verge of bankruptcy. Lennox, who became IH's boss in 1982, has made steady progress in building a new company from the disastrous situation in which IH found itself. At present, Navistar has a positive net worth, with a comfortable long-term debt of $800 million. By comparison, IH's debt in 1981 was $2.5 billion.

Navistar bears little resemblance to the old IH. In its heyday, IH employed 100,000 people in forty-eight plants—Navistar presently has seven plants. The most dramatic change occurred in 1985 when Lennox sold IH's agricultural business along with the Harvester name. That deal, worth $448 million, enabled IH to rid itself of an extremely burdensome financial drain.

Lennox is now able to focus Navistar's efforts on manufacturing medium- and heavy-duty trucks and truck engines. The truck business will continue to use the name "International," and it is doing quite well. It currently has 23 percent of the U.S. market, and its distribution system of 900 dealers is the envy of competitors.

This new, streamlined Navistar, however, does have problems lurking ahead. The deregulated trucking industry has caused a slump in medium- and heavy-duty truck sales, and most observers believe that such sales will remain flat for the rest of the decade. But because Navistar has reduced the old IH break-even point by 50 percent, Lennox is optimistic about truck and truck engine manufacturing. Moreover, Navistar is presently looking for acquisitions in industries that are not cyclical or capital intensive.

Should Navistar become too successful, it faces a not so unusual problem that large organizations have learned to face in the 1980s—it can become a takeover target. Navistar currently has more than $1 billion in tax-loss carryover credits, and its dealer system makes it attractive to foreign manufacturers. This dealer system is essential for selling large quantities of heavy-duty trucks, and Navistar's acquisition could provide a foreign manufacturer with an important foot in the door in the heavy-duty truck market.

Source: L. Freeman, "IH Reincarnated as Navistar," *Advertising Age* (January 13, 1986), 61; Kathleen Deveny, "Can Navistar Succeed Where Harvester Failed?" *Business Week* (January 20, 1986), 28.

Organizations can be reborn. Navistar and Chrysler Corporation are excellent examples. Living with and managing change are demanding requirements for managers of all organizations. Many organizations are unable to change fast enough to meet or stay ahead of competition and the external environment. Because they are unable to achieve a rebirth, they die.

This chapter deals with the "recycling" of organizations and how all organizations inevitably must deal with the imperative of change.

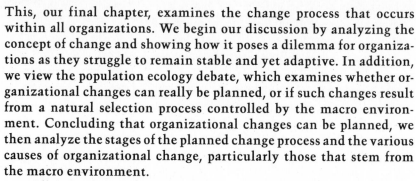

CHAPTER PLAN

This, our final chapter, examines the change process that occurs within all organizations. We begin our discussion by analyzing the concept of change and showing how it poses a dilemma for organizations as they struggle to remain stable and yet adaptive. In addition, we view the population ecology debate, which examines whether organizational changes can really be planned, or if such changes result from a natural selection process controlled by the macro environment. Concluding that organizational changes can be planned, we then analyze the stages of the planned change process and the various causes of organizational change, particularly those that stem from the macro environment.

Following this analysis, we perform a critical study of the organizational life cycle, which consists of five stages: birth, growth, maturity, deterioration, and death. We expand on the study of the last stage, death, by discussing its relationship to catastrophe theory.

There are many ways that an organization can manage change. For example, it can know and forecast, initiate, amplify, smooth, buffer, and stop. In this regard, we also discuss the necessity for a philosophy of innovation within modern organizations.

We devote considerable attention to the process of organizational development (OD). We define the process, stressing that OD first begins with a careful audit of the organization's operations, structure, mission, goals, resources, and so forth. In order to further understand OD, we next concentrate on the various OD strategies and intervention techniques.

The process of dynamic homeostasis, whereby organizations attempt to remain in a state of equilibrium with the environment, is analyzed as a lead-in to our study of the future of bureaucracy in order to determine if that type of organizational structure can remain viable in the future. Finally, our chapter closes with an examination of what we believe will be tomorrow's organizations and how they will be different from the traditional bureaucratic structure.

In this, our last, chapter, we present actions an organization can take to postpone and, some would argue, even prevent death. This chapter examines ways organizations can maintain their health and vitality. We focus on the change process since this is the process critical to organizational survival. We use the term *renaissance* in the chapter title to connote the concept of renewal and as a key element in the survival process.

THE CONCEPT OF CHANGE

Change is simply the alteration of the status quo. In a technical sense, it occurs continually; no moment is exactly like the one that preceded it. However, for our purposes we are interested in the kind of change that has a significant impact on organizational operation. This change may be generated in the environment or it may be generated from within the organization. Change generated within the macro environment of the organization is *exogenous* change. Change generated from within the organization itself is *endogenous* change. In many cases exogenous change will cause endogenous change. A new strict pollution-control law will cause the organization to change internally to deal with the law. The organization may choose not to obey the law, but such a choice will involve internally generated action or change. Sometimes endogenous change causes exogenous change. An organization may pressure a legislative body to pass a law such as a trade subsidy. Here, the internally generated change causes a change in the macro environment.

It is not always apparent at first glance where the change is generated. A group of employees may initiate a union-organizing campaign in order to become represented by a union for purposes of collective bargaining. However, whether this is initiated by the employees themselves or by an outside professional organizer may not be readily apparent. Yet organizations should be vitally interested in determining the source of a specific change. Understanding the source of change usually provides the organization with a better understanding of the reason for the change as well as its intensity, predicted permanency, and the background factors that caused it.

The Dilemma with Organizational Change

Organizations face a dilemma with respect to change. On the one hand, organizations desire change in order to remain competitive, adopt more effective and efficient technology and methods (e.g., electronic data processing), and to remain in harmony with their environment. On the other hand, organizations often resist change because they desire stability and predictability. Organizations must have relatively stable output, predictable costs, and protection of their financial integrity. The key question for the organization thus becomes, how can we achieve desired change without it disrupting our operations?

Thus, the organization tries to find its place along the following continuum:

Stability ←——————————→ Rapid change
Predictability   Unpredictability
Familiarity   Unfamiliarity
Certainty   Uncertainty

Another way to examine the consequences of this continuum is as follows:

Stability ←——————————→ Rapid change
Staleness   New challenges
Boredom   Opportunities for new markets
                            and growth
Atrophy   Opportunities for new methods
                            and technology

An organization that maintains the status quo may find that it generates boredom and staleness among its members; the organization may even atrophy as it becomes out of tune with its environment and die. Change can bring new challenges, new markets, and new technology. Finding the proper point on this continuum to balance the desirable and undesirable consequences of change is a very real challenge for managers in today's organizations. This is not an easy task. As we saw in Chapters 2, 3, and 4, the extent of environmental change faced by the organization will have a major impact on the amount of internal change required by the organization. Organizations facing stable environments will not need to change as much as organizations facing dynamic environments.

Planned versus Unplanned Change: The Population Ecology Debate

Do organizations actually determine their own fate with regard to change? Can organizations actually adapt to environmental change, or does environmental change occur in such a manner that many organizations cannot adapt and, therefore, they die? The central issue here is between environmental determinism and freedom of organizational choice and adaptation. This idea builds on Darwin's theory of natural selection, which holds that only those species that can adjust to environmental change survive; they are "selected" for survival by the environment. Those that are not so selected die.

Astley and Van de Ven argue that this "adaptation versus selection" issue is a central debate in organization theory.[1] *Population ecology*, that is, the totality or relationships between organizations and their environment, can be applied to organization theory to help explain the environment in determining the survival of organizations.[2] It is as if environmental factors select those organizations for survival that best fit the environment. The organization finds its niche and survives. This theory argues that there is little, if any, adaptation (i.e., planned change by the organization). The environment weeds out those organizations that do not fit.

If one accepts this environmental determinism approach, there is little hope that managerial action can control change. A key factor in environmental adjustment is *organizational inertia*. The stronger the inertia, the more difficult it is for management to manage change. Such factors as sunk costs, communication structures, internal politics, and institutional norms can create a high degree of inertia and little adaptability.[3] The organization can have a kind of pervasive momentum that causes "sluggish adaptation" to environmental changes, and so requires organizational adaptation of a different type than was intended initially.[4] Inertia and momentum both affect an organization's ability to adapt.

The General Motors Corporation, which we have cited several times throughout this text, is an example of an organization in a state of inertia. With 800,000 employees and an accompanying cumbersome bureaucracy, this company has had a very difficult time trying to revitalize itself in view of fierce foreign competition and the generally sluggish American economy of the 1980s. This inertia is well documented by the fact that, in 1986, although GM was of a size that could control 60 percent of the American automobile market, in reality, it controlled only 43 percent. In the words of H. Ross Perot, the former member of the GM board of directors, "Revitalizing GM is like teaching an elephant to tap dance."[5]

It is important to ask the question, to what extent does the population ecology argument apply to organizational change and adaptation? Can organizations change and adapt, or does the environment simply select those organizations that will survive? Research findings are sketchy, but Wholey and Brittain conclude that "although organizational ecology's main contribution is its dynamic environmental conceptualization, this does not displace all other explanatory variables."[6] Today in much of the research, ecological variables are combined with institutional and structural variables to explain organizational adaptation. Therefore, environmental determinism, with its emphasis on the ecological variables, does not appear to provide a complete explanation for organizational survival.

Our approach to the question of whether change can be planned or whether it is always unplanned is a managerial one. That is, we assume that the organizational change process can be managed to some extent. This means that *planned* change is possible.[7] To the extent that change can be planned, uncertainty and instability associated with change can be reduced. Of course, not all change an organization experiences can be planned or even significantly influenced. Sometimes external change comes so rapidly and with such severity that the organization is pushed along with the current like a rudderless ship. We saw this happen to many firms in the 1970s because of the Arab oil embargo and resultant energy shortage. And we see it happening today as organizations face fierce competition from foreign competitors and the threat of takeover. The same phenomenon may occur with regard to internal change in the organization if it does not monitor its internal operations carefully enough. For example, pent-up frustrations may explode in a prolonged strike.

In these cases, change will have unintended and unplanned effects. Yet even here managers should attempt to anticipate change and its effects and adapt or cope, even though they may believe they cannot manage or influence the change itself. This adapting and coping behavior also calls for a managerial approach.

Sources of Change and their Impact on the Organization

One way of viewing change is to classify it as to the impact it may have on the organization. As we see in Figure 16.1, change can impact the task, structure, technology (tools), or people (actors) in the organization.[8] Change that originates in the environment or within the organization can cause the task of the organization to change. A university offering primarily educational programs to eighteen to twenty-two year olds may establish a weekend executive M.B.A. program. It may also establish re-

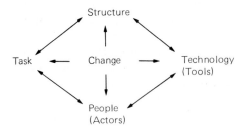

FIGURE 16.1

The Impact of Change on Aspects of the Organization

Source: Adapted from Harold J. Leavitt, "Applied Organization Change in Industry: Structural, Technical, and Human Approaches," in *New Perspectives in Organization Research*, edited by W. W. Cooper, H. J. Leavitt, and M. W. Shelly II (New York: John Wiley & Sons, 1964): 56.

search programs. This will depend in part on the opportunities and constraints that exist in the environment and on the philosophy and mission that pervade the organization, as we saw in Chapter 8.

Structure may change. Organization growth or retrenchment as well as new government actions often change structure. For example, affirmative action requirements may force the organization to establish a department of equal employment opportunity with a chief equal opportunity employment officer. We see many examples of changes in technology that immediately affect the tools and operations of a firm. Recall the major changes in the computer industry when the small microprocessing chips were developed. People, the actors, in the organization are obviously affected by change. Attitudes, emotions, skills, abilities, expectations, and interests all change. Often this change occurs because of general changes occurring in the environment. Some people argue that our generally permissive and affluent society has caused a deterioration of the traditional work ethic among today's youth. Others argue that social movements such as civil rights and women's liberation have developed a certain expectation of "entitlement" among all workers in organizations.[9]

Seldom is the impact of change neatly compartmentalized as affecting just one or two parts of the organization. The arrows in Figure 16.1 indicate that change usually has an interactive, dynamic effect on the parts of the organization.

Stages in the Planned Change Process

Examination of the source of change is but one stage in the change process. As we see in Figure 16.2, the process involves several additional stages. The first step in the process is stress. Stress results because of a problem either internal to or outside of the organization. It could be stress in terms of interactions, sentiments, or attitudes (behavioral stress) or in terms of procedures, programs, or ineffectiveness (technical stress). This second type of stress results from technical rather than behavioral factors. Actually, in any situation there are usually technical and behavioral factors at work, and it is often difficult to separate the two.

These two types of stress are readily apparent in modern organizations as they begin to feel the pressure to change. As we read in our analysis of the Apple Computer organization in Chapter 13, behavioral stress (and subsequent conflict) among Apple executives and employees led to a sequence of massive changes involving restructuring and high turnover among top executives in that company. We saw technical stress at work within Xerox when, during the mid-1980s, that company began to feel the effects of fierce competition by other copier manufacturers. This technical stress forced Xerox to take a long, hard look at the technical processes involved with its product design and how they could and should be

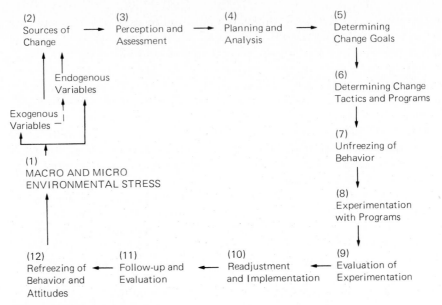

FIGURE 16.2

The (Planned) Change Process

changed. As a result, the company made design changes that made its products easier to service.

This stress, then, becomes a source for change. People recognize the problem and decide something should be done about it. In this perceiving and assessment stage, managers in the organization determine the type of change that is building, the importance of the change to the organization, and the speed of the change. This stage is very much affected by the management group's basic perceptual set. How do they view change in general? Do they find it threatening? Do they view it as a nuisance or as a challenge? How much experience have they had with change? All these questions come to bear as the managers attempt to assess the extent and type of change that may be building.

In the planning and analysis stage (the fourth step in the process), the management group actually becomes involved as a change agent. It is at this point that they decide how they will deal with the change. Are they going to try to stop it, redirect it, amplify it, or ignore it? Will they adopt a strategy of becoming actively involved or only tangentially involved in the change? This is the first step for the management group in designing a change strategy.

The fifth step involves the specification of change goals. These are the results management would like to achieve with the change. It may be to increase productivity, reduce costs, increase sales, reduce the number of employees, build a new factory or office, repeal a law or prohibit its passage, or assure full compliance with a law. This is an important step because not knowing where one wants to be after a change causes many problems in deciding what one should do to handle a change. These goals should be stated in output terms and should be subject to verification through some type of measurement process.

Once the goals have been determined, the organization now becomes concerned with developing ways to achieve the goals. This means the organization determines the tactics, programs, and activities required to achieve the goals.[10] It answers the question, how will the goals be achieved? Notice here that the activity and the programs that result in this step ought to be closely tied to the goals. These should help the organization to keep from foundering as it attempts to implement the change.

Once these programs have been decided on, the organization must focus on the behavioral change it desires of its employees. Any change involves unlearning old ways of doing things and learning new ways. This step is the unlearning or unfreezing step. Attempts must be made to ensure that employees will approach the change with open minds. Of course, in this step the organization needs to be sure that the employees know fully:

1. What the change is
2. Why it is needed
3. What will be expected from them
4. What the benefits for them will be
5. What disadvantages or problems might crop up and how they should be dealt with
6. What behavior change will be needed in programs, tasks, and activities

One way to bring this about is to have a participation strategy of adopting change. This would have employees affected by the change actually involved in determining the decisions required to carry it out. This should occur in an open, nonthreatening, supportive environment. Many employees oppose change because they feel threatened by it or do not fully understand it. Managers must try to overcome these concerns at this stage by involving employees in planning the decisions associated with the change.[11] Of course, this is easier said than done.

General Foods (GF) was an innovator in providing for worker involvement in the change process. At its Topeka, Kansas, dog food plant, GF decided to experiment with a participative management system whereby workers would be permitted to make their own job assignments, schedule breaks, interview prospective employees, and even decide pay issues. General Foods initiated this change as an experiment without being threatened by any undue pressure from the environment or from within the organization. But, at its Hoboken, New Jersey, coffee plant, GF did introduce a similar participative management system in order to stem rising production costs.

The introduction of this change at both GF plants has not met with complete success or approval by all parties concerned. The reasons for this include a lack of commitment from top management, lack of support from middle management members who did not want to lose control, and the perception among workers that they were really not being granted all the authority that was promised to them. Thus, as noted above, using a participation strategy to implement change is often more easily said than done.

Most organizational change is instituted incrementally. That is, it is evolutionary rather than revolutionary. One way to achieve incremental change while minimizing disruption is to implement change on an experimental basis. This allows the organization to monitor the change in a controlled environment. It can help the organization avoid instituting a large-scale change that may fail. This trial period on a limited basis reduces the costs of a failure. It also allows the organization to work out the problems in a change before it is widely adopted. Indeed, GF's use of a participative change strategy was initially begun as an experiment in its Topeka plant. Top-level management at GF had the foresight not to initiate such a drastic change organization-wide.

Suppose, for example, an organization decides to institute a new performance appraisal and development system substantially different from the present system. Since performance appraisal is a very sensitive issue in most organizations, it would be wise to institute this on a limited basis in one department or division of the organization. This experimentation, if carefully monitored, would indicate to the organization the likelihood that the proposed system would work throughout the organization. In choosing the unit for experimentation, however, the organization must be careful to select one that is representative of the rest of the organization. Choosing the largest or smallest unit, or the most progressive or conservative unit, may lead to an incorrect conclusion as to how well the change could be implemented throughout the organization.

The experiment should be thoroughly evaluated in as systematic, objective a fashion as possible. A date should be established for completing the evaluation so that it does not drag on. It is important in this phase to evaluate two areas: (1) the technical or performance output brought about by the change and (2) the attitude of the people involved in the change. We want to know whether the change has affected performance, and we want to know how people feel about the change.

In our performance appraisal process, we might find that the forms and system we designed do seem to work. That is, they do serve as a basis for making rewards on an objective basis, for improving job performance, and for developing training and development programs for employees. However, we may find out that most of the employees find some aspects of the process disagreeable. Perhaps they dislike the face-to-face interview required, or they find the time constraints too tight, or feel that the appeals process is unfair. Therefore, we should be concerned about dealing with these objections in order to make sure that the system remains effective in the future.

After the evaluation, steps should be taken to readjust the planned change (if needed), and the change should be implemented in the rest of the organization. The experience with the change when it was experimentally implemented will serve as the basis for readjustment and full implementation. Of course, this full implementation should be carefully monitored and evaluated to see that the original change goals are being met.

Finally, if all has gone well, the members in the organization affected by the change should become so familiar with it that a refreezing of behavior takes place. That is, the change now becomes part of the daily routine and is no longer viewed as something new and unusual. The process does not end here because this new behavior brought about by the change may cause internal or external stress that, in turn, can cause additional change. Thus, the cycle can repeat itself.

The change process is not as neat as we have indicated in this model. Often, it is not easy to separate one step from another when implementing or observing change in the real world. However, this model should give managers some framework by which to analyze change, and it should help managers to better identify the critical variables in dealing with change.

CHANGES IN THE MACRO ENVIRONMENT

Let us briefly revisit the sources of change. In particular, we need to focus on change as it occurs in the macro environment. Macro environmental change has a direct bearing on internal organization change. In Chapter 3 we examined the macro environment and briefly discussed some of the changes occurring in it. We do not repeat this examination here but do present a model for understanding the development of macro environmental change.

Since the mid-1970s there has been a drift to the right on the political spectrum. In 1980 and 1984 we elected Ronald Reagan, a conservative Republican, as president. And although the Republicans no longer control the Senate, they did for many years of the Reagan administration. The Supreme Court has seen the appointment of three conservative Justices, and the possibility of a fourth, during the Reagan years. Tensions in Central America and the Middle East and the rise of terrorism have added to the renewed interest in a strong military. A rekindling of the cold war with the Soviets in the early 1980s may be tempered somewhat by Gorbachev's new policy of *glasnost* and the Soviets' seeming willingness to negotiate an arms treaty. On the economic front, worries over the budget deficit and the balance of trade are on the minds of all U.S. businesspeople. What do the 1990s hold? Of course, no one knows, but political, social, and economic changes will have profound effects on organizations. As you can see, planning for one decade is not enough; an organization must constantly be taking the pulse of its dynamic macro environment if it hopes to succeed.

Causes of Environmental Change

Were the above-mentioned issues in the 1970s and 1980s the causes of environmental change or the results of it? This is difficult to answer. Social change arises because of tensions in the social fabric of a society. These tensions or stresses, however, are not enough to bring about the change. One way to view social change is to look at it from a social-movement standpoint. Much social change results from social movements. *Social movements* are organized actions to establish a new order of life. For example, the civil rights struggle, feminism, consumerism, and the antiwar, antibusing, and antiabortion efforts all can be viewed as social movements undertaken to change some aspect of society.

Smelser presents us with a model to analyze a social movement and the social change that results from it.[12] This model is summarized in Figure 16.3. The first requirement for social change is *structural conduciveness*. There are structural characteristics of society that permit

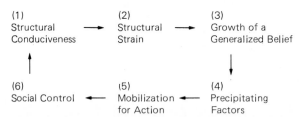

FIGURE 16.3

Smelser's Model of a Social Movement

Source: Adapted from Neil J. Smelser, *Theory of Collective Behavior* (New York: The Free Press, 1962).

or encourage episodes of collective behavior. In our society these include freedom of speech and the press, political action, lobbying, and freedom of assembly. Without this conduciveness, it would be difficult for people of similar persuasion to get together to work for change.

The second step is *structural strain*, which results from impairments of the relations among parts of a social system. These strains create demands to readjust the social situation. Such strains might be high levels of unemployment, poverty, deprivation, value inconsistencies, unpopular laws or court decisions, rising crime, or any other major issue.

For a social movement to begin, this strain must result in the third factor, a *generalized belief*. People must feel that they can do something about the strain. These beliefs activate people to participate in episodes of collective behavior. The beliefs identify the source of strain, attribute certain characteristics to the source, and specify responses to the strain as possible or appropriate. They provide a rallying cry for the movement. Some popular beliefs are equality, free enterprise, integration, education for all, peace, and individual freedom from government harassment.

The fourth stage is the occurrence of *precipitating factors*. These are events that create, sharpen, or exaggerate a condition of strain or conduciveness. They are the "straw that breaks the camel's back," and they set collective behavior in action. Some examples of such factors are court-ordered busing, a rapid increase in the price of a basic commodity such as meat or gasoline, the arrest or assassination of a popular group leader, or an attack or rebuff directed toward the group. These precipitating factors move the group to action.

In the fifth step this action becomes organized under the direction of a set of leaders. This *mobilization for action* brings the affected group into action. A structure and continuity to coordinate and guide the group are developed. Often a well-known person, such as Ralph Nader, Jerry Falwell, Lee Iacocca, or Edward Kennedy, will lend his or her name to the group and serve as a rallying point for leadership.

The final stage in the process is the resultant *social control* developed to deal with the change. At this stage the power groups in society (e.g., businesspeople, the courts, or government bodies) take action to implement, deflect, or inhibit change. It is in this stage that the change either becomes institutionalized or disappears from its former prominence. For example, the change may result in the passage of a new law or in some action that would be taken to prohibit the desired change from occurring, such as social ostracism or imprisonment of the movement's leadership.

Not all social change results from the activities of social movements. Changes in technology, for example, are almost completely institutionalized in U.S. society. Galbraith refers to the "technocrats" whose job it is to create and control knowledge for use by organizations.[13] The federal government funds much basic technological research through grants by the National Science Foundation and military and aerospace contracts. This kind of social change is best viewed as planned or controlled change because the change process itself is institutionalized in the society, although the change itself often has some unforeseen consequences.

Some social movements of the past have resulted in institutionalization of change. The development of unions and the general acceptance of collective bargaining in society have institutionalized much change fought for in the worker movements of the United States. Women's voting rights are the result of the suffrage movement, and many changes now advocated for women take place through existing political processes.

Other changes that take place in the macro environment come about not because of internal social movements or institutionalized changes, but because of political and economic actions of other countries. The oil cartel established by the OPEC nations in 1974 had a major impact on the U.S. economic and political systems because of the high oil prices that were established. The Soviet Union's massive wheat purchases in the mid-1970s directly benefited the farmer and food processors in the United States and led to further developments in detente. They also led to increased food prices for U.S. consumers. The terrorism sponsored by Libya in the mid-1980s caused a strong military action by the United States in bombing Libya, and a heightened sense of patriotism resulted.

These changes required much organizational adjustment such as the shifting of sources of energy to coal and the redesigning of products to make them more energy efficient. Changes that occur in other societies often cause social movements and organizational change in the United States. The Vietnam antiwar movement would not have occurred had there not been a civil war in Vietnam that ultimately led to U.S. involvement. Increasing protest to apartheid in South Africa has resulted in many U.S. companies divesting their holdings there. So, changes in other countries can have a direct impact on organizations in the United States or they can have an indirect impact by spawning social movements.

ORGANIZATIONAL CHANGE

In the previous section, we reviewed the causes of environmental change using Smelser's social movement model. In this section we examine the organizational change process. In Chapters 4 through 7, we examined how organizations interface and cope with their environment. We continue that discussion here by relating this change to the internal organization processes we examined in Chapters 8 through 15. In particular, we examine what organizations do to ensure that their internal processes are in tune with the environment.

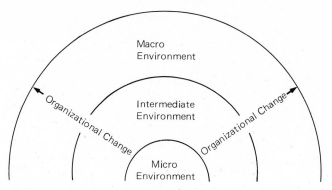

FIGURE 16.4

Organizational Renewal and Change and the Organization's Environments

In other words, we attempt to show what organizations do to ensure that their internal processes are consistent with environmental demands and conditions. Figure 16.4 shows the outward reach of the organization as it attempts to renew and change to keep in harmony with its outside environment.

Change and the Organization's Life Cycle

Because the outside environment is the source of life for an organization, we discuss the concept of the organization life cycle. The life cycle of an organization shows how the organization is dependent on the outside environment as it goes through its life-cycle stages.

Organizations are born, grow, mature, and die, as do all biological and social systems. The life cycle of an organization can be depicted as a series of five major stages: birth, growth, maturity, deterioration, and death.[14] Figure 16.5 depicts the life cycle for an organization. The curve is merely illustrative. Some organizations grow at faster rates and some at slower rates; others decline more rapidly or more slowly than those depicted. Note that the graph depicts growth as measured by total sales units produced, or number of employees for a time period (months, quarters, or years). Also note that as organizations die they usually do not have low total dollar sales, budgets, or outputs during their last years of life; they may still have high sales, budgets, and outputs even though the rates of growth in these items have begun to decline. However, at some point, organizations begin to lose their effectiveness and eventually deteriorate and die.

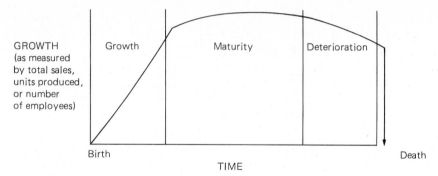

FIGURE 16.5
An Organization's Life Cycle*

BIRTH. An organization is born when a group of people get together for some common purpose. Generally, a mission or purpose exists on a consensus basis. Jobs are determined and assigned to people. Generally, there is much excitement with the new venture. The organization is quite informal. Usually there are no organization charts, written policies, or formal, written job descriptions. Much interaction is on a daily face-to-face basis. People know each other personally. They may even be good friends. We saw this situation occur in Chapter 11 where we showed how Celestial Seasonings began as a small enterprise among two friends who decided that collecting herbs and making tea was a "neat" way to make some extra money.

A hierarchy develops as operatives and top management are formed. Eventually a level of middle management forms. Even though this takes place, the style of management is usually informal, almost casual. In fact, managers and supervisors often do nonmanagerial work, helping out employees in this new exciting venture.

Usually the entrepreneurial role is strong at this stage. There is a dominant personality or two who have the vision and capital and are willing to risk it on the new venture. At this stage the organization is very much affected by the personalities of one or two key people.

When Holiday Inn first started out in the early 1950s, three dominant personalities controlled the fledgling organization: Kemmons Wilson, the founder; Wallace Johnson, his partner; and William Walton, the executive vice president. Even when the company had 100 franchises in 1959, the Holiday Inn organization could still be characterized as informal, with Wilson, Johnson, and Walton firmly in charge of all aspects.[15] This

---

*This concept is borrowed from the product life cycle concept developed in marketing.

feeling of family began to change, however, when the organization moved into the growth stage of the organizational life cycle.

GROWTH. The second stage occurs when the organization experiences its strongest growth. Increases of sales and profits in the hundreds of percent annually are not uncommon. Apple Computers in the late 1970s and early 1980s demonstrated this tremendous growth.

New people are hired, new products and services developed, and new markets cultivated. The dominant personalities involved begin to play a less important role. The face-to-face daily communication among all organization members begins to subside. The organization becomes more formalized and substitutes written policies and a formal hierarchy for the informal consensus once achieved through face-to-face interaction.

People begin to feel depersonalized as the organization gets larger and they become one of many faces. New jobs are constantly being created and role definition as well as role relationships become a problem. Consensus on goals or basic purpose may deteriorate as products, services, and markets proliferate.

Let us refer again to the Holiday Inn saga to show a real-life example of this stage. During the 1960s and early 1970s, Holiday Inn experienced tremendous growth. By 1969, there were over 1,100 franchises.[16] In addition, the company decided to diversify through the acquisition of a bus line, an ocean freighter, a campground chain, a meatpacking plant, and so on. As the organization grew and expanded into other areas, the managerial ranks correspondingly grew. Although Chairman of the Board and founder Wilson would still "get ideas," he would turn these over to his staff for development and implementation.

MATURITY. At maturity, growth begins to slow. There is usually some year-to-year growth but on a far less percentage basis than previously. The key task at this stage is to maintain viability. New products, services, and markets begin to become exhausted. The organization often becomes stale. The institutionalization process that began during the growth stage now threatens to harden into a rigid bureaucracy and strangle the organization. It is in this stage that the organization looks for other organizations to acquire in order to keep expanding.

By this stage the organization has developed a culture; that is, it has a tradition, a well-established way of doing things. There are values held dearly by the company. Norms or standards of behavior are usually both explicit (written) and implicit (generally understood).

Too strong a tie to tradition and existing culture can kill an organization. Maintaining viability is a very real challenge. Many organizations are able to stay in the maturity phase for years and years, experiencing some ups and downs along the way.

By the mid-1970s, Holiday Inn was at this stage. When OPEC turned off the spigot in 1973, thus curtailing travel, Holiday's profits dropped 78 percent, and its stock price dropped 90 percent.[17] Moreover, a host of competitors, such as Ramada, began to offer travelers new services and decor that far surpassed those offered at Holiday Inn. As consumers became more sophisticated and widely traveled, Holiday Inn did not change to meet their needs and expectations. Michael D. Rose, then head of the conglomerate's hotel division, noted, "The first generation of management was behind in the shift of the marketplace. They didn't see the need for a quality product."[18]

DETERIORATION. Eventually the organization begins to have trouble coping. Key people leave; markets and products no longer match; the reason why the organization formed no longer appears to fit the marketplace. The organization has trouble shifting gears to entirely new products and markets. Tradition appears to rule everything. People are valued for their time of service, not their ideas or performance. New people and new ideas are usually resisted.

The organization begins a process of withdrawal. A cocoon is formed to protect the organization from the now-threatening outside environment. Competitors with fresh ideas and products attack the organization. The organization attempts to fight back, not by developing new products but by trying to seal itself off from adverse consequences of the environment.

Within the lodging industry from the late 1970s through 1987, the consumer "inn" market thoroughly splintered, and, thus, specialty inns were developed by Holiday's competitors. It was Days-Inn for the budget-minded and Hyatt Regency for the upscale, thus leaving Holiday Inn squirming in the shrinking middle market. At Holiday, occupancy rates fell from 80 percent to 62.2 percent within a ten-year period.[19] This was a heavy price to pay for ignoring environmental developments.

Sometimes an organization is able to pull out of this stage through one of two means. First, the governing board can appoint a new top management group and give it a strong hand to clean house and redirect the organization. Holiday Inn opted for this approach. More professional managers, experienced in marketing strategies, were brought into the organization. The original founders and executives either retired or were bought out. Roy Weingarden, former vice chairman of the board, became chairman, and Michael D. Rose, former head of the hotel division, became president. They shed the Holiday conglomerate's less successful operations, sold unprofitable properties, ordered franchisees to "spruce up," and even entered the gambling business through Holiday's acquisition of Harrah's Casino in Atlantic City, New Jersey. In 1987, the Holiday Inn organization was still the world's largest lodging chain; however, it is not yet finished with the change process that will enable it to leave the deterioration stage of the organizational life cycle.

Second, the organization can make itself available as a merger candidate. A growing or mature organization may try to absorb the deteriorating one because it (the deteriorating one) has resources—plants, equipment, patents—that the growing one needs.

Either of these two methods can pull an organization out of its tailspin. Sometimes the deterioration phase exists for several years, and then the organization dies or rebounds, as did Chrysler Corporation. Sometimes it is only a matter of weeks, as it was with Air Florida when it filed for bankruptcy in 1984.

DEATH. At some point, an organization ceases to play a viable role in society. Deterioration progresses to the point of no return. Entropy is achieved as more energy is expended than is taken in. The organization uses itself up and burns itself out. It can no longer regenerate.

Not all organizations actually die in the sense that they cease to exist altogether. They may continue to exist but in a substantially different form. They may be merged or consolidated with a larger organization. The programs and services of a government unit may be combined with those of another. A new organization arrangement that takes over the products and services of a wide variety of different organizations might be established. In each of these cases, the original organization is said to have ceased to exist when the resultant organization is completely different from the original in terms of personnel, functions, outputs, and name.

One may suggest at this point that all organizations change through time. Major change through time is not a sufficient condition to indicate that the original organization has died. If the organization is still performing substantially the same functions and producing the same output, it still exists even though the people who made up the original organization are no longer there.

Another way to assess the death of an organization is to look at its legal status. A corporation, partnership, or sole proprietorship may cease to exist because it no longer exists as a legal entity. Southern Airways ceased to exist when it became part of Republic Airlines. People Express Airlines ceased to exist after being subsumed in Texas Air.

One final note on Figure 16.5—the maturity phase for an organization often is its longest phase. It is during this phase that the organization grows very slowly from year to year and is relatively stable. This period is also interspersed with spurts of growth and short periods of decline. For some organizations in the maturity phase, it may appear that they will last forever. However, they will eventually begin to deteriorate and finally die. We make the assumption at this point in the text that all organizations die. Later in the chapter we relax this assumption when we discuss the process of organization development.

Catastrophe Theory and Organization Death

A recent theoretical development in mathematics called *catastrophe theory* can help us understand the death stage in the life cycle.[20] It rests on the idea that continuously changing forces produce discontinuous effects. René Thom, the initial researcher in this area, labeled the theory "catastrophe" to emphasize the unexpected events that can come about as usually continuous causes produce discontinuous effects.[21] The writings of Drucker (*The Age of Discontinuity*) and Toffler (*Future Shock*) are popular versions of this theory, though without the rigorous analysis and mathematics. (Neither Drucker nor Toffler labeled their ideas catastrophe theory.)

Many common expressions reflect our intuitive belief in catastrophe theory. For example, "the straw that breaks the camel's back" and "reaching the end of one's rope" reflect the idea of a key precipitating factor occurring during normal change that causes a major unexpected change.

Firestone Tire and Rubber Company came very close to organizational death in 1979 because of a single catastrophe, the recall of *9 million* of its 500-model steel-belted radial tires due to defects. Although Firestone has managed to survive, it did so by closing nine of its seventeen plants and by slashing its work force from 107,000 employees to 55,000.[22]

Frequently catastrophe theory addresses the issue of death. For example, it has been brought to bear on endangered species and endangered institutions. Figure 16.6 shows catastrophe theory applied to an endangered species. At some point if the resources decrease beyond an initial threshold P, the population will collapse until the species reaches an endangered state, where it may be threatened by extinction. This is shown by the upper line in Figure 16.6. Note that it takes considerably more resources, represented by point Q, to rescue an endangered species than to maintain a viable one. Points P and Q are called *catastrophes* or *catastrophic jumps*.

The variation of catastrophe theory that is used to analyze organizations is called *cusp catastrophe*. The use of this technique results in a three-dimensional graph, considerably more complex than that shown in Figure 16.6, which for our purposes need not be reproduced here. Using this approach in studying organizations, we can measure the quality of a product or service provided by an organization. As the resources of the organization are cut, the quality will fall only slightly up to some point. However, if the cuts are too deep or too long, so great a loss of staff and other support services occurs that quality may suddenly collapse unex-

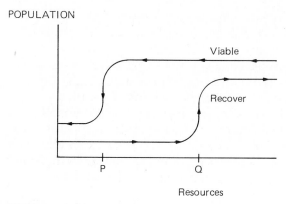

FIGURE 16.6

Catastrophe Theory and an Endangered Species

pectedly. A discontinuous or disproportionate change results from one
additional cut from the budget. The last cut becomes the "straw that
breaks the camel's back."

Catastrophe theory helps us understand why organizations may die
near the height of their sales, budgets, or total employees. Organizations
do not gradually die out; they die quickly as growth begins to decline, as
we saw in the graph in Figure 16.5.

The Organization's Life Cycle and Its Environment

As we discussed above, all organizations experience a life cycle of birth,
growth, maturity, deterioration, and death. As the organization passes
from one stage to the next in this life cycle, it changes. Not only does it
grow and then decline in terms of budget, assets, employees, sales or profits, but the structure, resource mix, and managerial skill mix also change.
Small, new organizations usually begin by serving a small market with a
limited product/service line. The structure and policy of the organization
are usually simple and quite informal. Since there is usually much face-
to-face interaction on a daily basis among employees and managers, there
is little need to issue complex operation and policy manuals. The managerial skills most valued at this stage of organizational growth are innovation and risk taking.

As the organization experiences its rapid growth period, it tends to
become more highly structured and to develop more comprehensive policies and procedures. This is done in order to assure managerial control
during a very dynamic time when many new employees, markets, and

products or services are being added to the organization. Structure often becomes more differentiated as the organization attempts to cope with growth. The managerial skills desired still include innovation but also include basic day-to-day administrative skills. The skills also begin to become more specialized, breaking into production, accounting, finance, marketing, sales, and personnel as the organization differentiates.

The maturity phase places great emphasis on marketing and sales skills as efforts are made to expand markets in order to continue the growth of the previous period. The manager who can consolidate and streamline operations is valued. Structure tends to become more firmly set, and policy may not be as flexible as before as the tenure and age of managers with the organization increase.

The deterioration stage finds the organization losing sales, profits, markets, and employees at a gradual rate. Efforts are made to change structure and policy to better meet the changing needs of the environment. Managers skilled in retrenchment operations and able to move established bureaucrats off their established positions are valued. A redefinition of role and mission of the organization usually occurs. The organization may attempt to adopt new management techniques and systems (e.g., MIS and MBO) to revitalize itself as it attempts to stave off death.

Should the organization be unable to reverse itself, it dies. A caretaker management team disburses the organization's resources back to society, and the organization ceases to exist as an entity. Death may also come through a merger or consolidation, which, while not ending the organization, significantly changes its image, identity, and perhaps even legal status.*

These life-cycle changes are major changes all organizations face. The way in which these changes affect a particular organization, however, is unique to that organization because there are so many different alternative strategies that can be adopted to deal with each of these major changes. Thus, while the thrust of major life-cycle changes occurs in all organizations, the specific types of changes and their effects will vary from organization to organization.

Adizes treats the organizational life cycle in a more complicated way than we do here and points out the role of organizational development at each stage of the organization's life cycle.[23] Using a ten-stage life cycle model of courtship, infancy, go-go, adolescence, prime, maturity, aristocracy, early bureaucracy, bureaucracy, and death, he points out that the unique needs of the organization at each stage require a different treatment. For example, in the go-go stage, the third stage of development, the

---

*A change in legal status could end the existing organization by abolishing it as a distinct legal entity.

organization needs sound, yet flexible, administrative systems to remain healthy. In later stages, such as maturity and aristocracy, the organization needs methods to generate innovative ideas in the organization.

Adizes's model reinforces our systems and contingency approach to organizations. Any effort at organizational development must understand the life-cycle stage of the organization. This holistic approach with relevant identification of inputs, throughputs, and outputs that are to be changed should help ensure the success of the organizational development program undertaken.

The environment provides the lifeblood for the organization by providing a market for its product and services and by serving as a source of resources. Even though we have assumed that all organizations eventually die, many organizations today are undertaking various programs and courses of action to ensure their continued growth and health.

An organization exists to meet a need in the environment. The environment is also the source of the organization's inputs or resources. Thus, to the extent that the environment can be accurately assessed and resources efficiently acquired, the system of linkages an organization establishes with its environment can do much to maintain the organization's health and growth. This system of linkages, which we discussed in Chapter 4, serves as the organization's lifeline with its environment. An organization sufficiently out of tune with its environment will have a difficult time surviving.

The effectiveness of these linkages is critical today. The rapid changes in most environmental sectors, coupled with the increasing heterogeneity found in environmental sectors, make it ever more difficult for an organization to stay in tune with its environment. Yet stay in tune it must if it is to avoid deterioration.

MANAGING ORGANIZATIONAL CHANGE

Much organizational activity in the area of change occurs in the growth and maturity stages. Efforts are undertaken to keep the organization a growing, healthy, viable institution in order to stave off deterioration and death. The material in this section focuses on how managers can implement change to maintain the optimum stage in the life cycle.

How Organizations Cope with External and Internal Change

Managers should try to encourage those external and internal changes that are viewed as best for the organization. While this may seem like a selfish organizational perspective, organizations are expected to act in their own self-interest. This process works if all organizations, acting in their own self-interest, serve as checks and balances on one another. In U.S. society, this works reasonably well most of the time as organizations compete in the marketplaces of ideas, products/services, resources, and causes. Even with large, powerful organizations, countervailing power often exists as large unions are offset by big business, or the federal bureaucracy by politicians and voters. This is known as *pluralism* and consists of a system of checks and balances among large, powerful groups.

The alternative to this pluralistic system is central planning. This may take the form of socialism, in which the government owns and plans the use of factors of production, or of communism, in which the government not only owns the economic resources but also controls society's means of political expression, or of fascism, in which the economic sectors are not controlled by the government but the political ideals are. Some argue that we are approaching a more centralized power system that is different from both pluralism and centralized government authority. Mills refers to the "power elite" whom he views as the real controllers of society.[24] This is a group of people who are heads of our major corporations, government agencies, banks, and universities. They are viewed as a select few who often move from government to business to academics, and really form the ruling class. If this system actually exists, the system of checks and balances is impaired.

However, assuming that organizations do act in their own self-interest in dealing with change and assuming that this is a healthy thing for society, what are some actions that organizations can take? Organizations can do at least one of the following in dealing with change: know and forecast it, initiate it, amplify it, smooth it, buffer it, or stop it.

KNOW AND FORECAST. Using internal and external sensors, organizations observe what change is occurring within the organization and in the organization's macro environment.* This is the first step in the change process, as we explained earlier. Regardless of the strategy taken, this is required to manage change. However, not only must the present change be known but future change must be predicted. We live today for tomorrow. One key ingredient for remaining in tune with the environment in the future is to predict what that future is to be. It is for this reason that so many organizations have added long-range planning and forecasting units. By the same token, forecasting internal change is also required. This also attempts to ensure that internal organizational processes will be in tune with the environment and that needed changes will be properly planned for.

Some argue that it is virtually impossible to plan for change because

---

*We discussed the use of sensors for forecasting change in detail in Chapters 4 and 7.

of the rapid pace and type of change now occurring in society. Toffler speaks of "future shock" and argues that future changes in U.S. society will result in shock for its organizations and people.[25] Drucker writes of the "Age of Discontinuity" and argues that future changes cannot be predicted from past and present trends because they will be of a different form and type.[26] While agreeing that these two authors and others have valid points, we argue that simply giving up is not the proper response to forecasting future changes. Rather, more appropriate and sophisticated forecasting techniques and processes are needed as are greater efforts to shape, guide, and buffer change.

INITIATE. Organizations may find it in their best interest to start change either internally or externally. Management might initiate and implement a new product, compensation system, information system, or performance appraisal system. Managers perceive stress or external and internal opportunities and respond to them with change. They take the initiative and are in control throughout the change process. This is what American Express did through the leadership and actions of its CEO, James Robinson, when he launched his "One Enterprise" strategy, which we discussed in Chapter 14. You will remember that Robinson saw a need for more cooperation and integration between his various business units in order to take advantage of opportunities created by the deregulation of the financial services industry.

The same may happen in the macro environment. Advertising, personal selling, and other promotion methods are change-initiation processes used to get a customer or client to buy the organizational product or service offered. Lobbying for the passage or repeal of a law is also a change-initiating approach to change in that it places the organization in an active rather than a passive or reactionary role with regard to change. It can give management the head start it needs to manage the change. It can place management at an advantage, but it does not guarantee success.

AMPLIFY. Organizations may not choose to initiate a change but, once started, may choose to amplify or encourage it. For example, a group of employees may suggest a cost-saving change in the production process. Management, through suggestion systems or other participative methods, encourages it or amplifies such changes even though it may not initiate them.

By the same token, a powerful client or customer group of the organization may initiate a new product/service warranty idea for the organization that the organization views as a desirable selling tool for its product/service. The organization may encourage the further development of the idea.

One disadvantage of adopting an amplification approach is that hopes and expectations may be raised and then dashed if the organization decides in the end that the proposed change cannot be implemented. Another disadvantage is that the organization may find it difficult to place itself in a controlling position with regard to the change.

As we saw in an earlier discussion in this chapter, these problems associated with amplification occurred in the GF organization as it tried to amplify the changes begun with the implementation of its participation strategy. On one hand, workers felt that management did not really fulfill its promises of delegating decision-making authority down to the lowest level, while on the other, many GF managers felt that, through this experiment, they had lost control over workers and production.

The advantage to this approach is that it can encourage new ideas for change because employees, customers, clients, and others may be willing to suggest change if they feel that such requests are welcome. These can be a rich source of creative ideas for the organization. The 3M Company stressed such an approach in its advertisements of the mid-1980s, and other companies often use such an approach in their campus recruiting advertising.

SMOOTH. Here the organization attempts to protect its technical core by controlling the rate or effects of change by reducing its variations. Inventories, whether they be raw material, in-process, or final product in the warehouse, are devices to protect the technical core from changes in supplier capabilities and deliveries, breakdowns in the production line, and variations in customer ordering. Such smoothing allows the organization to plan better and to deal with change by reducing uncertainty caused by fluctuations.

After Maytag purchased Magic Chef in 1986, this new, much larger organization was faced with the potential problem of having too bloated an inventory of major home appliances. Therefore, Maytag protected itself by smoothing, for example, by offering volume deals for a full line of products to large groups of major appliance dealers.

The disadvantage to this approach is that it can result in discouraging change that should be initiated or amplified. An organization may, in attempting to smooth change, discourage change that should be made. Organizations do this when they become fearful that change may overwhelm their technical core. The key to smoothing is to ensure that such smoothing is selective and does not smooth or postpone urgently needed change.

BUFFER. Similar advantages and disadvantages exist for buffering change. Buffering change is an attempt to place padding around decision-authority centers or the technical core so that the change is filtered or softened before it hits the center or core. This sometimes is done to isolate the center from bad news in order not to upset it. It may also be done in order to give the center or core a chance to prepare a plan for dealing with the change.

One additional disadvantage is that buffering can isolate the center or core from change, resulting in being shut off from reality. This was certainly the case at Puma AG, the German athletic shoe manufacturer. In 1986, Puma sales dropped from $443.6 million to $388 million.[27] This occurred because the organization's technical core and decision makers were isolated from the customer/client component of the macro environment, particularly within the United States. The reason for this isolation can be attributed to Puma's system of having independent, licensed distributors sell its products, while its main competition, Addidas, had direct control of its distribution rights. Therefore, Addidas decision makers were not buffered from information concerning changing consumer tastes in athletic shoes.

STOP. Organizations often choose to stop change if they perceive it as detrimental to their interests. Stopping change can take several forms. A climate that discourages internal change can be developed. Those who are viewed as "boat rockers" or "wave makers" are penalized or released from the organization. A more subtle form of stopping internal change involves initially encouraging change and then consistently finding ways to prevent its implementation.

At the macro level, organizations often lobby or advertise against certain changes. They may also initiate alternative courses of action to displace the suggested change. Or the change may be postponed in hopes that it will eventually die. This has been the tactic of the auto companies in attempting to prevent the implementation of the final stages of emission control standards mandated by Congress since 1977.

A Philosophy on Innovation

A key ingredient in managing organizational change and in achieving organization renaissance is the development of a managerial philosophy on innovation.[28] *Innovation* is the development and implementation of new processes or procedures that are substantially different from existing ones. Innovation implies a breakthrough in technological development or application. It also implies a change that has come about because of creativity, the putting together of ideas and concepts in a new way. It differs from simple change in implying that it results in something that has not been done or tried before, either within the particular organization or in other organizations. It is a new and fresh way to deal creatively with a problem or an issue.

In developing a philosophy on innovation, managers decide whether to encourage or discourage it; they form a clear understanding of the role of innovation and how to implement it. Too often managers in organizations do not develop such a philosophy and state it explicitly. Rather, one can only infer an implied philosophy based on behavior one observes in the organization.

Why is innovation important? It is important because it helps us get at the core issue of what exactly is change. If an organization adopts an MBO system, it is instituting a change, but it is not being innovative. MBO has been around for several years and is being used by hundreds of government and business organizations. So, even though it may be viewed as a change by the managers in that particular organization, it is not an innovative one. When managers decide what their philosophy on innovation is, they make a commitment to the type of change they wish to achieve.

VALUE APPROACHES TO INNOVATION. If the organization defines its role and mission as being a leader in the industry, it must have a philosophy of innovation that encourages creativity, open discussion of new ideas, development of technology, and research and inquiry. Such an organization will want to initiate and amplify change. It will want to have good internal and external sensors operating under an action-adaptation environmental strategy in order to receive and analyze important internal and external information. The reward system will encourage the "wave makers" and "boat rockers."

The Lotus Development Corporation exemplifies an innovative organization. It spends heavily on research and development in order to diversify its array of software products, has replaced many of its former top managers with individuals knowledgeable in the management of innovation, and keeps its sensor mechanisms alert and open to the demands of the marketplace as well as to technological opportunities.

Obviously, many organizations decide to be followers rather than leaders. Their position on innovation is much different from that described above. When change is adopted, it is change that has been developed and tested somewhere else and has proved successful. Organizations adopt this approach for several reasons. First, these organizations are low risk takers or even risk avoiders. Perhaps because they fear failure or lack resources to predict consequences of change, they want to adopt only proven changes. Something new and untried is too risky. To them, "nothing ventured, nothing gained" becomes "nothing ventured, nothing lost." Managers in these organizations may also find innovation threatening. They may question their and the organization's ability to cope with innovations, even fearing them because they see them not as an opportunity but as a threat. They may also have high anxiety levels because they are unable to cope with uncertainty and ambiguity. Innovation, because it results from new and untested arrangements of concepts, often produces ambiguous situations in which there are few "yes" and "no" answers and many "maybes."

By 1985, Texas Instruments, a former leader in innovation, had become a follower. Although Texas Instruments accelerated the computer age by perfecting the mass production of transistors thirty years ago, most of its products in recent years have been improvements of old inventions rather than the breakthroughs that characterized earlier strategic decisions that were firmly made.

Some managers and organizations do not seek the status that being known as an innovator can provide. Rather, they prefer to achieve status through other means—perhaps by consolidating existing power or by being regarded as a stabilizing influence in the community.

Finally, some organizations and managers are *stimulus avoiders*. They prefer a stable environment and fear stimulus "overload" or stimulus "addiction," which they may think results from high levels of innovation.

While these are some reasons why innovation may not be actively encouraged by the organization, the organization may have little choice in the matter. If the organization faces a dynamic, heterogeneous environment, the only way it may be able to cope and adapt to this environment is through innovation. Unable to innovate, the organization may soon deteriorate and die as it finds that past tried-and-true methods are no longer appropriate for future environmental opportunities and constraints.

CHANGE AND ORGANIZATION DEVELOPMENT

Organization development (OD) is the process whereby organizations attempt to improve and renew themselves. OD usually includes critical examinations of organization goals, work systems, strategies, policies, procedures, work group behavior, and structure. It also includes executive, management, professional, supervisory, and technical training and development. Often, outside consultants are brought into the organization to assist with the OD process and any training that might be involved. The goal of OD is to improve the functioning of the organization and of its managers and employees. It is planned renewal and development of the organization initiated by top decision-authority centers.

OD programs are becoming increasingly common, yet their components vary. For some organizations, OD is simply training and development. For others, it is a series of weekend executive retreats scheduled periodically for critical evaluation and renewal. For still others, it is a comprehensive program focusing on all aspects of organizational life and functioning. Figure 16.7 shows the various OD approaches that can be used to bring about planned change. Notice that some OD interventions

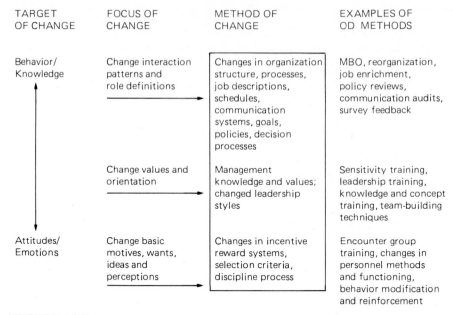

TARGET OF CHANGE	FOCUS OF CHANGE	METHOD OF CHANGE	EXAMPLES OF OD METHODS
Behavior/ Knowledge	Change interaction patterns and role definitions	Changes in organization structure, processes, job descriptions, schedules, communication systems, goals, policies, decision processes	MBO, reorganization, job enrichment, policy reviews, communication audits, survey feedback
	Change values and orientation	Management knowledge and values; changed leadership styles	Sensitivity training, leadership training, knowledge and concept training, team-building techniques
Attitudes/ Emotions	Change basic motives, wants, ideas and perceptions	Changes in incentive reward systems, selection criteria, discipline process	Encounter group training, changes in personnel methods and functioning, behavior modification and reinforcement

FIGURE 16.7

Some OD Approaches to Bring about Planned Change

Source: Adapted from P. Lawrence and J. Lorsch, *Developing Organizations* (Reading, Mass.: Addison-Wesley, 1969), 87.

focus on knowledge and behavior, while those at the bottom of the chart focus on attitudes and emotions.

The Organization Audit

A rather new development in OD programs is the organization audit. The purpose of this audit is to assess the present strengths and weaknesses of the organization. The goal is to determine where the organization is at a point in time so that an OD program can be built that capitalizes on the organization's strengths and overcomes the organization's weaknesses. The audit is the first step to building a sound OD program.

A typical audit would attempt to answer the following questions:

1. What operations of this organization seem to be most effective and efficient?
2. What operations are having problems?
3. Why do the problems exist?

4. What are the reasons some operations are so much more effective than others?
5. What are the most important assets of this organization (e.g., markets, name and reputation, land, key personnel, R & D)?

In answering these questions, the organization would need information on the following types of items:

1. The extent to which organization objectives are being met
2. Market share vis-à-vis competitors' shares and the organization's competitive advantage
3. Current and projected availability of key resources
4. Financial and accounting information including key ratios, costs, sales, and profit
5. Personnel utilization plans
6. Previous performance appraisals of personnel
7. Market research information
8. State of R & D in the organization

Managing Organization Development—Some OD Strategies

The literature is replete with articles explaining and expounding various OD techniques. In this section, we do not try to fully evaluate or even explain the many OD techniques in existence. Rather, we will highlight some of the more popular techniques.[*]

We take the approach of examining OD techniques based on the breadth of their focus. As shown in Figure 16.8, the initial focus on OD was on changing the individual and his or her relationship to a small group. Much of this came out of the National Training Laboratory group in Bethel, Maine. Clinical psychologists had a major impact on the development of OD, and many OD methods that focus on the individual are still heavily influenced by work done by clinical psychologists.

As time went on, the focus of OD expanded to include other group relationships within the organization (Level 2, Figure 16.8). Here the focus is on how to help one group work better with other groups. Social psychologists and their studies on group behavior had a major impact on OD techniques that focus on this level.

More recently, OD methods have looked at the organization as a

[*]Readers interested in a thorough discussion of the advantages and disadvantages of OD programs are referred to A. A. Armenakis, et al., "Research Issues in OD Evaluation: Past, Present, and Future," *Academy of Management Review* 8, no. 2 (April 1983): 320–328; and P. Hurley, "What in the Name of OD Do We Do?" *Training Development Journal* 37 (April 1983): 42–48.

FIGURE 16.8

The Broadening Scope of OD

whole (Level 3). What can be done to make the entire organization operate more effectively and efficiently? How can major organizational units
be integrated more effectively? Organizational sociologists and management professors and consultants have had a major impact on OD techniques at this level.

Finally, a fourth level of focus is developing in organizational development that looks at the organization and its relationship with other organizations in the environment. Some OD specialists might argue that
this is not the province of OD. Certainly, it is not the province of traditional OD approaches, but organizational sociologists and management
professors with a specialty in organization development have learned
that very often it is difficult to change and improve an organization unless interorganizational relationships are improved. For example, perhaps an organization needs to improve its relationship with its dealers or
suppliers in order to become more effective or efficient. Or perhaps the
organization needs to deal better with shareholders, government agencies, or major customers. If this is the case, then OD efforts should be focused on bringing about the change to improve these relationships. Or
perhaps the organization should merge with another organization to improve its position and strength in the market. OD efforts aimed at bringing about the attitude and behavior changes necessary to consummate a
merger would be appropriate.

Because Level 4 is an emerging level, there are few OD techniques available that focus specifically on interorganizational change. But there are techniques that examine the other levels of OD, some of which are described below.

INTERVENTIONS DIRECTED TOWARD INDIVIDUAL NEEDS AND ATTITUDES. Some of the earliest efforts in OD focused on individual attitudes, behavior, and beliefs. The basic purpose of these techniques is to attempt to change individual attitudes, behavior, and beliefs. Various methods are used, usually in conjunction with outside consultants and training experts. Most of these methods can be grouped under the title "laboratory training" since the change is attempted in an artificial or laboratory situation away from the job.

The most popular form of this laboratory training is called *sensitivity* or *"T"* (for training) *group training*. In this method, trainees are encouraged to become sensitive to their own and group member attitudes and beliefs. The idea is to recognize the biases, prejudices, and mistaken beliefs we all have and to try to change them. The group is used as a medium to bring about this change. Heavy group criticisms of each other's attitudes is supposed to result in a dropping of perceptual barriers. Through group suggestion and examination, new attitudes are then formed that are devoid of prior biases and prejudices. Because of the heavy emotional atmosphere and the use of the group in the method, it is also referred to as *encounter group training*.

Critics argue that there is little empirical evidence that what is learned in the laboratory is useful in the organization. That is, little transfer of training takes place. Furthermore, there is a risk that the technique itself threatens the mental health of some who participate in the experiments. But most important, critics indicate that sensitive, open, and trusting behavior may be unproductive in some organizations and can even result in people becoming suspicious, uncomfortable, and hostile toward the newly learned attitudes and behavior of recent graduates of sensitivity training classes.[29]

Proponents of sensitivity training readily admit the need for more systematic evaluation of laboratory methods in bringing about organization effectiveness. They indicate that most of the criticisms of the method result because of some inexperienced and incompetent people and consulting organizations who call themselves sensitivity training consultants when they are not. In the hands of an unskilled group leader, the process can fail miserably. Furthermore, these critics recognize that the value of the technique must be consistent with the values of the organization.

KNOWLEDGE AND CONCEPT TRAINING. This popular and integral part of OD focuses on improving the knowledge of individuals in organizations. Through classroom training, either in-house or at an off-organization site (often a university), training participants are exposed to a wide variety of topics in management, professional, and technical areas. These programs are usually conducted in a traditional classroom setting and primarily rely on a lecture-discussion format although case analysis, role playing, films, and group exercises are often used.

The programs are usually entitled something like "Executive Management," "Supervisory Management," "Engineering Development," or "New Trends in Accounting." Their focus is not on the interpersonal skills and attitudes emphasized in laboratory training but on the knowledge and concepts individuals need to perform their jobs better. The participant may be given an opportunity to practice some of these concepts and, hence, the skills involved, in role playing and case analyses sessions; however, the major thrust of the program is to impart concepts and knowledge. Some specific applications include Zenith Corporation's teaching the features of its color televisions to its wholesale sales representatives; Pfizer Laboratories' teaching its sales personnel the medical background of pharmaceuticals sold to doctors; and AT&T's training its telephone repair clerks how to deal effectively with customers.

This technique for OD has a major advantage in that it is widely accepted by members of organizations. The need for continual updating of knowledge in order to remain effective is a very popular idea. Another advantage is that there are many organizations that have the resources to specialize in this type of effort. These include consulting and training organizations such as the American Management Associations (AMA) as well as colleges and universities. In addition, many organizations have added their own in-organization trainers who instruct in these areas.

Its most serious disadvantage is the blockage of training transfer that often occurs between the classroom and the job. Achieving the linkage between the concepts learned in a training session and the practice of these concepts back on the job can be difficult. Another disadvantage is that training is often used as a reward for good effort and is not necessarily tied to a career development plan for an individual. Instead of an individual receiving a raise or promotion (because none are available), he or she may be sent to a three-day training program sponsored by AMA in New York. No effort is made to determine if the individual really needs the training.

Still, knowledge and concept training is an efficient way to impart a large amount of knowledge to individuals, and it is done on the premise that some of it is bound to "take" and thus will improve individual and organizational performance.

On-the-job training (OJT) can help overcome the blockage-of-training problem experienced in both knowledge and laboratory training.

Under this approach to OD, the individual is provided the knowledge, concepts, and skills needed to do the job while at the job site. The individual may work alongside an expert performer of the job, such as in an apprentice-journeyman relationship, or he or she may be periodically instructed by a superior on how the job should be performed. The individual also may practice the job in a training facility under the guidance of a competent trainer. The major assumption is that the person learns by doing and is guided in his or her efforts by someone in the organization.

OJT is a very popular form of training. It was first used to train individuals for semiskilled and skilled factory positions, but it is now being used for management, engineering, accounting, and sales trainees in organizations. Its major advantage is that it overcomes the blockage-of-transfer problem. Its most serious disadvantage is that it can provide trainees with a narrow range of skills and knowledge applicable only to one specific job and will not serve the individual well if he or she is promoted or moves to another organization. Thus, such training can become merely orientation to a specific job in a specific company. However, this disadvantage can be overcome if OJT is combined with episodes of classroom and laboratory training, and if it is tied to the individual's career plan so that additional OJT and classroom training are provided as the individual moves up the career ladder.

INTERGROUP TECHNIQUES. These techniques try to improve the interaction among groups that make up the various organization subsystems. One such technique, developed by Blake, Shepard, and Mouton, brings together the leaders of two or more related groups and attempts to get a commitment from them to try to improve their relationship.[30] Once the commitment is achieved, each group independently develops a list of likes and dislikes about the other group and a list that attempts to anticipate what the other group(s) will say about them. The leaders of each group then combine these lists into a single list of issues and problems to be resolved. Under the guidance of a trainer, the groups then develop a plan to resolve the issues and assign responsibility for action. Follow-up meetings are scheduled to see that the plans are being carried out.

Another approach attempts to resolve the conflict that results in organizations among groups that perform highly differentiated tasks.[31] Working with a consultant, the groups attempt to identify and resolve conflict that results from the way in which they are structured, their orientation toward the task, their time orientation (short or long), and the degree to which they focus on goals. Ways are developed to integrate the activities of related units by developing unit managers with broad perspectives, who rely heavily on open confrontation.

TEAM BUILDING. Partly in response to the criticism and shortcomings of sensitivity training, some behavioral scientists have turned to the notion of trying to increase organizational effectiveness by training with teams in laboratory settings.[32] Such work teams might include a middle manager, several first-line supervisors who report to the middle manager, and perhaps a few rank-and-file employees who work for one or more of the supervisors. The training group is often called a "family group" to connote these on-the-job relationships. The subject matter of the training class focuses on the group's day-to-day interaction with each other. This often includes their formal and informal communication patterns, what roles the members see themselves playing in the group, how the group makes decisions about goals and problem solving, and how effective the leadership processes are.

There are many team development strategies, but most efforts rely on an approach where the trainer first puts the group through exercises designed to diagnose problems in communication, leadership, decision making, or other group interactive processes. Once these problem areas have been identified, the trainer attempts to create a situation in the group that provides members with quick and accurate feedback about how their interpersonal behavior may be the source of the identified problems. The trainer also explores with the group how they might change their behavior to avoid the problem in the future. Frequently the trainer will provide laboratory situations in which group members can practice new behaviors with the group's encouragement. The trainer may even continue in a consulting role back on the job to assist the team and individual members in learning to interact in a new way.

As different organizations merge or are acquired, the team building aspect of OD has gained increasing importance. You will remember that in Chapter 14 we discussed the important role played by psychologists in this area when Sperry was acquired by Burroughs. Burroughs CEO Michael Blumenthal hired psychologists to work with managers from the two organizations in order to mold common organizational bonds between the heretofore different management groups.

One advantage of this approach over sensitivity methods is that the subject matter of the class is directly relevant to the job. Group interaction is emphasized over individual attitudes and values. There is also a greater likelihood that the group will reinforce the newly learned behavior back on the job. However, a serious disadvantage with the approach is the loyalty the "family group" members may form to each other rather than to the organization. They may actually form a closed group that excludes outsiders who did not participate in the training. This type of clique formation can destroy the effectiveness of the training.

There has been little systematic evaluation of these intergroup techniques, but, in the hands of a skilled consultant working with a group who wants to improve the integration of their activities, the technique can be successful in identifying and removing roadblocks to effective integration of tasks.

ORGANIZATION-WIDE TECHNIQUES. We discuss two organization-wide techniques: *MBO* and *survey feedback*. Even though we discuss these as organization-wide techniques, they can be used within one division or department. A very popular OD process, MBO, requires managers in organizations to explicitly formulate organization and unit missions, objectives, and plans of action for objective accomplishment, and to allocate resources toward the accomplishment of these objectives. We discussed MBO in Chapter 8 as a system of setting objectives. You should refer to that discussion for a review of the MBO process.

Survey feedback technique relies on attitude surveys that are used to assess various facets of the organization's operations. These surveys are distributed to members of the organization. The data from the survey are compiled and given to first-line management. They evaluate and discuss the data, pinpointing problems and what can be done about them. However, unlike typical morale surveys, the process does not stop here. Under the direction of an in-house or outside trainer, the data from the survey are passed up through the units of the organization where supervisors and subordinates meet in groups to discuss and interpret them. Recommendations are developed for overcoming organizational problems suggested by the data. The data are then passed to the top level of the organization. The role of the trainer in this process is to assist in interpreting the data and to help bring about the desired change.

The advantage of this approach is that it enables the organization to build problem-solving sessions on the basis of systematized attitudinal data that have been collected in the organization. This gives the organization a more objective approach for developing solutions for the perceived problem areas in the organization. The disadvantage to the approach is that there is little empirical evidence that these problem-solving sessions actually result in better decisions or improvements in individual and organizational performance. The sessions may simply end up being talking sessions, with little concrete action resulting.

Organizational Development and Bureaucracies

Can OD techniques have much effect on bureaucracies? Schein and Greiner maintain that "the millennium of organic organizations is not on the horizon" and that "bureaucratic structures are still the dominant organizational form."[33] For many organizations, the bureaucratic form is entirely consistent with the environment they face. Yet traditional OD efforts are geared to making organizations more organic/adaptive. Does this mean that OD has no place in a bureaucratic organization, assuming that bureaucracy is consistent with the environment faced by the organization?

Schein and Greiner argue that OD does have a role to play in bureaucracies. They state that ". . . by returning to an original cornerstone of the OD movement—its focus on dealing with emergent behavioral problems in organizations—it can make a significant contribution to the functioning of traditional organizations."[34] They argue for a contingency approach to OD that recognizes that the "diseases" of a bureaucratic organization are distinctly different from those of organic structures and, thus, should receive different treatments. For example, they cite the following problems, typical of bureaucracies, that are amenable to appropriate OD treatments:

1. *Functional myopia and suboptimization* caused by too much specialization and functional allegiance. *OD treatments*: team building, off-site planning and budgeting sessions, goal integration programs, and job rotation programs.
2. *Vertical lock-in and incompetency* caused by narrow promotion ladders and promotion based on seniority. *OD treatments*: assessment centers, career counseling and information systems, and wider job posting.
3. *Top-down information flow and problem insensitivity* caused by the hierarchical and mechanistic nature of bureaucracies. *OD treatments*: shadow structure made up of collateral or parallel management teams to recommend solutions to top management, junior boards of executives, corporate ombudsman to clear blocked channels, and MBO.
4. *Routine jobs and dissatisfaction* caused by heavy specialization. *OD treatments*: job enrichment, better supervisory training, extrinsic reward systems tied to incentives and performance.

Some would argue that some of the suggested treatments for the problems of a bureaucracy are not those traditionally offered in OD programs. Yet, if we broadly define OD as a structured intervention to bring about a planned organizational change beneficial to the organization, then junior boards of executives, job postings, corporate ombudsmen, and new reward systems can rightly be considered elements of OD programs. The point is that using OD techniques to turn bureaucratic organizations into organic/adaptive ones is not appropriate if not called for by the environment. This does not mean that OD cannot work in bureaucracies, but it does mean that OD techniques specifically amenable to bureaucracy should be used.

CHANGE AND THE FUTURE

Throughout this book we have indicated that organizations are a product of their environment. We assume that virtually all organizations will face an increasingly dynamic—less stable, more heterogeneous—environment in the future. The basic prescription thus becomes one of designing organization structures and processes that institutionalize the change process so that the organization *lives with* its environment in a dynamic interaction.

In facing this environment, organizations have to deal with a fundamental question: To what extent can the organization maintain consistency of action and coordination brought about by centralized decision making and policy formulation and yet be responsive and flexible enough (decentralized) to meet the changing environment? At the point of organization boundary interface, authority delegated to the boundary-spanning units provides quick response, but centralized authority offers more consistent response. How much delegation should be made to boundary-spanning units in view of this phenomenon?

Change and Homeostasis

Organizations face a dilemma with regard to change. On the one hand, they want to achieve internal stability because of the predictability that it provides. On the other hand, they want internal flexibility because it allows the organization to adapt to new situations as they arise. The job of the organization thus becomes one of finding the point on this stability–flexibility continuum that achieves an appropriate balance for the organization.

This process can be further examined by looking at the process of dynamic homeostasis. Organizations, like people, like to exist in a state of equilibrium. That is, they want to resolve major problems, overcome shortcomings, and resolve major conflict. When an organization is in a steady state internally and with its environment, it is in *equilibrium*. The process of achieving a new equilibrium different from a previous equilibrium is called *dynamic homeostasis* and allows the organization to achieve new equilibria (steady states) that are different from previous ones and are also compatible with the environment.

Figure 16.9 presents an example of this adjustment process. Assume that an automobile manufacturing company has faced the following environmental conditions over the years: periods of prosperous economic activity, periods of recession, periods of demands for style and horsepower, periods of demand for safety and fuel efficiency, periods of demand for lower pollution, the Arab oil embargo, changes in foreign competition, and changes in technology. The graph in Figure 16.9 shows a theoretical

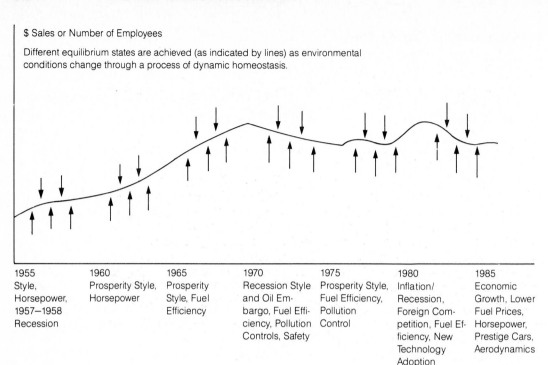

$ Sales or Number of Employees

Different equilibrium states are achieved (as indicated by lines) as environmental conditions change through a process of dynamic homeostasis.

1955	1960	1965	1970	1975	1980	1985
Style, Horsepower, 1957–1958 Recession	Prosperity Style, Horsepower	Prosperity Style, Fuel Efficiency	Recession Style and Oil Embargo, Fuel Efficiency, Pollution Controls, Safety	Prosperity Style, Fuel Efficiency, Pollution Control	Inflation/ Recession, Foreign Competition, Fuel Efficiency, New Technology Adoption (Robotics, Electronic Components)	Economic Growth, Lower Fuel Prices, Horsepower, Prestige Cars, Aerodynamics

FIGURE 16.9

An Auto Company and Dynamic Homeostasis

schedule of equilibrium states that the organization has achieved through the process of dynamic homeostasis. The lines in this figure represent the equilibrium states for the period. Movement to a new line or equilibrium state occurs through dynamic homeostasis. The arrows within each line segment represent movement around the line as the organization attempts to strike an equilibrium.

This figure is a theoretical example of the process. Not all organizations are able to continually strike the equilibrium states. Some cease to exist, such as Studebaker in the United States in the late 1950s. Some almost cease to exist only to revive, as did Chrysler in the 1980–1983 period. Furthermore, the auto company (or most organizations) does not simply adapt to the new environment; it also tries to influence it. For example, auto companies were successful in postponing the implementation of some of the EPA auto emission standards from the early 1970s to the late 1970s. Air bag restraints originally required by the federal government for the early 1980s may be postponed indefinitely. Thus, organizations that follow an action-adaptation strategy may influence the level of a future equilibrium state. Organizations with either an imperviousness or selective imperviousness strategy may be in an equilibrium state internally but may have a very difficult time determining whether they are in an equilibrium state with their environment. Of course, organizations following the strategy of adaptation seek to achieve an equilibrium state with their environment but are at the mercy of the environment, which dictates the state.* Unlike organizations following the action-adaptation strategy, they do not seek to influence the equilibrium state that the environment dictates for them.

What does the future hold? We believe more organizations will need to adopt the action-adaptation strategy in seeking new states of dynamic homeostasis. Organizations will not only need to know their environment thoroughly, but they will also need to influence it. Not knowing the environment (imperviousness and selective imperviousness) will cause disaster for tomorrow's organization since it will never know if it is in harmony with the environment. Simply trying to adapt to the environment without attempting to influence it will also be disastrous since the rapidity of environmental change will cause the organization perhaps to reach equilibrium with the environment but at a great cost of internal conflict and discord—internal disequilibrium—as the organization is continually changing internal structure and process to achieve external equilibrium.

Galbraith has already recognized this movement among organizations to an action-adaptation strategy when he speaks of "technocrats" within organizations whose job it is to plan and thereby reduce environmental uncertainty.[35] He goes on to say that with business organizations, these individuals are actually able to exercise some control over the environment (market) and thus negate or counteract some of the operations of a freely competitive market. They do this by expanding the boundaries of the organization through vertical and horizontal integration and through more sophisticated boundary-spanning units that impact more forcefully on the environment.

The dangers of wide adoption of the action-adaptation strategy are readily apparent. If organizations are able to significantly influence their environment, might some powerful organizations actually be able to *control* it? Galbraith recognizes this danger and indicates that it is a serious one for economic markets. Powerful business firms can be in the position of setting prices, output, and wage rates that may be at variance with

---

*See Chapter 7 for a review of these strategies.

what a competitive market might dictate. We can only hope that many competing, powerful organizations, each trying to control its environment, will offset the influences of one another so that no one organization or group of organizations achieves "too much" power or influence over the environment. Galbraith also alludes to this possibility in his theory of countervailing power, which states that large power blocks of sellers and buyers may counteract the power of each other.

THE FUTURE OF BUREAUCRACY

What does widespread acceptance of the action-adaptation strategy by organizations facing increasingly dynamic environments mean for the future of bureaucracy? Our basic belief is that the days of the traditional bureaucratic structure are numbered for many organizations, although there is likely to be increasing use of variations of the basic bureaucratic form. Traditional bureaucracy may still be appropriate for those organizations facing a stable homogeneous environment, but we are likely to see more experimentation with the bureaucratic form and even, in a few cases, experimentation with alternative organizational forms. However, we do not believe the days of the entire concept of bureaucracy are numbered. Bureaucracy is widely used and many organizations feel comfortable with it. Structure is not something organizations experiment with on a widespread basis. Yet, the pressures from the environment are likely to cause some limited experimentation with a variation of the bureaucratic form.

For example, as the Aston studies and later replications showed, it is possible to have bureaucracies with different characteristics. It is possible to have a bureaucratic organization with either centralized or decentralized decision making. In fact, there are many points along the centralization–decentralization continuum that the organization can select. Also, there are degrees of formalization and standardization that an organization following the basic bureaucratic form can select.

Bureaucracy is a multidimensional concept. Perhaps organizations of the future will structure boundary-spanning units and internal operations more than they do now so that decision making can actually be decentralized. In other words, if enough guidance and structure are provided through policy and rules, then lower units in the organization can make decisions on their own without asking for approval from higher units. In this way, decentralization can be achieved through a more structured internal environment.

The Bureaucratic Structure

We have described the characteristics of bureaucratic organization throughout the text. As we indicated, the concept of bureaucracy as stated by Weber was a rational response to the then all-too-common form of "rule-of-thumb" management found in the earlier part of this century. It essentially extended the field of scientific management to the whole area of organization design. It attempted to provide a rationale for the use of clear-cut policies, rules, procedures, reporting relationships, authority differentials, and location of decision points in organizations.

Few people would argue today that organizations should not have policies, rules, procedures, and so on. Bureaucracy is not criticized on these grounds. Rather, it is criticized for *rigid* practices and policies, extended reporting relationships, centralization, a closed-system perspective, and an inability to change when change is called for by the environment.

This criticism is summarized by the common complaints of too much "red tape," inflexibility, and impersonalization that are levied against bureaucracies. These situations, which often exist in bureaucratic structures, are not inherent in the concept of bureaucracy but rather result from the human failings in applying the concept.

Conditions Where Bureaucracy Works Best

Are these complaints justified? Yes, when a mechanistic or bureaucratic structure is not appropriate for the environment; yes, when people who hold slots in the bureaucracy are incompetent and are more concerned with passing the buck and protecting their own position than with getting the job done; and yes, when policies, procedures, rules, and structure are seldom (if ever) reviewed and changed. But this doesn't have to be the case. Bureaucracy is probably the best form of organization for organizations facing a stable, predictable, relatively homogeneous environment, as we pointed out earlier.

Kodak Corporation, which we discuss in the end case of this chapter, had a bureaucratic form of organization that served it very well until recent years. In the past, Kodak's environment was quite stable and predictable (e.g., Kodak held the patents for most major photographic processes and equipment); technology advanced at a steady pace; and international competition was negligible. Thus, the bureaucratic structure fit perfectly.

Bureaucracy can be very efficient in developing ways of handling common, recurring problems. There is no need to reinvent the wheel each time a problem recurs. Rather, the job of the manager is simply to apply an appropriate, carefully thought out, logical policy or rule, and the problem is solved. Decision points and decision rules are specified and established, and issues are passed to the proper point of responsibility (often high in the organization) where a decision is made and passed back down. Since the environment is stable, time for making a decision is of relatively little importance.

Conditions Where Bureaucracy Does Not Work Well

The more unpredictable the environment is, the less effective bureaucracy is. As the environment changes—especially as it changes in less predictable ways—the organization finds that previously determined policies and rules do not apply to new problems. It finds that centralized decision making takes too long to resolve issues. It finds that such functions as planning and monitoring the environment take on much greater importance. In short, it finds it cannot speedily adjust and adapt to new conditions. It experiences a crisis in coping. Again, we refer to the end case of this chapter to show how Kodak's bureaucratic structure was unable to cope with a dynamic and unpredictable environment.

Of course, this is the argument for the organic-adaptive organization, which is flexible, allows for planning and environmental monitoring, and makes decisions quickly. But does this mean that we must completely abandon the bureaucratic model?

An Evaluation of the Bureaucratic Model for the Future

Organic-adaptive organizations and bureaucratic organizations are not necessarily bipolar opposites on a continuum. Those who favor organic-adaptive organizations would not argue that organizations must abandon policy and rule formulation, clear-cut decision points, authority differentials, and clear structure. Any organization, to exist as an organization, needs some "glue" to hold it together. Policies, procedures, and structure are the glue. They give the organization some means of achieving integration. They also give the organization at least a moderate degree of consistency.

But organizations need to have less rigid policy. They need mechanisms that allow policy to be adaptable to differing shades of the same problem. They need internal systems that force a review of policy, procedures, and structure periodically so that they can be changed as needed. Clear decision points are needed but should be moved down in the organization. This decentralization of authority will allow more rapid decision making. The bureaucracy needs to monitor its environment. It needs to plan future courses of action based on the information obtained through this monitoring process. Planning becomes more important as the bureaucratic organization attempts to predict future environmental changes so that it will be prepared with goals, policies, procedures, and rules needed for tomorrow.

Do these characteristics required of an organization in the future destroy bureaucracy as an organizational form? We do not think so, although the organization will probably change its form. The tenets of bureaucracy might well be kept, but the organization will become more flexible and so be able to respond to a moderately changing environment, if not to a turbulent one.

Dr. J. Richard Hackman, a well-respected organization theorist from Yale University, suggests that the bureaucratic model for the future will take one of two routes.[36] Route One will focus on fitting jobs to people in organizations. That is, work will be enriched so that employees are internally motivated to perform well. Organizations will be viewed as places where people can grow and learn new things, and considerable attention will be spent on supporting and nurturing employees' aspirations for personal development. Should Route One be the one taken by organizations in the future, Hackman argues that organizational structures will be leaner, with fewer hierarchical levels and fewer managerial and staff personnel.

Route Two focuses on fitting people to jobs. That is, work will be designed for the maximum attainment of economic and technological efficiency. If Route Two should be the future reality for organizations, then it will be necessary to make people adapt in acceptable ways to their work experiences. Thus, bureaucracy will remain rigid as work performance and organizational production are closely monitored and controlled by managers. In short, the development and utilization of routine technologies will enhance, rather than erode, the rigidity and formalization aspects of bureaucracy.

Loosely Coupled Organizations

Organizations of the future may be held together in a more loosely coupled way than present organizations. This can happen in two ways. First, the internal bonds that hold together various units of an organization may not be as tight as they have been. In other words, there is likely to be more decentralization with local unit autonomy than there is now. Second, organizations may form loose alliances with other organizations for specific purposes. In other words, two or more organizations may form an agreement to work together on a certain project for a period of time much like the venture arrangement. In the framework of Chapter 6, we are likely to see more organizations in the coalitional and federative modes of interorganizational cooperation.

There are many examples illustrating the concept of loose coupling. DuPont created a separate automotive products division and moved it, along with its plastics operations, to Detroit in order to interact more effectively with automakers. Cincinnati Milagron, the machine tools manufacturer, works quite closely with aircraft manufacturers in its efforts to develop and sell entire, very versatile, manufacturing systems. Microchip manufacturers have entered into all sorts of technology exchange agreements with each other in order to survive in an environment characterized by rapidly expanding technology and fierce foreign competition.

This loose coupling will allow organizations to better meet contingencies in the environment and to build a temporary base of power. Of course, to do this, they will have to give up some of their autonomy. But they may be willing to do this in order to gain power in the environment.

CHARACTERISTICS OF TOMORROW'S ORGANIZATION

Just what form, then, will the organizations of tomorrow take? Will we have ad-hocracies, bureaucracies, venture arrangements? We believe that organizations will take many forms but that certain characteristics will be common among all forms. No doubt, organizations will lean to the organic/adaptive model more in the future than they do now, but they will also have other characteristics, which we detail below.

Temporary

Organizations of the future will likely be more temporary arrangements than they are today. This will happen in two ways. First, more organizations will adopt the ad-hocracy form. They will exist for a certain purpose and will cease to exist once that purpose has been achieved. Thus, the organization life cycle will be accelerated for these organizations. Second, internal arrangements within organizations are likely to be more temporary. The organization may very well act as a shell within which parts and arrangements are rapidly changed and rearranged.

The trend of people moving in and out of organizations will continue, if not accelerate. Reorganization of structure will occur more frequently. Tasks, goals, and, indeed, organization missions will change more frequently as organizations attempt to cope with dynamic environments. Reporting relationships will be temporary. Project and matrix management will be more commonly used within organizations.

This element of temporariness is already quite evident in many large organizations as circumstances in the environment force them to eliminate departments, cut back operations, and lay off employees. This does not mean that important functions are not performed. Rather, small service entities and individuals, not a part of the main organization, are now providing temporary help to large organizations that formerly had the staff and resources to conduct most, if not all, of their operations in-house. GM's Chevrolet division, whose engineering budget is larger than the sales of all but 200 of the country's largest companies, is increasingly spending this budget on small contractors and suppliers.[37] Many new organizations, such as Headquarters Companies of New York, are specifically set up to offer temporary services such as a $395-per-month package of telephone, typing, and secretarial services for work-at-home consultants.[38] If entire organizations are not yet completely temporary in nature, many of their very important functions are now conducted by external individuals or organizations working on a temporary, contractual basis.

Minimum Status Differentials

People will be judged on the basis of their competency rather than on the basis of the authority of their position. Status will accrue to individuals who demonstrate competency. Since demonstrated competency will vary with the required expertise for the task at hand, individual status will vary over time. Hence, we believe status differentials will be minimized in organizations.

Professional Managers

The trend toward more professionalism among managers has long been in existence. We see the trend intensifying in the future. Traditional managers will have an increasingly more difficult time managing tomorrow's complex, sophisticated organizations. The technical competencies required of tomorrow's managers—financial skills, EDP skills, marketing skills, planning skills, human resource skills—demand a trained and educated professional manager. Note that Holiday Inn had to recruit professional managers in order to cope more effectively with its environment as that organization progressed through the organizational life cycle.

Because the research and writing in management has mushroomed over the last twenty years, we are seeing the expansion of the knowledge base on which this professional training and education will be built. The number of M.B.A. programs has increased greatly, particularly in metropolitan areas. The amount of noncredit training and development sponsored by consulting, professional, and trade associations as well as universities will continue to expand because the need to keep current will expand.

Perhaps this professionalism will eventually be institutionalized and recognized through a certification program for managers. Already such certification exists for other professions and occupations—law, medicine, accounting, teaching, insurance, real estate, engineering—and there are indications it will soon exist for management. The American Society for Personnel Administration (ASPA) has developed a certification system for personnel managers. The Credit Union National Association (CUNA) has developed a certification procedure for credit union managers.

Certification requires that a person in a profession or occupation meet certain minimum standards of competence. This certification is usually achieved through passing a paper-and-pencil test to measure the applicant's knowledge. It can serve to ensure that all individuals within a profession or occupation meet basic performance criteria. (However, it can also be used to reduce or hold down the supply of individuals in an occupation or profession below market levels, thereby increasing wages for those in the profession.) Whether such a certification program is finally developed for managers will ultimately depend on whether widespread agreement can be reached as to what the required basic competencies of managers are, what minimum standards are acceptable, and how it can be determined whether individuals have these competencies.

Flexible and Adaptive

For the future, we see more organic/adaptive organizations and fewer mechanistic ones. Because of the changing nature of the environment and the necessity of organizational response to this environment, the organic/adaptive organizational model will become more widespread than it is today. This does not mean that the bureaucratic/mechanistic organizational form will cease to exist. It will not. But there should be fewer organizations of this type, and those remaining will be modifications of the original bureaucratic model.

Considerable Decentralization and Delegation

To achieve flexibility and adaptiveness, organizations of the future will decentralize decision-making authority farther down the organizational hierarchy so that decisions are actually made closer to the points of organizational operation. This will minimize the time for organizational action. Such decentralization does not mean that organizations will no longer make policy and rules. However, it does mean that overall policy making will set broader parameters for managerial action rather than specify detailed management activities.

When W. T. Stephens became CEO of Manville Corporation in September, 1986, one of his first priorities was to push decision-making authority down to the lowest possible level in order to "allow the best people to bubble to the top." Since Manville declared Chapter 11 bankruptcy due to asbestosis claims, it reorganized its structure and changed its basic mission from manufacturing asbestos products to manufacturing fiberglass, forest, and specialty products. As Manville changed its mission and core technology and interacted with new environments, it was essential that maximum flexibility be delegated to the organization's decision makers at the divisional and plant levels.

There is a countertrend to this decentralization process, however. The use of computers and the adoption of a systems philosophy of management, along with the greater demand by society for organizational accountability, often causes an organization to centralize. Computers enable organizations to centralize information. A systems approach often causes managers to view the organization as a total complex of parts (holism) that can, in turn, cause managers to attempt to "manage" these parts. Finally, the desire for accountability may cause managers to centralize so that control will be easier in order to reduce any deviations in accepted standards of performance.

Even though this countertrend exists, we believe that the complexity and large size of organizations will require considerable delegation if organizations are to meet the needs of their dynamic environment. Perhaps the watchword is more creative "centralized decentralization" whereby decentralized operating decisions are carried out under the umbrella of centralized policy decisions.* GM is one notable example of this approach.

Complexity

There is continually growing evidence of increasing organizational complexity. In order to reduce the uncertainties posed by the environment, organizations have become more vertically and horizontally differentiated. They buy their suppliers and their distributors; they buy their competitors; they buy producers of very dissimilar products in order to reduce the cyclical sales nature of many product lines. They get larger in order to have greater bargaining power with government, competitors, and financial institutions, and in order to achieve economies of scale. All these actions lead to greater complexity. Unless antitrust action on the part of government agencies becomes much more aggressive, we see this trend toward complexity continuing.

---

*Such a statement has been made to us on several occasions by the presidents of two of the nation's larger conglomerate corporations.

Supersensitive Sensors and Social Sensitivity

Organizations of the future will be much more sensitive to the needs of the society in which they exist; they will have more social sensitivity. They will be concerned about the necessity of society's legitimizing their rights to existence and operation. They will be more aware of their social responsibilities and, thus, more aware of the social impact as well as the economic impact of their actions. We see this now in demands being made for business responsibility with respect to the social issues of pollution, civil rights, power, international payments, and consumer protection.

The argument for "social audits" and "social reporting" by business organizations in order to measure the social impact of business behavior is increasing.[39] Perhaps such audits will eventually be required on an annual basis by the Securities and Exchange Commission (SEC) for all firms trading stock, much as financial audits are now required.

The net effect of this trend is that organizations will need supersensitive sensors that not only obtain and rapidly report environmental information to decision-authority centers but that also are given the authority to try to influence the environment more than they do now. It is not that organizations will become chameleons under an adaptive strategy, but that they are more likely to adopt an action-adaptation strategy under a social sensitivity umbrella.

Waste Management Corporation, which we discussed in Chapter 4, certainly exemplifies this growing organizational trend. Because the mission of this particular organization requires it to deal with a variety of government entities in relation to the disposal of a variety of wastes, the effective utilization of boundary spanners and sensors is imperative for successful operations.

Goal Directedness

Organizations of the future will be more goal directed than those of today. The widespread adoption of various MBO models by both business and government organizations, as well as charities, churches, volunteer associations, and other organization types, indicates that the focus on the organization mission and specific objectives will increase even though MBO currently is paid only lip service by many organizations now using it. Such goal-directed behavior may very well lead to greater organization efficiency and effectiveness as efforts become more focused on specific targets to be achieved.

To achieve greater goal-directed behavior within very complex organizations, the organization will have to develop better means of integrating individual and group output. This problem with integration likely augurs for more widespread use of project and matrix forms of management-integrating structures.

THE LARGE CONGLOMERATE: A MODEL OF TOMORROW'S ORGANIZATION?

There is some evidence that the model of the organization of tomorrow may be a large conglomerate made up of a number of semiautonomous, wholly owned, subsidiaries. We see this with Beatrice, the Conoco-Dupont merger, the Northwest-Republic Airline merger, and the GE-RCA merger. It will be interesting to see if Reagan's pro-business philosophy, which has resulted in less aggressive antitrust prosecutions, is continued by the next administration.

Such mergers allow a firm to grow by diversifying through takeovers of existing firms. For some firms, it is a matter of survival (e.g., American Motors and Renault). For others it is a means to expand into new markets (e.g., Conoco and Dupont). As these mergers occur, many of the ideas discussed in the previous section, such as complexity, decentralization, flexibility, and adaptiveness, will apply.

Corporate takeovers are not new; they have been occurring for decades. LTV is a prime example of a firm that grew rapidly in the 1960s through acquisitions. What is new, however, is the fact that takeovers seem to be occurring among already large firms. In the past, a firm would acquire a fast-growing, profitable upstart in the same or different industry. Today, firms seem to be acquiring firms as big as, if not bigger than, the acquiring firm. The takeover of Eastern Airlines by Texas Air and AMC by Chrysler are examples of this strategy. This is unusual but possible (indeed, some would say probable) as cash-rich firms buy the outstanding stock of cash-poor firms. Thus, we are likely to see mergers made by highly profitable firms wishing to expand markets.

In the future, we are likely to see an increase in both friendly and hostile takeovers as firms try to increase their power in the marketplace. Corporate takeovers have many advantages. First, a takeover would reduce uncertainty in the market, as we discussed in Chapter 6. Second, it would allow the firm to grow by entering new markets, thus increasing assets and profitability.* Third, it would allow the firm to compete better in international markets when dealing with the large firms and cartels often found in other countries. Fourth, for the takeover firms, it is an attempt to ensure survival. (For the firms that are acquired it means death since

---

*Some analysts report that as many as one-third of acquisitions are unprofitable. See Thomas Petzinger, Jr., "To Win a Bidding War Doesn't Ensure Success of Merged Companies," *The Wall Street Journal* (September 1, 1981), 1FF.

they no longer exist as separate legal entities.) Fifth, certain economies of scale may be achieved in using fixed assets such as an electronic data system or large plants.

The acquisition strategy for coping is likely to result in fewer organizations of the traditional business form and more organizations of the large, complex, diversified form with widely dispersed semiautonomous operating units. Of course, this strategy may change if the federal government decides to tighten up in its antitrust activities.

Whatever the forms the organizations of the future take, one thing is certain: The knowledge we gain as students of organization theory will be ever more crucial for success.

SUMMARY

In this chapter we have viewed organizational change by addressing the issue, how can an organization stay in tune with its environment? Organization change and development is a complex process that we have presented in a somewhat simplified model. The focus of such change is the changes that occur in the macro environment (exogenous change). The organization attempts to adapt to and influence these changes, and, in the course of doing so, modifies its internal structure and processes. Often the change is a response of the organization to extend the growth and stability periods of its life cycle.

As the population ecology debate points out, there is even some argument as to whether organizations are masters of their own fate. One argument in this debate states that organizations are free to make whatever choices are necessary in order to adapt to their environment and survive. The argument on the other side of the debate proposes that it is the environment itself that determines an organization's fate. Those that the environment "selects" survive; those that it does not wither away and die.

The management of organization change can take one or more of six major forms. Organizations can know and forecast, initiate, amplify, smooth, buffer, or stop change. Organizations will adopt different actions depending on their basic posture toward the environment, as we discussed in Chapter 4 (imperviousness, selective imperviousness, adaptation, or action-adaptation). However, regardless of the strategy or tactic taken with regard to environmental change, most organizations will at least want to know and forecast change. This is a prerequisite for developing a posture toward the change-management tactic employed. Also, most organizations will adopt several tactics. They will encourage some changes, deflect some, and stop others. Although it may be possible to identify one basic tactic used by an organization, it is often difficult.

Regardless of the tactic taken, the organization must try to do certain things to maintain, improve, and renew itself. This strategy of renewal is organization development. Under OD, organizations examine their goals, work systems, strategies, policies, and intergroup and intragroup behavior and structure. This is usually done with the assistance of an internal or external consultant or trainer in a learning environment. Because of the learning associated with many OD programs, OD is often viewed simply as training. While training is a major part of OD, it is by no means the whole story. OD also includes organization self-assessment and examination, task forces, problem-solving groups, as well as various forms of training and development.

There are several OD techniques. One common technique is management by objectives (MBO), which involves assessment and development and can result in useful objectives and programs the managers can follow in their daily work routine. Another consists of various laboratory methods aimed at changing an individual's attitudes and beliefs. These include sensitivity training (T group) and encounter group dynamics. Team-building techniques are also used in laboratory settings that emphasize the development of "families" within the organization.

Knowledge and concept training provided through college courses, seminars, workshops, conferences, and institutes are very popular and stress the knowledge and conceptual tools individuals need to perform the job effectively, rather than focusing on individual attitudes and beliefs. A serious disadvantage of this approach is blockage of training transfer between the training site and the job site. For this reason on-the-job training (OJT) has been widely used to give participants job skills required in a specific job.

Survey feedback techniques rely on attitude surveys to discover problems and solutions in a systematic fashion among an organization's managers. Intergroup techniques are used to identify and remove problems between differentiated work groups. Both these techniques suffer from a lack of empirical data indicating their effectiveness or ineffectiveness, but, in the hands of a skilled trainer/consultant and willing participants, the techniques can be helpful in identifying and removing organizational roadblocks.

We have also examined how organizations may significantly change in the future. The organizations of tomorrow will be less bureaucratic and more organic/adaptive than those of today. This does not spell the end of bureaucracy but does mean that bureaucratic organizations will exist in modified forms. They will be less bureaucratic than those of today and will have more flexible policy, rules, and procedures carried out under a decentralized decision process.

Alternatives to bureaucratic organizations will continue to develop and will be more in the organic/adaptive mold. Regardless of the form of organization in the future, we believe that all organizations will have certain common characteristics. They will be more temporary arrangements than they are today, and some organizations will be shells in which resources move freely in and out. There will be minimum status differentials within organizations, and status will be based on competency. Professional, perhaps even certified, managers will direct organizations of the future. Flexibility and adaptability will be two key, overriding qualities that organizations will attempt to achieve, and they will be considerably decentralized in order to achieve them. This will cause organizations to be more complex in the future. Supersensitive sensors will keep the organization in touch with its environment and will even attempt to influence the environment. Finally, organizations will be more goal directed as they respond to increasing demands for social accountability.

QUESTIONS FOR REVIEW AND DISCUSSION

1. What is change? What is organizational change?
2. Can change be managed? If so, how? If not, why not?
3. How does change relate to an organization's life cycle? Must all organizations die? Why or why not?
4. What do we mean when we say the organization faces a dilemma with respect to change?
5. What is OD? How is it related to organizational change?
6. Can OD programs be used in bureaucratic organizations? Why or why not? If so, how?
7. How would you go about determining the actual effectiveness of various OD techniques?
8. Will there be a place for the bureaucratic structure in tomorrow's society? Explain your answer.
9. What is meant by creative "centralized decentralization"? Is this likely to become more common? Why?
10. Can any organization ever achieve a pure equilibrium state? Explain your answer.
11. Pick an organization with which you are familiar and critique its structure. Is it bureaucratic? Is it likely to prosper in the future? Why or why not? What must it do to assure its continued existence and environmental viability?
12. If all organizations adopt an action-adaptation strategy, won't the largest, most powerful organizations simply dominate society? Do they now? Make a case for both the affirmative and negative answers to each of these questions.
13. How will tomorrow's organizations be different from those of today?

14. What characteristics do you look for in an organization's design and structure when contemplating a job with the organization?

ENDNOTES

1. W. Astley and A. Van de Ven, "Central Perspectives in Organization Theory," *Administrative Science Quarterly* 28, no. 2 (June 1983): 245–273.

2. John Betton and Gregory G. Dess, "The Application of Population Ecology Models to the Study of Organizations," *Academy of Management Review* 10, no. 4 (October 1985): 750–757.

3. M. T. Hannon and J. Freeman, "The Population Ecology of Organizations," *American Journal of Sociology* 82, no. 5 (March 1977): 929–964.

4. D. Miller and P. Friesen, "Momentum and Revolution in Organizational Adaptation," *Academy of Management Journal* 23, no. 4 (December 1980): 591–614.

5. Todd Mason, Russell Mitchell, and William J. Hampton, "Ross Perot's Crusade," *Business Week* (October 6, 1986), 60–65.

6. Douglas R. Wholey and Jack W. Brittain, "Organizational Ecology: Findings and Implications," *Academy of Management Review* 11, no. 3 (July 1986): 513–533.

7. Larry E. Short, "Planned Organizational Change," *MSU Business Topics* 21, no. 4 (Autumn 1973): 53–61.

8. Harold J. Leavitt, "Applied Organization Change in Industry: Structural, Technical and Human Approaches," in *New Perspectives in Organization Research*, ed. W. W. Cooper, H. J. Leavitt, and M. W. Shelby II (New York: John Wiley & Sons, 1964): 55–71.

9. David W. Ewing, *Freedom Inside the Organization: Bringing Civil Liberties to the Workplace* (New York: E. P. Dutton, 1977).

10. Bernard Taylor and Roscoe Davis, "Implementing an Action Program via Organizational Change," *Journal of Economics* 28, no. 3 (Spring–Summer 1976): 203–208.

11. Paul Hersey and Kenneth Blanchard, "Change and the Use of Power: The Management of Change, Part I," *Training and Development Journal* 26, no. 1 (January 1972): 6–10.

12. Neil J. Smelser, *Theory of Collective Behavior* (New York: The Free Press, 1962).

13. John K. Galbraith, *The New Industrial State* (Boston: Houghton Mifflin, 1967), 57–59.

14. Ichak Adizes, "Organizational Passages: Diagnosing and Treating Life Cycle Problems of Organizations," *Organizational Dynamics* (Summer 1979): 2–25.

15. John Heylar, "Altered Landscape: The Holiday Inn Trip," *The Wall Street Journal* (February 11, 1987), 1, 18.

16. Ibid., 18.

17. Ibid.

18. Ibid.

19. Ibid.

20. E. C. Zeeman, "Catastrophe Theory in Administration," invited address, Forum of the Association of Institutional Research, Atlanta, Ga., April 1980; and E. C. Zeeman, *Catastrophe Theory: Selected Papers 1972–1977* (Reading, Mass.: Addison-Wesley, 1977).

21. René Thom, *Structural Stability and Morphogenesis* (Northampton, Mass.: Benjamin, 1972).

22. Stephen Koep, "A Tire Maker Lags," *Time* (February 16, 1987), 48.

23. Adizes, "Organizational Passages."

24. C. Wright Mills, *The Power Elite* (Oxford: Oxford University Press, 1967).

25. Alvin Toffler, *Future Shock* (New York: Random House, 1970).

26. Peter F. Drucker, *The Age of Discontinuity: Guidelines To Our Changing Society* (New York: Harper & Row, 1969).

27. Terence Roth, "Puma Hopes Superstar Will Help End U.S. Slump, Narrow Gap with Addidas," *The Wall Street Journal* (February 5, 1987), 24.

28. William Gruber and John Niles, "How To Innovate in Management," *Organizational Dynamics* 3, no. 2 (Autumn 1974): 31–47.

29. Clayton Olderfer, "Understanding Laboratory Education: An Overview," *Monthly Labor Review* 93, no. 12 (December 1970): 18–27.

30. R. P. Blake, H. A. Shepard, and J. S. Mouton, *Managing Intergroup Conflicts in Industry* (Houston: Gulf, 1965).

31. Paul R. Lawrence and Jay W. Lorsch, *Organization and Environment: Managing Differentiation and Integration* (Homewood, Ill.: Richard D. Irwin, 1969).

32. James Owens, "Organizational Conflict and Team Building," *Training and Development Journal* 27, no. 8 (August 1973): 32–39.

33. Virginia E. Schein and Larry E. Greiner, "Can Organizational Development Be Fine Tuned to Bureaucracies?" *Organizational Dynamics* (Winter 1977), reprinted in *The Dynamics of Organization Theory*, eds. John F. Veiga and John N. Yanouzer (St. Paul, Minn.: West, 1979), 400.

34. Ibid., 401.

35. Galbraith, *The New Industrial State*.

36. J. Richard Hackman and Greg R. Oldham, "Work Redesign in Organizational and Society Context," in *Perspectives on Behavior in Organizations*, 2d ed., eds. J. Richard Hackman, Edward E. Lawler III, and Lyman W. Porter (New York: McGraw-Hill, 1983), 586–598.

37. Amanda Bennett, "Growing Small: As Big Firms Continue to Trim Their Staffs, 2-Tier Setup Emerges," *The Wall Street Journal* (May 4, 1987), 1, 12.

38. Ibid., 12.

39. Arthur Elkins and Dennis W. Callaghan, *A Managerial Odyssey: Problems in Business and Its Environment*, 3d ed. (Reading, Mass.: Addison-Wesley, 1981), 201–212.

ANNOTATED BIBLIOGRAPHY

Ackerman, L. S. "Transition Management: An In-depth Look at Managing Complex Change." *Organizational Dynamics* 11, no. 1 (Summer 1982): 46–66.

The author sees change as a matter of determining the degree of disruption that can be tolerated by the organization's structure and process components. Ackerman believes that the commitment of top-management expertise, resource availability, and an organizational willingness to take risks are key factors in the success of a change effort.

Beckhard, Richard. *Organization Development Strategies and Models.* Reading, Mass.: Addison-Wesley, 1969.
  Beckhard, in a very readable book, presents an anthology of OD intervention strategies available to the practitioner. On the theoretical side, lucid explanations of the basic models are covered. Good examples accompany the discussion.

Beer, Michael, and Huse, Edgar. "A Systems Approach to Organization Development." *Journal of Applied Behavioral Science* 8, no. 1 (January–February 1972): 79–101.
  OD approaches too often concentrate on a single method. In an applied study, the following conclusions are reached: (1) OD efforts need not begin at the top; (2) structural and interpersonal changes must be complementary; (3) behavioral change precedes cognitive change; and (4) the selection of change leaders as initial targets is a good strategy for OD.

Britan, Gerald. *Bureaucracy and Innovation: On Ethnography of Policy Change.* Beverly Hills: Sage, 1981.
  This is a study of the dynamics of the federal bureaucracy. Britan focuses specifically on the government's efforts to stimulate technological innovation through policy experiments that represent innovations within the bureaucracy itself. While describing the operations of the Experimental Technology Incentives Program (ETIP) of the U.S. Department of Commerce, Britan is concerned with the larger question of the personal understanding and relationships through which policies develop and change.

Brown, J. L., and Agnew, N. M. "Corporate Agility." *Business Horizons* 25, no. 2 (1982): 29–33.
  This article focuses on the idea of corporate responsiveness as a key factor in change management. The authors identify four basic conditions of responsiveness related to goal clarity, knowledge, and energy for innovation within the organization: clear goals/adequate knowledge (optimal state); clear goals/crude knowledge (trial-and-error approach); vague goals/adequate knowledge (system rigidity); and vague goals/crude knowledge (system failure).

Chahravarthy, B. S. "Adaptation: A Promising Metaphor for Strategic Management." *Academy of Management Review* 7, no. 1 (January 1982): 35–44.
  The author sees change as a key management function involving the choice of an appropriate strategy and design of a matching structure. He delineates a complicated model of strategy and structure to account for the various states within which organizations move during change.

Denhardt, Robert B. *In the Shadow of Organization.* Lawrence, Kans.: Regents Press of Kansas, 1981.
  This short, innovative contribution explores individual freedom in an age of organization. Conflict between self and society and between autonomy and domination serves as the basis for recommended future reforms of modern organizations.

Goodman, Paul S.; Pennings, Johannes M.; and associates. *New Perspectives in Organizational Effectiveness.* San Francisco: Jossey-Bass, 1977.

A collection of papers on organizational effectiveness that deals with definitional and methodological issues, the text points out the linkage of OD efforts with effectiveness. It shows substantive insight into organizational effectiveness issues.

Jones, Thomas M., and Goldberg, Leonard D. "Governing the Large Corporation: More Arguments for Public Directors." *Academy of Management Review 7*, no. 2 (April 1982): 603–611.

Government-appointed public directors may or may not make corporations behave in a socially acceptable manner, but they would make an appropriate response to three corporate governance problems: (1) the vagueness of the social responsibility doctrine, (2) the legitimacy of corporate social decision making, and (3) the compatibility of corporate governance with democratic principles.

Kimberly, John R.; Metes, Robert H.; and associates. *The Organizational Life Cycle: Issues in the Creation, Transformation, and Decline of Organizations.* San Francisco: Jossey-Bass, 1980.

New businesses, public agencies, and other organizations are created each day. Why are some successful while others never get off the ground? How do organizations change as they grow, and how can they successfully manage new problems? Why do many organizations stagnate and decline? These questions are important for all organization and management specialists. Yet, until now, organizational research and theory have assumed that organizational structures are relatively fixed. This book remedies these deficiencies by reporting findings from extensive longitudinal field studies of organizations as they began, grew, and in some cases declined. The authors demonstrate that organizational development can be successfully conceptualized as following a life cycle.

Kirkpatrick, Donald L. *How to Manage Change Effectively: Approaches, Methods, and Case Examples.* San Francisco: Jossey-Bass, 1985.

This book shows how to plan, implement, and manage change in the workplace successfully, while gaining needed acceptance and commitment from employees. The author explains why change is a constant element in the successful organization—and he examines the kinds of change managers encounter, what role managers should assume during change, and how to deal with problems during the change process.

Lippitt, Gordon L. "Quality of Work Life: Organizational Renewal in Action." *Training and Development Journal 32*, no. 7 (July 1978): 4–10.

This article points out how organizational renewal can be used to improve the quality of work life in organizations. Managers and human resource specialists can bring together the skills and resources needed to bring about sufficient, timely renewal in organizations to meet challenges of the future.

Lippitt, Gordon L.; Langseth, Peter; and Mossop, Jack. *Implementing Organizational Change: A Practical Guide to Managing Change Efforts.* San Francisco: Jossey-Bass, 1985.

This book gives practical, step-by-step advice on how to analyze the changes needed within an organization to increase effectiveness, solve problems, adapt to new conditions, and achieve goals. The authors discuss how to determine exactly what changes are required and how to implement those changes efficiently, effectively, and with the support of all involved.

Mansfield, Roger. "Bureaucracy and Centralization: An Examination of Organizational Structure." *Administrative Science Quarterly* 16, no. 4 (December 1973): 477–488.

The coming death of bureaucracy has been a recurrent recent theme in management literature. This article does some empirical examination and finds this conclusion to be premature. Some implications are made for the continued successful use of bureaucracy in the future.

Miller, Danny, and Friesen, Peter H. "Structural Change and Performance: Quantum Versus Piecemeal-Incremental Approaches." *Academy of Management Journal* 25, no. 4 (December 1982): 867–892.

The effectiveness of different approaches to changing organization structure is examined. Two dimensions of structural change are explored. The findings show a tendency for quantum change, that is, change that is both concerted and dramatic, to be more associated with high performance than are piecemeal and incremental changes.

Nord, Walter, and Durand, Douglas. "Beyond Resistance to Change." *Organizational Dynamics* 4, no. 2 (Autumn 1975): 2–19.

The authors conducted an in-depth study of a single organization that had tried several OD techniques, all of which met with resistance to change and subsequent failure. The discussion of the reasons behind the resistance to change is enlightening.

Pondy, Louis R., and Huff, Anne S. "Achieving Routine in Organizational Change." *Journal of Management* 11, no. 2 (Spring 1985): 103–116.

The authors preconceived that uncertainty and the need to discover new framing concepts would frequently face school decision makers trying to significantly alter their domain. In contrast, however, the authors found that familiar administrative mechanisms were used to channel consideration of a major decision—that of the computerization of the curriculum. These familiar administrative mechanisms were used in combination with inspired use of language to reinforce the routine frame. Thus, for organizational participants, the very routineness symbolized the unexceptional nature of a change that might otherwise have aroused considerably more attention.

Nystrom, Paul C., and Starbuck, William H., eds. *Handbook of Organizational Design.* Vols. I and II. Oxford: Oxford University Press, 1980.

The editors and sixty-five contributing authors draw on research from a broad range of fields to examine the interdisciplinary nature of organizational behavior in different industries, organizational forms, nations, and a wide spectrum of social sciences. Volume 1 examines the philosophy underlying the ways organizations do and should adapt to the characteristics of societies. Volume 2 addresses questions concerning ways organizations operate from within and how they do and should alter their environments. The authors, predominantly American, bring together findings from many areas of research: industrial psychology, management science, economics, political science, industrial engineering, policy, history, sociology, strategic planning, and anthropology.

Redburn, F. Stevens. "On Human Services Integration." *Public Administration Review* 37, no. 3 (May 1977): 264–269.

This article looks at "human services integration"—the structural changes, including centralization and decentralization of authority—pointing out that this process may facilitate better service delivery in public organizations.

Richetto, Gary. "Organizations Circa 1990: Demise of the Pyramid." *Personnel Journal* 49 (July 1970): 598–603.

This article is representative of the theme of the decline of the bureaucratic form. Various reasons for the expected decline and some potential replacements are discussed.

Sarason, Seymour B. *The Creation of Settings and the Future Societies.* San Francisco: Jossey-Bass, 1972.

More new enterprises, ventures, organizations, and societies—Sarason calls them settings—have been created in the past thirty years than in the entire history of the human race: new businesses, universities, schools, clinics, research institutes, government agencies, communes, and a bewildering array of others. The problems involved in creating these new settings are strikingly similar. Studies show that 75 percent of the new ventures fail within the first five years. Why? What are the main factors to consider in creating any new enterprise or venture? Sarason comes to grips with the problem and sets its boundaries for the first time.

Schein, Edgar. *Process Consultation: Its Role in Organization Development.* Reading, Mass.: Addison-Wesley, 1969.

Schein gives a thorough discussion of the OD technique of process consultation. Various strategies of application, as well as the finer points of the practice of the method, are discussed. Examples and cases are also included.

Scott, William G. "Organization Theory: A Reassessment." *Academy of Management Journal* 17, no. 2 (June 1974): 242–253.

In a classic article of foresightedness, Scott examines the appropriateness of the present systems model of organization. He concludes that, in light of current and future environmental forces, the systems paradigm may require replacement with a radical model that he outlines.

Seashore, Stanley, and Bowers, David. "Durability of Organizational Change." *American Psychologist* 25 (March 1970): 227–232.

Do OD intervention improvements last? Do organizations retain and practice the OD method or do they revert to old ways? In a concentrated study of an organization, the authors found (somewhat to their surprise) that the organization's change was durable. Various explanations for this outcome are discussed.

Sullivan, Jeremiah J. "A Critique of Theory Z." *Academy of Management Review* 8, no. 1 (January 1983): 132–142.

Ouchi's Theory Z prescribes how employees should be motivated for increased productivity. Based on the theoretical work of Emile Durkheim, it views the modern large corporation as a communal alternative to the shortcomings of other institutions in industrial mass societies. Ouchi's assertion that Japan is the only industrial society in which Theory Z has flourished receives limited support from research findings. Moreover, Ouchi's grounding of the theory of humanistic management seems unwarranted.

Weiss, Carol H., and Barton, Allen H., eds. *Making Bureaucracies Work*. Beverly Hills: Sage, 1980.

This work examines reforms that have been instituted or advocated to improve government agency performance in the United States. The contributors identify strategies that hold promise for making public bureaucracies more effective, and mechanisms that generate more negative consequences than gains. Together, they offer directions to efforts to make government agencies more effective, efficient, and responsive to the needs of the citizenry.

ADDITIONAL REFERENCES

Anthony, William P. *Participative Management*. Reading, Mass.: Addison-Wesley, 1978.

Argyris, Chris. *Organization and Innovation*. Homewood, Ill.: Richard D. Irwin, 1965.

Armenakis, A. A., and Feild, H. S. "Evaluation and Organizational Change Using Nonindependent Criterion Measures." *Personnel* 28 (1975): 39–44.

Basil, D. C., and Cook, C. W. *The Management of Change*. New York: McGraw-Hill, 1974.

Beckhard, Richard. "Strategies for Large System Change." *Sloan Management Review* (Winter 1975): 45–55.

Benne, K. D., and Birnbaum, M. "Principles of Changing." In *The Planning of Change*, edited by W. G. Bennis, K. D. Benne, and R. Chin, 222–230. New York: Holt, Rinehart and Winston, 1969.

Bergey, J., and Slower, R. "Administration in the 1980s." *Advanced Management Journal* 34, no. 2 (April 1969): 25–33.

Dunbar, R. L. M., and Dutton, J. M. "Crossing Mother: Ideological Constraints on Organizational Improvements." *Journal of Management Studies* 19, no. 1 (1982): 91–108.

Ferguson, Marilyn. *The Aquarian Conspiracy: Personal and Social Transformation in the 1980s*. Los Angeles: J. P. Tarcher, 1980.

Galbraith, J. *Organizational Design*. Reading, Mass.: Addison-Wesley, 1977.

Galbraith, J. R. "Designing the Innovating Organization." *Organizational Dynamics* 10, no. 3 (1982): 5–26.

Gannon, Martin, and Kopchick, Charles. "The Percentile Approach to OD Assessment." *Business Horizons* (October 1974): 81–87.

Growler, D., and Legge, K. "Participation in Context: Towards a Synthesis of the Theory and Practice of Organizational Change." In *Journal of Management Studies* 15 (May 1978): 149–175 and 16 (May 1979): 139–171.

Harris, Kenneth. "Organizing to Overhaul a Mess." *California Management Review* 17, no. 3 (Spring 1975): 23–31.

Huber, George H. "The Nature and Design of Post Industrial Organizations." *Management Science* 30, no. 8 (August 1984): 928–951.

Jacobs, Bruce A. "Does Westinghouse Have the Productivity Answer?" *Industry Week* 208 (1981): 95–98.

Jenkins, John A. *Creating the Future: Corporate Strategists Shape the 21st Century.* Washington, D.C.: Bureau of National Affairs, 1979.

Jones, Thomas E. *Options for the Future: A Comparative Analysis of Policy-oriented Forecasts.* New York: Praeger, 1980.

Kahn, Herman, et al. *The Next 200 Years: A Scenario for America and the World.* New York: William Morrow, 1976.

Kilmann, R. H., and Mitroff, I. I. "Problem Defining and the Consulting/Intervention Process." *California Management Review* 21 (Spring 1979): 26–33.

Kimberly, J. R., and Miles, R. H. *The Organizational Lifecycle: Issues in the Creation, Transformation, and Decline of Organizations.* San Francisco: Jossey-Bass, 1980.

Lawrence, P. R., and Lorsch, J. W. *Developing Organizations: Diagnosis and Action.* Reading, Mass.: Addison-Wesley, 1969.

Lippitt, Gordon. *Organizational Renewal.* New York: Appleton-Century-Crofts, 1969.

Nicholas, John M. "The Comparative Impact of Organization Development Interventions on Hard Criteria Measures." *Academy of Management Review* 7, no. 4 (December 1982): 531–542.

Newton, Grant. "Management Account: Catalyst for Change." *Management Accounting* 58 (July 1976): 52–56.

Ouchi, William G. *Theory Z: How American Business Can Meet the Japanese Challenge.* Reading, Mass.: Addison-Wesley, 1981.

Schiff, Frank W. *Looking Ahead: Identifying Key Economic Issues for Business and Society in the 1980s.* New York: Committee for Economic Development, 1980.

Toffler, Alvin. *The Third Wave.* New York: William Morrow, 1980.

Walters, Roy W. "Organization Change—A New Model." *Personnel Journal* 54, no. 11 (November 1975): 573–574.

Wholey, Douglas R., and Brittain, Jack W. "Organizational Ecology: Findings and Implications." *Academy of Management Review* 11, no. 3 (July 1986): 513–533.

Zand, Dale E., and Sorenson, Richard E. "Theory of Change and the Effective Use of Management Science." *Administrative Science Quarterly* 20, no. 4 (December 1975): 532–545.

Zmud, R. "Diffusion of Modern Software Practices: Influence of Centralization and Formalization." *Management Science* 28, no. 12 (December 1982): 1421–1431.

Zmud, R. W., and Armenakis, A. A. "Understanding the Measurement of Change." *Academy of Management Review* 3, no. 3 (July 1978): 661–669.

```
C    A    S    E
```

16.5 Million Yellow Boxes

On January 9, 1986, a federal court ordered Eastman Kodak out of the instant camera business as a result of its violation of Polaroid patents. Kodak warehouses were filled with 16.5 million yellow boxes containing its instant cameras—collecting dust. Two weeks later, Kodak announced its return to the 35 mm camera business, but with a difference—the cameras are not manufactured in Rochester, New York, but in Japan. And a month after that, Kodak announced that its profits were the lowest in ten years.

Since its founding by George Eastman, Eastman Kodak has prided itself on technical know-how, manufacturing expertise, and consistent profitability. During the past ten years, however, while other organizations produced myriad innovations in the camera/film/film processing field, the Rochester corporation laid back as a result of its tradition-bound management that insisted on doing everything the "old way." The company was organized along functional lines, with manufacturing, marketing, and research and development operating as separate and isolated entities. Decisions were delayed until they percolated to the executive suite. Innovation and ability on the part of Kodak managers did not count nearly as much

Source: Alex Taylor III, "Kodak Scrambles to Refocus," *Fortune* (March 13, 1986), 34–39.

as seniority and fealty to the organization; hence, lethargy and stagnation.

Change is in the wind in Rochester. New Kodak Chairman Colby H. Chandler has reorganized the business and focused attention on diversification and acquisitions. These actions are necessary to bring Kodak's technology up to date as the industry has shifted from chemical-based to electronics-based photography. Moreover, Chandler has deemed it imperative for his company to market products made by others until it develops adequate technology to design and manufacture its own.

This new direction will not be easy for a company thrown into businesses where it has little experience, but big rivals. As a historical leader in the photography industry, Kodak was used to stability and insulation from the environment. Now it finds itself competing directly with such firms as RCA, GE, Xerox, and so on, not to mention the Japanese firms like Minolta, Fuji, and Nikon that have significantly eaten away at Kodak's share of the camera and film market.

Management professor E. Kirby Warren of Columbia University doubts that the Kodak organization can change quickly enough to keep up with its competition. He believes that Kodak needs to bring in more outside managers because the "stolid" people at Kodak cannot get it in their minds that they've been beaten by the Japanese.

Of course, the Polaroid patent suit was *the* decisive blow to Kodak's complacency. Refusing to accept Polaroid inventor Edwin Land's offer to Kodak years ago, the company stagnated in this specific area until technological advances made the instant camera a mass consumer item. Rushing to catch up, Kodak managers told employees not to be "constrained" by potential patent infringements. Now, Kodak is not only out of the instant camera business, but has lost $800 million from the cameras it cannot sell. That figure is not the bottom line—damages have yet to be determined by the court, and that figure could be in the billions.

Kodak used to be a leader. Now it is a follower. Its manufactured-in-Japan 35 mm camera is no better than those of its rivals, and Kodak's goal in marketing this item is to sell more film. The company believes that people who buy its camera will also buy its film. But that may not happen, because Kodak's chief film competitor, Fuji, has captured most of the growth in this market by keeping its film prices 10 percent below Kodak's. What is Kodak to do? The great majority of its profits rest with film sales.

Chairman Chandler, in order to put some propulsion into Kodak, has reorganized his company's photographic division. In 1985, he broke this division into seventeen business units. Younger managers have skipped the traditional pecking order to run fifteen of these units, and responsibility for key decisions has been pushed from the executive suites to the unit heads. Chandler hopes that this change in management style and organization will promote innovation, speed reaction time, and establish clear profit goals.

This reorganization of the photographic division may get results. J. Philip Sampler, the division head, says of the old way: "There was a feeling that everyone did his own job, and if something went wrong, it was somebody else's problem ... We haven't been able to show numbers yet, but we've cut waste and improved production. And products *are* [emphasis added] moving faster to market." Moreover, by breaking Kodak into smaller business units, the company has become more entrepreneurial, as opposed to its previous risk-aversiveness.

Another key change in Rochester has been the search for acquisitions to fill in gaps in product lines and obtain technological knowhow. In addition, Kodak has formed a venture board within the company to underwrite small projects and make venture capital investments. This new venturesomeness has brought in a multitude of entrepreneurs, venture capitalists, and investment bankers to Rochester. The company now has an "office of submitted ideas" designed to screen outside projects.

The marketing of other organizations' products is another quantum change for Kodak. For years, it was one of the most fully integrated manufacturers in the United States. It even had its own stockyards as a source of gelatin for its photographic paper. Now, it sells video cameras by Matsushita and markets one-hour film processing labs made by Noritsu Koki and Copal, also from Japan. Of course, having to sell others' products means thinner profit margins. But, states Chandler, "Our manufacturing skills haven't disappeared. If and when it's economically attractive to produce here, we will."

One other major change at Kodak merits attention—increased research and development efforts in the electronic imaging field, which will most certainly replace chemical film processing in the years to come. Should Kodak become successful in these efforts, it has a chance to regain its leadership role in the photography/film/film processing market.

Kodak is a different company now. Says one analyst, "I think it is quite a different corporation. It is less paternalistic and less isolated in terms of attitude."

QUESTIONS FOR DISCUSSION

1. How can an organization, such as Kodak, keep from getting out of touch with its environment(s)?
2. How can Kodak know when it is again in harmony with its environment?
3. What changes, if any, would you suggest in Kodak's organization structure that could help the company adapt? Provide a suitable rationale for your suggestions.
4. Can an organization outgrow its structure? In other words, can an organization become so large as to be unmanageable, regardless of its organization structure?
5. What are the implications of today's environment for "yesterday's" organizations?

Integrative Cases

I n this, the last section of the book, you are asked to synthesize and integrate the concepts that have been covered in the text. Six cases are presented. Each case requires you to apply various organization theory concepts in an analytical framework.

Each case is based on actual incidents experienced by real organizations and is followed by a series of questions for analysis. These questions do not address all of the issues in the case, but should help you analyze the case within the framework of the text material. Try to answer each question and then formulate a list of additional points that need to be addressed. Expand your analysis to include an examination of these points.

The cases cover a variety of different types of organizations, including a federal agency, an information processing/manufacturing/research and development company, an automobile manufacturer, an airline, a financial services company, and a multinational conglomerate. Each organization faces a unique set of circumstances to which it must respond. Our open-systems environmental framework should allow you to identify and analyze the important variables involved in order for you to develop appropriate solutions.

NASA:
Mission Aborted

INTRODUCTION

On January 28, 1986, the shuttle *Challenger* exploded in a ball of fire twelve miles above the Atlantic Ocean off Cape Canaveral, Florida. The explosion of *Challenger* and death of her crew were more than a national tragedy or an unforseeable and inexplicable aberration. This tragedy exposed the weaknesses and inefficiencies that had been eating away at the NASA organization like an uncontrolled cancer. That a similar tragedy had not occurred during an earlier shuttle launch was more due to luck and timing rather than to the mythical careful planning, emphasis on safety, engineering wizardry, and excellent management practices heretofore attributed to NASA.

Three months after *Challenger* exploded, a Titan rocket exploded over Vandenberg Air Force Base in California, and one month later, on May 3, 1986, a Delta rocket carrying a hurricane-spotting satellite had to be be destroyed over Cape Canaveral. NASA and the U.S. space program in general were in deep trouble.

This case will examine the incidents and controversy concerning NASA operations, particularly vis-à-vis the shuttle program. In addition, we will analyze various commentaries put forth by experts and the findings of the Rogers commission, the organization charged with investigating the *Challenger* tragedy. We will focus particularly on the dysfunction within the NASA system, with special emphasis on such areas as authority relationships, accountability, boundary spanning, integration, and NASA goals and the means used to achieve them.

BUREAUCRATIC/SYSTEMS PROBLEMS

By examining the findings of the Rogers commission, in addition to other information, it becomes apparent that NASA had become an ineffective and inefficient organization during recent years.

First, budget constraints during the past decade had forced a *70 percent* cut in safety and quality-control personnel.[1] Therefore, these two significant functions within NASA were severely understaffed, and they were no longer (at least in a de facto sense) important goals to be achieved.

Second, in order to cope with its dual role as both a passenger and cargo service, NASA significantly decentralized its organization structure. According to the findings of the Rogers commission, NASA headquarters in Washington, D.C., lost control of its widespread operations at the Johnson Space Center in Houston, the Marshall Space Flight Center in Huntsville, Alabama, and the Kennedy Launch Center in Florida. In turn, these three critically important NASA centers were unaware of their relationships with each other; thus, communications and coordination of activities were severely lacking. Indeed, this lack of control extended to NASA suppliers and contractors, who often fell behind in their delivery of vital hardware for the shuttle. This latter problem was compounded when these private entities succumbed to pressure from NASA bureaucrats to produce and deliver, even if testing and quality had to suffer.

Hard examples of these problems will be shown below as we trace the history of the now famous O-ring seal, the direct cause of the *Challenger* explosion.

History of the O-ring

The organizational reporting system within NASA is as complex as the organization itself. The system is comprised of elaborate reporting channels; however, in practice, these channels, particularly those concerning the O-ring seal and shuttle booster rockets, produced reams of paper that masked, rather than uncovered, problems.

The paper trail began in January, 1979, when John Miller, chief of the solid motor branch at Marshall, warned his superiors that the O-ring seal was malfunctioning. On May 29, 1980, a NASA engineering panel noted that the O-ring seals of a shuttle booster rocket failed during a ground test. Continuing to follow this problem, NASA, on December 17, 1982, added the O-ring seal to its criticality-1 list, ". . . meaning that it lacked a reliable back-up part and, if the joint failed, it would lead to a loss of mission and crew."[2] Although placement on this list should have alerted top-level NASA management to the urgency of this matter, there were already 748 parts on this list; therefore, the O-ring did not stand out. Dutifully, Lawrence Mulloy, the booster manager at Marshall, slapped a formal launch constraint on shuttle launches as a result of the information he had concerning the O-ring; however, he also routinely removed this constraint prior to each shuttle launch. During the Rogers commission hearings, Mulloy's superiors within NASA stated that they did not know about these constraints and their subsequent lifting each time a shuttle was launched.

In 1984, John Miller again warned his superiors at Marshall about the O-rings. During the same year, George Morrow, chief engineer for United Space Boosters, a private company, wrote to Mulloy, stating that the Titan rockets produced by his company had joint problems similar to those associated with the shuttle boosters.

Certainly, NASA managers, particularly those at Marshall, knew of the O-ring problems. However, rather than seek a solution itself, NASA top-level management at Marshall asked the prime contractor for the booster rockets, Morton-Thiokol, to seek a solution to this recurring and nagging problem.

MORTON THIOKOL'S ROLE. Upon being requested by NASA officials at Marshall to investigate the O-ring problems, Morton-Thiokol set up a task force to investigate this recurring "irritation." When a shuttle was launched on January 24, 1985, following the coldest overnight temperature of any flight to date, Thiokol engineers noted and dutifully reported that this launch produced the most extensive O-ring damage ever. Thiokol's post-flight summary to NASA stated that "low temperatures enhanced the probability of seal erosion,"[3] and, moreover, on August 9, 1985, Thiokol officials told NASA that the O-rings did not even do their jobs when the temperature was as cold as 50° F.

Although the Thiokol task force certainly seemed to be doing its job in investigating the O-ring problem, top-level managers at that company seemed to have the same "hearing" problems that their counterparts at NASA were having. Bob Ebeling, the manager of booster-ignition systems at Thiokol, wrote an interoffice memorandum on October 1, 1985, in which he stated, "HELP!! The seal task force is constantly being delayed by every possible means. . . . The allegiance of the O-ring investigation task force is very limited to a group of engineers numbering 8–10. . . . We wish we could get action by verbal request, but such is not the case."[4]

To make matters worse, Marshall managers, tiring of problems associated with the shuttle, asked Thiokol to "winnow" any and all problems associated with the shuttle booster rockets. In spite of spending $2 million attempting to correct the O-ring problem, Brian Russell, Thiokol's manager of special projects for the booster rockets, recommended on December 6, 1985, that the O-ring problem be dropped from the critical problems list. Indeed, just six days prior to the fatal *Challenger* launch, an unsigned memo at Marshall stated that "this problem is considered closed."[5]

Morton-Thiokol's last appearance in this drama occurred on the eve of the *Challenger* launch. Aware of the problems that cold weather could cause with the O-ring, four Thiokol vice presidents held a teleconference with NASA managers. Although the Thiokol people told the NASA people about their fears for the *Challenger* considering the cold weather and associated O-ring problems, the NASA people objected quite strongly to anything that might delay the launch. The Thiokol vice presidents then took a "management vote" (ignoring the advice of their own engineers seated right next to them) and elected not to oppose the launch.

PRESSURES TO LAUNCH

Our previous discussion has described some of the various events and decisions (or lack of decisions) that led to the *Challenger* launch. However, the question of "Why?" still remains unanswered.

Organizations do not exist in a vacuum. Rather, they exist in an environment that exerts pressure from all angles. Such is certainly the case with an organization like NASA that is public, considered "glamorous," and constantly in the limelight. Jerome Lederer, founder of the private Flight Safety Foundation and a former NASA safety expert, offered this explanation: "There was social pressure: they had thousands of school kids watching for the first school lesson from space. There was media pressure: they feared if they didn't launch, the press would unfavorably report more delays. And there was commercial pressure: the Ariane [European launcher] was putting objects in space at much lower cost. NASA was also trying to show the Air Force that it could launch on schedule. The pressures were subtle, but they acted upon them."[6]

Competition

As Lederer noted, the forces of competition also pressured NASA to launch *Challenger*. Although NASA is a government agency, one of its functions has been to launch commercial payloads for private organizations, with the goal of making a profit for NASA. Ariane directly competes with NASA for this commercial business, and some U.S. companies have shifted their business from NASA to Ariane, not only because of the latter's cheaper prices, but also because its launch schedules have been more dependable.

NASA's potential competition is not only foreign. General Dynamics, with a wealth of experience in providing rockets for the Air Force, stated that it wished to enter the space launch business. Basically, General Dynamics, if given the opportunity, planned to rent government launching facilities and use its own rockets to get payloads into space.

Thus, we can see how the competitive component of the macro environment exerted pressure on NASA to launch *Challenger* despite the wealth of information available to that organization concerning the safety implications of the O-ring seal in the booster rockets.

The Military/SDI

No discussion of external pressures on the NASA organization would be complete without a short analysis of its relationship to the military. In addition to its many launches of military satellites, NASA (at the time of this writing) is one of the primary organizations charged with making the Strategic Defense Initiative (SDI) operational; that is, NASA is responsible for getting military hardware into space. Thus, it is required to work closely with the armed forces, particularly the Air Force, on technological developments such as sensors, computers, laser mirrors, and satellite battle stations.

NASA has tentative plans to begin launching this military hardware by the mid-1990s. However, NASA and the military are already constrained in this endeavor by the sheer physical weight and size of the assorted hardware. In its first year of SDI launch operations, NASA is expected to launch a total of 2.6 million pounds of equipment, and over 4.4 million pounds of equipment by the year 2000.[7] The problem is the availability of the shuttle and other launch vehicles (Deltas and Titans) for carrying this much weight into space. In short, the present SDI strategy demands *considerable* use of the shuttle, the Deltas, and the Titans in order to get everything in place. Therefore, from NASA's point of view, it was imperative to get in as many shuttle launches as possible in order to prove the validity of this means of getting hardware into space.

OFFICIAL CONCLUSIONS AND RECOMMENDATIONS

The basic recommendation made by the Rogers commission was that NASA take firm control of its sprawling and decentralized bureaucracy and, moreover, cut back on meaningless paper flow. Concerning the all-important safety function, the commission recommended that anyone in the NASA system holding a strong view regarding a safety issue *must* be permitted to express his or her opinion *at any level*, rather than be limited to communicating his or her concerns only through departmental channels.

Conversely, the commission felt that top-level managers in NASA should take the initiative to raise oral questions, rather than simply send paper inquiries down through the ranks where they can be lost, ignored, or merely given lip service.

In addition, the commission recommended the adoption of new rules for launch. First, all preflight discussions of whether a launch should or should not go will be recorded. Second, the astronauts themselves will be involved in the decision-making process.

Concerning the redesign of the O-ring, the task will be supervised by independent experts.

The current NASA chief, James Fletcher, has stated his priorities: the improvement of NASA's management practices (without being specific); the setting up of a panel of experts from the National Academy of Sciences to oversee the shuttle redesign; the employment of outside management experts to review the management structure at NASA; and the issuance of a directive to all top-level managers within NASA that they talk to each other on a regular basis.

Indeed, the job at NASA is *not* simply to identify the "failure of a human being within the system"; rather, according to commission chairman Rogers, "It was a little more than that. It's [sic] a failure of the whole system."[8]

GOALS

Before NASA can redesign its system and fix its management structure and practices, it must first rethink its overall mission and corresponding goals. Moreover, after determining its mission and goals, NASA must develop a variety of means to achieve them. Indeed, some experts state that the *Challenger* disaster occurred because ". . .the Shuttle has become a substitute for a goal instead of a means of obtaining a goal."[9]

There has been considerable soul-searching at NASA since January 28, 1986; however, there has been little concrete agreement as to what exactly NASA's mission and goals should be. To make a complex situation even more complex, there are a plethora of outside entities, such as the military, the president, Congress, the National Academy of Sciences, and the National Commission on Space, offering suggestions and directives as to what exactly the NASA organization should do. Some say that the *Challenger* should be replaced with another shuttle and that (with changes in management practices) NASA should continue as it has in the past. Others say that NASA should refocus its efforts on using only crewless launch vehicles to deliver payloads into space. The Reagan administration wants NASA to dedicate the bulk of its efforts toward military (SDI) programs. And there are those who believe that NASA should retreat from or even abandon the launching of foreign and commercial payloads. Finally, there are arguments stating that NASA should be, first and foremost, a research and development organization. Whatever the point of view, most knowledgeable sources strongly believe that NASA must have a vision supported by realistic goals; otherwise, vast sums of resources and technology will be wasted on aimless wandering.

Almost simultaneous with the *Challenger* explosion, NASA published a book, *NASA Space Plans and Scenarios to 2000 and Beyond*, in which it listed its formal, long-term explicit goals and the means to achieve them. At the time of this writing, this book still remains the official, long-term vision of the NASA organization.

National Space Strategy

On August 15, 1984, the president approved a National Space Strategy designed to implement the national policy for space. The strategy, as applied to *civil* space programs, is comprised of the following elements:

Insure routine, cost-effective access to space with (via) the Space Transportation System.

Establish a permanently manned presence in space.

Foster increased international cooperation in civil space activities.

Identify major long-range national goals for the civil space program.

Insure a vigorous and balanced program of civil scientific research and exploration in space.

Encourage commercial Expendable Launch Vehicle activities.

Stimulate private sector commercial space activities.[10]

NASA's Eight Major Goals

In 1986, NASA published the following eight overall goals, based on its original mandate from the National Aeronautics and Space Act of 1958:

Provide for our work force a creative environment and the best of facilities, support services, and management support so that they can perform with excellence NASA's research, development, mission, and operational responsibilities. Provide for the development of employees so as to enhance and sustain an integrated work force of highest quality at NASA.

Make the Space Transportation System fully operational and cost effective in providing routine access to space for domestic and foreign, commercial, and government users.

Develop within a decade (by 1996) a permanently manned space station.

Conduct an effective and productive aeronautics research and development program which contributes materially to the enduring preeminence of U.S. civil and military aviation.

Conduct an effective and productive space and earth sciences program which expands human knowledge of the earth, its environment, the solar system, and the universe.

Conduct effective and productive space applications and technology programs which contribute materially toward U.S. leadership and security.

Expand opportunities for U.S. private sector investment and involvement in civil space and space-related activities.

Establish NASA as a leader in the development and application of advanced technology and management practices which contribute to significant increases in both Agency and national productivity.[11]

Space Flight Goals

Because this case has dealt primarily with NASA problems involved with its space flight program, it is important to list NASA's long-term goals regarding this activity.

Maintain a Shuttle launch schedule with reserve capacity, while conducting safe, successful Shuttle missions having progressively lower operational costs and shorter turn-around times.

Help in meeting NASA's objectives of developing and putting into routine operation in low Earth orbit by the early 1990s a manned permanent space station facility.

Define, design, and provide a second-generation space transportation system, including unmanned cargo vehicles and second-generation orbiters.

Develop and operate on a routine basis, beginning in the mid-1990s, geosynchronous orbit space platforms that are manned, permanent, and multifunction.

Develop and put into routine operation by 2000 geosynchronous orbit facilities that are permanent, multifunction, and able to be periodically manned.

Develop technology and techniques to construct, deploy, or assemble such facilities in space, and to test and service them in orbit.

Encourage and support NASA and industry development technology to improve concepts for space boosters that significantly reduce launch costs.[12]

Other NASA Goals

Without listing them specifically, NASA has set for itself myriad other goals pertaining to such areas as the development of space tracking and data systems, a space communications network, a ground communications network, research and development for advanced systems, solar system exploration, and the obtainment of new knowledge in astrophysics, life sciences, materials processing, and communications capabilities.

Staff Requirements

In order to achieve its plethora of official goals, NASA believes that it must create a work environment that will enable the agency to achieve and maintain a work force of the highest excellence. Therefore, NASA has undertaken a priority activity recruitment of recent college and university graduates of distinction in engineering and the sciences. In 1986, NASA announced that its current scientist and engineering complement of 10,900 is expected to grow to 11,500 by the end of fiscal year 1989.[13] Nowhere does NASA mention its need to recruit personnel knowledgeable in the art and science of management.

Information Processing

In order to handle the vast quantities of information that will be necessary for NASA to accomplish its mission, the agency will establish the "Automated Information Management Program."[14] Specifically, this program will combine administrative data processing, telecommunications, and office automation into a comprehensive system of computer-based tools to handle a variety of tasks. It will ensure maximum information exchange with great flexibility for accommodating growth and changes in needs. In order to ensure that this program attains maximum benefit, NASA has established a council to provide program direction and quality. This council includes representatives from each headquarters program office, the comptroller, and each field center.

At the time of this writing, NASA still has not been able to resume its shuttle operations and many questions remain concerning the future nature and direction of the agency.

QUESTIONS FOR DISCUSSION

1. What type of strategy did NASA adopt in dealing with the shuttle problem? Why do you suppose that its management did this?

2. From this case, do you believe NASA is applying sound organization theory components to resolve its dilemma? Specifically, identify the components of organization theory most involved with this case.
3. Evaluate NASA's approach to meeting its staff needs.
4. Evaluate NASA's approach to meeting its information needs.
5. What suggestions would you make if you were called on to help NASA at this point?

ENDNOTES

1. Ed Magnuson, "Fixing NASA: As a Tough Report on 'Challenger' Is Readied, the U.S. Debates Its Space Future," *Time* (June 9, 1986), 17.
2. Ibid., 18.
3. Ibid.
4. Ibid.
5. Ibid., 19.
6. Ibid., 20.
7. Ibid., 24.
8. Ibid., 20.
9. Ibid., 17.
10. Office of External Relations, NASA, *NASA Space Plans and Scenarios to 2000 and Beyond* (Park Ridge, N.J.: Noyes Publications, 1986), 3.
11. Ibid., 4–5.
12. Ibid., 14–15.
13. Ibid., 32.
14. Ibid., 238.

IBM:
Blue Skies

INTRODUCTION

IBM Corporation (nicknamed "Big Blue" by its employees because of the blue logo it puts on all of its products) reorganized its sprawling structure in 1981–1982 to better meet the needs of its myriad customers and to better adapt to the demands of a complex and heterogeneous environment.

This reorganization was necessary for a variety of reasons. First, the organization had been losing out to its competition, particularly Apple Computers, in the personal computer (PC) field and to other companies in the areas of microcomputers and minicomputers. IBM's market share in the computer and office products industry, which was 60 percent in 1967, had fallen to 40 percent by 1980.[1] Although the company's gross revenues had been rising at 13 percent per year throughout the 1970s, this revenue growth did not come close to matching the expanding market opportunities created by new computer and information-processing technology.

Second, although IBM was well known for its marketing zeal and savoir faire in providing service to its customers, the 1970s found the organization in a performance distress situation regarding these two functions. There were many late deliveries of products, and the marketing staff, divided among various divisions and groups, was unable to sell IBM products in an integrated, across-the-board manner. In other words, customers could not buy a full line of products from one sales representative;

rather, they had to contact several representatives to complete their orders.

This case will examine the corporate reorganization of IBM that resulted from the conditions described above. In order to accomplish this, we will first discuss the history and resultant corporate culture within this particular organization, because these two areas had (and still do have, for that matter) a direct bearing on IBM's ability to adapt to new situations with a minimum of pain. Second, we will examine the old corporate structure and the problems it presented regarding such functions as innovation, integration, and differentiation. Third, we will study the new structure with a view toward determining how it better suits IBM's needs. Finally, we will present a short discussion of the multiple benefits that have accrued to IBM since its reorganization.

HISTORY AND CULTURE OF IBM

Today, IBM enjoys success because of the actions it took in the early 1980s, and there can be little doubt that this success can be traced to the principles and beliefs of its five chief executive officers, particularly those of Thomas Watson, Sr., the founder. Concerning these principles and beliefs, one analyst has noted that "IBM created an environment that is unique because of its strong set of beliefs and principles. It's almost overwhelming how it affects employees and rubs off on customers."[2]

Thomas Watson, Sr.

In 1913, Thomas Watson, Sr., was hired as the general manager of Computing, Recording, Tabulating (CRT) Company. Watson had been hired to "clean up" this firm, particularly its financial problems. He was successful in this endeavor, particularly because he believed in working with and through his employees. Indeed, "loyal and happy" employees was one of the three main beliefs set forth by Watson, the other two being "customer service" and "striving for excellence."

While the organization was still called CRT, Watson promulgated rules for just about everything in order to reinforce his beliefs and values. Employees were told what to wear (dark suits, white shirts, striped ties) and what to drink (no alcohol), and "THINK" signs were posted everywhere in order to instill a striving for excellence in employees' work efforts. Watson's great respect for the individual was reflected by his "no lay off" policy, even when times were hard. His personal involvement with employees and belief in excellence could be seen years later when CRT became known as IBM. He commissioned the company song book, and personally led company sing-a-longs, particularly the rendition of

IBM's theme song, "Ever Onward." The lyrics are an excellent depiction of the corporate culture created by the founder:

> Our products are known
> In every zone.
> Our reputation sparkles like a gem.
> We've fought our way through.
> And new fields we're sure to conquer too.
> For the ever onward IBM.[3]

By 1924, Watson had become CEO and changed the name of the company to International Business Machines (IBM). During the next twenty years, IBM came to dominate the mechanical/electrical business machine market, so much so that in 1932 an antitrust suit was filed. In 1934, IBM signed a consent decree, in which it agreed to change its practices without admitting any monopolistic behavior.

Under Watson, IBM missed out on being the first organization to introduce a working computer. Its competitor, Remington-Rand, accomplished this with the introduction of UNIVAC in 1951. One year later IBM did enter this market, and, following his principle of customer service, Watson made rapid headway in this new market by dispelling customers' fears of computers. "Buyers were promised that IBM service engineers would keep a close watch over the machines and quickly fix any glitches. The salesmen were so knowledgeable and thoroughly trained that their very presence inspired confidence. UNIVAC representatives, by contrast, were seen to dwell on technical details that customers could barely follow."[4] By 1956, IBM had an 85 percent share of the computer market.[5]

Thomas Watson, Jr.

Thomas Watson, Jr., the son of the founder, became president of IBM in 1952 and CEO in 1956. As had occurred twenty years before, IBM was slapped with another antitrust suit, and in January 1956, Watson, Jr.'s first act as CEO was to sign another consent decree similar to the one his father had signed in 1934.

Among Watson, Jr.'s most notable achievements was his decentralization of the IBM organization in order to enhance innovation and push decision making down to the lowest possible level. Previously, the structure was a functionalized, very formal bureaucracy in the traditional sense. This decentralization was particularly beneficial for IBM's marketing function. Local sales managers, because of their special knowledge of customer needs, now had the authority to make many of their own decisions. Goals and budgets were set by the corporate headquarters; otherwise, the sales managers decided how, what, and when.

In addition, Watson, Jr., made the important strategic decision of manufacturing a single family of computers that could speak the same language, use the same software, and be appropriate for both business and scientific use. His decision resulted in the introduction of the 360 line of computers in April 1964. Within five years, almost $1 billion worth of these computers had been sold and 100,000 employees were added to the corporation. IBM was so successful in this field that *another* antitrust suit was filed in 1969, and this one was to be in and out of court until January 1982.

Concerning the son, one should note that he held firmly to the three basic principles set forth by his father—concern for the individual employee, customer service, and a striving for excellence.

T. Vincent Learson

This individual's tenure as IBM CEO (1971–1973) has been the shortest in the history of the organization. Learson's major contribution was his encouragement of different groups within IBM to bring forward proposed designs and compete against other proposals in a "shoot-out." As intended, this decision ensured that IBM would maintain its innovative environment and manufacture the finest products for the market.

Frank Carey

During Carey's reign (1973–1980), IBM entered a period of relative stagnation. The primary reason for this can be traced to the continuing antitrust suits that had been plaguing IBM since the early 1930s. Under Carey, IBM avoided price reductions for its products, shied away from diversification, and, most significantly, hesitated to develop and introduce new products. According to analysts, the IBM organization became very conservative because every move had to be evaluated in terms of its effect on the pending antitrust suit.

John Opel

Opel, who had been an IBM employee for thirty years before becoming CEO in 1980, is the current leader of the organization. He is credited with making IBM the marvel of the modern business world.

Opel can be considered a reincarnation of the founder, Watson, Sr. His shirts are buttoned-down white oxfords, his ties are impeccable, and his shoes are the standard corporate cordovan. Opel claims that he became CEO because he molded himself to just what the company wanted him to be, and, moreover, that he is an "interchangeable" part of IBM. "I'm a product of the culture of IBM, of the way we do things,"[6] he said.

Opel is to be credited, first and foremost, for the IBM reorganization of 1981–1982. He formed a corporate management committee (CMC), comprised of top-level managers from the various subunits within the company, and charged it with a two-fold mission: (1) Redesign the IBM structure to better meet the demands of the marketplace; and (2) formulate a corporate growth strategy. (IBM was able to redirect its efforts toward innovation and market growth partially as a result of the lifting of the antitrust suit in January 1982.)

Because we will discuss the actual reorganization in the next section of this case, we will devote our efforts here to describing the new corporate strategy developed by Opel and his CMC.

THE NEW STRATEGY. This strategy was built around three main areas (excluding structure): (1) low-cost production, (2) low-cost distribution, and (3) penetration of high-growth markets.

Concerning low-cost production, IBM began to upgrade its facilities in the late 1970s, with heavy emphasis on this upgrading occurring during the early 1980s. From 1977–1983, IBM invested nearly $10 billion in new plants and equipment.[7] The corporation is now the lowest-cost producer in all areas of data processing. In addition, IBM has spent $500 million in employee education and training.[8] This latter effort reflects IBM's and Opel's continuing concern for the individual employee.

In order to be the lowest-cost distributor in the business, IBM began to use nearly every conceivable sales channel—its own retail stores, wholesalers, and even independent retailers. These latter two alternative distribution channels were required because direct sales costs were considered to be too high in relation to incoming sales revenues. As a result, IBM has been able to reach millions of small businesses (under 200 employees), which are prime users of its multitude of office and computer products.

IBM has been extremely successful in penetrating high-growth markets. In the late 1970s, IBM missed out in the PC market. However, in 1983, two years after "Big Blue" entered this market, it managed to control 21 percent of all PC sales with a value of $7.5 billion.[9] (The reason for IBM's rapid success in this area can be attributed to its new, innovative management structure, which we will discuss in the next section.) We should add here that IBM is a great "listener" to the market in order to identify new opportunities. It subscribes to virtually every major computer market-research service, and uses its worldwide intelligence-gathering network that includes economists and market analysts.

One of the most promising new fields to be explored by IBM under its new strategy is the automated office. Working toward dominating this emerging market, the corporation purchased 15 percent of Rolm Corporation in 1983. Rolm, which makes switches that are used to direct the flow of voice and data communications between office workstations, was an essential acquisition if IBM truly wished to be successful in this endeavor. (IBM purchased all of Rolm in 1984.)

Recognizing the international nature of the computer/information processing market, IBM, under Opel's leadership, has entered into cooperative agreements with foreign firms such as Matsushita Electrical of Japan. This venture will permit IBM to produce a PC that can transform phonetic symbols into Kanji, the ideograms that are the basic unit of the written Japanese language.

ORGANIZATION RESTRUCTURING

Before discussing the structural changes brought forth by Opel and his CMC, it is first necessary to examine the structure that governed IBM authority relationships and functions throughout the late 1960s and entire 1970s.

The Old Structure

As can be seen in Figure 1, the old IBM structure was basically a hybrid group/division structure, with the most important units being the Data Processing (DP) Marketing Group, the DP Product Group, and the General Business Group.

DP MARKETING GROUP. This group is comprised of three divisions, Data Processing, Federal Systems, and Field Engineering. Only the first division, Data Processing, actually had marketing responsibilities.

The Data Processing Division had marketing responsibility within the United States for those customers having large, centralized systems. These systems included information-handling, computer programming, auxiliary equipment, engineering, and educational.

Federal Systems was the division that provided information-handling and control systems to various federal agencies, particularly those involved with seaborne, airborne, spaceborne, and ground-based operations.

The Field Engineering Division provided maintenance and support services for those products marketed by Data Processing and manufactured by the DP Product Group, described below.

DP PRODUCT GROUP. This group was comprised of four divisions and focused its activities on development and manufacturing functions.

The Data Systems Division had worldwide development responsibility for large, complex systems in addition to U.S. manufacturing

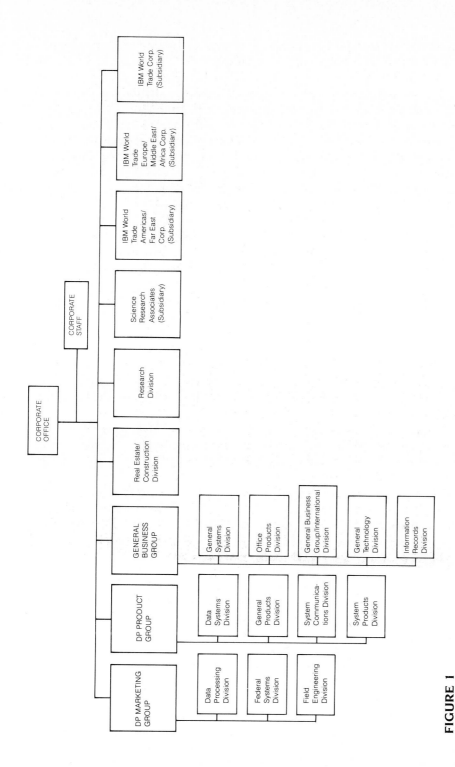

FIGURE 1

IBM Organization Chart (Before 1981–1982 Reorganization)

Source: Adapted by the authors from a prose narrative of the IBM organization structure, *IBM Annual Report, 1979.*

responsibility for those systems. Products included component parts, specifically logic and memory components.

The General Products Division had worldwide development responsibility for high-performance storage systems in addition to U.S. manufacturing responsibility for those items, including disk products, tape units, printers, and so on.

System Communications was the division within the DP Product Group that had worldwide responsibility for systems and products that prepare and process information for communication purposes. As with the other two divisions previously discussed within this group, it also had U.S. manufacturing responsibility for these products.

The fourth division within the DP Product Group was System Products. This division, like the other three, had worldwide development and U.S. manufacturing responsibilities for its products, which included intermediate range processors, related programming, and impact printers.

GENERAL BUSINESS GROUP. In terms of number of divisions (five), this was the largest group within the old IBM organization. You will note that the divisions within this group had a mixture of development, manufacturing, and marketing responsibilities for a wide range of products.

The General Systems Division had worldwide product management and development responsibilities in addition to U.S. manufacturing, marketing, and service responsibilities for low-to-moderate-priced information-handling systems.

The Office Products Division had worldwide product management and development responsibilities in addition to U.S. manufacturing, marketing, and service responsibilities for products such as typewriters, copiers, and related supplies. This division also had worldwide product management and U.S. marketing and service responsibilities for products such as magnetic media typewriters, information processors, dictation equipment, and direct-impression composing products.

Marketing, service, manufacturing, and overall performance responsibilities for both General Systems Division and Office Products Division products in twenty-one foreign countries were vested in a third division, General Business Group/International Division.

The fourth division, General Technology, had worldwide development and U.S. manufacturing responsibilities for the component technology requirements of the low-to-moderate-priced computers manufactured by the General Systems Division and the various items manufactured by the Office Products Division.

The Information Records Division, the last in the General Business Group, had U.S. marketing responsibility for products such as magnetic tape, diskettes, data modules, and disk packs in addition to U.S. manufacturing and marketing responsibilities for a variety of other products, including data-processing cards, business forms, ribbons, and other consumable products used in information-handling systems.

OTHER DIVISIONS. IBM had two separate divisions reporting directly to the corporate office as opposed to being classified as members of a larger group. The Real Estate/Construction Division was, of course, concerned with site acquisition and construction of IBM facilities. The Research Division conducted scientific research on the development of various technologies that would have long-range potential importance for the company.

SUBSIDIARIES. Four independent subsidiaries occupied special niches within the IBM empire. Science Research Associates had worldwide development production, and marketing responsibilities for a wide range of educational materials and services for schools, colleges, universities, and so on. The other three subsidiaries, depicted on the right side of Figure 1, were responsible for maintaining and supporting IBM operations in foreign countries.

The New Structure

IBM's current organization structure is depicted in Figure 2. The most striking change is the use of the words "Information Systems" to designate the three major groups. This reflects IBM's commitment to the development, manufacture, and marketing of total information systems in comparison to its prior concentration on data-processing (a more limited term) equipment. CEO Opel has noted that while people have limited needs for certain commodities, they have an insatiable demand for information. "I have yet to hear somebody say they could not use more information. Hence, the demand for information processing, though perhaps not infinite, is enormous,"[10] said the IBM CEO.

In terms of actual functional responsibilities, the most noticeable change from the old structure is the creation of the National Accounts (NA) and National Marketing (NM) Divisions within the Information Systems Group. As you read the description of these divisions' activities below, you will realize that the all-important marketing function at IBM has been consolidated into these two divisions (with a few minor exceptions). Compare this to the old structure where marketing was splintered among multiple divisions within several large groups.

Similar to the old structure, the new IBM structure is a hybrid group/ division structure. Most functions are carried on within three groups, Information Systems, Information Systems and Technology, and Information Systems and Communications.

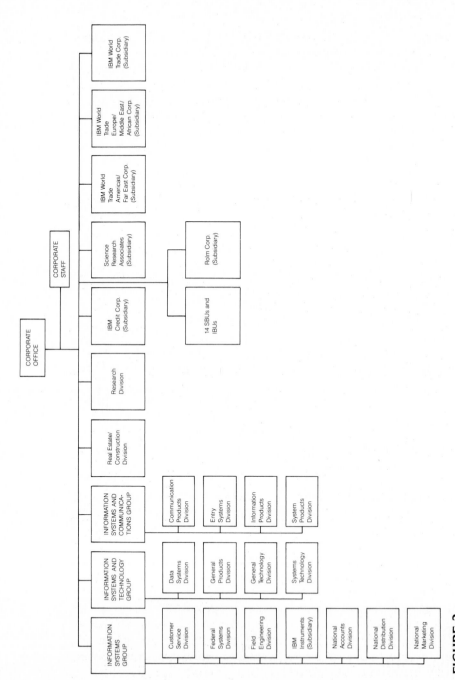

FIGURE 2

IBM Organization Chart (After 1981–1982 Reorganization)

Source: Adapted by the authors from a prose narrative of the IBM organization structure, *IBM Annual Report, 1983.*

INFORMATION SYSTEMS GROUP. This is the largest group within IBM today and is comprised of seven divisions. The first, Customer Service, is responsible for maintenance, related support, and programming services within the United States. The Federal Systems Division remains unchanged from the 1970s organization structure, other than the fact that the group to which it belongs has undergone a name change. While the Field Engineering Division still provides maintenance and support, its role has been expanded to include distribution of *all* hardware and software products.

IBM Instruments is a new subsidiary reporting directly to the group, rather than to the corporate office. It is responsible for developing, servicing, and marketing specialized analytical instruments.

The NA Division has both marketing and field administration duties within the United States for the *full line* of IBM products. It is market-segment focused in that it serves the needs of large accounts with complex information-processing needs.

Because IBM is now selling its products through multiple distribution channels, it has set up a special division, National Distribution, which is responsible for supervising the distribution of selected systems and high-volume products through these multiple and alternative distribution channels. This division also has some manufacturing and procuring responsibilities in addition to marketing responsibility for selected IBM accessories.

NM is the division entrusted with the responsibility for marketing and servicing the *full line* of IBM products. However, unlike NA, this division is market-focused on smaller firms.

INFORMATION SYSTEMS AND TECHNOLOGY GROUP. This group, comprised of four divisions, is mainly concerned with developing and manufacturing IBM's most complex equipment.

The Data Systems and General Products divisions have the same basic responsibilities that they had under the old structure; however, the group to which they report has been changed from DP Product Group to Information Systems and Technology Group. The General Technology Division's scope of operations has been expanded to include worldwide development of U.S. manufacturing of logic, memory, special semiconductors, and multilayer ceramics. In addition, the group to which this unit reports has obviously been changed.

The final division within this group is Systems Technology. It has worldwide development, product assurance, and U.S. manufacturing responsibilities for the circuit packaging utilized in IBM computer systems. This division also develops and manufactures intermediate processors and printers in addition to developing programming systems.

INFORMATION SYSTEMS AND COMMUNICATIONS GROUP. As the name implies, this group supervises a number of divisions responsible for the operations associated with communications. This group is comprised of four divisions, the most prominent of which is Communication Products. This division has worldwide development and U.S. manufacturing responsibilities for telecommunications systems, display products, and distribution industry systems. As IBM enters the world of automated offices, this division will serve as the worldwide focal point for office systems and systems network architectural activities.

The Entry Systems Division has U.S. manufacturing, worldwide development, and product management responsibilities for general purpose, low cost PCs and related software.

The information needs of the banking industry are served by this group's Information Products Division. It develops and programs specialized typewriters, copiers, and a variety of systems for banks.

The final division within this group, Systems Products, has U.S. manufacturing responsibility for small and intermediate-sized general purpose systems and related programming.

OTHER DIVISIONS. These are exactly the same as those that existed prior to the 1981–1982 reorganization.

IBUS AND SBUS. In order to stimulate technological innovation and new product development, IBM created Independent Business Units (IBUs) and Special Business Units (SBUs). IBUs, being totally independent, manage their own finances, manufacturing, and marketing functions, while SBUs depend on support from one or more of the official groups (or divisions within them) for some support. IBM, as far as these units are concerned, considers itself a venture capitalist, and these units are, in effect, companies within a company.

IBM currently has a total of fourteen IBUs and SBUs. Among other accomplishments, these units have led IBM into building industrial robots and electrocardiagraphs, writing customized software, and developing, manufacturing, and selling directory assistance equipment to telephone companies. The most notable achievement of one of these units was the development of IBM's extremely successful PC. The development of the IBM PC was accomplished by a twelve-man SBU group in Boca Raton, Florida. This team, assembled in July 1980, was told to develop a competitive and easy-to-use machine within a year. The tremendous success of this venture was documented in our previous discussion concerning the accomplishments of CEO Opel.

SUBSIDIARIES. Besides the Rolm Corporation, there is one new subsidiary in this category, the IBM Credit Corporation. This entity provides for lease financing of IBM products and finances installment receivables resulting from sales of IBM (and other manufacturers') equipment to U.S. customers. The other independent subsidiaries are the same as depicted in Figure 1.

Implementation of the New Structure

Before we leave our discussion of the IBM reorganization, we should note that the restructuring was effected very quickly and with a minimum of involvement by lower-order employees at IBM. This, however, does not contradict one of the basic tenets of the IBM culture—concern for the individual employee. The task force charged by the CMC with designing the new structure had specific instructions to consider the needs of each and every IBM employee. In order to deal with potential worker displacement, training programs were made available to individuals needing them.

Second, because the IBM culture can be considered thick and homogeneous, most employees' attitudes did not need to be changed because loyalty to the organization and its management is a basic tenet of this culture. Thus, any difficulties or resistance encountered in changing worker attitudes were minimal.

Third, as a direct result of IBM's promote-from-within policy, the top-level managers involved with the new organization design had worked their way through the ranks. Therefore, these individuals were aware of the problems and attitudes of lower-level employees.

POST-REORGANIZATION PERFORMANCE

We have already mentioned some of the results of this reorganization during our discussion of Opel's tenure as CEO. However, we will now examine in greater detail some of the phenomenal success experienced by IBM during the immediate period following reorganization.

In terms of market share, IBM's performance since the end of the 1970s has been remarkable. By viewing Figure 3, one can see how IBM's slide has been reversed from its 1970s stagnation period. This turnaround significantly correlates with the reorganization.

By examining IBM's growth in three major markets, mainframes, minicomputers, and business microcomputers, the results are striking, particularly in the latter category. Figure 4 graphically illustrates this point.

By the end of 1982, IBM's profits had soared to $4.4 billion on sales of $34.4 billion, thus making it the most profitable company in America for that year.[11] For stockholders, equity rose 22.1 percent in 1982, top among

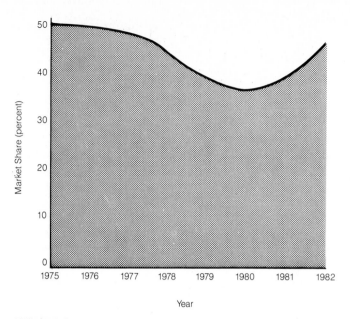

FIGURE 3

IBM's Overall Market Share (Market includes top fifty computer manufacturers)

Source: Peter D. Petre, "The New Lean, Mean IBM," *Fortune* (June 13, 1983), 74. Copyright © 1983 Time Inc. All rights reserved.

the nation's twenty largest corporations. Stock prices rose from $62 a share in 1981 to $114 a share in 1982.[12]

We have already stated the success that IBM has had with its SBUs and IBUs. Some analysts believe that IBM will soon dominate the automated office market. Through its acquisition of the Rolm Corporation, IBM now has the technology to develop such systems. In addition, the new organization structure recognizes the importance of these products. Refer to Figure 2 and note that a new division, Communication Products, was established to develop precisely such systems.

We have already shown how most of the overlap in the marketing and the service functions has been resolved through the new organization structure. Under the old structure, there was confusion among IBM and its customers concerning which group or division would actually handle a particular product. Now, with a few exceptions, any business entity will deal with either the NA or NM division, thus indicating the success of the organization structure that was born of IBM's desire to provide one-sales-representative customer contact.

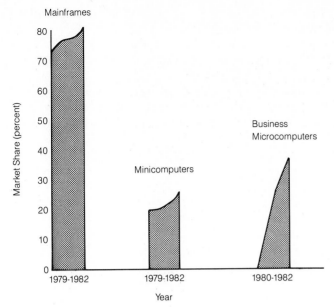

FIGURE 4

IBM's Share of Three Market Segments

Source: Peter D. Petre, "The New Lean, Mean IBM," *Fortune* (June 13, 1983), 74. Copyright © 1983 Time Inc. All rights reserved.

In conclusion, it was essential for IBM to develop a structure that would enable it to adapt to the highly volatile, yet challenging, environment of the 1980s. The reorganization that occurred in 1981–1982 was the vehicle that IBM chose, and evidence suggests that this reorganization has proven highly successful. This has been demonstrated by the elimination of organization overlap, increased revenues, expanded market share, and increased customer satisfaction. Indeed, IBM appears to be the "Big Blue" of old.

QUESTIONS FOR DISCUSSION

1. Evaluate carefully IBM's approach to dealing with its overall situation that it faced during the 1970s. What alternatives could it have chosen?
2. Enumerate those organization theory concepts found in this case and show how IBM dealt with each.

3. Using organization theory concepts, show how IBM can go about retaining its current market position.

4. What difficulties might IBM have had in its reorganization efforts if it had not had a thick and homogeneous culture? Be thorough in your answer.

5. For each integration device mentioned in the text, show how it can/should be used in the new IBM organization. Would each of these uses have been different in the case of the old IBM organization?

ENDNOTES

1. Peter D. Petre, "The New Lean, Mean IBM," *Fortune* (June 13, 1983), 69.
2. John Greenwald, "The Colossus that Works," *Time* (July 11, 1983), 45.
3. Ibid., 46.
4. Ibid.
5. Ibid.
6. Ibid., 48.
7. Ibid., 49.
8. Ibid.
9. Ibid., 44.
10. Ibid., 51.
11. Ibid., 44.
12. Petre, "The New Lean, Mean IBM," 69.

Chrysler:
You *Would* Buy a Used
Car from This Man

INTRODUCTION

In 1980, the Chrysler Corporation, then the nation's number three automaker, was on the verge of bankruptcy. Many local dealerships had closed their doors; literally thousands of Chrysler products were collecting rust and dust in huge outdoor storage areas; and, at the height of the energy crisis and ever-increasing gasoline prices, Chrysler products still resembled the behemoths of the 1950s and 1960s.

Within five years, Chrysler's turnaround was one of the most dramatic, well-publicized events in the history of American business. Buoyed by federally backed loans and led by the charismatic Lee Iacocca, Chrysler at the time of this writing is one of America's most successful large corporations. Table 1, which depicts Chrysler financial data from 1979 to 1985, demonstrates the enormity of this turnaround.

The purpose of this case is to examine Chrysler's renaissance in terms of the organization theory concepts found within the text. This case will focus on four main areas: (1) the history of Chrysler Corporation with a view toward showing how this particular organization suffered from a long series of problems that culminated in its near-bankruptcy of 1980; (2) the actual renaissance process, with particular emphasis on the various means used to revitalize the organization. (These means included cost savings, revenue increases, and a redesign of the organization structure); (3) Iacocca's use of power; and (4) speculation as to Chrysler's future without Iacocca.

TABLE 1

Chrysler Corporation's Financial and Market Share Data (1979–1985)

Year	Annual Sales (millions of dollars)	Earnings per Share	Dividends (full year)
1979	12,002	−17.18*	$.20
1980	9,225	−26.00*	—
1981	10,822	−7.18*	—
1982	10,045	−1.28*	—
1983	13,240	2.86	—
1984	19,573	7.83	$.40
1985	21,256	9.38	$.67

Year	Common Stock Price (year-end)	Retail Market Share (North America)
1981	$ 2¼	9.8%
1982	$11⅞	10.3%
1983	$18⅜	10.4%
1984	$21⅜	11.6%
1985	$31⅛	12.2%

*Computed loss

Source: "Chrysler Corporation," *Value Line Investment Survey* (June 1986), 104.

HISTORY OF THE CHRYSLER CORPORATION

Since its founding in 1925, Chrysler has undergone a series of ups and downs. By examining its history and the actions of its CEOs, we will observe how its crisis of the late 1970s and early 1980s had precedent in the past.

Walter Chrysler

After viewing his first automobile in 1908, Walter Chrysler, a railroad locomotive designer and plant superintendent, borrowed some money from a friend to buy his first auto; thus began Chrysler's romance and involvement with automobiles and the automobile industry. As he was to write later, "I did not simply want a car to ride in it. I wanted a machine so I could learn all about it. Why not? I was a machinist, and these self-propelled vehicles were by all odds the most astonishing machines that had ever been offered to man."[1]

Shortly after buying this car, Chrysler accepted a job offer from Charles Nash, the president of Buick (later to become part of GM). Nash's challenge to Chrysler was to convert what was merely a refined carriage-building company into a modern automobile manufacturing organization. By borrowing techniques that he had learned from his experience in the locomotive manufacturing industry, such as a moving production line, Chrysler made Buick so successful that it became the cash cow of its parent organization, GM. By 1919, Chrysler was made vice president of Buick, and his salary had risen to the then (and still) astonishing figure of $500,000 per year.[2]

Because Chrysler did not see eye to eye with Wil Durant, the GM chairman, he quit Buick and soon became the chairman of the reorganization and management committee of Maxwell Motor Company, a "sick" organization. While in this position, Chrysler developed the "Chrysler Six," the first U.S.-produced high compression six-cylinder-engine motor vehicle. This automobile was so successful that Maxwell Motor Company was able to obtain badly needed financial credit from the banks in order to mass produce the vehicle. In 1923, Chrysler was named president of Maxwell, and two years later, on June 6, 1925, Maxwell Motor Company became Chrysler Motors, with Walter Chrysler becoming chairman of the board and CEO.[3]

Chrysler took it upon himself to make Chrysler Motors competitive with GM and Ford. In 1928, two new models, the DeSoto and Plymouth were introduced, and by the end of the year the third model, the Dodge, came into being with the Chrysler purchase of Dodge Brothers. Thus, in three short years, Chrysler Motors had become the third largest automaker in the United States.[4]

During the Great Depression of the 1930s, Chrysler Motors had the distinction of being the only U.S. automaker to sell more cars and trucks than it had in the prosperous 1920s. This can be credited to a critical cost control scheme developed by Walter Chrysler whereby his organization shifted from a "make-to-stock" production system to a "make-to-order" one. Thus, delays and inventory surpluses were significantly ameliorated. In addition, Chrysler practiced "parts integration," the use of common/identical parts for the construction of different cars. This was another critical variable that enabled Chrysler to be profitable during the Great Depression.

K. T. Kellor

After Walter Chrysler died in 1940, K. T. Kellor took over the reins of power within the Chrysler organization. Chrysler retooled itself during World War II and produced scores of different armaments (particularly tanks); however, after the war, the organization entered its first stagnation period.

By the end of the 1940s, a hardened corporate culture at Chrysler prevented the organization from experimenting with new ways of designing and selling cars. Practical rather than fashionable cars were the mainstay of Chrysler production lines, even though the American public after the war desired fashion. In addition, Chrysler engineers would first determine the size, styling, and content of cars, top-level management would then approve the design, and, after this, accountants would determine detailed costing. Conversely, the competition at GM and Ford would first determine a suitable rate of return for an automobile and *then* work backward from that point in terms of design, styling, and content.

Chrysler's imperviousness to the post-war environment, particularly to the customer/client component of that environment, can be further evidenced by its sales organization. Basically, the sales functions were vested in local dealerships, without direction and goals being set by corporate headquarters. Thus, corporate-level decision makers did not have ready access to adequate information concerning what was happening in the marketplace without that information first being filtered, and perhaps even distorted, by the dealers. According to A. Vanderzee, head of Chrysler sales during that period, "What we knew about retailing we learned from the dealer and we encouraged him to be self-sufficient in every respect."[5] Some critics characterized these dealers as "greedy, insensitive, and unethical."

The final problem facing the post-war Chrysler Corporation was its ineffective organization structure. The company was run by an operations committee comprised of Kellor and seven vice presidents. In turn, each division within Chrysler had very little decision-making authority, and, moreover, there was little or no integration between divisions. One former official likened this situation to a "rimless wooden wheel," with Kellor at the center being the only person to know what was going on.

L. L. Colbert

Colbert became president of Chrysler in 1951 and chairman of the board in 1956. He tried to decentralize the decision making that had been vested for too long within the top-level operations committee. But because of stiff opposition from his top-level managers, he met with little success. Indeed, under Colbert, the organization became even more centralized. For example, the sales representatives were taken from the divisions and placed within corporate headquarters, and all division engine production was consolidated within a newly established central manufacturing unit. In addition, in order to reduce development time for new models, Colbert cut twelve months from the thirty-six-month cycle for the development of new cars; thus, quality suffered.

Problems associated with the Chrysler dealerships also continued to hurt the company. There was little or no concern for showroom standards or the accumulation of inventory at the dealerships. Colbert had reversed the make-to-order principle back to a make-to-stock one without regard for market demand. In short, his philosophy was to produce as many cars as possible and then let the dealers sell them.

Finally, labor unrest plagued the organization in the 1950s. In an attempt to improve productivity, Colbert laid off thousands of employees, thus incurring the wrath of the United Auto Workers (UAW). Unlike Ford and GM, Chrysler plants were not widely scattered throughout the United States. Most operations took place in Michigan, where the UAW was most powerful. Colbert retired in 1961 and was replaced by Lynn Townsend.

Lynn Townsend

Under Townsend's leadership, some problems were alleviated but others became compounded. His emphasis on volume production rather than quality added to the company's inventory problems. Also, by following styling trends established by GM and Ford, Chrysler ceased to be the innovator it had once been.

Townsend did, however, reduce costs by cutting back by 20 percent his white-collar work force.[6] He also closed several unprofitable plants and sold off the fleet of corporate airplanes. In addition, he combined two inefficient transmission plants into one efficient one.

Townsend's main achievement was the hiring of American Motors's highly regarded sales executive, Virgil Boyd. Boyd reorganized the organization's sales function, which heretofore had been overly independent and sluggish. New standards, directions, and goals were set for the dealers, who, in turn, were now more accountable to Chrysler headquarters for their performance. Boyd also established Chrysler's overseas marketing strategy, which was very successful in selling Chrysler products, particularly in Latin America.

In terms of innovation to stimulate sales, Townsend formed Chrysler Credit Corporation. Chrysler Credit provided financing to consumers wishing to purchase Chrysler products. Townsend also diversified the Chrysler Corporation with the founding of the Amplex, Chemical, Marine, Airtemp, Mopar Parts, Defense, and Space divisions in addition to the founding of Chrysler Realty. These diversifications, however, never amounted to more than 5 percent of the company's total revenues.[7]

To reflect his efforts at turning the organization around, Townsend changed the corporate logo to the "pentastar," which is still the Chrysler trademark.

In 1973–1974, the oil shock hit the nation and Chrysler Corporation. Because Townsend believed that this would be a temporary situation, he ordered Chrysler to continue full production of its large cars. Meanwhile, his competitors at GM and Ford began to develop smaller, more fuel-efficient cars and trucks. And, of course, the Japanese were beginning to penetrate the American market at this time.

Whatever progress Townsend had made for his organization during the 1960s and very early 1970s was to be doomed by Chrysler's inability to change in response to the oil crisis of the 1970s.

John Riccardo

Riccardo can best be remembered as the "caretaker" of the Chrysler Corporation from 1975 to 1979. Riccardo knew that his company had to drastically change its ways; however, it simply did not have the resources to do so, nor did he have a vision of what Chrysler should become in view of the changed environment in which it existed. In 1978, Lee Iacocca, a Ford vice president, left that organization and joined Chrysler. Thus, the stage was set for the renaissance that brought Chrysler out of the doldrums that had plagued it on and off since the end of World War II.

THE IACOCCA RENAISSANCE

When Iacocca was hired as the new Chrysler president by Chairman Riccardo in 1978, the company had just suffered a $205 million loss.[8] For Iacocca, who became chairman at the end of 1979, a four-fold challenge faced him and his organization: (1) obtain emergency funding; (2) cut costs; (3) increase revenues; and (4) transform Chrysler into a new organization, one characterized by pride, quality, and efficiency.

Emergency Funding

Perhaps no business story received as much news attention from 1979 through 1981 as Chrysler's successful attempt to obtain federally backed loans. The crisis within Chrysler was so grim that the organization teetered on the edge of bankruptcy. Using his own personal appeal and friendship with then-President Carter, Iacocca managed to obtain $1.5 billion in federally backed loan guarantees. Most analysts believe that this decision was politically rather than economically motivated. Had the loan deal not been approved by the president and Congress, Chrysler most certainly would have had to declare bankruptcy. The ripples from the subsequent unemployment would have had profound effects in the states where Chrysler had its plants, particularly Michigan, Indiana, Ohio, Illinois, and Missouri. These are large, crucial states in election years, and 1980 *was* an election year, both for the presidency and for Congress. Certainly, events within the political component of the macro environment had a profound effect on the future of Chrysler! (As you will read below, Chrysler was so successful in its revitalization efforts that in 1985, Iacocca paid back *all* the federally guaranteed loans several years early, thus saving his company millions in interest payments.)

Cost-Cutting

The federal government did not agree to back the $1.5 billion to Chrysler with no strings attached. A loan guaranty board, comprised of Chrysler creditors and federal officials, was responsible for overseeing Chrysler's cost-cutting/revenue-producing programs, with the goal of ensuring that this organization would be a going concern no later than December 31, 1983. Had this board determined that Chrysler's plans were not feasible, it is quite possible that the organization would not have received all of the loans it requested. Of the $1.5 billion approved, Chrysler received $1.2 billion in two installments in 1980 and 1981.[9]

Cost-cutting measures took a variety of forms. Iacocca managed to wring $1 billion in wage concessions from the UAW, a 5 percent reduction in prices charged by suppliers for ninety days in 1981, a $575 million cut in proposed expenditures for new plant capacity, and most surprisingly, managed to persuade Chrysler's lenders to convert $572 million in debt to preferred stock, thereby reducing interest payments by $100 million a year.[10]

Furthermore, Iacocca cut costs by reducing his organization's blue-collar work force from 160,000 employees to 80,000 in 1982 and by closing many unprofitable dealerships.[11]

Perhaps one of the best ways to cut overall costs in the automobile manufacturing (or any other) industry is to boost productivity. That Chrysler managed to do this is well evidenced by the fact that its break-even point has been cut from 2.4 million to 1.2 million units per year.[12]

Chrysler employed two major methods to increase its overall productivity (cost per unit). First, Iacocca returned to the concept of parts integration first used by his predecessor, Walter Chrysler. By using a single platform (drivetrain, floorpan, and suspension), the company was able to manufacture a wide variety of vehicles ranging from convertibles to minivans. By being able to make more vehicles from a single, common platform, the automaker significantly cut labor, production, and inventory costs. Concomitant with the single-platform technique was the introduction and utilization of automated manufacturing equipment (as improving financial conditions permitted).

Second, it was imperative that Chrysler obtain more work output from employees. That Chrysler accomplished this can be seen by the actions undertaken at the organization's Detroit Trim plant where automobile upholstery is manufactured. Management worked together with the UAW to discard inflexible work rules, provide for employee participation in decision making, lay off unnecessary employees, lower wages, streamline jobs, and increase work quotas. Even though many of these actions were unpopular, workers wanted to keep their plant open and thus understood the necessity for these actions. Not only has Detroit Trim remained open, but productivity has increased from 11,460 units produced per day to over 14,000.[13] Similar methods were used and similar results obtained at other Chrysler plants.

Where costs could not be cut in operations such as those described above, plants were shut down. This had the effect of *lessening* Chrysler's vertical integration and thus saving it money. This is because all Chrysler plants are UAW-unionized, with workers being paid relatively high wages. On the contrary, independent suppliers can provide different parts to Chrysler at a lower price because they are *not* unionized. This is another example of the two-tier system being used ever increasingly by American organizations in order to cut costs.

These and other efforts at increasing productivity have been able to save the Chrysler Corporation between $300 to $500 per car.[14]

Chrysler's strategy of cost-cutting has worked extremely well for the organization. The firm's net operating income had risen from a loss of over $1 billion in 1980 to a profit of $250 million by 1983.

Revenue Increases

Cutting costs was only half the battle. Chrysler had to make money as well. One way Chrysler Corporation raised money was by selling off some of its more dubious assets. For example, in 1982 it sold Chrysler Defense Systems to General Dynamics for a hefty $336 million, thus raising badly needed revenues.[15]

However, Chrysler's main thrust toward raising revenues was, simply put, to sell more cars. The organization has managed to accomplish this quite well, and by referring to Table 1, you will note that the organization's market share rose from 9.8 percent in 1981 to 12.2 percent by 1985.

This increase in sales began in 1981 when Chrysler sold large numbers of its subcompacts Omni and Horizon and compacts Aries and Reliant. Rebates, tied to the prime interest rate, helped pull the sales of these vehicles to a respectable level. Moreover, the use of the 2.2 liter engine in the subcompacts was considered a plus because this type of engine is considered by engineers to be a marvel of power and versatility, and consumers seemed to agree with the engineers.

New products such as the Shelby, a souped-up Dodge Charger, the Laser, and convertibles also appealed to consumers and helped increase Chrysler's overall sales volume during the early 1980s. The most successful new products developed and introduced by the organization were its minivans, the Plymouth Voyager and Dodge Caravan. Chrysler sold

135,391 of these vans from January, 1984, through November, 1984.[16] Chrysler is also 15 percent owner of Mitsubishi of Japan, the manufacturer of the Dodge Colt. Because of solid engineering and performance, tens of thousands of Colts have been sold in the United States since 1983.

Before leaving this section, we should note that both cost savings and increased revenues are often associated with the introduction and use of the best technologies. Cognizant of this, Iacocca instituted Chrysler Technologies, a division whose mission is to seek future acquisitions for the company in high-tech fields. Complementing Chrysler Technologies is Chrysler's Liberty project. Liberty is a future plan comparable to GM's Saturn project, that is, a "factory of the future" producing the highest-quality goods with the latest technology. Finally, in order to ensure that Chrysler workers are trained to use and manage new technology, the organization has instituted training programs to keep workers technically sophisticated.

Reorganization

One of the problems associated with the old Chrysler was its ineffective organization structure. As we have mentioned several times in our discussion of Chrysler's history, this structure has hampered integration and coordination of activities, blurred authority relationships, and compounded the decision-making process. Figure 1 depicts Chrysler's organization structure as it existed in 1979.

As can be seen in Figure 2, the 1986 Chrysler organization has undergone significant structural changes, particularly in terms of differentiation and integration. Analysts now note that the bureaucratic infighting that characterized the old Chrysler appears to have gone, and decisions seem to flow faster. Joseph M. Byers, automotive sales manager for Aluminum Company of America, said, "There are fewer people you have to go to for a decision. From a vendor's standpoint, that's the single biggest improvement."[17]

One of the most noticeable changes depicted in the 1986 organization chart has been the grouping of all automotive functions within the Chrysler Motor Group. Compare this to Figure 1, which shows how spread out all automotive operations were. Figure 3 further breaks down the Chrysler organization structure by examining the different functions and relationships within the Chrysler Motors Group.

LEE IACOCCA AND THE USE OF POWER

No discussion of the Chrysler renaissance would be complete without an analysis of the personal power used by the chairman, Lee Iacocca, to get

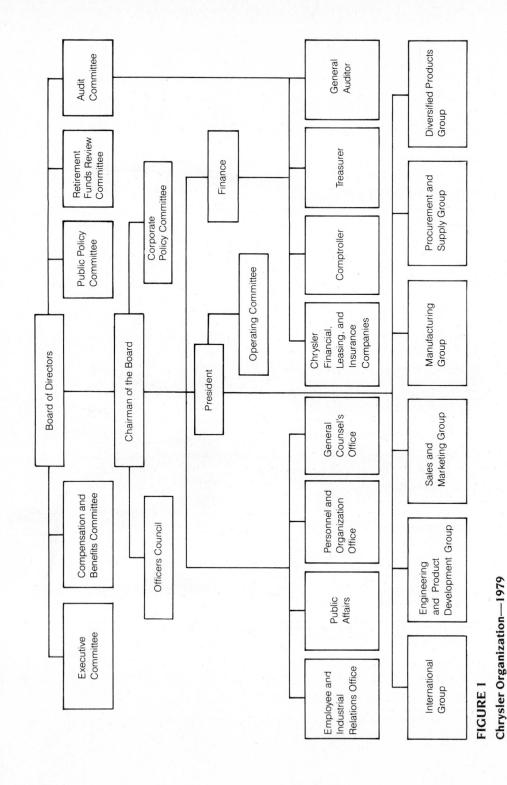

FIGURE 1

Chrysler Organization—1979

Source: Adapted from Chrysler Corporation, *Corporate Organization Chart* (October 2, 1979).

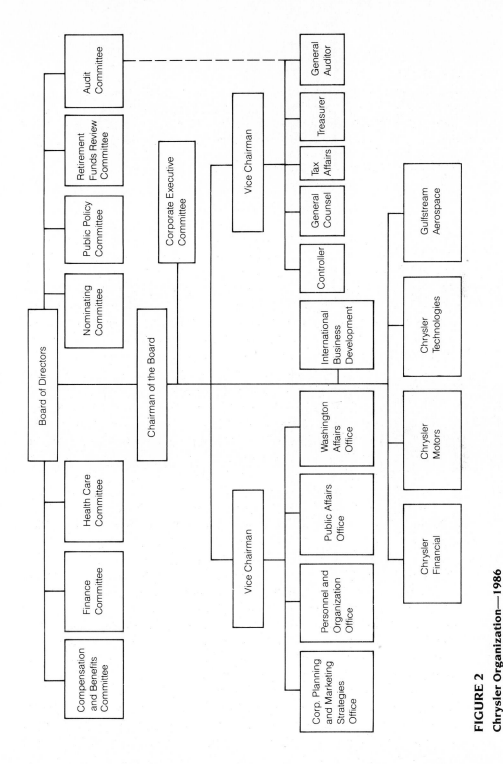

FIGURE 2

Chrysler Organization—1986

Source: Adapted from Chrysler Corporation, *Corporate Organization Chart* (February 6, 1986).

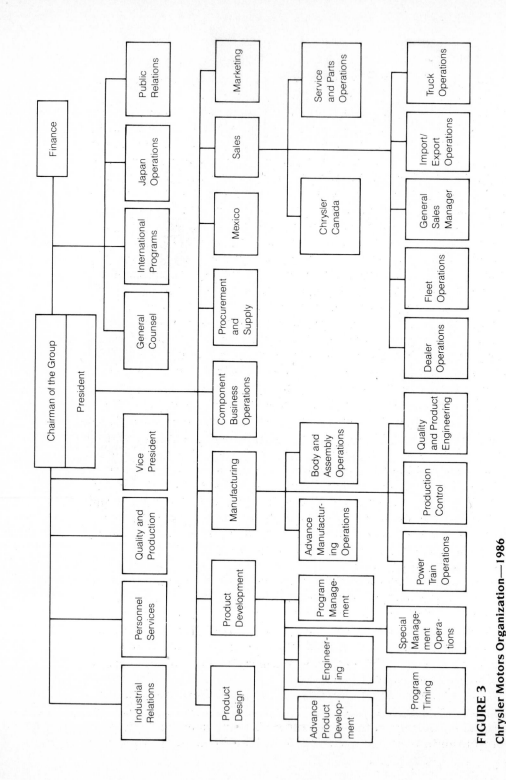

FIGURE 3

Chrysler Motors Organization—1986

Source: Adapted from Chrysler Corporation, *Chrysler Motors Organization Chart* (February 6, 1986).

things accomplished within his organization and to build cohesive teams of Chrysler managers and employees.

There are many ways an individual can obtain and exert power within an organization. As chairman, Iacocca certainly possesses tremendous legal power as vested in him by the stockholders and board of directors. However, other CEOs of near-to-failing organizations have held and used legal power to the fullest, only to see their organizations end up in bankruptcy proceedings. What Iacocca had and still has is a combination of referent and charismatic power.

Iacocca's referent power is based on the fact that he is an engineer by profession and had considerable experience with the Ford organization before coming to Chrysler. As an engineer, he possessed a basic understanding of the technological and manufacturing processes that go into the making of an automobile; it was no surprise that he came up with the idea of a single platform for manufacturing a wide variety of vehicles. His experience at Ford not only provided him with extensive knowledge of automobile manufacturing and marketing operations in general, but also provided him with an insider's knowledge of what Ford, one of Chrysler's main competitors, had planned to do in terms of styling, engineering, and marketing strategy. Iacocca's knowledge of Ford operations certainly gave Chrysler a keen competitive edge. It was no coincidence that the Omni and Horizon entered the market the same time as the Escort and the Lynx.

Even more central to the Chrysler success has been Iacocca's charisma—the sheer strength of his personality. As a charismatic leader, Iacocca created a vision for his organization—what it could be and how it could achieve its long-term goal of once again becoming a successful American business institution.

Many of us have witnessed Iacocca's charisma through his television ads. He let the public know (and apparently the public believed him) that Chrysler had a good product, was correcting past mistakes, and was going to be around for a long time.

In terms of team-building and getting the job done through subordinates, Iacocca is unsurpassed. He pulled together a solid management team, opened up communication channels between management and labor, and instilled confidence, enthusiasm, and pride throughout the ranks of lower-order employees. Had Detroit Trim, discussed earlier in this case, been part of another near-to-failing organization, the workers might not have made the necessary concessions in order to keep their plant open.

In short, much of the impetus behind the Chrysler renaissance cannot be explained in terms of production costs, increased sales, technology, or restructuring. Rather, it must be attributed to the charismatic power and leadership abilities of one man—Lee Iacocca.

CONCLUSION

It is obvious that Chrysler must continue to keep its costs down and sales up in order to remain viable. In this regard, programs already undertaken should be maintained and expanded.

Cost savings and increased sales, by themselves, however, are not the crucial issues on which the Chrysler future rests. The crucial issue is, what happens after Iacocca leaves?

Certainly, Chrysler can never return to its old strategy of imperviousness to changes in the environment. It is imperative that it maintain open lines of communication and information flow between the customer/client component of the macro environment and the corporate headquarters. It must never lose the spirit of innovation that has enabled it to develop such "hot" models as the convertible and minivan.

The main point to be considered here is the possibility of a power vacuum and resultant anarchy/conflict occurring after Iacocca's departure. However, as we have previously discussed, Iacocca is adept at team-building. At the time of this writing, a triumvirate rules directly under Iacocca. Chrysler Motors chairman, Gerald Greenwald (Iacocca's probable successor), is in charge of finances; Chrysler Motors president, Howard Sperlich, is in charge of new car design and manufacturing; and Chrysler Corporation vice chairman, Ben Bidwell, guides the marketing and sales efforts.

So, what are the chances of politics, conflict, and disruption occurring after Iacocca? According to Bidwell, "Three guys go into a room and there's some noise, but three come out, one guy maybe a step ahead. We get along pretty well. We have a reasonably good sense of our turf. The balance is pretty good."[18]

Thus, Iacocca's legacy to Chrysler might very well be the sense of unity and purpose that he has provided. Perhaps this legacy will help ease the aftershock of his inevitable departure.

QUESTIONS FOR DISCUSSION

1. Using the concepts of differentiation and integration as your focus, analyze the organization chart of Chrysler Motors shown in Figure 3.
2. Evaluate thoroughly Iacocca's high visibility profile in terms of organization theory.
3. Evaluate the boundary-spanning network of the Chrysler sales organization when it was composed primarily of independent dealerships.
4. Evaluate Chrysler's information-processing/decision-making processes. How would you improve them?

5. Speculate on the current culture at Chrysler. Trace, again speculatively, its history and impact on the organization. *REGONDOSE*

6. Trace the history of Chrysler's strategy for dealing with the environment and evaluate its current choice. *SELECTIVE IMPERVIOUSNESS*

ENDNOTES

1. Chrysler Corporation, *Plymouth: Its First Fifty Years* (June 11, 1978), 8.

2. Michael Moritz and Barrett Seaman, *Going for Broke: The Chrysler Story* (Garden City, N.Y.: Doubleday, 1981), 30.

3. Chrysler Corporation, *Chronological History of the Chrysler Corporation* (1953), 1.

4. Chrysler Corporation, *1914–1964: Dodge Brothers First Fifty Years* (April 1973), 12.

5. Chrysler, *Chronological History*, 49.

6. Chrysler, *Plymouth*, 20.

7. Peter J. Schuyten, "Chrysler Goes for Broke," *Fortune* (June 19, 1978), 55–56.

8. Irwin Ross, "Chrysler on the Brink," *Fortune* (February 9, 1981), 39.

9. Ibid.

10. Ibid., 41.

11. Ibid.

12. "Can Chrysler Keep Its Comeback Rolling?" *Business Week* (February 4, 1983), 133.

13. Jeremy Main, "Anatomy of Plant Rescue," *Fortune* (April 4, 1983), 113.

14. "Comeback Rolling," 135.

15. Ibid., 136.

16. "Give Me a K," *Forbes* (November 19, 1984), 339.

17. "Comeback Rolling," 135.

18. Barry Stavro, "Is There Life After Iacocca?" *Forbes* (February 8, 1985), 76.

Eastern Airlines: Clipped Wings

INTRODUCTION

By the summer of 1986, Eastern Airlines (EAL) had ceased to be an independent business entity. Though maintaining its name, logo, and old routes, EAL had become a unit of Texas Air, Frank Lorenzo's airline conglomerate that had just gobbled up People Express Airline and Continental Airline before the EAL acquisition.

With a few exceptions, EAL had been a highly successful and profitable airline since its founding in 1938 until 1980. However, the problems it suffered during the early 1980s caused EAL's top-level management and stockholders to decide to sell out for two reasons. First, hostile labor-management conflict within EAL had disrupted the organizational system to the point where profits had nosedived, operating costs skyrocketed, and, most important, the organizational climate within EAL had become "poisoned," thereby precluding any hope for successful labor-management conciliation. Second, as a result of the airline deregulation that had come into being in 1978, competition in the industry had become so fierce that EAL simply could not compete against the plethora of small airlines that squeezed it from one side and the "supercarriers" that squeezed it from the other.

The purpose of this case is to examine EAL's decline in light of these two forces by focusing on organization theory concepts such as conflict and the supremacy of the external environment in determining an organization's fate.

SETTING THE STAGE

Frank Borman, former USAF colonel and astronaut, became president of EAL in 1975. At that time, EAL was undergoing a financial crisis similar to the one it experienced in the early 1980s; however, the 1975 crisis was less severe and was the result of an economic recession that was hurting all airlines, not just EAL.

Within four years, Borman and his management team did much to turn EAL around. Management was streamlined; routes were improved; and Borman, believing that his airline's future rested on the acquisition of new, fuel-efficient aircraft, invested heavily in new planes, particularly the Airbus A300 and the Boeing 757. This buying binge put EAL heavily into debt, and by 1982 EAL's long-term debt was over $2 billion, or more than 63 percent of its assets.[1]

Throughout the late 1970s and into the 1980s, labor-management conflict had been stewing within EAL. During this time, the majority of the company's employees belonged to one of three unions. The International Association of Machinists (IAM) had 12,500 EAL members who were machinists, mechanics, and ground crews. As we will see throughout this case, the IAM and its leader, Charles Bryan, were the sharpest thorns in EAL's side. The Airline Pilots Association (ALPA) represented EAL's 4,600 pilots and became militant toward the end of EAL's existence as an independent business. Eastern's third union, the Transport Workers Union (TWU), represented the 6,000 flight attendants within EAL, and, like the ALPA, became militant. Finally, there were 11,000 employees within EAL who did not have union representation. These employees consisted of first-line supervisors, management, and ticket agents.

Throughout the 1970s and into the 1980s, EAL had been able to buy labor peace with its unions by agreeing to the latters' wage and benefit demands. Thus, by 1979, EAL's labor costs were 43 percent of its total revenues, an amount significantly higher than that of its competitors.[2] As increased competition began to pressure EAL when the decade changed, these high labor costs became unrealistic for the company to maintain.

A few examples will demonstrate these unrealistic labor costs. In 1983, senior pilots at EAL averaged an annual income of $140,000 per year for only 564 hours of flying. Their counterparts at People Express were paid $55,000 per year for 900 hours of flying.[3] Although the mechanics' wages did not vary much from airline to airline, work rules did. At Delta, for example, nonunion mechanics could double as baggage handlers at peak periods, while at EAL, the mechanics would not work in any other capacity, no matter what their work load was. For example, when a latch broke on a baggage bin, the gate agent had to call his or her supervisor, who, in turn, would call the lead IAM representative (union shop steward). The steward would then assign a mechanic to fix the bin. Not only did this work rule rigidity exist at EAL, but the company, through its IAM union contract, was not permitted to hire part-time employees. This was economically disastrous for the EAL organization, particularly during slow periods when full-time employees had nothing to do. Finally, management contracted out many projects, such as engine overhauls, to outside firms despite the fact that its machinists were theoretically able to handle this work. Management argued that outside firms could do this cheaper and more efficiently. Thus, EAL paid its full-time machinists for doing nothing while it simultaneously paid millions of dollars for contract work that should have been accomplished in-house.

One of the ways EAL was able to buy labor peace was through its implementation of the Variable Earnings Program (VEP) in 1975. Because 1975 was a recession year in which EAL lost $95.6 million, the company demanded that employees "give back" 3.5 percent of their wages to the company.[4] In return for this, employees would receive a share of the profits in any year in which net earnings exceeded 2 percent of gross revenues. Although EAL enjoyed profitable years from 1976 through 1979, the VEP actually provided lower wages to employees, particularly the members of the IAM, who accused management of "tinkering" with its pension set-asides and depreciation formulae. Thus, the failure of the VEP to put money into workers' pockets after they had agreed to wage decreases set the stage for the acrimonious confrontations that would plague the organization until it lost its independence in 1986.

Airline deregulation and subsequent increased competition set the rest of the stage for the EAL drama. As new routes, new competitors, and airfare wars came into being, EAL suffered worse than its rivals. Indeed, from 1981 to 1983, the airline industry in general lost $1.8 billion,[5] while EAL lost $65.9 million in 1981 alone. EAL's losses can be partially explained by its bad planning in face of environmental uncertainty in addition to its high labor costs. Borman opted to combat his company's financial losses by focusing solely on lowering labor costs, and this tactic led to the "fatal" conflict situation that is the cornerstone of this case.

LABOR-MANAGEMENT CONFLICT

1981 not only saw a huge loss for EAL, but it also marked the end of the contract between the company and the IAM. Then, for almost two years, bargaining produced no new contract between the IAM and EAL, and as EAL's financial situation worsened, new contract talks started in early 1983.

The EAL-IAM Crisis

By 1983, EAL was in its deepest trouble ever as it suffered staggering losses of $183 million.[6] The failure of the VEP had caused the loss of a great deal of the commitment Borman might have had from his organization's employees, particularly those who were members of the IAM.

At the corporate headquarters in Miami, Borman was under pressure from his lenders to turn the company's fortunes around, and, as was suggested by the banks, the primary means for accomplishing this turnaround was to be wage concessions, particularly from the IAM.

During the 1983 labor-management contract talks, Borman demanded a two-year wage freeze, which, according to Borman, was necessitated by the threat of *immediate* bankruptcy for the company. The IAM did not believe Borman and threatened to strike. Borman, realizing that a strike *would* bankrupt the company within twelve days should it occur, did a complete turnaround and agreed to a 32 percent wage hike for IAM members during an eighteen-month period from March 1983 through September 1984.

Within two months of this announcement, Borman did another turnaround. EAL needed an *immediate* $60 million in cash in order to operate.[7] Therefore, in May 1983, Borman cancelled his wage-hike promises and demanded immediate "give backs" from labor.

The union demanded access to the company books because, simply stated, the leaders did not believe Borman's new threat of bankruptcy, although by the summer of that year, EAL's income was well below previous projections; operating losses were mounting; and the pressure from the banks for a complete financial restructuring of the company had increased. By September 1983, the company's condition had worsened to the point that a 20 percent wage cut was deemed necessary by Borman.

Fortune magazine, in its issue of October 17, 1983, graphically depicted the importance of this 20 percent wage concession. By examining Figure 1, we see that *Fortune* estimated the company's losses to exceed $300 million in 1984 without the concession; however, with the concession, net income for 1984 would be several million dollars.

In an unprecedented move, EAL permitted the IAM leader, Charles Bryan, and the IAM's independent financial consultants to view the company's books. After a careful examination, the IAM agreed with Borman's dire prediction. Wage concessions totaling 18 percent were agreed to by the IAM.

Personal feelings between Borman and Bryan were so hostile that third parties, representing both labor and management, handled the 1983 contract negotiations. Under this unusual arrangement, Raymond J. Minella of Merrill Lynch represented the IAM and Frederick W. Bradley of Citicorp represented the airline.

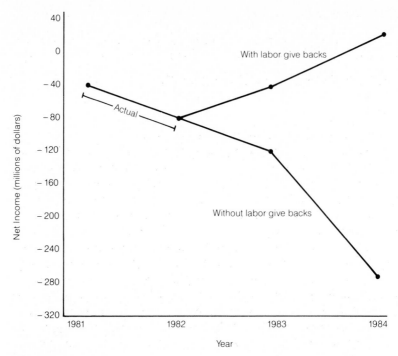

FIGURE 1

***Fortune*'s Estimate of EAL's Immediate Future (with and without Wage Concessions)**

Source: Adapted from Stratford P. Sherman, "Eastern Airlines on the Brink," *Fortune* (October 17, 1983), 104. Copyright © 1983 Time Inc. All rights reserved.

The New Contract

The IAM and the other unions did not agree to this concession without getting some concessions of their own. On December 7, 1983, a three-year contract was signed by the parties. In return for the 18 percent wage concession, EAL employees received 25 percent of EAL common stock and four seats on the board of directors. Through these four seats (one of which was held by Bryan), the IAM became involved in nearly all aspects of wielding power within the company. This included scrutinizing financial data, corporate planning, analyzing routes, monitoring capital investments, and, of course, organizing the work effort.

Under this contract, a new employee involvement program, Programs for Positive Action, gave mechanics and machinists expanded authority over their own work efforts. In addition, the company reduced by one hundred the number of first-line supervisors who formerly directed the mechanics and machinists. Mechanics and machinists took over such routine but important functions as filling out flight forms, certifying flight weight, verifying attendance, and communicating with flight operations—all tasks formerly handled by the first-line supervisors. In addition, IAM stewards took over such supervisory duties as assigning jobs, directing the work effort, and even signing time cards.

For its part, the IAM agreed to more flexible job assignments. Throughout 1984–1985, a flight was no longer delayed until an electrician could be found to change a light bulb or a ramp attendant found to locate a stray piece of luggage. Whoever was available handled simple tasks such as these, regardless of his or her union affiliation.

The Honeymoon

Throughout 1984 and the first quarter of 1985, it appeared that EAL had found profitability and labor peace. In terms of revenue increases, lowering unit costs, improving operating profits, and making its debt load more manageable, EAL did quite well, particularly in comparison with other large airlines.

EAL had an excellent 1984. The good times of 1984 even continued into the first quarter of 1985 as EAL earned profits of $53.2 million, with $28.9 million being set aside for employee profit-sharing.[8] Additionally, EAL was managing to fill a hefty 60 percent of its seats.[9]

During the good year of 1984, EAL expanded its Kansas City hub to better compete for east-west traffic, while simultaneously it reduced flights out of its ailing Houston hub where it had been consistently beaten by Continental because of fare differentials. By moving twelve planes out of Houston (where passengers paid 11.5¢/mile) to Atlanta (where they paid 16¢/mile) EAL's profitability soared.[10]

The atmosphere of bitter conflict that had plagued labor-management relations gave way to one of cooperation and common effort. All supervisors and mid-level managers at Eastern underwent a week of participatory management training in early 1985, and lower-level employees increased their efforts to be productive, thus saving the company millions of dollars. Concerning the latter efforts, a few examples will demonstrate these changes.

An EAL machinist called a friend at Delta and learned that Delta was paying $1,400 for a barrel of hydraulic fluid that cost EAL $1,600. The machinist notified the right people at EAL and saved the airline $177,000. Joseph Leonard, executive vice president for operations at EAL, noted, "Before the fall of '83, that wouldn't have happened. The employee wouldn't have had a strong stake in the company. He would have felt that nobody would listen to him."[11]

Another employee, an engine shop mechanic, started collecting worn out fan blades that are part of the intake section of a jet engine. Instead of selling the old blades for scrap, the employee devised a plan to reweld and remachine the blades, thus saving the company $306,000 a year.[12] These are just two examples out of many that show how changed employee attitudes at EAL in 1984–1985 improved productivity and saved the company enormous sums.

During the 1984–1985 "honeymoon," conditions at the airline had improved to the point where Borman announced in February 1985 that IAM members would receive a 13 percent wage increase and pilots a 7.5 percent increase over the next two years. In addition to these announced raises, the IAM wrung from Borman promises to reduce management ranks by 5 percent, to implement a profit-sharing plan, and to maintain employee health benefits at the then-current level. And the honeymoon continued as flight attendants promised to work longer hours with no increase in pay. Indeed, by mid-1985, it appeared that EAL was well on the road to recovery.

The Honeymoon Is Over

The labor-management honeymoon at EAL experienced a slight setback even during the good year of 1984 when Borman asked for more wage concessions (ostensibly as a result of pressure from the banks). However, IAM President Bryan threatened to take EAL to court because further concessions would violate the 1983 contract. Again, Borman backed down and announced the wage increases discussed in the previous section. Within weeks, however, of his promises to the IAM and ALPA, Borman partially reneged. The 13 percent raise for the IAM was reduced to 5 percent, and the 7.5 percent raise for the pilots was done away with completely.

The dormant labor-management conflict at EAL reawakened as the company returned to net operating losses after the first quarter of 1985. These losses were caused primarily by fierce fare wars between the various airlines, disappointing levels of traffic, and hundreds of flight cancellations that were caused by a pilot shortage. By the end of 1985, Borman was again threatening bankruptcy and the unions were again threatening strike. EAL was headed for serious trouble. According to Randy Barber, a financial analyst, "But when you're in default, suppliers and customers get very nervous. Travel agents cancel bookings. Other carriers don't forward money until the ticket is pulled. Vendors demand cash on the barrelhead."[13] In other words, the public began to lose confidence in the airline.

At the end of 1985, Borman called for a new round of contract negotiations. He stated that the company's survival depended on a *permanent* restructuring of labor costs as opposed to the year-to-year concessions that had managed to save the carrier during previous years. For 1986, Borman wanted a 25 percent cut from the company's projected $2 billion in labor costs. This was anathema to the IAM, whose members, only nine months earlier, saw their promised pay increases drop from 13 to 5 percent. Moreover, to further complicate the issues, during the spring of 1985, Borman promised both the IAM and ALPA that he would provide 14.5 percent pay raises to their members in 1987. These constant changes between promised raises and demands for concessions seriously undermined the credibility of Borman, the patience of EAL employees, and the public's confidence.

By the beginning of 1986, it was no longer a simple case of Frank Borman versus the IAM. The other two unions, the TWU and the ALPA, were joining ranks with the IAM in order to form a common bargaining strategy for all unionized employees at EAL. The members of the TWU became militant after Borman announced plans at the beginning of 1986 to lay off 1,010 of its members in addition to requesting a 20 percent wage cut from the membership. The ALPA became furious at the same time when Borman requested that they too take a 20 percent wage cut.[14] Keep in mind that the ALPA had been promised two wage increases, 7.5 and 14.5 percent, during 1985, only to have these promises rescinded. Therefore, it was no surprise that all three unions were in a conflictful mood during early 1986.

THE POWER ISSUE

From a labor-management point of view, the problems at EAL during the 1980s can be traced to the power struggle between Borman and the IAM. For Borman, power had come from two sources. First, there was the rational/legal power he possessed by sheer virtue of the number of positions he held (often simultaneously) within his organization. These positions included chairman of the board, chief executive officer, president, and chief operating officer. Certainly, within the very top levels in the EAL hierarchy, practically all power had become vested in the person of Frank Borman.

The second source of Borman's power was his personal qualities, his charisma. As a former USAF colonel and astronaut, Borman believed in the prerogative of absolute command. He honestly believed that, because he was Frank Borman, he had "the moxie, the reflexes, the experience, and the coolness,"[15] to put EAL back in the forefront of the airline industry. As one Eastern executive put it, "This is a very centralized company . . . Frank Borman makes the decisions."[16]

At the other end of the power spectrum were the three labor unions.

The IAM wielded tremendous power at EAL because of its control of critical labor resources. And when official power was granted to the IAM by the 1983 contract, it became even stronger. In terms of hierarchical power relationships, Borman's power over his employees became continually weaker as a result of his constant flip-flopping over wage concessions/increases. In other words, employees simply did not believe what he had to say, and thus there was very little or no commitment to Borman from his lower-level subordinates.

The group with the least power at EAL was the nonunion employees, consisting of ticket agents, first-level supervisors, and mid-level management. This loose group of employees once supported Borman; however, by 1986, their support weakened for two reasons. First, this group perceived that its power over lower-order employees, particularly machinists, mechanics, and baggage handlers (IAM members) had been considerably lessened as a result of the 1983 contract. Second, because this group of employees was not organized, it received inequitable pay vis-à-vis the unionized groups.

Indeed, by viewing Figure 2, we observe how polarized the power situation was at EAL during the 1980s. As the figure shows, Borman and top-level management exerted pressure on the unions and the nonunion employees. The unions, through their considerable power, returned the

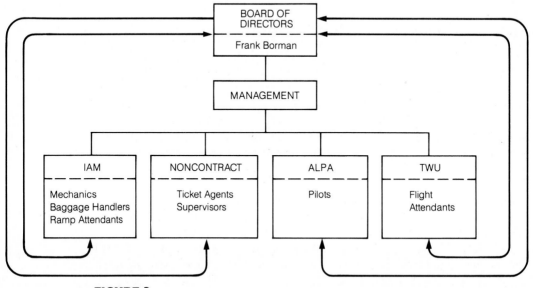

FIGURE 2
Power Chart of EAL

pressure to Borman and his board. Management and the nonunion employees had no real power to influence anyone in the organization. In short, power was not diffused throughout the organization in any manner that paralleled authority relationships.

ENVIRONMENTAL PRESSURES

As we have discussed several times throughout this case, EAL has suffered not only because of union problems. It has also suffered because of forces from the external environment over which it had very little, if any, control.

When the Airline Deregulation Act of 1978 was signed by then-President Carter, competition exploded in the industry. For a profit-making organization, competition is probably the most critical component of the external environment with which it must deal. Within EAL's competitive environment, two phenomena that significantly hurt the organization occurred.

First, after deregulation, a plethora of low-cost, nonunionized airlines came into existence to serve both minor and major transportation hubs. In Florida, where Eastern had historically been very strong, many newcomers, such as PBA, ASA, Gulf Air, and a host of others, competed directly for passengers. Likewise, already existing small airlines, such as Piedmont, have expanded their routes in Florida and have certainly taken away some of EAL's market share.

Second, in response to deregulation and subsequent competition, many medium-sized and large airlines have merged or been acquired. In this sense, the number of competitors has decreased; however, these much-larger supercarriers, such as Northwest/Republic, TWA/Ozark, Texas Air/Continental, now have significant economies of scale in their operations and, thus, a strategic advantage over other airlines such as EAL. For example, when Northwest acquired Republic, the former took control of the latter's very profitable Minneapolis hub. Also, the combination of fleets makes for more efficient operations, particularly in the areas of scheduling, maintenance, and ticketing.

Thus, EAL has been squeezed from two competitive directions. Smaller airlines confront EAL in regional operations while the larger supercarriers have been able to attack EAL in the area of national/international flights.

Finally, EAL has had a spotty record in predicting and providing for environmental changes. As we have discussed, the airline borrowed heavily in the late 1970s to purchase advanced, fuel-efficient aircraft. EAL expected the fuel crisis to worsen, and thus thought it would have a competitive advantage over other airlines because it would use larger, fuel-efficient planes. Because fuel prices actually dropped in the 1980s, this strategic move proved to be erroneous. Indeed, Borman and his staff have been simply horrible at projecting their own company's quarterly financial condition.

CONCLUSION

By the first quarter of 1986, EAL suffered a record loss of $110.6 million.[17] Indeed, bankruptcy did seem an imminent probability. At that time, the company had four limited alternatives.

First, Borman could continue to press for more labor wage and work rule concessions. This approach, however, was not feasible in view of the fact that all three labor unions had joined together in their refusal to accede to any more concessions.

Second, EAL could have sold off various assets (e.g., routes and/or aircraft). This alternative was impractical because selling off routes would only strengthen the competition and the used aircraft market had become glutted as the supercarriers placed their excess planes on the market.

Third, the airline could declare Chapter 11 bankruptcy, thereby voiding union agreements and gaining extra time to pay off its creditors. However, this would be a very bad choice from a public relations point of view. As we have already discussed, EAL's business dropped sharply during the second half of 1985 when rumors were rife about its possible bankruptcy. Should EAL have chosen this route, it is quite probable that it never would have regained the public's confidence.

The fourth alternative (and the one actually chosen by EAL) was to allow the company to become a friendly takeover target. This was the best alternative for several reasons. First, the new ownership would enable both management and labor to renew negotiations from a fresh start. Perhaps different top-level personnel would lessen some of the traditional hostility that had hampered cooperation between Borman and the unions. Second, such a move would bring in badly needed cash. And, finally, by being acquired by another airline, EAL would gain the competitive advantage that had accrued to other supercarriers.

Whatever EAL's future fortunes might be, they will lie with those of Texas Air, of which EAL is now a part. Texas Air's fortunes will certainly rest on the actions of its chief, Frank Lorenzo, who has a reputation as a union buster. Indeed, when Lorenzo took over New York Air and encountered union problems, he declared bankruptcy for the company, thus voiding union contracts and negating union power. Should tensions develop at EAL between the unions and Lorenzo, they will certainly be handled in a different manner than they were under Borman's leadership.

QUESTIONS FOR DISCUSSION

1. Describe and analyze the form(s) of conflict that were present at EAL during the period covered by the case.
2. If you were Frank Lorenzo, how would you go about managing the culture of EAL? Would you expect the culture to be thick or thin? Why?
3. Evaluate EAL's ability to scan and adjust to the external environment. Which components most affected EAL? Illustrate the latter by example.
4. The case makes the point that power relationships and authority relationships did not coincide. Show some examples of this and indicate why this incongruity was important.

ENDNOTES

1. Robert Kuttner, "Sharing Power at Eastern Airlines," *Harvard Business Review* (November–December 1985): 92.

2. Ibid.

3. Stratford P. Sherman, "Eastern Airlines on the Brink," *Fortune* (October 17, 1983), 104.

4. Kuttner, "Sharing Power," 92.

5. Sherman, "Eastern Airlines," 104.

6. Kuttner, "Sharing Power," 92.

7. Ibid.

8. Reggi Ann Dubin, "Why Frank Borman Finally Has Something to Smile About," *Business Week* (April 29, 1985), 54.

9. Ibid.

10. Ibid.

11. Kuttner, "Sharing Power," 96.

12. Ibid., 97.

13. Ibid., 99.

14. Pete Engardio and Chuck Hawkins, "Frank Borman Faces a Crucial Countdown," *Business Week* (February 3, 1986), 29.

15. Sherman, "Eastern Airlines," 103.

16. Ibid.

17. Eric Morgenthaler, "Eastern Air Posts Record Quarterly Loss of $110.6 million, Blaming Labor, Fares," *The Wall Street Journal* (April 30, 1986), 10.

Shearson/American Express: A Leg to Stand on

INTRODUCTION

When Howard Clark resigned as CEO of American Express Corporation (Amex) in 1975, that company was well known for maintaining an impeccable record of continuous growth and profitability since 1946. Indeed, this record was of such paramount importance to the firm that Clark's successors, CEO James D. Robinson, III, and President Roger H. Morley, considered maintaining it to be the primary goal of the organization.

That this record has been maintained and even expanded by Amex is evident twelve years later. Shearson/American Express (as it is now known) is one of the most successful "financial supermarkets" in the world arena. Its total net income *exceeded* $1 billion in 1987,[1] and the company's heretofore limited operations (travel services, credit cards, and insurance) have been greatly expanded to include all aspects of financial services serving all market segments.

How Shearson/American Express arrived at its pinnacle of success is the focus of this case. More specifically, through examining this organization's recent history, you will be able to observe how many of the constructs of organization theory that we discuss throughout the text (e.g., strategy, boundary spanning, environmental imperatives, interorganizational relationships, culture, power, conflict, and so on) are more than mere theoretical abstractions; rather, they are everyday realities within actual organizations.

SEARCHING FOR THE "FOURTH LEG"

When Robinson and Morley took control at Amex, the company was facing problems from all three of its core businesses. The first of these, Fireman's Fund Insurance, like all property and casualty insurance companies, produced fantastic earnings during some times and intolerable losses during other periods. The second core business, Amex's International Bank, had been doing poorly. In 1977, its return on assets nosedived to a below-average .6 percent.[2] Also, many of its loans were to Third-World countries, notorious for their loan defaults to American lending institutions. The third operation, Travel Related Services (TRS), was doing very well with its travelers checks and credit cards. However, many experts both inside and outside Amex considered these products "mature," with very little potential growth. Moreover, Amex was suffering from the competitive pressures unleashed by its rivals: VISA and Master Charge (now Master Card) in the credit card field, and Citicorp in the travelers check market.

Robinson and Morley found themselves as heads of a company that could be compared to a "chair with three legs," and some of the legs were starting to rot. A "fourth leg" was needed to stabilize the company and enable the two young executives to maintain, and perhaps even surpass, the profitability record. The vehicle for obtaining this fourth leg was to be an acquisition. Of course, this would cost the company millions of dollars, but Robinson and Morley looked on this new venture with an eagerness that is often found in young executives who have suddenly risen to power and want to make a name for themselves.

The McGraw-Hill Debacle

As Robinson and Morley set off on their hunt for a fourth leg toward the end of 1977, a critical question remained to be answered: What was American Express and what did it want to become? In other words, should it be a company serving people who like to travel, a financial services company, an insurance company, or even a communications company? These two young men answered this question with the vague answer that Amex should become a "broadly defined service company."

At first, Amex thought it would be best to acquire another insurance company, despite the fact that insurance company profitability, as it had learned with Fireman's Fund, was cyclical and/or unpredictable. Focusing efforts on life insurance companies in particular, Robinson and Morley sought to acquire the Philadelphia Life Insurance Company for $230 million. However, plans for this acquisition were discarded after Tenneco, owner of 24 percent of Philadelphia stock, refused to sell.[3]

Shortly thereafter, Robinson and Morley realized that Amex needed a new department within their organization structure "to act as a catalyst (for) and to develop and evaluate opportunities for new and important sources of earnings."[4] Thus, the Office of Strategic Program Development was formed. George Waters, the Amex executive vice president who was responsible for running the successful credit card operations, was chosen to head this new office.

Right after this new department was formed, the two Amex co-leaders decided that their next acquisition attempt would be McGraw-Hill, the publishing and information services company. This decision turned out to be one of the most embarrassing failures in the history of corporate America, and, moreover, it was made by Morley and Robinson without first consulting Waters and his new department.

Robinson and Morley regarded McGraw-Hill as an information company, and they both believed that its acquisition would "fit in nicely" with Amex's own highly sophisticated data and communications services. (Amex had previously acquired the controlling interest in Warner Communications, the name having been changed to Warner-Amex Communications.) Although McGraw-Hill might be best known to the average person for the plethora of education texts it publishes, the company made (and still makes) millions from selling specialized information through other means (e.g., *Business Week* magazine, Standard and Poor financial services, and the Dodge Construction Data-base services).

In addition to the "fit" between Amex and McGraw-Hill, the latter was a winner. Its earnings had risen steadily from 1971 through 1978, exceeding $63 million by the end of 1978.[5] Moreover, the leaders at Amex knew McGraw-Hill better than any other information company because Morley sat on its board. Trouble had been brewing at McGraw-Hill due to interpersonal conflict between Chairman Harold McGraw, Jr., and his two cousins, John and Donald, who were also McGraw-Hill executives in addition to being major shareholders. This conflict situation appeared to make conditions ripe for an acquisition.

After several meetings (with vague results) between McGraw, Robinson, and Morley, the two Amex heads decided to mount a takeover, even if such an action were resisted by McGraw-Hill. A takeover committee was formed within Amex and was comprised of investment bankers, corporate attorneys, and board members. The charge to the committee was to develop an appropriate takeover strategy.

What Robinson, Morley, and members of the committee failed to foresee was the determination of Harold McGraw *not* to sell his company. After Amex made two offers to McGraw-Hill in 1979 that were refused, the latter company went on the offensive against the former by engaging a consultant to help undermine Amex's image. This offensive resulted in Amex's public embarrassment and cessation of its takeover attempts.

THE MCGRAW-HILL OFFENSIVE. Harold McGraw wasted no time in hiring "big gun" Martin Lipton to attack Amex in the arena of public opinion. Lipton realized at once that Amex was vulnerable in two areas. First, because Amex operated in highly regulated businesses, insurance and banking, a host of potential problems could be generated for the company by federal and state regulatory agencies. Second, because Amex earned millions from its travelers checks and credit cards, Lipton believed that he could tarnish the company's *image* of integrity.

Lipton and his cohorts at his public relations firm went after Amex with a vengeance. On the legal front, petitions were brought before the Federal Communications Commission (to ascertain if Amex should be allowed to run McGraw-Hill's television stations should the merger occur) and before the New York supreme court (to determine if such a merger would violate New York's antitrust laws). In addition, Lipton had friends in Congress, such as Representative Henry Reuss of the House banking committee. Reuss soon announced plans to investigate conglomerates that "hurt the public interest."

Lipton, however, was most effective in attacking Amex's public image. Through an open letter published in major newspapers throughout the country, McGraw-Hill "questioned the morality of the travelers cheque because Amex didn't pay any interest on the funds."[6] This letter also raised the issue of whether *Business Week* should be owned by a company that would be the focal point of many of its articles. And, the letter suggested that, by Amex's owning of Standard and Poor, which rated bonds held by Amex, the latter organization could abuse its ownership by adjusting its portfolio on learning that a rating change was about to occur.

Hostilities between these two organizations grew to the point where Amex threatened to sue McGraw-Hill for libel. McGraw-Hill, in return, threatened to sue Amex President Morley because of a "breach of trust." (Remember that Morley was a member of McGraw-Hill's board of directors.)

The powers at Amex soon realized that this battle could only damage (perhaps irreparably) both companies in the long run; therefore, Amex withdrew its offers. Morley was the scapegoat responsible for this debacle, and so he resigned his position at Amex. Robinson remained as CEO because the company was still making money and, thus, the all-important profitability record was still intact.

The Shearson Acquisition

Shortly after the failed McGraw-Hill takeover attempt, Robinson had breakfast with a friend, Sandy Lewis. Lewis explained to Robinson his vision of the future financial world where the financial services industry would soon be dominated by large companies able to offer a wide range of services such as stock brokerage, real estate, insurance, lending, and so on. Lewis felt that Amex could play a leading role in this new environment and suggested that Robinson seriously consider acquiring Shearson Loeb Rhoades, the second largest and most profitable publicly owned brokerage firm in the nation.

Though at first cool to the idea, Robinson and his fellow Amex executives soon warmed up to it. The main question to be answered was whether Amex's customers would buy a wider variety of financial services through the company should they acquire Shearson. They soon reasoned that the answer was yes. The American Express Card itself was a financial instrument, and studies indicated that card holders held 70 percent of the financial assets in the country.[7] Thus, Shearson's financial offerings could be sold to card holders; likewise, cards could be sold to Shearson account holders.

ARGUMENTS FOR THE ACQUISITION. In addition to the argument stated immediately above, many other arguments were put forth favoring the acquisition. First, Shearson was *the* most profitable brokerage house in the nation. It had tremendous potential to add to Amex's earnings; thus, the record would be maintained. Shearson's profit curve paralleled that of Amex from 1972 to 1980. Indeed, toward the end of the decade, Shearson's profit curve was actually much steeper than Amex's. Certainly, such an acquisition would turn into a valuable asset for Amex.

Not only did Shearson wish to grow, but its CEO, Sandy Weill, admired Amex. "He liked its reputation, its wealth, and the potential tie-in between Amexco's and Shearson's products, and even the fact that Amexco was in close physical proximity to Shearson and all of Wall Street."[8] Weill was a firm believer in the philosophy of acquisition. He had previously tried, and failed, to merge with another New York brokerage house, Kuhn Loeb. That did not stop his determination to expand Shearson through the acquisition process. In fact, the reason for much of Shearson's success could be attributed to the very wise acquisitions accomplished by that company during the 1960s and 1970s. These can be seen in Table 1.

Therefore, might not Shearson benefit as the acquiree in this particular instance as opposed to being the acquirer, particularly if the acquisition were redefined as a merger? Certainly, the idea that millions of American Express card holders might shift their savings from banks to Shearson accounts was very, very attractive.

The general notion of a brokerage firm, such as Shearson, joining forces with a much larger service firm, such as Amex, was gaining adherents at this time. While Amex was courting Shearson, other brokerage firms, such as Dean Witter Reynolds, the fifth largest in the country, actually asked Amex to acquire it. Therefore, should Shearson not allow it-

TABLE 1

Shearson Acquisitions (1967–1979)

Year	Company Acquired	Type of Business
1967	Bernstein McCauley, Inc.	Investment management
1970	Hayden, Stone, Inc.	Brokerage
1973	H. Hentz and Company	Brokerage
1973	Saul Lerner and Company	Brokerage
1974	Shearson, Hammill and Company	Brokerage
1976	Lamson Brothers and Company	Commodities
1978	Faulkner, Dawkins & Sullivan, Inc.	Regional brokerage
1979	Western Pacific Financial Corporation	Mortgage banking
1979	Landauer Associates (25% interest)	Real estate
1979	Reinholdt and Gardner	Midwestern brokerage
1979	Loeb, Rhoades, Hornblower and Company	Investment bankers

Source: Adapted from "The Everything Financial Service: Can Amex and Shearson Live Happily After the Merger?" *Business Week* (May 18, 1981), 110.

self to be acquired by Amex, another brokerage firm most certainly would, thereby gaining the competitive advantages discussed above.

ARGUMENTS AGAINST THE ACQUISITION. Despite the potential wealth that would accrue to both organizations should an acquisition/merger occur, many arguments were put forth by some executives in both companies against such a move.

First, Shearson CEO Weill and many analysts believed that a clash of corporate culture might preclude success should Shearson become a part of Amex. Weill had created a corporate culture at Shearson that was characterized by entrepreneurial thinking and innovation. Moreover, within the Shearson organization, open lines of communication were maintained between all ranks and the external environment. The result of this culture was a very young, dynamic company with a cadre of young managers who believed that their ideas were valued and could be realized through the Shearson system created by Weill. Amex, on the other hand, was a one-hundred-year-old company that many thought to be too large and set in its ways. It had been characterized as being too conservative, too formal, and too bureaucratic. If these assertions were true, then cultural conflict and all its resultant maladies could become a reality should the two organizations join together.

Closely related to the different cultures were the different customers that each organization had. Through its travelers checks and credit cards, Amex sold "security." By contrast, because it was a brokerage house, Shearson catered to risk takers. Could these cultural and customer differences be resolved once the two organizations became one?

Problems with the banks were another issue to be considered, particularly from the Amex side. Amex had heralded itself throughout the years as a "partner" of banks. Indeed, its travelers checks and credit cards were mostly sold *through* banks. However, the Shearson acquisition/merger would draw customers away from the banks and poison Amex's relationship with these entities. Of course, what Amex could do (and actually did do) was to offer its travelers checks and cards through its own and Shearson's outlets.

Another doubt concerning the Shearson move came from those within Amex who feared that the company's entrance into the cyclical brokerage business might cause revenues to fall and thus mar the record. As we have previously pointed out, Amex shied away from cyclical businesses in the past because of their unpredictability.

Finally, there was the problem of precedent. No one had ever acquired a publicly owned brokerage firm before, and after the McGraw-Hill disaster, no one at Amex wanted to be a ground breaker. And, of course, there were legal considerations, particularly potential antitrust suits. Indeed, in 1980, the Independent Bankers Association of America began to put pressure on both the Justice Department and the Federal Trade Commission to ban the merger on antitrust grounds.

Despite the arguments against the acquisition/merger, the external environment, that determinant of many organizational successes and failures, precipitated the actual joining together of the two companies.

Amex's Office of Strategic Program Development, ignored during the McGraw-Hill fiasco, was now actively utilized by Robinson during his courtship of Shearson. The office pointed out that the newly elected president (Reagan) and his administration intended to loosen regulatory strings and encourage investment. Thus, it was believed by Amex decision makers that this change in Washington, D.C., would lead to a rebirth of investments in a wide range of financial products. Certainly, the favorable winds blowing from the political component of the external environment helped persuade Amex officials to pursue the acquisition/merger.

It was an event within the competitive component of the external environment, however, that catalyzed the actual merger between Amex and Shearson. On March 20, 1981, Prudential Insurance purchased Bache securities. The new organization, Prudential-Bache, could now offer an enormous variety of financial products to all types of customers. In short, a giant financial supermarket suddenly appeared on the scene and, moreover, merger precedent had been broken because Bache had been a publicly owned company. It became suddenly apparent that in the new world of financial services, giant companies such as Prudential-Bache would be in control.

Negotiations concluded quickly between Amex and Shearson, with the final deal being signed on April 21, 1981. For James Robinson, he had found the fourth leg for Amex, and had clearly redefined his company as a financial services organization. For Sandy Weill, this was the alliance that would enable Shearson to maintain and even expand its presence in the financial services industry.

SHEARSON/AMERICAN EXPRESS

The new company, known as Shearson/American Express, is now a state-of-the-art financial conglomerate. Indeed, Shearson/American Express made more money in the first quarter of 1986, $321 million, than it made in 1977 when Robinson became CEO.[9] In terms of its assets and revenues, as depicted in Figure 1, the company has shown unparalleled growth. By viewing this figure, you will note that Shearson/American Express had over $100 billion in assets that produced revenues of nearly $20 billion during the first half of 1987.

The Shearson acquisition/merger in 1981 was the catalyst that turned this organization into a highly successful financial services conglomerate. Since that time, through additional acquisitions in the financial services area, Shearson/American Express has been able to gain more assets, produce more revenues, and earn even greater profits. These post-Shearson acquisitions include the Trade Development Bank in 1983; Investors Diversified Services in 1983; another brokerage firm, Lehman Brothers Kuhn Loeb in 1984; and 25 percent of First Data Resources in 1985. Complementing these acquisitions, the financial conglomerate has divested itself of various businesses that no longer fit in its financial services niche. These included most (85 percent) of Fireman's Fund Insurance in 1985 and 1986 and Warner-Amex Communications in 1985.[10]

The corporate culture at Shearson/American Express has undergone a dramatic change that was the exact opposite of what critics of the acquisition/merger thought would happen. Rather than having subsumed the innovative Shearson culture in its stodgy bureaucracy, Amex's culture has been transformed by Shearson's. Since 1981, thousands of new employees have joined the ranks, either through internal growth or acquisitions, and these new people have brought in flexibility, innovation, a broad outlook, and dynamism to Shearson/American Express. This new blood, coupled with success, has created a "new company," one that has a well-deserved reputation for opportunism and adaptability, not only in the United States but throughout the world. This opportunism and adaptability are well evidenced by the new fields Shearson/American Express has entered during the last several years. For example, the company moved into the consumer lending business in 1986 by starting a nationally chartered bank in Delaware and a state-chartered bank in Minnesota. Travel Related Services introduced the new Optima card,

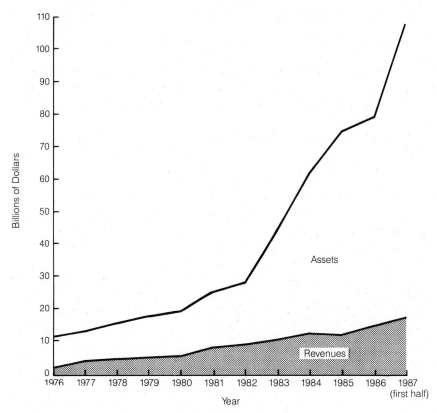

FIGURE 1

AMEX Assets/Revenues (1976–1987)

Source: Peter Z. Grossman, "James D. Robinson, III Takes Charge," *Best of Business Quarterly* 9, no. 2 (Summer 1987): 90. Figures taken from Value Line.

which gave customers revolving charge privileges. This and other innovations by TRS have been so successful that this division's contribution to Shearson/American Express's overall earnings jumped to 57 percent from 40 percent during 1981–1986.[11]

Sandy Weill left the company in 1986 due to his disagreement with Robinson concerning the fate of Fireman's Fund Insurance, which Weill wanted to keep. This would seemingly be an irreplaceable loss for the company because Weill had become a driving force within Shearson/American Express, just as he had been for Shearson when that company was an independent entity. However, Robinson has surrounded himself with a cadre of strong managers two and three layers deep that provide him and the board of directors with a breadth and depth of knowledge and opinion that keep the company viable and vibrant. These managers represent professions such as investment banking, real estate, marketing, finance, professional administration, and so on. The collision of their various values and points of view works together to produce a synergy that has put Shearson/American Express at the top of the business world.

When Robinson first took over as CEO of Amex in 1977, colleagues referred to him as "Jimmy Three Sticks" (after the "III" following his full name). He is now referred to as Mr. James D. Robinson, III.

QUESTIONS FOR DISCUSSION

1. Evaluate Amex's approach to setting its organizational mission.
2. Evaluate Amex's strategic decision making. Specifically, how would you have advised Amex officials to proceed had you been called in as a consultant in 1977?
3. What culture-management problems would you have anticipated when Shearson was acquired in 1981? How would you have prepared both companies for them?
4. Discuss the conflict issue that resulted in Sandy Weill's resignation.
5. To improve its boundary-spanning efforts, Amex established a department, the Office of Strategic Program Development. Do you think this was a good idea? What other approaches/techniques might Amex have used instead?

ENDNOTES

1. Peter Z. Grossman, "James D. Robinson, III Takes Charge," *Best of Business Quarterly* 9, no. 2 (Summer 1987): 90.

2. Ibid., 84.

3. Ibid., 85.

4. Ibid.

5. Ibid.

6. Ibid., 87.

7. Ibid., 89.

8. Anthony Bianco, "American Express: A Financial Supermarket that Works," *Business Week* (June 2, 1986), 78.

9. Ibid.

10. Ibid., 79.

11. Ibid.

Bayer: Take Two Aspirin and . . .

INTRODUCTION

West Germany's Bayer GmbH. (Corporation), best known in the United States for one of its products, Bayer Aspirin, is one of the world's largest and most successful conglomerates. In 1982, its annual sales topped $14 billion.[1] Two years later, its sales neared 43 billion deutschmarks ($20 billion ±) and it had over 175,000 employees.[2] The Bayer organization and its subsidiaries have established a commercial presence throughout the world by developing, manufacturing, and selling a wide range of chemical, health care, agricultural, and photographic products.

Bayer has come a long way since its factories and offices lay in ruins at the end of World War II. And as the world has changed during the past forty years, so has Bayer changed with it. The giant conglomerate of today bears little resemblance to the organization that struggled to rebuild itself during the immediate post-war era. This is because Bayer has managed to adapt itself to both opportunities and threats in the external environment, the primary vehicle for adapting to these changes being its well-thought-out and planned structural changes. The purpose of this case is to examine four major structural changes that occurred within the Bayer organization from the mid-1950s to 1984.

THE FUNCTIONAL STRUCTURE

By viewing Figure 1, you can observe the functional structure that existed at Bayer from the mid-1950s to 1965. A functional structure was appropriate for Bayer during this period for several reasons: (1) The organization was still rebuilding from World War II, and this structure focused organizational efforts on the basic functions that had to be accomplished if Bayer was to become a viable entity; (2) technology, although accelerating, was still relatively stable; (3) Bayer's product line was relatively small; and (4) Bayer operations were basically focused on doing business in West Germany; that is, Bayer was not the international conglomerate that it is today.

As you see in Figure 1 (and the other figures), Bayer has two boards. The first, the supervisory board, is required by West German law and is comprised of labor representatives, major stockholders, and other outside interests. Serving as a watchdog, the supervisory board appoints the members of the management board (comprised of functional heads) and either approves/disapproves the latter's major decisions.

The members of the management board, however, wielded (and still do) the real power. Each member gets one vote on decisions such as capital investments, takeovers, plant closing, layoffs, and dividends. Moreover, within the old Bayer functionalized structure, each member also served in a line capacity as the head of a specific function. As can be seen in Figure 1, these functions included production, sales, research, application technology, personnel, finance and accounting, and so on. The purpose of this dual role for management board members was similar to that of members of the U.S. Congress. Each member of the board casts his or her vote in the best interests of the corporation; yet, he or she was also responsible for arguing the best interests of his or her particular functional area.

SPECIALIST COMMITTEES/FUNCTIONAL STRUCTURE

In 1965, as a result of growth, resultant complexity, and the need to better control certain functions, Bayer modified its existing structure by establishing "specialist committees" to integrate the work of those functions concerned with the organization's primary mission. These all-important functions were production, sales, research, and application technology. As can be seen in Figure 2, these functional areas were further differentiated into the type of product involved, for example, organic chemicals, dyestuffs, rubber, fibers, and so forth. Each product was represented by a specialist committee comprised of the heads of the respective product units within each functional area. These committees, along with the functional heads, constituted a matrix-like structure. Thus, the head of

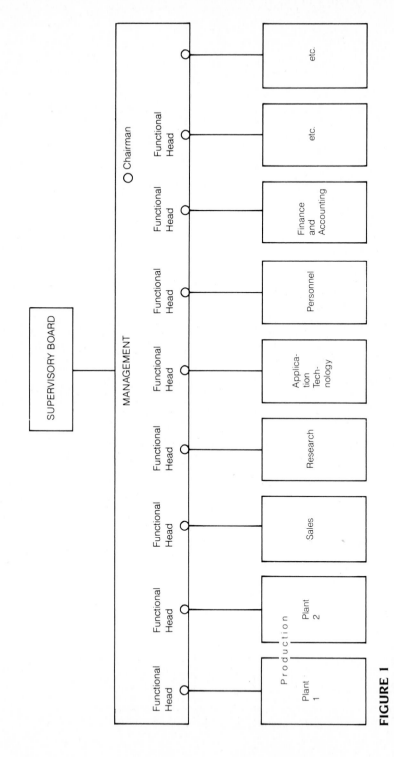

FIGURE 1

Functional Organization Structure at Bayer (1950s–1965)

Source: Reprinted with permission from Heinrich Vossberg, "Bayer Reorganizes in Response to Growth," *Long Range Planning* 18, no. 6 (December 1985): 14. Copyright © 1985, Pergamon Journals Ltd.

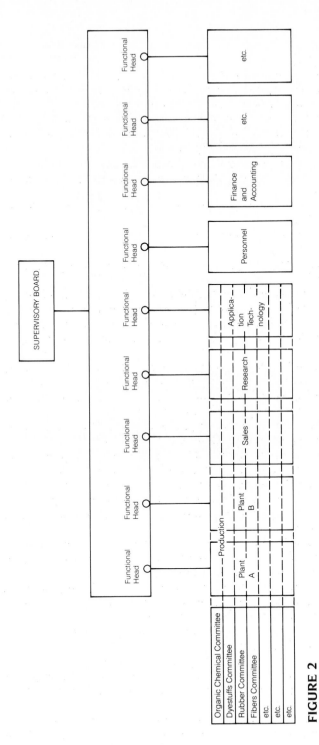

FIGURE 2

Specialist Committees/Functional Structure at Bayer (1965–1971)

Source: Reprinted with permission from Heinrich Vossberg, "Bayer Reorganizes in Response to Growth," *Long Range Planning* 18, no. 6 (December 1985): 14. Copyright © 1985, Pergamon Journals Ltd.

the dyestuffs unit within sales would not only be responsible to the corporate sales manager, but to the dyestuffs specialist committee (of which he or she was a member) as well.

THE DIVISIONAL STRUCTURE

A radical revamping of the Bayer organization structure occurred in 1971 when the company moved to a divisional structure. By 1971, Bayer's product line and geographic dispersion had increased significantly, and the old functionalized structure, even with its specialist committees, was no longer applicable to the internal and external realities of the day.

The most noticeable change, as can be seen in Figure 3, is that the management board members delegated their line authority to the division/plant managers. This move freed up the board members' time so that they could devote more attention to corporate-wide issues; however, each board member *still* acted as the spokesperson for a particular division or plant in board proceedings.

The division structure grouped the industrial activities of the various operations according to product and then differentiated each product operation according to function (e.g., production, sales, research, and application technology). This resulted in the formation of nine operating divisions, each being run as a semi-independent profit center with worldwide responsibility for its individual business operations. Each operating division (based on either product or market considerations) was headed by *two* division managers with *equal* status.

The central service functions (e.g., personnel, finance and accounting, and so on) for the rapidly expanding Bayer were vested within nine corporate divisions and served the entire organization. Staff functions that were geared *specifically* for the management board were delegated to a corporate staff section. Finally, each of Bayer's four main plants became a separate unit on the same level as the operating and corporate divisions.

SECTOR/DIVISIONAL STRUCTURE

In 1971, when the divisional structure was introduced, Bayer's sales stood at $4 billion and its overseas operations accounted for less than one-half of this figure.[3] However, within ten years, the Bayer organization not only expanded its West German operations, but its acquisitions and foreign operations grew at such a rapid rate that these latter units and operations became responsible for 57 percent of Bayer's $14 billion in sales during 1982.[4] Therefore, the company needed to develop and implement

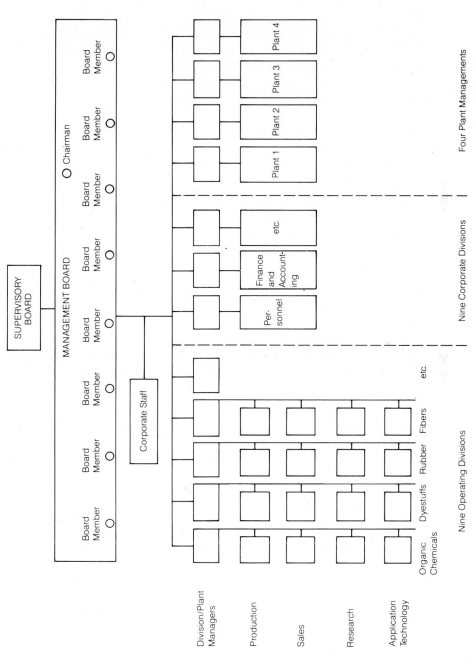

FIGURE 3

Divisional Structure at Bayer (1971–1984)

Source: Reprinted with permission from Heinrich Vossberg, "Bayer Reorganizes in Response to Change," *Long Range Planning* 18, no. 6 (December 1985): 15. Copyright © 1985, Pergamon Journals Ltd.

a structure that would cover the geographic and product-line spread that it had acquired.

By viewing Figure 4, you can see that all business activities are now grouped within six sectors, which, in turn, are comprised of between two and six business groups. Similarity of product or technology appears to be the basis for this design. In addition, many central staff functions have been combined into a corporate staff division that serves Bayer on a worldwide basis. These various central staff functions are depicted in the figure. The remaining service functions are depicted at the bottom of the figure.

The Management Board

Under the sector/divisional structure, the board members no longer represent the specific interests of a sector or service division; rather, they now act as a spokesperson for different geographic regions. For example, board members represent such areas as Latin America, the Benelux countries, Eastern Europe, North America, and so on. Also, within the management board, various committees have been formed to assist the board in its dealings with the five service divisions. These committees include corporate coordination; logistics and services; finance; research and development; investment and technology; ecology, and personnel and law. Each sector head is now required to attend one board meeting per month.

Sectors

Each sector is led by a sector head. The responsibilities of a sector head include the coordination and monitoring of the activities of the various business groups under him or her and interpreting and implementing corporate policy for the sector. As with the units under the old division structure, each business group within a sector acts as a semi-independent profit center, responsible for developing and expanding its own particular set of activities.

One of the reasons for combining these groups into sectors was because many of these business groups are newly acquired subsidiaries. By combining and integrating these subsidiaries with the older business units into groups and sectors, Bayer expects to "achieve greater integration and flexibility" for the entire organization and to ". . . achieve greater efficiency by combining functional resources more effectively to achieve corporate objectives."[5] In short, the feeling at Bayer is that each subsidiary's relative value to the corporation will become more visible under the business group/sector structure. This particularly applies to the more recent acquisitions, for which there were no slots under the old division

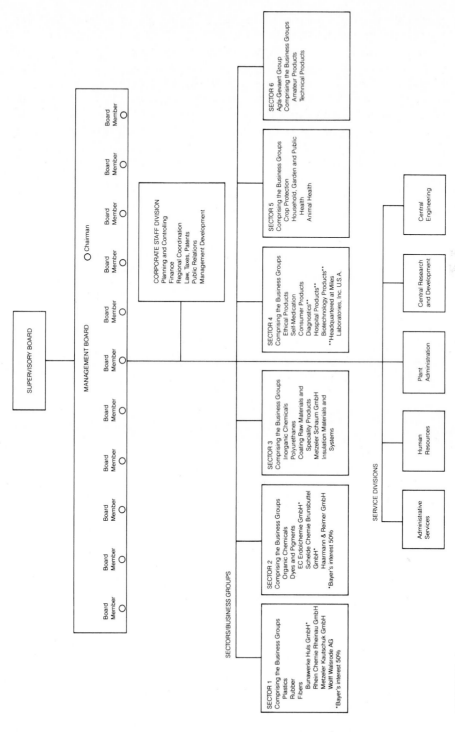

FIGURE 4

Sector/Divisional Structure at Bayer (1984–Present)

Source: Reprinted with permission from Heinrich Vossberg, "Bayer Reorganizes in Response to Growth," *Long Range Planning* 18, no. 6 (December 1985): 17. Copyright © 1985, Pergamon Journals Ltd.

structure. In other words, to add another division would have been chaotic from a coordination point of view.

Let us take the example of Sector 6 at the far right of Figure 4 to illustrate this point. This sector, known as the Agfa-Gavaert group, includes a subsidiary of the same name and, in turn, two other business groups, amateur products and technical products. Before restructuring, Agfa-Gavaert, as an independent subsidiary, earned $2.3 billion for the parent company; however, it was too loosely controlled because, simply stated, there was no place for it in the old division structure.[6] Now, this subsidiary is well integrated with two in-house business groups (of which its products are related) via the formation of Sector 6. Agfa-Gavaert now has a sector chief to argue for its future to the entire management board, while simultaneously, its needs are weighed against those of the organization as a whole. Likewise, other subsidiaries have been integrated into other business groups and sectors.

Corporate Staff Division

This division combines all the staff and service functions necessary for the planning, integration, and control of all the company's worldwide activities. The six activities comprising this division include planning and controlling; finance; regional coordination; law, taxes, patents; public relations; and management development.

The corporate staff department heads and sector heads have *equal* status—neither group can override the other. Should they be unable to reach a mutual decision, then the management board will decide the issue. The regional coordination department within the corporate staff division is a particularly powerful body because its responsibilities include the integration of all plans and operations of all business groups and sectors for inclusion in the corporate master plan.

Service Divisions

The activities of the remaining staff and service functions are vested in the five service divisions. Basically, many diverse functions, formerly the responsibility of units under the old division structure, have been centralized here. For example, the activities of the four main Bayer plants are now combined into one plant administration division. Whereas each operating division in the 1971 structure had its own research and application technology functions, these are now combined and coordinated within the central research and development division. The administrative services division is responsible for purchasing, traffic and distribution, advertising, accounting, and MIS. Human Resources handles personnel and insurance matters for all of Bayer (previously, subsidiaries handled their own personnel and insurance activities). The last division, central engineering, handles corporate-wide project engineering, utilities, process control systems, and industrial safety for the organization worldwide.

CONCLUSION

Large, complex organizations that operate internationally face a dilemma in terms of organization design. On one hand, their geographic and product diversities demand that some authority be delegated to the various subunits. On the other hand, there is some need for centralized decision making and a tremendous need for integration and coordination of activities. The Bayer organization, through its 1984 restructuring, seems to have solved this dilemma by grouping its myriad business functions into business groups and sectors. Because these business groups are run as semiautonomous profit centers, decentralization has been achieved. Members of the management board and the various departments within the corporate staff division ensure that the activities of the business groups and their sectors are harmonious with each other, thus providing for integration and coordination. And, of course, there are certain functions and activities that can be centralized, as evidenced by the formation of the five service divisions.

QUESTIONS FOR DISCUSSION

1. Describe the environment best addressed by a <u>functional structure.</u> Do you think the reasoning employed by Bayer was appropriate for adopting this structure? (W WII)

2. Evaluate Bayer's decision to add specialist committees to its structure in 1965. Specifically, what problems does such a matrix structure create and what type of problems does it appear to solve best?

3. Why wasn't a functional structure suitable for the 1971 environment in which Bayer found itself? (larger environ.) Division Structure

4. Suggest and apply, by way of examples, some means that Bayer can use to integrate its large and complex structure. Prod, Region, Tech Structure

5. Do you believe that Bayer has developed its ultimate organization design? Provide the *proper* organization theory concepts/rationale for your answer. No, ...

ENDNOTES

1. "How Bayer Is Revamping Its Corporate Structure," *Chemical Week* (November 2, 1983), 25.

2. Heinrich Vossberg, "Bayer Reorganizes in Response to Growth," *Long Range Planning* 18, no. 6 (December 1985): 13.

3. "How Bayer Is Revamping," 25.

4. Vossberg, "Bayer Reorganizes," 13.

5. "How Bayer Is Revamping," 25.

6. Ibid., 26.

G L O S S A R Y

Abstract system. A system that does not have physical characteristics; a system composed of ideas or concepts.

Acceptance of information. The process of receiving and accepting information by the proper organizational unit.

Accessibility of information. The degree to which information used by the organization's decision makers is easy to obtain.

Accountability. The obligation that a subordinate has to keep his or her superior informed of the execution of responsibility.

Acquisition. The combining of two companies where one organization acquires, or subsumes, another.

Action-adaptation. A strategy in which the organization adapts to significant existing environmental opportunities or threats while it simultaneously attempts to create environmental opportunities.

Adaptiveness. A strategy in which the linking systems adjust the organization to the environment; the organization changes itself to adjust to the environment.

Adaptive structure. See *Organic structure.*

Ad-hocracy. A temporary organization that exists to reach a certain goal or set of goals and disbands once the goal is achieved.

Analysis. An approach to differentiation that looks at the overall work of the organization and splits it up into increasingly more specialized tasks, moving from top to bottom.

Analysis of information. The process of determining the usefulness of information.

Analyzability of problems (Perrow). A technology classification criterion based on the ability of the organization's decision makers to solve problems associated with the use of technology. Simple, routine technologies present problems that are easy to analyze and solve, while nonroutine, complex technologies present problems that are quite difficult to analyze and solve.

Analyzers. Firms having one product in a stable market and another in a changing market.

Antecedent conditions (Rahim). Behavioral, demographic, and structural conditions that exist among parties prior to conflict's occurring.

Anticipating. The process of forecasting resource availability on the input side and demand on the output side of the organization's production system.

Aston studies. Studies done by Pugh and associates of the University of Aston in England to test various characteristics of bureaucracy in real organizations.

Authority. The formal right to make decisions and to take action to implement those decisions based on formal organizational relationships.

Automation of equipment (Aston studies). A technology classification criterion that distinguishes between technology that is "self-operated" and that which requires a high degree of human interaction and control.

Avoidance. A means of dealing with conflict whereby one or more parties attempts to divert attention from the conflict.

Bargaining model of conflict. Organizational conflict that occurs when members of an organization compete for scarce resources.

Bases for design. The criteria that are used to differentiate and classify organizational tasks.

Behavioral changes (Rahim). Aggressive behavior (accompanied by a reinforcing attitude) that occurs after conflict is initiated.

Behavioral School of organization theory. The school of theory that extended the Classical School by applying the disciplines of psychology, social psychology, and sociology to the study of organizations.

Bottom-up approach (organizational culture). A technique used for changing an organization's culture that depends on involvement of group members in the change process.

Boundary-spanning role. The set of behaviors of an informal boundary spanner. For example, CEOs of major organizations often play the role of boundary spanners when dealing with members of the political component of the macro environment.

Boundary-spanning units. Those units whose primary purpose is to adjust the organization to the constraints and contingencies found in the environment that are not controlled by the organization; boundary-spanning units form a link between the organization's environment and decision-authority centers within the organization.

Boundary framework. The system through which the organization maintains harmony with its environment by gathering the necessary inputs for decision making, the implementation of decisions, and the distribution of organizational outputs.

Boundary maintenance. The management of boundary-spanning units to ensure their permeability and resilience.

Bounded rationality. The notion that an organization's decision makers must make decisions with limited information; thus, "rational" decisions are limited by the "boundaries" of available information. See *Satisficing*.

Brand manager. A product manager in a multiproduct, multibrand consumer organization who is given authority to ensure that sufficient quantities of a product will be available, that distribution will occur, and that dealers will promote the product.

Budget. A plan for the commitment of resources to support activities required for goal accomplishment.

Buffering. Methods used by the organization to protect the technical core from fluctuating levels of inputs and fluctuating market demand.

Bureaucratic model. A model focusing on the formal operations of organizations; it examines such subjects as principles of specialization, hierarchical arrangements, delegation, and responsibility structure.

Bureaucratic model of conflict. Conflict that occurs when a superior attempts to control the behavior of subordinates.

Bureaucratic organization. A form of organization first proposed by Max Weber that was built around rational decision making; knowledge and ability were seen as superior to favoritism as the basis for organization.

Bureaucratic structure. A system based on rational organizational principles.

Business-level strategies. Strategies undertaken by the organization to promote one of its particular product or service lines.

Cash cows (Boston Consulting Group matrix). Products with high market share and low growth rate as the market becomes saturated.

Catastrophe theory. A mathematical theory based on the idea that continuously changing forces produce discontinuous effects.

Centralization. A condition in which there has been little delegation.

Ceremonial. A system of several cultural rites connected with a single occasion or event.

Characteristics of the parties (Deutsch). The personalities and belief patterns of parties to a conflict.

Charismatic power. Influence based on personality.

Classical School of organization theory. A school of thought concerned with attempting to build a set of rational techniques that would help in building structure and process, and to provide a coordinated set of relationships among the components of the organization.

Client group. That group which the organization was specifically designed to serve in the provision of goods and services.

Closed system. A system that does not interact with its environment.

Coalitional context. Context for organizational dependencies in which issue-specific interorganizational relationships occur while the organizations retain autonomy in areas other than the specific issues.

Coercive power. The power that comes from the ability to coerce or punish another.

Combination strategies. The simultaneous use of different strategies for different units within an organization.

Commitment. A condition in which members of a group entrust their abilities and loyalties to an organization in return for satisfaction. The degree of commitment shown by organization members is often a reflection of the strength of an organization's culture. In addition, members with high degrees of commitment to their organization are more tolerant of direction and control.

Competition. A major component of the macro environment in which different organizations offer similar products or services.

Complexity. The degree of sophistication and specialization that results from differentiation, integration, and spatial dispersion.

Compromise. A strategy for dealing with conflict in which both parties yield somewhat from an original position that is part of the conflict.

Concentration. The extent to which power and authority are dispersed in the environment.

Concentration growth strategy. A strategic plan developed by an organization that focuses growth on a single product or group of closely related products.

Concentric diversification. A strategic plan whereby the organization moves into products or services that are different, yet somewhat related, to its original products or services.

Concrete system. A system that has physical characteristics.

Conflict. A condition that occurs when two or more individuals or groups that have opposing goals, ideas, philosophies, or styles confront each other in some form.

Conflict aftermath (Pondy). The fifth and final stage of the conflict episode that occurs after manifest conflict has been exhibited. This stage can be characterized by either resolution of the conflict or it can be the basis for the recycling of the episode into further conflict.

Confrontation. The objective recognition that conflict exists and the attempt to deal with it based on facts rather than emotions.

Confrontation of intimacy/role differentiation/and peer relationship issues. The second stage in the formation of group culture, during which the members of the group seek normative consensus and harmony.

Conglomerate diversification. A strategic plan whereby the organization diversifies by obtaining products and services totally unrelated to its original products and services.

Conglomerate merger. Type of horizontal integration in which an organization acquires a firm in a noncompeting industry (diversification).

Consumer client group. The end users of an organization's products and services; the group whose wants and needs the organization seeks to fill.

Consumer needs. The needs of the consumer group that the organization exists to serve; the basis for definition of primary objectives.

Contingency plans. Plans constructed by strategic managers for the most-likely-to-occur scenarios developed from scenario analysis.

Contingency School of organization theory. The school of theory that puts forth the idea that the organization's relationships with its environment should be flexible and prescriptive rather than static and patent; based on the open-systems concept.

Continuous technology (Woodward). Type of technology in which production runs continuously, with no start-ups or down times on a daily or weekly basis.

Control. The function of a system that provides adjustments according to a plan; the maintenance of deviations from a system's objectives within allowable limits.

Control of the agenda. The right certain individuals have to decide the agenda for action.

Cooptation. A condition that occurs when one organization or group of people absorbs another.

Core technology. The system the organization employs for the production of primary utility.

Corrective action. The action taken to remove the cause of deviation between actual performance and standards.

Cost-benefit. See *Inducement-contributions.*

Cost centers (multidimensional matrix). The functional entities of a company (e.g., marketing, manufacturing, research) as well as supportive activities, that are grouped together in order to track costs.

Cost leadership. A business-level strategy used by the organization, which is based on the organization's producing the product or service cheaper than the competition.

Craft structure. A type of organization exemplified by an informal group of friends that start a small business.

Creativity/stability issue. The third stage in the formation of group culture, during which the members of the group become concerned with team continuity and accomplishment. The group seeks to be simultaneously innovative and stable.

Cultural flexibility. The ability of an organization's culture to accommodate both internal and external environments.

Culture. The sum total of learned behavior traits characteristic of the members of a society; the values, norms, artifacts, and accepted behavior patterns of a society.

Culture audit (formal). A ten-step methodology developed by Schein that external consultants use to identify and define an organization's culture.

Culture audit (informal). The methods a newcomer to an organization uses to learn and adopt the prevailing culture.

Culture conflict. Conflict that occurs between individuals or groups because of different values, norms, and behavior patterns.

Customer/market analysis. A stage in the strategic planning process whereby the organization analyzes the customer and client groups it serves in addition to surveying the general nature of the market.

Cybernetic system. A system with a communication and control system that operates to maintain a steady state.

Daily beliefs. Rules and feelings about the everyday behavior in an organization. Daily beliefs are an integral part of an organization's culture and can be extensions of its guiding beliefs that form the basis for the culture.

Decentralization. A condition in which there has been a considerable amount of delegation and, thus, a considerable vesting of responsibility and authority in the hands of subordinates.

Decision-authority center. The place/position in the organization that can act on the information provided by the boundary-spanning unit.

Decision process (Rahim). The use of a substitute process or structure for decision making that conflicting parties use to take the place of usual decision making.

Decision support system (DSS). An interactive computer system that can easily be used by noncomputer specialists to assist them in decision making.

Decisions. Choices based on authority, power, or a combination of both that are intended to affect behavior in some manner.

Defenders. Organizations with a relatively narrow line of products and market domains.

Delegation. The passing of duties and rights (responsibility and authority) from a superior to a subordinate.

Democratic process. Conflict-resolution process in which individuals can debate opposing views and, after discussion, vote on the issues, with the majority vote prevailing.

Dependency/authority issue. The first stage in the formation of group culture, during which members of the group select a leader who will guide the group to its maximum benefit.

Desensitization. A condition that occurs when the sensors become so used to environmental stimuli that the stimuli have little effect on the sensors.

Differentiation. The creation of organizational divisions through task specialization.

Differentiation strategy. See *Product/service differentiation.*

Diffusion. The rapidity with which organizations adopt new technology.

Divestiture. A defensive strategy used by the organization whereby the organization sells or divests itself of a business or a part of a business.

Division of labor. The proper allocation of work to people and machines; specialization of task performance.

Divisional structure. The type of organizational structure that occurs when the organization expands into other markets or begins operations at different geographical sites, thereby making it imperative that the organization create divisions within the structure in order to hold the entire organization together.

Dogs (Boston Consulting Group matrix). Products with low growth and low market share.

Domain consensus. The defining of the expectations of members of the organization and those with whom they interact concerning the activities and client groups of the organization.

Dominant coalition. The existing authority holders of an organization; a group of key decision makers whose influence on the system is the greatest.

Dynamic homeostasis. The process of achieving a new equilibrium different from the previous equilibrium.

Dynamic system. A system that changes over time.

Early adopters. Leaders who are the second group to adopt innovations and who are respected in their communities; the people viewed as the ones to check with by others who later adopt innovations.

Early majority. The third group of adopters of new ideas who deliberate a long time before adopting a new idea.

Economic model. An organizational model based on economic rationality.

Economic system. The system a society uses for allocation and distribution of scarce resources.

Effectiveness. A condition in which a focal organization, using a finite amount of resources, is able to achieve stated objectives as measured by a given set of criteria.

Efficiency. A relative measure of the relationship between resource use and results; input/output ratio; generally, the value of the results from an expenditure and resources should be greater than the value of the resources expended.

Enacted environment. The relevant environment that the organization creates for itself by aggressively scanning, scoping, and narrowing the macro environment to its pertinent parts.

Encounter group training. A radical form of sensitivity group training.

Endogenous change. Change generated from within the organization.

Entrepreneurial structure. The type of organization structure that occurs when labor specialization appears in its basic form.

Entropy. A point at which a system expends more energy than it is able to replace from the outside.

Environment. All groups, norms, and conditions with which an organization must deal; the total set of outside forces surrounding and tending to shape the behavior of the organization and its members.

Environmental analysis and forecast. This is the beginning of the strategic management and planning process whereby the organization: (1) determines the present state of the environment and (2) forecasts what is likely to happen.

Environmental homogeneity. The degree to which variables in an organization's task environment are similar.

Environmental interface. The act of linking the organization to its environment; specifically, the means by which organizations interact with their environment.

Environmental scanning. Assessing and projecting changes in various macro environmental components over a short- to long-term period in order to forecast and plan.

Environmental stability. The certainty of the range of variation found in the environment over time.

Equifinality. The ability of a system to produce the same outputs using diverse means.

Equilibrium. A state of balance or equality between opposing forces; a state of balance or adjustment of conflicting desires or interests.

Equilibrium objectives. Objectives (such as preserving relative market share) that serve to maintain the organization in a steady state with its environment.

Equipment based design. Differentiation based on the equipment that is used or worked on in a given process.

Ergonomics. The study of the problems of people in adjusting to their environment; the study of how tools and equipment can be adapted to human use.

Estimates of outcomes (Deutsch). The tendency of parties to a conflict to pursue the conflict based on their estimate of either winning or losing.

Exception principle. Each level of management is only concerned with performance that deviates greatly from the expected performance; review is done on the basis of the exception.

Exceptions (Perrow). A technology classification criterion based on the number of exceptions allowed by the technology. Technologies with high routines have few exceptions while those with a varied routine have many exceptions.

Exogenous change. Change that originates in the outside environment.

Expert power. Influence resulting from knowledge or special skills.

Expert systems (ES). Knowledge-based computer information systems that utilize artificial intelligence (i.e., the computer acts as if it were actually thinking through a problem or an issue).

Explicit objectives. Formal objectives, not necessarily the actual objectives, of an organization.

External dependency. The extent to which an organization is dependent on its external factors.

Federative context. A context for interorganizational relationships in which a supraorganization authority controls and monitors interdependent activities of the federated organizations.

Feedback. The return to the input of a part of the output of a machine, system, or process.

Felt stage (Pondy). The third stage in the conflict episode, in which emotions are excited and feelings become hostile.

Field theory (Lewin). The expression of social and psychological concepts and events in terms of physical science field force concepts.

Flat organization. An organization that has large or wide spans of control and few levels of management.

Focus strategy. See *Market/segment focus*.

Forecasts. Estimates of future conditions that are likely to affect goal accomplishment.

Formal organization. The de jure organization (i.e., the structure of the organization that can be depicted by a formal organization chart); the official structure.

Formal theory of authority. The right of the manager to make decisions and to issue orders and instructions that comes from the ownership and control of property.

Formalization. The process whereby management attempts to deal (through the use of policy, procedures, directives, and so forth) with the problems of control and coordination that occur as a result of increased size in organizations.

Friendly takeover. A merger in which the firm to be acquired has no objection to the acquisition, and might even encourage it.

Functional differentiation. The classification of work into the primary functional components (such as production, marketing, and so on) that need to be carried out for the organization to operate.

Functional myopia and suboptimization. Bureaucratic problems in organizations caused by too much specialization and functional allegiances, characterized by shortsightedness and less-than-optimum levels of efficiency. These problems can be treated by OD techniques such as team building, offsite planning and budgeting sessions, goal integration programs, and job rotation programs.

Functional process. Horizontal growth achieved by adding more personnel to a work unit without creating a new organizational level(s).

Functionalism. The examination of a system in terms of the interrelationships between its structure, processes, and functions.

Functionalized structure. A line-and-staff structure that has been modified by the delegation of authority to personnel to use outside their normal spans of control.

Geographical areas (multidimensional matrix). The geographic segmentation of an organization, with its segments being considered to be both profit and cost centers for matrix structure purposes.

Geographical differentiation. Separation of functions based on the physical location of the work that is done; often found within the sales and marketing functions of the organization.

Goal. An unrealized state or condition that the members of an organization do not possess, but which they deem desirable.

Goal attribution. A condition in which an observer assigns or ascribes a goal to a particular undertaking.

Goal displacement. A situation in which an original goal is given a different place in the hierarchy or is substituted for by some other goal.

Goal hierarchy. An array of goals for an organization arranged by priority.

Goal-seeking system. A system that produces different reactions to a given internal or external event to attain different external or internal states.

Group model. See *Human relations model.*

Guiding beliefs. The philosophical roots and principles on which the organization is built. Guiding beliefs are the core of an organization's culture.

Harvest strategy. A stability strategy used by the organization that milks the investment (i.e., retrieves the value of earlier investments).

Hierarchy of human needs. A motivational theory developed by Maslow that maintains that humans have a five-level array of needs that determine behavior; the most basic need is physiological, then safety, social, ego or self-esteem, and self-actualization, the highest order need.

Holism. A view of organizations in which the organization is viewed as a functioning whole; a change in any element of the system will thus change the entire system.

Homeostasis. The state of equilibrium.

Horizontal differentiation. The division of work into tasks and subtasks that does not result in more organizational levels.

Horizontal integration. Form of interorganization integration in which one organization obtains a firm in the same industry or obtains a firm in a noncompeting industry.

Hostile takeover. Merger in which the firm to be acquired vigorously resists being taken over by another company.

Human relations model. A model of organization that examines organizational operations in terms of group as well as inter- and intra-action processes; concerned with social relations, satisfaction, and other aspects of the informal organization.

Humanism. A concern for the human element when designing, utilizing, and evaluating an organization.

Imperviousness. An environmental strategy that an organization uses to seal itself off from the environment.

Implicit objectives. Attributed objectives that an organization works toward; these can be different from the formally stated objectives.

Improvement objective. A goal that the organization perceives is better than the present state or condition.

Individual behavior model. A model of behavior centered on the individual.

Inducement-contributions. Basis of the cost-benefit interorganizational relationship; organizations will join other organizations when inducements (benefits) to do so outweigh the costs (contributions) necessary to be part of a larger whole.

Industrial democracy. An organizational state based on the concept of participation; authority flows from the bottom up, and managers exist to carry out the wishes of various constituent groups.

Informal organization. The de facto organization (i.e., relationships among organizational members that are not necessarily sanctioned by the de jure organization).

Information audit. A process used to determine if and how information is actually being used.

Information processing and choice. The process of scanning the organization's environment, both micro and macro, in order to obtain vital information necessary for decision making.

Information system. The system of gathering, reporting, analyzing, accepting, storing, retrieving, and using information in the organization.

Infrastructure technology. The various organizational buffers that organizations use to incorporate and mediate the influence of technology in the macro environment.

Innovation. The development and implementation of new processes or procedures that are substantially different from existing ones; implies change through creativity.

Innovator. Someone who introduces new ideas, methods, or devices; the first to adopt a new technology.

Input. The resources coming into a system.

Integration. The condition in which all the parts of the total organization are held together in a state of dynamic equilibrium; concerned with the means organizations use to coordinate the work between differentiated task groups.

Intensive technology. The technology used to assemble a variety of techniques and methods for a specific time period to accomplish a specific goal.

Interaction conflict. Conflict that results from the interaction of group members, particularly when the outcome of the group's actions meets with failure, thus causing resentment and finger-pointing by the members.

Interconnectedness. The number and pattern of linkages or connections among organizations.

Interdependency. The conditions that exist when elements, objects, or events within a system are all dependent on the other elements, objects, and events within the system.

Intergroup conflict. Conflict that occurs between two or more units or groups within an organization.

Intergroup techniques. OD techniques that attempt to improve the interaction among groups that make up the various subsystems within an organization.

Interlocking directorates. The condition that exists when one or more individuals serve on two or more boards of directors.

Internal organization assessment. The part of the strategic management process where the organization examines its own internal operations in order to determine its strengths and weaknesses.

Interpersonal conflict. Conflict that occurs between two or more organizational members at the same or different levels.

Intragroup conflict. Conflict that occurs among members of a group or between two or more subgroups within a group.

Intrapersonal conflict. Conflict that occurs within an individual as a result of intrarole pressures.

Issue conflict. Conflict that occurs between members of a group that centers on making a decision or solving a problem. This type of conflict is exacerbated when the individuals' values and goals are different.

Job content (Herzberg). Recognition, promotion, professional growth, and so on that affect how people behave in organizations.

Job context (Herzberg). Working conditions, pay, quality of supervision, and so on that affect how people behave in organizations.

Job design. The appropriate grouping of duties, functions, and responsibilities to be performed.

Joint venture arrangement. An organization formed by two or more organizations to accomplish a specific project or venture and that is dissolved once the project is completed.

Knowledge and concept training. An OD technique that focuses on improving the knowledge and skills of individuals working within an organization.

Laggards. The last group to adopt innovations; traditionalists.

Laissez-faire structure. A loose collection of people brought together for a period of time under a relatively loose style of management and control; usually exists solely to satisfy the desires of the members of the organization rather than to satisfy the needs of some client group.

Language. A daily jargon used by organization members that is particular to the organization and a manifestation of its culture.

Late majority. The group that adopts new ideas only after public opinion favors the innovations.

Latent stage (Pondy). The first stage in the conflict episode, in which conditions that breed conflict exist.

Liaison position. A horizontal linking position that is given authority to link two units in the organizational hierarchy for information sharing and task coordination.

Line-and-staff structure. A form of organization structure that results from the addition of a staff element(s) to the line structure in order to handle secondary operative work.

Line operative work. Nonmanagerial work that is concerned with the production and distribution of primary utility necessary to satisfy the needs and desires of the primary consumer group (also called primary operative work).

Line structure. The structure of an organization that forms around the tasks involved in producing or distributing the primary utility it creates.

Linkage. The communication channel between a boundary-spanning unit and a decision-authority center.

Linking-pin structure. A structure that emphasizes the vertical and horizontal linkage role that a manager plays in integrating the tasks of an organization.

Long-linked technology. The technology used when steps are sequential in nature.

Long-term objectives. Those objectives that cannot be accomplished within a short period, such as a year; generally, long-term objectives range up to twenty years in time span.

Loosely coupled systems. Systems with a low level of connectedness or interdependency among their member organizations.

Lower-order-participant power. Power possessed by people occupying lower levels in an organization structure through their control of information, persons, or instrumentalities.

Machine bureaucracy (Mintzberg). A centralized, formal organizational structure characterized by very formalized procedures, a proliferation of rules and regulations, and formalized communications.

Macro environment. The network of systems in which organizations exist; composed of culture, political forces, economic forces, competition, technology, skill mixes, and consumer/client groups; a source of opportunities and constraints for the organization.

Management behavior. The things a manager does in carrying out responsibilities.

Management by objectives (MBO). A system of management aimed at improving managerial planning and control by providing for systematic involvement of organization members in the goal-setting process and for ensuring that proper action is taken to monitor progress and to take corrective action when necessary; the system is composed of missions, forecasts, objectives, programs, schedules, budgets, standards, measurements, and corrective actions.

Management information system (MIS). A formalized organizational process for making information available to managers on a timely, accurate, and relevant basis.

Management theory. The explanation of management practice, that is, how managers behave.

Managerial authority. Authority composed of the right of choice among alternatives and the right of enforcement based on official organizational position.

Managerial philosophy. A basic set of values that provides a general guide or framework for managerial behavior.

Managerial work. Work consisting of decision making and influence.

Manifest stage (Pondy). The fourth stage in the conflict episode, in which adversarial behavior is exhibited.

Market differentiation. A basis for differentiation founded on the customer served.

Market/segment focus. A business-level strategy used by the organization as it attempts to carve out a niche in the market. Organizational efforts then focus on serving that niche.

Mass technology (Woodward). Type of technology in which many units are produced at one time.

Matrix structure. An organization structure that is based on units of responsibility that cut across the vertical and horizontal units in the organization.

Measurement. The comparison of actual performance with standards to determine if goals are being accomplished.

Mechanistic model. See *Bureaucratic model.*

Mechanistic structure. A type of organization structure that is based on decision-authority relationships and rules to the point of virtual mechanization.

Mediating technology. The technology used to bring together organizations with complementary abilities.

Merger. A combining of several companies or corporations into one, as by issuing stock of the controlling corporation to replace the greater part of the subsumed organization.

Micro environment. The internal components and systems of the organization.

Mini-max strategy. The reaching of a solution to a conflict that can be acceptable to both parties, based on the proposition that people are willing to give up something in order to get and/or keep something they prefer.

Mission. An organization's basic purpose; in MBO, purpose provides an overall sense of direction needed for coordination.

Model building. The graphic presentation of ideas that specifies variables and makes explicit their interrelationships.

Multidimensional matrix. A variation of the project, product, and program matrix structures that was developed by Dow Corning.

Multigoal-seeking system. A system that seeks different goals in at least two different external or internal environmental conditions.

Munificence. Excessive amounts of critical resources in the environment.

Myth. A dramatic narrative of imagined events used to explain origins and transformations within an organization. Myths are vehicles used by the organization to convey its culture to members.

Nature of the conflict (Deutsch). The extent to which parties to a conflict stand rigid on the issues. The more rigid the parties, the more difficult it is to manage the conflict.

Negative entropy. The opposite of entropy, this involves taking in more energy than is expended so that the system builds rather than dissipates energy.

Neutral strategy. A stability strategy used by the organization to keep it doing what it has always been doing without a growth goal in mind.

Objectives. Short-term goals that are developed from the mission; they provide the foundation for the measurement of accomplishment.

Open system. A system that interacts with its environment; an organization is an open system.

Operations analysis (information processing). The examination of an organization's operations by flowcharting information flows.

Operative authority. A type of authority made up of two basic subrights: the right to carry out responsibility and the right to determine, within reason, how and when it will be done.

Operative work. The basic activity that directly enables the organization to realize its objectives.

Organic structure. A structure that tends to have the opposite characteristics of those associated with the bureaucratic structure; it is flexible and adaptive to its environment.

Organization. An open, dynamic, purposeful social system of cooperation designed to enhance individual effort aimed at goal accomplishment; consists of the human element, the physical element, the work element, and the coordination element; transforms resources into outputs for users.

Organization audit. An investigation that assesses the present strengths and weaknesses of an organization.

Organization boundary units. Those responsibility centers that surround the organization's technical core, and that moderate the flow of inputs to the technical core and the flow of outputs from that core; links organization to its environment.

Organization design. The structure and process in the organization. Includes structure as well as policies, work flows, and other aspects of organization operations.

Organization development. The process whereby organizations attempt to improve and renew themselves; refers to the changes an organization makes so that it can better state its goals and achieve them effectively and efficiently.

Organization domain. An area of the macro environment that consists of organizational claims in terms of the range of products offered, population served, and services rendered.

Organization life cycle. The birth, growth, maturity, deterioration, and death of an organization.

Organization size. The number of employees, or members, in an organization.

Organization theory. Concepts, principles, and hypotheses used to explain the components of and behavior in and of organizations.

Organizational culture. The mix of values, beliefs, assumptions, meanings, and expectations that members of a particular organization, group, or subgroup hold in common and that they use as behavior and problem-solving guides.

Organizational gap. An organizational condition in which a task or function of the organization that is necessary for goal achievement goes unassigned.

Organizational inertia. The inability of an organization to change because of such factors as sunk costs, inadequate communication structures, disruptive internal politics, and dysfunctional institutional norms.

Organizational overlap. An organizational condition in which a task or function is performed by two or more organizational units or persons.

Organizational parallelism. A condition in which the status and power of a given organization's sensors are matched with the status and power of other organizational sensors in the environment.

Organizational politics. The structure and process of the use of authority and power to affect definitions of goals, directions, and so on; the management of influence to obtain ends not authorized by an organization; pragmatic ways to advance in an organization.

Organizational renaissance. Organizational renewal; rebirth.

Output. The end results of a system.

Overall cost leadership. See *Cost leadership.*

Perceived conflict (Pondy). The second stage in the conflict episode, in which one or more of the parties becomes aware of the potential for conflict.

Permeability. A relative measure of the flow of resources and information between the organization and its environment; the degree to which the organization's boundary permits interaction with the macro environment.

Personal qualities. Qualities such as knowledge, charisma, and skill possessed by some actors in an organization that make these actors more important and powerful than others in the organization.

Physical structure. The actual design of an organization's buildings and one's location in them, including furniture, office design, physical stimuli, and artifacts. The physical structure of an organization is often a reflection of its culture.

Policy. A guide to action that should be followed by individuals in the organization in order to provide consistency of decisions.

Political model of organizations. A view of organizations from the basis of decisions that stem from power rather than on the basis of decisions that stem from authority. See also *Power model.*

Political system. The form and role of the government and the political processes of a society.

Population ecology. The totality of relationships between organizations and their environment. Population ecology is the basis for the adaptation versus selection (social Darwinism) debate within organization theory.

Position power. The amount of power that attaches to the various offices in an organization.

Power. The ability (potential or actual) to impose one's will on others outside formal organizational relationships; the ability of one person to affect the behavior of another by the use of some means other than authority.

Power consequences. The assessment of power in an organization through the examination of the effects or consequences of the decisions made by various actors.

Power model. An explanation of organizations as social systems in which power differentials determine a major part of organizational behavior.

Power symbols. The trappings of office, such as offices, carpets, or reserved parking spaces.

Preemptive strategies. Strategies used by organizations to disrupt the normal state of affairs in an industry or product line.

Primary beneficiaries. A group of people that the organization is basically established to serve (e.g., customers/clients); the needs and desires of this group set the basis for defining the organization's basic purpose and objectives.

Primary objectives. The end-states that are tied directly to the satisfaction of the needs and desires of the organization's primary client group; the primary objective of an organization is to produce and distribute those goods and services that have the ability to satisfy the primary client group of the organization.

Primary operative work. The production of goods and services that will satisfy consumer needs.

Prior relationship between the parties (Deutsch). The prior experiences that parties to a conflict have had with each other in terms of competition or cooperation.

Process (Deutsch). The kind of tactic used by parties to a conflict.

Process differentiation. A type of organizational arrangement based on the process that is performed.

Product differentiation. A type of organizational arrangement based on the product produced.

Product matrix structure. Structure in which personnel and other resources are assigned to work on major promotional efforts for various products.

Product/service differentiation. A business-level strategy used by an organization whereby the organization creates a belief in the market that the product or service it offers is unique.

Professional bureaucracy. A very complex, informal, and decentralized organizational structure that is characteristic of such organizations as hospitals, universities, law firms, and school systems. These organizations are termed "professional" because they are comprised predominantly of professionals.

Professionalism. The attainment of professional recognition by an actor in an organization (e.g., a CPA certificate) that increases the actor's importance and power within the organization.

Profit centers (multidimensional matrix). The different units in an organization, frequently defined along product lines, grouped together in order to track profits.

Program matrix structure. Structure used by an organization to coordinate a number of programs across a number of functional areas for an unspecified period of time.

Programs. Major activities required to accomplish objectives under an MBO system.

Project matrix structure. Structure in which people are assigned to various projects based on the stage of project development and the project director's need for personnel and other resources for a specified period of time.

Prospectors. Organizations that are always looking for new market opportunities.

Purposeful system. A system that can change its goals under constant conditions; it can produce the same outcome in different manners and produce different outcomes in the same way.

Quality of information. The degree to which information used by the organization's decision makers is accurate.

Quantity of information. The degree to which the amount of information used by the organization's decision makers is sufficient to make an informed decision.

Question mark products (Boston Consulting Group matrix). Products with low market share and high growth possibilities.

Rational power. Influence that stems from one person's acceptance of its legitimate exercise by another.

Rationing. The process of limiting the distribution of resources on the input side and sales on the output side of the organization's production system.

Reactors. Organizations having top managers who frequently perceive changes and uncertainty in their outside environments, but who cannot marshal organizational resources to respond effectively to them.

Reciprocity. Interorganizational relationships characterized by mutual action, dependency, exchange, or agreements among organizations.

Referent power. Influence that stems from a person's identifying with its possessor.

Relevance of information. The degree to which information used by the organization's decision makers pertains to the organization's domain and task environments. The most relevant information needed by the organization is that needed for strategic decisions.

Reliability. A quality of information referring to the degree to which information is consistent.

Reporting of information. The process whereby information is communicated to the proper decision-authority center in an organization.

Representational indicators. Measures that assess the position of social actors in critical organizational roles such as membership on influential boards, committees, or occupancy of key administrative posts.

Reputation of actors. The reputations that employees have which affect the possession and use of influence.

Required confirmation control. A control principle that maintains that no action may be undertaken without first getting specific approval from another unit or management level in the organization.

Resilience. The degree to which the boundary-spanning units respond to changes in the mission and goals of the organization.

Resource dependence. A condition whereby the scarcity of resources in the environment forces organizations to take actions to control these resources, one of these actions being the formation of interorganizational relationships.

Resource-exchange network. A form of reciprocity in which network members trade available resources among themselves without relying on outside funding or agency support.

Resource scarcity/performance distress. A condition in which organizations have difficulty obtaining resources or achieving their goals; thus, they are more apt to form interorganizational relationships in order to alleviate these problems.

Responsibility. The obligation that organizational members assume to carry out their duties to the best of their ability and in accordance with directions.

Reward power. Influence that stems from one person's ability to control and dispense benefits to another.

Rich information. Type of information that helps clarify ambiguous situations.

Ritual. A standardized, detailed set of techniques and behaviors that manifests an organization's culture.

Role conflict. Conflict that occurs between individuals in a group that results from the various and often different expectations that the individuals have of one another.

Routine jobs and dissatisfaction. Bureaucratic problems in organizations caused by heavy specialization resulting in boredom and lack of job satisfaction. These problems can be treated by OD techniques such as job enrichment, supervisory training, and the use of extrinsic reward systems tied to incentives and performance.

Routinization. The development of set routines for the performance of work.

Satisficing (Simon). The search for solutions based on the concept of bounded rationality. Objective decisions are based on a kind of triangle of rationality limited by one's skills, values, and knowledge of the decision subject, and thus, decisions made inside these limits are called satisficing decisions.

Scalar process. Vertical organizational growth that occurs by the addition of more levels in an organization structure.

Scenario analysis. The construction of alternative future events and the probability of their occurrence.

Schedule. Specific time required for the sequential execution of the activities required to accomplish organizational goals.

Secondary beneficiaries. All those outside the primary beneficiary group that the organization seeks to satisfy; this group includes suppliers, government, and so forth.

Secondary objectives. The needs and desires of secondary beneficiaries of the organization.

Selective imperviousness. A linkage model that permits the organization to be discriminating in its linkage systems; only key areas of the task environment are allowed to penetrate the organization.

Sensitivity group training. A method of training in which trainees are encouraged to become sensitive to their own and to group member attitudes and beliefs.

Sensor distortion and filtration. The process of perceiving and interpreting information by the organization's sensors who are biased because of their unique backgrounds or personal characteristics; thus, information can be distorted or filtered by the sensors.

Sensor isolation. The cutting off of the organization's sensors from the organization's decision-authority centers.

Sensor misplacement. The process whereby the organization's sensors interact with inappropriate parts of the task environment while simultaneously ignoring the appropriate parts of that environment.

Sensors. The points of contact of the boundary-spanning unit with the environment; they keep the organization in contact with, and determine its sensitivity to, the environment.

Servo-mechanism. A part of a system that serves to effect system correction when deviations occur.

Short-term objectives. Desired end-states that can be attained in a relatively short time, such as a year or one accounting cycle.

Simple structure (Mintzberg). An informal and highly centralized organization characterized by little or no support staff, little differentiation, a loose division of labor, and a very small managerial hierarchy.

Situational authority. A type of hybrid authority that contains elements of both managerial and staff authority; generally delegated to a staff person who is given the right to make binding decisions about a given function throughout the organization structure.

Skill mix. The kinds and amounts of abilities possessed by the available work force.

Slogan. A verbal message or statement that an organization uses as a means of ready recognition of the organization and its products, thereby reflecting the organization's culture.

Smoothing (conflict). A means of dealing with conflict by consoling the conflicting parties.

Smoothing (technology). Methods used by the organization to protect the technical core by leveling or smoothing out the flow of incoming raw materials and departing products.

Social choice context. A condition that exists when there is little, if any, organizational cooperation (i.e., organizations act autonomously without any regard for any common goals or transcending values).

Social interlocking. A form of interorganizational relationship; informal relationships form as a result of the social interactions of key managers.

Social movement (Smelser's model). A six-phase model consisting of structural conduciveness, structural strain, growth of a generalized belief, precipitating factors, mobilization for action, and social control.

Sociotechnical systems. The field that recognizes both the human factor (socio) and the technical factor (technology) in designing jobs.

Space and time (multidimensional matrix). The fluidity and movement through time of the multidimensional matrix structure. This characteristic refers to the ability of the organization to adapt to environmental influences over time.

Span of control. The number of immediate subordinates who report to a given superior.

Specialization. The development of a set of job skills that is required by increased, and perhaps more diversified, work loads.

Specificity of evaluation (Aston studies). A technology classification criterion that refers to the degree to which work flow can be measured quantitatively.

Staff authority. The right to make recommendations, suggestions, and so on about the implementation of decisions.

Staff operative work. Nonmanagerial activity concerned with producing and distributing secondary utility.

Stakeholders. Groups of people who have a vested interest in the operation and outcomes of the organization.

Standards. Criteria used to determine the degree of success in goal accomplishment.

Star products (Boston Consulting Group matrix). Products with high growth rates and market share.

State-maintaining system. A system that reacts in a specific manner to an internal or external event in order to produce a given external or internal state.

Static system. A system in which no changes take place over time.

Storing of information. The process of keeping or accumulating information for some future use by the organization's decision makers. Information can be stored by the use of traditional files or by computer tapes or disks.

Story. A narrative based on true events that organizations use to convey culture to the organization's members.

Strategic business unit (SBU). An organizational unit established primarily for strategic planning/decision-making purposes. SBUs are used mainly in diversified multiproduct/services organizations and are comprised of groups of related products or services directed to a distinct customer group.

Strategic decisions. Those decisions that tie the organization's mission and purpose to environmental opportunities and constraints.

Strategic management. The process of decisions and their implementation that adapts the organization to its environment to better accomplish organizational purposes and to sustain the organization's long-term viability by enhancing the value of its products or services.

Strategic planning premises. A set of key assumptions the organization makes about the future after it has performed a variety of environmental analyses and forecasts.

Strategy-culture conflict. Conflict that results from the incompatibility of a group's cultural values with the main strategic direction of the organization.

Structural conduciveness of the environment. The degree to which the structure of society permits or even encourages organizations to form interorganizational relationships.

Structure. The hierarchical pattern of authority, responsibility, and accountability relationships designed to provide coordination of the work of the organization; the vertical arrangement of jobs in the organization.

Structure formation (Rahim). The reliance on rules and written communications by parties to a conflict (i.e., the conflict is institutionalized and relations between the conflicting parties are as formal as possible).

Subsystems. A group of functioning elements within a larger system.

Superordinate goal/Outside force. An outside threat or goal that compels different organizations to form interorganizational relationships.

Suppression. The use of power and/or authority to put down conflict.

Survey feedback technique. An intervention technique, using attitude surveys, by which a consultant/change agent can obtain data about an organization and its problems through working collaboratively with organizational members.

Survival/growth issues. The fourth and final stage in the formation of group culture, in which the members' attention is focused on preserving the status quo within the group and resisting change.

Symbol. Any object, act, event, quality, or relationship that serves as a vehicle for conveying cultural meaning within an organization.

Synergism. The interactive effect of parts of a system that, when working together, produce a product that is greater than the sum of the effects of the parts when acting separately.

Synthesis. An approach to differentiation that builds from the bottom up, focusing on combining specialized tasks into even larger sets of tasks.

System. An organized or complex whole; an assemblage or combination of things or parts performing a complex or unitary whole.

Systems model of conflict. Lateral conflict in organizations that stems from situations requiring a high degree of cooperation and coordination.

Systems School. An explanation of organizations that is built on the works of both the Classical and Behavioral Schools and which applies systems and mathematical theories to the study of organizations.

T group training. See *Sensitivity group training.*

Tall organization. An organization that has relatively narrow spans of control and many levels of management.

Task environment. Those components of the environment that are relevant (or potentially relevant) for goal setting and attainment; composed of customers, suppliers of equipment, materials, labor, capital, work space, competitors for both markets and resources, and regulatory groups, including government agencies, unions, and interfirm organizations.

Task force structure. See *Matrix structure*.

Team building. An intervention process in which group members diagnose how they work together and plan changes to improve the group's effectiveness.

Technological model. A model of organization that is based on the technology used by the organization as the explanation of how the organization develops and operates.

Technology. The techniques and science of production and distribution of goods and services found in a given society.

Theory. An explanation of some phenomenon; consists of principles that describe relationships observed in association with that phenomenon for the purpose of explaining and predicting the phenomenon.

Theory of countervailing power. The theory that as a particular organization becomes powerful in the environment, other organizations will coalesce to build a competing power base, resulting in a balance of power among the interested organizations in that enacted environment.

Theory X. An approach to management that characterizes people as believing work is undesirable, that people will only do enough to avoid punishment, and thus the best motivation is fear or threats.

Theory Y. A management approach that assumes that work is natural, that people are creative and have initiative, and are self-motivated, and thus the best motivation is anything other than fear or threats.

Thick culture. The predominant culture within an organization or group that is widespread and accepted by the members.

Third party (Deutsch). An outsider to a conflict episode who has the resources and skills to encourage the parties to resolve their differences.

Timeliness of information. The degree to which information used by the organization's decision makers is recent. Usually, the more recent the information, the more valuable it is.

Thin culture. The culture within an organization or group that is not widely spread or accepted by the members.

Top-down approach (organizational culture). A technique used by management to change an organization's culture whereby top-level managers "decree" that different norms of behavior are to be observed.

Top-down information flow and problem insensitivity. Bureaucratic problems in organizations caused by the hierarchical and mechanistic nature of bureaucracies. In these conditions, there is basically a one-way information flow accompanied by a lack of appreciation for problem solving. These problems can be treated by OD techniques such as the formation of shadow structures comprised of collateral management teams, junior boards of executives, and corporate ombudsmen. In addition, MBO can also be used to rectify these problems.

Transformation. The process of a system that changes inputs into outputs.

Trend analysis. The graphical presentation of a future trend in the environment based on a historical trend extrapolated from a set of data.

Turnaround strategy. A defensive strategy used by the organization to reverse a negative trend that usually entails such cost-cutting measures as layoffs, reduction of expense accounts, and wage cuts.

Two-factor theory of motivation (Herzberg). A tenet of the Behavioral School stating that there are two determinants of behavior in organizations—job context and job content.

Type I error. A piece of information that is regarded as true, when, in fact, it is false.

Type II error. A piece of information that is regarded as false, when, in fact, it is true.

Types of design. Organizational models of ways in which differentiation patterns are integrated in the organization.

Unit technology (Woodward). Type of technology in which production runs consist of only a few units at a time.

Unitary context. A context for organizational dependencies in which the supraorganization exercises authority over the organizations under its control and governs the interdependencies among the organizations.

Unk-unk. An unknown-unknown, that is, a piece of information that is unknown; the need to know this information is also unknown.

User-based information. Information that is specifically designed to meet the needs of its users.

Validity. A quality referring to the degree to which the information measures what it is purported to measure.

Vertical differentiation. The division of work by level of authority; often referred to as the scalar process.

Vertical integration. Form of interorganizational cooperation in which an organization makes its intermediate environment part of the organization by taking control of its suppliers or dealers.

Vertical lock-in and incompetency. Bureaucratic problems in organizations caused by narrow promotion ladders and promotions based on seniority. These conditions cause undue functional specialization and inbreeding and can be treated by OD techniques such as career counseling, the use of assessment centers, and wider job postings.

Work. An activity that can be clearly distinguished from any other activity and which, when executed, produces or distributes utility; types include operative (both primary and secondary) and managerial.

Work flow rigidity (Aston studies). A technology classification criterion that is concerned with the degree of flexibility in both human skills and machine capabilities.

Zone of indifference (Barnard). An area of concern in which the projected and realized effects of a superior's decisions are inconsequential to subordinates attitudes and behavior.

N A M E   I N D E X

SUBJECT INDEX